About This Book

Why is this topic important?

The term *instructional design* has two possible meanings. One meaning refers to a field of practice. A second meaning refers to a rigorous way of creating good training called the instructional systems design (ISD) process. Instructional design is, first and foremost, about how to get good work results from human beings in organizational settings.

The U. S. military originally invented the ISD process to organize efficient, effective, systematic, and results-oriented troop training. In recent years, however, the term instructional design has gained a broader meaning associated with the myriad ways by which to achieve improvement in human performance. Many of those ways transcend mere training. But a key focal point of interest for many instructional designers remains on how to improve human performance in organizational settings through effective training.

What can you achieve with this book?

How do you troubleshoot problems with human performance? When problems stem from individuals who lack knowledge, skill, or attitude to carry out the work effectively, how do you go about establishing rigorous training that gets results? This book is primarily, though not exclusively, about how to get results from training. It is based on research by seasoned practitioners on what it takes to analyze human performance problems and then—when training is an appropriate solution—to design and develop effective training, implement that training, and evaluate it.

How is this book organized?

The book is divided into five distinct parts. Part One provides a conceptual foundation for the book by showing how to detect and solve human performance problems. Part Two focuses on analyzing instructional needs, learners, work settings, and work. Part Three centers on performance objectives and measurements to guide the remaining steps in the instructional design process by describing precisely what targeted learners should know, do, or feel on completing a planned learning experience. Part four rounds out the discussion on the steps in a systematic approach to instructional design by covering instructional strategies, materials, and evaluation. Part Five examines how to manage instructional design, demonstrate effective communication skills, and develop oneself professionally in instructional design. Many chapters follow a common format that describes how to demonstrate competencies linked to effective instructional design, how to explain and judge them, and how to address key ethical and cross-cultural challenges in demonstrating those competencies. The last chapter sums up some lessons that the authors have learned about what it means to perform effectively as an instructional designer.

The book concludes with two appendices. One appendix permits you to self-assess yourself against research-based competencies of effective instructional designers. The second appendix reports the results of a survey conducted with instructional designers about real-world issues. A website accompanies the book. It provides slides to accompany each chapter. It also provides many practical worksheets (denoted in the book with the web icon) from the text. Further, it provides activities based on—or meant to enhance reader understanding of—each chapter. Please see the Contents of the Website at the end of this book for additional information. The materials are available FREE with the purchase of this book at

www.pfeiffer.com/go/masteringid

How is the fourth edition different from the third edition?

This book is updated with new references, new slides and exercises for the accompanying website, and new sections on knowledge management, wikipedias, blogs, instant messaging, and a host of new technologies and applications available to instructional designers.

About Pfeiffer

Pfeiffer serves the professional development and hands-on resource needs of training and human resource practitioners and gives them products to do their jobs better. We deliver proven ideas and solutions from experts in HR development and HR management, and we offer effective and customizable tools to improve workplace performance. From novice to seasoned professional, Pfeiffer is the source you can trust to make yourself and your organization more successful.

Essential Knowledge Pfeiffer produces insightful, practical, and comprehensive materials on topics that matter the most to training and HR professionals. Our Essential Knowledge resources translate the expertise of seasoned professionals into practical, how-to guidance on critical workplace issues and problems. These resources are supported by case studies, worksheets, and job aids and are frequently supplemented with CD-ROMs, websites, and other means of making the content easier to read, understand, and use.

Essential Tools Pfeiffer's Essential Tools resources save time and expense by offering proven, ready-to-use materials—including exercises, activities, games, instruments, and assessments—for use during a training or-team-learning event. These resources are frequently offered in looseleaf or CD-ROM format to facilitate copying and customization of the material.

Pfeiffer also recognizes the remarkable power of new technologies in expanding the reach and effectiveness of training. While e-hype has often created whizbang solutions in search of a problem, we are dedicated to bringing convenience and enhancements to proven training solutions. All our e-tools comply with rigorous functionality standards. The most appropriate technology wrapped around essential content yields the perfect solution for today's on-the-go trainers and human resource professionals.

Pfeiffer
www.pfeiffer.com   *Essential resources for training and HR professionals*

William J. Rothwell dedicates this book to his wife, Marcelina V. Rothwell. She is the wind beneath my wings.

H.C. Kazanas dedicates this book to his wife, Nuria Kazanas.

MASTERING THE INSTRUCTIONAL DESIGN PROCESS

A Systematic Approach

FOURTH EDITION
A REVISED EDITION BASED ON AN ADAPTATION OF
INSTRUCTIONAL DESIGN COMPETENCIES: THE STANDARDS (3RD ED.)
AND *INSTRUCTIONAL DESIGN COMPETENCIES: THE STANDARDS* (2ND ED.)

William J. Rothwell and H.C. Kazanas

Pfeiffer
A Wiley Imprint
www.pfeiffer.com

Library of Congress Cataloging-in-Publication Data

Rothwell, William J.
  Mastering the instructional design process : a systematic approach / William J. Rothwell and H.C. Kazanas. — 4th ed.
     p. cm.
  Includes bibliographical references and index.
   ISBN 978-0-7879-9646-8 (cloth)
    1. Employees—Training of.   2. Instructional systems—Design.   I. Kazanas, H. C.   II. Title.
  HF5549.5.T7R659   2008
  658.3'12404—dc22

                                                                          2008016488

Printed in the United States of America
Printing   10 9 8 7 6 5 4 3 2 1

CONTENTS

Tables, Figures, and Exhibits   xi

Preface to the Fourth Edition   xv

Acknowledgments   xxxv

About the International Board of Standards for Training, Performance, and Instruction   xli

About the Authors   xxxvii

Pre-Test About Instructional Systems Design (ISD)   xliii

PART ONE: DETECTING AND SOLVING HUMAN PERFORMANCE PROBLEMS

1 What Is Instructional Design?   3

2 Alternatives to Instructional Solutions: Five Frequent Options   17

3 Determining Projects Appropriate for Instructional Design Solutions   36

PART TWO: ANALYZING NEEDS, LEARNERS, WORK SETTINGS, AND WORK

4 Conducting a Needs Assessment   59

5 Assessing Relevant Learner Characteristics   89

6 Analyzing Relevant Work Setting Characteristics   112

7 Performing Work Analysis   130

PART THREE: ESTABLISHING PERFORMANCE OBJECTIVES AND PERFORMANCE MEASUREMENTS

8 Writing Performance Objectives   169

9 Developing Performance Measurements   190

10 Sequencing Performance Objectives   210

PART FOUR: DELIVERING THE INSTRUCTION EFFECTIVELY

11 Specifying Instructional Strategies   229

12 Selecting or Designing Instructional Materials   257

13 Evaluating Instruction   288

PART FIVE: MANAGING INSTRUCTIONAL DESIGN PROJECTS SUCCESSFULLY

14 Designing the Instructional Management System   313

15 Planning and Monitoring Instructional Design Projects   332

16 Communicating Effectively   350

17 Interacting with Others   367

18 Promoting the Use of Instructional Design   391

19 Developing Yourself   405

20 Being an Effective Instructional Designer: Lessons Learned   410

Appendix I: Online Instructional Design Resources   417

Appendix II: What Is Knowledge Management (KM), and How Does
KM Relate to Instructional Design?   423

Appendix III: Learning Theory and Instructional Design   427

References   433

Name Index   459

Subject Index   465

Contents of the Website   479

TABLES, FIGURES, AND EXHIBITS

Tables

P.1   Comparison Between Books   xxii

1.1   Factors Affecting Performance   8

3.1   The Performance Engineering Matrix   43

4.1   Strengths and Weaknesses of Selected Data Collection Methods   77

5.1   Summary of Stages in the Classic Dalton, Thompson, and Price Model   98

7.1   Summary of Approaches to Task Analysis   146

7.2   Content Types: Definitions and Examples   149

8.1   Verbs Associated with Objectives in the Cognitive Domain   181

8.2   Verbs Associated with Objectives in the Affective Domain   182

8.3   Verbs Associated with Objectives in the Psychomotor Domain   182

9.1   Purposes of Performance Measurement   194

9.2   Behaviors Specified in Instructional Objectives and Corresponding Test Items   201

11.1   Instructional Events and the Conditions of Learning They Imply for Five Types of Learned Capabilities   238

11.2   Instructional Strategies and Tactics   241

14.1   An Example of a Simplified Decision Chart   325

17.1   A Model for Selecting Techniques to Establish and Maintain
       Rapport in Instructional Design Projects   371

Figures

P.1   Model of the ISD Process   xix
P.2   Revised Model of the ISD Process   xx
1.1   A Comprehensive Model of Human Performance in Organizations   7
1.2   A Situation-Specific Model of Human Performance   10
1.3   The Basic Components of an Organization as an Open System   11
3.1   Components of a Problem   38
4.1   A Model of Steps in the Instructional Design Process   60
5.1   A Model of Steps in the Instructional Design Process   90
6.1   A Model of Steps in the Instructional Design Process   113
7.1   A Model of Steps in the Instructional Design Process   131
7.2   Uses for Results of Task or Content Analysis   152
8.1   A Model of Steps in the Instructional Design Process   170
8.2   Steps for Converting Results of Task or Content Analysis into
       Performance Objectives   175
8.3   Levels of Objectives in the Cognitive Domain   178
8.4   Levels of Objectives in the Affective Domain   179
8.5   Levels of Objectives in the Psychomotor Domain   180
9.1   A Model of Steps in the Instructional Design Process   191
10.1   A Model of Steps in the Instructional Design Process   211
10.2   Rules for Sequencing Performance Objectives: A Flowchart   217
11.1   A Model of Steps in the Instructional Design Process   230
11.2   Algorithm for Selection of Instructional Mode   249
12.1   A Model of Steps in the Instructional Design Process   258
12.2   An Algorithm for Deciding Whether to Produce Your Own
       Instructional Materials   261
12.3   A Flowchart for Judging the Accuracy, Completeness,
       and Appropriateness of Selected Instructional Materials   283
12.4   A Flowchart for Judging the Accuracy, Completeness, and
       Appropriateness of Prepared Instructional Materials   284
13.1   A Model of Steps in the Instructional Design Process   289
14.1   An Example of a Simplified Instructional Flowchart   325
15.1   Planning, Scheduling, and Controlling Instructional Design Projects   337
16.1   Types of Verbal-Visual Image Relationships   353

Exhibits

1.1   Ten Key Assumptions About Instructional Design and Instructional
        Design Competencies   4
3.1   The IBSTPI Code of Ethical Standards for Instructional Designers   51
5.1   A Worksheet on Learner Characteristics   100
8.1   A Worksheet for Preparing Instructional Objectives   184
8.2   A Worksheet for Judging Performance Objectives   186
9.1   A Worksheet for Judging Performance Measurements   206
10.1 A Worksheet for Judging the Sequencing of Performance Objectives   223
11.1 A Worksheet for Judging the Appropriateness of a Specified
        Instructional Strategy   252
12.1 A Portion of a Representative Learner Guidesheet   268
12.2 A Portion of a Representative Lesson Plan   272
12.3 An Interview Guide for Collecting Case-Study Information   278
12.4 A Framework for Preparing a Role Play   280
12.5 An Interview Guide for Gathering Information on Critical Incidents   281
13.1 A Worksheet on Instructional Materials and Methods for
        Expert Reviewers   300
13.2 A Checklist About Instructional Materials and Methods for
        Expert Reviewers   301
13.3 A Checklist for Judging the Appropriateness, Comprehensiveness,
        and Adequacy of Statements of the Evaluation Plan and Revision
        Specifications   305
14.1 A Worksheet on the Instructional Management System   316
14.2 A Survey Questionnaire to Assess Learner Motivation   322
14.3 A Checklist for Judging the Appropriateness, Comprehensiveness, and
        Adequacy of the Instructional Management System   330
15.1 A Standardized Format for a Progress Report   343
15.2 A Checklist for Judging the Appropriateness and
        Comprehensiveness of a Project Plan   347
16.1 A Worksheet for Assessing Appropriate Answers to Questions   359
16.2 A Worksheet for Assessing Your Writing for Grammatical Correctness   362
17.1 A Checklist for Judging the Appropriateness and Effectiveness of
        Behaviors Used in Specific Interactions with Other People   388

PREFACE TO THE FOURTH EDITION

Some would say that the world of instructional design has changed dramatically yet again since the third edition of this book appeared in 2004. Those changes were just as dramatic as what happened between the first edition of this book in 1992 and its second edition in 1998. While it is probably not possible to be comprehensive in reviewing all those changes, certainly some of them include: (1) a burgeoning number of standards and studies have appeared about what instructional designers (or their professional equivalents) do and what kind of people they should be (see, for instance, Bernthal, Colteryahn, Davis, Naughton, Rothwell, and Wellins, 2004; (2) a growing emphasis on competencies as the characteristics that underpin performance (Dubois and Rothwell, 2004); (3) increasing interest in learning objects ("A Field Guide," 2002; Barron, 2002; Merrill, 1996); (4) increasingly louder cries for reforms in the instructional design process and complaints about so-called traditional approaches to instructional design; (5) growing use of media blends by which to deliver instruction (Barbian, 2002a); (6) increasing sophistication among instructional designers on the application of human performance technology, which some call *performance consulting* and others call *human performance improvement;* (7) increasing emphasis on values and ethics as factors that do—or should—affect performance (Hultman, 2002); and (8) continuing awareness of the importance of cross-cultural issues in instructional design–as well as international comparisons of training (Marquardt, King, and Ershkine, 2002).

Managers in the United States, and in other nations as well, are trying harder than ever to improve human performance. In some respects, this pursuit of improvement has become the modern business world's equivalent of the medieval quest for the Holy Grail. Of course, there are good reasons for improving performance. The competitive environment has never been more fierce. The outsourcing of products and services—including instructional design work itself—is taken for granted in many settings. And there is increasing willingness to outsource services offshore as well as manufacturing. E-learning grew popular, and it made many instructional designers feel like they needed to relearn their profession from scratch (Alden, 1998). Then it, too, has undergone dramatic reformation (Shank, 2001; Taylor, 2002), transformed into blended learning, and more recently into a growing preoccupation of the instructional design world with such newfangled modalities as iPods, wikipedias, blogs, social networking, and uploaded personal videos. But one thing has not changed: the long-term success of organizations continues to hinge on improvements in human performance. That is important to bear in mind even as new forms of technology are used and experimented with in delivery. Media use remains only the means to the end of improved performance (Bernardez, 2003), and instructional designers are still subject to the pointed complaint by managers that they are too interested in the media and not interested enough in finding learning that aligns with achieving business strategy.

For some managers, efforts to improve human performance have led to headlong plunges into flashy fads and quick fixes—modern-day snake-oil remedies. Other managers, however, are meeting the challenges they face by taking a more thoughtful approach: supporting and participating in the systematic analysis of human performance problems, identifying the root causes of those problems, considering various solutions to them, and carrying out the solutions in ways designed to reduce the unintended consequences of corrective action. It is true that there is a desire to accelerate this process, but many people have grown wiser about what it takes to make change happen, even as they have tried to do things faster.

Instructional designers are often the standard-bearers of these calculated efforts to improve human performance. They continue to work under the guise of many job titles. They are sometimes called performance technologists, performance consultants, trainers, training and development specialists, workplace learning and performance professionals, learning and performance professionals, instructional developers, staff development specialists, performance consultants, or instructional designers. Whatever their titles, they share a common goal of improving human performance. Perhaps training remains as the best-known performance improvement strategy, although many people are experimenting with approaches that integrate employee development with work processes so that people learn as they work (and work as they learn) in real time. Management solutions that do not include training range from the preparation and use of job aids, the redesign of organizational structures and reporting relationships, the redesign of work, the refocusing of employee selection methods, the reengineering of work-related feedback methods, and the design and implementation of employee reward systems. There are literally thousands of ways to solve human performance problems, and the sheer choice of solutions is as daunting as discovering root causes.

The examples and references incorporated in this book grow out of our own experiences in instructional design. Since our experiences have not been universal, we have attempted to focus on what we know. Generally, our goal is to give instructional designers a tool for developing their own skills in down-to-earth ways.

But one theme should be clearly stressed from the outset: *instructional systems design (ISD) is not about the mindless application of step-by-step schemes or new technology.* Analyzing human performance problems, designing and developing solutions, implementing those solutions, and evaluating results is hard work. It requires a blend of intuitive and analytical thinking. And it requires a willingness to meet client needs to solve organizational problems, which (in turn) may demand that instructional designers skip steps in the traditional ISD model, multi-task to do several steps at once, rearrange steps, add steps (such as translation), or even reinvent steps to meet the unique needs of unique clients in unique situations. (For additional theoretical and practical perspectives on the study of ISD, see Ertmer and Quinn, 2002, and Reigeluth, 1999.)

The Foundation of the Book

In the past, books on instructional design have often reflected the personal opinions of the authors and have not been based on an underlying foundation of solid research. However, *Mastering the Instructional Design Process: A Systematic Approach, Fourth Edition* is based on Richey, Fields, and Foxon's *Instructional Design Competencies: The Standards* (3rd ed.) (2001) as well as on the predecessor to that work–which was Foshay, Silber, and Westgaard's *Instructional Design Competencies: The Standards* (1986). The third edition of this work is abbreviated throughout this book as *The Standards*. Prepared through the cooperation of highly respected professionals in the instructional design field, *The Standards* was sponsored by the International Board of Standards for Training, Performance, and Instruction (IBSTPI).

The Standards, in its third edition, identifies twenty-three competencies for instructional design work. Each competency consists of component performances. Performances are the behaviors that instructional designers can carry out to demonstrate each competency. In *The Standards*, each competency and component performance is labeled as "essential" or "advanced" to indicate the level of expertise required. While the competencies and their component performances may vary among organizations because of differences in corporate cultures, *The Standards* provides a solid foundation for describing the instructional design field. The relationship between the chapters of this book and the second and third editions of *The Standards* is presented in Table P.1. Of course, the competencies identified in each edition of *The Standards* implies a model of the Instructional Systems Design (ISD) process. (See Figures P.1 and P.2.) Although we have chosen to retain the structure of the second and third editions for this book because of their clarity and popularity, readers are advised to note the relationship shown in Table P.1 between the chapter titles of this book and the competencies of *The Standards*, 3rd ed. Figure P.1 shows the instructional systems design process from Foshay, Silber, and Westgaard and Figure P.2 shows the model from Richey, Fields, and Foxon.

The fourth edition of *Mastering the Instructional Design Process: A Systematic Approach* is intended to take up where *The Standards* leaves off. While *The Standards* focuses on *what instructional designers do*, this book focuses on *how to demonstrate competencies of instructional design work*. Its purpose is thus to point the way toward building instructional design competencies.

The Audience for the Book

This book is for instructional design professionals and professionals in the making, whatever their formal job titles. It is intended as a desk aid to help professionals carry out their work and as a text for students. A comprehensive list of references appears at the end of the book. We suggest that readers use it to pursue subjects of interest to them.

Mastering the Instructional Design Process: A Systematic Approach, Fourth Edition, should also be of interest to others, such as human resource professionals and operating managers, who have reason to analyze human performance problems systematically, pinpoint the root causes of those problems, consider various solutions to the problems, and carry out the solutions in ways designed to reduce the unintended side effects of corrective action.

Overview of the Contents

This book is adapted from *The Standards*. The chapters do not follow the sequence of competencies in *The Standards*. That is necessary because print media is, by its nature, linear. Some may want to follow a step-by-step approach. But others, more wisely, will know to adapt their project approach to meet specific client and learner demands and project constraints.

FIGURE P.1. MODEL OF THE ISD PROCESS.

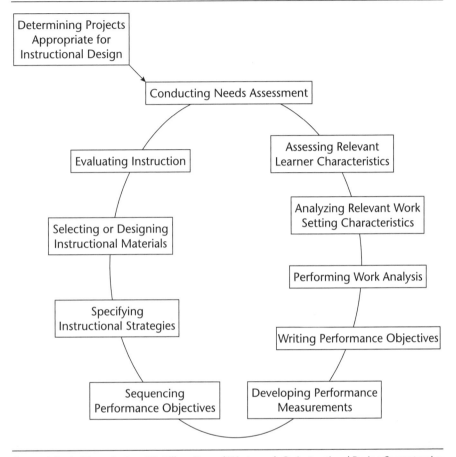

Source: Adapted from Foshay, W., Silber, K., and Westgaard, O. *Instructional Design Competencies: The Standards.* Iowa City, IA: International Board of Standards for Training, Performance, and Instruction, 1986.

The book opens with a pre-test about instructional systems design. That Pretest may be regarded as an advance organizer to help readers assess their own grasp of instructional systems design.

Part One consists of Chapters One, Two, and Three. It provides a conceptual foundation for the book. Its focus is on detecting and solving human performance problems.

Chapter One serves as an introduction. It sets the stage for the remainder of the book by defining instructional design, describing instructional design as an emerging profession, and summarizing key issues that affect human performance in organizations. It also addresses several important critiques of traditional instructional design approaches.

In Chapter Two, we review several management solutions—what some call *non-instructional solutions*—to human performance problems. Not based on *The Standards*,

FIGURE P.2. REVISED MODEL OF THE ISD PROCESS.

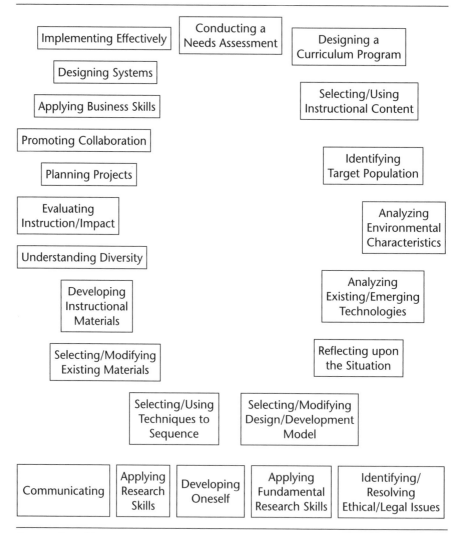

Source: Adapted from Richey, R., Field, D., and Foxon, M. *Instructional Design Competencies: The Standards* (3rd ed.). Syracuse, NY: ERIC Clearinghouse on Information and Technology, 2001.

the chapter properly emphasizes the importance of getting clear what the cause (or the causes) of performance problems are. However, we discuss them because instructional designers must be capable of solving human performance problems and not just using training to solve every problem. Moreover, individuals working as instructional designers must increasingly become familiar with human performance improvement strategies other than instruction (Rothwell, 2000; Rothwell, Hohne, and King, 2007).

Chapter Three, the last chapter in Part One, focuses on determining which projects are appropriate for instructional design solutions. After defining what we mean by a performance problem and discussing the ways of labeling the parts of a problem, we distinguish between comprehensive and situation-specific models for analyzing human performance problems. *A comprehensive problem-solving model* is useful to scan the "big picture" of an organization; a *situation-specific model* guides instructional designers to deal with common symptoms of human performance problems that prompt managers to request the aid of instructional designers. The chapter concludes by addressing key ethical and cross-cultural challenges in applying performance analysis.

Parts Two, Three, and Four comprise Chapters Four through Thirteen. They are unified by a common, but simplified, model of the instructional design process.

Part Two consists of four related chapters, which, respectively, focus on analyzing instructional needs, learners, work settings, and work. Chapter Four focuses on conducting a needs assessment. Appropriate only when an employee performance problem has been attributed to a deficiency in knowledge, skills, or attitudes and can be most cost-effectively addressed through instruction, needs assessment is an evaluation of instructional requirements. The chapter addresses developing a needs assessment plan, conducting a needs assessment, identifying instructional problems, judging needs assessment plans, justifying needs assessment, addressing ethical and cross-cultural issues in needs assessment, and reviewing recent developments in needs assessment.

Assessing the relevant characteristics of learners is the topic of Chapter Five. In this chapter we explain how to select, carry out, judge, and justify learner characteristics for assessment. The chapter also addresses key ethical and cross-cultural issues in assessing relevant learner characteristics and describes a recent development affecting learner assessment.

Closely related to Chapter Five, Chapter Six focuses on analyzing characteristics of a work setting. In this chapter, we explain how to achieve a better match between learners and the settings in which instruction is designed, delivered, and applied. To that end we cover methods of determining work-setting resources and constraints and judging and justifying setting analysis. We also address key ethical and cross-cultural issues in analyzing work-setting characteristics.

TABLE P.1. COMPARISON BETWEEN BOOKS.

Chapter in *Mastering the Instructional Design Process,* Fourth Edition	Competency/Standard from *Instructional Design Competencies: The Standards,* 2nd ed.	Competency/Standard from *Instructional Design Competencies: The Standards,* 3rd and 4th editions.**
Part One: Detecting and Solving Human Performance Problems		
1	*None*	*None*
2	*None*	*None*
3	Determining Projects Appropriate for Instructional Design Solutions	• Conducting a needs assessment • Identifying and resolving ethical and legal implications of design in the workplace
Part Two: Analyzing Needs, Learners, Work Settings, and Work		
4	Conducting Needs Assessment	• Conducting a needs assessment • Applying fundamental research skills to instructional design projects
5	Assessing Relevant Learner Characteristics	• Identifying and describing target population characteristics
6	Analyzing Relevant Work Setting Characteristics	• Analyzing the characteristics of the environment
7	Performing Work Analysis	• Selecting and using a variety of techniques for determining instructional content
Part Three: Establishing Performance Objectives and Performance Measurements		
8	Writing Performance Objectives	*None*
9	Developing Performance Measurements	*None*
10	Sequencing Performance Objectives	*None*

Part Four: Delivering the Instruction Effectively

11	Specifying Instructional Strategies	• Selecting and using a variety of techniques to define and sequence the instructional content and strategies • Analyzing the characteristics of existing and emerging technologies and their use in an instructional environment
12	Selecting or Designing Instructional Materials	• Selecting or modifying existing instructional materials • Developing instructional materials • Designing instruction that reflects an understanding of the diversity of learners and groups of learners
13	Evaluating Instruction	• Evaluating and assessing instruction and its impact

Part Five: Managing Instructional Design Projects Successfully

14	Designing a Learning Management System	• Designing instructional management systems • Designing a curriculum or program
15	Planning and Monitoring Instructional Design Projects	• Planning and managing instructional design projects • Applying business skills to managing instructional design • Reflecting on the elements of a situation before finalizing design solutions and strategies • Selecting, modifying, or creating a design and development model appropriate for a given project
16	Communicating Effectively	• Communicating effectively in visual, oral, and written form

(continued)

TABLE P.1. COMPARISON BETWEEN BOOKS. (cont'd.)

Chapter in *Mastering the Instructional Design Process*, Fourth Edition	Competency/Standard from *Instructional Design Competencies: The Standards*, 2nd ed.	Competency/Standard from *Instructional Design Competencies: The Standards*, 3rd and 4th editions.**
17	Interacting with Others	• Promoting collaboration, partnerships, and relationships among the participants in a design project
18	Promoting the Use of Instructional Design	None
19	None	• Updating and improving one's knowledge, skills, and attitudes pertaining to instructional design and related field • Applying current research and theory to the practice of instructional design
20	None	• Providing for the effective implementation of instructional products and programs

*Foshay, W., Silber, K., and Westgaard, O. *Instructional Design Competencies: The Standards.* Iowa City, IA: International Board of Standards for Training, Performance, and Instruction, 1986.

**Richey, R., Fields, D., and Foxon, M. *Instructional Design Competencies: The Standards* (3rd ed.). Syracuse, NY: ERIC Clearinghouse on Information and Technology, 2001. Copyright 1993 by the International Board of Standards for Training, Performance and Instruction. All rights reserved. Used with permission.

Chapter Seven defines work analysis. Work analysis is conceptually related to needs assessment, since both are centered on work-related requirements. The chapter also reviews competency assessment and provides an introduction to it. The chapter then describes how instructional designers may judge and justify a job, task, or content analysis. The chapter concludes with a few words about key ethical and cross-cultural issues in work analysis.

Part Three comprises three chapters on performance objectives and measurements. Performance objectives and measurements are, of course, developed from the results of needs assessment, learner analysis, setting analysis, and work analysis. They are intended to guide the remaining steps in the instructional design process by describing precisely what targeted learners should know, do, or feel on completing a planned learning experience. Writing statements of performance objectives is the topic of Chapter Eight. The chapter explains how instructional designers can distinguish performance objectives from instructional-organizational goals or learner-trainer activities, state objectives in performance terms, judge performance objectives prepared by others, justify objectives that have been prepared, and address key ethical and cross-cultural issues in writing performance objectives.

Developing performance measurements is the topic of Chapter Nine. Established to monitor learner achievement, performance measurements build accountability for results into instruction from the outset. In this chapter, we explain how performance measurements and performance objectives are related, how to generate performance measurements, how to state a rationale for the way a measurement instrument is constructed or a judgment about a performance measurement is made, and how to address key ethical and cross-cultural issues in developing performance measurements.

Chapter Ten addresses the sequencing of performance objectives—a step of instructional design that should occur after work tasks have been analyzed and inventoried, performance objectives have been formally stated, and performance measurements have been established. The purpose of this step in the instructional design process is to ensure that, during instruction, workers are introduced systematically to what they must know or do. We explain how to state rules for sequencing performance objectives, how to apply the rules, how to judge the sequencing of performance objectives, how to justify decisions made about sequencing performance objectives, and how to address key ethical and cross-cultural issues associated with sequencing performance objectives.

Part Four comprises three chapters that cover, respectively, instructional strategies, materials, and evaluation. Part Four rounds out the discussion of steps in the instructional design process. Specifying instructional strategies is the topic of Chapter Eleven. Building on earlier chapters about preceding steps in the instructional design process, it defines instructional strategy, distinguishes between instructional strategy and instructional tactics, and describes how to conceptualize instructional strategy. The chapter also offers advice on how to choose strategy and tactics, choose media and delivery methods, and judge and justify strategy, once it is chosen. It also provides an overview of cognitive strategy. Finally, the chapter identifies ethical and cross-cultural issues in specifying instructional strategies.

Selecting or designing instructional materials, a familiar and important topic to many instructional designers, is the topic of Chapter Twelve. In this chapter, we advise instructional designers to follow six simple steps when designing these materials: (1) prepare a working outline, (2) conduct research, (3) examine existing instructional materials, (4) arrange or modify existing materials, (5) prepare tailor-made instructional materials, and (6) select or prepare learning activities.

Evaluating instruction is the topic of Chapter Thirteen. We devote primary attention to formative evaluation conducted before instruction is delivered on a large scale to the targeted learners. We describe how to develop a formative evaluation plan, carry out the plan, generate ideas for revising instruction, judge and justify formative evaluation, and address key ethical and cross-cultural issues in evaluating instruction.

Part Five consists of seven chapters. Two chapters focus on managing instructional design, three center on communication skills for instructional designers, one focuses on professional development, and one sums up the lessons learned about being an effective instructional designer. Chapter Fourteen summarizes important issues associated with designing an instructional management system. We focus on methods of ensuring that entrance into instruction is quick and easy, that learners entering instruction are diagnosed for their readiness, and that learners are directed to appropriate sections with a minimum of time and effort. We also discuss ways of making sure that each step, section, or experience within the instruction is provided with transitions and references, that each instructional element is easily identified in terms of both content and purpose, and that competence is documented.

Planning and monitoring instructional design projects is our focus in Chapter Fifteen. We describe how to develop a project management plan for an instructional design project. We also describe how to judge and justify project plans.

In Chapter Sixteen, we provide helpful hints about ways to cultivate and apply effective visual, oral, and written communication skills. Like many professionals, instructional designers must be capable of formulating and articulating their thoughts. However, their need to exercise communication skills is probably greater than in many other fields. Chapter Sixteen is divided into three sections: (1) using effective visual communication, (2) using effective oral communication, and (3) using effective written communication.

In Chapter Seventeen, we describe methods that instructional designers can use to interact effectively with others. More specifically, the chapter focuses on techniques for establishing rapport with others, stating the purpose of interpersonal interactions, asking questions, providing explanations, listening actively, dealing with conflict, handling resistance to change, keeping people on track, securing commitment, and selecting appropriate behaviors for effective interpersonal interaction.

In Chapter Eighteen, we offer suggestions about promoting the use of instructional design in organizational settings. We open the chapter with a brief case study to dramatize important issues in promoting instructional design. We then turn to describing ways to make others aware of instructional design. We conclude the chapter with a few words of advice about justifying these promotional efforts.

In Chapter Nineteen, we offer some suggestions about professional development. And, in Chapter Twenty, we offer six key points—lessons, if you want to call them that—about what it takes to be effective in the instructional design field.

The book ends with three appendices. The first is a brief summary of online resources on instructional design. Not intended to be exhaustive, it points readers to a few key online resources that may be useful in building their understanding of instructional design. The second appendix summarizes the relationship between knowledge management and instructional design. The third appendix provides an overview of learning theories and their implications for instructional design. As in appendix one, appendix three is not intended to be exhaustive but merely representative of some key learning theories of value to instructional designers.

A website (www.pfeiffer.com/go/masteringid) accompanies the book. It provides slides to accompany each chapter of the text. It also provides a syllabus for an introductory course in instructional design, many practical worksheets from the text, and activities based on, or meant to enhance reader understanding of, each chapter.

Important Issues, Trends, and Changes Influencing the Fourth Edition

Three major changes have occurred in the years since the second and third editions of this book were published. These changes may be categorized as follows: (1) issues affecting this book, (2) trends affecting the world scene, and (3) trends primarily affecting the instructional design field. We think that here in the Preface to the Fourth Edition we should review those changes and discuss what they mean. The changes provide an important rationale for the revisions we made in this edition.

Two key issues directly affect this book. First, we have been told at professional conferences, on international trips, over the Internet, and in many discussions with colleagues that the book has been widely adopted as a graduate text and as a corporate instructional design handbook. For this we thank our many readers for their compliments and for their suggestions for improvement. Second, we have both made changes since the second and third editions were published. William Rothwell has continued his work on competency modeling, conducting research on what CEOs expect of trainers and what learners must do to make themselves more competent in the learning process (Rothwell, 2002; Rothwell, Lindholm, and Wallick, 2003) . He has also traveled to China more than forty times since the first edition of this book appeared. H.C. Kazanas continues his more relaxed lifestyle in retirement as a professor emeritus, although he often travels internationally.

Macrotrends

We would be remiss if we did not acknowledge the influence of large-scale trends affecting the settings in which instructional designers work. These large-scale trends are called *macrotrends,* meaning that they are driving forces for change that influence events worldwide. Six such macrotrends have been identified (Rothwell, Prescott, and Taylor, 1998 and 2008), and they continue to exert influence.

First among them are breaking new technologies (constituting a macrotrend), which have become the order of the day; they affect modes of working, learning, and instructing. Long synonymous with improvements in work output or speed, technological applications are worth intensive scrutiny. One reason is the so-called *productivity paradox* (Krohe, 1993): technological change does not necessarily lead to improvements in production quantity, quality, or customer satisfaction levels. Nor does it always reduce production costs or time. Instructional designers must know how to take proper advantage of new technology to increase productivity. They must know how to apply performance analysis to new technology as it is introduced and how to apply their skills to rapidly changing work methods and new instructional media.

Second among the macrotrends is rapid change, which has become the only constant. The most obvious consequence of this macrotrend is that effective instructional designers must possess not only fundamental instructional design competencies for individually oriented change efforts to be effected through learning but also more advanced competencies designed to effect group-oriented change through learning (Rothwell and Sullivan, 2005). Indeed, instructional designers must influence organizational activities beyond the instructional setting if they are to be successful. They must also help their clientele avoid the perils of chasing fads for their own sake.

Third, a focus on cost control has prompted organizations to downsize their workforces, outsource activities transcending their core competencies, and increase the number of strategic, synergistic partnerships. Many instructional design projects have, as a consequence, been outsourced in whole or in part. While this macrotrend has been a godsend to external consultants, it has been a bane to instructional designers employed as internal consultants because it intensifies their fears about long-term job security.

Fourth, *knowledge capital*—a term synonymous with *intellectual capital* that refers to the collective economic value of the education, experience, and institutional memory embodied in an organization's workforce—has at last been recognized as critical to organizational success (see the classic treatment by Nonaka and Takeuchi, 1995). Indeed, "human resources are the only remaining source of competitive advantage for organizations. Most other major components of competitiveness are universally available: natural resources can be bought; capital can be borrowed; and technology can be copied. Only human resources—the people in the workforce, with their skills and commitment—and how they are organized are left to make the difference between economic success and failure" (Rosow and Hickey, 1994, p. 1). By what they do, instructional designers build knowledge or intellectual capital and bench strength in their organizations. Their role will thus become more important, as will the role of instructional design in meeting the key global HR challenges of leadership development, performance management, recruitment, retention, organizational values, and corporate culture (Wellins and Rioux, 2000).

Fifth, speed in market change as a macrotrend means that products and services must be delivered faster, better, and cheaper if organizations are to survive and thrive in a global marketplace. Consumers and stakeholders worldwide have grown to expect immediate responses to their preferences in ways that individualize products and services while simultaneously taking advantage of economies of scale—a phenomenon requiring *mass customization* (Pine, 1993). As in other high-skill and high-wage fields, instructional design work must also be performed faster, better, and cheaper and must be adapted to the fluctuating tastes of discriminating consumers.

Sixth and finally are globalization and diversity—taken together. This macrotrend has led many instructional designers to build their competencies for managing or celebrating diversity (ASTD Multicultural Forum, 1996) and for functioning internationally or cross-culturally. Of special note is the increasing importance of knowledge about how to translate instruction, both for different languages and for different cultural contexts, in instructional design work.

Microtrends

We must acknowledge the influence of other trends uniquely affecting instructional design work. We call these activity-specific trends *microtrends,* and they are driving forces for change within the instructional design field. Several microtrends are shaping the future of instructional design. They serve as a counterpoint to the six macrotrends described in previous paragraphs.

The first microtrend is a demand for increasing speed in analyzing, designing, developing, implementing, and evaluating instruction by such stakeholders as top managers and operating managers. Instructional designers are under pressure as never before to slash instructional design time while sacrificing nothing in quality. This microtrend has led to just-in-time training methods—and to assessments of how quickly instruction is designed. It has prompted instructional designers to find creative ways to balance rigor and speed. It has also led to *rapid prototyping.* "In this approach, borrowed from engineering design," explains Donald Ford (1996, p. xviii) in his useful instructional design casebook, "the ISD [instructional systems design] model is telescoped so that analysis, design, and development occur simultaneously rather than sequentially. This is facilitated by use of design prototypes that are constructed and implemented while needs assessment continues. The results of prototype tryouts can then provide further data for needs assessment."

A second microtrend is a growing focus on the performance (work) setting rather than on the instructional setting. Exemplary instructional designers have long known that the work environment exerts far more influence on performance change than the instructional environment does. One result is a systematic search for ways to make the work environment more supportive to applying what people learn off the job in instructional environments. This microtrend has prompted interest in the characteristics associated with learning organizations (Senge, 1990), high-performance workplaces (Dubois and Rothwell, 1996), and learning support embedded in and around the work—so-called situated learning. It has also led to a fundamental reexamination of what can be done to surround performers with what they need to perform at the time they need it and in the place they need it through the creation of manual or electronic performance support systems.

A third microtrend is increasing awareness of how people learn and what instructional designers should do to encourage learning. More attention is now being paid to the views of cognitivists and constructivists. Cognitivists, on the one hand, have infused the instructional design field with a new and sometimes bizarre nomenclature, consisting of such esoteric terms as *internal representations, schemata, bundles or files, and strategies* (Brien and Eastmond, 1994; Clark, 1992).

"The latest developments in instructional design," as Ford (1996, p. xx) explains, "are generally drawn from cognitive psychology, including information processing, learner analysis, and the use of higher level thinking processes and instructional strategies to develop designs." Constructivists, however, regard reality as determined by the knower's experiences. For constructivists, the mind is a builder of symbols. Both cognitivism and constructivism have important implications for instructional design because they focus more attention on what learners know or do to make meaning of what they are learning (Rothwell, 1996c, 1996d, and 2002).

A fourth microtrend is the increasing expectation of stakeholders that instructional designers will direct their attention beyond merely designing instruction (*an activity*) to improving, enhancing, or engineering effective human performance (*an outcome*). That means instructional designers are assuming new roles as performance consultants and internal consultants rather than playing the restricted roles of Johnny-one-notes whose abilities are limited to designing instruction alone. Indeed, instructional designers are not alone. Many people, including operating managers, can apply the competencies of human performance improvement (Rothwell, 2000).

A fifth microtrend is the emergence of an expansive view of performance-related issues transcending traditional knowledge, skills, and attitudes. Many instructional designers have thus begun to focus on assessing and modeling competencies. While the term competency has about as many definitions as authorities writing on the subject, it usually refers to the characteristics underlying successful performance. Competencies are discovered by studying work outputs produced by successful performers and stem from *who the performers are* and not so much from *what work they do*. Competencies include bodies of knowledge, individual personality traits, and levels of individual motivation that transcend knowledge, skill, and attitude (Dubois and Rothwell, 2000).

A sixth microtrend is a fundamental reexamination of the accountabilities of all stakeholders in the instructional design process. Despite the desires of stressed-out operating managers, instructional designers should not shoulder all the work or responsibility for effective instruction. Others have important roles to play before, during, and after instructional delivery. One result of this microtrend is increased attention to emphasizing what managers should know about instruction. A second result is more attention focused on what learners can do to plan and implement their own learning projects (Rothwell, 2002). A third result is a contingency-based view of instructional planning that adapts instructional design to such situational variables as the learners, the learning contexts, and the instructional designers' competencies.

A seventh microtrend is an increasing awareness of what experienced, exemplary instructional designers actually *do* and what skills and knowledge they need in order to perform. From research we now know what we have long suspected: to accelerate the process, experts in instructional design creatively add, subtract, resequence, combine, or simultaneously perform parallel steps in the instructional systems design (ISD) model to fit the situation (Wedman and Tessmer, 1993). Variables influencing these decisions include the instructional designers' skills, client-stakeholder needs or preferences, and project constraints on time, money, and people. One result: many are taking a *contingency-based view* of the instructional planning process that eschews linear, one-size-fits-all approaches (Rothwell and Cookson, 1997). That calls for special knowledge and skills from instructional designers.

An eighth microtrend is increased financial accountability for instructional designers. Clients, both internal and external, are asking for convincing evidence that instructional design projects have favorable cost-benefit ratios and that instructional interventions make good financial sense. Some instructional designers must forecast the financial value of projects *before* they are authorized. Instructional designers must therefore become highly skilled in estimating the costs of human performance problems and solutions and the benefits accruing from those solutions. Additionally, they must learn to involve their clients in analyzing the financial results of instruction, calculating the time value of money linked to these results, and forecasting the variable costs and benefits associated with designing instruction across a range of media.

A ninth and final microtrend is increased interest in older learners and increased interest in tapping the retiree base to address expected talent shortages in the United States and in other nations. While androgogy has traditionally focused on middle-age and younger workers, growing interest exists in addressing the unique needs of older—and often post-retirement—workers. While much research disproves the old notion that "you can't teach an old dog new tricks," many negative stereotypes about older workers and older learners remain prevalent in the management ranks and even among learners (Moseley and Dessinger, 2007). Some differences do exist with older learners, but much research supports the notion that people can continue to learn—and perform— effectively at almost any age. What is dangerous is to accept stereotypes without considering vast differences in individual ability at any age. Older learners can do just about anything that younger learners can. But they may require encouragement, because even they sometimes buy into negative stereotypes about their own abilities.

Taken together, the trends make the instructional design field more challenging than it was when the third edition of this book was published. The structure of the fourth edition is largely unchanged from the second edition. Many readers asked us to retain the structure because it was effective, but we made some changes to address the trends we just mentioned and the new version of *The Standards*. We have also updated many references to help readers find detailed discussions of topics treated in the text and the important issues described earlier.

ACKNOWLEDGMENTS

We wish to thanks members of the International Board of Standards for Training, Performance, and Instruction (IBSTPI) for their encouragement of this project and their permission to use *The Standards* as the foundation for this book. (A description of IBSTPI appears on page xli for those who are curious about what the board is and what it stands for.) While any mistakes in this book are entirely our responsibility and not that of the International Board, we are indebted to the board members for their support.

William J. Rothwell also thanks his graduate research assistant Lin Gao for her assistance in helping to secure and repeatedly follow up on necessary copyright permissions.

William J. Rothwell
University Park, Pennsylvania
February 2008

H. C. Kazanas
Naples, Florida

ABOUT THE AUTHORS

William J. Rothwell is a professor of workplace learning and performance in the Workforce Education and Development program in the Department of Learning and Performance Systems on the University Park campus of the Pennsylvania State University. In that capacity, he heads up a graduate emphasis in workplace learning and performance (WLP). He is also president of Rothwell & Associates, Inc. (see www.rothwell-associates.com), a full-service consulting firm that specializes in all facets of human performance improvement.

Rothwell completed a B.A. in English at Illinois State University, an M.A. (and all courses for the doctorate) in English at the University of Illinois at Urbana-Champaign, an M.B.A. at the University of Illinois at Springfield, and a Ph.D. degree with a specialization in employee training at the University of Illinois at Urbana-Champaign.

Before entering academe in 1993, Rothwell had been a training director in the public and private sectors since 1979. In that capacity he designed or supervised the design of countless instructional programs.

Rothwell has authored, co-authored, or edited numerous books, book chapters, and articles. Among his most recent publications are *Human Resource Transformation* (with R. Prescott and Maria Taylor, 2008); *Working Longer* (with Harvey Stearn, Joel Reaser and Diane Spokus, 2008); *Human Performance Improvement: Building Practitioner Performance* (2nd ed.) (with Carolyn Hohne and Stephen King, 2007); *Instructor Excellence: Mastering the Delivery of Training* (2nd ed.)

(with Bob Powers, 2007); *Next Generation Management Development: The Complete Guide and Resource.*(with Bob Cecil, 2007); *Handbook of Training Technology: An Introductory Guide to Facilitating Learning with Technology—from Planning Through Evaluation* (with Marilynn Butler, M., Cecilia Maldonado, Daryl Hunt, D., Karen Peters, Jie Li, and J. Stern, 2006); *Effective Succession Planning: Ensuring Leadership Continuity and Building Talent from Within* (3rd ed.) (2005), and *Career Planning and Succession Management* (with R. Jackson, S. Knight, and J. Lindholm, with Wei Wang and Tiffani Payne, 2005). Rothwell is also North American editor for an academic journal, *The International Journal of Training and Development.*

H.C. Kazanas is professor emeritus of education in the College of Education at the University of Illinois, Urbana-Champaign. He received his B.Sc. and M.Ed. degrees from Wayne State University in industrial education and his Ph.D. degree from the University of Michigan in education.

Kazanas' present professional interests as a consultant are management development, training of employees on the job, and the effects of work values on productivity. He has been an active member of several professional organizations, including the American Society for Training and Development and the International Society for Performance Improvement; he has served on many committees and has held leadership roles, including that of president of the National Association of Industrial and Technical Teacher Educators. He received several outstanding service awards. Kazanas has published eighty articles in twenty different journals in education and human resource development. He has contributed several book chapters and monographs and has authored or co-authored eleven books relating to technical training in manufacturing and human resource development. One of his technical books has been translated into Spanish and Arabic.

With William J. Rothwell, he has co-authored *Planning and Managing Human Resources: Strategic Planning for Human Resource Management* (2nd ed.) (HRD Press, 2003) and *The Strategic Development of Talent* (2004).

Kazanas worked for ten years in the manufacturing industry as a machinist and production supervisor and for thirty years as an educator in human resource development. He has been a consultant in human resource development with such national and international organizations and agencies as the U.S. Department of Labor, the U.S. Department of Education, the U.S. Agency for International Development, Motorola, Westinghouse, the World Bank, the United Nations Development Program, the International Labor Office, and UNESCO. He has worked in Asia, Africa, Europe, and South America. Kazanas has taught at Eastern Michigan University, the University of Missouri-Columbia, and the University of Illinois. He has served as graduate program coordinator and department chair at the University of Missouri-Columbia and the University of Illinois, respectively. During his academic career he has coordinated and directed many research studies in such areas as work values, attitudes, and productivity, strategic human resource planning, on-the-job training, management job rotation programs, and individualizing instruction.

ABOUT THE INTERNATIONAL BOARD OF STANDARDS FOR TRAINING, PERFORMANCE, AND INSTRUCTION

The International Board of Standards for Training, Performance, and Instruction (IBSTPI) is a professional service organization to the instructional design, training, and performance improvement communities. The board serves these communities through research, publications, and conferences.

The board consists of fifteen professionals, selected to be broadly representative of the communities we serve. Members are from universities, government, large businesses, and consulting firms. In recent years, the board has begun to live up to its name as an international board, with directors from Australia, Canada, England, Norway, and The Netherlands, in addition to members from the United States. The board grew out of the work of the Joint Certification Task Force, which was composed of the Association for Educational Communications and Technology (AECT) and the National Society for Performance and Instruction (NSPI, now the International Society for Performance Improvement, ISPI). Created in 1977, the task force included over thirty professional practitioners and academics with expertise in various facets of training, performance,

Source: Adapted from T. Spannaus, "Foreword" (pp. xi-xiii). In R. Richey, D. Fields, and M. Foxon, *Instructional Design Competencies: The Standards* (3rd ed.). Syracuse, NY: ERIC Clearinghouse on Information and Technology, 2001. Copyright 1993 by the International Board of Standards for Training, Performance and Instruction. All rights reserved. Used with permission.

and instruction. The task force developed the initial set of competencies for the instructional design professional, published an index linking current publications to competencies, and created a prototype assessment procedure. Also during this period, members of the task force spoke at professional meetings and published articles on professional competence and certification. Further information about IBSTPI and its activities can be found at www.IBSTPI.org.

PRE-TEST ABOUT INSTRUCTIONAL SYSTEMS DESIGN (ISD)

Complete the following pre-test before you read the book. Use it as a diagnostic tool to help you assess your own need for instruction in instructional systems design (ISD). You may also use it as an advance organizer to refer you directly to topics in the book that are of special importance to you at this time.

The Pre-Test

Directions: Read each item in the Pre-Test below. Circle a True (T), a Not Applicable (N/A), or False (F) in the left column opposite each item. A T should represent that you feel fully competent; an F should indicate that you feel that you need more professional development on the topic. Spend about ten minutes on the pre-test. Be honest! Think of what you know about instructional design. When you finish, score and interpret the results using the instructions appearing at the end of the pre-test. Then be prepared to share your responses with others as a starting point for organizing your own development in ISD. If you would like to learn more about one item below, refer to the number in the right column to find the chapter in this book in which the subject is discussed.

The Questions

Circle your response
for each item below   *Chapter in the book in which the topic is covered*

How competent are you in:

T	N/A	F	1. Defining instructional systems design (ISD)?	**1**
T	N/A	F	2. Describing alternatives to instructional design?	**2**
T	N/A	F	3. Determining projects that are appropriate for instructional design?	**3**
T	N/A	F	4. Conducting a needs assessment?	**4**
T	N/A	F	5. Assessing relevant learner characteristics?	**5**
T	N/A	F	6. Analyzing relevant work setting characteristics?	**6**
T	N/A	F	7. Performing work analysis?	**7**
T	N/A	F	8. Writing performance objectives?	**8**
T	N/A	F	9. Developing performance measurements?	**9**
T	N/A	F	10. Sequencing performance objectives?	**10**
T	N/A	F	11. Specifying instructional strategies?	**11**
T	N/A	F	12. Selecting or designing instructional materials?	**12**
T	N/A	F	13. Evaluating instruction?	**13**
T	N/A	F	14. Designing the instructional management system	**14**
T	N/A	F	15. Planning and monitoring instructional design projects?	**15**
T	N/A	F	16. Communicating effectively?	**16**
T	N/A	F	17. Interacting with others?	**17**
T	N/A	F	18. Promoting the use of instructional design?	**18**
T	N/A	F	19. Developing yourself?	**19**
T	N/A	F	20. Being an Effective Instructional Designer?	**20**

_____ **Total**

Scoring and Interpreting the Pre-Test

Give yourself *1 point for each T* and a *0 for each F or N/A* listed above. Total the points from the *T* column and place the sum in the line opposite to the word **TOTAL** above. Then interpret your score as follows:

Score

Above 19 points	You feel fully competent in instructional design. While you can still develop professionally, you feel that you understand the basics quite well.
15 to 18 points	Improvements could be made to your feelings of competence in instructional design. On the whole, however, you feel that you are fairly well prepared.
12 to 14 points	You need to improve your understanding of points of instructional design. You should plan significant professional development.
Below 12 points	You need to plan significant professional development.

PART ONE

DETECTING AND SOLVING HUMAN PERFORMANCE PROBLEMS

CHAPTER ONE

WHAT IS INSTRUCTIONAL DESIGN?

Instructional design means more than literally creating instruction. It is associated with the broader concept of analyzing human performance problems systematically, identifying the root causes of those problems, considering various solutions to address the root causes, and implementing the solutions in ways designed to minimize the unintended consequences of corrective action. Instructional design usually encompasses not just the preparation of work-related instruction but also the selection of such management solutions to human performance problems as the preparation and use of job aids, the redesign of organizational structure and reporting relationships, the redesign of jobs and tasks, the refocusing of employee selection methods, the reengineering of job-related and task-related feedback methods, and the design and implementation of employee reward programs (Jacobs, 1987; Rothwell, 1996 and 2000; Rothwell, Hohne, and King, 2007).

As we use the term, instructional design is (1) an emerging profession, (2) focused on establishing and maintaining efficient and effective human performance, (3) guided by a model of human performance, (4) carried out systematically, (5) based on open systems theory, and (6) oriented to finding and applying the most cost-effective solutions to human performance problems and discovering quantum leaps in productivity improvement through human ingenuity. We follow the International Board of Standards for Training, Performance, and Instruction (IBSTPI) by making ten basic assumptions about instructional design and competencies associated with it. (See Exhibit 1.1.) In this chapter, we will explore each of the six characteristics identified above to lay the groundwork

EXHIBIT 1.1. TEN KEY ASSUMPTIONS ABOUT INSTRUCTIONAL DESIGN AND INSTRUCTIONAL DESIGN COMPETENCIES.

Assumption 1:	Instructional designers are those persons who demonstrate design competencies on the job regardless of their job title or training.
Assumption 2:	ID competencies pertain to persons working in a wide range of settings.
Assumption 3:	Instructional design is a process most commonly guided by systematic design models and principles.
Assumption 4:	Instructional design is most commonly seen as resulting in transfer of training and organizational performance improvement.
Assumption 5:	Instructional design competence spans novice, experienced, and expert designers.
Assumption 6:	Few instructional designers, regardless of their levels of expertise, are able to successfully demonstrate all ID competencies.
Assumption 7:	ID competencies are generic and amenable to customization.
Assumption 8:	ID competencies define the manner in which design should be practiced.
Assumption 9:	ID competencies reflect societal and disciplinary values and ethics.
Assumption 10:	ID competencies should be meaningful and useful to designers worldwide.

Source: R. Richey, D. Fields, and M. Foxon, *Instructional Design Competencies: The Standards* (3rd ed.). Syracuse, NY: ERIC Clearinghouse on Information and Technology, 2001, pp. 36–42. Copyright 1993 by the International Board of Standards for Training, Performance and Instruction. All rights reserved. Used with permission.

for the remainder of the book. We shall also address important recent critiques of traditional instructional design approaches.

Instructional Design: An Emerging Profession

Instructional design is an emerging profession. People can—and do—enter jobs as instructional designers and work in that capacity for their entire careers.

Employment advertisements for instructional designers and closely aligned jobs frequently appear in print and online. (See, for instance, the job search websites run by the International Society for Performance Improvement at www.ispi.org and by the American Society for Training and Development at www.astd.org.)

Many organizations across a broad spectrum of industries employ instructional designers. Jobs bearing this title are quite often positioned at the entry level. They occupy the first rung on a career ladder leading to such higher-level jobs as instructor, project supervisor of instructional design, and Chief Learning Officer (CLO). But variations of this career ladder do exist. Job titles also vary. Alternative job titles may include performance technologist, performance consultant, human performance improvement specialist, human performance enhancement professional, instructional developer, education specialist, employee educator, trainer, staff development specialist, instructional technologist, or instructional systems specialist. Because variations do exist in work duties, in modes of occupational entry, in educational preparation, and in career paths, instructional design should be regarded as an emerging rather than an established profession.

However, the recent trend has been toward certification in the field. That trend suggests increasing professionalism. For instance, the International Society for Performance Improvement has unveiled a program leading to the Certified Performance Technologist (CPT) designation (for a description, see www.certifiedpt .org/WhatisCPT.htm). It is being offered in cooperation with the American Society for Training and Development as well (see www.astd.org/CPT/). That follows a growing trend for certification of many kinds, ranging from individual (such as the CPT) to e-learning product certification (see www .astd.org/ecertification/). ASTD has also unveiled the Certified Performance and Learning Professional (CPLP) designation to certify in a broad range of areas of expertise in the field.

Instructional Design: Focused on Establishing and Maintaining Efficient and Effective Human Performance

The chief aim of instructional design is to improve employee performance and to increase organizational efficiency and effectiveness. For this reason, instructional designers should be able to define such important terms as performance, efficiency, and effectiveness.

What Is Performance?

Performance is perhaps best understood as the achievement of results, the outcomes (ends) to which purposeful activities (means) are directed. It is not synonymous with behavior, the observable actions taken and the unobservable decisions made to achieve work results. However, behavior can contribute to results and is therefore important in considering those results.

There are several types of performance, of course. *Human performance* is the result of human skills, knowledge, and attitudes. *Machine performance* is the result of machine activities. Capital performance is about financial results. *Company performance* is the result of organizational activities.

When asked to think about performance, most people in the United States think first of individual performance. There are at least two reasons why. First, people are sensitized to appraisals of individual performance because most organizations make evaluating performance an annual ritual, often linked to pay decisions. This practice has made a lasting impression on nearly everyone. Second, U.S. culture has long prized rugged individualism, implying that very little lies beyond the reach of determined heroes (and heroines) exerting leadership and acting alone. However, continuing trends point toward a sustained emphasis in the future on the performance of teams, groups, departments, divisions, or organizations. Those trends are as evident in the instructional design field—where team-based, and even virtual team-based (Bell and Kozlowski, 2002), instructional design is becoming more commonplace—as in other fields. That trend is likely to grow as global virtual teams work continuously, and often collaboratively through concurrent software, to design and deliver instruction.

Defining Efficiency and Effectiveness

Traditionally, two aspects of performance have been considered—efficiency and effectiveness. These terms have no universally accepted definitions. However, *efficiency* is usually understood to mean the ratio between the resources needed to achieve results (inputs) and the value of results (outputs). Some have said that the central question of efficiency can be posed simply: Are we doing things right? In this question, the phrase "doing things right" means "without unnecessary expenditures of time, money, or effort."

Effectiveness, on the other hand, usually means the match between results achieved and those needed or desired. Its central question is this: Are we doing the right things? In this question, the phrase "right things" typically means "what others, such as customers or key stakeholders, expect or need from the organization, group, or individual."

Instructional Design: Guided by a Model of Human Performance

Instructional design is guided by a model of human performance. In the most general sense, of course, a *model* is a simplified or abstract representation of a process, device, or concept. A model of any kind is designed to help understand a problem, situation, process, or device. It provides a basis for a common understanding, and common labels, for people to discuss the issue. This applies to a model of human performance, which is a simplified representation of factors involved in producing work results. It is intended to provide labels to key factors involved in performance and clues to pinpointing underlying causes of human performance problems.

Many human performance models have been constructed. They can be categorized as comprehensive or situation-specific. A *comprehensive performance model* includes as many factors as possible affecting human performance in organizational settings. An example is shown in Figure 1.1. Table 1.1 defines and briefly describes the factors appearing in Figure 1.1.

A *situation-specific performance model* focuses on an existing or suspected problem. One of the best known was first described in a classic treatment by

FIGURE 1.1. A COMPREHENSIVE MODEL OF HUMAN PERFORMANCE IN ORGANIZATIONS.

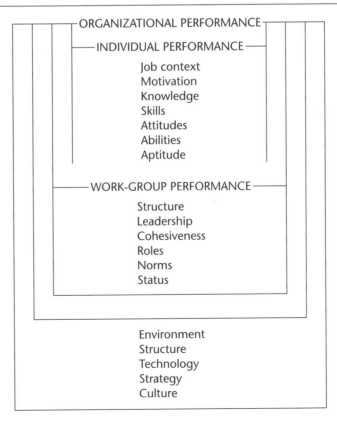

ORGANIZATIONAL PERFORMANCE

INDIVIDUAL PERFORMANCE

Job context
Motivation
Knowledge
Skills
Attitudes
Abilities
Aptitude

WORK-GROUP PERFORMANCE

Structure
Leadership
Cohesiveness
Roles
Norms
Status

Environment
Structure
Technology
Strategy
Culture

TABLE 1.1. FACTORS AFFECTING PERFORMANCE.

Factor	Brief Definition	Questions to Consider about the Influence of the Factor on Performance
Individual Performance		
Job context	The environment of the job, including supervisor(s), equipment and tools to be used, customers, and co-workers.	Do people have the necessary equipment, tools, and resources to perform?
Motivation	The desire to perform.	Do people want to perform?
Knowledge	Facts and information essential to performing a job or task.	Do people have the necessary facts and information they need to take action and make decisions?
Skills	Abilities to do things associated with successful job performance.	Can people do the things associated with successful job performance?
Attitudes	Feelings about performance that are voiced to other people.	How do people feel about their behavior?
Abilities	Present capabilities to behave in certain ways.	Do people possess the necessary talents and mental or physical characteristics?
Aptitude	The future capability to behave in certain ways.	Are people physically and/or mentally capable of learning how to perform?
Work-Group Performance		
Structure	The way work is allocated to members of a work group.	Is responsibility for results clearly assigned? Are people aware of what they are responsible for? Are they held accountable for achieving results?
Leadership	The way directions are given to members of a work group.	Is it clear who is in charge? Does the leader consider how people feel (attitudes) as well as what must be done to achieve results (tasks)?
Cohesiveness	The extent to which members of a work group are unified, pulling together as a group.	Are people willing to work together to achieve desired results?
Roles	The pattern of expected behaviors and results of each member of a group.	Do members of a group understand what they are responsible for doing?
Norms	Accepted beliefs of the work group.	How do members of a work group feel about the results they are to achieve? Methods of achieving those results?

(Continued)

Factor	Brief Definition	Questions to Consider about the Influence of the Factor on Performance
Status	The relative position of people in a group.	Do people have the formal authority to act in line with their responsibilities? Are other people willing to follow the lead of those who know what to do?
Organizational Performance		
Environment	The world outside the organization.	How well is the organization adapting to—or anticipating—changes outside it that affect it?
Structure	The way work is divided up and allocated to parts of the organization.	Is work divided up appropriately?
Technology	Actions taken by people to change objects, people, or situations. Often refers to "how the work is done."	Is the organization applying work methods that reflect current information about how to do the work?
Strategy	The means to achieve desired ends. It denotes an organization's long-term direction.	Is the organization competing effectively?
Culture	Beliefs and attitudes shared by members of an organization.	Do members of the organization share common beliefs and attitudes about what they—and the organization—should do?

Rummler (1976). (See Figure 1.2.) According to Rummler in a classic model, five factors should be considered whenever a human performance problem is identified. They are (1) the job situation, (2) the performer, (3) the behavior, (4) the consequence, and (5) the feedback of the consequence back to the performer. Rummler (1976, p. 14–23) observes that "in any job there is a situation or occasion requiring a particular performer to make a particular response or take some action, which results in some consequence to the performer. The performer may consider that consequence to be positive or negative or to have little value. And last, information on that consequence is fed back to the performer."

Rummler's classic model remains useful in analyzing human performance problems. After all, the root cause of the problem must be determined, and each factor in this simple model can be examined as a possible root cause. If it is not clear when the desired performance is necessary, the cause stems from the *job situation*. If performers are physically or mentally unable to perform, the cause stems from the *performers*. If performers lack the necessary skills or tools or

FIGURE 1.2. A SITUATION-SPECIFIC MODEL OF HUMAN PERFORMANCE.

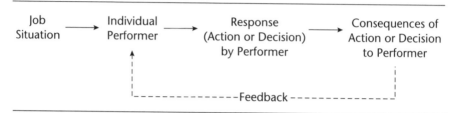

Source: Rummler, G., "The Performance Audit." In R. Craig (Ed.), *Training and Development Handbook: A Guide to Human Resource Development* (2nd ed.). New York: McGraw-Hill, 1976, pp. 14–23. Reproduced with the permission of McGraw-Hill, Inc.

other resources, the cause stems from the *response (behavior)*. If the consequences of performing are punishing or do not exist, the cause of the problem stems from the *consequences*. If performers are given no information about the value of their performance, then the problem's cause stems from *inadequate or nonexistent feedback*.

We will discuss models for analyzing human performance in greater detail in Chapter Two. For now, suffice it to say that instructional designers base what they do on a human performance model. Applying such a model to problem solving is the foundation of instructional design. After all, the field is associated with analyzing human performance problems systematically, identifying the root cause or causes of those problems, considering various solutions to address the root causes, and implementing the solutions in ways designed to minimize the unintended consequences of corrective action (Rothwell, 1996; Rothwell, Hohne, and King, 2007).

Instructional Design: Carried Out Systematically

Instructional design is not just a field. It may also be regarded as a process for examining human performance problems and identifying solutions. The process should not be carried out intuitively; rather, its success depends on systematic application. Instructional designers place their faith in an iterative and systematic process that, viewed holistically, is more powerful than any single part. At the same time, that process is not necessarily linear or step-by-step (Richey, 1995; Troha, 2002). Many different systematic instructional design models have been constructed to guide instructional designers in their work (see Harris and Castillo, 2002).

Instructional Design: Based on Open Systems Theory

Instructional design is based, in part, on open systems theory (Richey, 1993). An *open system* receives inputs from the environment, transforms them through operations within the system, submits outputs to the environment, and receives feedback indicating how well these functions are carried out. To survive, any open system must gain advantages from its transactions with the environment.

Inputs include raw materials, people, capital, and information. *Operations* are activities occurring within the organization that add value to raw materials. *Outputs* are services or finished goods released into the environment by the organization. Figure 1.3 illustrates these basic components of an open system.

All open systems share common characteristics. First, they are dependent on the external environment for essential inputs and reception of their outputs. Second, there is a pattern to the flow of inputs and outputs. Third, all but the simplest open systems are composed of subsystems and interact with environmental suprasystems. A subsystem is a system within a system. A *suprasystem* is an overarching system that includes more than one system.

As Katz and Kahn (1978) explain in their classic treatment of open systems theory, most organizations consist of four generic subsystems. (They are called "generic" because they are found in most organizations, regardless of industry or reporting relationships.) The first is the *production subsystem*, which focuses on getting the work out. The second is the *adaptive subsystem* that includes any functions concerned with helping the organization change its internal operations to adapt to external environmental change. The third is the *maintenance subsystem*, which is concerned with streamlining internal operations and increasing efficiency. The fourth and last is the *managerial subsystem*, concerned with directing

FIGURE 1.3. THE BASIC COMPONENTS OF AN ORGANIZATION AS AN OPEN SYSTEM.

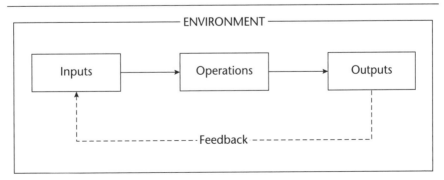

and coordinating the other three subsystems. Although organizations vary, in most firms the production or operations department exemplifies the production subsystem, the marketing department exemplifies the adaptive subsystem, the human resources department exemplifies the maintenance subsystem, and the top management team exemplifies the managerial subsystem.

Most organizations function within many suprasystems. Perhaps the most obvious is the *industry suprasystem*, composed of all organizations involved in the same basic type of work. There are also other, equally important, suprasystems. The *governmental-legal suprasystem*, for instance, is made up of all government agencies regulating the industry of which one organization is part. It also includes the applicable laws, rules, and regulations with which the organization must comply. The *marketing competitive suprasystem* is made up of all competitors, present and future. The *economic suprasystem* consists of the national and international economic environment within which the organization functions. The *technological suprasystem* is composed of the tools, state-of-the-art know-how, and work methods used in delivering the organization's services or producing goods. The *supplier suprasystem* comprises all suppliers providing inputs to an organization. Each suprasystem exerts influence on organizational performance.

Open systems theory is important to instructional designers for two reasons. First, instructional designers recognize the critical importance of adapting to, and even anticipating, changes in the environment. Organizational and individual effectiveness depends on how well work results match environmental demands. Hence, one question that should be asked in any performance improvement effort is this: How much will this project contribute to the organization's ability to adapt to changing environmental conditions? If the answer is "not much" or "we don't know," then it could well be that performance improvement activities should be directed to other projects.

Second, instructional designers recognize that any corrective action taken to change one subsystem will affect others. The parts of any organization (system) are as interdependent as the strands of a spider web. It follows, then, that a change in one part will affect others, just as an entire spider web vibrates when one strand is disturbed. For example, if a change is made in the kinds of people selected into a job category, it will affect the kind of training they should receive. Large system changes in organizations will have effects that are partially predictable—and partially unpredictable.

However, order exists even amid apparent random disorder, a central view held by advocates of complexity theory (Olson and Eoyang, 2001; Titcomb, 1998; You, 1993). Observers of the instructional design field have repeatedly emphasized that much can be learned from complexity theory. More specifically, complexity theory enriches the traditional open systems orientation of instructional design by "assuming a more holistic orientation, rather than one of uni-directional causality" and by "reflecting the dynamic and unpredictable aspects of the learning process" (Richey, 1995, pp. 100–101).

Instructional Design: Oriented to Finding and Applying the Most Cost-Effective Solutions to Human Performance Problems

Instructional designers sometimes assume, mistakenly, that their role is to "offer job-oriented instruction." Sometimes others in the organization share the same misconception of their role. In fact, human performance problems cannot always be solved by instruction. In fact, instruction should only be used when the performance problem stems from a lack of knowledge or skills or the wrong attitudes and when instruction is the most cost-effective solution. Since we will use the terms knowledge, skills, and attitudes throughout this book, perhaps some definitions are in order at this point. *Knowledge* is simply "what the employee knows. It is important in terms of jobs and training because people usually perform better if they understand what they are doing and why" (McArdle, 1989, p. 34). *Skills* involve the abilities to do something—such as operate a machine. "Skills imply actions; others can observe them" (McArdle, 1989, p. 34). The term *attitudes* denotes how people feel about what they do and how they express their feelings. Instructional designers "generally accept that how people feel about what they are doing and the organization for which they are working has some effect on their performance" (McArdle, 1989, p. 34). As work becomes more focused on making decisions, processing information, and servicing customers, attitudes—traditionally neglected by instructional designers in favor of knowledge and skills—are becoming more important in the mix of what leads to effective performance (Rothwell and Lindholm, 1999).

Instruction should not be used as the solution when a performance problem stems from lack of motivation, feedback, incentives, or some other cause. It is also a costly solution because it demands substantial investments of time and money to prepare effective instructional materials, test them, revise them, deliver them, and evaluate them. Employees receiving off-the-job instruction lose time doing work and are usually paid while learning, which adds to the cost. At the same time, instructional designers and others involved in the preparation of instructional materials must be paid, which further adds to the cost.

For all these reasons, work-oriented instruction is a costly way to improve performance. It should only be used as a solution of last resort. Indeed, instructional designers should be certain that there will be a favorable return on any investment in performance improvement efforts. To this end, they may apply any one of many different methods of cost-benefit forecasting and analysis to estimate the expected return (payoff) on the investment. First they estimate the cost of the performance problem. Then they estimate the expected costs to rectify the problem. Finally, they compare the two. If a return on investment takes too long, instructional designers should direct their attention to other projects in which the benefits are more certain, payoffs are higher, or results can be achieved faster.

Criticisms of Traditional Instructional Design Approaches

No field of endeavor is immune to criticism. That is as true of instructional design as it is of any field. Critics of traditional instructional system design (ISD) approaches have grown increasingly strident in their complaints about its real and perceived shortcomings. It is thus worthwhile to discuss early in this book the most serious concerns they have voiced.

In a classic article that launched a continuing debate, Merrill, Li, and Jones (1990) distinguished between First Generation Instructional Design, which they designate ID_1, and Second Generation Instructional Design, which they designate ID_2. ID_1 "assumes a cumulative organization of learning events based on prerequisite relationships among learned behaviors" (p. 7). ID_1 has long dominated the field but suffers from many limitations, according to the article's authors. For example, they believe it focuses on parts rather than integrated wholes, provides superficial advice for organizing instruction, adopts a closed-system view of instruction that disregards the environment in which instruction is carried out, asserts an unrealistic approach to instructional development, and produces instruction that is to learners passive (and thus boring) rather than active (and thus motivating).

To solve these problems, the authors argued that a new ID_2 paradigm is needed in the instructional design field. ID_2 will lend itself to "analyzing, representing, and guiding instruction to teach integrated sets of knowledge and skills." It will also suggest ways to select "interactive instructional strategies" and will be "an open system" that is "able to incorporate new knowledge about teaching and learning and to apply these in the design process." In addition, ID_2 should—among other innovations—"organize knowledge about instructional design and define a methodology for performing instructional design," provide "a series of intelligent computer-based design tools for knowledge analysis/acquisition, strategy analysis and transaction generation/configuration," and make use of "a collection of mini-experts, each contributing a small knowledge base relevant to a particular instructional design decision or set of such decisions" (Merrill, Li, and Jones, 1990, p. 10). More recently, Merrill has recommended a "pebble in the pond" approach that relies on key principles to guide instructional design (Merrill, 2002).

Other authorities in the instructional design field have joined the chorus calling for innovative new approaches to meet the daunting challenges facing today's instructional designers (see, for instance, Clark, 2002; Dick, 1993; Gustafson, 1993; Richey, 1993; Sink, 2002). One central dilemma, however, may not be that the field is in need of new models to guide instructional design but that existing models are not effectively applied. As Richey (1995, p. 97) succinctly frames the question: "Do the difficulties [with traditional approaches] stem simply from a pervasive need for more expertise in the use of the ISD models, or do they stem from the models themselves, or from the feasibility of their practical application?" Richey's view is that "the field is conservatively leaning in the direction of enhanced models" to meet future challenges. These models, while retaining essential and proven components of ID_1, will be designed and applied in ways that will minimize its shortcomings.

Additional critiques of the traditional ISD model have surfaced since year 2000 (Gordon and Zemke, 2000; Zemke and Rossett, 2002). Zemke and Rossett (2002) summarize the criticisms of the ISD model as boiling down to several key complaints. The first complaint is about the process. The point here is that "the ISD process itself is flawed." It is, the critics contend, too slow and overly analytical for a frenetically paced world. The second complaint is about the practice. Here the criticism is that "[ISD] is pushed beyond rational utility," write Zemke and Rossett (2002), "and made into a lock-step straitjacket. That, critics say, is exactly the problem." Of course, ISD does not need to be treated that way–but, the critics assert, it too often is treated that way. Third, technological innovations have rendered the ISD model out of touch. What may have worked for classroom-based training is not appropriate, or even desirable, for e-learning and many emerging instructional technologies. Indeed, the emergence of social networking websites in which individuals can communicate in real-time leads to increased pressure for real-time, instant-messaging-style instruction. (Popular social networking sites include MySpace.com, Facebook.com, hi5.com, Friendster.com, orkut, Bebo.com, and Netlog.com, many of which are available with multiple language versions.) As Zemke and Rossett (2002) note, "if traditional training is a challenge for ISD, there are those who believe it is more so for the new creative blends of online learning and performance support that are becoming prevalent today." Zemke and Rossett quote San Diego State University (SDSU) assistant professor Vanessa Dennen, who said that "ISD in the traditional sense looks tired . . . while the rest of the world is getting wired." But that view is not shared by everyone. Some believe that the problem with e-learning and other forms of technologically-dependent instruction, itself under attack, is its tendency to truncate necessary steps of analysis, design, development, implementation, and evaluation. The result is that sometimes, critics contend, instruction is thrown at problems that it can never solve because management action is needed instead.

But one thing is clear: there is considerable pressure to reduce the time it takes to deliver effective learning experiences. To the extent that the instructional design process appears to be slow and ponderous—which it does not have to be—the pressure is on to slash through slow turnaround times and experiment with rapid approaches to instructional design.

Conclusion

The instructional design field is an exciting one that has real potential to improve employee performance and thus enhance organizational productivity, increase competitiveness, and eliminate the problems faced by workers who lead lives of quiet desperation amid sometimes chaotic and irrational organizational settings. Instructional designers view their roles as more than just "preparing instruction." Instead, they see what they do as linked inexorably to one of continuous improvement of organizational conditions and operations. Their challenging role is to analyze human performance problems systematically, identify root causes of those problems, consider various solutions to address the root causes, and implement solutions in ways designed to minimize the unintended consequences of corrective action. While traditional instructional design models have been under attack for some time, almost everyone agrees that a systematic approach to instruction is better and more effective than unplanned, haphazard, or seat-of-the-pants approaches.

Our goal in the following chapters is to describe the competencies of instructional design work and provide the means by which practitioners can develop, or sharpen, their abilities.

CHAPTER TWO

ALTERNATIVES TO INSTRUCTIONAL SOLUTIONS

Five Frequent Options

The world is full of many problems. But solving those problems can be reduced to two key options. One option is to change individuals by equipping them with new knowledge, skills, or attitudes. That approach is the *instructional solution*. Another option is to change the organizational environment in which individuals carry out their work. Since management does (or should) control most environmental factors of organizations in which people carry out their work and strive to achieve results, any solution that is not an instructional solution may be properly regarded as a management solution. *Management solutions* thus include everything that could be done to affect human performance in organizations other than offering instruction or training.

Management solutions–which are sometimes called *noninstructional* or *non-learning solutions*—address human performance problems through means other than training, education, or development. While most books on instructional design do not treat these solutions, stakeholders of the instructional design process such as senior executives and operating managers are demanding that instructional designers broaden their focus to provide performance consulting and avoid restricting themselves to instructional solutions alone. We include this chapter to give instructional designers a rudimentary knowledge of management solutions. Our goal is not to be comprehensive in our scope, since there are myriad ways that an organization's decision-makers could address performance problems through means other than by offering instruction (see, for instance, Langdon, Whiteside, and McKenna, 1999; Rothwell, Hohne, and King, 2007). Nor can instructional designers expect to become specialists in all methods. Nobody can be everything to everyone. But instructional designers should know enough to diagnose root cause(s) and discover a list of possible solutions. From that point, competent assistance from other specialists may be warranted.

Many management solutions have been identified. But, for purposes of this chapter, we shall focus on five only: (1) feedback methods, (2) job performance aids, (3) reward systems, (4) employee selection practices, and (5) organizational redesign. These five solutions were chosen because instructional designers have often used them—in isolation or in combination (Jacobs, 1987). However, as many as fifty interventions have been well-documented (Langdon, Whiteside, and McKenna, 1999). In our summary of each of the five key noninstructional solutions, we will (1) describe what it is, (2) explain when it should be used, and (3) summarize how to apply the solution to human performance problems.

Feedback Options

Feedback is a continuous process of providing information about an activity, sometimes during the activity itself (Nadler, 1977). It serves two primary purposes. First, by stimulating people to continue doing more or less of what they are already doing, it influences the quantity of performance (Tosti, 1986). Second, by stimulating people to change how or what they do, it influences the quality of performance (Tosti, 1986). Feedback can be either *incidental*, that is, growing out of specific situations in a spontaneous way, or *intentional*, that is, growing out of situations deliberately designed to provide people with evaluative information about how or what they do. Substantial research evidence exists to support the value of improving feedback (Dean and Dean, 1994; Deterline, 1992; Jacobs, 1988; Kiger, 2001; Swinburne, 2001).

When Should Feedback Be Used to Address a Performance Problem?

Use feedback after thoughtfully pondering these questions (Rummler, 1983, p. 14): (1) Do employees receive enough information on the consequences of performing as desired? If the answer is no, provide feedback. (2) Are employees receiving accurate information on the consequences of performing as desired in a way that leads them to believe that their performance is correct? If the answer is no, improve the clarity and accuracy of feedback performers are receiving. (3) Are employees receiving timely information on the consequences of their performance so that it can be used in time to improve what they are doing or how they are doing it? If the answer is no, improve the timeliness of the feedback.

How Should Feedback Be Used in Solving Performance Problems?

The quantity and quality of feedback can be addressed through coaching, production wall charts, memorandums, team meetings, performance appraisals, 360-degree feedback, customer surveys, or even instant messaging. Each of these methods, and others, can affect the quantity or quality of feedback that employees receive about what they do, how well they do it, what results they achieve, or how well their work results match up to desired results. Any approach that can improve the clarity and timeliness of feedback ranks as significant in solving human performance problems.

Coaching occurs during work activities and is thus appropriate for improving employee behavior on a short-term—even minute-by-minute—basis. Although employees can (and sometimes do) coach each other, coaching is often done by supervisors, who offer their employees timely, immediate, and concrete feedback about performance. Coaching sessions may last between a minute and many hours. Effective coaches are supportive, expressing through body language as well as spoken word their confidence that the employee is capable of superior performance. Effective coaches are also able to make a point quickly, reinforce the importance of the point, establish (perhaps on the spot) a plan for improvement with the employee, gain employee commitment and willingness to change, deal effectively with excuses, describe the consequences of human performance problems, and maintain confidence in employee abilities over time (Stowell and Starcevich, 1987). That may include improving acces to informal social networks (Lahti, Darr, and Krebs, 2002). *Executive coaching* has emerged in recent years as an important performance improvement intervention to increase the interpersonal effectiveness of those in leadership positions.

Production wall charts are visual displays that provide immediate, concrete feedback to employees about their performance, often on a daily basis. They are thus appropriate for increasing feedback on how much or how well individuals or work groups are producing. The typical wall chart in a manufacturing firm, as one example, might illustrate individual or work-group piece rates, error rates, scrap rates, and various other information on a graph. The typical wall chart in a service firm, as another example, might illustrate the results of customer perception surveys about the quality of customer service or the incidence of customer complaints. With the feedback provided by these charts, employees are thus able to see tangible results from their work and can improve or change it based on the feedback they receive.

Memorandums are short, written directives to employees. They provide practical, how-to-do-it guidance on handling common or unique problem situations. In many cases, they are prompted by a mistake made by an otherwise good, experienced performer and thus serve as feedback intended to change what employees do or how they do it. They may be delivered via print or electronic media such as email.

Team meetings are vehicles for giving feedback to all members of a work group about what they are doing or how well they are performing. Team meetings also provide a means of increasing group cohesiveness by building a sense of "psychological closeness" among members of a group. High group cohesiveness is equated with increased group performance when group goals coincide with organizational goals. Much attention has been focused on methods of conducting successful team meetings—and "team building," which is the process of increasing the work group cohesiveness.

Performance appraisal is an excellent tool, in theory at least, for providing individuals with structured feedback. Just as job descriptions outline major job activities, appraisals measure how well employees carried out those activities in a given time period. Performance appraisal is continuous—people are always appraising employee performance—even when no formal performance appraisal process exists in an organization. In many organizations, formal appraisals are often conducted on a cycle, usually once a year. While too infrequent to substitute for the spontaneous feedback provided by supervisors or co-workers to employees on daily work performance, appraisals are appropriate for uncovering and highlighting long-term performance trends and developmental opportunities.

Unfortunately, performance appraisals are not always effective in providing structured feedback to employees. There are many reasons why, and those reasons may provide clues to why nearly one-third of all HR practitioners were identified in one study to be unhappy with their organizations' appraisal programs (Joinson, 2001). Some appraisal systems are designed to accomplish too much. They may be intended to provide evaluative feedback on past performance, plan future career advancement, justify salary actions, and assess training needs. Sometimes the appraisal systems themselves lack top management support, fail to provide a method for establishing performance standards at the beginning of the appraisal cycle, discourage give-and-take discussions between employee and supervisor in favor of one-sided meetings led by the supervisor, and lack clear job relatedness. To be effective, an appraisal system must be designed to overcome these common problems.

A recent trend has been to move away from isolated performance appraisal to adopt an entire performance management system. While *performance management* is sometimes a term in search of meaning, it can mean "an ongoing communication process, undertaken in partnership, between an employee and his or her immediate supervisor that involves establishing clear expectations and understanding about the essential job functions the employee is expected to do, how the employee's job contributes to the goals of the organization, what 'doing the job well' means in concrete terms, how employee and supervisor will work together to sustain, improve, or build on existing employee performance, how the job will be measured, and identifying barriers to performance and removing them" (Bacal, 1999, pp. 3–4). The implications of that approach are clear: to avoid performance problems by creating a system by which good performance is planned, tracked, and followed up.

One special approach to gathering and giving feedback, used by 90 percent of Fortune 1000 companies (Atwater and Waldman, 1998), is *360-degree feedback*. It takes its name from the number of degrees in a circle. Many approaches to 360-degree feedback rely on written or electronic instruments to collect perceptions about individuals from those surrounding them in a circle of acquaintances, including their supervisors, co-workers, subordinates, customers, and even family members (Dubois and Rothwell, 2000). However, the same idea can be applied by other means, such as by using group activities and even electronic groupware. A key strength of 360-degree feedback is its face validity. Its results are often compelling evidence to those receiving them, and it can often motivate people to want to change. A key weakness of 360-degree feedback is that it is only as effective as the quality of information available to those recording their perceptions. In other words, if people do not know enough about you to offer good feedback, then their views may be flawed.

Customer surveys provide feedback to all members of the organization—managers and employees alike—about how well the organization is meeting the needs of people it is intended to serve. This information can be most useful in planning for future performance improvement, for both the individual and the organization. Customer surveys can be conducted by enclosing written questionnaires with products, telephoning customers some time after product (or service) delivery, visiting customers on-site, offering toll-free hot-line numbers for questions or help, or providing large-scale written questionnaires to an organization's mailing list of past customers. Of course, an entire range of strategies going well beyond mere customer surveys may be used to obtain information about customer satisfaction, since customers often do not know the precise causes of the poor or suboptimal service they receive. Hunger for feedback has prompted organizations in addition to service-oriented firms to seek such customer information.

Job Performance Aids

According to Joe Harless (1986) in a classic treatment, a *job performance aid* is "a mechanism that stores information external to the user, guides the performance of work, and meets these requirements: (1) Can be accessed and used in real time (employed during actual performance of the task); (2) Provides signals to the performer when to perform the task or increments of the task (stimuli); (3) Provides sufficient direction on how to perform each task (responses); and (4) Reduces the quantity and/or time the information may be recalled (reduces access of memory)" (p. 108). In a memorable quotation that emphasizes the simplicity and value of job performance aids—sometimes simply called job aids—Harless (1985, p. 5) once remarked that "inside every fat course is a thin job aid crying to get out."

Job aids provide employees with guidance on how to perform in the work context (Finnegan, 1985). They cost significantly less to prepare and use than training, and some experimentation has even been done in using job aids during instruction to accelerate the learning process to reduce training time (Spaulding, 1997). Job aids are easier than training to revise under swiftly changing work conditions. Of course, job aids can be used in conjunction with training to help ensure transfer of training from classroom to job. This is why canny instructional designers sometimes deliberately create "trainee workbooks" or "job checklists" that lend themselves easily to being taken out of a training classroom and used immediately on the job (Harless, 1986).

When Should Job Performance Aids Be Used to Address Performance Problems?

Job aids are appropriate when the consequences of errors are great, procedures are complicated, work tasks are not frequently performed, the time for training is limited, and the budget for training is also limited (Finnegan, 1985). But they are inappropriate when employees have no time during work tasks to refer to them or when an employee's credibility with customers will be undercut by referring to a job aid during performance of a work task. Nor are they appropriate when the consequences of errors are not great, work procedures are simple, and employees frequently perform the task.

How Should Performance Job Aids Be Designed and Used?

Virtually anything that provides on-the-spot, practical guidance can be considered a job aid, such as cues built into the questions on an application form that explain what information is being requested (Rossett and Gautier-Downes, 1991;

Smillie, 1985). Examples of job aids include cleaning instructions sewn into clothing, lights on automobile instrument panels, operators' manuals provided with personal computers, and warnings on medicine bottles (Rothwell and Sredl, 2000). However, the most familiar job aids include checklists, decision aids, algorithms, procedure manuals, and work samples (Jacobs, 1987; Lineberry and Bullock, 1980; Tilaro and Rossett, 1993). Recent attention has also focused around simple online job aids (Strandberg, 1999) and around real-time performance support provided by instant messaging, ipods, wikipedias, or other aids.

Checklists are simple to design and are widely applicable to any activity (such as an organization's procedures) that must be performed in a sequence. To create a checklist, begin by listing tasks of an activity or procedure in the order they are supposed to be performed. Label the column above the tasks "Tasks to Perform." Then add another column for responses, such as "yes," "no," and "not applicable to this situation." Label the column "Responses: Did You Do?" Be as short in your task descriptions as possible to keep the checklist simple. If most employees are making the same mistakes, add notes for clarification of tasks.

Algorithms are usually visual representations, often resembling flowcharts, of steps to take in an activity or procedure (Horabin and Lewis, 1978). If employees follow an algorithm precisely, they should not be able to deviate easily from correct performance. Developing an algorithm closely resembles the process of developing a checklist. Start with a task analysis and identify alternative actions in each step of an activity or procedure. Then flowchart the steps, depicting precisely what choices are available to a performer and what consequences will result from each choice. Use an algorithm only for short procedures, since lengthy ones will require many pages to flowchart.

Procedure manuals are step-by-step instructions for carrying out work activities. They are intended to serve as practical "how to" references, organized around typical work duties or problem situations, and are meant to be consulted by performers as need arises. To develop a procedure manual, begin with a comprehensive list of organizational policies or work-related problems. Conduct a separate task analysis or procedure analysis on each policy or problem activity. Then write step-by-step guidelines on what to do to comply with each policy or solve each work-related problem.

Procedure manuals are often written with the aid of the *playscript technique*, which takes its name from the highly structured scripts used in theatrical productions. A procedure that is described by means of the playscript technique lists steps in chronological order from beginning to end and uses columns with headings such as "When?," "Who?," and "Does What?" Items in the "When" column describe the conditions under which action should be taken or the time it should be taken. Items in the "Who" column affix responsibility for taking action. Items in the "Does What" column describe what steps should be taken.

While potentially useful for providing on-the-spot guidance to workers, procedure manuals are often tough to keep up-to-date. (When out of date, they create more of a performance problem than they solve.) Of course, they can always be computerized for ease in updating. When they are computerized and placed online, they become a computer-based referencing system.

Work samples are examples of work that can be used by employees to save time or imitate a previously successful work product. It is easy to cite examples of them. Lawyers use work samples when consulting books filled with prewritten contracts. Secretaries use work samples when they pull a letter from a disk and revise it to handle a similar situation. Auditors use work samples when they prepare an "exemplary audit report" and then follow it when subsequently asked to prepare reports. If employees can see an example of something that has been done correctly, they can often replicate it closely in similar situations in the future. That saves time, money, and effort while obtaining reliable results. Employee performance can be documented through work samples contained in online or paper work portfolios.

Reward Systems

A *reward system* is the organization's way of tying employee actions to positive consequences. You might think of it as the means by which an organization attracts people to join, keeps them working, and motivates them to train or perform (Bishop, 1988b). Rewards are the positive consequences that (presumably) greet individual performance that is consistent with organizational goals. Motivation means simply "the desire to perform." It governs human choices of behavior and action (Vroom, 1964), and it is related to rewards because people choose to perform what they are rewarded for doing. While theories of rewards and human motivation differ, almost everyone agrees that employees tend to do what they are rewarded for doing, will avoid what they are punished for doing, and will neglect what they are neither punished nor rewarded for doing (Kerr, 1975). And managers are sometimes too limited in their thinking about how to reward performers for what they do (Falcone, 2002).

Managers do not always consider employee rewards or motivation when carrying out such typical management functions as planning, organizing, scheduling, delegating, controlling, budgeting, communicating, or staffing (Lawler, 1977). As a result, rewards do not always match up with desired performance, and the impact on performance is predictably negative. In contrast, organizations typified by a culture of "excellence" tend to match rewards to organizational goals and desired results (Kerr and Slocum, 1988). At the same time, care must be taken to avoid unethical manipulation of human beings by using a mechanistic "carrot-and-stick" approach that promises rewards for performance and punishments for nonperformance ("Rethinking Rewards," 1993). Several important works have been published about reward systems in the last few years (Chew and Chong, 1999; Kerr, 1999; Lei, Slocum, and Pitts, 1999; Zingheim and Schuster, 2002).

When Should Rewards Be Used in Addressing a Performance Problem?

Rewards or work consequences should be reviewed when planning any change that will affect the organization, work group, individual, or job. Instructional designers should be sure to pose the following question before the change is implemented and consider the answer carefully: "What's in it for the performer if he or she does what is asked?" To perform successfully, people must feel they will be able to succeed. They must also expect to receive some reward—and must value this reward (Vroom, 1964). To complicate matters, individuals may vary in their perceptions of these issues, however.

When troubleshooting existing human performance problems, instructional designers should pose these questions to identify a problem caused by a poorly designed reward system: (1) Is the problem caused by obstacles in the work environment rather than by a lack of skills on the part of the individual? (2) Before performing, does the employee expect not to be rewarded—or even to be treated negatively—as a result of performing as desired? (3) Are the consequences of performing without much perceived value to the employee? (4) Do employees find the consequences of performing as desired negative (punishing), or neutral (no results), or positive (important)? If the answer to any of these questions (with the exception of the last part of question 4) is yes, then the performance problem is attributable, in whole or part, to a poorly designed reward system.

How Should Incentive Systems Be Used to Address a Performance Problem?

In a classic article on incentive systems, Kemmerer and Thiagarajan (1989, p. 11) note that all incentive systems "should be intentional, external, and standardized." By intentional, they mean that incentives should be deliberately designed to encourage a performance that is consistent with job or organizational goals. By external, they mean that rewards should generally be controlled and monitored by management levels within the organization. By standardized, they mean that all reward systems "should specify a standard procedure that identifies the employees, activities, and incentives—and the relationships among them" (p. 11). Employees in an organization may be categorized into groups or teams, the activities and accomplishments of each group or team may be identified as they contribute to organizational goals, and each group or team may be rewarded in line with its accomplishments.

Whenever approaching a performance problem, instructional designers should always consider the consequences to performers of achieving results desired by an organization. Any intentionally designed incentive system may have been established to achieve from one to four possible goals: (1) contribute to attracting people to an organization, (2) encourage people to remain with the organization, (3) encourage people to behave in certain ways—such as follow standard operating procedures or apply creativity, or (4) encourage people to achieve work results desired by an organization. If the consequences of performing result in none of these, then it is unlikely that the performance is being intentionally encouraged by the organization. But it should be, if the performance is valued.

Various incentives may be matched to desired work results (Nelson, 1994; Robinson, 1994). In general, they can be classified as monetary incentives (sometimes called extrinsic rewards) or nonmonetary incentives (or intrinsic rewards).

Employee Selection Practices

Effective *employee selection practices* involve matching people to work for which they are qualified. Employee recruitment, a related activity, involves seeking individuals who are qualified for the work and encouraging them to participate in the selection procedure. In these processes, managers in most organizations begin by analyzing work activities. They then infer from those activities the knowledge, skills, and attitudes necessary for applicants to learn the job quickly, recruit people from sources where they can acquire the necessary knowledge or skills, and screen individuals until the best-qualified candidate is matched to the work (Arvey and Faley, 1988). Human resource managers are particularly well equipped to provide insight into methods of improving selection and recruitment practices.

If there is a single step that most organizations can take to improve human performance, improving selection and recruitment methods might well be it (Burk and Birk, 2001). Employee selection is an excellent leverage point to begin averting human performance problems. Instructional designers can help to do that by describing the work and/or the most successful people who perform it, analyze that work and/or the most successful performers, and establish selection criteria appropriate for choosing people best able to do the work.

Selection methods influence training because the knowledge, skills, and attitudes that individuals bring to work influence what they must learn to perform competently. If experienced people are hired, training time should be reduced. Of course, the organization will generally have to pay a premium on salaries for experienced people. If inexperienced people are hired, training time should be increased. The organization will also be able to pay less for salaries.

When Should Selection Practices Be Used to Address a Performance Problem?

Corrective action should be taken to improve organizational selection practices when most or all of the following symptoms are evident: (1) turnover is high; (2) involuntary termination rates are increasing from their historical rates in the organization; (3) employees are complaining that, at the time they were recruited for or placed in their current positions, they were not expecting the work activities they subsequently encountered; and (4) supervisors and managers are complaining that their employees are ill-equipped, even after training, to perform duties for which they are accountable.

How Should Selection Methods Be Used to Address a Performance Problem?

If instructional designers have reason to believe that human performance problems in an organization stem in whole or in part from selection methods—or believe changes in selection methods can contribute to solving existing human performance problems—then they should focus their attention on each major step in the organization's selection process. They should begin by examining recruitment, job or work analysis, selection tools, and selection results.

Recruitment is the process of attracting people to the organization. There are two labor pools from which to recruit: (1) inside the organization, and (2) outside the organization. Examine methods presently being used to recruit from both sources. Is any long-term, continuous effort being made to identify and target sources of talent, both internal and external, for entry-level vacancies in the future, or do decision makers wait until vacancies exist and then scurry around madly looking for people to fill them? If the latter is the case, work to improve external recruitment by establishing internship programs with local schools, work-study programs with government agencies, and adopt-a-school efforts to build ties with local sources of talent. Run employment advertisements even when no vacancies exist simply to keep a large and current inventory of applications on file to use as the need arises. Make sure that recruitment efforts are targeted, as much as possible, at sources of talent appropriate for meeting the organization's needs. Establish an employment brand by exploring why people remain with an organization, rather than focusing solely on exit interviews as an indicator of why people leave. At the same time, establish internal job posting and career improvement programs so that employees can gradually qualify for advancement in the organization.

Recruitment may also be focused on two kinds of employment opportunities: long-term and short-term. Long-term workers are hired for extended time spans. Short-term workers are employed on a temporary or contingent basis. Examine methods used to select people for each kind of employment opportunity. Be sure to look closely at how short-term workers are matched up to work assignments and are briefed on what to do, how to do it, and why it is worth doing. If the work performance of short-term workers differs dramatically from that of long-term workers, then take steps to improve screening procedures.

Job analysis is the process of identifying work activities in the organization (McCormick, 1979). The result of a job analysis is a job description, which literally describes what people should be responsible for doing and what results they should achieve. When addressing a performance problem that may be caused by poor selection methods, examine the completeness, accuracy, and currency of existing job descriptions (Bishop, 1988a). Do they provide clues, as they should, for identifying the knowledge, skills, and attitudes needed for successful job performance? Do they provide criteria for evaluating the education and experience of applicants relative to the knowledge, skills, and attitudes needed for successful job performance? If not, work toward updating job descriptions or making them more complete or accurate. Start by consulting the *Dictionary of Occupational Titles* (1991) or its online equivalent o'net (at www.onet.gov). Then refer to other print and online references that can be helpful in preparing job descriptions.

Although job analysis has traditionally (and unfortunately) been associated with rigidly defined and bureaucratically administered notions of "jobs" as "finite boxes full of work activities," it can still be most useful in team-based organizations or in other settings where traditional notions of jobs are being supplanted by more flexible views of work design. In the latter settings, job analysis can be directed to team rather than to individual responsibilities and outputs.

Selection tools are methods for structuring information or evaluating applicants relative to work requirements. They include application blanks, selection tests, and structured guides for interviewing job applicants. Written pre-employment tests, in particular, have been the subject of substantial litigation since the Civil Rights Act of 1964 because the results may "exhibit a sizeable mean difference in test scores between black and white employees" (Arvey and Faley, 1988, p. 317). Even though recent court cases have made the legal status of pre-employment tests equivocal, there is research evidence to support the desirability of using multiple selection tools instead of relying simply on unstructured job interviews. In some cases, major improvements can be made in selection practices simply by substituting highly structured for unstructured employment interviews through the use of a job performance aid called an employment interview guide.

Selection results are consequences of recruitment and selection methods. Typical results may include separation (firings or resignations), retention in the present position, or movement within the organization. Take care to examine separations, both voluntary and involuntary, before and after any change in selection procedures. Try to predict, in advance, what effects will be created by a change in selection methods.

Selection results may also include the proportion of protected groups within the organization compared to those in the general population from which the organization recruits and hires. While United States Supreme Court rulings have raised doubts at this writing about the future of disparate impact—defined as otherwise neutral selection practices that have a consequence of adversely affecting employment of protected groups—socially responsible organizations support voluntary diversity-enhancing efforts to seek out and employ members of protected labor groups such as women, minorities, and the disabled.

For this reason, many organizations take affirmative action to recruit, hire, train, and promote people in protected labor categories. Organizations may also support diversity programs to build appreciation for differences among workers. Any changes in selection practices should be made only after considering what effects (if any) they will have on efforts to support social equality in human resources practices.

Approaches to selection have been complicated by a tendency to use more part-time or contingent workers. Some observers believe that "jobs"—in the sense of finite clusters of work activities—are a thing of the past (Bridges, 1994). In some organizations, self-directed teams undertake an entire work process, and each worker is responsible for achieving all goals established for the team. While that generally produces enlarged jobs, it also complicates the process of defining what people should learn and how their individual performance should be judged.

Organizational Redesign

Organization design refers to the process of establishing reporting relationships and command structure. It determines who has authority to make what decisions and who is responsible for achieving what results. *Organizational redesign* is the process of changing "assigned goals, responsibilities, and reporting relationships within a given organization" (Rummler, 1986, p. 212). Although typically connoting changes in the organization's structure (reporting relationships), organizational redesign in a broader sense may include any change in the structure of an organization, division, department, work unit, team, or job (Conference Board, 1989). It may thus incorporate *job* or *work redesign*, which is the process of changing "the contents, methods, and relationships of jobs to satisfy both organizational and individual requirements" (Gibson, Ivancevich, and Donnelly, 1985, p. 16). Job or work redesign can be synonymous with work restructuring.

There is a substantial body of literature on organizational design and redesign, including much impressive research (Campion and McClelland, 1993; Carr, 1990; Chase and Tansik, 1983; Conference Board, 1989; Duncan, 1994; Galbraith, Downey, and Kates, 2001; Jewell and Jewell, 1992; Lawler, 1996; Morabito, Sack, and Bhate, 1999; Nystrom and Starbuck, 1983; Pearce and David, 1983; Rummler, 1986; Rummler and Brache, 1995.). This research leaves little doubt that organizational design affects organizational and individual performance. Less certain is what the relationship is, how much it is affected by the personal motives of those establishing organizational designs, and what unpredictable results can stem from changes made to those designs.

When Should Organizational Redesign Be Used to Address a Performance Problem?

Consider organizational redesign as a possible solution to human performance problems when the following symptoms are evident: (1) confusion about job responsibilities; (2) vague or unclear job descriptions; (3) outdated organization charts; (4) unclear relationships between the organization's stated strategic goals and its structure; (5) complaints from supervisors and managers about overseeing too many people or too many different jobs; (6) pockets of "burned out" employees doing boring work, too much work, or too little work; (7) inefficient workflow, resulting in inefficient steps, unnecessary complexity, or other wasteful uses of resources; or (8) inability by the organization to adapt swiftly to dynamic conditions in the external environment, such as new competitors or unusual requests from customers or suppliers.

How Should Organizational Redesign Be Used
to Address a Performance Problem?

Rummler (1986), in a classic treatment, outlines specific steps for instructional designers to follow in organizational redesign that remain very useful. First, he suggests determining where there is a need to redesign the structure of jobs in the organization or the collection of activities a job is made up of. Redesign should be considered, he notes, only when the organization is experiencing a performance problem in responding to external demands or in using resources efficiently.

Second, he recommends examining the primary responsibilities of each major structural component of the organization—division, department, or work unit—to identify key problems affecting each component and describe the flow of work passing through the organizational system. Third, he suggests preparing alternate and improved models of workflow. Fourth, he emphasizes the importance of establishing a mission (purpose statement) and goals (desired results) for the new, major structural components illustrated on the organization chart. Fifth, he recommends drawing up a new organization chart (structure) for the organization based on environmental demands and efficient workflow. Sixth and finally, he urges that the process of establishing new missions and goals down the organization's chain of command be continued until each division, department, and job is included.

Rummler's suggestions for organizational redesign are quite logical. Similar suggestions are offered in the literature of strategic business planning, business process reengineering, and job redesign. Unfortunately, organizational redesign is as much a political issue affecting the power of individual managers as it is an efficiency issue affecting an organization's ability to survive in its environment. Consequently, logical approaches do not always prevail and are sometimes sacrificed to the whims of self-interested managers.

Jacobs (1987), in a classic treatment, describes several ways to carry out organizational redesign. He suggests (1) changing reporting relationships; (2) improving information sharing; (3) defining job responsibilities; (4) changing job responsibilities; (5) changing goals, objectives, or standards; and (6) increasing information available about workflow systems.

Changing reporting relationships, or reorganization, means altering who reports to whom. It is the one method most commonly associated with organizational redesign. It should be used carefully because changing the leaders of various organizational components can have unintended and negative side effects. For instance, subordinating one activity or department or manager to another inevitably reduces the emphasis placed on the subordinated activity or department and can create another management layer through which approvals must pass.

Improving information sharing means finding ways to increase relevant, job-related information about workflow in an organization. To achieve this goal, conduct a communication audit. Using a standardized questionnaire and approach to analyzing organizational communication, examine what information—and how much—flows between work units. In addition, examine how and when information is communicated. Conducting such examinations can be easier at a time when computerized communication, such as electronic mail, is on the increase and lends itself to analysis more easily than interpersonal communication does.

Defining job responsibilities has to do with analyzing what people do, how they do it, and what results are desirable in line with organizational goals. When responsibilities or work goals are vague, employee and organizational performance can be improved simply by describing what people do. In practical terms, it means creating job descriptions when they do not exist, revising those that are outdated, or communicating to employees for what job responsibilities they are accountable.

Changing job responsibilities is sometimes appropriate to address human performance problems caused by boring jobs. Use job enrichment to add tasks to jobs so that they will become more interesting and will require employees to exercise increased responsibility. Job enrichment is a method of creating a qualitative change in responsibilities. To address human performance problems caused by jobs with a limited range of tasks, use job enlargement to add more of the same kinds of tasks to the job. This is a means of creating quantitative change in responsibilities. To address human performance problems caused by shortages of staff in key positions—a common problem as organizations downsize—use job rotation to relieve monotony and cross-train several workers for key jobs.

Changing goals, objectives, or standards is a means of shifting accountability for a job, work unit, department, division, or organization. A *goal* is derived from a statement of purpose that addresses the reason for the existence of a job or organization. It is usually expressed in general, rather than in specific and measurable, terms. An *objective* is derived from a goal. It is specific and measurable. It describes what must be achieved in a given period of time and how good achievement is defined. A *standard* is a minimum expectation of performance, usually expressed in measurable terms. By changing goals, objectives, or standards, decision makers can also change the direction of an organization or organizational component.

Increasing information available about workflow systems means helping people understand how each part of an organization contributes to the products made or services delivered. There are many ways to achieve this purpose. In some organizations, for instance, managers provide their employees with published "directories" that list "who to call for help" on specific, common problems. In other organizations, expert systems have been established to guide nontechnical workers through the steps of answering a customer's technical question or through troubleshooting common problems with equipment. In still other organizations, company newspapers run articles periodically on each department so that employees will know what each department does and how work flows through it.

What Is New in Alternatives to Instructional Design?

It just makes sense to ask, if traditional instructional design has such flaws and is prone to so much criticism, what might be a workable alternative to it?

Several ideas have been proposed.

One alternative to traditional instructional design is to substitute another instructional design model for the ISD model, described in later chapters. The goal is to place more of the burden for the instructional design process on training participants and on their managers. For example, Rothwell (1999) proposed reinventing the action learning model so that it could be used both as a format for employee development and as an alternative model to instructional design. In this approach, a team is formed of individuals to attack a business problem, formulate a vision, address an issue, or meet or formulate a goal. By this definition, for instance, a team would be formed to develop a new company orientation program—a task traditionally left to instructional designers and to HR professionals. The team members would include both those needing development and those who could contribute to the goal of the team. In designing an orientation program, for instance, new hires and supervisors who oversee many new hires would be good candidates to include on that team. The reason: They are keenly aware of the problems faced by new hires and highly motivated to solve those problems. While working with an instructional designer on the team to benchmark other orientation programs and learn about instructional design, they would both accomplish a goal—that is, creating a new program—while also learning about what is necessary to build effective training. When the training program is eventually rolled out, it would gain much credibility from the participation of new hires and key supervisors. Hence, the effort would gain in two ways: (1) individuals on the team would be developed by learning about training; and (2) the organization would gain because the training would have more credibility. The advantage of this approach is to build involvement and thereby gain buy-in from key stakeholders. It has been shown anecdotally to work best with so-called soft skills training, such as diversity training or sexual harassment avoidance training. But the disadvantage is that workers and their managers may resist efforts to participate on action learning teams. Without proper persuasion about the value of the effort beforehand—and proper accountability or rewards established—workers and their managers may believe that they do not need designers because they are doing the training department's job. That is not true, but it may be what is perceived. Care must be taken to avoid that perception and demonstrate that action learning results in two benefits, rather than one. Participation on the team itself is a way of building competencies.

A second alternative to traditional instructional design is rapid prototyping. In rapid prototyping it is assumed that early efforts on any new venture will fail. The goal is to reduce the time it takes to introduce an innovation, try it out, learn from it, and let it fail. But then subsequent efforts, in accelerated fashion, are introduced. The goal is to accelerate practical experience in solving a problem by speeding up the learning curve. Eventually, the theory goes, a subsequent experiment in prototyping will lead to success. This approach has been tried in instructional design project. New training is rapidly prepared, field-tested, and then a new enhancement is quickly rolled out. The advantage of this approach is speed; the disadvantage is that using this approach could undermine the credibility of instructional designers by showing that many efforts are required for them to achieve a successful instructional design. Multiple efforts may be perceived as wasteful of time and resources by those who do not understand or appreciate the value of the approach.

A third alternative to traditional instructional design is to rely on increasingly available software to produce so-called concurrent instructional design. Using software that permits many people to participate at the same time in writing or designing the same training needs assessment procedures, develop instructional plans, select or prepare instructional materials, or devise evaluation procedures and instruments, concurrent instructional design usually involves a virtual team that works together—often in real-time—to produce the same learning experience. For instance, instructional designer could meet online to produce an e-learning program. Working together—and perhaps over vast geographical distances—they produce a product together online. This approach has the advantage of diminishing the time it takes for individual team members to produce a product or finish an entire project. The disadvantage is that it requires a careful project plan and effective ongoing group facilitation so that an online free-for-all is avoided and the group members approach their tasks in a focused way.

The goal of most alternatives to traditional instructional design is to cut the cycle time needed to finish effective instructional projects. Much experimentation is going on to that end. Some experimentation focuses on using new, popular developments on the web, such as blogs and wikipedias. Some leverage technology so that people can meet online with concurrent software or use videoconferences or teleconferences so as to avoid the difficulties of scheduling face-to-face meetings with people who are rarely available at the same time. Some leverage new technologies such as iPods, iPhones, cell phone screens, or other recent technological developments to deliver instruction to busy participants who may not have time to participate in classroom or even online instruction.

Conclusion

Management solutions should be chosen when human performance problems are caused by deficiencies in the environment. They should also be used when they are more cost effective than such instructional solutions as training, education, or development for addressing deficiencies in knowledge, skills, or attitudes. As we pointed out in this chapter, five management (noninstructional) solutions are frequently used: (1) feedback methods, (2) job performance aids, (3) reward systems, (4) employee selection practices, and (5) organizational redesign. However, many others are available for consideration when warranted by the root cause of a human performance problem (Langdon, Whiteside, and McKenna, 1999). Each management solution is appropriate for addressing only certain human performance problems, and we provided guidelines for selecting when to use each noninstructional solution. We also described specific ways to improve feedback methods, prepare job performance aids, redesign reward systems, reexamine employee selection practices, and redesign organizational reporting relationships.

CHAPTER THREE

DETERMING PROJECTS APPROPRIATE FOR INSTRUCTIONAL DESIGN SOLUTIONS

This chapter focuses on analyzing human performance problems systematically and identifying their root causes, activities that instructional designers typically call performance analysis or front-end analysis. (For simplicity's sake, we use the term *performance analysis* throughout.) Performance analysis is carried out to distinguish problems, situations, or projects appropriate for instructional solutions, such as job-specific training, from those that are more appropriately addressed through management (noninstructional) solutions. It is often regarded as an important role for anyone in the field whose focus is on getting results (Rothwell, 2000).

According to *The Standards* (Richey, Fields, and Foxon, 2001, pp. 48–49), one competency for instructional design is to "conduct a needs assessment." It is regarded as an essential competency. The performance statements associated with this competency indicate that instructional designers should be able to (Richey, Fields, and Foxon, 2001, pp. 48–49):

a. Describe the problem and its dimensions, identifying the discrepancies between current and desired performance (essential).
b. Clarify the varying perceptions of need and their implications (essential).
c. Select and use appropriate needs assessment tools and techniques (essential).
d. Determine the possible causes of the problem and potential solutions (essential).

e. Recommend and advocate non-instructional solutions when appropriate (advanced).

f. Complete a cost benefit analysis for recommended solutions (advanced). (pp. 48–49))

While some of these performance statements are actually repeated in the chapter on needs assessment, we begin the chapter by defining human performance problems and labeling their most common features. We then distinguish between two types of problem-solving models—comprehensive and situation-specific—and describe how to apply them. A simple example of a problem-solving situation is provided. We also offer brief discussions about judging and justifying performance analysis. Finally, we address key ethical and cross-cultural challenges in applying performance analysis.

Defining Human Performance Problems and Labeling Their Parts

The word *problem* is formed from two Greek words—*pro*, meaning "forward," and *ballein*, meaning "to throw" (McCall and Kaplan, 1985, p. 10). It literally means "something thrown forward," a result of a discrepancy between the actual (what is?) and the ideal (what should be?) that requires present or future action. The actual is called *condition*, meaning "the existing state of affairs." The ideal is called *criterion*, meaning "the desired state of affairs." The difference between condition and criterion is a *gap*. The reason (or reasons) for the gap is the problem's root cause; the consequences of the gap are the problem's *symptoms*. These components of a problem are illustrated in Figure 3.1.

To be successful in determining which human performance problems are appropriately addressed through instruction, instructional designers must be able to distinguish among these components. And they often must reach these conclusions fast (Rossett, 1999).

First, collect information about the condition. It should be easily identified. Simply ask people about the problem. When people describe what is happening or how employees are performing, they are providing information about condition. Second, identify criterion. It may not be as easily identified as condition. Criterion refers to the desired or ideal state, what should be happening, or how people should be performing. There are essentially two kinds of criteria: (1) performance standards, which are minimally acceptable job performance benchmarks (Springer, 1980) and (2) performance objectives, which are desirable job performance targets

FIGURE 3.1. COMPONENTS OF A PROBLEM.

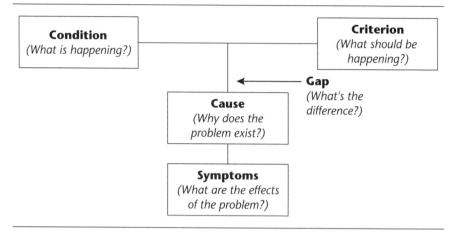

Source: Rummler, G. "The Performance Audit." In R. Craig (Ed.), *Training and Development Hand-book: A Guide to Human Resource Development* (2nd ed.). New York: McGraw-Hill, 1976, pp. 14–11. Reproduced with the permission of McGraw-Hill, Inc.

(Odiorne, 1979). Inexperienced employees usually require training to perform to standard; experienced employees are expected to perform at least to standard. In contrast, performance objectives require results exceeding minimal requirements. Performance standards, like objectives, should be measurable and expressed as results to be achieved in an identifiable time period. Standards are usually established from historical information, organizational plans, or management expectations. Objectives should be established by mutual agreement of employees and their immediate supervisors.

Unfortunately, managers do not always establish clear expectations for performance—that is, for performance standards or objectives. Nor do they always communicate their expectations to workers. In these situations, the performance problem results from a lack of criteria. Employees cannot perform competently when managers do not know what they want, employees do not know what results are desired, or desired results have not been communicated. In these cases, instructional designers can often solve the problem by helping managers establish and communicate performance standards or objectives to workers. In settings where workers are more empowered, as on self-directed work teams, the workers themselves may reach consensus on what the work standards should be and then communicate them to management.

After identifying condition and criterion, identify the gap (difference) between them. What is the difference? How important is it? If it is not important, time and resources should be devoted to other, more significant projects; if it is important, then consider the problem's cause. Always remember that the only effective solution to any problem must address its cause. While human performance is complicated, and many causes for a performance problem are possible, all causes can be reduced to three fundamental ones (Rummler, 1983): (1) a deficiency of knowledge, (2) a deficiency of environment, or (3) a combination of the first two.

A *deficiency of knowledge* exists when people do not know how to perform or know what results they seek. For example, newly hired or newly transferred employees frequently experience deficiencies of knowledge because they are not aware of what they are supposed to do or how they are expected to perform.

A *deficiency of environment*—sometimes called a *deficiency of execution*—exists when people face barriers to performance. Such barriers include poor or inadequate feedback, poorly designed jobs, or negative (punishing) consequences for good performance. For example, a deficiency of environment may be created when an employee is asked to perform her job while, at the same time, performing the job of a vacationing employee. In this case, she has been burdened with double duty and may not perform either job successfully. The results of a large-scale, award-winning study of International Society for Performance Improvement members revealed that more experienced instructional designers usually begin by assuming that human performance problems stem from a deficiency of environment rather than from a deficiency of knowledge (Meyer, 1995). Important research has also been conducted to identify the characteristics of workplaces that are especially conducive to performance, and these are called high-performance workplaces (see Dubois and Rothwell, 1996; Office of the American Workplace, 1995). Closely related is the notion of performance management, which sets out to establish a systematic approach to planning, tracking, and following up on work (Bacal, 1999).

A combination of deficiencies of knowledge and environment exists when part of a performance problem results from an employee's lack of knowledge or skills or poor attitude, and part results from obstacles posed by the environment. Suppose that, in the example in the previous paragraph, the employee is asked to perform someone else's job but has never been trained to do it. In that case, she will experience both a deficiency of knowledge (the other job) and a deficiency of environment (performing two jobs at once). Such a combination of deficiencies is increasingly common in today's complex workplace and calls for sophisticated troubleshooting approaches.

One way to think about analyzing performance problems is to examine each of seven key performance drivers (Ross, 2003). First, think about conditions. Under what working conditions do people perform? Second, think about standards. How well do people understand their performance expectations? Third, consider incentives. How are people rewarded for performing? Fourth, think about capacity. Do performers have the ability to do, or learn, the work? Fifth, consider knowledge and skill. Do they know what to do and why?

Do they know how to do it? Sixth, think about measurement. How is performance measured? Seventh and finally, consider feedback. How quickly and specifically do people hear about the results they produce? How well are they guided to understand how to align what they do to the performance expectations of those they serve?

Symptoms are the consequences of a performance problem. Quite often, managers confuse a symptom with a problem. Typical symptoms include (Rummler, 1983, p. 10):

- Tasks are not being performed to standards.
- Employee performance gets worse over time.
- Employees do not believe there is reason for them to perform as desired.
- Deadlines are not being met.
- There is a work backlog.
- Employees are performing up to standard, but work is rejected because of a mismatch with quality requirements.
- Some work tasks are "forgotten" or "fall through the cracks."
- Employees perform successfully only when they are observed by their supervisors.
- Managers have reason to believe employees are deliberately exerting less effort than they are capable of.

Each item in this list is a symptom because underlying cause(s) will only be revealed after further investigation. However, these symptoms typically result from a deficiency of environment, not a deficiency of knowledge. Hence, instruction will not be appropriate as a solution because it addresses deficiencies of individual knowledge. To solve these problems, instructional designers should apply management solutions.

Models for Performance Analysis

Over the years, several well-known people have devoted considerable attention to performance analysis. Through experience they have developed classic models for troubleshooting human performance problems. These classic models differ somewhat because their creators were not always trying to achieve the same results. Several case books have also been prepared that describe how performance analysis works (see, for instance, Phillips, 2000; Rothwell and Dubois, 1998).

Two Categories of Models

There are two categories of problem-solving models (Rothwell, 1996): (1) comprehensive models, which are useful for scanning "the big picture" of an organization to identify problems, and (2) situation-specific models, which provide guidance in dealing with the kind of run-of-the-mill symptoms that prompt managers to request the aid of instructional designers. A *comprehensive model* is appropriate for those occasions on which much information must be reviewed quickly, such as full-scale instructional design projects involving an entire organization. For example, if a consultant enters an organization for the first time, she may need to get a quick overview of the whole organization. A comprehensive model is appropriate for that. But a *situation-specific model* is appropriate for troubleshooting management requests to solve immediate operational problems. If a manager calls a consultant by phone and requests a training program, that may be indicative of the need to apply a situation-specific model.

Applying a Comprehensive Problem-Solving Model: Gilbert's Performance Matrix

Perhaps the best example of a comprehensive model is Gilbert's performance matrix. It is well-known. In a classic book published by McGraw-Hill in 1978 and republished again by the International Society for Performance Improvement in 1996, Gilbert describes it as "a way to organize our points of view so we shall set first things first when we design a performance system . . . and troubleshoot problems in existing systems" (p. 110). It is called a matrix because it allows instructional designers to examine six different hierarchically ordered performance levels. Each level corresponds to a different value system or vantage point by which performance can be viewed. Each level contains three related "cells"—models, measures, and methods. Gilbert uses the term model to mean a criterion, ideal, goal, expectation, standard, or objective. A measure is analogous to condition or actual results. A method is a solution, a way to narrow or close a gap between what is (measure) and what should be (model).

When the matrix is applied to organizational settings, Gilbert suggests using only the three bottom levels of the matrix: policy (institutional systems), strategy (job systems), and tactics (task systems). Gilbert (1996, p. 136) believes these levels are "most demanding of detailed analysis when we design such subcultures as schools or institutions in the world of work." Gilbert calls this modified matrix the performance engineering model (PEM).

Gilbert's famous disciple, Geary Rummler (1976), has described in a classic and detailed treatment how to apply the PEM. He suggests that instructional designers begin their analysis at the policy level, asking questions about models, measures, and methods to determine which performance improvement programs will have the highest possible payoffs. They should then ask questions about the strategy level to identify how to define and improve jobs. Finally, they should ask questions about the tactics level to determine what specific actions must be taken to help people become more efficient in their jobs. The appropriate questions to ask appear in the modified performance engineering matrix presented in Table 3.1.

Begin the investigation by asking the questions appearing at the top left of the PEM. Then work to the right and down. There is one important reason for applying this top-down approach: "The source of performance problems usually originates from the organizational level just above where the problem is first perceived to exist" (Jacobs, 1987, p. 29). For instance, many job problems at the strategy level stem from organizational, departmental, or division problems at the policy level. Similarly, many task problems within jobs at the tactical level stem from job problems at the strategy level. To solve these problems, the causes at higher levels must be addressed first.

Applying a Situation-Specific Problem-Solving Model: Mager and Pipe's Performance Analysis

Gilbert's performance engineering model is a powerful tool, but it is not the only one useful in troubleshooting performance problems. In fact, the problem-solving model of Mager and Pipe may actually be better known than Gilbert's. Mager and Pipe's model, summarized in their classic book, *Analyzing Performance Problems or "You Really Oughta Wanna"* (1999), is particularly useful to instructional designers as they field daily requests for assistance they receive from managers, supervisors, and workers. Their model has undergone revision in recent years. But the current version of that model follows the same basic logic as the classic original.

Review this model step by step. First collect as much information as possible about the performance problem. Ask questions such as these:

- What is the problem?
- How many people are affected?
- When did the problem first become evident?
- What are the consequences of the problem?
- What is happening at present?

TABLE 3.1. THE PERFORMANCE ENGINEERING MATRIX.

Levels	Models *What Should Be?*	Measures *What Is?*	Methods *How Can Performance Gaps Be Closed?*
POLICY (Organizational, Division, Departmental, and Work-Unit Level)	• How should work be organized? • How should work be allocated? • How should work flow into, through, and out of the organization, work unit, or job? • How can economic benefits be maximized?	• What are present conditions? • What gaps exist between what is and what should be? • What gaps are of most economic importance?	• What general methods could be used to solve the performance problem(s)? • What are the estimated costs of each general method that can be used to solve the problem? • What performance improvement method is likely to have the greatest worth?
STRATEGY (Job Level)	• What are the most important work outputs of the job? • How should the job be structured? • What are the requirements associated with major duties/results of the job? • What are the standards for each work output?	• What is the present status of the job? • What deficiencies exist in job outputs? • What are the causes of important discrepancies between what is and what should be?	• What performance improvement method(s) can be used to narrow or close performance gaps? (Consider information, training, guidance, motivation, reward systems, etc.)
TACTICS (Tasks-Within-Jobs Levels)	• What do people have to know or do to achieve desired results and carry out desired tasks? • What environment is needed for the job? • What can be done to match the right people to the right jobs?	• What media should be used? • What time schedules should be used to develop designs? • What are the costs of implementing solutions?	• What materials, tools, and resources are needed to solve performance problems (that is, narrow or close gaps between what is and what should be)?

Source: Rummler, G. "The Performance Audit." In R. Craig (Ed.), *Training and Development Handbook: A Guide to Human Resource Development* (2nd ed.). New York: McGraw-Hill, 1976, pp. 14–21. Reproduced with the permission of McGraw-Hill, Inc.

- How do you know there is a problem?
- Who is affected by it?
- Where is the problem evident?
- Are some locations affected more than others?
- What should be happening?
- How wide is the gap between what is and what should be?

Use the answers to these questions to describe the performance discrepancy.

Next, consider the relative importance of the performance problem. Continue to pose questions to people familiar with it:

- Why is the discrepancy important?
- How much will it cost to fix the problem? (Estimate cost of training in salaries, lost work time, and preparation of training materials.)
- What will happen if no action is taken to correct the problem?
- How much is the discrepancy costing the organization in lost production, wasted materials, lost time, or employee turnover?
- What is the estimated benefit of correcting the problem? (Subtract the estimated cost of correcting the problem from the estimated benefit to the organization of correcting the problem.)

Use the answers to these questions to compare the expected benefits (savings) of correcting the problem less the cost of solving it. If the problem does not meet the test of importance, ignore it and devote attention to other problems that do meet the test of importance. If the problem meets the test of importance, however, go on to the next step.

Next, consider whether the performance discrepancy is caused by deficiencies in knowledge, skills, or attitudes, or deficiencies in the environment. Ask this question: *Could people perform properly if their lives depended on it?* The answer to this question is crucial and can provide guidance in selecting an appropriate way to close the performance gap.

If it is a deficiency in knowledge, skills, or attitudes—that is, people could not perform competently even if their lives depended on it—then ask another series of questions to identify an appropriate solution. First, are people accustomed to performing? If not, consider formal training. For example, training is appropriate when reducing the unproductive breaking-in period of new employees. If people are accustomed to performing, determine whether they are used to performing often. If not, address the performance problem by giving employees the opportunity to practice. If they are performing often, the problem may be solved by improving the quantity and quality of feedback that employees receive about what they do.

Before deciding on a final solution, double-check the analysis. Consider: Is there a simpler way to address the problem than has been identified to this point? For instance, would it be easier and faster to change the job? Or to provide employees with checklists, procedure manuals, or other job performance aids that can be used as the job is performed? Would on-the-job training solve the problem more quickly and inexpensively?

Finally, analyze the performer before offering off-the-job training, arranging practice, arranging feedback, changing the job, or arranging on-the-job training. Do all performers have the ability to benefit from the corrective action that is contemplated? If not, transfer employees who are unable to learn work requirements. These performers may require retraining for other work first. As a solution of last resort, terminate people who cannot be matched to available work in the organization.

If a performance problem is caused by a deficiency of environment, that is, people could perform if their lives depended on it but are not doing so for some reason, then ask other questions to find the best solution. Begin with this one: Why are people not performing? First, consider whether people are punished in some way for performing. For example, does their good performance yield them nothing but more work or the sneers of co-workers? (If so, they will not perform as desired until the punishment is removed.) If people are not punished for performing, are they rewarded in some way for not performing as desired? For example, are they praised by co-workers for devoting their energies to other activities? If so, then nonperformance is rewarding, and the consequences should be changed. Make it so that performance is rewarding. Finally, consider whether employees face obstacles that prevent them from performing. If they do, remove the obstacles. Obstacles might include lack of time or proper equipment to perform, for instance.

At this point, select and implement solutions to the performance problem. As part of this process, prepare detailed estimates of the benefits expected to result from correcting the performance problem. In addition, estimate the likely costs of taking corrective action.

Quite often the means of implementing a solution is as important as the results to be achieved. For this reason, take pains to brief key decision makers about the cause of the performance problem and gain their support for implementing an appropriate solution. Encourage them to participate in this process, recognizing that their participation will be time-consuming and will undoubtedly add to the time and cost of solving the problem. However, their support will also increase the likelihood that the solution will enjoy long-term success because it will have garnered their ownership.

Performance Analysis: An Example

Joel Finlay is an instructional designer employed by the XYZ Corporation. Working out of the corporate training department, Joel is a troubleshooter who responds to special requests for assistance made by any of the corporate divisions. His primary function is to diagnose human performance problems and identify appropriate solutions. Based on his recommendations, division or corporate management will either ask for additional assistance from the training department or will contract externally with vendors for help in rectifying a performance problem.

Joel was recently asked for assistance by XYZ pharmaceuticals—manufacturers and marketers of many popular over-the-counter cold remedies. Joel was told this division was experiencing a decline in sales. The director of human resources for this division, who initially contacted Joel, felt that the problem was caused by high turnover among the salesforce and that the problem could be solved by intensive sales training. Before Joel arrived at the division's headquarters, he asked the director of human resources to schedule meetings with the vice president of marketing and several other key managers in the division so that, when Joel arrived, he could use his time economically.

In that initial meeting, Joel explained to the managers that his purpose was not solely to deal with the (purported) turnover problem, which might only be a symptom of some other problem, but rather to help the managers identify opportunities for performance improvement in the division. He went on to explain that, to be of maximum value, he needed to collect background information about the division.

Joel began his questioning at the top left of Gilbert's performance matrix. He asked the managers to describe for him how the division is structured, how work flows into and out of it, and what activities are of greatest economic value to it. He then went on to ask them about present conditions (sales, turnover, profits, and so on) and desired conditions (sales standards and targets). From this quick overview, Joel could see that the division's primary source of revenues depended on the salesforce. Each salesperson was given an exclusive territory, worked solely on commission, and made commissions by servicing all product outlets in the assigned area.

Switching to the strategy (job) level of Gilbert's performance matrix, Joel then asked about the outputs of the salesperson's job. From detailed questioning,

Joel was able to determine that the managers could not identify important outputs. They tended to speak in terms of activities (behaviors) rather than results. Joel also learned that some salespersons had territories so large, such as the entire Chicago area, that one person could not possibly service it effectively. By this point, Joel had gathered enough information to recommend (1) clarifying work standards by outputs and (2) restructuring the salespersons' jobs so that their territories could be handled effectively.

Not wishing to disappoint his clients, Joel then shifted his attention to salesforce turnover. Joel called this the presenting problem. (For Joel, a presenting problem is one that triggers an initial plea for help from managers.) Joel examined the turnover issue by using Mager and Pipe's performance analysis model. He asked the managers to describe the nature of the problem, how present turnover differed from historical rates, what locations (if any) were affected by turnover most, what information had been collected through exit interviews with departing salespersons, when turnover rates had begun increasing, and what corrective actions had already been taken to deal with turnover.

From answers to these and similar questions, Joel determined that turnover was an important problem for the XYZ pharmaceutical division. However, it did not stem from a deficiency in knowledge or skills or an attitude problem; rather, it seemed to stem from many obstacles faced by salespersons in their jobs. Joel made a note to himself to check that tentative conclusion against written exit interview questionnaires completed by terminating salespersons.

Joel found the managers receptive to his initial conclusions. They agreed to work with him to verify his conclusions—or arrive at new ones based on a review of exit interview questionnaires and talks with experienced salespersons.

Judging Performance Analysis

Instructional designers should be able to judge the quality of decisions made by others. There are several reasons why. First, the ability to think critically and thus evaluate decisions and actions made by others is usually a demonstration of proficient skill. Second, and more to the point, instructional designers must occasionally review the work of their professional colleagues to ensure that it was performed properly.

Judging performance analysis is particularly important because it is essential that human performance problems be analyzed systematically and their causes determined before appropriate solutions can be identified.

On occasion, instructional designers do find themselves assigned to the middle—or even near the end—of a project rather than at the beginning. In these cases, a performance analysis has usually been completed by others. How do newcomers to a project know, then, that the performance analysis was properly completed? The answer is that they do not, at least not without reviewing, and critically evaluating, the steps in the performance analysis that was conducted.

In some instances, instructional designers who are assigned late to a project may need to conduct their own abbreviated performance analysis, a condensed version of a complete performance analysis. This is also an excellent way for a newcomer to be oriented to the project. To conduct an abbreviated performance analysis, instructional designers should begin by asking a number of important questions:

1. What was happening at the time the performance problem was first noticed?
2. What should have been happening?
3. How important was the gap between what was happening and what should have been happening?
4. What was the cause of the gap? Why was it happening?
   a. Was the problem attributable to deficiencies in knowledge, skills, or attitudes?
   b. Was the problem attributable to a deficiency in the environment?
   c. Was the problem caused by a combination of knowledge and environmental deficiencies?
5. What actions have been taken to solve the problem?
6. What has happened on the instructional design project?
7. When did the project begin?
8. Who has been working on the project?
9. What important decisions have been made on the project?
10. How committed is management to achieving results?
11. What are the history, structure, and pertinent policies of the organization or group within the organization?
12. Who are the key decision-makers associated with this instructional design project? What preferences do they seem to have for solving the problem?

An abbreviated performance analysis helps a team of instructional designers avoid groupthink—the deterioration of mental efficiency, reality testing, and moral judgment resulting from a group's desire to minimize interpersonal conflicts and preserve solidarity (Janis, 1973). By raising questions, a newly assigned instructional designer can bring out concerns and doubts that may be shared by several team members who have been reluctant, for fear of starting group conflict, to voice their opinions. This can be an effective way of preventing groupthink.

Justifying Performance Analysis

Instructional designers should always be able to explain the underlying rationale for their decisions and actions. At least two approaches can be used by instructional designers to justify the results of their performance analyses. They are compatible and can thus be used together.

The first approach is to educate clients about instructional design. This approach works best when there is extended contact between instructional designers and their clients. To use this approach, instructional designers should take every opportunity to brief their clients on the theory of performance analysis and the distinction between human performance problems that lend themselves to solution through training, education, and development and problems that better lend themselves to other solutions. There are many opportunities for such briefings, such as during an initial meeting with a prospective client, during problem identification interviews, and in written project status reports. Instructional designers may also circulate articles on performance analysis, send electronic mail messages to key people, give talks to organizational groups, and write short articles for in-house publications. It is usually easier to justify results of performance analysis if managers, workers (and, when appropriate, union officials) have been educated about the process.

A second approach is to explain the assumptions underlying the decisions made in analyzing a specific problem, in identifying its causes, and in determining appropriate solutions. This approach seems to work best when the time for client contact is limited. Instructional designers using this approach should state their assumptions about problem solving up-front, describe the steps taken to analyze the problem, and explain the reasons for choosing an appropriate solution. This approach appears to work best in written reports or oral presentations.

Acting Ethically in Applying Performance Analysis

"Ethics," writes Peter Dean (1993, p. 7), "can be defined as the rules or standards that govern the conduct of the members of a group. They distinguish between right/wrong and good/evil." They are closely associated with morals, understood to mean rules governing individual conduct. They are also associated with values, defined as the "core beliefs or desires that guide or motivate the individual's attitudes and actions" (Dean, 1993, p. 7).

Ethical issues were identified as a competency area for instructional designers in *The Standards* (Richey, Fields, and Foxon, 2001, p. 48). One competency for instructional design is to "identify and resolve ethical and legal implications of design in the workplace." It was identified as an advanced competency. The performance statements associated with this competency indicate that instructional designers should be able to (Richey, Fields, and Foxon, 2001, p. 48):

a. Identify ethical and legal dimensions of instructional design practice (advanced).
b. Anticipate and respond to ethical consequences of design decisions (advanced).
c. Recognize and respect intellectual property rights of others (essential).
d. Recognize the ethical and legal implications and consequences of instructional products (advanced).
e. Adhere to regulatory guidelines and organizational policies (essential).

In light of the Enron scandal and the others that followed in its wake it is likely that ethical and moral issues will play a high-profile role in the life of anyone in organizations today (Hultman, 2002; Ulrich and Smallwood, 2003). Simpson (2002) reported a 22 percent growth in the number of companies providing ethics training in 2000, and best practices in ethics training may (arguably) be found among defense contractors ("Defense Contractors Create Gold Standard for Ethics Training and Compliance," 2002). The International Board of Standards for Training, Performance, and Instruction has issued ethical guidelines for instructional designers, and they are worth reviewing (Spector, 2001). See Exhibit 3.1.

Instructional designers, like all those who work in organizations, face ethically conflict-laden situations called ethical dilemmas (Rothwell, Sanders, and Soper, 1999). Typical ethical dilemmas include situations in which individuals face:

• Capricious application of policies.
• Disregard for individual rights or safety.
• Misrepresentation of individual qualifications.

But the classic ethical dilemma is, of course, the situation in which individuals must choose between what they know is right and what they know will benefit them personally.

Consider a simple example to see how an ethical dilemma might arise in instructional design. Suppose, for instance, that an instructional designer is called in to help a manager troubleshoot a performance problem. Let us say that the manager is mediating between two workers who ceaselessly argue

EXHIBIT 3.1. THE IBSTPI CODE OF ETHICAL STANDARDS FOR INSTRUCTIONAL DESIGNERS.

I. Guiding Standards: Responsibilities to Others

    A. Provide efficient, effective, workable, and cost-effective solutions to client problems.

    B. Systematically improve human performance to accomplish valid and appropriate individual and organizational goals.

    C. Facilitate individual accomplishment.

    D. Help clients make informed decisions.

    E. Inform others of potential ethical violations and conflicts of interest.

    F. Educate clients in matters of instructional design and performance improvement.

II. Guiding Standards: Social Mandates

    A. Support humane, socially responsible goals and activities for individuals and organizations.

    B. Make professional decisions based on moral and ethical positions regarding societal issues.

    C. Consider the impact of planned interventions on individuals, organizations, and the society as a whole.

III. Guiding Standards: Respecting the Rights of Others

    A. Protect the privacy, candor, and confidentiality of client and colleague information and communication.

    B. Show respect for copyright and intellectual property.

    C. Do not misuse client or colleague information for personal gain.

    D. Do not represent the ideas or work of others as one's own.

    E. Do not make false claims about others.

    F. Do not discriminate unfairly in actions related to hiring, retention, and advancement.

IV. Guiding Standards: Professional Practice

    A. Be honest and fair in all facets of one's work.

    B. Share skills and knowledge with other professionals.

    C. Acknowledge the contribution of others.

    D. Aid and be supportive of colleagues.

    E. Commit time and effort to the development of the profession.

    F. Withdraw from clients who do not act ethically or when there is a conflict of interest.

with each other to the point that it is disrupting work-group performance. The manager believes that the two workers require interpersonal skills training. But after applying skillful performance analysis, the instructional designer discovers that the problem stems from poor work design that has given the two workers conflicting work responsibilities. If, at the same time, the instructional designer is rewarded in the organization only for how many individuals attend training sessions, he or she may experience an ethical dilemma rooted in the conflict between doing what is right (telling the truth about the cause of the problem and seeking an appropriate solution) and doing what will benefit himself or herself most (recommending interpersonal skills training for people even when not needed).

A key ethical challenge in applying performance analysis, then, can be expressed as a question: *Can the performance analysis withstand charges that the instructional designer acted from self-interest only?*

It should be recognized that instructional designers, whether serving as internal or external consultants, can be accused of—and sometimes are—acting from self-interest. Both internal and external consultants may stand to benefit, after all, if a performance analysis reveals that their services are required. It is unethical to manipulate a performance analysis so that the results reveal a need for internal or external consulting services when that need is not supported by compelling evidence, when other services are called for, or when other consultants are better qualified to address them.

To withstand this challenge, instructional designers should be prepared to describe how they carried out the performance analysis and how they reached the conclusions they reached. If the same performance analysis can be replicated by others with the same or similar results, then instructional designers should be confident that they have acted ethically and served their client to the best of their ability. Instructional designers may find it helpful to train employees, supervisors, and managers on performance analysis. In that way, they can effectively distinguish instructional from management projects on their own.

In the survey conducted by Rothwell (2003) for the third edition of this book, several respondents described ethical challenges they face when undertaking performance analysis. One respondent wrote that "management does not want to be improved." A second respondent pointed to problems stemming from an organizational culture that "does not support management action [against the norm]." A third respondent indicated that he or she faces an ethical challenge every time the recommendation is made to solve a problem using any means other than training. A fourth respondent commented that "people think training solves everything when clearly it does not," and a fifth indicated the requests for training frequently stem from "what is really an accountability issue."

A common theme running through the respondents' remarks is that managers sometimes want to shove their problems onto the desks of instructional designers rather than assume responsibility for issues that the managers themselves should deal with. Of course, such situations call for tactful, but firm, management coaching by the designers. Maslak (2003) calls these problems "the performance improvement dilemma." As he notes, instructional designers must be prepared to deal with clients who fail to recognize that a problem exists, confuse symptoms with root causes, and lack the willingness to take the tough-minded management actions necessary to solve problems.

Applying Performance Analysis Cross-Culturally

All elements of instructional design should be examined for their cross-cultural applications and implications. Doing so is just good business practice at a time when globalization has become a reality. For these reasons, instructional designers and others have been paying more attention to cross-cultural issues in recent years (see, for example, Borman, 2001; Laroche, 2000; Mullins, 2000; Sitze, 2000; VanLeeuwen, 2001; Wederspahn, 2002; and Weech, 2001).

Consider performance analysis. It may not work equally well in all cultures, unless special care is taken. While the process itself is logical, cultural issues may complicate applications. For instance, in some parts of the world individuals take risks if they are outspoken about their opinions. They may be interrogated, imprisoned, and even tortured if they speak their minds. Under these conditions, instructional designers who question managers and workers about human performance problems may unintentionally resemble political interrogators. As a consequence, they may experience unique difficulties in applying performance analysis and may occasionally obtain unreliable results.

While no one approach can be used universally to overcome this problem, instructional designers should verse themselves in the political climate of the cultures in which they function. If the local political climate is a closed one, then instructional designers may find it helpful to enlist a cultural informant—an individual who is trustworthy, is familiar with local cultural conditions, and is able to understand why a performance analysis is important. The cultural informant should be able to suggest ways to set managers and employers at ease about the performance analysis or offer ideas about innovative approaches that may be used to carry out the same or equivalent process in the culture.

What Is New in Determining Projects Appropriate for Instructional Design Solutions?

Performance analysis has historically focused on identifying gaps between desired (ideal) and actual (real) results. Some authorities distinguish between performance analysis (finding the gaps) and cause analysis (identifying the root causes of why the gaps exist). Other authorities make no distinction and regard finding gaps and their root causes as a single process rather than different but related processes.

But one thing is clear: critics of performance analysis point out that it is reactive, focusing on problems only after they occur or someone notices them. They also point out that performance analysis has historically been focused on what is going wrong and is thus focused on the negative. But recent writings on positive change theory, sometimes called appreciative inquiry, suggest that solving problems may miss more energizing approaches to identifying and leveraging strengths (Cooperrider and Whitney, 2005). Positive change theorists do not ask "What is going wrong?" so much they ask "What is going right? and How can that be carried so far that competitors will need have a prayer of reaching us?"

When managers are first introduced to positive change theory, they often find fault with what they perceive to be an overly optimistic approach that focuses solely on the good and ignores the bad. That is a misrepresentation of positive change theory. Advocates point out that overemphasizing the negative, and problem solving, tends to lead to much attention focused on finding someone to blame rather than on solving the problem. Finger-pointing becomes the first order of the day in too much problem solving. And they may have a point. Furthermore, advocates of positive change theory assert, people tend to be demotivated and de-energized by criticism and fault-finding. But when the emphasis is on identifying and leveraging strengths, people become more motivated and more highly engaged.

What does positive change theory mean for performance analysis? The short answer is that it has profound implications. Instead of asking "What's the gap?" and "Why is it happening?" (traditional questions in performance analysis) instructional designers would ask "What is going right?" and "How could that be leveraged to greatest advantage?" They could pose those questions individually through interviews, in small groups through focus groups, by survey or by any of the means by which performance analysis is carried out. Samples of positive questions could include any of the following:

- What does the organization do best?
- What makes the organization uniquely competitive and different from others in the industry?

- What are the strengths of the organization's people?
- What are individuals' unique talents?
- How can strengths be leveraged to best advantage?
- If the organization were able to take advantage of its greatest strengths as far as they could be pushed, what would be different? What would that vision of the ideal future look like?

In a specific situation, a performance analyst might ask:

- What is going right?
- What are the unique strengths of the current situation?
- What motivates people the most about the organization?
- What good things do people take for granted?
- What unique talents do individuals or the team possess? What would it be like if those talents were pushed as far as they could go?

Many other such positive questions could be selected from an encyclopedia of positive questions (Whitney, Cooperrider, Kaplin, and Trosten-Bloom, 2001).

Advocates of positive change usually do not suggest combining gap-finding (a negative or problem-solving emphasis) and opportunity-finding (a positive emphasis). Just as two wrongs do not make a right, a positive and a negative do not equal a neutral. Instead, the result is usually negative, as people fall into finger-pointing, blame-placing, and defensiveness. But it is possible to combine the approaches through skillful practice. One way to do that is to focus on identifying strengths and then invite managers or others to compare their organizational practices to Identified best practices. That makes the comparison different from a simple focus on troubleshooting problems.

In the future, it is very likely that a positive approach will be used more frequently In performance analysis. The focus will not solely be on troubleshooting problems. An equal or greater emphasis is likely to center on leveraging existing strengths, talents, and competitive advantages.

Conclusion

As we have noted in this chapter, any employee performance problem consists of several parts. Condition means "the existing state of affairs"; criterion means "the desired state of affairs." The difference between condition (what is happening?) and criterion (what should be happening?) is a gap. The reason for the gap is the problem's cause; the consequences of the gap are the problem's symptoms.

Various problem-solving models have been devised to provide guidance in troubleshooting. A comprehensive model is appropriate for large-scale examinations of organizations or work units. Some instructional designers use a comprehensive model when entering an organization for the first time. Perhaps the best example of a comprehensive model is Gilbert's performance engineering model. A situation-specific model is useful to instructional designers as they handle the daily requests for help they receive from managers, supervisors, and workers. It is appropriate for small-scale examinations of problems stemming from operations. Perhaps the best known is Mager and Pipe's performance analysis model.

By applying these models appropriately, instructional designers can determine the causes of human performance problems. All human performance problems stem from just three possible root causes: (1) deficiencies in knowledge, skills, or attitudes; (2) deficiencies in the environment; and (3) a combination of these. There are two classes of solutions: instructional and noninstructional. Instructional solutions rely on training, education, or development to address human performance problems. They should be chosen only when (1) performance problems are caused by deficiencies in individual knowledge, skills, or attitudes and (2) alternatives have been ruled out. On the other hand, noninstructional solutions rely on methods other than training, education, and development to address performance problems. They should be chosen when human performance problems are caused by environmental deficiencies or when they are less costly to use than instruction. In the future, however, more focus may be devoted to examining strengths and what is going right, rather than simply focusing on solving problems.

PART TWO

ANALYZING NEEDS, LEARNERS, WORK SETTINGS, AND WORK

CHAPTER FOUR

CONDUCTING A NEEDS ASSESSMENT

Following our discussion of management and instructional solutions to human performance problems discussed in Chapters Two and Three, let us turn now to needs assessment. As we do so, we should begin by explaining that, over the years, instructional designers have devised many models to guide the process of developing instruction. But most boil down to the well-known ADDIE model, which takes its name from the first letter in each step of the process—*A*nalysis, *D*esign, *D*evelopment, *I*mplementation, and *E*valuation (see Rothwell and Cookson, 1997).

The ADDIE model was essentially invented by the U.S. military to ensure efficient and effective training for soldiers, and it has been widely adapted by many organizations—both in the United States and in other nations. These models share at least one common feature: they base instruction (training) on performance requirements in a dynamic, sequential, and multistage process. Once the cause of an employee performance problem has been pinpointed and a management solution has been ruled out, instructional designers then prepare workplace training. One model for this process is shown in Figure 4.1. This chapter—and the nine chapters following it—describe the model.

At this point, allow us to emphasize two key points.

First, the steps depicted in Figure 4.1 are intended to serve as a road map and not as an inflexible list of rules or required, sequential steps. Just as a compass provides general guidance to a destination, so too does the model shown in Figure 4.1. But travelers can use a compass to arrive at their destinations on many routes. So, too, can instructional designers use the model depicted in Figure 4.1 in

FIGURE 4.1. A MODEL OF STEPS IN THE INSTRUCTIONAL DESIGN PROCESS.

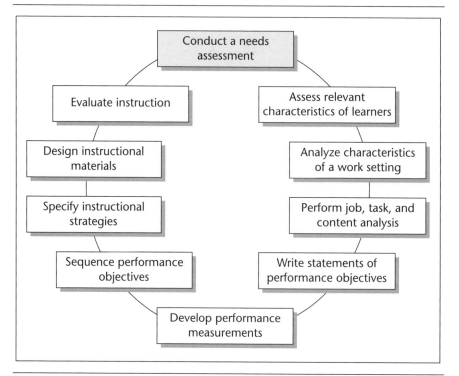

many ways to design instruction. The model is shown as a circle to indicate that any step may serve as a starting point and that any other step may follow.

Second, while the traditional ISD model has been criticized–and some say it is inappropriate for e-learning or other technologically based instruction–we believe it still serves as a reliable guide. That is a view others share (Beckshi Doty, 2000). Indeed, the ISD model may be even more important with e-learning and with blended learning than it has been historically for classroom-based instruction (Barbian, 2002). One reason is that designing effective e-learning can be costly and time-consuming, and it is thus important to be sure that problems to be solved really are suitable for an instructional solution.

Conducting a needs assessment is usually the first step in the ISD model. The purpose of needs assessment is to uncover, more precisely than performance analysis does, what the performance problem is, who it affects, how it affects them, and what results are to be achieved by training. Needs assessment is very important because all subsequent steps in the ISD model depend on its results (Rothwell, 2000; Rothwell and Sredl, 2000). However, daunting obstacles must be overcome to perform needs assessment successfully. One obstacle is the perception of top managers that instructional designers or trainers are self-interested parties in the needs assessment process who may stand to benefit from the results by justifying their existence (Bengtson, 1994; Rothwell, Lindholm, and Wallick, 2003).

A second obstacle is that needs assessment is sometimes thought to take too much time in an age of dynamic change (Lewis and Bjorkquist, 1992). That issue figures prominently in recent writings about needs assessment (Barksdale and Lund, 2001; Gupta, 1999; Lee and Owens, 2001; "Quick, Consultative Approach to Training Needs Assessment," 2001). A major challenge is balancing rigorous with speedy analysis–despite a growing array of online approaches to provide support for conducting needs assessment (see, for instance, www .hr.com/icg).

A third obstacle is the view expressed by some operating managers that instructional designers do not possess adequate skills to perform needs assessment because they lack in-depth business or technical knowledge of how the work is done or firsthand knowledge of individual workers (Bengtson, 1994). Of course, many other obstacles to effective needs assessment have been identified.

Recall from Chapter Three that, according to *The Standards* (Richey, Fields, and Foxon, 2001, pp. 48–49), one competency for instructional design is to "conduct a needs assessment." It is an essential competency. The performance statements associated with this competency indicate that instructional designers should be able to (Richey, Fields, and Foxon, 2001, pp. 48–49):

a. Describe the problem and its dimensions, identifying the discrepancies between current and desired performance (essential).
b. Clarify the varying perceptions of need and their implications (essential).
c. Select and use appropriate needs assessment tools and techniques (essential).
d. Determine the possible causes of the problem and potential solutions (essential).
e. Recommend and advocate non-instructional solutions when appropriate (advanced).
f. Complete a cost-benefit analysis for recommended solutions (advanced).

Research skills are, arguably, related to conducting needs assessment–and evaluating instruction. After all, research can be understood here to mean the systematic investigation of issues. Research is necessary to discover needs and evaluate results. According to *The Standards* (Richey, Fields, and Foxon, 2001, pp. 47–48), one competency for instructional design is to "apply fundamental research skills to instructional design projects." It is regarded as an advanced competency. The performance statements associated with this competency indicate that instructional designers should be able to (Richey, Fields, and Foxon, 2001, pp. 47–48):

a. Use a variety of data collection tools and procedures (advanced).
b. Apply appropriate research and methodologies to needs assessment and evaluation (advanced).
c. Use basic statistical techniques in needs assessment and evaluation (advanced).
d. Write research and evaluation reports (advanced).

In this chapter, we define terms associated with needs assessment, describe essential steps in developing needs assessment plans, review typical problems likely to arise during needs assessment, suggest ways of overcoming these problems, explain how to identify instructional problems based on needs assessment results, provide a simple case study highlighting important issues in needs assessment, offer some advice on judging and justifying needs assessment, address key ethical and cross-cultural issues in conducting needs assessment, and review some recent developments in needs assessment.

Defining Terms

To understand needs assessment, instructional designers should first understand the meaning of key terms associated with it. Such terms include need, needs assessment, needs analysis, training requirements analysis, needs assessment planning, and needs assessment plan.

A Definition of Need

A *need* has traditionally been defined as a performance gap separating what people know, do, or feel from what they should know, do, or feel to perform competently. The word need should be used as a noun, not as a verb (Kaufman, 1986). The reason: when need is used as a verb in the sentence, "We need some training on time management," it implies something merely desirable (a want) rather than something essential to competent performance. A need should always be linked to the essential knowledge, skills, and attitudes an individual must possess to perform work competently and thereby accomplish the desired results.

A Definition of Needs Assessment

A *needs assessment* "identifies gaps in results, places them in order of priority, and selects the most important for closure or reduction" (Watkins and Kaufman, 1996, p. 13). It is undertaken to "identify, document, and justify gaps between what is and what should be and place the gaps in priority order for closure" (Kaufman, 1986, p. 38). Although such gaps are a traditional starting point for developing instruction (Rothwell and Sredl, 2000), analyzing gaps is sometimes fraught with the problem of overlooking the performance levels of experts in a group or organization (Lewis and Bjorkquist, 1992).

In a classic discussion that has withstood the test of time, Kaufman and English (1979) identify six types of needs assessment arranged in a hierarchical order of complexity. The first, and least complex, is alpha assessment. It focuses on identifying the nature and cause of a performance problem. (An alpha assessment is synonymous with performance analysis.) A beta assessment is the second type. It is based on the assumption that an employee performance problem exists but that alternative solutions must be weighed for their relative cost-benefit and practicality. A gamma assessment, the third type, examines differences between alternative solutions to a performance problem. The fourth type is a delta assessment, and it examines specific performance gaps between what is and what should be. An epsilon assessment, the fifth type, examines discrepancies between desired and actual results of an event. A zeta assessment is the sixth type. It involves continuous assessment and evaluation in which regular feedback is used to monitor solutions and make corrective changes if they are necessary.

A Definition of Needs Analysis

A *needs analysis* discovers the underlying causes of gaps between the ideal or desirable and the actual. It is usually carried out following a needs assessment. It goes beyond a needs assessment, which merely shows that a performance gap exists, to pinpoint the root cause(s) leading to that gap. Of course, identifying root causes is essential for discovering the best solutions (Rothwell, Hohne, and King, 2000).

A Definition of Training Requirements Planning

Care should be taken to avoid making assumptions too quickly about the causes of gaps. As Watkins and Kaufman (1996, p. 13) point out, "Although the term 'training needs assessment' is popular in the field, it seems to be an oxymoron. If you know that training is the solution, why do a needs assessment? A more accurate label for what is called a 'training needs assessment' is 'training requirements analysis.' A training requirements analysis can be a useful and important approach to designing training that will respond to your needs after you have defined them." A training requirements analysis (TRA) thus specifies exactly what training is necessary.

A Definition of Needs Assessment Planning

Needs assessment planning is the process of developing a blueprint for collecting needs assessment information. It should not be confused with a needs assessment plan. Planning is a process, while a plan is a product (Rothwell and Cookson, 1997). For needs assessment planning to be handled successfully, key line managers and other interested groups should participate in each step of designing the needs assessment plan and interpreting the results. Participation in needs assessment, as in many organizational activities, is essential to building ownership among key stakeholders.

In the broadest sense, needs assessment planning can be categorized into two types: comprehensive and situation-specific.

Comprehensive needs assessment planning is broad, covering large groups inside or outside an organization (Rothwell and Kazanas, 1994a). Sometimes called macro needs assessment (Laird, 1985), it is appropriate for determining the continuous and relatively predictable training needs of all newly hired workers, since they must be oriented to their jobs. The results of a comprehensive needs assessment are used to establish an organization's curriculum—an instructional plan—covering basic training for each job category. A curriculum provides long-term direction to organized learning activities (Rothwell and Kazanas, 1994a, 1994c; Rothwell and Sredl, 2000).

Situation-specific needs assessment planning is narrower. Sometimes called micro needs assessment (Laird, 1985), it is appropriate for correcting a specific performance problem that affects only a few people. For instance, a microtraining need exists when one supervisor reveals no knowledge of "progressive discipline" in the firing of an employee, but other supervisors possess that knowledge.

More often than not, instructional designers devote their attention to situation-specific needs. There are several reasons why. First, relatively few organizations establish an instructional plan or training curriculum across all job categories. As a result, they lose the advantages that could be gained by pursuing a long-term direction for instructional activities in the organization. Second, situation-specific needs often have built-in management support. Since the performance problem already exists, has visible symptoms, and affects an identifiable target group, instructional designers find they already have a constituency of interested stakeholders who are eager to support efforts—and furnish resources—to solve the problem.

A Definition of Needs Assessment Plan

A *needs assessment plan* is a blueprint for collecting information about instructional needs. By its very nature, a needs assessment plan assumes that sufficient justification already exists to solve a human performance problem. In form it usually resembles a research plan, a proposal for conducting a research study.

A needs assessment plan should usually address seven key issues (Foshay, Silber, and Westgaard, 1986, p. 27):

1. *Objectives.* What results are desired from the needs assessment?
2. *Target audience.* Whose needs will be assessed?
3. *Sampling procedures.* What methods will be used to select a representative group of people from the target audience for participation in the needs assessment?
4. *Data collection methods.* How will information about needs be gathered?
5. *Specifications for instruments and protocols.* What instruments should be used during needs assessment, and how should they be used? What approvals or protocols are necessary for conducting the needs assessment, and how will the instructional designer interact with members of the organization?
6. *Methods of data analysis.* How will the information collected during needs assessment be analyzed?
7. *Descriptions of how decisions will be made based on the data.* How will needs be identified from the results of data collection and analysis?

However, the anecdotal evidence available about needs assessment consistently shows that such issues are given varying degrees of emphasis—depending on project constraints and stakeholder requirements and expectations.

Steps in Developing Needs Assessment Plans

To develop a needs assessment plan, instructional designers should first clarify why they are doing the assessment. Beyond that, the appropriate place to start depends on the problem that is to be solved, the number of people affected by it, and the time span available for the intended solution. For example, the appropriate starting point for an alpha needs assessment is not the same as that for a delta assessment. Likewise, the starting point for a comprehensive needs assessment differs from a situation-specific needs assessment.

Instructional designers who set out to develop a plan for a comprehensive needs assessment that is adequate for establishing a long-term instructional plan for an organization or an employee job category are embarking on an ambitious undertaking akin to corporate strategic business planning. They should begin by locating a current organization chart and information about strategic business plans, job categories in the organization, common movements from each job category to others, existing human performance problems in each job category, and individual training needs. They should then identify, for each job category, the knowledge, skills, and attitudes necessary for employees to perform competently. They should use the skills list as the basis for a curriculum by job category, team, department, or geographical site. More information on this challenging but difficult process can be found in Rothwell and Sredl (2000).

Instructional designers who are developing a situation-specific needs assessment plan that is designed to close a performance gap through instruction should begin by clarifying what they know about it. For example:

Question	*Related Issues*
What is happening now?	How are people presently performing?
	What results (levels of outputs and quality) are now being achieved?
What should be happening?	What are the relevant work standards or performance objectives?
	What relationship, if any, exists between the organization's Strategic Business Plan and employee performance?
	How do managers and others (such as customers) want people to behave or perform?
	What results should be achieved by employees?
	How much does management or other stakeholders (such as customers or shareholders) want this ideal state to exist?
How wide is the performance gap between "what is" and "what should be"?	How can the gap be measured?
	What historical trends are evident?
	Is the gap increasing over time?
How important is the performance gap?	What effects (consequences) of the gap are evident in the organization?
	How does the gap affect individuals inside the targeted group? outside the targeted group?

How much of the performance gap is caused by deficiencies in knowledge, skills, or attitudes?	Can the problem be broken down into parts?
	Are some parts of the problem (that is, sub-problems) caused by deficiencies in knowledge, skills, or attitudes, while others are caused by deficiencies in the environment?
What solutions are cost-effective and feasible?	How should sub-problems caused by environmental deficiencies be solved?
	How should sub-problems caused by deficiencies in knowledge, skills, or attitudes be solved?
What unintended side effects of taking corrective action can be predicted?	Will efforts to investigate problems or sub-problems change them because people will modify their behaviors during the investigation process?
	Will data collection efforts create expectations, realistic or otherwise, about management actions or solutions?
	Will decision makers interpret results of needs assessment in conformity with logical conclusions reached, or will they impose their own personal interpretations on results?

Having answered these questions, instructional designers should then move on to establish objectives, identify the target audience, select sampling procedures, decide on appropriate data collection methods, specify instruments and protocols, choose methods of data analysis, and describe how decisions will be made based on the data. We now turn to a discussion of each step.

Establishing Objectives of a Needs Assessment

Needs assessment objectives spell out the results sought from needs assessment. In a written needs assessment plan, they should appear immediately after a succinct description of the performance problem to be investigated. Needs assessment objectives, much like instructional objectives, provide direction. They reduce the chance that instructional designers might get sidetracked studying tangential issues during the assessment process. In addition, they also clarify why the problem is worth solving and what the ideal assessment outcomes will be.

To establish needs assessment objectives, instructional designers should begin by clarifying what results are to be achieved from the needs assessment. This is a visioning activity that should produce a mental picture of the desired conditions existing at the end of the assessment process. Once the vision has been formulated, instructional designers should then write a short (one- to two-page) proposal for conducting the needs assessment. This proposal should be used as a selling tool and as a formal request. Most important, it should be used to build ownership for the assessment among key decision makers.

Results can be thought of in several ways. One desirable result of needs assessment is agreement among stakeholders about what the needs are and what instruction should meet them. A second desirable result is a sense of what learners must know, do, or feel to overcome the deficiency of knowledge causing the performance problem. A third and final result is a clear sense of the final work product of the needs assessment. By thinking about the final work product, instructional designers begin to clarify just how the results should be presented to stakeholders. For example, should the needs assessment results be described in a detailed report, a memo, a letter, an executive briefing, an electronic mail message, a Web site, or some combination?

Objectives can take different forms in a needs assessment plan. For example, they can be presented as questions about a performance problem, statements of desired results, or statistically testable hypotheses. Questions are appropriate when the aim is to use information collected during needs assessment to stimulate organizational change. Statistically testable hypotheses are appropriate only when assessment will be carried out with extraordinary rigor and the information collected during assessment will be subjected to statistical analysis. Any good book on social science research will contain sections on establishing "research objectives," a topic that can be readily translated into advice about preparing "needs assessment objectives."

Identifying the Target Audience

Whose instructional needs are to be addressed in solving the performance problem? Who must be persuaded by the results of needs assessment to authorize instructional projects and provide resources for carrying them out? To answer these questions, instructional designers have to identify target audiences. Of course, any needs assessment really has at least two target audiences—performers and decision-makers.

Performers are employees whose instructional needs will be identified through the needs assessment process. They correspond to subjects in a research project. Any needs assessment will have to identify who is presently affected by the performance problem, how much they are affected, and where they are located. In microtraining needs assessment projects focusing on a single work unit, it may be possible to identify only a few individuals whose needs should be examined. But in most macrotraining needs assessment projects, it will be necessary to consider instructional needs by employee job categories or departments. Each job class may be viewed as a different market segment for instruction, and each segment may differ in needs. For example, if human performance problems stem from lack of employee knowledge about such organizational "rules" as dress code or hours of work, employees may lack knowledge of them, while supervisors, managers, or team members may lack knowledge of how to deal with the corrective action stemming from those problems.

Decision makers are the individuals whose support will be crucial if the needs assessment plan is to be carried out successfully. They may include instructional designers who will use results of the needs assessment and supervisors of employees who will receive instruction. It is essential to identify who will receive results of the needs assessment, because their personal values and beliefs will affect the interpretation of the results.

Establishing Sampling Procedures

A *sample* is a small, representative group drawn from a larger group called a population. Sampling is the process of identifying smaller groups for examination. It is used to economize the time and expense of gathering information about needs, and it is often the focus of some questions (Kish, 1995; Thompson, 2002).

Any sample will deviate to some extent from the "true" nature of the population from which it is drawn, a principle known as sampling error. Sampling error cannot be eliminated, but it can be predicted and conclusions can be reached in a way that takes its effects into account. A sampling procedure is the method used to select a sample.

Instructional designers commonly use any of four types of sampling procedures: (1) convenience or judgmental sampling, (2) simple random sampling, (3) stratified sampling, and (4) systematic sampling. To determine which one to use, instructional designers should consider the objectives of the needs assessment, the degree of certainty needed in the conclusions, the willingness of decision makers in the organization to allow information to be collected for the needs assessment study, and the resources (time, money, and staff) available.

Convenience or judgmental sampling is probably used more often than many instructional designers would care to admit. It is a type of non-probability sampling in that the subjects for review are chosen for convenience or accessibility rather than representativeness. Sampling of this kind is tempting because it is usually fast and inexpensive. Unfortunately, convenience or judgmental samples do not necessarily yield unbiased results because the choice of cases may be biased from the outset. To carry out convenience or judgmental sampling, instructional designers (1) select some number of cases to include in the sample based on convenience (they are easiest to obtain), access (capable of examination), or intuition (best guess of appropriate number to sample), and (2) choose the sample based on the results of Step 1.

Simple random sampling is a type of probability sampling in which each subject in the population has an equal chance of being selected for study. This sampling procedure is appropriate when the population is large, and it does not matter which cases in the population are selected for examination. To carry out simple random sampling, instructional designers should (1) clarify the nature of the population, (2) list the population, (3) assign an identification number to each member of the population, and (4) select the sample by using any method that permits each member of the population an equal chance of being selected (for example, use a random number table or the random number feature on certain calculators).

Stratified sampling is more sophisticated. It is appropriate when the population is composed of subgroups differing in key respects. In needs assessment, subgroups may mean people in different job classes, hierarchical levels, structural parts of the organization, or geographical sites. They may also mean classifications of people by age group, level of educational attainment, previous job experience, or performance appraisal ratings. The important point is that stratified sampling ensures that each subgroup in a population is represented proportionally in a sample. For instance, suppose 10 percent of an organization consists of salespersons. If it is important in needs assessment to ensure that 10 percent of the sample consists of salespersons, then stratified sampling is appropriate. In simple random sampling, that may not occur. To carry out stratified random sampling, instructional designers should (1) clarify boundaries of the population, (2) identify relevant subgroups within the population, (3) list members of each subgroup, (4) assign numbers to each member of each subgroup, (5) determine what percentage of the population is made up of members of each subgroup, and (6) select the sample at random (each subgroup should be represented in proportion to its representation in the population).

Systematic sampling is an alternative to other methods. It is very simple to use. Suppose that it is necessary to assess the training needs of 10 percent of all employees in an organization. First make a list of everyone in the organization. Then divide the number of persons by 10 percent. Finally, select every tenth name on the list. If names are listed in random order, the resulting sample will be as good as a simple random sample. But if there is any order to the list whatsoever, the resulting sample may be biased as a result of that order.

Many novices—and, on occasion, even those who are not novices—express concern about sample size. On this subject, misconceptions are common. For instance, some people claim a sample size of 5 or 10 percent of a population is adequate for any purpose. Others may (jokingly) claim that any needs assessment is adequate if at least 345 cases are reviewed—because 345 is the minimum number of cases necessary to achieve a representative sample of the entire U.S. population at a low confidence level! However, population size has nothing to do with appropriate sample size.

Three issues should be considered when selecting sample size. First, consider degree of confidence. To be 100 percent certain, examine the entire population. But if lower degrees of confidence can be tolerated, the percentage of the population to be examined can be reduced. Second, consider maximum allowable error, indicating what number it may not exceed. Third, consider standard deviation. It measures variations in the population. When these numbers have been computed, appropriate sample size can be determined.

Determining Data Collection Strategy and Tactics

How will information about instructional needs be collected? Answer this question in the needs assessment plan, making sure that the data collection methods chosen are appropriate for investigating the performance problem. Five methods are typically used to collect information about instructional needs: (1) interviews, (2) direct observation of work, (3) indirect examination of performance or productivity measures, (4) questionnaires, and (5) task analysis. Other possible data collection approaches include (1) key informant or focus groups, (2) nominal group techniques, (3) Delphi procedure, (4) critical incident method, (5) competency assessment, (6) assessment center, and (7) exit interviews. In her classic book on training needs assessment, Rossett (1988) also lists others.

Interviews are structured or unstructured conversations focusing on needs. They are relatively simple to plan and conduct. Instructional designers should usually focus these conversations on key managers' perceptions about the performance problem and the planned instruction necessary to solve it. A key advantage of interviews is that they allow instructional designers the flexibility to question knowledgeable people, probing for information as necessary (Holstein and Gubrium, 2001). On the other hand, a key disadvantage of interviews is that they may be time-consuming and expensive to carry out, especially if travel is required. To plan interviews, instructional designers should

1. Prepare a list of general topics or specific questions.
2. Identify people who are knowledgeable about training needs.

3. Meet with the knowledgeable people and pose questions about training needs.
4. Take notes during or immediately following the interview.

Direct observations of work are, as the phrase implies, first-hand examinations of what workers do to perform and how they do it. They may be planned or unplanned; they may or may not rely on specialized forms to record the actions or results of performers–and may even focus on behavior (Thompson, Felce, and Symons, 1999).

Indirect examinations of performance or productivity measures are called indirect because they are unobtrusive and thus do not require instructional designers to observe workers performing; rather, they judge performance from such tangible results or indicators of results as production records, quality control rejects, scrap rates, work samples, or other records about the quantity or quality of work performed. Indirect examinations may be structured (in which results of observations are recorded on checklists) or unstructured (in which the researcher's feelings and perceptions about results are recorded).

Questionnaires, sometimes called mail surveys or web-based surveys, consist of written questions about instructional needs. They solicit opinions about needs from performers, their supervisors, or other stakeholders. They are sometimes developed from interview results to cross-check how many people share similar opinions or perceptions about needs (Dillman, 1999). They may be structured (and use scaled responses) or unstructured (and use open-ended essay responses). In recent years, many people have moved from so-called paper-and-pencil questionnaires to web-based or web-supported questionnaires. However, following the anthrax scare of recent years, response rates for both paper-and-pencil and web-based questionnaires have been far from impressive for many researchers. Anecdotal evidence suggests that response rates as poor as 5 percent are not uncommon, and such low response rates are not helpful for drawing generalizations—although they may provide intriguing information for subsequent data collection efforts.

Task analysis is a general term for a series of techniques by which work procedures or methods are carried out (Annett and Stanton, 2001; Watson and Llorens, 1997). We will have more to say about this approach to data collection in Chapter Seven.

Key informant groups or focus groups rely on highly knowledgeable people or committees composed of representatives from different segments of stakeholders (Bader and Rossi, 2002; Krueger and Casey, 2000). Key informant groups are especially knowledgeable about a performance problem or possible instructional needs; focus groups are committees, usually created informally, that are established to identify instructional needs through planned participation of representatives from key stakeholder groups.

The nominal group technique (NGT) takes its name from the formation of small groups in which the participants do not, during the earliest stages of data collection, actively interact. Hence, they are groups in name only, that is, they are only nominal groups. To use NGT in data collection, instructional designers should

1. Form a panel of people representative of the targeted learners (or their organizational superiors).
2. Call a meeting of the panel.
3. Ask each panel member to write opinions about training needs on slips of paper.
4. Permit no discussion as the opinions are being written.
5. Record items on a chalkboard or an overhead transparency for subsequent panel discussion.
6. Combine similar responses.
7. Solicit discussion from panel members about what they have written.
8. Ask panel members to vote to accept or reject the opinions about training needs recorded on the chalkboard or transparency.

The Delphi procedure takes its name from the famed Delphic Oracle, well-known during ancient Greek times. Similar in some ways to NGT, the Delphi procedure substitutes written questionnaires for small-group interaction as a means of collecting information about training needs. To use the Delphi procedure to collect data, instructional designers should

1. Form a panel of people representative of the target group.
2. Develop a written questionnaire based on the training needs or human performance problems to be investigated. Posing open-ended questions is acceptable at the outset.
3. Send copies of the questionnaire to panel members.
4. Compile results from the initial round of questionnaires and create scales to assess levels of agreement among the experts.
5. Prepare a second questionnaire and send it and the results of the first round to the panel members.
6. Compile results from the second round.
7. Continue the process of feedback and questionnaire preparation until opinions converge, usually after three rounds.

The critical incident method takes its name from the process of collecting information about critically important (critical) performance in special situations (incidents). Critical incidents were first used as a method of collecting information about the training needs of pilots during World War II and have subsequently been used to identify special training needs of CIA agents (Johnson, 1983). To use the critical incident method, instructional designers should

1. Identify experts such as experienced performers or their immediate supervisors.
2. Interview the experts about performance that is critical to success or failure in performing a job.
3. Ask the experts to relate anecdotes (stories) from their first-hand experience about situations in which performers are forced to make crucially important decisions.
4. Compare stories across the experts to identify common themes about what performers must know.
5. Use this information to identify training needs.

Alternative approaches to this critical incident process may be used, of course, and may focus on the most difficult situations encountered, common daily work challenges, or the most common human performance problems observed with newcomers.

Competency assessment has been growing in popularity in recent years (Rothwell and Lindholm, 1999). Its purpose, according to one of many views, is to identify and isolate the characteristics of ideal (exemplary) performers (Dubois and Rothwell, 2000). Those characteristics are, in turn, used as a foundation for preparing instruction that is designed to raise average performers to ideal performers. A major advantage of competency assessment is that it is targeted toward achieving ideal performance more than rectifying individual performance problems or deficiencies. But a major disadvantage is that needs assessments using this form of data collection may be quite expensive and time-consuming to do if they are to be legally defensible. To use the competency assessment method, instructional designers should

1. Form a panel of managers or experienced performers.
2. Identify the characteristics of ideal performers. (In this context, characteristics may mean behaviors, results achieved, or both.)
3. Pose the following questions to the panel members: What characteristics should be present in competent performers? How much should they be present? Answering these questions may involve behavioral events interviewing

in which exemplary performers are asked to relate a significant work-related story from their experience and describe exactly what they did, how they felt as they did it, and even what they thought as they did it.

4. Devise ways to identify and measure the characteristics.
5. Compare characteristics of actual performers to those described in the competency model.
6. Identify differences that lend themselves to corrective action through planned instruction.

Numerous alternatives to this approach exist. The reason: Views about what should be used as the basis for competencies may differ. According to one view, for instance, competencies are derived by studying the results (outputs) produced by performers; according to another view, competencies are derived from examining common characteristics shared by exemplary performers.

An assessment center is not a place; rather it is a method of collecting information (Thornton, 1992). Assessment centers are expensive to design and operate, which is a major disadvantage of this approach to data collection. However, their results are detailed, individualized, and job-related, and that is a chief advantage of the assessment center method. To use the assessment center, instructional designers may have to rely on the skills of those who specialize in establishing them. The basic steps in preparing an assessment center are, however, simple enough. They require a highly skilled specialist, familiar with employee selection methods and testing validation, to

1. Conduct an analysis of each job category to be assessed.
2. Identify important responsibilities for each job.
3. Use the results of Step 2 to develop games or simulations based on the knowledge and skills needed to perform the job successfully.
4. Train people to observe and judge the performance of participants in the assessment center.
5. Provide each individual who participates in the assessment center with specific feedback from observers about training needs.

Exit interviews are planned or unplanned conversations carried out with an organization's terminating employees to record their perceptions of employee training needs in their job categories or work groups. Exit interviews are relatively inexpensive to do and tend to have high response rates. However, they may yield biased results in that they tend to highlight perceptions of employees who have decided to leave the organization.

Many instructional designers wonder when to choose one or more of these data collection methods. While there is no simple way to reach a decision about choosing a method, several important issues identified by Newstrom and Lilyquist (1979, p. 56) in their classic treatment of this topic are still quite relevant:

1. *Incumbent involvement.* How much does the data collection approach allow learners to participate in identifying needs?
2. *Management involvement.* How much does the data collection approach allow managers in the organization to participate in identifying needs?
3. *Time required.* How long will it take to collect and compile the data?
4. *Cost.* What will be the expense of using a given data collection method?
5. *Relevant quantifiable data.* How much data will be produced? How useful will it be? How much will it lend itself to verifiable measurement?

In considering various data collection methods, instructional designers are advised to weigh these issues carefully. (See Table 4.1.) Not all data collection methods share equal advantages and disadvantages.

Specifying Instruments and Protocols

What instruments should be used during the needs assessment, and how should they be used? What approvals or protocols are necessary for conducting the needs assessment, and how will the instructional designer interact with members of the organization? These questions must be addressed in a needs assessment plan. The first has to do with specifying instruments; the second has to do with specifying protocol.

Many instruments may be used in needs assessment. Common methods of collecting information about instructional needs rely on commercially available or tailor-made questionnaires, interview guides, observation guides, tests, and document review guides. Commercially available instruments and online data collection methods have been prepared for widespread applications, although some consideration of how to use an instrument or groupware program in one organizational setting is usually necessary and should be described in the needs assessment.

Tailor-made instruments are prepared by instructional designers or others for assessing instructional needs in one organization or one job classification. The process of developing a valid, reliable questionnaire may require substantial work in its own right, and this process should be described in the needs assessment plan. The use of groupware necessitates establishing an approach to data collection.

TABLE 4.1. STRENGTHS AND WEAKNESSES OF SELECTED DATA COLLECTION METHODS.

Methods	Criteria				
	Incumbent Involvement	Management Involvement	Time Required	Cost	Relevant Quantifiable Data
Interviews	High	Low	High	High	Moderate
Direct observation of work	Moderate	Low	High	High	Moderate
Indirect examinations of performance or productivity measures	Low	Moderate	Low	Low	High
Questionnaires	High	High	Moderate	Moderate	High
Task analysis	Low	Low	High	High	High
Key informant or focus groups	High	Moderate	Moderate	Moderate	Moderate
Nominal group technique	High	Moderate	Moderate	Moderate	Moderate
Delphi procedure	Low	Moderate	Moderate	Moderate	Moderate
Critical incident method	Moderate	Moderate	Low	Low	Low
Competency assessment	Low	High	High	High	High
Assessment center	High	Low	High	High	High
Exit interviews	Low	Low	Low	Low	Low

Source: Newstrom, J., and Lilyquist, J., 1979, p. 56. Reprinted from *Training and Development Journal.* Copyright 1979. The American Society for Training and Development. Reprinted with permission. All rights reserved.

Protocol generally means diplomatic etiquette and must be considered in planning needs assessment. It stems from organizational culture—the unseen rules guiding organizational behavior. In this instance, "rules" should be interpreted as the means by which instructional designers will carry out the needs assessment, interact with the client, deliver results, interpret them, and plan action based on them. In the process of developing the needs assessment plan, instructional designers should seek answers to such questions as these:

- With whom in the organization should the instructional designer interact during the needs assessment? (How many people? For what issues?)
- Whose approval is necessary to collect information? (For example, must the plant manager at each site grant approval for administering a questionnaire?)

- To whom should the results of the needs assessment be reported? To whom should periodic progress reports be provided, if desired at all?
- How have previous consultants, if any, interacted with the organization? What did they do particularly well, or what mistakes did they make, according to managers in the organization?
- What methods of delivering results are likely to get the most serious consideration? (For instance, will a lengthy written report be read?)

Instructional designers should always remember that the means by which needs assessment is carried out can influence the results and the willingness of the client to continue the relationship. For this reason, it is important to use effective interpersonal skills (described in Chapter Seventeen).

Determining Methods of Data Analysis

How will results of the needs assessment be analyzed once the information has been collected? This question must be answered in a needs assessment plan. It is also the one question that instructional designers may inadvertently forget. But if it is not considered, then subsequent analysis will be difficult because instructional designers may find that they did not collect enough information, or they collected the wrong kind to make informed decisions about instructional needs.

Selecting a data analysis method depends on the needs assessment design, corresponding to a research design, that has been previously selected. They include: (1) historical, (2) descriptive, (3) developmental, (4) case or field study, (5) correlational, (6) causal-comparative, (7) true experimental, (8) quasi-experimental, and (9) action research (Isaac and Michael, 1984).

Historical and case or field study designs usually rely heavily on qualitative approaches to data analysis. The instructional designer simply describes conditions in the past (historical studies) or present (case or field study). Hence, analysis is expressed in narrative form, often involving anecdotes or literature reviews. Anecdotes have strong persuasive appeal, and they tend to be selected for their exceptional or unusual nature. They are rarely intended to be representative of typical conditions or situations.

Descriptive designs include interview studies, questionnaires, and document reviews. Data are presented either qualitatively as narrative or quantitatively through simple frequencies, means, modes, and medians. A frequency is little more than a count of how often a problem occurs or an event happens. A mean is the arithmetic average of numbers. A mode is the most common number, and the median is the middle number in a sequence. Perhaps examples will help to clarify these terms. Suppose we have a series of numbers: 1, 4, 9, 7, 6, 3, 4. The frequency is the number of times each number occurs. Each number occurs one time, except for 4. The mode of this series of numbers then is 4, since it occurs most frequently. The median is the middle number, found by arranging the numbers in order and then counting: 1, 3, 4, 4, 6, 7, 9. The median in this array is 4, since it is the middle number. To find the mean (arithmetic average), simply add the numbers and then divide by how many numbers there are. In this case, the sum of $1 + 4 + 9 + 7 + 6 + 3 + 4$ equals 34 divided by 7 equals 4.8 (rounded). Frequencies, means, modes, and medians are used in analyzing needs assessment data because they are simple to understand and are also simple to explain to decision makers. In addition, they lend themselves especially well to the preparation of computerized graphics.

The analysis used in other needs assessment designs—developmental, correlational, experimental, quasi-experimental, or causal-comparative—requires sophisticated statistical techniques. For these designs, the most commonly used data analytical methods include the analysis of variance, chi square, and the t test. When these methods must be used, instructional designers should refer to detailed descriptions about them in statistics textbooks.

Assessing the Feasibility of the Needs Assessment Plan

Before finalizing the needs assessment plan, instructional designers should review it with three important questions in mind: (1) Can it be done with the resources available? (2) Is it workable in the organizational culture? and (3) Has all superfluous information been eliminated from the plan?

It makes little sense, of course, to prepare an ambitious plan that cannot be carried out due to lack of resources–or accelerated project timelines with ridiculously short fuses. For this reason, careful thought must be given to the available resources. More specifically, instructional designers should ponder these issues: Given the draft needs assessment plan, what resources will be necessary to implement it successfully? How many and what kind of people will be required to staff the effort? What equipment and tools will they need? How long will it take to conduct the needs assessment? What limitations on staff, money, equipment, or access to information are likely to be faced, and is the needs assessment plan realistic in light of available resources and likely constraints?

Just as it makes little sense to establish an ambitious needs assessment plan that cannot be carried out with the resources available, it also makes little sense to plan a needs assessment that will not be supported by the organizational culture. For this reason, the following questions are also worth consideration: How are decisions made in the organization, and how well does the needs assessment plan take the organization's decision-making processes into account? Whose opinions are most valued, and how well does the needs assessment plan take their opinions into account? How have organizational members solved problems in the past, and how well does the needs assessment plan take the organization's past experience with problem solving into account?

Finally, superfluous information should be eliminated from the needs assessment plan, needs assessment processes, and reports on the results. The acid test for useful information has to do with the amount of persuasion that is necessary. Complex plans are unnecessary when decision makers do not require much information to be convinced of an instructional need. Indeed, too much information will only distract decision makers, drawing their attention away from what is important. Simplicity is more powerful and elegant.

Developing a Needs Assessment Plan: A Case Study

Josephine Smith is the training director at a large Midwestern bank. She was recently hired for this job. As her first assignment, she was asked to review correspondence leaving the bank. Key officers of the bank have a problem of (in the words of one) "providing a tone in our correspondence that we put customer service first in whatever we do."

Josephine conducted an initial performance analysis (an alpha needs assessment) and found that the "problem" has several components. Each component she calls a "sub-problem."

First, the bank uses form letters for most routine correspondence. Loan officers commonly send out these form letters, which were not written with an emphasis on a good "customer service tone." This sub-problem is a deficiency in the environment, and Josephine has asked the key officers to form a committee to review the letters and eventually revise them. They have agreed. Second, Josephine's investigation reveals that employees at the bank do not know how to write correspondence with an adequate "customer service" tone. This sub-problem is a training need.

Josephine set out to assess training needs by analyzing common problems appearing in nonroutine correspondence sent from the bank. She will use the results of this situation-specific, gamma-type needs assessment to identify the gap between what is (letters as written) and what should be (letters as they should be written). She will, in turn, use that information in establishing instructional objectives for training that will furnish loan officers—her target audience—with the knowledge they need to write letters in desired ways.

Josephine begins needs assessment planning by proposing to her immediate superiors a review of special letters recently mailed from the bank by loan officers. These letters will be compared to criteria, set forth on a checklist, for letters exhibiting an adequate customer service tone. This checklist (an instrument) will be prepared by a committee consisting of Josephine and several key managers in the bank. (The first step in developing the checklist will involve clarification of just what does and what does not constitute a good customer service tone, a phrase too vague to provide guidance in establishing concrete instructional objectives.) The same committee will then use the checklist to review letters and identify the frequency of common problems of tone in the letters. It will use the results to prioritize training objectives for loan officers.

Solving Problems in Conducting Needs Assessment

Planning a needs assessment poses one challenge. Conducting the needs assessment—implementing the plan—poses another. While logic and research rigor are typically emphasized in the planning stage, everyday pressures to achieve quick results and hold down costs most keenly affect instructional designers during the implementation stage. However, implementation problems can usually be minimized if the plan has been stated clearly and key decision makers have received advance notice of the plan and its pending implementation. Indeed, the chances for success increase even more if key decision makers participated in developing the plan and feel ownership in it.

When implementing the needs assessment plan, instructional designers should at least be able to apply appropriate tactics to ensure successful implementation. Tactics, perhaps best understood as specific approaches used in day-to-day operations, are necessary for dealing with common problems typically arising during implementation of a needs assessment plan. These problems include (1) managing sample selection, (2) collecting data while not creating false expectations, (3) avoiding errors in protocol, and (4) limiting participation in the interpretation of needs assessment results.

Selecting a sample is usually simple enough. But actually contacting people or finding the "cases" selected is not always so simple. Sometimes people selected are not available because of absences from the job, pressures from work assignments and deadlines, or unwillingness to participate. "Cases"—such as documents or work samples—may be unavailable because they are being used for other reasons or are geographically beyond easy reach.

Perhaps the best way for instructional designers to handle sampling problems is to anticipate them. Sample sizes can be enlarged beyond what is minimally needed so that allowances have been made for unavailable people or cases. Lack of cooperation can be avoided by communicating with others about the purpose of the study, why and how they were chosen to participate, whether their names will be used in the presentation of results, and what will happen with the results.

The more employees who provide data about instructional needs, the higher people's expectations will be that corrective action in the organization will take place. This expectation of change can be a positive force—an impetus for progressive change—when action quickly follows data collection and is visibly targeted on problems that many people believe should receive attention. However, the reverse is also true: the act of collecting data can be demoralizing when corrective action is delayed or when key managers end up appearing to ignore the prevailing views of prospective learners about the direction for desired change. To overcome this problem, instructional designers can choose to limit initial data collection efforts to small groups or to geographically restricted ones so as to hold down the number of people whose expectations are raised.

Errors in protocol can also plague needs assessment efforts. Perhaps the most common one is the instructional designer's failure to receive enough— or the right kind of—permissions to collect data. To overcome this problem, instructional designers should be sure to discuss the organization's formal (or informal) policies on data collection with key decision makers in the organization before sending out questionnaires, interviewing employees, or appearing in work units to observe job activities. They should double-check to make sure they have secured all necessary approvals before collecting data. Failure to take this step can create significant, and often unfortunate, barriers to cooperation in the organization. Indeed, it may derail the entire needs assessment effort.

Some instructional designers like to think of themselves as powerful change agents who are technically proficient in their craft and who, like skilled doctors, should "prescribe the right medicine to cure the ills" of the organization. Unfortunately, this approach is not always effective because it does not allow decision-makers to develop a sense of ownership in the solutions. Indeed, they may think of the solution as "something dreamed up by those instructional designers." To avoid this problem, instructional designers may form a committee of key managers to review the raw data and detailed results of their needs assessment before proposing a corrective action plan. Committee members go over the data and the analytical methods used. They are then asked for their interpretations and suggested solutions.

This approach serves several useful purposes. First, it builds an informed constituency among the audience for the needs assessment report. Members of that constituency will grasp, perhaps better than most, how conclusions were arrived at. Second, they have an opportunity to review raw data. (On occasion, striking anecdotes or handwritten comments on questionnaires have a persuasive force that statistical results do not.) Third, by giving members of the committee an opportunity to interpret results on their own, instructional designers build support for the needs assessment's results.

Identifying Instructional Problems

Instructional designers should be capable of pinpointing instructional problems based on needs assessment results. Of course, the key to identifying instructional problems is the needs assessment plan itself. It should clarify what performance is desired and provide criteria by which to determine how well people are performing, how well people should be performing, and how much difference there is between the two. By keeping in mind what results are sought throughout the needs assessment process, instructional designers can prepare themselves for identifying instructional needs.

One way to identify instructional needs is to focus, over the course of the needs assessment, on tentative needs that are discernible during the data collection process. To keep track of them, instructional designers may wish to use a needs assessment sheet. It is a structured way of recording instructional needs for subsequent review. Accountants use similar sheets when conducting financial, compliance, management, or program results audits. While the final results of the needs assessment may or may not confirm these needs, the needs assessment sheets do provide a means by which instructional designers can communicate with team members. They are also very helpful because they often suggest ways to organize the needs assessment report.

Judging Needs Assessment Plans

Instructional designers should be capable of judging needs assessment plans prepared by themselves or others. Their judgment should be based on the contents and feasibility of the needs assessment plan and the match between instructional problems and data about them. Some observers call this an auditing process (Kaufman, 1994).

Judging Contents and Feasibility of a Needs Assessment Plan

Instructional designers should always review their own needs assessment plans—or plans of other instructional designers—to be sure that they contain at least the following: (1) needs assessment objectives, (2) identification of the target audience, (3) procedures for sampling the target audience and organizational objectives, (4) strategy and tactics for data collection, (5) specifications of instruments or protocols to be used, (6) data analysis methods, and (7) a description of how decisions will be made based on the data.

Instructional designers should then review the details in the needs assessment plan. Are they adequate to guide implementation? Are they feasible? Does the plan possess sufficient detail so that someone knowing little about the organization can understand why the needs assessment is necessary? Are there reasons given for the selection of instructional objectives, targeted audience, sampling procedures, data collection strategy and tactics, instruments and protocols, and analytical methods and decision-making methods?

Judging the Match Between Instructional Problems and Data About Them

Instructional designers should also evaluate the match between the results of needs assessment and the conclusions about instructional problems based on them. To address these issues, instructional designers may find it helpful to prepare a simple chart indicating the needs assessment results and the conclusions drawn from them. If there is a match, this chart should be easy to prepare. Otherwise, it may be necessary to backtrack—or advise others to do so—in order to collect additional data or revise conclusions.

Justifying Needs Assessment

Instructional designers should also be able to justify needs assessment. They should thus be able to explain the reason the needs assessment was conducted and justify the objectives, target audience, sampling procedures, data collection methods, instruments and protocols, methods of data analysis, methods of conducting the assessment, and methods of identifying human performance problems appropriately solved by instruction. In short, they should be able to explain why the needs assessment was carried out, why it was planned as it was, why the plan was implemented as it was, and what the results mean. If instructional designers cannot justify what they do, they will find it difficult to answer the questions raised by operating managers or clients. It is also wise at this point to gain agreement with the client about the relative costs and benefits of designing and delivering the instruction, since it is usually more convincing to forecast expected results first than to try to prove them after project close-out.

To provide good justification, instructional designers should keep track of their reasons for making decisions about needs assessment plans, objectives, target audience, sampling procedures, data collection methods, instruments and protocols, methods of data analysis, methods of conducting the assessment, and methods of identifying human performance problems appropriately solved by instruction. All team members assigned to an instructional design project team should be briefed on these issues so that they can field questions about them.

At the end of the needs assessment, instructional designers should do a postmortem, reflecting on the project from the beginning. They should discuss why the needs assessment was carried out and what was learned from the process. Did team members include all essential elements of a needs assessment plan, such as objectives, target audience, sampling procedures, data collection strategy and tactics, instruments, protocols, data analysis methods, and descriptions of how decisions will be made based on the data? Did they ensure that the needs assessment plan was practical to implement? Were they able to identify instructional problems congruent with data on discrepancies between what is happening and what should be happening?

Acting Ethically in Conducting Needs Assessment

A key ethical challenge in applying needs assessment can be expressed by this question: *Can the needs assessment withstand charges that it was not cost-effective, timely, or rigorous?*

Most instructional designers will find that their internal or external clients are not well-versed on what needs assessment is, why it should be conducted, how it should be conducted, or how long it should take. In fact, one manager told an instructional designer of the authors' acquaintance that "If you have to take time to investigate the problem, then you are not aware of our business challenges and should seek employment elsewhere." While that view may be wrongheaded, it does underscore the need for instructional designers to educate their clients about what they do and to justify every step.

To make the case for a needs assessment, instructional designers should brief their clients on the instructional design process at the outset of their engagement. Needs assessment should be described for what it is—a way to economize efforts by targeting only the instruction that is necessary to solve or avert human performance problems. That will save time and money by avoiding investments in "sheep dip training" that exposes all people to the same instruction despite unique individual or group needs.

In Rothwell's (2003) survey conducted for the third edition of this book, one respondent pointed to needs assessment and needs analysis as a frequent cause from which ethical challenges stemmed. The respondent bewailed that "it is often described as something that should be relentlessly and systematically done, but we are often pushed to action without the minimum analysis information." There is thus a difference between what is contractually required and what is "right" (Hatcher, 2002)–a major ethical dilemma encountered by those working in today's frenetically paced organizations.

Assessing Needs Cross-Culturally

Needs assessment is prone to the same cross-cultural issues as performance analysis. Just as political climate can help or hinder performance analysis, so too can it help or hinder needs assessment. While no silver bullet exists to avoid all problems in all settings, a cultural informant should be identified and consulted before a needs assessment is conducted in a culture with which the instructional designer is unfamiliar. Recall from the last chapter that cultural informants should be trustworthy and familiar with the local culture. In addition, they should understand why a needs assessment is important.

Cultural informants should also be consulted about the language abilities of those targeted for participation in needs assessment and other cultural variables. For instance, if an instructional designer wants to administer a written needs assessment questionnaire, it will usually be necessary to determine in advance what language skills are possessed by those targeted to complete the question- naire. It will also be necessary to determine whether the questionnaire should be written in English, the native tongue of the targeted participants, or both. (Translated questionnaires, of course, introduce a host of new requirements, too, such as the need to check translation accuracy.) Similarly, local customs–or the availability of technology—may also affect applications of other data col- lection methods. For instance, observation may prove distracting and trouble- some to individuals in some cultures, so special steps may be necessary to make it work as intended. If web-based questionnaires are administered, care must be taken to ensure that it does not take eight minutes to turn a web page—as it does in China when the server is located in the United States.

Recent Developments in Needs Assessment

Since the third edition of this book was published, needs assessment has become the focus of increased attention in many disciplines. Instructional designers are well advised to remain vigilant to new approaches to needs assessment, since those approaches are likely to affect their work more in the future.

One development is the increasing sophistication of technologically based methods to conduct needs assessment. As special approaches to collecting data from groups become available, watch for the emergence of real-time needs assess- ment. Also watch for more creative applications of tried-and-true approaches. For example, one author of this book has conducted a focus group by conference call that worked surprisingly well. It was also done at much lower cost than would have been possible if a group of people had to travel to one location.

A second development is the inclusion of benchmarking, and the consideration of best practices, in needs assessment. Early approaches to needs assessment directed attention to performance expectations inside organizations only. But, as the principles of process improvement have become commonplace, instructional designers are comparing internal performance expectations to external best-practice examples, to performance expectations in other organizations, and to customer expectations of targeted learners. As a consequence, benchmarking methods are being combined with needs assessment to identify best, not better, performance requirements. However, care should be taken when benchmarking to avoid central tendency error—the fallacy of promoting mediocrity instead of best practices, as many organizations focus their attention exclusively on what is done in a few blue-chip firms rather than seek unusual but highly innovative approaches that may exist in smaller, more entrepreneurial organizations.

A third development is the recognition that change is occurring so quickly that traditional needs assessment results date too rapidly. Instructional designers must adopt dynamic approaches to address this moving target effect. They must lead the target, taking action to help learners anticipate rather than react to changing performance expectations. One way to do that is to develop future scenarios—descriptions of conditions prevailing in alternative futures—and base instruction around them.

A fourth development is that instructional designers are increasingly tasked to look for performance improvement opportunities based on strengths rather than on deficiencies (gaps). As a result of positive change theory, many managers and others would rather focus on leveraging strengths rather than on solving problems. To do that requires a special mindset, one that begins with first asking people what motivates them in their work and progresses into inviting them to conceptualize ways to increase that feeling. While it may sound different, the approach does have much to recommend it—particularly in successful organizations in which it is difficult to excite people to want to solve problems.

What Is New in Conducting a Needs Assessment?

Needs assessment and needs analysis, like performance analysis, have historically focused on performance gaps between what people know, do, or feel and what they should know, do, or feel to perform their jobs successfully. Critics of traditional needs assessment, like critics of traditional performance analysis, tend to take issue with gap analysis—that is, a focus on deficiencies—as a foundation for needs assessment. By doing that, instructional designers seem to be finding fault. That makes participation in training a form of punishment because it appears to emphasize what people do not know. The critics would further contend that such an emphasis on deficiencies is past-oriented because those deficiencies are based on historical knowledge about what needs to be known, done, or felt to be successful. But the future may be quite different from the past.

Those emphasizing positive change—that is, appreciative inquiry—will tend to focus on the future and gear training as a means of preparing people for the future and building on their strengths, rather than emphasizing deficiencies based on the past alone.

Another development in needs assessment and analysis is growing interest in competency identification, modeling and assessment. The focus should not be so much on the work to be done, as task analysis and job analysis tradition-ally focus, but on differences between the characteristics of the best performers and other performers. In a classic treatment, Gilbert indicated that performance improvement potential (PIP) involved comparing the outputs or productivity of the most productive people to that of the whole work group. PIP was intended to demonstrate the realistic productivity gap that existed between all workers or average workers compared to those who are the most productive. That thinking has led to one way to think about the value of competency modeling as a means of leveraging performance for an entire workforce (Dubois and Rothwell, 2003).

Finally, another new development is the increasing use of online and other virtual methods to facilitate training needs assessment. Many organizations now offer web-based survey software. Videoconferencing makes online focus groups and virtual face-to-face interviews possible. In short, there is growing interest in using technology-assisted methods to pinpoint training needs with a view toward cutting the time and cost involved in doing so. The future is likely to see more such methods being used.

Conclusion

In this chapter we described the first step in the systematic design of instruction— conducting a needs assessment. The purpose of needs assessment, as we explained, is to uncover precisely what the human performance problem is, whom it affects, how it affects them, and what results are to be achieved by instruction. In the next nine chapters, we will continue to describe steps in the model of instructional design introduced in this chapter. As we do so, readers should remember along the way that the instructional systems design model is intended to serve as a road map and not as an inflexible list of rules or required steps.

CHAPTER FIVE

ASSESSING RELEVANT LEARNER CHARACTERISTICS

Learners are not all alike. Members of different occupations and individuals differ in the ways they learn best. As instruction is prepared, these differences must be taken into account. To do that successfully, instructional designers should be aware of the characteristics of the targeted learners. The process of identifying these specific characteristics is called *assessing relevant characteristics of learners*, although we will call it simply *learner assessment*. It is the second box in the model of the instructional design process we introduced in Chapter Four. (See Figure 5.1.) It is also the second of several related forms of analysis that may be performed before instructional materials are prepared. The first analysis, needs assessment, was described in the last chapter.

According to *The Standards* (Richey, Fields, and Foxon, 2001, p. 49), one competency for instructional design is to "identify and describe target population characteristics." It is regarded as an essential competency. The performance statements associated with this competency indicate that instructional designers should be able to (Richey, Fields, and Foxon, 2001, p. 49):

a. Determine characteristics of the target population influencing learning and transfer (essential).
b. Analyze, evaluate, and select learner profile data for use in a particular design situation (advanced).

FIGURE 5.1. A MODEL OF STEPS IN THE INSTRUCTIONAL DESIGN PROCESS.

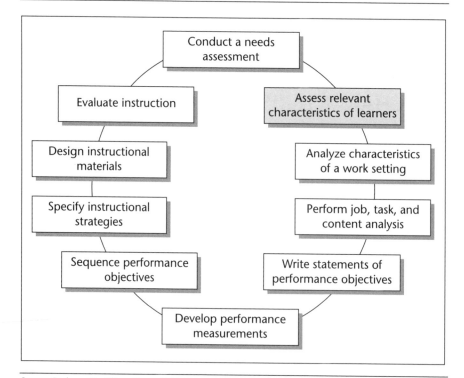

Source: Foshay, W., Silber, K., and Westgaard, O. *Instructional Design Competencies: The Standards.* Iowa City, IA: International Board of Standards for Training, Performance, and Instruction, 1986, p. 3. Copyright 1993 by the International Board of Standards for Training, Performance and Instruction. All rights reserved. Used with permission.

In this chapter, we describe selecting learner characteristics for assessment, suggest methods of identifying appropriate learner characteristics, discuss ways of conducting learner assessment, provide suggestions about developing learner profiles, describe cognitivism as it affects learner assessment, and offer helpful hints for judging and justifying learner assessment. We conclude the chapter by describing key ethical and cross-cultural issues in assessing relevant learner characteristics.

Selecting Learner Characteristics for Assessment

Before preparing instructional or training materials, instructional designers should be able to answer this simple question: *Who is the intended and appropriate learner?* The answer helps define the target population, target group, or target audience. Traditionally, writers on this subject have advised instructional designers to direct their attention to typical or representative learners so as to maximize the number (and success rates) of people who subsequently participate in instruction (Blank, 1982). However, growing sensitivity to the needs of atypical learners, such as those possessing physical, mental, or learning disabilities, may require instructional designers to pay increasing attention to a broader range of learner characteristics. Indeed, somewhere between 3 to 16 percent of all adults in the United States experience learning problems (Hallowell and Ratey, 1993; Smith, 1994; Tracey, 1995), and that group is too large to ignore. Employers are also expected to provide reasonable accommodation for learning disabilities under the Americans with Disabilities Act.

What Learner Characteristics Should Be Assessed?

Assessing learner characteristics resembles *segmentation*, the process used to categorize consumers by similar features. A well-known technique in the advertising and marketing fields, segmentation gives advertisers the ability to target messages to the unique needs and concerns of their audiences. In similar fashion, learners are consumers of services provided by instructional designers. Consequently, many fundamental marketing principles apply to the process of assessing learner characteristics. Much as an organization competes against other organizations in the marketplace, so instruction must compete with other priorities for the attention of learners and their supervisors. The key to success in instructional design, as in marketing, is "to make selling superfluous. The aim is to understand the customers so well that the product or service fits them and sells itself" (Drucker, 1973, pp. 64–65).

Three basic categories of learner characteristics are relevant to a specific situation, performance problem, or instructional need: situation-related characteristics, decision-related characteristics, and learner-related characteristics.

Situation-related characteristics stem from events surrounding the decision to design and deliver instruction. The chief focus of the instructional design effort should be directed to those most affected by it. The reason: subsequent delivery of instruction to that group will presumably have the greatest impact. It will also be substantially more cost-effective than delivering instruction to all employees when only some really need it.

For example, suppose that customers of one organization complain that they are not being treated courteously over the telephone. Performance analysis reveals that it is a problem caused by a lack of knowledge about phone courtesy. In this simple example, the performance problem itself suggests an important learner characteristic: training should be designed only for employees using telephones and dealing directly with customers. Since not all employees in the organization use phones or deal with customers, this learner characteristic alone is helpful in narrowing down the target audience. Moreover, it raises additional questions. For instance, what do these employees have in common that (perhaps) others do not? Why do they talk to customers, for example?

When assessing situational characteristics of learners, instructional designers should begin by asking this question: What are the possible relationships between the performance problem and the learner? Does the performance problem itself suggest unique characteristics of the learners who should receive instruction? If so, what are they? Will those characteristics remain the same—or change—over time? If they will change, in what ways will they change?

Decision-related characteristics pertain to those making decisions about learner participation in instruction. When assessing these characteristics, instructional designers should ask the following question: Who makes decisions about permitting people to participate in instruction? After all, instructional designers may prepare instruction for a targeted group, but others often decide who actually participates. If this fact is ignored, much time may be wasted preparing instruction to meet the needs of one group, only to find that other groups actually participate.

Instructional designers should thus clarify, before preparing training materials, who will make decisions about participation. There are several ways to do that. One way is to establish a formal committee of people from inside the organization. The members of the committee can give advice about who should participate, predict who is likely to participate, and offer practical guidance for attracting appropriate participants by targeting the needs of decision makers.

Learner-related characteristics stem from learners themselves. There are two kinds: (1) prerequisite knowledge, skills, and attitudes, and (2) other learner-related characteristics. Prerequisite knowledge, skills, or attitudes is sometimes called simply a prerequisite. In a classic treatment, Blank (1982, pp. 44–45) defines a prerequisite as "a characteristic, trait, or ability that students should possess to be successful on the job—but one that they will not get as a result of a training program." Blank identifies four types: (1) physical traits, (2) previously learned skills, (3) previously learned knowledge, and (4) previously learned attitudes.

Physical traits include manual dexterity, grip strength, lifting ability, visual acuity, hearing ability, tolerance to extreme conditions, height, weight, sense of balance, and sensitivity to chemicals or other substances. Employers must take care to make reasonable accommodation, too, for workers with physical and other disabilities who can perform various jobs, but perhaps with modifications. Previously learned skills include the ability to read, write, and compute at a certain minimum level, the ability to use certain types of machines or tools, the ability to drive specific vehicles (forklift, road grader, tractor), and the ability to type. Previously learned knowledge includes awareness of rules such as those associated with arithmetic, grammar, pronunciation, electricity, chemistry, or medicine. Previously learned attitudes include basic employability skills, such as awareness of the importance of appropriate dress, punctuality, interpersonal relations at work, and organizational policies and procedures (Carnevale, Gainer, and Meltzer, 1988).

There is no foolproof method for establishing instructional prerequisites; rather, it is often a trial-and-error process. In many cases, instructional designers must simply ask themselves what knowledge, skills, and attitudes they think participants will bring with them to instruction. Later, when instructional materials and methods are tested on small groups of learners chosen as representative of the targeted audience, assumptions made about prerequisite knowledge, skills, and attitudes can also be tested. Another approach is to select at random a few prospective participants to see if they do, in fact, possess the necessary prerequisites.

Instructional designers should remember two key points as they identify prerequisites. First, if trainees enter instruction lacking essential knowledge or skills, then these essentials must be furnished to them. Second, competent legal advice should be sought before people are screened out of instruction that is necessary for job advancement or security, particularly when physical traits are the prerequisites. The reason is that using physical requirements in screening, while superficially appearing to have a neutral effect on the selection of protected labor groups, may actually screen out higher proportions of females and others. When instruction is necessary for job entry or advancement and is denied to some individuals solely because they do not meet previously established prerequisites about physical ability, then it functions as a selection device. As a result, instruction is subject to the laws, regulations, and court decisions affecting equal employment opportunity and equal access for the disabled.

Other learner-related characteristics are also worthy of consideration. They center around the learners' demographic characteristics, physiological characteristics, aptitudes, experience, learning styles, attitudes, job categories, value systems, life cycle stages, or career stages. The following provides an overview of the terms designating these important characteristics.

Demographic characteristics include age, gender, and race; physiological characteristics include heart condition, lung capacity, and general physical condition. Experience characteristics include length of service with the organization, length of service in the job, experience with present job activities prior to job entry, and similar experience; learning style characteristics are classified according to standardized categories.

Aptitude includes talents and skills; knowledge includes education, basic skills, and specialized previous training. Attitudinal feelings include feelings about the topic, training, the job, performance problems, and the organization.

A more in-depth look at these terms follows.

Demographic characteristics are associated with learners' race, gender, and age. Two demographic issues are worthy of special consideration. First, instructional designers should ask whether the instruction they design will be geared to the needs of a particular racial group, gender, or age group, as is sometimes the case in specialized seminars on career planning, communication, retirement, or other subjects. If it will be, then any assumptions made about the learners should be double-checked. These assumptions may be based, knowingly or unknowingly, on stereotypes about the needs or beliefs of the targeted audience and thus may be erroneous. To avoid this problem, some instructional designers may establish an ad hoc panel of advisers to clarify or check the assumptions made about the learners before instruction is designed. Much interest lately is beginning to focus around the needs of older learners, people over the traditional retirement age, since Baby Boomers are aging and may soon become a central focus of interest to many employers who are strapped for talent (Moseley and Dessinger, 2007).

Learner sensitivity to special issues is a second matter to be considered. In recent years, for instance, much attention has been devoted to establishing gender-neutral language so as to avoid stereotypes or other objectionable implications about the gender of employees. Are there other issues to be addressed in the instruction that need to be considered from the standpoint of unique employee groups? If so, they should be identified. Further, means should be established, before instruction is designed, to make sure that learner sensitivities are not violated and that human diversity is celebrated.

Physiological characteristics pertain to the most intimate aspects of the learner. They may include sensitivity to chemicals, prior medical history, and genetic heritage, including a tendency to certain forms of disease. As medical science has advanced, it has become more than a science fiction writer's dream to assess—and even predict—human sensitivity to substances and inclinations to disease.

Relatively little attention in the literature has been devoted to making assumptions about learners' physiological conditions. Nevertheless, if learners will be exposed to chemicals during instruction, then their physiological characteristics should be considered. Should they be given medical examinations before exposure? Have all government requirements been met so that employees are aware of their "right to know" about the substances to which they will be exposed?

Aptitudes are the future capabilities to perform in certain ways. Some individuals are gifted with talents that others do not possess, and those talents are synonymous with aptitudes. Employers sometimes administer aptitude tests before or after employee selection to assess individual potential. When test scores are available, they can be a rich source of information about learners. While this information may be used in designing instruction, it should be examined with due consideration to organizational policies on employee confidentiality and rights to privacy.

Experience means the amount of time the targeted learners have spent in the employing organization, in their jobs, and in their chosen occupations. It is frequently one of the most important learner characteristics to consider in designing instruction. There are several reasons why. First, experience sometimes affects motivation to learn. When people first enter an organization, job, or occupation, they are often highly motivated to learn. They want to reduce the tension existing between themselves and the unfamiliar surroundings (organization) or unfamiliar activities and expectations they face. When instruction will be designed for those with limited experience, there is a greater likelihood that the targeted learners will be motivated to learn. These learners are willing to take instruction very seriously indeed and may (in fact) be depending on it to help them make essential transitions in their lives. Second, experience affects the selection of appropriate instructional methods. Learners with the least experience need the most guidance. Since they "do not know what they do not know," they are prime candidates for directive methods or simulated experiences. However, learners with the most experience generally rebel against directive instructional methods or unrealistic simulations.

Knowledge is associated with what learners know about the subject of instruction, the performance problem, learning needs, and organizational policies and procedures. What, if anything, is known about the learners' knowledge of these subjects? What assumptions, if any, are safe to make about what they know before they enter instruction? Have learners had much or little formal education generally? Have they had specific, previous instruction on the subject at another institution? If so, how was the subject treated?

Learning style refers to the ways people behave and feel while they learn. Several classic questionnaires are available for assessing the learning style of individuals. They may be administered to representatives of the expected target group before instruction is designed, and then the results of the questionnaires can be used in preparing instruction. Alternatively, learners may be asked at the outset of instruction how they learn best, and the results can be used at that stage to modify instruction. Related to learning style is *learning competence*, how well individuals have learned how to learn. It is a topic of growing importance (see Rothwell, 2002), and it should not be assumed that education alone indicates success in learning competence. People may need to be trained on how to learn better.

Attitudinal characteristics refer to learners' feelings about performance that they voice to other people. The term specifically denotes what learners think about a subject, the performance problem that instruction is designed to solve, their own learning needs, the organization, and other important issues. One way instructional designers can assess attitudes is to prepare and administer a simple attitude survey to representatives of the targeted audience. Another way is to field-test instructional materials and then administer an attitude survey to participants in a small-group session.

Geographical location may affect learners' needs and willingness to participate in instruction. It may also influence their attitudes about the performance problem and the instruction designed to address it. After all, learners in different parts of the world may report to different supervisors and may face problems differing in degree or type from learners in other locations. Marketing specialists stress the importance of geographical dimensions as a basis for segmenting markets. Instructional designers may wish to target instruction to one geographical area first and then, in time, to spread out to others. This method is frequently used in marketing products or services.

Job category means the learners' job duties and responsibilities within the organization. It can be an important determinant of what employees need to know and do to perform satisfactorily. Job categories often become the basis for establishing long-term instructional plans to make it easier to orient people to new jobs, upgrade their knowledge and skills as job requirements change, and prepare individuals for promotion or other movements. Of course, in some organizations, team or individual assignments—or some other method—may be substituted for job category if they are the primary means by which work is organized.

There is good reason for placing heavy emphasis on job or work categories when assessing learner characteristics. The work performed is a key link between individual and organizational needs. Individual needs and characteristics also tend to vary somewhat by job or by work responsibilities. Hourly employees may not need the same instruction as supervisors, managers, or executives on a given organizational policy or procedure. Consequently, instruction targeted for one employee category should take the duties and responsibilities of that category into account.

However, jobs may be categorized in several ways. For instance, some instructional designers prefer to use a general job classification scheme. Examples of general job categories include executives, managers, first-line supervisors, technical employees, salespersons, professionals, and skilled workers. An alternative classification scheme, established by the Equal Employment Opportunity Commission for mandatory government reports on hiring, training, and other employee activities, lists the following job categories: officers and managers, professionals, technicians, sales workers, office and clerical workers, skilled craft workers, semiskilled operatives, unskilled laborers, and service workers. The actual job titles placed in each job category may vary across organizations but should remain consistent within one organization.

Value systems are, according to one classic definition, "enduring organizations of beliefs concerning preferable modes of conduct or end-states of existence along a continuum of relative importance" (Rokeach, 1973, p. 5). They are closely associated with organizational culture, perhaps best understood as the taken-for-granted assumptions about the "right" and "wrong" ways of behaving and performing in a particular setting (Schein, 1985). To be effective, instruction should be designed with multiple value systems taken into account (Zemke and Zemke, 1981). Rokeach included a questionnaire in his classic book The Nature of Human Values (1973) that remains very useful in assessing the value systems of people in organizational settings. Instructional designers may administer this survey before instruction is designed or before it is delivered to a specific group in one instructional session. Another classic book, by Francis and Woodcock (1990), also provides information for assessing individual values.

Life cycle stage pertains to the individual's age and stage of development. In each stage of development, the individual experiences central life crises that stimulate interest in learning about issues related to those crises. Consequently, the life cycle stages of prospective participants in instruction are worth some consideration by instructional designers.

The crucial importance of life cycles was first recognized by the developmental psychologist Erikson (1959). It has since been popularized by Levinson (1978) and Sheehy (1974). The importance of life cycle stage in designing instruction was first recognized by Havighurst (1970), described more completely by Knox (1977), and reinforced by Knowles (1984) and Knowles, Swanson, and Holton (2005). Knowles, for instance, identifies three specific stages of adulthood and describes typical "life problems" associated with them, based on vocation or career and home and family living. The three stages are early adulthood (age eighteen to thirty), middle adulthood (age thirty to sixty-five), and later adulthood (age sixty-five and over).

During early adulthood, as Knowles points out, most people are exploring career options, choosing a career, getting a job, learning job skills, and making career progress. They are also usually dating, selecting a mate, preparing for marriage and family, and accepting many responsibilities of adulthood, such as purchasing a home, raising children, and making repairs. They are thus primarily interested in learning about improving their employment-related skills, clarifying their personal values, and coping with the responsibilities of the first stage of adulthood. During middle adulthood, most people face somewhat different life problems. They learn advanced job skills and move beyond technical and into supervisory work. They cope with the challenges of teenage children, adjust to aging parents, and plan for retirement. They are chiefly interested in self-renewal and in dealing with change. During later adulthood, most people encounter challenges very different from those of the middle years. They must adjust to retirement. They may have to adjust to the death of a spouse or learn how to deal with grandchildren. Their central learning issues have to do with keeping up-to-date and coping with retirement.

Career stages or career prospects may also influence learners. Several career theorists have suggested that individuals progress through identifiable career stages (for example, Dalton, Thompson, and Price, 1977). Examples of such stages include apprentice, colleague, mentor, and sponsor. These stages and their potential influence on instruction are described in Table 5.1. Recent attention has focused on integrating career planning and succession management, and that attention can have implications for what development programs are needed to build competencies (Rothwell, Jackson, Knight, Lindholm, with Wang and Payne, 2005).

TABLE 5.1. SUMMARY OF STAGES IN THE CLASSIC DALTON, THOMPSON, AND PRICE MODEL.

Stage	Focus	Affects Instruction
Apprentice	Performs technical work Deals with authority Learns from others about work and about dealing with others	Interest in techniques and technical issues Interest in dealing with others
Colleague	Begins to specialize Regarded as competent Makes contacts	Interest in maintaining professional competence
Mentor	Provides leadership Develops more contacts Demonstrates ability to get things done	Interest in dealing with others Interest in guiding/influencing others
Sponsor	Initiates programs Guides others Continues to develop contacts	Interest in exerting long-term impact by influencing "up-and-coming" people

Source: Rothwell, W., and Kazanas, H. *Human Resource Development: A Strategic Approach,* © 2004, p. 362. Reprinted by permission of Human Resource Development Press, Amherst, MA.

Consider the career stages of the targeted learners. After all, learners who view instruction as a vehicle for career advancement—as those in the apprentice stage are likely to do—will tend to want practical, hands-on instruction that can help them advance in their careers. Other learners will not. They will see instruction as serving other purposes. In one classic treatment, for instance, Houle (1961) found that some people regard instruction as a vehicle for socializing with others, while others focus on acquiring knowledge for its own sake.

Selecting Learner Characteristics: A Case Study Example

Georgeanna Lorch is an instructional designer who has been hired as an external consultant to design and implement a new management performance appraisal system for Ajax Vending Company, a wholly owned subsidiary of a much larger corporation. The new appraisal system will be used with all supervisors, managers, executives, professionals, and technical workers at Ajax. As part of her contract, Lorch is preparing instruction on appraisal for managers and executives in the company.

Lorch begins assessing relevant learner characteristics by brainstorming, more specifically by completing the Worksheet on Learner Characteristics appearing in Exhibit 5.1. When she has completed the worksheet, she has identified most of the crucial learner characteristics that will affect her project. Later, she discusses—and double-checks—the learner characteristics with members of the organization and randomly selected representatives of the targeted audience.

Determining Methods for Assessing Learner Characteristics

Instructional designers should know when and how to assess learner characteristics.

When Should Learner Characteristics Be Assessed?

Learner characteristics should be assessed at three different points in the instructional design process.

First, instructional designers should consider the targeted learners before instruction is prepared to meet identified instructional needs and solve specific human performance problems as they exist at the present time. As they do that, they should clarify exactly what assumptions they make about the knowledge,

EXHIBIT 5.1. A WORKSHEET ON LEARNER CHARACTERISTICS.

Directions: Use this worksheet to help you structure your thinking on learner characteristics that may—or should—influence your instructional design project. For each learner characteristic listed in column 1 below, identify in column 2 what learner characteristics are unique to the situation. Then, in column 3, describe how the characteristic(s) should be addressed or considered in the instruction that you subsequently design.

Column 1	Column 2	Column 3
What learner characteristics . . .	What are the characteristics?	How should the characteristics be addressed (or considered) in the instruction you subsequently design?
Are targeted directly at the area of need?		
Pertain to organizational policies?		
Pertain to learner/organizational needs?		
Can be addressed with available resources?		
Pertain to existing constraints on the instructional design project?		
Are feasible to collect data about in terms of resources and logistical limitations?		
Are translatable into design specifications?		
Are related to the performance problem that instruction is intended to solve?		
Other		

skills, and attitudes typical of intended learners. Instruction should be designed accordingly, but it should be made clear how prospective participants may satisfy necessary prerequisites through means other than instruction. These assumptions can be tested later during formative evaluation of the instruction.

Second, instructional designers should consider targeted learners who may need to participate in future instruction, perhaps on a regular basis. These learners will be affected by the selection and promotion practices of the organization, which will (in turn) determine the appropriate entry-level knowledge, skills, and attitudes of people moving into the jobs. After all, future learners may have needs—and the organization may experience human performance problems—uniquely different from those existing at the time instruction is first designed or delivered. For instance, job duties may change. Likewise, the organization may shift strategic direction and thereby change performance requirements of every position. Then, too, new technology and work methods may be introduced. These changes (others can be identified as well) may dramatically affect the appropriate learner characteristics to be considered. Hence, instructional designers should forecast learner characteristics that may need to be considered for designing effective instruction in the future (Rothwell and Kazanas, 2003).

Third, instructional designers should consider characteristics of a specific targeted group of learners each time the instruction is delivered (Knowles, 1980). After all, one group or one individual may have a unique profile, perhaps one radically different from the typical or representative characteristics of most learners in the organization. If radical differences between an actual targeted group of learners and the average or typical learners are ignored, major problems will be experienced during delivery.

How Should Learner Characteristics Be Assessed?

Instructional designers may assess learner characteristics using either of two methods: the derived approach or the contrived approach.

The derived approach is simplest to use. Can instructional designers identify learner characteristics of obvious importance to a given performance problem, instructional need, or organizational constraint simply by brainstorming? If so, they can derive relevant learner characteristics. If relevant learner characteristics can be identified in this way, then a list of learner characteristics to consider during instructional design will usually suffice. The process can be quite simple.

However, the contrived approach may not be as simple to use. If learner characteristics cannot be identified easily through the derived approach, then instructional designers should contrive a list of characteristics worthy of consideration. They should then go through the general list item by item, asking themselves whether each item is related to the performance problem to be solved, the instructional needs to be met, or the organization's policies and procedures. Unrelated items on the list can be ignored; related items must be pinpointed.

Expensive and time-consuming methods of assessing learner characteristics are simply unnecessary in most cases. Very often, instructional designers and line managers already have a firm knowledge of the people for whom instruction is being designed. All that is necessary, then, is to write out that profile of the prospective learner and verify its accuracy with others such as line managers, supervisors, prospective learners, and members of the instructional design team. Once formalized in writing, it should be reviewed periodically to make sure it remains current.

Developing a Profile of Learner Characteristics

Instructional designers should be able to summarize the results of a learner assessment in a learner profile. Simply stated, a learner profile is a narrative description of the targeted audience for instruction that sets forth key assumptions that will be made about them as instruction is prepared. To be adequate, this learner profile should be consistent with the results of the learner assessment and complete enough to be used for making instructional decisions.

What Should Be Included in a Learner Profile?

A *learner profile* should clarify exactly what assumptions will be made about individuals who will, or should, participate in an instructional experience that is intended to rectify a performance problem. It can be thought of as a "role" (or even "job") specification of the learner that summarizes

- *Necessary background knowledge, skill, attitudes, and physical traits.* What should the learner already know or be able to do at the time he or she begins instruction? What should he or she feel about it? What minimum physical traits, if any, are necessary for success in the instructional experience?
- *Other necessary learner characteristics.* These include any assumptions made about learners' demographic or physiological characteristics, aptitudes, experience, learning styles, attitudes, job categories, value systems, life cycle stages, or career stages.

It is also wise to indicate reasonable accommodation that can be made for the physically or mentally disabled and those experiencing special learning problems.

How Should a Profile of Learner Characteristics Be Developed?

There are three basic ways to develop a profile of learner characteristics for instruction: normatively, descriptively, and historically. The *normative profile* is established judgmentally, without necessarily considering the existing "market" of learners. Instead, it summarizes characteristics of the "ideal" or "desired" learner. To develop such a profile, instructional designers—or instructional designers working along with operating supervisors and managers—may make arbitrary assumptions about what knowledge, skills, attitudes, physical traits, and other characteristics learners should possess before they enter instruction.

The *descriptive profile* is established by examining the characteristics of an existing group and simply describing them. It thus summarizes characteristics of the probable or likely learner. To develop such a profile, instructional designers—working alone or in tandem with experienced job incumbents and supervisors—select a representative random sample of a "targeted group of learners" and describe their knowledge, skills, attitudes, physical traits, and other relevant characteristics.

The *historical profile* is established by examining characteristics of those who actually participate in instruction over a period of time. It thus summarizes characteristics of the historical learner. To develop such a profile, instructional designers should track the knowledge, skills, attitudes, and physical traits of those who participated in instruction and who then went on to become exemplary (excellent) performers. With this information, it is possible to develop a predictive profile of those most likely to succeed following instruction.

A Recent Development in Learner Assessment: Cognitivism

How much is learning affected by changing a learner's environment alone? How much is it controlled by the interaction between the learner's environment and his or her internal (cognitive) processes?

These questions express a central focus of concern among many instructional design theorists in recent years. Behaviorists believe that environmental change alone shapes learning. Their thinking was the foundation for the earliest views of instructional design (Lamos, 1984). Cognitivists focus on interactions between the external environment of the learner and the internal (mental) world of the learner (Clark, 1992). Cognitivism, although the idea has existed in some form for some time, is a recent development in learner assessment. Cognitivists focus as much on what learners do in the learning process (which follows from their orientation) as on what instructional designers should do to shape an environment conducive to learning. This section provides a simple primer on cognitivism and some implications for instructional designers. Cognitive strategy is reviewed in Chapter Eleven.

The Importance of the Learner

According to cognitivists, learners create their own interpretations of instruction based on their experiences, expectations, and beliefs. As a result, the nature of those experiences, expectations, and beliefs is fundamentally important to helping learners make meaning of new information or ideas.

Types of Knowledge

Cognitivists believe that knowledge content is classified into two categories:

- *Procedural knowledge.* Knowledge of this kind addresses the question, How is something accomplished?
- *Declarative knowledge.* Knowledge of this kind addresses the questions, Why do things work the way they do? and What is the name of an object or place?

Understanding the difference between types of knowledge content is important because each type of knowledge is learned and applied differently.

Procedural knowledge, on the one hand, is used with ideas or tasks lending themselves to step-by-step analysis and discrete decision points. It thus helps people learn what to do. Over time, people exercise most procedural knowledge unthinkingly, even automatically. Learning to ride a bicycle requires step-by-step (and thus procedural) knowledge. Once learned, riding a bicycle is performed unselfconsciously. Expert performers in most jobs carry out most of their work automatically, since they have learned what to do in step-by-step fashion.

Declarative knowledge, on the other hand, is used with ideas or tasks requiring creativity. More versatile than procedural knowledge, it helps people learn why an idea is worth pursuing or why a task is worth accomplishing. Different forms of declarative knowledge exist but, unlike procedural knowledge, are never exercised unthinkingly. People must always remain vigilant and self-conscious if they are to apply declarative knowledge, because it is complex.

As individuals do complicated tasks, they apply both procedural and declarative knowledge. To that end they develop schemata—models of processes lending themselves to analysis and improvement. Researching the acquisition and application of schemata is an important issue for the future of instructional design. So, too, is researching metacognition, understood to mean strategies used by learners to solve problems for which previous experience is inadequate.

Using Cognitivism in the Instructional Design Process

What good does it do an instructional designer to be aware that learners apply their own strategies to learning? How can that affect the instructional design process?

The most important single contribution of cognitivism is that learners develop their own strategies for learning. Instructional designers should thus build into the design of instruction "help systems" that link into learner strategies. Understanding individualized learning styles, while helpful, is insufficient to the task because most learning style assessments are limited in the advice and prompting they provide to learners. What is more powerful is the development of a total performance support system that gives learners access to appropriate procedural and declarative knowledge content just in time to be used. The compelling question is this: How can learners be provided with the knowledge they need to perform at the time they need it and in the form they need it? Answering that question leads to the development of a so-called performance support system. (If computerized, it becomes an electronic performance support system.) A performance support system surrounds learner-performers with immediate access to help that can be applied to pressing problems. A performance support system can be constructed before, during, and after the instructional process itself and integrated with work performance itself. Planning such support, during and after instruction, expands the role of instructional designer beyond mere "preparer of instruction" to "orchestrator of on-the-job and off-the-job learning." That is a challenging—and creative—role.

Constructivism: A Recent Critique of Cognitivism

No idea is immune to criticism. The same principle applies to cognitivism, which itself began as a reaction to—and criticism of—behaviorism (Cooper, 1993). Cognitivism has been criticized for not going far enough in valuing the learner's role in the learning process. While behaviorism ignored the learner's role and emphasized the external environment in effecting change, cognitivism presented a view that balanced the learner's internal and external worlds.

Constructivism, however, goes beyond cognitivism to emphasize the learner's internal world exclusively. Learners make their own meaning. Instructional design has limited value if its role is to structure the external world or to structure the learner's world without learner involvement. More helpful, assert constructivists, is discovery learning or problem-based learning in which people discover their own knowledge and their own strategies for applying it and receiving feedback about it. Individuals should be challenged with problems to elicit learning, supplied with the resources to solve them, and given access to helpful feedback. Resources for learning should be embedded in (or situated in) the environment. The burden of learning and experimentation rests with them. One approach might be to train learners on the instructional systems design model and then have them tackle the problem of training others on an issue. Supplied with ample resources, they would then undertake a discovery learning process in which they would attack the problem (in this case, training others) while learning about the instructional design process as a side effect of the process.

Judging Learner Assessments

Instructional designers should be capable of evaluating learner assessments performed by themselves or other designers. As they do so, they should give special emphasis to the means by which learner characteristics were chosen for assessment, the way information was collected about them, and the quality of the learner profile that was subsequently developed.

To judge learner assessment, instructional designers may begin by first making sure that an assessment was conducted! Beyond that, they can question those who performed the assessment. A good approach is to try to get them to spell out the assumptions they made so that it is clear what the learner should already know, do, or feel at the time he or she begins instruction. Then they can be asked what provisions, if any, have been made for those lacking prerequisite abilities and those with physical disabilities or special learning problems.

Second, if a learner assessment has been made, instructional designers should ask the following questions:

1. What learner characteristics were assessed?
2. How were they assessed?
3. What philosophical consideration underlies existing learner profiles (are they descriptive, normative, or historical)?
4. Was the learner assessment well designed?
5. Should more information about learners be collected?
6. Should additional refinements be made to learner profiles?

What happens if learner assessments are not undertaken? Consider the following vignette, described by a respondent to Rothwell's (2003) survey that was conducted in preparation for the third edition:

> [The most difficult situation I ever faced was in] designing a "new hire to retirement" skill promotion and pay scale using "pay-for-skills" criteria in a U.S. manufacturing plant in Mexico. That was to include the screening and hiring of the new employees in a computation of vacation time, aguinaldo [special employer pay], taxes, school stipends, employer provided transportation, employer provided cafeteria services, etc. This was then folded in to the research completed on education levels of the average Mexican employee in similar endeavors and technical schools available in the local area. We also looked at high school and post-high school opportunities to ascertain how much and what type of training was needed for each classification level being hired for. The initial footprint was established by using a unionized U.S. plant as the database for the skill levels required to operate the various types of equipment being installed at the Mexican facility. It became evident at an early stage that many of the complicated pieces of equipment being purchased for the Mexican facility required a much higher level of skill, knowledge, and experience than the vast majority of new hire Mexican workers would have.

The point to the vignette, of course, was that mistakes were made by not establishing an early profile of the kind of person who would be participating in instruction and in the selection process. The result, no doubt, was much lost time and money. The vignette dramatizes the importance of thinking through a learner profile in advance. (For instance, it might be pointless to establish an e-learning course for technologically challenged learners.)

Justifying Learner Assessments

Instructional designers should be capable of explaining why a learner assessment was necessary, why some learner characteristics were identified as relevant, and why the assessment was carried out as it was. Competent instructional designers should thus be prepared to explain the work they have done with other people—other instructional designers, operating managers, or learners. Often, this requires keeping notes of steps taken during the instructional design process. In many cases, the rationale for selecting learner characteristics for assessment and the methods used in this process should be explained in instructional catalogues or other sources available to users of the instruction.

To make this rationale simple and complete, many instructional designers prepare a brief checklist about the learner assessment. It is retained in files about each instructional design project and is thus available to future designers. It is also readily available to those who may have questions about the assessment.

Acting Ethically in Assessing Relevant Characteristics of Learners

A key ethical issue in assessing relevant characteristics of learners can be expressed by this question: *Is the learner assessment free of bias and stereotyping?*

In justifying assessments of learner characteristics, instructional designers should take care to avoid intentional or unintentional bias. One way to do that is to use sampling methods effectively, keeping assessments strictly focused on learner characteristics that are essential to work success. After all, training is a selection method. It is thus subject to the same legal safeguards as other selection methods (see Arvey and Faley, 1988).

Respondents to Rothwell's (2003) survey, conducted for the third book, indicated that assessments of learner characteristics can sometimes be a source of ethical challenges. One respondent wrote that, too often, assessments of learner characteristics are nothing more than "basic socio-demographic data of little relevance." A second respondent pointed to problems that can surface when managers "feel that unit performance issues reflect poorly upon themselves personally." A third noted, without explanation, that "learning styles are not valid in our work," and a fourth bewailed the tendency of his or her organization to "try to put into one method an approach to testing everyone." These comments from the real world reflect some key challenges faced by instructional designers as they try to apply theory and demonstrate instructional design competence.

Applying Assessments of Relevant Characteristics of Learners Cross-Culturally

Cultural beliefs can affect learners' views about instruction. Consequently, targeted learners should be assessed for relevant cultural views that may affect instruction as it is designed, developed, delivered, and evaluated. Key cultural dimensions about people are listed in the left-hand column in the list to follow. Important questions to consider about the targeted learners' cultural views are listed in the right-hand column.

Cultural Dimension	*Important Questions to Consider*
The individual	How much is individualism valued over groups or families?
	How widely do laws, rules, and regulations apply?
	Do they apply to everyone, or are exceptions made based on other considerations?
Age	How much respect is accorded to age in the culture?
	How is age regarded? Is increasing age associated with experience or with being out of touch?
Height and weight	How is physical size and weight regarded in the culture?
	What are the physical requirements associated with the work, and how are those regarded in the culture?
Education and experience	How well-respected is education in the culture?
	How well-respected is experience in the culture?
Gender	How much does gender affect expectations about what people may or may not do, or who may or may not speak, and when?

By considering the list of cultural issues, instructional designers may more effectively tailor instruction to learners in a specific culture.

What Is New in Assessing Learner Characteristics?

Three issues seem to be of growing interest about learners in recent years. They are also likely to be of growing interest in the future.

The first issue centers around addressing the needs of older workers and learners. As the workforce ages globally, instructional designers around the world are asking "How are older workers different from middle-aged and younger adults?" Of course, the first issue is to define what is meant by an older worker. There is no standard definition. Some define it as anyone over age sixty. Others indicate that it should be tied to the traditional retirement age, which the Social Security Administration currently defines as age sixty-five, but which will increase to age sixty-seven.

Very little is known about the specialized learning issues of older adults or older workers, however older is defined, compared to the research results currently available for young people or for the middle-aged. But a few facts can be gleaned from research. One finding is that older adults, contrary to popular stereotypes, are not that much different from middle-aged adults.

While they may experience some decline in their sense of sight and hearing, which will of course have a bearing on the reasonable accommodations that should be made for them during instructional delivery, it Is not true that older workers are less productive than the young. Nor do they find it more difficult to learn than younger workers (Charness and Czaja, 2006).

The second issue focuses on differences between learners in their comfort with technology-mediated instruction. Those learners before the so-called digital divide are generally less comfortable with online learning experiences than younger people, who grew up with it. Of course, generalities are dangerous because they are not universally true. For this reason, it is worth asking a targeted group of learners about their preferences in learning experience delivery. Do they prefer onsite to online instruction? Would they rather have a live instructor than find information available at any time? But it is clear that older adults generally are less likely to access the Internet than other key groups ("A nation online," 2004).

The third issue has to do with learner independence. Some authorities are making note of the emergence of a free agent learner (Short and Opengart, 2000). Just like a free agent in the athletic world, a free agent learner is one who has little loyalty to anyone. Free agents are like self-directed learners on steroids. They look for learning-on-demand and want to find information readily available, in a form they can immediately apply, when they need it to solve work-related problems. They do not care where it comes from, and so they have less loyalty to sources of information than to the immediate applicability of that information. For this reason, free agent learners prefer tools and job aids that can be used in real time to solve the immediate work problems they face. They are less willing to wade through lengthy training courses to find the answers to their questions.

As the web expands in scope and sophistication, it is likely that more people will be free agent learners. They will grow adept at surfing the web, seeking the information they need when they need it. That will mean growing impatience with long courses and more demand for real-time performance support in a form that can be immediately used on the job. An extensive overview of learner analysis theories and approaches appears on the web at www.angelfire.com/la2/learners/learners.html.

Conclusion

Learner assessment addresses the following deceptively simple question: Who is the intended and appropriate learner? The answer to this question helps define the target population, target group, or target audience. In this chapter, we described selecting learner characteristics for assessment, suggested methods of identifying appropriate learner characteristics, discussed ways of conducting learner assessment, provided suggestions about developing learner profiles, described a recent development affecting learner assessment (cognitivism), and offered helpful hints for judging and justifying learner assessment. We concluded the chapter by describing key ethical and cross-cultural issues in assessing relevant learner characteristics. In the next chapter, we turn to methods of analyzing the settings in which learners must apply what they learn.

CHAPTER SIX

ANALYZING RELEVANT WORK SETTING CHARACTERISTICS

Analyzing the characteristics of a work setting is the process of gathering information about an organization's resources, constraints, and culture so that instruction will be designed in a way appropriate to the environment. For simplicity's sake, we will call it setting analysis. It is the third box in the model of the instructional design process we introduced in Chapter Four (see Figure 6.1). Setting analysis is also one form of analysis performed before instructional objectives and materials are selected or written. The first analysis—needs assessment— was described in Chapter Four; the second analysis—learner assessment—was described in Chapter Five; and the fourth analysis—work analysis—will be described in Chapter Seven.

According to *The Standards* (Richey, Fields, and Foxon, 2001, p. 50), one competency for instructional design is to "analyze the characteristics of the environment." It is regarded as an essential competency. The performance statements associated with this competency indicate that instructional designers should be able to (Richey, Fields, and Foxon, 2001, p. 50):

a. Identify aspects of the physical and social environments that impact the delivery of instruction (essential).
b. Identify environmental and cultural aspects that influence attitudes toward instructional interventions (advanced).

FIGURE 6.1. A MODEL OF STEPS IN THE INSTRUCTIONAL DESIGN PROCESS.

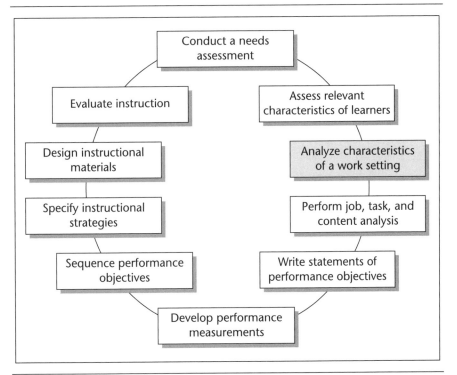

c. Identify environmental and cultural factors that are influencing learning, attitudes, and performance (advanced).
d. Identify the nature and role of varying work environments in the teaching and learning process (advanced).
e. Determine the extent to which organizational mission, philosophy, and values influence the design and success of a project (advanced).

In this chapter, we explain the importance of setting analysis; we identify key environmental factors; and we describe how to carry out this form of analysis. We also offer advice about judging and justifying setting analysis. Finally, we conclude by identifying key ethical and cross-cultural challenges affecting work setting analysis.

The Importance of Setting Analysis

Twenty-five years ago, and in a classic description, Steele (1973) emphasized the importance of physical settings in planned organizational change efforts. He noted, "If one attempts to make changes in the social functioning of an organization, one must pay attention to the physical systems which form part of the context for the social system" (p. 6). As he defined it, physical system means setting or environment. It is "the total surrounding context for the person or the subject of interest" (p. 6).

Theorists have also more recently emphasized the importance of the setting in which people apply what they learn (Dubois and Rothwell, 1996; Senge, 1990; Watkins and Marsick, 1993). A dynamic interaction exists when knowledge is applied to a situation by an individual. Ignoring the environment and the situation in which knowledge is applied is metaphorically akin to focusing on a hammer but not considering the nail to be used or the board to which the nail is to be affixed.

Those who set out to change organizations require what Steele (1973, p. 8) called environmental competence, meaning "(1) the ability to be aware of one's environment and its impact; and (2) the ability to use or change that environment." To demonstrate environmental competence, managers—or such other change agents as instructional designers—should "be more aware of the setting," "ask themselves what they are trying to do there," "assess the appropriateness of the setting for what is to be accomplished," and "make appropriate changes to provide a better fit between themselves and the setting" (p. 8). Detailed examinations have been conducted to determine the competencies required to facilitate organizational change, and instructional designers increasingly find that they must demonstrate these competencies as well as those linked specifically to instructional design work.

Indeed, the instructional design process is a change effort that is intended to meet or avert deficiencies in knowledge, skills, or attitudes. It should therefore be carried out with due appreciation for the environments in which instruction will be designed, delivered, and subsequently applied. If this step is ignored, instructional designers may experience stiff resistance from managers and prospective participants as they prepare instruction. Worse yet, participants in instruction may later experience much frustration if, when they return to their job settings, they are not allowed to apply what they learned because their managers or co-workers do not support it.

Identifying Factors and Carrying Out Setting Analysis

Instructional designers should make systematic examinations of the development, delivery, and application environments at the outset of the instructional design process. The development environment is the setting in which instruction will be prepared; the delivery environment is the setting in which instruction will be presented; and the application environment is the work settings in which learners will be expected to apply what they learn. Each of these environments should affect instructional development, delivery, and application.

What Characteristics of the Development Environment Should Be Assessed, and How Should They Be Assessed?

Begin a setting analysis by focusing initial attention on the development environment, since it will affect how the instructional design project proceeds. First, list characteristics of the setting that may affect the instructional design assignment. Examples may include any or all of the following characteristics that are listed in the left column and briefly described in the right column:

Developmental Characteristics	*Brief Description*
The (apparent) nature of the change desired	The prevailing desire to improve consistency or change the way the organization functions.
The organization's mission	The primary reason for the organization's existence. A short description of the organization's products and service lines, customers, philosophy of operations, and other relevant characteristics that affect why the organization exists and how it interacts with the external environment.
Organizational philosophy and perceived values	Fundamental beliefs about the way the organization should function with its customers, employees, the public, and other key stakeholders. Includes not only what management says "should be done" but also what is "really done."
The organization's goals and plans	Beliefs about what the organization should do in the future and assumptions about the environments in which it is or will be functioning.
The organization's structure	The way that duties and responsibilities have been divided up in the organization— that is, reporting relationships.

Developmental Characteristics	*Brief Description*
Results of a needs assessment and analysis	The difference between what is and what should be, stemming from lack of employee knowledge or skills or poor attitudes.
Resources available for the development effort—people, money, time, equipment, and facilities	The resources available for carrying out instructional development.
Pre-selected instructional design methods	Managers' predisposition to approach an instructional need in a specific way, regardless of results yielded by analysis.

Other developmental characteristics of the setting may also be considered. For instance, Weisbord (1993, p. 754) suggests that organizations may be examined by asking questions about six key issues, and each question may be adapted to focus on developmental issues: (1) What business are we in, and how does instruction contribute to that? (2) How is the work divided up, and how does division of labor affect instruction? (3) Do all needed tasks have incentives, and what incentives exist for participating in—and applying—instruction? (4) Does the organization possess coordinating technologies, and does the instruction being designed also possess coordinating technologies? (5) How is conflict among people and technologies managed, and how is such conflict addressed in instruction? and (6) How are these issues kept in balance in the organization, and what part does instruction play in maintaining that balance?

Second, determine how many of these development characteristics may affect the present instructional design assignment and how they may, or should, affect it. Given the culture of the organization and the performance problem that instruction is intended to solve, consider three major questions:

1. Based on what is known of the organization, how many of these characteristics are relevant to the present assignment?
2. How are the characteristics relevant? What is known about them?
3. How should information about these characteristics be used in such subsequent steps of the instructional design process (depicted in Figure 6.1) as analyzing tasks? Writing statements of performance objectives? Developing performance measurements? Sequencing performance objectives? Specifying instructional strategies? Designing instructional materials? Evaluating instruction?

Third, conduct a reality check to make sure that the most important developmental characteristics have been identified, their key implications noted, and the information recorded for appropriate use during the instructional design project. To do that, discuss the questions above with key decision-makers in the organization, other members of the instructional design team, and experienced or exemplary performers in the organization. Analyze their responses carefully and make the changes they suggest when warranted.

What Characteristics of the Delivery Environment Should Be Assessed, and How Should They Be Assessed?

Focus attention next on the delivery environment, since it will affect how instruction is received by managers and employees of the organization. First, decide how the instruction will probably be delivered. While final decisions about delivery strategies are not usually made until later in the instructional design process, determine whether managers in the organization have predetermined notions—and justifications for them—about how instruction should be delivered, who should participate in it, when it should be delivered, why it should be delivered, and what needs or whose needs are to be met by it.

There are, of course, many ways to deliver instruction. It may be delivered on or off the job; it may be delivered to individuals (for example, through computer-based or web-based training, e-mail attachment, audiotapes or audioconference, videotapes or videoconference, print-based programmed instruction, self-study readings) or to groups. The appropriate choice of what to examine in the delivery environment depends on how instruction will be delivered.

Most instructional designers and other training and development professionals, when asked about delivery, usually think first of the classroom, although that is by no means the best, least costly, or most effective alternative. When instruction is delivered on the job, relevant characteristics are the same as those in the list following for the application setting. When instruction is delivered off the job and in a meeting (informal) or classroom (formal) setting, relevant characteristics to consider may include any of the following listed in the left column and briefly described in the right column (Crowe, Hettinger, Weber, and Johnson, 1986, p. 128):

Delivery Characteristics	*Brief Description*
Learner involvement	The extent to which participants have attentive interest in group activities and participate in discussions.
	The extent to which participants do additional work on their own and enjoy the group setting.

Delivery Characteristics	*Brief Description*
Learner affiliation	The level of friendship participants feel for each other, that is, the extent to which they help each other with group work, get to know each other easily, and enjoy working together.
Instructor support	The amount of help, concern, and friendship the instructor directs toward the participants.
	The extent to which the instructor talks openly with students, trusts them, and is interested in their ideas.
Task orientation	The extent to which it is important to complete the activities that have been planned. The emphasis the instructor places on the subject matter.
Competition	The emphasis placed on participants' competing with each other for successful completion of the tasks and for recognition by the instructor.
Order and organization	The emphasis on participants' behaving in an orderly and polite manner and on the overall organization of assignments and classroom activities.
	The degree to which participants remain calm and quiet.
Rule clarity	The emphasis on establishing and following a clear set of rules and on participants' knowing what the consequences will be if they do not follow them.
	The extent to which the instructor is consistent in dealing with participants who break the rules or disrupt the group in its activities.
Instructor control	The degree to which the instructor enforces the rules and the severity of the punishment for rule infractions. The number of rules and the occurrence of students' getting into trouble.
Innovation	The extent to which participants contribute to planning classroom activities, as well as the number of unusual and varying activities and assignments planned by the instructor.
	The degree to which the instructor attempts to use new techniques and encourages creative thinking on the part of the participants.

Other characteristics may also be considered. Use these lists as a starting point for identifying important characteristics of the delivery environment and determining how they may be relevant to delivering instruction. Also refer to the lists in deciding how these characteristics should be considered while you analyze tasks, write statements of performance objectives, sequence performance objectives, specify instructional strategies, design instruction materials, and evaluate instruction. Be sure to conduct a reality check at the end of these steps and when instruction is subsequently delivered.

What Characteristics of the Application Environment Should Be Assessed, and How Should They Be Assessed?

Characteristics of the application environment may affect the instructional design process just as much as, if not more than, characteristics of the development and delivery environments. The application environment should be considered before instruction is designed to maximize the likelihood that learners will transfer what they learn from instruction to their jobs (Baldwin and Ford, 1988).

Historically, instructional designers have seldom paid as much attention to the application environment as they could have, concerning themselves instead with results at the end of the instructional experience (Rothwell and Sredl, 2000). One unfortunate result is that not more than 10 percent of the estimated $100 billion spent on workplace instruction in the United States each year produces on-the-job change (Broad and Newstrom, 1992). To the extent that instructional designers have paid attention to the application environment, they are usually aware that learners are more likely to transfer what they learn from instruction to their jobs when conditions in the two environments are similar, if not identical (Thorndike and Woodworth, 1901a, 1901b, 1901c). Results of research also indicate that it may be possible to focus training on broad, underlying skills that can be applied in different but related work tasks (Fleishman, 1972).

Any or all of the following characteristics listed in the left column and briefly described in the right column may influence on-the-job application of instruction (Crowe, Hettinger, Weber, and Johnson, 1986, p. 146).

Application Characteristics	*Brief Description*
Involvement	The extent to which employees are concerned about and committed to their jobs.
Peer cohesion	The extent to which employees are friendly and supportive of one another.

Application Characteristics	*Brief Description*
Supervisor support	The extent to which management is supportive of employees and encourages employees to be supportive toward one another.
Autonomy	The extent to which employees are encouraged to be self-sufficient and to make their own decisions.
Task orientation	The degree of emphasis on good planning, efficiency, and getting the job done.
Work pressure	The degree to which the press of work and time urgency dominate the job milieu.
Clarity	The extent to which employees know what to expect in their daily routine and how explicitly rules and policies are communicated.
Control	The extent to which management uses rules and other pressures to keep employees under control.
Innovation	The degree of emphasis on variety, change, and new approaches.
Physical comfort	The extent to which the physical surroundings contribute to a pleasant work environment.

Additional characteristics of the application environment may also be worthy of consideration (Fitz-Enz, 1984, p. 210).

Application Characteristics	*Brief Description*
Leader behavior	The supervisor's way of dealing with people, workflow, and resource issues.
Work behavior	Work-related interactions with co-workers and supervisor.
Delegation	Extent to which and manner in which the learner's supervisor delegates and encourages new ideas.
Worker capability	Skills, knowledge, experience, education, and potential that the worker brings to the job.
Strictness	Firm and equitable enforcement of the company rules and procedures.
Equipment design	Degree of difficulty experienced in operating equipment.

Job satisfaction	Each worker's general attitude and amount of satisfaction with the job.
External influences	Effects of outside social, political, and economic activity.
Safety	The organization's efforts to provide a safe and healthy working environment.
Self-responsibility	Workers' concern for quality and their desire to be responsible.
Resources	Availability of tools, manuals, parts, and material needed to do the job.
National situation	Impact of national conditions on the worker and the company.
Co-workers	Mutual respect and liking among members of the work group.
Pay and working	Performance reviews, promotions, pay, and work conditions scheduling.
Job stress	Environmental effects such as temperature and ventilation, plus feelings about job security.
Personal problems	The impact of overtime on personal life and other issues concerning personal life.
Self-esteem	The sense of self-respect—and respect from others—that learners derive from doing the job.
Work problems	Physical and psychological fatigue resulting from work.
The organization	General attitudes toward the organization, its style of operation, and its stability.
Economic needs	Degree to which the work satisfies workers' needs for food, clothing, and shelter.
Responsibility accepted	Desired workload and responsibility versus actual workload and responsibility.
Organizational policies	Rest periods, training, work layout, and departmental characteristics.

Since the publication of the first edition of this book, the U.S. Department of Labor sponsored a research study that identified eight categories of a High Performance Workplace (HPW)—defined as a work environment that is conducive to high performance by management and workers. The study pinpointed fifty-five criteria organized in eight key categories (Office of the American Workplace, 1995):

High-Performance Workplace Characteristics	*Brief Description*
Training and continuous learning	Employees are encouraged to maintain current skills
Information sharing	Communication in the organization is effective, contributing to high performance.
Employee participation	Employees are given a say in important decisions affecting them and the organization.
Organization structure	The organizational structure supports effective decision making.
Worker-management partnerships	Workers and management partner effectively to achieve exemplary customer service.
Compensation linked to performance and skills	Workers and management are rewarded in line with their contributions.
Employment security	Employees are treated equitably by the organization and do not fear for their jobs.
Supportive work environment	The environment surrounding workers on their jobs is safe, family-friendly, and encourages high performance.

Dubois and Rothwell (1996) have developed a survey instrument to collect employee and management perceptions about how important and how well these HPW characteristics are evident in the organization. Other researchers have identified related HPW characteristics (Appelbaum and Batt, 1994; Bassi, Gould, Kulik, and Zornitsky, 1993; Osterman, 1990; Wallace, 1994). More recent attention has focused around so-called employee engagement, an organizational environment in which people feel a close connection emotionally between themselves and the organization's mission, purpose, and goals. Concerns have been raised because a diminishing number of workers—only about 29 percent of workers in the United States—are fully engaged (Crabtree, 2007).

Research by Rothwell (2002) indicates that specific barriers may face learners in the learning process. Rothwell has published an assessment instrument that is useful in examining the learning climate to assess how well learners may be able to learn based on organizational conditions. That is, of course, a key issue in facilitating individual learning and transfer of training.

Use these lists of characteristics to analyze the application environment. First, determine how many of these application characteristics are relevant to the present instructional design assignment and how they may (or should) affect it to improve the chances that instruction will subsequently be applied by learners on their jobs. Given the culture of the organization and the performance problem that instruction is intended to solve, consider the following questions:

1. Based on what is known about the organization, how many of these characteristics are relevant to the present assignment?
2. How are the characteristics relevant? What is known about how each characteristic affects on-the-job performance?
3. How should information about these characteristics subsequently be used in the instructional design process to improve the chances that learners will apply on the job what they learned during instruction? How should this information influence subsequent steps in the instructional design model?

As in the analysis of characteristics affecting the development and delivery environments, conduct a reality check to ensure that these questions have been answered appropriately. In addition, make notes to use during the instructional design process. When necessary, recommend that managers make non-instructional changes to the work environment to encourage on-the-job application of learning.

Judging a Setting Analysis

Instructional designers should be capable of evaluating a setting analysis to determine whether it was conducted at the appropriate time and was focused on appropriate issues. Take a few simple steps to make these judgments.

First, make sure to begin with that a setting analysis was conducted. Instructional designers assigned to a project at the middle or end of the work should ask their teammates what environmental characteristics were examined, why they were chosen, and why other characteristics were ignored. A few other simple questions are also worth asking:

1. What are the constraints, if any, on the project?
2. What resources are available?

3. How have the constraints and available resources of the project been taken into account on the project thus far?

4. How do the resources available and constraints affecting the project influence the development of instruction?

5. How will the available resources and constraints affect delivery?

6. How may they affect application of the instruction by learners?

7. What is the culture of the organization, and how may it affect instructional development, delivery, and application?

If other members of the instructional design team are unable to answer these questions, then set out to investigate characteristics of the work setting and apply the resulting conclusions to subsequent steps in the instructional design process.

Second, check whether the analysis was conducted properly. If the characteristics of the work setting have been investigated, be sure they have been verified. Look for evidence of agreement from independent sources—members of the instructional design team, line managers, and experienced employees—on assumptions that have been made about the development, delivery, and application settings. If the assumptions cannot be verified, then be prepared to review and revise instruction.

On occasion, instructional designers may wish to wait until a rehearsal of the instructional materials or delivery methods to verify some important points. At this time, for example, they can question knowledgeable members of the organization concerning the assumptions made about the learners and delivery or application environments. If these members of the organization confirm the assumptions upon close questioning, then there is no reason to make changes. However, if they point out additional issues for consideration, then be prepared to make appropriate changes to the instruction.

Third, make sure that the results of analysis are used during instructional development, delivery, and application. To this end, periodically ask members of the instructional design team how they are using what they know about the settings and how they feel they should be using this information.

Justifying a Setting Analysis

Instructional designers should be capable of explaining why they conducted a setting analysis and the reasons they chose to focus on certain features of the design, delivery, and application environments. To explain the reasons for conducting a setting analysis, instructional designers should be prepared to point out to line managers and others that instruction must be tailored to the unique needs of learners and the unique conditions in the organization. There is no one right way to do that. Instead, instructional designers must take their cues from what managers talk about and say they want. The setting analysis can be explained as a way to ensure that instruction matches up to their expectations, organizational goals, and other requirements.

To explain the features of the environments chosen for consideration, instructional designers should be prepared to point to information they have collected from credible sources in the organization. That is why reality checks are worth conducting. They provide support—and ownership—among key decision makers. They also give the setting analysis legitimacy and grounds for justification.

Acting Ethically in Analyzing the Characteristics of a Work Setting

A key ethical issue in analyzing the characteristics of a work setting can be expressed by this question: *Were the unique cultural differences of work settings considered as they may affect instruction?*

As the old saying goes, "Think globally, but act locally." The same principle should be followed in analyzing needs, designing and developing instruction, and evaluating results. It also applies to developing instruction that lends itself to application in the workplace.

One way to take cultural differences into account is to design an "instructional shell" at a central site and then send it to a regional site for enhancement to add local examples and ensure consistency with local customs, practices, needs, examples, and applications. That approach strikes a balance between thinking globally and acting locally. It also ensures that instruction is tailored to the unique requirements of a work setting, whether that setting represents a location in another culture or a location in another facility.

To ensure that instruction is realistically tied to practices and conditions in the work environment, instructional designers should involve supervisors, co-workers of targeted learners, and others who play key roles in the work environment. That facilitates transfer of learning from an instructional setting to a work setting.

To address these issues, instructional designers may need to pay special attention to transfer-of-training strategies to ensure that instruction is carried back to the work setting. They may also be called on to apply the theories and principles of organization development (Rothwell and Sullivan, 2005). The reason: OD helps to create a corporate culture that is conducive to the transfer of learning from off-the-job to on-the-job applications.

In Rothwell's 2003 survey, conducted in preparation for the third edition of this book, he asked respondents about the biggest ethical challenges they faced when analyzing relevant work environment characteristics. To cite a few relevant remarks from the survey results, which should be self-explanatory:

> "I work in a regional training center where we are responsible for twenty-four countries. Our budget has been shrinking every year for the past five years. We are losing touch with our audience, stakeholders, and becoming an ivory tower."
>
> "We are attempting to use Human Performance Technology without the requisite foundation and background information to justify our decisions."

The common theme here is that the work environment is creating its own barriers to achieving the results sought.

Applying Analysis of Work Settings Cross-Culturally

Specific cultural beliefs can often affect learners' views about instruction and about applying what they have learned. Consequently, work settings should be analyzed for the role played by culture and how that role may affect instruction as it is designed, developed, delivered, and evaluated. Key cultural dimensions about work settings are listed in the left-hand column to follow. Important questions to consider about the targeted learners' cultural views are listed in the right-hand column.

Cultural Dimension	*Important Questions to Consider*
Improvement	Do people in the culture generally equate change with progress or with decline? On what basis is improvement assessed?
Time	How committed are individuals to one task at a time?
	Are they capable of doing more than one thing at a time?
	Is punctuality defined strictly or loosely?
	What is the orientation to time in the culture?
	How is it viewed?

	How much are traditions valued over current times?
	How much are current times valued over the future?
	How much is the future valued over the present or past?
Place	How much space is preferred between individuals?
	Do close friends function in close physical proximity, or do they remain apart?
Competition	How much emphasis is placed on "winning over others"?
	How much emphasis is placed on success through relationships, teamwork, and family?
Communication	How much of a message is inferred from the context in which it occurs, and how much of a message must be stated explicitly for it to be understood?
Learning	How much preference exists for analysis (breaking problems down into smaller parts)?
	How much preference exists for learning by doing?
	How much preference exists for viewing "the big picture"?

By considering this list of cultural issues, instructional designers may more effectively tailor instruction to the cultural conditions prevailing in the work setting.

What Is New in Analyzing Relevant Work Setting Characteristics?

Where people work has more impact than just about anything else on how they perform and how much they apply what they learn. For this reason, instructional designers are becoming increasingly interested in finding ways to build a supportive learning climate in the workplace and to ensure that learning transfers back to the job. At the same time, many organizational leaders are growing more interested in organization development and change management, ways of managing change in work settings. They realize that training alone will rarely, if ever, lead to corporate culture change.

Employee engagement programs are perhaps the most important development in work settings in recent years. Research conducted by the Gallup organization has shown a troubling increase in two of three distinct employee groups: the not engaged and the actively disengaged. *Engaged employees* are passionate about what they do and where they work. *Not engaged workers* just go through the motions of working but do not really care. *Actively disengaged workers* undermine their organization's efforts. According to *Gallup Management Journal's* semi-annual employee engagement index (Crabtree, 2007), American work-places fully engage only 29 percent of U.S. workers. Most workers (54 percent) are *not engaged*. Most shocking, 17 percent of workers are actively disengaged. That means they work deliberately to undermine the mission, objectives, and efforts of their organizations.

For instructional designers, employee engagement—or lack of it—can have a profound impact on the effectiveness of learning experiences. If learners do not care about the organization, they will not be motivated to learn. Training will be something that they do not care about any more than anything else. They will participate if required, but will hardly be involved. And if the learn-ers are actively disengaged, they are quite likely to undermine, sabotage, and subvert learning efforts for others. They will do that by making fun of the train-ing, trying to undermine the trainer or other learners, asking questions that are intended to cause disruptions, and will in all respects demonstrate a lack of civil-ity or respect for other people.

What can be done about these issues? One strategy is to launch a planned employee engagement program to identify the root causes of behaviors asso-ciated with "not engaged" and "actively disengaged" workers (Swindall, 2007; Townsend and Gebhardt, 2007). Alternatively, instructional designers can mea-sure employee engagement before instruction and take steps to try to modify instruction to make it more engaging. They can also field-test it to minimize the chances to subvert the training and train instructors on strategies to deal with those who are actively disengaged. While no strategy is foolproof, it may be necessary to pay more attention to ways of motivating the learners in a work setting with a higher-than-average percentage of "not engaged" or "actively dis-engaged" workers. Wlodkowski (1999) offers many strategies for doing that.

Another issue in today's work settings is that many workers are approach-ing burnout. There are too few workers chasing too much work. According to one source, "workers in the United States do not lead the world in dedicated hours at work, Korea holds the top spot in 2005. However, stateside profes-sionals log 100 hours per year more than those professionals in Japan, and 389 hours more than professional workers in Europe. The average workweek in the United States puts workers behind the desk for 44 hours" ("United States vs. France," 2005). The result is that people are stressed out. Some demand more of a work/life balance. That can impact their willingness to learn—and apply what they learn—on the job. There is a crowding out effect that affects learning transfer. If people are so busy that they do not know what they are doing from one minute to the next, they will hardly be able to think long enough to apply what they learned. Nor will they be able to concentrate on e-learning at their desks if distracted from it every few minutes.

Instructional designers should consider the impact of a stressed out workplace on learners, encouraging the learners themselves to suggest ways that they can integrate what they learn on the job. At the same time, designers should also provide on-the-job tools that will make it easier for people to apply what they learned on the job.

Conclusion

In this chapter, we described the third step in the systematic design of instruction—setting analysis. The purpose of setting analysis, as we explained, is to ensure that instruction is prepared with due regard to the available resources, constraints, and culture of the organization. Setting analysis must focus on three related environments: (1) the development environment, meaning the setting in which instruction will be prepared; (2) the delivery environment, meaning the setting in which instruction will be presented; and (3) the application environment, meaning the work settings in which learners will be expected to apply what they learn. Each environment has its own unique characteristics that may affect subsequent steps in the instructional design process. In the next chapter, we turn to the last of four related forms of analysis that should be conducted before performance objectives are written.

CHAPTER SEVEN

PERFORMING WORK ANALYSIS

The process of gathering detailed information about the work that people do in organizations is called work analysis. A general term, work analysis encompasses three different kinds of investigation—job analysis, task analysis, and content analysis. Taken together, they are probably the most technical activities of the instructional designer's job because carrying them out requires specialized skills.

Work analysis for training can be expensive and time-consuming. For this reason, it is warranted only after performance analysis reveals a performance problem lending itself to an instructional solution and after a needs assessment provides information about the performance gap. Work analysis takes up where needs assessment leaves off. Its results become the basis for developing performance objectives to guide later steps in the instructional design process. Work analysis is the fourth box in the model of the instructional design process we introduced in Chapter Four (see Figure 7.1). Work analysis is also the last of four related forms of analysis carried out before performance objectives are written and instructional materials are prepared. The other three forms of analysis were described in Chapters Four to Six.

In this chapter, we define job, task, and content analysis. Moreover, we explain how to carry out each of them and offer advice to instructional designers about judging and justifying work analysis. Competency modeling is a relatively new development relevant to instructional design, and it is summarized briefly in this chapter (Rothwell and Lindholm, 1999). Finally, we briefly address key ethical and cross-cultural issues in conducting job, task, and content analysis.

FIGURE 7.1. A MODEL OF STEPS IN THE INSTRUCTIONAL DESIGN PROCESS.

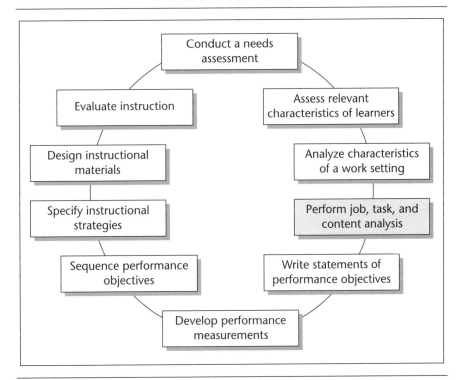

Source: Foshay, W., Silber, K., and Westgaard, O. *Instructional Design Competencies: The Standards.* Iowa City, IA: International Board of Standards for Training, Performance, and Instruction, 1986, p. 3. Copyright 1993 by the International Board of Standards for Training, Performance and Instruction. All rights reserved. Used with permission.

Job Analysis

Work is important to employee performance, satisfaction, and morale. What people do—their work—is central to organizational structure and performance. Successful performance (results or outcomes) can be attributed to many causes, of course. But one major cause is work design, the way in which work activities and responsibilities are allocated to individuals, teams, and other groups in organizational settings. Most people spend significant portions of their lives performing their work, so what they do and how they do it can have a major impact on their mental and physical well-being. Work, sometimes organized into jobs and sometimes organized in other ways, also determines an individual's, and often an entire family's, standard of living.

In the last ten years, the traditional bureaucratic notion of job has been supplanted by a more flexible view of work (Bridges, 1994). In the words of one articulate manager, "Jobs go away, but work never seems to do that. If anything, work is growing more challenging in process reengineered and downsized work settings. Older notions of lifetime employment, rigidly defined jobs and top-down decision making have been replaced by less stable employment relationships, team work structures, and contingent workers." However, it is worth emphasizing that the time-tested principles of job analysis are generally applicable whether the focus is on jobs, job categories, teams, or more innovative approaches to work design.

Defining Job Analysis

A job analysis is a systematic examination of what people do, how they do it, and what results they achieve by doing it (Denis, 1992). The results of job analysis can usually become a starting point for more detailed task or content analysis. It is performed to clarify work titles, responsibilities, activities, and entry qualifications (Brannick and Levine, 2002; Clifford, 1994; Hartley, 1999).

Defining Terms Associated with Job Analysis

Instructional designers should devote some time to familiarizing themselves with the nomenclature of job analysis; otherwise, they may become confused quickly. Job means simply a collection of related activities, duties, or responsibilities. More than one person occupies a job. Defined another way, a job means—according to a classic source—"a group of positions which are identical with respect to their major or significant tasks" (McCormick, 1979, p. 19).

Position usually does not mean the same thing as job. A position connotes tasks and duties performed by only one person (McCormick, 1979). For instance, an organization may employ four people in the job of internal auditor; however, each person is assigned different duties, so there are really four internal auditor positions. Incumbents are persons presently sharing one job title.

The Importance of Job Analysis

Job analysis is important because it identifies what people do—or should do—and thereby provides information for selecting, appraising, compensating, training, and disciplining employees. Indeed, job analysis helps (Werther and Davis, 1985, p. 117):

- Evaluate how environmental challenges affect individual jobs.
- Eliminate unneeded job requirements that can cause discrimination in employment.
- Discover job elements that help or hinder quality of work life.
- Plan for future human resource requirements.
- Match job applicants and job openings.
- Determine training needs for new and experienced employees.
- Create plans to develop employee potential.
- Set realistic performance standards.
- Place employees in jobs that use their skills effectively.
- Compensate jobholders fairly.

Without the results of job analysis, it would not be clear what activities employees should be held accountable for doing, what results they should be achieving, or how their work activities contribute to achieving organizational objectives. Job analysis can also reveal obstacles to performance that transcend the control of job incumbents and require corrective action by management.

When Should Instructional Designers Perform Job Analysis?

In most cases, instructional designers should perform job analysis only when job descriptions are nonexistent, outdated, inconsistent with information desired by decision makers, or inadequate for guiding more detailed task analysis. It should also be carried out when job descriptions are subject to dramatic future revision as a result of technological, regulatory, or other changes in the job environment. If none of these conditions exists, the time and expense necessary to perform a job analysis may be more effectively devoted to other projects. In addition, job analysis should be focused on the targeted audience for instruction, since broad-scope analysis of all jobs in an organization will lead instructional designers far astray from efforts of immediate, practical value for improving human performance.

An Overview of the Steps in Performing Job Analysis

When conducting a job analysis, instructional designers should

1. Identify the jobs to be analyzed.
2. Clarify the results desired from the analysis.
3. Prepare a plan that answers these questions:
   a. Who will conduct the job analysis?
   b. What is the purpose of the analysis?

     c. How will the results be used?

     d. What sources or methods will be used to collect and analyze job information?

  4. Implement the job analysis plan.

  5. Analyze and use the results of the job analysis.

We now turn to a discussion of each step.

Step 1: Identifying the Jobs to Be Analyzed

Identifying the jobs to be analyzed is the first, and simplest, step in job analysis. If the job bears no title because it does not yet exist in the organization, then assign a tentative job title after consulting relevant sources from the industry and from government. A good place to begin any job analysis is with a review of *The Dictionary of Occupational Titles* (1991), which lists titles and paragraph-length job descriptions for hundreds of jobs. Each job is classified according to a unique scheme indicating the skills it requires.

Step 2: Clarifying the Results Derived from the Analysis

The second step of any job analysis is clarification of the desired results. Instructional designers should focus their attention on two questions: (1) Why is the job analysis being conducted? and (2) What results are sought from it? Always begin by addressing the first question, thus clarifying the purpose of the investigation.

Job analysis serves four possible purposes (Walker, 1980), and each implies a different approach. One purpose is to determine what people actually do in their jobs and thereby clarify reality. A second purpose is to determine what people believe job incumbents do in their jobs and thereby bring out perceptions. A third purpose is to determine what people, or their immediate supervisors, believe that job incumbents should do and thereby identify job norms. A fourth and final purpose is to determine what people—or their supervisors—believe job incumbents are or should be planning to do in their jobs in the future if changes in the workplace are expected to occur (Rothwell and Kazanas, 2004). Job analysis of this kind thus focuses on plans or future change.

Unfortunately, most job analysis focuses on perceptions, since "finding out what individuals actually do is more time-consuming and costly than finding out what individuals and managers think they do" (Walker, 1980, p. 147). However, instructional designers should more often focus their attention on reality or plans and future change. This is because instruction needs to be centered around what job incumbents actually do to perform successfully or what they should do to meet future objectives of their organization.

Once the purpose of job analysis has been clarified, instructional designers should next decide what results are desired. Four are possible: (1) a job description literally describes the activities, duties, and responsibilities of a job as well as other relevant aspects; (2) a job specification literally specifies essential qualifications for successful entry into the job; (3) a task listing delineates, in detail, the activities performed by job incumbents; and (4) job performance standards identify targeted or minimum expectations for performance, sometimes in measurable terms. Hence, the results of job analysis may be expressed in job descriptions, job specifications, task listings (sometimes called task inventories), job performance standards, or all four.

The results desired from the job analysis will affect the approach used to carry out the analysis. For instance, if the aim is to prepare a job description, the instructional designer should select a job title (What should the job be called?), prepare a purpose statement for the job of no more than one or two sentences (Why should the job exist?), identify reporting relationships (What job titles report to the job? and What job title do incumbents report to?), and summarize major or representative job tasks (What tasks are customarily performed by job incumbents?). Experienced job incumbents or their supervisors are often able to prepare a job description based on perceptions in a few minutes.

Most organizations already have job or work team descriptions on hand. Job descriptions can be essential starting points for designing job-specific instruction (Rothwell and Kazanas, 1994b), although they are rarely detailed enough to provide all the information needed by instructional designers.

There is no one "right" format for job descriptions. Most organizations establish their own format, and instructional designers should use that format when conducting job analysis. Many books set forth sample job descriptions, and software packages exist on the market that will help write such descriptions. In some organizations, decision-makers may prefer that instructional designers go beyond the basics of job descriptions. In other words, they may be asked to list more than job title, purpose statement, reporting relationships, and representative tasks. They may also wish to list work standards for each task; knowledge, skills, and attitudes required to perform each task; estimated time percentages devoted by job incumbents to each task; the most critical tasks that are essential to job success; physical, mental, and learning requirements; or minimum entry requirements.

A job specification usually appears at the end of a job description. When preparing a job specification, focus attention on what people should know, do, or feel in order for them to learn—that is, train for—the job. Establish only essential, minimum entry requirements. Avoid unnecessary references to general experience or education so as to ensure that the organization engages in fair employment practices for protected labor groups. More appropriately, list only specific skills needed by job incumbents to perform—or learn—a job. To cite a simple example, indicate that a secretary should have "a demonstrated ability to type thirty-five words per minute with three errors or less" rather than "a high school diploma."

Most job descriptions also contain a list of representative tasks called a task listing. Preparing such a list can be relatively simple if it is based largely on perceptions, or it can be time-consuming and expensive if it is based on reality or plans. This list can be a starting point for more detailed task analysis (discussed in the next section). If the desired result of a job analysis is a detailed task listing, sometimes called a task inventory, then focus attention on detailed work results or work activities of job incumbents. For more information about task analysis, see the classic books by Jonassen, Hannum, and Tessmer (1989) and Khalifa (1993).

If job or work performance standards are the desired results of a job analysis, then clarify precisely how to measure performance on each job task and how well each task should be carried out by an experienced job incumbent. Although it is common for managers and workers to complain that job performance standards cannot be measured for tasks in their jobs, the fact is that standards can be established for any job. Simply examine each task for quantity, quality, cost, time, or customer service requirements. The following list, on which the first three categories are adapted from a classic discussion by Jacobs (1987), suggests possible criteria:

Quality

- How well does the performance match a model?
- How superior is one performance to another based on market value or expert opinions?
- How many items are produced in a given time?
- How timely is task completion?
- How much is produced in a given time?

Cost

- How much is the labor cost relative to what is produced?
- How much do the materials cost to achieve desired work results?
- How much are the managerial or administrative costs for achieving desired results?

Time

- How many items are produced in a given time compared to best practice organizations?
- How fast is product or service cycle time (from innovation to market)?

Customer Service Requirements

- How satisfied are customers with the end results?
- How many and what kind of complaints or compliments are received from customers inside and outside the organization?

Step 3: Preparing a Plan to Guide the Job Analysis

The third step is preparation of a plan to guide the investigation. That plan should address at least the following questions: (1) Who will conduct the job analysis? (2) What is the primary purpose of the analysis? (3) How will the results of the analysis be used? (4) Who is depending on the results of the analysis? and (5) What sources or methods should be used to collect and analyze job information?

First, decide who will conduct the job analysis. Will it be human resource professionals, external consultants, instructional designers, supervisors, or others? The answer to this question is very important, since the credibility of the job analysis is influenced by who performs it. Those perceived to have a self-interest in the results will not be credible.

Then clarify why the analysis is being conducted. Is the purpose primarily to determine what job incumbents really do? If so, then instructional designers will have to ensure that the data collected represent reality. Or is the purpose to determine what job incumbents should do in the future? If so, then it will be necessary to establish ways to forecast or scan the future. Next, identify who is depending on the results. Is it instructional designers alone, or do others have an interest in the results for such other reasons as improved compensation practice or process reengineering? If job analysis results are of value to others, and not just to instructional designers, then their interests must be determined at the outset so that the results will answer their questions and address their key concerns.

Finally, decide on the sources and methods that should be used to collect and analyze job information. Sources of information may include job incumbents, supervisors, those familiar with work performed by job incumbents, and others. Methods may include such standard social science data collection vehicles as written surveys, interviews, observations, work diaries, and work records. The earliest methods of job analysis, called time-and-motion studies, relied on highly detailed observation of blue-collar workers in manufacturing settings. More recently, surveys and interviews have tended to be used about as often as observation. One reason is that survey or interview results can often be obtained much more quickly than observation results, and often at substantially lower cost. A second reason has to do with the fact that the U.S. economy is moving away from blue-collar manufacturing to white-collar service jobs. Surveys and interviews are sometimes more appropriate for studying jobs requiring specialized cognitive (knowledge) and affective (feelings and attitudes) skills than for those involving psychomotor (manual) skills (Zemke and Kramlinger, 1982).

Step 4: Implementing the Job Analysis Plan

The fourth step of job analysis is implementation. At this point, instructional designers carry out the job analysis plan, collecting information about the jobs under investigation. In many respects, the problems faced in this step resemble the problems faced in collecting data about training needs. More specifically, instructional designers should avoid creating false expectations and avoid errors in protocol during data collection.

False expectations arise when job incumbents believe that job analysis will produce results of immediate advantage to themselves. For instance, they may believe that a review of what they do will lead to a higher salary, a lofty job title, or some other advantage. Instructional designers should avoid the problems stemming from building false expectations by clarifying from the beginning of the analysis precisely why it is being performed, and what will and will not happen as a result of it.

Errors in protocol stem from inappropriate interaction between the instructional designer and job incumbents or their immediate supervisors. Imagine, for instance, how a job incumbent will treat an instructional designer who shows up to perform a job analysis unannounced. To avoid the consequences stemming from that error and similar ones, instructional designers should at least (1) identify who needs to give permission for a job analysis to be conducted, (2) clarify how permissions are given, and (3) allow sufficient time for those permissions to be given.

Step 5: Analyzing and Using the Results of the Job Analysis

Instructional designers select methods for analyzing the results of the job analysis during Step 3, but they carry out the analysis in Step 5. As in needs assessment, this selection will depend on how the information is to be collected. The results of job analysis are expressed as job descriptions, job specifications, task listings, or job performance standards.

Summary

Job analysis is the most general form of work analysis. It lays the foundation for related, but more detailed, analysis of tasks or content. We turn next to task analysis.

Task Analysis

To design job-specific instruction, instructional designers must know in precise detail exactly what workers do, how they do it, why they do it, what mental, physical, and learning requirements are essential to doing it, and what equipment or other resources they must have to perform. The results of job analysis are too general to provide this amount of detail. Consequently, task analysis is necessary as a starting point for preparing performance objectives to guide results to be achieved by instruction.

Defining Task Analysis

A task analysis is an intensive examination of how people perform work activities. It can sometimes involve a critique and reexamination of work activities as well. Task analysis is carried out to (1) determine components of competent performance; (2) identify activities that may be simplified or otherwise improved; (3) determine precisely what a worker must know, do, or feel to learn a specific work activity; (4) clarify conditions (equipment and other resources) needed for competent performance; and (5) establish minimum expectations (standards) for how well job incumbents should perform each task appearing in their job descriptions. Task analysis is not limited to any single method or technique and can be carried out in many ways.

Defining Terms Associated with Task Analysis

To understand task analysis, instructional designers should begin by familiarizing themselves with such terms as task, subtask, element, and task listing.

A task is, according to one classic definition, "a discrete unit of work performed by an individual. It usually comprises a logical and necessary step in the performance of a job duty, and typically has an identifiable beginning and ending" (McCormick, 1979, p. 19). A task does not always involve observable behavior; rather, it may also involve an unobservable mental action such as "making a correct decision." Yet a task can be clearly understood to mean "a group of related activities directed toward a goal" that "includes a mixture of decisions, perceptions, and/or physical (motor) activities required of one person." It "may be of any size or degree of complexity as well" (U.S. Air Force, 1973, p. 63).

The following examples of tasks from Reddout's classic article "What Is a Task?" (1987, pp. 5–6) will help to clarify these points:

Introduction

Training literature is full of information on developing task-oriented training documents, such as training manuals. However, little is said about what a task is or how a trainer can identify a task.

Task Types

A task is a series of actions or behaviors which accomplishes a goal. Tasks are divided into two major types: Cognitive tasks are performed mentally. A cognitive behavior such as evaluating, deciding, or discriminating is not observable. These mental processes do not have a set of steps which follow a precise order. They are difficult to define and difficult to teach.

Action tasks have a set of clearly defined steps that are observable. Action tasks have a performer and another person who is changed by the actions of the performer. Sometimes an object may be changed by the action.

Example—Cognitive Task

Select a personal computer.

In this task, although the decision may be based upon specific criteria, the selection is made mentally. Two individuals, given the same circumstances, may follow two sets of actions and select two different computers.

Example—Action Task

Replace a burned-out bulb on an overhead projector.

In this task, each step can be observed, and the performer must follow a particular order of actions (the new bulb cannot be put in until the old one is removed). Also, each person who performs the task follows the same set of actions to achieve the same outcome or goal.

Definition

An action task, then, is a series of actions or behaviors that
- Involves interaction between a person (the performer) and an object or another person
- Changes the object or person in some way
- Accomplishes a goal

Criteria

An action task can be further defined by applying the following criteria. An action task

- Has a definite beginning and end
- Is performed in relatively short periods of time
- Can be observed
- Can be measured
- Is independent of other actions

Examples of Action Tasks

- Dial a long-distance telephone number.
- Perform a needs analysis.
- Measure and record vital signs.
- Pitch a softball.
- Build a bookcase.
- Update a computerized mailing list.

Nonexamples

- Display the main menu for a data base management system.
  - Is not independent of other actions.
- Collect stamps.
  - Does not have a definite beginning and ending.
  - Is not performed in relatively short periods of time.
- Know how to fill out an expense report.
  - Cannot be observed. ("Know" is not an overt behavior.)
  - Cannot be measured. ("Know" cannot be demonstrated.)

A subtask is one step in a task. It "is sometimes considered the smallest step into which it is practical to subdivide any work activity without analyzing the separate motions, movements, and mental processes involved" (McCormick, 1979, pp. 19–20).

An element is a step-within-a-step of a task. It "consists of very specific separate motions or movements" in time-and-motion studies conducted by industrial engineers (McCormick, 1979, p. 20). An element can be detected by detailed photographic studies of manual operations. For instance, an element within the task of "shoveling coal into a furnace" is "placing a hand on the shovel."

A task listing means quite literally what the phrase implies: it is a list of tasks. The aim of a task listing is to answer this question: What do people do as they carry out their work? The result of a task listing becomes the starting point for developing a task analysis, since a task listing describes what people do but not how they do it. Task listings are sometimes included in job descriptions, although more detailed task listings can be developed using each major task in a job description as a starting point.

An Overview of the Steps in Performing Task Analysis

Instructional designers should begin a task analysis study in essentially the same way they begin a job analysis:

1. Identify jobs or tasks to be analyzed.
2. Clarify the results desired from the task analysis.
3. Prepare a plan to guide the task analysis.
4. Implement the task analysis plan.
5. Analyze and use the investigation's results.

We now turn to a step-by-step discussion of this procedure.

Step 1: Identifying Tasks to Be Analyzed

The first step is to identify the tasks to be analyzed. Using a task listing, instructional designers identify what tasks within a job are to be analyzed. They must first decide what kinds of tasks are involved, because the nature of the tasks determines which of several approaches to task analysis should be selected.

There are four kinds of tasks: procedural, process, troubleshooting, and mental (Swanson and Gradous, 1986).

Procedural tasks are synonymous with action tasks, as described in the preceding examples from Reddout's article "What Is a Task?" They involve interactions between people and materials or machines. They are completely observable and occur in an identifiable sequence. Examples of procedures include riding a bicycle, filling an automobile's gasoline tank, or changing a light bulb.

Process tasks are partially observable, are bound to a particular process, occur within a preexisting system, and involve interactions between people and a process. Examples of processes include an organization's purchasing practices, a company's manufacturing methods, or a management information system. Processes usually lend themselves especially well to flowcharting or algorithms (Horabin and Lewis, 1978).

Troubleshooting tasks are quite similar to process tasks, except that the flow works in reverse. If a machine or system is not functioning as it should, then human beings must work backward from what should be to what is to determine the problem's cause. Suppose instructional designers wish to find out why a computer will not run a program. (Computer manuals frequently contain "troubleshooting guides" to help novices figure out why these marvelous machines sometimes have trouble working for their less-than-machine-perfect owners.) To perform this troubleshooting task, instructional designers must know how the program "should" work before they can determine why it is not working. Experts are frequently able to do troubleshooting quicker than novices (Johnson, 1988).

Mental tasks are unobservable. Synonymous with cognitive tasks as described in the preceding examples from Reddout's article, they involve people-idea or people-people interactions (Swanson and Gradous, 1986). While they may occur in a predictable sequence, that sequence occurs within the mind of the performer.

Step 2: Clarifying the Desired Results

The second step of any task analysis should clarify the desired results. Always consider two key questions for that purpose: (1) Why is the analysis being conducted, and (2) What results are sought from it? To answer the first question, decide whether the purpose is to analyze how people actually perform, how they think they perform, how they should perform, or how they should perform in the future. Most task analysis combines two of these purposes, focusing both on how people actually do perform and on how they should perform.

Next, direct attention to determining what results are desired. How detailed does the task analysis really have to be? It makes no sense to be extremely detailed when that is unnecessary. Indeed, it makes much more sense to start out with the fewest details and add to them over time (Jackson, 1986). Jackson advises instructional designers to "begin by getting general information about all tasks—typically inputs and outputs first, then major steps. This will help clarify relationships among tasks and ensure that the information gathered is both accurate and necessary" (p. 92). Results of task analysis can be expressed in terms of application of intellectual skill, cognitive strategy, verbal information, or motor skill or attitude (Gagné, Briggs, and Wager, 1992). Some task analysts prefer to progress beyond simple analysis (How is the task performed?) in order to address performance measurements (How well should the task be performed?) and conditions necessary for performance (What tools, equipment, and other resources must be available to the performer for the task to be conducted?).

Step 3: Preparing a Plan to Guide the Task Analysis

The third step is to prepare a plan to guide the task analysis. Put in writing how the task analysis will be conducted, complete with statements of the purpose and desired results. Be sure to answer three important questions: (1) Who will conduct the task analysis? (2) Whose task performance will be examined? and (3) What approach will be used to collect and analyze task information?

Task analysis is a time-consuming activity, and the detailed results it typically generates are not often needed by human resource professionals in the way that job analysis results usually are. Consequently, it will usually be conducted by instructional designers from inside or outside an organization, although industrial engineers are also quite capable of carrying out these investigations in blue-collar industrial settings. Instructional designers are thus the most likely to collect—and use—task listing and analysis information.

A key issue to consider at the outset of a task analysis is the amount of time and money it will take to perform. That depends, of course, on the number of tasks to be analyzed and the detail required. If many tasks will be scrutinized or the detail required is great, one or two in-house instructional designers can rarely handle the assignment in a brief time span. For this reason, managers of instructional design projects may request contractual assistance from outside groups—vendors, local college faculty, or other instructional designers—to perform task analysis, particularly in large settings such as nuclear power stations.

When outside instructional designers are used, they should be selected with the same care as in-house staff. Check their references carefully. Request samples of their work. To reduce the time it will take to orient them to the project, furnish them with examples to show the detail that is required.

It should be relatively easy to specify whose task performance will be examined. However, the sources to use in gathering task information can sometimes be debated. There are four possible sources of information about tasks: performers, non-performers, documents, and environmental features (Jackson, 1986).

Performers are those who do the work. Much valuable information can be collected by observing what they do, asking them what they do, and examining their work results. However, there are different categories of performers—as shown in the list following. Each category of performer furnishes a unique source of information.

Types of Performers	*What They Can Tell You*
Master performers	Master performers can provide information about the most efficient and effective way to perform a task. Normally, task analyses should be based on the way the most successful people perform the task.
Average performers	Information about the way average performers behave and the results they obtain can provide opportunities for improvement. A comparison of average and master performers will provide information about the size of the gap.
Low performers	Information from low performers can be useful for making training decisions, and comparisons with average or master performers can provide information about opportunities for improvement.

Analyst as performer   Analysts can also gather information by performing the tasks themselves. This can confirm information from others as well as help identify gaps in information.

Non-performers are those who have reason to be familiar with work tasks but who do not actually perform them. They can often provide important perspectives about what results should be achieved but are not being achieved. Examples of non-performers include supervisors, internal customers of a work process, external customers of the organization, the organization's suppliers or distributors, subordinates, peers, resource or staff personnel, subject-matter experts, and future performers. The nature of the information they provide is summarized here (Jackson, 1986, p. 89).

Documents are references used by performers to carry out work tasks or by non-performers to find out about those tasks. Examples of documents include procedure manuals, training manuals, and forms. They can be valuable sources of information about how work tasks should be performed, how they should be measured, and what resources are needed for performance.

Environmental features are the conditions under which instruction is to be developed or applied. (Key features of these environments have already been described at length in Chapter Six.) In the task analysis plan, be sure to consider what approach to use in collecting and analyzing task information. Base the selection of an approach on the task to be examined, as shown in Table 7.1. If a procedural task is to be examined, then use procedural analysis; if a process or troubleshooting task is to be examined, then use process and troubleshooting analysis; if a mental task is to be examined, then use content analysis (Swanson and Gradous, 1986).

Steps 4 and 5: Implementing the Task Analysis Plan and Analyzing and Using Results

Implementing a task analysis plan should be simple enough, even if actually conducting task analysis can be a time-consuming and tedious process. Carlisle (1986, p. 5) summarizes these steps succinctly. "First, the job or task is broken down into its component parts. Second, the relationships between the parts are examined and compared with correct principles of performance. Third, the parts are restructured to form an improved job or task, and learning requirements are specified." The first step is the task listing component of the study. The outputs of a task listing become the basis for task analysis, and the outputs of a task analysis become the basis for performance objectives and test items. Of course, performance objectives provide descriptions of what learners should know, do, or feel at the end of an instructional experience.

TABLE 7.1. SUMMARY OF APPROACHES TO TASK ANALYSIS.

Approach to task analysis	Use the approach under the following conditions	Description
Procedure analysis	Interaction between person-material or person-machine Step-by-step procedure Observable activity	List the steps in a procedure from the standpoint of a performer of it, beginning each task statement with a verb. Describe how to measure the quality of the task. Describe how to recognize cues indicating when a task should be enacted. Identify instances in which tasks can be more effectively or efficiently performed.
Process and troubleshooting analysis	Interaction between person and system	Flowchart the system, showing how work should progress through it. Identify ways to improve the flow of work through the system, eliminating redundancy and unnecessary steps.
Content analysis	Interactions between person and system	Identify the subject or topic. Investigate what experienced performers know about the topic. Investigate how people perform the mental (covert) activity by asking them, observing results of work activity, or other methods. Conduct a search of literature on the topic. Synthesize results using any one of several methods. Describe the subject/content.

Source: Adapted from Swanson, R., and Gradous, D. *Performance at Work: A Systematic Program for Analyzing Work Behavior.* New York: Wiley-Interscience, 1986

Content Analysis

Content analysis, sometimes called subject matter analysis, "is intended (1) to identify and isolate single idea or skill units for instruction, (2) to act as an objective decision rule for including or excluding topics from instruction, and (3) to provide guidance to sequence topics in instruction" (Gibbons, 1977, p. 2).

According to *The Standards* (Richey, Fields, and Foxon, 2001, p. 49), one competency for instructional design is to "select and use a variety of techniques for determining instructional content." It is regarded as an essential competency.

The performance statements associated with this competency indicate that instructional designers should be able to (Richey, Fields, and Foxon, 2001, p. 49):

a. Identify content requirements in accordance with needs assessment findings (essential).
b. Elicit, synthesize, and validate content from subject-matter experts and other sources (advanced).
c. Determine the breadth and depth of intended coverage given instructional constraints (advanced).
d. Determine prerequisites given the type of subject matter, the needs of the learners, and the organization (essential).
e. Use appropriate techniques to analyze varying types of content (essential).

This competency is, of course, relevant to content analysis.

When Should Instructional Designers Perform Content Analysis?

Content analysis need not follow job or task analysis. It may be performed by itself, or it may follow task analysis as a means of relating work activities and results to the knowledge necessary for individuals to perform. Defined as "the process of breaking large bodies of subject matter or tasks into smaller and instructionally useful units" (Gibbons, 1977, p. 2), content analysis can be used in developing instruction or conducting consumer research (Sayre, 1992). These "instructionally useful units" may include facts, concepts, processes, procedures, or principles (Clark, 1986). For example, "If you make notes or prepare an outline of information for a lesson, a speech, or a paper, you list subject content" (Kemp, 1971, p. 44). Content analysis thus differs from job or task analysis because it stems from an examination of information or knowledge requirements rather than from sequences or procedures in conducting work activities or achieving work results.

Importance of Content Analysis

To perform, workers require information that they have translated into knowledge, skills, and attitudes and that they have organized in ways they can apply in a work setting. Of course, competent performance requires more than appropriate knowledge, skills, and attitudes. For instance, workers must be able to recognize the cues that signal when performance is appropriate or inappropriate. They must also be motivated to perform when they recognize the cues signaling an appropriate occasion to perform. Yet it is clear that workers will never be capable of performing competently if they lack the requisite knowledge, skills, and attitudes.

Content analysis is important, then, because it is a process of identifying the essential information that learners should translate into work-related knowledge, skills, and attitudes through planned instructional experiences. Instructional designers play an important role in organizing information in ways that will be meaningful to learners and that will help them translate information (facts, concepts, processes, procedures, principles) into work-related knowledge, skills, and attitudes.

Assumptions Underlying Content Analysis

Three key assumptions provide a theoretical foundation for content analysis. One assumption is, "Learning experiences are based on subject content" (Kemp, 1971, p. 43). In other words, learners must know before they can do. They must be familiar with a body of knowledge, skills, and attitudes associated with performance before they can perform competently.

A second assumption is that work tasks are not always the appropriate basis for instructional design because "it is not always the case that the end-purposes [objectives of instruction] reduce to a single task or set of tasks" (Gibbons, 1977, p. 4). Task analysis is not always an appropriate means of examining the components of effective performance because performance cannot always be reduced to step-by-step processes or procedures. Indeed, effective performance may on occasion depend on a learner's familiarity with facts, concepts, processes, procedures, or principles. Definitions and examples of these terms, all of which are important for understanding content analysis, appear in Table 7.2.

A third assumption underlying content analysis is related to the second: "instructional content and tasks vary across a set of categories [and] there are indeed different types of content" (Gibbons, 1977, p. 4). One implication of this statement is that "different types of content are likely to require methods of analysis suited to them individually. Hence, one type of analysis is not sufficient to handle all types of content adequately" (p. 4).

Instructional designers should not, of course, perform content analysis because it is intrinsically fascinating or satisfying in its own right. (Some perverse, highly technical instructional designers may find that it is!) Instead, it should be performed because it provides useful information for organizing instruction and developing objectives to guide information. As Kemp (1971, p. 44) succinctly explains in a passage that remains relevant:

> In the pattern of the instructional design plan we should proceed from statements of general purpose to objectives and then to subject content. In actual practice we often find it easier to begin with a statement of general purposes, follow it with a list of content to be taught and learned, and then backtrack to

TABLE 7.2. CONTENT TYPES: DEFINITIONS AND EXAMPLES.

Content	Definition	Example
Fact	An arbitrary association among concepts.	The editor of *Performance and Instruction* was Sivasailam Thiagarajan.
Concept	A category of items that share common characteristics.	Editor —A person —Responsible for articles written by others
Process	A series of steps whereby several individuals, departments, or objects accomplish a task.	How the company collects bills. How a generator works.
Procedure	A series of steps whereby an individual completes a task.	How to log on a computer.
Principle	A predictive relationship among concepts.	Goals that are specific and difficult yield more productivity than easy or vague goals.

Source: Clark, R. "Defining the 'D' in ISD, Part 2: Task-Specific Instructional Methods." *Performance and Instruction*, 1986, *25*(3), 13. Reprinted with permission of the International Society for Performance Improvement.

work on objectives, as suggested by the content. In one sense we might say that "objectives are what you want content to do." [Later] if you start with the content you will probably find that there is a sequence of order that indicates that certain parts of the content must be mastered as a basis for subsequent learning.

The question is, How is this "sequence of order" identified? The answer to that question is the basis for content analysis.

An Overview of the Steps in Performing Content Analysis

Instructional designers should take the following steps to perform a content analysis described in a classic treatment by Swanson and Gradous (1986):

1. Identify the subject or topic.
2. Investigate what experienced performers know about the topic.
3. Investigate how people perform the mental (covert) activity by
   a. Asking them.
   b. Observing results of work activity.
   c. Using other methods.
4. Conduct a literature search on the topic.

5. Synthesize results using any one of several methods to develop a model of the subject.
6. Describe the subject or content.

We now turn to a summary of each step.

Step 1: Identifying the Subject or Topic

First, identify the subject or topic. Try to link it to existing databases. For example, use the *Library of Congress Subject Index,* available in most libraries, and see how the topic is classified by libraries. Numerous other reference sources and databases can be consulted to identify keywords for use in identifying subject titles.

Step 2: Investigating What Experienced Performers Know About the Topic

Second, investigate what experienced performers know about the topic. Use questionnaires, interviews, observations of performers, document reviews, and Internet queries. Collect background information to clarify what the subject is. Ask experienced performers to explain what the subject is, how it relates to the work, and how they would orient a new employee to the subject.

Step 3: Investigating How People Perform the Activity

Third, investigate how people perform the mental (covert) activity by asking them, observing results of work activity, or using other methods. Analyze what was learned about the topic from experienced performers in Step 2, and then organize that information. Next try to clarify what knowledge is applied in the work setting, how it is applied, and how people organize and structure it themselves. If possible, establish categories for observation. If that is not possible, sit with performers as they work, and ask them what they do as they do it (Zemke and Kramlinger, 1982).

Organize information based on problems or situations encountered in the work setting and how performers respond to them. This process is called information processing analysis. For each behavior ask, What should a learner know or do to perform?

Step 4: Conducting a Literature Search on the Topic

Fourth, conduct a search of literature on the topic. Use any of the numerous sources of information available to instructional designers. Identify key references—organizational, occupational, governmental, industrial, or academic—during discussions with experienced performers. Other professional instructional designers may also be a valuable source of information about literature on the topic, since they may have had occasion to research the topic in the past.

Step 5: Synthesizing Results of the Content Analysis

Fifth, synthesize results of the content analysis. Use one of several methods to develop a synthesis model, defined by Swanson and Gradous (1986, p. 207) as "a structure on which to organize and fit the ideas and information on any subject matter relevant to performance at work." To develop a synthesis model, instructional designers must approach the subject matter creatively, using innovative problem-solving techniques to impose organization where there may appear to be none (Ulschak, Nathanson, and Gillan, 1983; Van Gundy, 1981).

Swanson and Gradous list eight techniques to develop synthesis models: (1) reflection, which compresses a subject into a "metaphor, cartoon, or narrative that somehow 'says it all'" (p. 195); (2) a two-axis matrix, in which two ideas are juxtaposed graphically to form a series of cells, each representing a different fact, concept, procedure, or principle; (3) a three-axis matrix, in which three ideas are juxtaposed graphically to form a cube, and each cell of the cube represents a fact, concept, process, procedure, or principle; (4) a flowchart, which "organizes and synthesizes information that contains input-process-output items, decision points, direction of flow, documentation or preparation steps, confluence and divergence, and extraction" (p. 199); (5) an events network, which "will help you take into account all the activity paths and events by which work toward an organizational goal is accomplished" (p. 199); (6) dichotomy, which divides subject matter into two completely different parts that are then contrasted and compared; (7) argumentation, which is a "synthesis method aimed at resolving two or more theses, positions, or valuations of a subject matter" (p. 201); and (8) graphic models that organize information visually through charts, maps, and other methods.

Step 6: Describing the Subject or Content

Sixth, describe the subject or content in a way that will facilitate learning by others. Remember that imposing organization on subject matter does not necessarily mean that the resulting arrangement will facilitate the learning of those unfamiliar with the subject. To organize subject matter for learning, perform an instructional analysis that identifies what learners should know in order to demonstrate knowledge or perform a task or other activity. This topic will be treated at the beginning of the next chapter, because instructional analysis is the link between what is to be learned and how instruction should be designed.

The results of content analysis, like the results of task analysis, provide the basis for preparing performance objectives to guide development of instruction and test items. To emphasize this point, this principle is illustrated in Figure 7.2.

FIGURE 7.2. USES FOR RESULTS OF TASK OR CONTENT ANALYSIS.

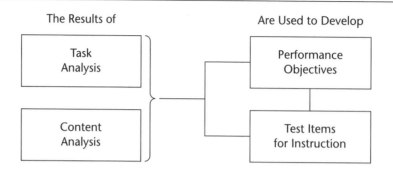

SCORM

Any discussion of content should also at least reference sharable content object reference model (SCORM). While space here is probably insufficient to describe it in great detail, readers should be advised that the goal of SCORM is to "make it so neither the content nor the delivery system relies on the other's special properties to create learning experiences that can adapt to the learner and that follow decent instructional design principles. The e-learning standards community is creating standard properties that can be used by all content and any learning platform. This work is incorporated into SCORM" (Robson, 2002, p. 48).

Judging Work Analysis

Instructional designers should be capable of evaluating work analysis studies conducted by themselves or others. The evaluation should focus on three central issues: (1) Was the procedure selected and carried out appropriately? (2) Was the analysis carried out with sufficient detail and in sufficient depth? and (3) Are the results useful for writing performance objectives to guide instruction?

Judging the Adequacy of an Analytical Method and Its Results: A Few Simple Steps

If job, task, or content analysis studies have been conducted poorly, it will be difficult—if not impossible—to design effective instruction tailored to work-related performance needs. After all, detailed analysis results in a thorough breakdown of a job, task, or subject-matter area so that it can be reassembled instructionally. If the analysis is wrong, then the instruction based on it will also be wrong, and the effects on workers may be devastating to their performance and morale, not to mention the effects on the organization's productivity.

- To judge whether the procedure was selected and carried out appropriately, study the plan for the work analysis to make sure it clearly sets forth each of the following:
- The purpose, goals, and objectives of the analysis.
- The analytical procedure selected.
- The reasons why the instructional designers chose the analytical procedure they chose.
- The constraints on time and resources that the instructional designers faced.
- The assumptions, if any, that the instructional designers made about the jobs, tasks, or content they analyzed.
- The methods used to collect and analyze data.
- The findings that resulted from the analysis.
- The background information available to instructional designers as they conducted the analysis. Did they research and then apply to the analysis information about the organization's mission, goals, structure, perceived values, and specifications derived from a needs assessment and analysis? Did they apply any additional information they were able to obtain from subject-matter experts or from documentation?

Obtain this information before evaluating the work analysis.

Second, review the documentation and clarify the constraints and resources available to carry out the analytical assignment. Then interview the instructional designers assigned to the project. Ask a few simple "acid test" questions:

- What was the purpose of the analysis? What were the objectives? Was the analysis carried out primarily to (1) describe the job, task, or content? (2) describe how the job or task is done or how content is used? (3) identify ways to improve the job or task or improve content application in work performance? or (4) identify how to instruct others on the job, task, or content?
- What constraints, if any, were faced on this project? What necessary resources were not available?
- How would you perform the analysis differently if you were asked to do it now?
- How did the culture of the organization affect analysis? How much cooperation did you receive from members of the organization?

Base part of the evaluation of the work analysis on the answers.

Justifying Work Analysis

Instructional designers should also be capable of justifying the work analysis conducted and the conclusions reached from it. Before, during, and after the work analysis, then, be prepared to explain and defend it against those who may have economic or political stakes in the outcomes. Detailed work analysis may sometimes seem threatening to workers and even their supervisors, and the results may have implications affecting workers' wages, salaries, and job security. For these reasons, some job incumbents and their supervisors may feel impelled to challenge job or task analysis results if they fear they may lose something valuable. These problems of acceptance can usually be averted if workers and supervisors actively participate at every stage of analysis. Greater participation will also tend to increase the likelihood that workers and supervisors will accept the results and will use them in subsequent instruction, both on and off the job. However, the greater the degree of participation and the larger the group of participants, the longer it will take to perform the analysis.

If constraints on time limit worker or supervisor participation, then be prepared to support the results of the work analysis against those who feel they may lose something. If possible, hold an "exit conference" at the end of the assignment with representatives of workers and management. Have documentation from the work analysis prepared and thoroughly organized for this conference, and do not expect to be treated cordially during the assignment. Prepare an outline to guide presentation of the results, and spell out how the investigation was conducted, who participated in it, how long it was conducted, what assumptions were made, and what the results do not mean as well as what they do mean. Find out, in advance of the assignment or the exit conference, whether the results will be used in any way that may later have an effect on workers' wages or future job security. If not, say so at the beginning of the assignment and repeat it again at the end; otherwise, ask representatives of the organization to attend the conference and discuss what impact the results may have.

Competency Models: What Are They?

Competency models have become a topic of major interest in many organizations (Cooper, 2000; Langdon and Marelli, 2002; Lucia and Lepsinger, 1999). Competency modeling has supplemented, and sometimes has supplanted, traditional task analysis. It therefore warrants description here because many instructional designers will probably increasingly encounter situations in which they must assess or use competencies as the basis for developing instruction. And it is also likely that, in the future, identifying—and finding ("Skills Inventories," 2002)—talent will grow more important.

What key definitions are associated with competencies? Why has competency modeling suddenly attracted such attention? What methodologies can be used to carry out competency modeling? While a complete description of competency modeling is beyond the scope of this book, this section serves as a primer on competency modeling.

Key Definitions

It is important to understand at the outset that competency is not a trademark, so meanings associated with the word vary dramatically. When confronted with the term, instructional designers should immediately ask these questions: How is that term being used? and What is its meaning in context? Answers to these questions should help clarify how the word is being used, since people can—and often do—associate it with varied meanings.

Some educators use the word competency as a shorthand term to refer to knowledge, skill, or attitude. But that is not the only way that the term can be used. According to Harvard psychologist David McClelland (1973, 1976), who is often credited with coining the term, a competency is a characteristic underlying successful performance. It transcends mere knowledge, skills, and attitudes and includes bodies of knowledge, theories, or motivation. Competency identification is a process of discovering the competencies distinguishing high performers (called exemplars) from average performers (Dubois and Rothwell, 2000). A competency model is the result of a competency identification process. Competency models may be prepared for job categories (such as supervisors), for departments (such as accounting), for occupations (such as nurses), for divisions (such as "the aerospace division"), or for entire organizations. Behavioral events interviewing (BEI) is the key methodology used to assess competencies. BEI usually involves asking one or several exemplary performers to describe what they did, what they thought, and how they felt as they were confronted with a difficult situation in their work, or with the singularly most difficult situation with which they have ever been confronted in their work.

Another school of thought describes what are called organizational core competencies (Campbell and Luchs, 1997; Prahalad and Hamel, 1990; Ulrich and Lake, 1990). These terms should not be confused with individual competencies, though they bear similarities. An organizational core competency is essentially a strategic strength, something one organization does better than its competitors. It might even perform better in that area than any organization in any industry and therefore be regarded as a world-class benchmark organization for its unique strength. As examples, IBM is known to have an organizational core competency in marketing; Motorola is known to have an organizational core competency in training; and FedEx is known to have an organizational core competency in the rapid transportation of materials. Identifying organizational core competencies is worthwhile because organizations should not completely outsource areas in which they perform better than others. They should also work to build on their strength, using it to maximum competitive advantage. For that reason, some observers believe that organizations should do training for core competencies, meaning that they should develop instruction to enhance an existing strength. The motto is, "Let's do better what we already do better than anyone else." The rationale is that a core competency may be what keeps the business competitive—and successful.

Why the Interest in Competencies?

Individual competencies have attracted much attention in recent years. Jobs have changed so much that decision making, and the often hard-to-define characteristics linked to the affective (feeling) domain, have become more important to work success. A simple-minded focus on knowledge, skills, and attitudes alone is not enough to capture these critically important intangibles that distinguish successful from unsuccessful performance. Competencies provide the fuzzy logic necessary to get at these intangibles. Competency models provide a blueprint for building these intangibles in organizational settings and may thus become foundational for future HR systems (Dubois and Rothwell, in press).

Methodologies for Competency Modeling

Competency modeling may be carried out using any one of numerous methodologies. To understand competency modeling, readers need some grounding in these methodologies or approaches. It is therefore worthwhile describing current competency modeling methodologies. Of course, each methodology has its distinct advantages and disadvantages, and no methodology is immune to criticism.

Traditional competency modeling methodologies can be classified into four major approaches: the borrowed approach, the borrowed-and-tailored approach, the process-driven approach, and the outputs-driven approach. Three newer approaches can be added to these: the invented approach, the trends-driven approach, and the rapid results assessment approach. The names for these approaches are, of course, arbitrary and are useful only as shorthand descriptors to capture the essence of each.

The borrowed approach to competency modeling is the easiest to conduct and is also the least expensive. It involves simply "borrowing" a competency model devised by another organization. It does not require the application of a methodology, since no investigation is required beyond finding and applying another organization's existing, proven, and validated competency model. Competency models are widely available. They can be found through published sources, purchased from consulting firms, or accessed through Internet-based or World Wide Web-based searches.

The borrowed-and-tailored approach requires a minimalist methodology. The reason: another organization has already conducted the study. Using that organization's study involves borrowing. However, to tailor the approach to another occupation or a unique corporate culture requires modifying the competency model to fit another organization or occupation. That may be conducted in such simple ways as surveying members of the targeted group or holding a focus group meeting composed of exemplary performer-practitioners.

The process-driven approach was made famous by the prominent consulting firm, McBer, now known as Hay/McBer. It is the oldest of the valid and reliable approaches to conducting competency modeling. It is labeled the process-driven approach here because it attaches much weight to the work (process) that is performed by exemplary job incumbents.

Basic steps in applying the process-driven approach include

- Investigating the work duties, tasks, responsibilities, roles, and work environment of the job, work, team, or occupation that is the target.
- Isolating the characteristics unique to exemplary performers.
- Verifying the model.

During the investigation stage a focus group is formed of experienced and exemplary job incumbents. Members of the focus group express work requirements as job outputs, work activities or responsibilities, personal characteristics, and behaviors associated with what is necessary to demonstrate successful performance. Focus group members also nominate exemplary job incumbents—an approach that is methodologically valid and reliable. Those exemplary job incumbents are, in turn, shown the results of the initial focus group and are asked to rate the results.

Subsequent steps in the process-driven approach involve isolating the characteristics of exemplary performers and verifying the model. Isolating the characteristics of exemplary performers is done by observing them, interviewing them, or both. Two lists are prepared. One list identifies competencies of exemplary job incumbents; another identifies competencies of average performers.

Competencies appearing on both lists are minimum competencies; those that are characteristic of exemplary performers only become the basis for complete competency model development.

Verifying the model can be carried out in three ways (Dubois, 1993). One way is to replicate the original approach to determine whether an identical model can be developed. A second way is to survey job incumbents. A third way is to test job incumbents using the model. All three major approaches to verification can be time-consuming and (potentially) expensive. The cost of verification is usually warranted only when the competency model will be used as a basis for hiring and terminating, as well as developing, members of the targeted group.

The outputs-driven approach was made famous by Patricia A. McLagan. Its name reflects its focus on work outputs, that is, on what successful performers produce—the outcomes or results of their work. Competencies are, in turn, derived from those outputs.

Basic steps in applying the outputs-driven approach include (Dubois, 1993)

- Compiling all available information about the duties, tasks, responsibilities, roles, and work environment of the job, work, team, or occupation that is the target of the competency modeling study.
- Establishing an expert panel consisting of individuals who supervise those in the targeted category and exemplary performers or exemplary job incumbents (as best they can be systematically identified).
- Expressing explicit assumptions about changes likely to affect the job, work, team, or occupation that is the target of the competency modeling study in the organization or field of endeavor.
- Compiling a menu of work outputs.
- Developing a menu of work quality requirements associated with the work outputs.
- Devising a list of work competencies and behavioral anchors or indices associated with each competency.
- Listing work roles developed through cluster analysis of the work outputs.
- Developing the draft competency model.

Compiling all available information about the duties, tasks, responsibilities, roles, and work environment of the job, work, team, or occupation that is the target of the competency modeling study is carried out by reviewing extant competency studies of the field. Establishing an expert panel of individuals supervising those in the targeted category and exemplary performers or job incumbents (as best they can be systematically identified) is carried out by clarifying the criteria to be used in selecting experts and by following through by applying those criteria. Expressing explicit assumptions about changes likely to affect the job, work, team, or occupation is conducted by isolating the trends or changes most likely to affect the job, work, team, or occupation. Compiling a menu of work outputs is carried out by calling together the expert panel to brainstorm the results of performing the work that is the target of investigation. Developing a menu of work quality requirements associated with the work outputs is carried out by asking members of the expert panel to describe the characteristics of successful work outputs. Devising a list of work competencies and behavioral anchors is also carried out by asking members of the expert panel. Members of such a panel may, for instance, be supplied with a list of competencies derived from previous competency studies and asked to rate them. Listing work roles is conducted by performing cluster analysis of the work outputs to identify related areas of work. Descriptive labels (role names) are then arbitrarily assigned to them. Finally, reviewing the draft competency model is handled by the expert panel or other groups. Validation and verification are performed by repeating the study with a different group or by surveying many job incumbents—surveying exemplary performers is even better—about the results.

Although the process-driven and outputs-driven approaches are the classic and traditional competency modeling and modeling methodologies, three newer approaches have appeared within the last three to five years. They are the invented approach, the trends-driven approach, and the work-responsibilities-driven approach.

The invented approach, while very low in validity and reliability, is faster than other methods. Decision makers are guided through a process of developing a competency model by "making it up out of the blue." This approach works best when job incumbents are not the most reliable source of information about the desirable changes that must be made for the job incumbents, team, or members of the occupation to change dramatically what they do or how they do it.

The trends-driven approach focuses attention on the future issues or trends affecting the job, work, team, or occupation. Instead of placing primary emphasis on what people do (as the process-driven approach does) or on the work products they make (as the outputs-driven approach does), the trends-driven approach focuses attention on what people must know, do, or feel to respond to emerging environmental changes. To carry out that approach, it is first necessary to isolate the key trends or changes affecting the organization, work, job, or occupation. It is then necessary to isolate what people should know, do, or feel to manage those trends in their work.

The rapid results assessment approach derives outputs, competencies, roles, and quality requirements from work functions, responsibilities, or behaviors (Rothwell, 1994). Basic steps in applying the rapid results assessment approach include

1. Targeting one occupational group or job category.
2. Selecting a panel of eight to twelve exemplary (star) performers from the group or job category to be examined and two or three immediate organizational superiors (also exemplary) of the targeted group to be examined.
3. Inviting the panel to a session to focus attention on the duties and responsibilities of the targeted group or job category.
4. Selecting a group facilitator and two assistant facilitators to conduct the session.
5. Assembling participants in a large room with a blank wall for one or two days.
6. Beginning the process by briefing participants on the process and on job challenges facing them in the future.
7. Asking participants to list their functions or responsibilities and the behaviors they perform.
8. Writing the statements on sheets of paper and taping the sheets to the wall.
9. Continuing the process until participants can no longer think of functions and responsibilities or behaviors.
10. Calling a break.
11. Creating exclusive categories in which to group the functions or responsibilities and behaviors.
12. Asking participants to return from break.
13. Verifying the function and responsibility categories by asking participants to review them.
14. Reviewing each function or responsibility and behavior that participants previously listed to ensure that it is placed under the proper category and to ensure that it need not be revised, deleted (because other functions or responsibilities overlap with it), or other functions or responsibilities added (because they were initially forgotten).
15. Calling another break.
16. Grouping function or responsibility categories and behaviors in sequential order.
17. Asking participants to return from break to verify or modify the sequential order proposed.
18. Adjourning the meeting.
19. Removing the chart from the wall and having it typed.
20. Verifying the chart devised by the participants by circulating it back to them in survey format for review.

21. Preparing surveys based on the chart to identify work roles, outputs, competencies, quality requirements, future trends, and ethical challenges related to each function or responsibility or behavior appearing on the chart.
22. Conducting the surveys, compiling results, and presenting them for review to another group of exemplary job incumbents and their immediate supervisors as a form of validation.

This approach can be computerized using group decision-support software.

This approach—as is true of others—has limitations. Rigor is often a function of time, since conducting and validating a competency study can require as long as several years. Faster results can be obtained, of course—but usually with sacrifices made to the rigor of the study.

Conducting Behavioral Events Interviewing

Most competency modeling methodologies rely on behavioral events interviewing (BEI) as a key way to isolate competencies. Some vendors offer courses lasting many weeks on how to conduct behavioral events interviewing.

But the basic approach is easily described. First, identify an exemplary (best) performer in a group targeted for competency modeling. Second, arrange to interview him or her for three to six hours, and have the interview videotaped or audiotaped. Ask the individual to describe the singularly most difficult situation with which he or she has ever been confronted at work. If the focus of attention is a job category, such as middle managers, then the situation should be related to that job category in the targeted organization; if the focus of attention is a department, such as accounting, then the situation should be related to that department.

Third, set the respondent at ease, and ask a question like this: "Tell me about a time when you were confronted with the singularly most difficult situation in your job that you have ever encountered in this organization. Be sure to tell me what led up to the situation, who was involved, what you did, and what happened as a consequence of what you did. Please do your best during the interview to record what you said, did, thought, and felt in each stage of the situation." Fourth, probe the respondent during the interview to ensure that all these issues have been addressed.

Fifth, have the interview transcribed. Review it for key themes. List them.

Sixth, and finally, conduct interviews with others in the job category or department. Repeat the interviewing process just described. When you finish, analyze the results of all interviews using content analysis to isolate the competencies leading to success.

Acting Ethically in Job, Task, and Content Analysis

A key ethical issue in analyzing the characteristics of a work setting can be expressed in this question: *Has a job, task, or content analysis been carried out in a way that maintains the realistic expectations of everyone involved?*

As noted in the chapter, the danger exists that a job, task, or content analysis will stray from the intended purpose into other areas such as job reclassification or salary studies of a given occupation, job, task, or content analysis. Even when that is not the purpose, it is sometimes perceived to be the purpose by incumbents or by their immediate supervisors. Confidentiality, when promised, must be preserved.

For this reason, it is very important that instructional designers make the purpose of the job, task, or content analysis clear to those who are targeted for such studies as a basis for instructional development. Further, instructional designers should also reemphasize the purpose of the study as it is carried out and when it is completed. To do otherwise is to risk creating a misunderstanding or raising unrealistic expectations.

In Rothwell's (2003) survey, conducted in preparation for the third edition of this book, he asked respondents about the ethical challenges they faced when performing job, task, or content analysis. Their comments are revealing, dramatizing the so-called "real world" dilemmas faced by instructional designers as they do their work. Here are a few select comments from the survey, told in the exact words of the respondents:

> "We often lack accurate and updated job descriptions to start with. Most people receive verbal instructions and one page of yearly goals. Each goal is limited to 150 characters due to the MIS system, and only four goals exist according to the worldwide balanced scorecard."
>
> [I face an ethical problem with this issue on] "every project."
>
> [It is too] "time-consuming."
>
> [My biggest problem is getting] "access to people in the field. This is a worldwide operation."
>
> [The problem with job analysis is] "keeping records from being disciplinary in nature."
>
> [In our organization, we do] "just enough to cover our efforts, not a quality job."

The common theme, then, is that instructional designers are often faced with too little time, or not enough management support, to do needs assessment.

Of course, that raises questions about the quality of the instruction that can be subsequently designed, developed, and delivered.

Respondents to Rothwell's (2003) study pointed to other ethical dilemmas they faced when performing task or content analysis. Here are some comments to reflect dilemmas in performing task analysis:

> "This is expensive and time-consuming for salespeople, actually takes days and impacts clients for real life observations. [It is] hard to sell to managers and rarely done."
>
> [We run into trouble with this on] "every project."

And here are two particularly pointed remarks about dilemmas that arise when dealing with content:

> "Management wants increased content delivered in a decreased time period. For example: two-day courses reduced to one day."
>
> "All the time we face a situation in which someone sends out an e-mail with slides attached. Then we are asked to 'put some training around it. '"

It is worthwhile pondering what strategies might be used to deal with this common problem of being asked to do too much, in too little time, with not enough planning. While there are no easy answers, some approaches might include explaining the need to do it, asking the client to choose what to cut out, and demonstrating the need for what is done.

Applying Job, Task, and Content Analysis Cross-Culturally

As in analyzing learners and work settings, instructional designers will find that cross-cultural issues can and do affect job, task, and content analysis. The most important questions to ask are these: How much does culture affect the job, task, or content? and In what ways are they affected?

Often, culture is integrally related to performance. Doing business in China is not the same as doing business in Western Europe or in the United States. Cultural issues do affect the way the work is done. That (in turn) affects performance. Instructional designers bear the responsibility to pose questions about culture and its possible impact on carrying out the work and achieving results. The time to do that is during job, task, or content analysis. Gaining insight into cross-cultural issues should be built in as the job analysis is planned and should be investigated more completely when it is an issue. Care should be taken, for instance, to compare time percentages devoted to different activities, incumbents' perceptions about the most important activities performed, and descriptions of how successful performance is defined.

What Is New in Work Analysis?

Work analysis has been revolutionized, like so much else, by the easy availability of relevant technology and by new methods that emphasize speed.

More information is available on the web about the work that people do. For example, instructional designers can find many government-researched job descriptions online. (See, for instance, job genie.) Functional evaluation information is also available online. (See, for instance, ProComp, 2005). The U.S. government is gradually moving away from the *Dictionary of Occupational Titles* and moving toward an online resource at O*NET (see O*NET, 2007). O*NET is meant to be a comprehensive, one-stop resource that will eventually provide job descriptions, breakdowns of job activities by knowledge, skill, and attitude, and much more. The private sector has also unveiled software such as Descriptions Now™ (see www.biztrain.com/products/descriptionsnow.htm), and various vendors provide specialized job descriptions for various industries. Instructional designers should be aware that the Sarbanes-Oxley Act and the Americans with Disabilities Act do have implications for writing job descriptions.

In conducting job analysis and writing job descriptions, instructional designers should beware of a common mistake. That is to rely on information from the manager only without consulting job incumbents. That may work for speed, but it ignores the vital information for job descriptions that can be provided only by those who actually do the job. Recognize that managers do not know everything that their workers do. It is thus important to capture information from both managers and experienced job incumbents. If time permits, better information yet can be obtained by securing input from stakeholders of the job, such as customers, suppliers, distributors, teammates, and other relevant interest groups.

Instructional designers would be well-advised to consider using electronic group decision support systems in preparing detailed job descriptions. An *electronic group decision support system* (EGDSS) is software that supports collaborative decision making by a group. When an electronic group decision support system is used in job analysis, the job description is posted online. Many people can participate in updating it. Since groups are more creative than individuals, that will often yield more complete information about work duties, responsibilities, and tasks than the perspective of one individual would. That can also facilitate synchronous and asynchronous discussions of what people do, what they should do, how they should do it, what outputs they should obtain, and how to measure their results.

Conclusion

In this chapter, we defined job, task, and content analyses and briefly explained how to carry out each of them. We offered advice to instructional designers about judging and justifying work analysis. We also summarized competency modeling and briefly reviewed how to handle key ethical issues in conducting job, task, and content analysis as well as cross-cultural issues in those activities. This chapter concludes our treatment of four related forms of analysis that are conducted before performance objectives are written and instructional materials are prepared.

In the next three chapters, we turn to the process of converting information about needs, learners, work settings, and work into objectives (results) desired from instruction. In Chapter Eight we show how to write statements of performance objectives; in Chapter Nine, we explain how to develop performance measurements, and in Chapter Ten, we clarify how to sequence performance objectives.

PART THREE

ESTABLISHING PERFORMANCE OBJECTIVES AND PERFORMANCE MEASUREMENTS

CHAPTER EIGHT

WRITING PERFORMANCE OBJECTIVES

Once work analysis has been performed, instructional designers should be ready to write statements of performance objectives. (See Figure 8.1.) Sometimes used synonymously with instructional or behavioral objectives, performance objectives are necessary for one very important reason: they guide remaining steps in the instructional design process by describing precisely what the targeted learners should know, do, or feel on completion of a planned learning experience. It is also highly desirable if they can also communicate the on-the-job results sought from the learning experience.

In a sense, performance objectives create a vision of what learners should be doing after they master the instruction. Objectives focus on the results of instruction, what learners should know, do or feel upon completion of a learning experience (Mager, 1997d). Objectives do not focus on what instructional designers should do or what activities trainers should use to effect changes in learners' work performance. Of course, as with many other topics in the instructional design field in recent years, some critics have weighed the pros and cons of objectives, questioning what they are for and why (Choi and Jonassen, 2000; Langdon, 1999).

In this chapter, we will explain how to distinguish performance objectives from goals and activities, summarize how to derive performance objectives from analytical results, describe how to write performance objectives, and provide advice about judging and justifying performance objectives. We will conclude by discussing a key ethical issue in writing performance objectives and applying cross-cultural awareness in writing performance objectives.

FIGURE 8.1. A MODEL OF STEPS IN THE INSTRUCTIONAL DESIGN PROCESS.

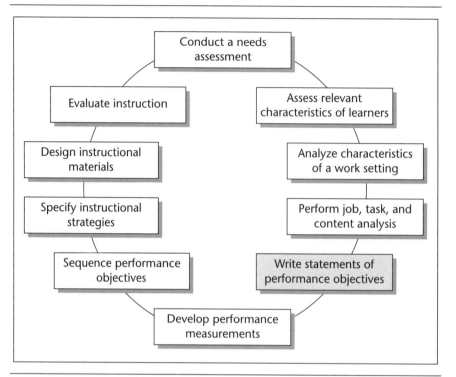

Distinguishing Performance Objectives from Goals and Activities

Performance objectives should not be confused with goals or activities. But what are instructional or organizational goals? What are learner or trainer activities? How do they differ from performance objectives? Let us begin the chapter by answering these questions.

What Are Instructional and Organizational Goals?

Instructional goals are simply expressions of the general results desired from instruction. Unlike performance objectives, they are not measurable. In a famous explanation, Mager (1997a) calls them warm fuzzies because they sound desirable (warm) but are so vague (fuzzy) that achieving them is unclear. In fact, different people may assign their own meanings or significance to them. Examples of instructional goals are easy enough to point out and include such lofty efforts as "improving customer service," "improving quality," "increasing profitability," and "increasing learner understanding." However, they are warm fuzzies, as Mager uses that term, because they do not clarify precisely what a learner must do or how a learner should perform.

Organizational goals are results desired from an organization. Often included as part of an organization's formal mission statement, they articulate philosophy, embody management values, and imply an organization's general direction. Their achievement is rarely restricted to a specific time. Nor do goals lend themselves, as organizational objectives do, to specific measurement methods (Rothwell and Kazanas, 1994a; Rothwell and Kazanas, in press). As expressions about an organization, their link to individual job performance is often unclear. Examples of organizational goals include "serving the community," "maintaining a safe and productive workplace for employees," and "making a reasonable return on investment." To become measurable, organizational goals must be translated into organizational objectives (Rothwell and Kazanas, 1994a). To focus on individuals, organizational goals must be translated into terms that are directly related to what employees do and how well they do it.

What Are Learner-Trainer Activities?

A *learner activity* refers to what a learner is doing during a planned learning experience. For example, "listening to a lecture"—admittedly a passive activity because it implies more action by a trainer than by a learner—is a learner activity. Another example: "answering the questions at the end of a case study." Activities emphasize behaviors; in contrast, performance objectives emphasize results. A trainer activity refers to what a trainer is doing during a planned learning experience. For instance, one trainer activity is "defining terms." Other examples include lecturing, introducing a learning activity, showing a videotape, or passing out evaluations. Trainers sometimes focus on what they should do during a learning experience rather than on what learners can do by the end of instruction.

How Do Performance Objectives Differ from Goals and Activities?

A *performance objective* is an expression of a desired result of a learning experience. It differs from a performance goal in that it is measurable and is an expression of what should be achieved. It differs from activities in that it describes desired results, not behaviors leading to results.

Deriving Performance Objectives from Goal Analysis and Task or Content Analysis

Instructional designers can derive performance objectives from goal analysis, carried out with instructional and organizational goals and learner-trainer activities, or from task or content analysis results. But what is goal analysis, and how is it carried out? How are the results of task and content analysis used to write performance objectives? Let us turn to these questions next.

Defining Goal Analysis

Goal analysis is a means of transforming laudable but otherwise vague desires into specific and measurable targets for learner accomplishment (Mager, 1997a). Goal analysis is appropriate to use on those many occasions when instructional designers are approached by their clients to work miracles. Clients often speak in terms of vague and ill-defined goals, and instructional designers must use methods such as performance analysis to decide what kind of performance problem exists. Goal analysis is a later step, intended to determine precisely what measurable results are desired from an instructional design solution.

Performing Goal Analysis

To perform goal analysis, instructional designers should carry out five simple steps:

1. Identify the goal, the warm fuzzy, and write it down. Clarify the vague goal that instruction intends to achieve.
2. Write down examples of what people are saying or doing when they are behaving in a way corresponding to the goal. In short, identify behaviors associated with the goal.
3. Sort out unrelated items and polish the list developed in Step 2. Eliminate duplications not clearly associated with achieving the goal.
4. Describe precisely what learners should be doing to demonstrate goal achievement. Statements of this kind become performance objectives.
5. Test the performance objectives to ensure that they are linked to the goal and, when enacted, will lead to the desired instructional results.

These five steps can help convert otherwise vague instructional or organizational goals—or learner or trainer activities—into precise and measurable performance objectives.

A simple description of the process should clarify it. Suppose a team of instructional designers has been assigned the daunting task of "improving customer service." (Clients sometimes speak vaguely when they identify perceptions of learner needs.)

First, the team members would have to make sure the aim is improving customer service, not some other goal. They would do that by analyzing the performance problem and assessing learner needs. Second—assuming a justifiable instructional need was identified—the team members would list specific employee behaviors associated with effective customer service. They would ask these questions: What will people be doing when they are serving customers effectively? What will they be saying? Examples of appropriate behaviors might include answering customer phone calls quickly and courteously, approaching customers politely when they arrive in a store to look at merchandise, and identifying customers' problems or needs quickly and accurately. (These are just a few examples of behaviors associated with the goal.) Note that even these behaviors can be made more specific if the instructional designers described precisely what an employee does to "act courteously" or "identify customers' problems." And the examples just given could easily swell if the team members applied various methods of creative problem solving to identify more behaviors and worker statements associated with "improved customer service" (Michalko, 1991). Once the previous steps have been completed, the instructional designers should then eliminate duplicative behaviors from the list. Finally, team members would write performance objectives and try them out to see whether learners who achieved them would indeed demonstrate "improved customer service" as defined by the clients.

Converting Results of Task or Content Analysis into Performance Objectives

Goal analysis is just one of two primary methods used to identify the specific results desired from instruction. The second, and perhaps more commonly used, method is conversion of task or content analysis results into performance objectives.

Recall that the results of task analysis reveal how work is, or should be, performed. As we have seen, the results of content analysis also create a logical organizational scheme for subject matter that can be used as a starting point for developing instruction. But there is quite a difference between doing the work—or organizing subject matter—and engineering instruction that will produce learners who can do the work or demonstrate the desired knowledge. For this reason, it is not enough just to analyze how the work is done or how subject matter can be logically organized. Some consideration must also be given to the related, but different, issue of how to produce the desired results of instruction.

Instructional designers convert the results of task or content analysis into specific performance objectives by

1. Establishing instructional purpose.
2. Classifying learning tasks.
3. Analyzing learning tasks.

These steps are depicted in Figure 8.2.

First, instructional designers should establish purpose. Purpose means the primary reason for a planned instructional experience. There are typically four choices: (1) increasing learners' knowledge, (2) changing attitudes or feelings, (3) building skills, or (4) combining one or more of the other three choices.

Second, instructional designers should classify learning tasks by examining each work task and asking this question: What kind of instruction will be necessary to instruct people to perform this task or demonstrate this knowledge? Only four answers to this question are possible. Instruction can be designed for (1) knowledge, (2) feelings, (3) skills, or (4) some combination of the first three. Here are a few examples of ways to classify tasks:

Work Task	*Classification of Learning Tasks*
Explaining a procedure to others	Knowledge
Serving customers courteously	Feelings
Typing letters	Skills

Instructional designers should bear in mind that the appropriate way to carry out the instructional design process depends on the results to be achieved. Classifying work tasks into learning tasks is important because it can suggest the best ways to design instruction that is intended to bring about particular results. Of course, more than one classification scheme for work or for learning tasks or content has been devised.

For example, in a classic treatment, Gagné, Briggs, and Wager (1992) distinguish among intellectual skills, cognitive skills, verbal information, motor skills, and attitude. As they define them, intellectual skills are equated with the ability to read, write, and compute, as well as capabilities needed to perform tasks in special occupational fields. Cognitive skills underlie learning how to learn, that is, knowing how to get to the heart of problems. Verbal information is linked to summarizing or stating a principle. "You can usually spot a verbal information goal by the verb that is used," explain Dick and Carey (1990, p. 34). "Often the learner must state, list, or describe something." Motor skill is associated with body movement

FIGURE 8.2. STEPS FOR CONVERTING RESULTS OF TASK OR CONTENT ANALYSIS INTO PERFORMANCE OBJECTIVES.

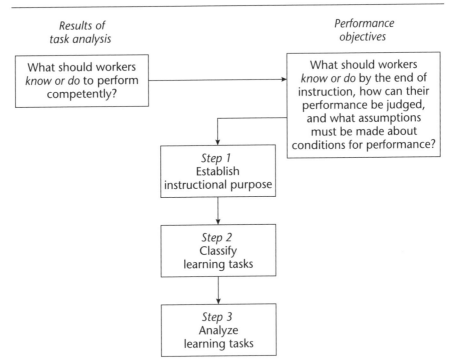

of any kind, ranging from moving a pen to using a computer keyboard. Attitude means a persistent set of beliefs. Since each of these learning tasks is intended to evoke a different result, each calls for different instructional strategies.

The third step is to analyze learning tasks, a process called learning task analysis (Gagné, Briggs, and Wager, 1992). Not to be confused with work task analysis, its purpose is to identify prerequisite knowledge. A prerequisite describes what learners should know before participating in instruction. Instructional designers use three methods to identify prerequisites: (1) learning hierarchies, (2) cluster analysis, and (3) procedural analysis (Dick and Carey, 1990).

Instructional designers develop a learning hierarchy by repeatedly asking this question of each work task and subtask: What does a learner need to know to do that? (Davis, Alexander, and Yelon, 1974). This process is called *hierarchical analysis*. To cite a simple example: to fill an automobile's tank with gasoline, a learner must first know what an automobile is, what a gasoline tank is, where the gasoline tank is located, where gasoline may be purchased, how to remove the gas cap, and so on. Each task implies a learning hierarchy. Hierarchical analysis is applied to intellectual, psychomotor, and attitudinal skills—but not to verbal information. To perform hierarchical analysis, instructional designers should simply flowchartthe relationship between the work task and the required prerequisite knowledge. They then develop performance objectives from the hierarchy.

Cluster analysis is appropriately used with verbal information or attitudes. It is particularly useful in developing performance objectives from results of content analysis and is based on categories of information. For instance, categories might include the number of letters in the alphabet (a fact) or the number of component parts in a social theory. (A social theory is a principle based on opinions of various experts.) To perform a cluster analysis, instructional designers begin by drawing a chart. They place an instructional goal at the top. They then list below it "the major categories of information that are implied by the goal" (Dick and Carey, 1990, p. 58). Instructional designers should try to be creative as they categorize information, but they should remember that one aim is to be as complete as possible. They must succeed in developing a scheme to organize the information. Quite often this process can economize the instructional effort.

Procedural analysis is the process of identifying what learners should know to perform one task or a series of related tasks (a procedure). It is appropriately applied to developing performance objectives for intellectual skills, motor skills, and attitudes. But it does not work with verbal information, for which no "step-by-step list of activities" can be created. To perform procedural analysis, instructional designers should first identify an instructional goal and then flowchart steps in the procedure. For each step (task) in the procedure, they should answer this question: What must the learner know, do, or feel to perform? They should then express the answer by stating precise performance objectives.

Linking Work Activities and Performance Objectives

Performance objectives must always be tied to work activities. However, they may be linked to different expressions of work activities, for instance, as work tasks are presently performed or as they could be more efficiently and effectively performed at present or in the future. Performance objectives can also be linked to subject matter as related to job performance. When learners achieve performance objectives by the end of a planned learning experience, they should be able to perform in the application environment, or at least be familiar with the verbal information on which work performance depends. Instructional designers generally direct their attention to demonstrating learner change by the end of instruction, not on the learner's return to the application environment, though that view has been changing (Rothwell, 1995b, 1996a, 1996b).

To demonstrate achievement of performance objectives in the application environment rather than merely at the end of instruction, they would probably have to devise more than one type of performance objective. Indeed, Briggs (1977) has identified four types of performance objectives. Each reflects a different time span. But instructional designers have seldom expressed performance objectives in terms of on-the-job changes; rather, the traditional focus has been on end-of-instruction changes. On-the-job change requires instructional designers to consider more than just what learners will be able to do: it also requires consideration of what the organization and the learners' supervisors must do to support the learners' application of knowledge, skills, and attitudes.

Stating Objectives in Performance Terms

Instructional designers should describe the desired results of instruction in performance-based terms. They should be able to classify the type of performance objectives that must be written and then state performance objectives that are directly or indirectly linked to work requirements. The objectives should thus clarify, in measurable terms, what learners should be able to do at the end of instruction, how well they should be able to do it, and what conditions have to exist or equipment must be available for them to exhibit the performance. To write performance objectives, however, instructional designers must have a task or concept analysis and a learner analysis.

Classifying Performance Objectives

Instructional designers begin the process of stating performance objectives by identifying the kinds of objectives that must be written. Referring to the task classification prepared earlier in the instructional design process, they should clarify whether each objective will focus on knowledge, skills, or attitudes.

The most commonly used classification scheme for performance objectives was first described in 1956. That year, Bloom and his colleagues published the *Taxonomy of Educational Objectives* and defined three domains of learning—knowledge, attitudes, and skills. Objectives focused on increasing learner knowledge are called cognitive objectives; objectives focused on changing learners' attitudes are called affective objectives; and objectives focused on building skills are called psychomotor objectives. Knowledge, as we defined it in Chapter One, means "facts and information essential to performing a job or task"; skills involve the "ability to behave in ways associated with successful job performance"; and attitudes are "feelings about performance that are voiced to other people."

Each "domain" of learning consists of increasingly complicated levels, as shown in Figures 8.3, 8.4, and 8.5. Instructional designers begin classifying performance objectives by identifying the level of the domain that they are trying to reach. When they have done that for the end results desired from a planned learning experience, they are ready to begin writing performance objectives.

Describing Parts of Performance Objectives

Performance objectives make tangible a vision of what learners should know, do, or feel at the end of a planned instructional experience. They should contain statements about at least two of the following three components (Mager, 1997d):

1. Performance
2. Criterion
3. Condition

FIGURE 8.3. LEVELS OF OBJECTIVES IN THE COGNITIVE DOMAIN.

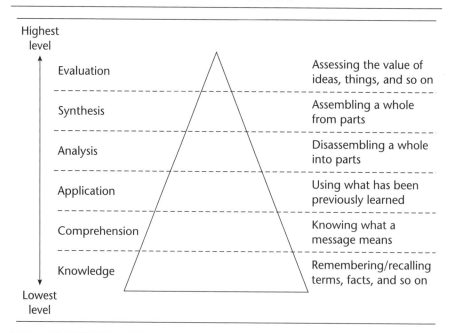

Source: Rothwell, W., and Kazanas, H. *Human Resource Development: A Strategic Approach.* Copyright 2004, p. 204. Reprinted by permission of Human Resource Development Press, Amherst, MA.

FIGURE 8.4. LEVELS OF OBJECTIVES IN THE AFFECTIVE DOMAIN.

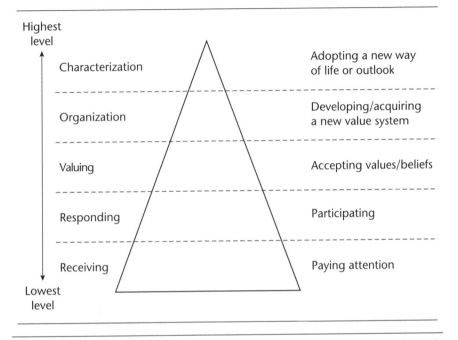

Source: Rothwell, W., and Kazanas, H. *Human Resource Development: A Strategic Approach.* Copyright 1994, p. 205. Reprinted by permission of Human Resource Development Press, Amherst, Mass.

Other components could also be included in performance objectives. They may include targeted participants (Mager, 1997d). They may even include a description of how instruction will be carried out (Mager, 1997d).

The *performance* component of an objective describes how a learner will demonstrate proficiency (Mager, 1997d). It is an activity or behavior to be learned during instruction and demonstrated afterward. A statement of performance always begins with a verb, and the choice of verb is typically linked to the type of task to be learned. Lists of verbs associated with cognitive, affective, and psychomotor performance are provided from a classic source in Tables 8.1, 8.2, and 8.3.

The *criterion* component of an objective describes, in measurable terms, just how well participants must perform to demonstrate competence (Mager, 1997d). It is worth emphasizing that a criterion must be measurable. Measures may be expressed by quantity, quality, cost, time, or customer requirements. Criteria may be derived from past work practices, present performance needs, future organizational plans, academic and government research, customer-focused research, benchmarking with best-in-class organizations, and other sources.

FIGURE 8.5. LEVELS OF OBJECTIVES IN THE PSYCHOMOTOR DOMAIN.

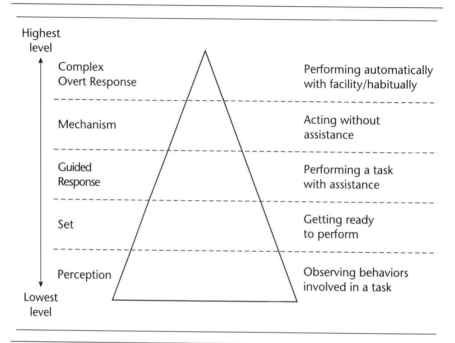

Highest level

Complex Overt Response	Performing automatically with facility/habitually
Mechanism	Acting without assistance
Guided Response	Performing a task with assistance
Set	Getting ready to perform
Perception	Observing behaviors involved in a task

Lowest level

Source: Rothwell, W., and Kazanas, H. *Human Resource Development: A Strategic Approach.* Copyright 1994, p. 206. Reprinted by permission of Human Resource Development Press, Amherst, Mass.

They should be tied to historical performance standards or future organizational plans (Rothwell and Kazanas, 1994a).

There are two different kinds of criteria: process and product (Blank, 1982). A *process criterion* describes how well the learner should perform the task; a product criterion describes the product of the task. Examples of process criteria include "following company procedures," "conforming to the organization's safety practices," and "within ten minutes." Product criteria include any of the following: "to the client's satisfaction," "with fewer than three errors," and "ready for sale."

To establish criteria, instructional designers should ask questions such as the following:

- How has competent work performance historically been identified through measurable means?
- How well must the work task associated with this performance objective be performed for the organization to meet its present competitive needs?

TABLE 8.1. VERBS ASSOCIATED WITH OBJECTIVES IN THE COGNITIVE DOMAIN.

I. Knowledge **Recall information**		*II. Comprehension* **Interpret information in one's own words**		*III. Application* **Apply knowledge or generalize it to a new situation**	
arrange	name	classify	recognize	apply	operate
define	order	describe	report	choose	practice
duplicate	recognize	discuss	restate	demonstrate	prepare
label	recall	explain	review	dramatize	schedule
match	repeat	identify	sort	illustrate	solve
memorize	reproduce	indicate	tell	interpret	use
		locate	translate		

IV. Analysis **Break down knowledge into parts and whole relationships**		*V. Synthesis* **Bring together parts of knowledge to form a whole and ubild relationships for new situations**		*VI. Evaluation* **Make judgments on basis of given criteria**	
analyze	differentiate	arrange	manage	appraise	judge
appraise	discriminate	assemble	organize	argue	predict
calculate	distinguish	collect	plan	assess	rate
categorize	examine	compose	prepare	attack	score
compare	experiment	construct	propose	choose	select
contrast	inventory	create	set up	compare	support
criticize	question	design	synthesize	estimate	value
diagram	test	formulate	write	evaluate	

Source: from *The Instructional Design Process* by J. Kemp, p. 84. Copyright © 1985. Published by Allyn and Bacon, Boston, MA. Copyright © 1985 by Pearson Education. Reprinted/adapted by permission of the Publisher.

- How can these organizational needs be expressed as measurable results to be achieved?
- How well must the work task be performed in the future to help the organization achieve its strategic business plans?
- How can performance be measured?
- How will the consequences of task performance be measured?

In some cases, there will be a difference between existing and possible criteria. In other words, workers can simply perform better than they have been

TABLE 8.2. VERBS ASSOCIATED WITH OBJECTIVES
IN THE AFFECTIVE DOMAIN.

I. Receiving **Paying attention**	*II. Responding* **Minimal participation**	*III. Valuing* **Internalizing preferences**
Listen to	Reply	Attain
Perceive	Answer	Assume
Be alert to	Follow along	Support
Show tolerance of	Approve	Participate
Obey	Continue	

IV. Organization **Development of a value system**	*V. Characterization* **Practice of a total philosophy of life**
Organize	Believe
Select	Practice
Judge	Continue to
Decide	Carry out
Identify with	

Source: from *The Instructional Design Process* by J. Kemp, p. 84. Copyright © 1985. Published by Allyn and Bacon, Boston, MA. Copyright © 1985 by Pearson Education. Reprinted/adapted by permission of the Publisher.

TABLE 8.3. VERBS ASSOCIATED WITH OBJECTIVES IN THE
PSYCHOMOTOR DOMAIN.

I. Reflexes **Involuntary movement**	*II. Fundamental Movements* **Simple movements**	*III. Perception* **Response to stimuli**
Stiffen	Crawl	Turn
Extend	Walk	Bend
Flex	Run	Balance
Stretch	Reach	Catch

IV. Physical Abilities **Developed psychomotor movement**	*V. Skilled Movements* **dvanced learned movement**	*VI. Nondiscursive* **Most advanced learned movement**
Move heavy objects	Play instrument	Dancing
Make quick motions	Use a hand tool	Changes in expression
Stop and restart movement		

Source: from *The Instructional Design Process* by J. Kemp, p. 84. Copyright © 1985. Published by Allyn and Bacon, Boston, MA. Copyright © 1985 by Pearson Education. Reprinted/adapted by permission of the Publisher.

performing. One way that instructional designers can gauge the possibility for productivity improvement is to subtract the difference between the work output of the highest and lowest performers. This difference is called the *productivity improvement potential,* or PIP (Gilbert, 1996). It too can serve as the basis for criteria in performance objectives.

The *condition* component of a performance objective explains what working conditions must exist when the performer demonstrates his or her knowledge, skill, or ability (Mager, 1997d). Conditions may include essential or desirable situations in which performance is necessary. Condition statements usually begin with the word "given," as in the following phrase: "given a ruler, the learner will be able to measure inches." In this context, "given" means "the learner is provided with some equipment, resources, or information with which to function and cannot perform competently without them."

Writing Performance Objectives

To write performance objectives, instructional designers should begin with the following sentence or some variation of it: "On completion of instruction, learners should be able to. . . ." They should then list the performance objectives, beginning each phrase with a verb. The portion of the objective that begins with the verb is the performance component. It is usually followed by statements about criterion and condition. Of course, criterion addresses this question: How well should the performance be done? It should always be measurable. The condition component addresses the following question: What equipment or other resources are necessary for the performance to be demonstrated by the learner? Some instructional designers may find this process easier if they use a worksheet like that shown in Exhibit 8.1.

Avoiding Common Mistakes in Writing Performance Objectives

Writing performance objectives is more difficult than it may appear at first blush. Some mistakes are relatively common. They are worth describing so they can be avoided.

1. Avoid making objectives long-winded. Try to make them as concise as possible.
2. Do not use vague language. Words and phrases such as "understand," "demonstrate familiarity with," or "know" should usually be avoided because they are vague.
3. Try to avoid descriptions of criteria that are linked to instructor (or supervisor) satisfaction, as in the phrase "will perform to the satisfaction of the

EXHIBIT 8.1. A WORKSHEET FOR PREPARING INSTRUCTIONAL OBJECTIVES.

Directions: Use this worksheet as a job aid whenever you draft performance objectives. In column 1 below, write a description of the work task or subject-matter topic on which the objective is to be based. Then, moving across the worksheet, complete columns 2 to 4.

Work task or subject-matter topic:	Performance objectives On completion of instruction, learners should be able to . . .		
Column 1	Column 2	Column 3	Column 4
	Performance	*Criterion*	*Condition*
Begin with a verb.	Answer this question: What will the learner know or do?	Describe how well the learner should know or be able to do the performance. (Make sure it is measurable.)	Begin with "given" or "when" and describe the conditions that must exist for the learner to perform.

instructor." The reason: performance objectives of this kind lead to arbitrary differences in assessments of learner achievement.

4. Avoid lengthy "laundry lists" of required equipment and other resources when describing the conditions necessary for performance. List only the equipment and other resources that would not be obvious to a reasonable person.

Judging Performance Objectives

Instructional designers should be able to evaluate the performance objectives written by themselves or others. In this process, they should be able to judge the accuracy, comprehensiveness, and appropriateness of the objectives. One of the easiest ways to evaluate performance objectives is to use a worksheet like that shown in Exhibit 8.2. Examine each objective with the aid of the worksheet and revise objectives whenever a "no" is checked.

Judging and Justifying Performance Objectives

Instructional designers should be capable of explaining why they have written performance objectives the way they have. Indeed, as in all steps of the instructional design process, instructional designers are accountable to their colleagues and to clients for what they do. This accountability is particularly important for identifying the results sought from instruction.

Once performance objectives have been written, instructional designers should be prepared to answer the following questions about them:

1. Who will be expected to achieve them?
2. What do the objectives mean?
3. When should they be achieved?
4. Where will they apply?
5. Why are they necessary?

To answer the question, Who will be expected to achieve the performance objectives?, instructional designers should be sure to clarify their targeted learners. In addition, they should be sure to determine precisely what those learners should already feel, know, or do before they enter the instruction. In short, important prerequisites must be clarified.

To answer the question, What do the performance objectives mean?, instructional designers should clarify the targeted results of instruction. They should be able to explain the objectives in the everyday language of the workplace. Objectives should become touchstones, so to speak, to determine whether the end results sought by instructional designers match those expected by learners and clients.

To answer the question, When should the performance objectives be achieved?, instructional designers need to explain to others that the focus of performance objectives is always on results, that is, on what learners can do on completion of the instructional experience. Instructional designers should also emphasize that they do not necessarily assume that the performance objectives can be applied in the work setting—and they should be prepared to explain why they make that assumption. If possible, instructional designers should enlist

EXHIBIT 8.2. A WORKSHEET FOR JUDGING PERFORMANCE OBJECTIVES.

Directions: Use this worksheet to judge performance objectives written by yourself or others. For each objective, consider each question appearing in the left column below. Mark a check (✓) for the appropriate response to each question in the center column. Then make notes to yourself for revision in the right column. If you answer yes to all questions, the objective meets all required criteria and it will not need to be revised. If you answer no to any question, the objective does not meet all required criteria. It should be revised.

Make copies of this worksheet as necessary, depending on the number of objectives that you will review.

Question	Response		Notes for Revision
Does the objective . . .	Yes (✓)	No (✓)	
1. Describe observable behaviors?	( )	( )	
2. Describe measurable behaviors?	( )	( )	
3. Match behaviors in the task?	( )	( )	
4. Describe or imply conditions . . .			
a. affecting the job, task, or content to be taught?	( )	( )	
b. in terms of information provided to the performer?	( )	( )	
c. in terms of the situation of performance?	( )	( )	
d. by means of which information is provided?	( )	( )	
e. in terms of tools available?	( )	( )	
5. Describe or imply criteria that			
a. are measurable?	( )	( )	
b. require performance in the same sequence as the task being taught?	( )	( )	
c. require performance to the level of precision appropriate to the learner?	( )	( )	
d. require performance to the level of the ultimate requirements of the task specification?	( )	( )	
6. Represent at least one task or relevant subject-matter topic?	( )	( )	

management support to examine the application environment and create support for application of instruction when learners return to their work settings.

To answer the question, Where will the performance objectives apply?, instructional designers should emphasize that the focus is on the instructional setting. They should continue to build support from management to create an application environment in which learners can apply what they learned.

To answer the question, Why are performance objectives necessary?, several points should be brought out. Instructional designers need to emphasize that they establish accountability for learners, draw learner attention to the expected results of instruction, provide indicators to the learners' supervisors about the benefits resulting from instruction, and establish targeted results for the instructional design process.

These explanations about performance objectives should be discussed with the client after goal analysis or task-content analysis has been performed but before preparation of test items or instruction itself. They provide the client with an early indication of the results that will be produced by instruction. If the client disagrees with these results, any concerns should be addressed before additional time is devoted to the project. If instructional designers progress further without client agreement and support, they may waste substantial time and work.

Acting Ethically in Writing Performance Objectives

A key ethical issue in writing performance objectives can be expressed by this question: *Do the performance objectives written match up to the performance expectations of the job, task, or content that was analyzed?* The key ethical issue in writing performance objectives is thus to ensure that performance objectives of instruction, when realized, will effectively meet job, task, or content requirements. Therefore, it is essential that instructional designers make sure that this match exists. If it does not, then learners who achieve performance objectives because of instruction will be unable to demonstrate effective performance.

In Rothwell's (2003) survey, conducted in preparation for the third edition of this book, respondents pointed to several common ethical dilemmas they face when preparing performance objectives.

Here is what they said, in their own words:

"I think [doing this] is key, but I get to do less than I'd like to."

[We face a problem with this on] "every project."

"We do this with subject-matter expert input but [with] no empirical evidence. [There is just] too much hearsay."

The picture drawn from these (admittedly sketchy) remarks is that instructional designers have a tough time establishing clear objectives. One reason may be that the client–management does not understand why it is critically important to clarify desired outcomes before preparing instruction to achieve those outcomes. Another reason may be the time it takes to prepare good, measurable objectives is not viewed as worthwhile.

Applying Cross-Cultural Awareness to Writing Performance Objectives

In Western culture, most instructional designers understand the logic of stating performance objectives first and then working to help learners achieve them. That logic, while usually workable in most other cultures, is not always as well-accepted in cultures that view change as an iterative process rather than one targeted in advance to achieve results. In cultures where stating objectives first is not considered desirable, an alternative is to reveal and emphasize performance objectives gradually. That approach may work better when learners are more sensitized to an evolutionary view of change and learning. Use a cultural informant to decide the approach likely to work best in each cultural context.

What Is New in Writing Performance Objectives?

Objectives are important in the work of any instructional designer. As with so much else in the business world, a growing number of websites provide information on objectives, and that includes support in writing them. (See, for instance, "Instructional Objective Helper," 2007). And at least some authors suggest that the components of objectives should be revisited.

More attention should be devoted to the metrics in objectives, which are called the criteria. How will the learners' success in achieving each objective be measured at the end of training? back on the job? It is difficult to hold learners accountable if the desired results cannot be somehow measured effectively. And criteria are often forgotten, or are ill-defined, in many objectives. The result is that it is unclear what results should be obtained from instruction, what learners should do upon completion, and how results of learning can or should be applied back on the job.

Heinich, Molenda, Russell, and Smaldino (2002) have suggested that the components of instructional objectives should be revisited. The parts of an objective should include four (rather than the classic three) key components: (1) audience, the targeted learners; (2) behavior, what people will do by the end of instruction; (3) conditions, the circumstances in which behaviors should be demonstrated; and (4) degree, the standard by which results will be measured. The advantage of this approach is, of course, that it stipulates exactly for whom the learning experience is intended.

Conclusion

In this chapter, we explained how to write performance objectives. The next chapter focuses on the related subject of developing performance measurements.

CHAPTER NINE

DEVELOPING PERFORMANCE MEASUREMENTS

Instructional designers should usually develop performance measurements during or immediately following the preparation of performance objectives. Measurements of all kinds—sometimes called metrics—have been commanding some attention in recent years (Brown, 1999; Hatten and Rosenthal, 2001). One reason has been growing demand by stockholders and stakeholders for accountability, generally from all organizational levels. Another reason is that instructional designers are being held accountable for showing results for whatever training investments are made by their organizations.

In this chapter, we consider the development of performance measurements. (See Figure 9.1.) We will then define performance measurements, explain their importance, and provide advice to instructional designers about developing them, judging them, and explaining them. We will also address important ethical and cross-cultural issues in developing performance measurements.

What Are Performance Measurements?

Performance measurements are various means established by instructional designers for monitoring learner achievement. Paper-and-pencil tests are perhaps the most common. Test items may be developed directly from performance objectives before instructional materials are prepared. In this way, accountability for results is built into instruction from early in the process.

FIGURE 9.1. A MODEL OF STEPS IN THE INSTRUCTIONAL DESIGN PROCESS.

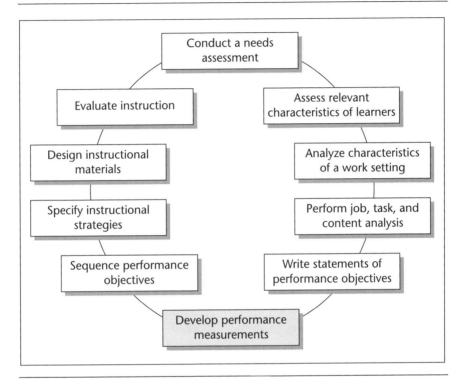

Source: Foshay, W., Silber, K., and Westgaard, O. *Instructional Design Competencies: The Standards.* Iowa City, IA: International Board of Standards for Training, Performance, and Instruction, 1986, p. 3. Copyright 1993 by the International Board of Standards for Training, Performance and Instruction. All rights reserved. Used with permission.

However, paper-and-pencil testing is not the only way to assess learner achievement. Other methods may also be used. For instance, trainees can be observed on the job as they perform the tasks they have learned. Computerized skills assessment is also becoming common (Lee and Mamone, 1995a, 1995b). So is portfolio analysis in which work samples are assessed.

Why Are Performance Measurements Important?

Performance measurements become benchmarks that, along with performance objectives (discussed in the previous chapter), provide guidance in the preparation of instructional programs. They help answer an age-old question about every instructional experience: "What should be taught?" (Egan, 1978, p. 72). They are thus important for three major reasons. First, they ensure economical choice of instructional content. Indeed, establishing performance measurements is part of the preliminary work that is to be completed before instructional materials are developed; it helps identify the content that should be included and the success level expected of learners upon completion of instruction. Second, performance measurements provide a basis for learner accountability to ensure that learner progress toward predetermined performance goals can be monitored during and after instruction. Third, performance measurements can help link up learner achievement to organizational strategic plans (Brown, 1995).

Developing Performance Measurements

Instructional designers should be capable of developing tests, written questionnaires, interviews, and other methods of measuring performance. The performance measures should be written clearly and correspond to performance objectives, rely on appropriate methods of measuring learning outcomes, comply with time and instructional constraints, and meet requirements for validity and reliability. Instructional designers should be able to develop performance measurements when they are furnished with necessary information on the characteristics of learners, the settings in which they are expected to perform, constraints on performance and instructional development, instructional objectives, and plans for analyzing needs and evaluating results as applicable.

Stated more simply, instructional designers should be able to answer two basic questions before they prepare instructional materials: (1) What should be measured? and (2) How should it be measured? To answer the first question, instructional designers should determine the purpose of the measurement and focus on appropriate methods of measuring instruction. To answer the second question, they should be able to design appropriate instruments—and write appropriate items for the instruments—to achieve the intended purpose.

Deciding on the Purpose

Once performance objectives have been written based on work requirements, instructional designers should decide

- What purpose will guide their performance measurement efforts.
- What performance measurement methods should be used to assess learners' progress.
- How performance should be measured.

Instructional designers should always begin by clarifying their purposes for measuring performance. There are at least four possible purposes (Kirkpatrick, 1996):

1. *Participant reaction.* How much do participants enjoy what they are learning? How much do they enjoy the instructional methods used?
2. *Participant learning.* How well are participants meeting performance objectives? How well have they learned?
3. *On-the-job performance change.* How much change is evident on the job, based on what participants have learned? How well has the learning transferred from the instructional to the application environment?
4. *Organizational impact.* How has the organization been affected by the results of an instructional experience?

These purposes are summarized in Table 9.1.

Determining Sources of Information

After determining the purpose of performance measurement, instructional designers should next determine the sources of information that will be used in measurement. There are three major sources of information. Performance objectives are the first. They should provide clues about what to measure because, as explained in Chapter Eight, each objective needs to contain a measurable criterion for assessment. To measure performance, then, instructional designers should simply consider how well learners have met the criterion set forth in each objective. Each objective should be directly tied to meeting job-related learning needs. Hence, the process of measuring objectives provides information about how well learning needs are being met by instruction.

Learner (worker) performance is the second source of information. Since instruction is—or should be—intended to improve individual performance in the workplace, information about what to measure should result from analysis of worker responsibilities, work standards, historical patterns of experienced workers' performance problems on the job, and forecasts of likely future job changes. Using job descriptions, performance appraisal data, work standards, and such other information as emerges from the results of participant reaction sheets (Dixon, 1990), instructional designers should be able to develop performance measures that are linked directly to successful job performance.

Stakeholder preferences are the third source of information. Stakeholders are people having a vested interest in instructional outcomes. Consider, for instance, what top managers and other interested parties want to know about

TABLE 9.1. PURPOSES OF PERFORMANCE MEASUREMENT.

Purpose	Description	Advantages	Disadvantages	Examples	Guidelines for Development
Participant reaction	Measure student feelings about a program/course	Easy to administer Provides immediate feedback on instructors, facilities, and program design	Subjective Provides no measurement of learning, transfer of skills, or benefit to the organization	"Happiness reports" Informal student/instructor interview Group discussion	Design a form which can be easily tabulated Ask questions which provide information about what you need to know: instructor effectiveness, facility quality, relevance of program content, etc. Allow for anonymity and opportunity to provide additional comments
Participant learning	Measure the amount of learning that has occurred in a program/course	Provides objective data on the effectiveness of the training	Requires skill in test construction Provides no measurement of skills or benefit to the organization	Written pre/post tests Skills laboratories Role plays Simulations Projects or presentations Oral examinations	Design an instrument which will provide quantitative data Include pre- and post-level of skill/knowledge in design Tie evaluation items directly to program learning objectives

On-the-job performance change	Measure the transfer of training	Data can be collected before students leave the training program Provides objective data on impact to job situation	Requires task analysis skills to construct and is time-consuming to administer Can be a "politically" sensitive issue	Performance checklists Performance appraisals Critical incident analysis Self-appraisal	Base measurement instrument on systematic task analysis of job Consider the use of a variety of persons to conduct the evaluation Inform participants of evaluation process
Organizational impact	Measure impact of training on the organization	Provides objective data for cost-benefit analysis and organizational support	Requires high level of evaluation design skills; requires collection of data over a period of time Requires knowledge of organization needs and goals	Employee suggestions Manufacturing indices —Cost —Scrap —Schedule compliance —Quality —Employee donations Quality-of-worklife surveys Union grievances Absenteeism rates Accident rates Customer complaints	Involve all necessary levels of organization Gain commitment to allow access to organization indices and records Use organization business plans and mission statements to identify organizational needs

Source: U.S. Department of Labor and U.S. Department of Education. *The Bottom Line: Basic Skills in the Workplace.* Washington, DC: U.S. Government Printing Office, 1988, pp. 38–39.

instruction or its results. Quite often, instructional designers find that two key questions merit special consideration when measuring instruction or its results: (1) Who wants to know? and (2) What do they want to know? (Brandenburg and Smith, 1986). A third question that may be addressed is, Why do they want to know?

Some instructional designers find it helpful to consult a menu of general questions about performance measures when deciding what to measure. Rae (1986, pp. 9–10) developed such a menu, shown below, that remains very useful.

Issue	*Questions*
Content of instruction	Is it relevant and in step with the instructional needs? Is it up-to-date?
Method of instruction	Were the methods used the most appropriate ones for the subject?
	Were the methods used the most appropriate for the learning styles of the participants?
Amount of learning	What was the material of the course?
	Was it new to the learner? Was it useful, although not new to the learner, as confirmation or revision material?
Instructor skills	Did the instructor have the necessary attitude and skill to present the material in a way that encouraged learning?
Length and place of instruction	Given the material essential to learning, was the learning event of the appropriate length and pace?
	Were some aspects of instruction labored and others skimped?
Objectives	Did the instruction satisfy its declared objectives?
	Was the learner given the opportunity to try to satisfy any personal objectives?
	Was this need welcomed?
	Were personal objectives actually satisfied?
Omissions	Were any essential aspects omitted from the learning event?
	Was any material included that was not essential to the learning?

Learning transfer	How much of the learning is likely to be put into action when the learner returns to work?
	If it is to be a limited amount only or none, why is this?
	What factors will deter or assist the transfer of learning?
Accommodation	If course accommodation is within the control of the instructor or is relevant to the type of instructional event, he or she may wish to ask whether the hotel or conference center training center was suitable.
	Was the accommodation acceptable? Were the meals satisfactory?
Relevance	Was this course/seminar/conference/workshop/ tutorial/coaching assignment/project the most appropriate means of presenting a learning opportunity?
Application of learning	Which aspects of your work now include elements which are a direct result of the learning event?
	Which new aspects of work have you introduced as a result of your learning?
	Which aspects of your previous work have you replaced or modified as a result of the learning?
	Which aspects of your learning have you not applied? Why not?
Efficiency	How much more efficient or effective are you in your work as a result of the instructional experience? Why or why not?
Hindsight	With the passage of time and attempts to apply the learning, are there any amendments you would wish to make to the training you received?

Select appropriate sources of information for performance measurement based on learner characteristics, setting resources and constraints, statements of performance objectives, and needs assessment or analysis or evaluation plan.

Deciding How to Measure

When deciding how to measure performance, instructional designers should apply the same classic criteria that Newstrom and Lilyquist (1979) have suggested in selecting a data collection method for needs assessment. The following issues may thus warrant consideration:

1. *Learner involvement.* How much learner involvement is desired or feasible?
2. *Management involvement.* How much management involvement is desired or feasible?
3. *Time required.* How much time is available for measurement?
4. *Cost.* How much is the organization willing to spend to measure performance?
5. *Relevant quantifiable data.* How important is it for instructional designers to devise quantifiable measurements that are directly linked to on-the-job performance?

Different methods of measuring performance earn high, moderate, or low ratings on each of these criteria. For this reason, it is usually necessary to identify priorities—that is, determine which one is the most important, second most important, and so on.

An Overview of Steps in Preparing Instruments

Having decided on a purpose (what is to be measured) and a measurement method (how it will be measured), instructional designers are then ready to begin developing measurement instruments. Instruments may be classified into three general types: (1) questionnaires, interview guides or schedules, observation forms, simulations, and checklists, (2) criterion-referenced tests, and (3) others. There are ten basic steps to be taken during the preparation of a measurement instrument:

1. Clarifying the purpose of measurement and selecting a type of instrument.
2. Giving the instrument a descriptive title.
3. Conducting background research.
4. Drafting or modifying items.
5. Sequencing—or reviewing the sequence of—items.
6. Trying out the instrument on a small-group representative of the learner population.
7. Revising the instrument based on the small-group tryout.
8. Testing the instrument on a larger group.
9. Using the instrument—but establishing a means of tracking experience with it.
10. Revising the instrument—or specific items—periodically.

These steps are summarized in the following paragraphs.

Step 1: Clarifying the Purpose of Measurement and Selecting a Type of Instrument

Instructional designers should start developing performance measurements by thinking through exactly why they are measuring instruction and, more important, what results they wish to achieve. Performance objectives are one starting point, since one purpose of measurement should usually be to determine how well learners have met instructional objectives by the end of the instructional experience. Instructional designers should ask themselves, among other questions, this one: How can I find out whether these results are being achieved during the instructional experience and whether they were achieved following the instructional experience? At this point they can select or prepare an instrument well suited to helping answer this question.

Step 2: Giving the Instrument a Descriptive Title

If performance will be measured using an instrument developed by someone else, instructional designers should consider the title to see if it accurately describes what they wish to measure. On the other hand, if the instrument will be tailor-made, the title should be chosen with great care. The reason: by selecting a title, instructional designers focus their thinking on exactly what will be measured.

Step 3: Conducting Background Research

Instructional designers can often save themselves considerable time and effort by locating previously prepared instruments. One way to do that is to network with other instructional designers to find out whether they have developed instruments for similar purposes. In addition, instructional designers can sometimes successfully track down elusive instruments or research studies by using specialized reference guides. Tests in print can be located through the impressive library of the Educational Testing Service in Princeton, New Jersey, which maintains a collection of 10,000 tests. Additional information about testing can be found in Smith and Merchant (1990) and Sullivan and Elenburg (1988). Manufacturers may also wish to consult Kaplan (1990) and the "National Skills Standards" (1995). (See the publications of the National Skills Standards Board on the board's website for detailed, and free, guidance on how to use the standards.)

Background research on instrumentation will rarely be a complete waste of time. Even when instructional designers are unable to locate instruments that measure exactly what they want, they may still be able to locate examples that will stimulate new ideas about item layout or item sequence.

When previously prepared instruments are found, instructional designers should decide whether to use them as they are or modify them to meet special needs. If previously prepared instruments can be easily modified, instructional designers can reduce the time and effort necessary to prepare and validate an instrument. But if efforts to locate instruments or research are to no avail, then it will be necessary to prepare a tailor-made instrument. Begin instrument development by addressing several important questions: Who will be measured? Who will conduct the measurement? What will be measured? When will the measurement occur? Where will the measurement be conducted? How will the measurement be conducted?

Step 4: Drafting or Modifying Items

Relying on instructional objectives or other sources as a starting point, instructional designers should next decide what questions they need to ask to measure the changes wrought by the instructional experience. If a previously prepared instrument was located, each item must be reviewed to ensure that it is appropriate. On the other hand, drafting original items or questions for interviews, questionnaires, observation forms, simulations, or checklists is a highly creative activity. Generate items or questions using focus groups or other creative methods (Michalko, 1991).

When drafting items, instructional designers should be sure to consider item format. Item format refers to the way performance is measured. Questionnaires or interview guides, for instance, may rely on open-ended items, closed-ended items, or some combination. Open-ended items produce qualitative or essay responses. The question "What do you feel you have learned in this instructional experience?" is an open-ended item. Closed-ended items produce quantifiable responses. Respondents asked to "rate how much you feel you learned during this instructional experience on a scale from 1 to 5, with 1 representing 'very little' and 5 representing 'very much,'" are answering a closed-ended item. An instrument relies on a combination when it contains both open-ended and closed-ended items.

Open-ended items are frequently used in conducting exploratory measurement studies. While the information they yield is difficult to quantify and analyze, they may also be used to establish response categories for closed-ended instruments. In contrast, closed-ended items are frequently utilized in analytical measurement studies. Although the information they produce is easily quantified and analyzed, it can sometimes be misleading if respondents are not given appropriate response categories. When that happens, respondents will select an approximation of what they believe and reply accordingly. Item format has a different, although related, meaning for observation forms, simulations, or checklists. These instruments are usually designed around observable behaviors associated with the instructional objectives or competent on-the-job performance. Instructional designers may prepare these instruments to count the frequencies of a behavior (How often did the learner do something?), assess the quality of a behavior (How well did the learner perform?), or both. The instrument user may exercise considerable flexibility in identifying what behavior to count or assess. Alternatively, the user may not exercise flexibility in assessing behaviors, because categories are predefined or methods of assessment have been provided on the instrument itself.

Item format has yet another meaning with regard to tests. Indeed, developing criterion-referenced tests poses a challenge somewhat different from developing questionnaires, interviews, simulations, or other measurement instruments. Test preparation is an entire field of its own (Krieger, 1994; Tenopyr, 1996). When developing criterion-referenced tests, "the verb component of the instructional objective indicates the form that a test item should take" (Kemp, 1985, p. 161). Examples of behaviors specified in instructional objectives and appropriately matched test item formats are shown in Table 9.2.

TABLE 9.2. BEHAVIORS SPECIFIED IN INSTRUCTIONAL OBJECTIVES AND CORRESPONDING TEST ITEMS.

Type of test item	Brief description of test-item format	Behavior (verb specified in the instructional objective)
1. **Essay** (*Example:* "What are the chief advantages and disadvantages of the essay format as a test item?")	A type of test item requiring a learner to respond in essay format. This type of item is appropriate for assessing higher levels of cognition—such as analysis, synthesis, and evaluation.	Construct Define Develop Discuss Generate Locate Solve State
2. **Fill-in-the-blank** (*Example:* "The_____ -in-the-blank is a type of test item.")	A type of test item requiring the learner to fill in the blank with an appropriate word or phrase. Scoring can be objective because the required response is quite specific—often only one word is correct.	Construct Define Identify Locate Solve State

TABLE 9.2. BEHAVIORS SPECIFIED IN INSTRUCTIONAL OBJECTIVES AND CORRESPONDING TEST ITEMS, cont'd.

Type of test item	Brief description of test-item format	Behavior (verb specified in the instructional objective)
3. **Completion** (Example: "A type of test item that requires the completion of a sentence is called the_____ .")	A type of test item that closely resembles the fill-in-the-blank type, except that the learner is asked to complete a sentence stem.	Construct Define Develop Discuss GenerateIdentify Locate Solve State
4. **Multiple-choice** (Example: "A type of test item requiring the learner to choose from more than one possible answer is the (a) multiple-choice; (b) essay; (c) completion.")	Kemp (1985, p. 162) calls multiple-choice "the most useful and versatile type of objective testing." Learners must choose between three and five options or alternatives as the answer to a question.	Discriminate Identify Locate Select Solve
5. **True-false** (Example: "A true-false test item is less versatile than a multiple-choice one." True-False)	A type of test item in which learners are asked to determine whether a statement is true or false.	Discriminate Locate Select Solve
6. **Matching** (See the example below.)	A type of test item in which learners are asked to match up items in one column with items in another column.	Discriminate Locate Select

For each item in column 1 below, select a corresponding item in column 2 by placing the number of the item before the item in column 1. Use items only once.

Column 1	*Column 2*
_____ 1. Essay	1. A type of test item in which learners have only two possible answers
_____ 2. Multiple-choice	2. A type of test item in which learners have between three and five alternatives
_____ 3. True-false	3. A test item requiring a narrative response

Type of test item	Brief description of test-item format	Behavior (verb specified in the instructional objective)
7. **Project** (Example: "Write an essay question to describe ten steps in preparing an assessment instrument.")	A type of test in which learners are asked to demonstrate the ability to perform a task they have (presumably) learned through participation in an instructional experience.	Construct Develop Generate Locate Solve

Step 5: Sequencing—or Reviewing the Sequence of—Items

One choice is to sequence items in a logical order based on work tasks. Another choice is to sequence items according to a learning hierarchy.

Step 6: Trying Out the Instrument on a Small-Group Representative of the Learner Population

Sometimes called instrument pre-testing, this step should not be confused with learner pre-testing. If possible, instructional designers should select a sample of people representative of the learner population to participate in the instrument pre-test and ask for their help in identifying wording that is unclear or is otherwise inappropriate. Instructional designers should explain the instrument items to the group rather than ask them to answer the questions. Their responses should be noted for use during the next step.

Step 7: Revising the Instrument Based on the Small-Group Tryout

If a complete revision is necessary, which should rarely be the case, another small group should be selected for the purpose of a second instrument pre-test. Otherwise, instructional designers should revise items, based on their notes from the previous step, to improve clarity.

Step 8: Testing the Instrument on a Larger Group

The next step is a field test of the instrument on a larger group under conditions resembling, as closely as possible, those in which the instrument will later be used. The results of the field test should be noted.

Step 9: Using the Instrument—But Establishing a Means of Tracking Experience with It

Instructional designers should use the instrument but should also establish a way of tracking future experience with it. The results need to be monitored over time. If tests are administered, instructional designers should periodically conduct item analysis to determine what questions the learners are missing and how often they are missing them. If questionnaires or interviews are used to measure performance, instructional designers need to note the response patterns they receive to determine whether specific questions are yielding useful answers. If instructional designers are using structured observation, they should periodically review the categories they initially created.

Step 10: Revising the Instrument—or Specific Items—Periodically

As performance measurements are made using instruments, instructional designers gain experience. They can take advantage of that experience by periodically revising the instrument, or specific items on it. Of course, revisions should also be made whenever changes are made to performance objectives or when new performance objectives are added.

Other Methods of Measuring Performance

Apart from questionnaires, interviews, simulations, and checklists, other methods may be used to measure participant reactions, participant learning, on-the-job performance change, or organizational impact. However, not every method is appropriate for every purpose. These methods (note that we do not call them *items* or *instruments*) include advisory committees, external assessment centers, attitude surveys, group discussions, exit interviews, and performance appraisal.

An advisory committee is a group consisting of stakeholders in instructional experiences (Rothwell and Kazanas, 1993a, 1994a). A committee may be established as standing (permanent and formal) or ad hoc (temporary and informal). One way to use an advisory committee is to ask its members to observe an instructional experience and assess how well they feel its objectives are achieved. Another way is to direct results of participant tests or other measures to committee members for interpretation.

An external assessment center is a process of measuring individual knowledge and skills. It is an extended simulation of job or group work. It could be used—although it would admittedly be expensive to do so—to determine what measurable change resulted from an instructional experience (Uretsky, 1989–1990).

An attitude survey is usually intended to assess individual perceptions about working conditions, co-workers, work tasks, and other issues. It could be used to determine people's perceptions of what changes or how much change resulted from instructional experiences.

A group discussion is simply a meeting. It could be used to identify relevant measurement issues or assess a group's perceptions about what changes or how much change occurred as a result of an instructional experience.

An exit interview is a meeting with an employee just prior to the individual's departure from an organization, department, or work unit. In some cases, exit interviews may be combined with questionnaires mailed to terminating employees some time after they leave the organization. Exit interviews may be used to identify relevant measurement issues or assess an individual's perceptions about what changes or how much change occurred as a result of an instructional experience.

A *performance appraisal* is an assessment of an individual's job-related activities and results over a predetermined time frame. It could be used to document a supervisor's perceptions of what changes or how much change occurred as a result of an individual's participation in an instructional experience.

Judging Performance Measurements

Instructional designers should be capable of judging performance measurements they or their colleagues have developed when they are provided with a performance measure and are furnished with necessary information on the characteristics of learners, the settings in which they are expected to perform, constraints on performance and instructional development, instructional objectives, and plans for analyzing needs and evaluating results as applicable.

As in the case of performance objectives, instructional designers may find it useful to rely on a worksheet when judging performance measures (see Exhibit 9.1). Every time an answer of no is given, instructional designers should reexamine the performance measurements and, when necessary, revise them.

Justifying Performance Measurements

Instructional designers should also be capable of explaining their reasons for developing performance measurements and instruments as they did. As in most instructional design activities, they should consider themselves accountable for what they do. Consequently, they should be prepared to answer questions posed by other stakeholders.

Acting Ethically in Developing Performance Measurements

A key ethical issue in developing measurements can be expressed by this question: *Are the learners involved in the process?* Performance measurements devised by management alone may not enjoy the ownership of workers—and may not even be realistic. Further, workers may be concerned about how the results of performance measurements will be applied to them as managers make future employment decisions.

EXHIBIT 9.1. A WORKSHEET FOR JUDGING PERFORMANCE MEASUREMENTS.

Directions: Use this worksheet to judge a performance measurement you or others have prepared.

First complete Part I to ensure that you have everything you need to judge a performance measurement properly. For each question in the left column, place a check (✓) in the center column to indicate an answer. If you are missing something necessary for proper judgment, make notes to yourself in the right column.

Second, complete Part II to judge each performance measurement. For each question appearing in the left column below, place a check (✓) in the center column. Each performance measurement should lend itself to a yes response. If you answer yes to all questions, the performance measurement should meet all required criteria. It should not need to be revised. If you must check no, make notes for revision in the right column. Use N/A (for "not applicable") when the performance measurement does not lend itself to the conditions set forth in the question.

Make copies of this worksheet as necessary, depending on the number of performance measurements you will review.

Part I. Conditions				
Question	**Response**			**Notes for Revision**
	Yes	No	N/A	
Do You have available . . .	(✓)	(✓)	(✓)	
1. A performance measure?	( )	( )	( )	
2. Appropriate information on				
a. Learner characteristics?	( )	( )	( )	
b. Setting resources and constraints?	( )	( )	( )	
c. Statements of performance objectives?	( )	( )	( )	
d. Needs assessment/analysis or evaluation plan (as applicable)?	( )	( )	( )	

To act ethically in the use of performance measurements, then, instructional designers must accept responsibility for working with their internal and external clients to ensure that performance measurements are established fairly and that workers are briefed in advance about how the results of performance measurements will be used.

In Rothwell's (2003) survey, conducted in preparation for this book's third edition, respondents were asked about challenges they face when developing

EXHIBIT 9.1. A WORKSHEET FOR JUDGING PERFORMANCE MEASUREMENTS, cont'd

Part II. Judgments of Performance Measurements

Question	Response			Notes for Revision
Dose the Performance Measurement . . .	Yes (✓)	No (✓)	N/A (✓)	
1. Show a one-to-one correspondence with the conditions being measured (when the instrument is designed to measure learning outcomes)?	( )	( )	( )	
2. Show a one-to-one correspondence with performance of the learning outcomes being measured (when the instrument is designed to measure learning outcomes)?	( )	( )	( )	
3. Use item types appropriate to objectives and the requirements of the performance environment.	( )	( )	( )	
4. Use development time efficiently, considering course length and project parameters?	( )	( )	( )	
5. Use respondent time efficiently, considering course length and project parameters?	( )	( )	( )	
6. Have acceptable reliability?	( )	( )	( )	
7. Have acceptable Validity?	( )	( )	( )	
8. Show acceptable item-writing style?	( )	( )	( )	

Mastering the Instructional Design Process: A Systematic Approach, Fourth Edition. Copyright © 2008 by John Wiley & Sons, Inc. Reproduced by permission of Pfeiffer, an Imprint of Wiley. www.pfeiffer.com

performance measurements. They pointed to common problems. Among them: "performance [*is*] not being measured"; "true performance measures are still new here"; [*doing this is difficult because*] management [*does not want to accept*] responsibility."

Applying Cross-Cultural Awareness to Developing Performance Measurements

In many Asian and European cultures, students advance through formal schooling only by demonstrating competence through paper-and-pencil testing. That practice is unlike the educational system in the United States. For that reason, testing in training contexts may be regarded much more seriously in Asian and European cultures than in the United States. Instructional designers should thus be aware that, by measuring learner performance through testing, they may exert on workers tremendous (and perhaps undue) pressure to excel. As a consequence, special care should be taken to clarify why testing is worthwhile and how the results will be used in making employment decisions.

What Is New in Developing Performance Measurements?

Perhaps the most recent development in performance measurement is the growing use of key performance indicators (KPIs) or key results areas (KRAs) in many organizations. A *key performance indicator* specifies the most important results or outcomes for a given job incumbent. They go beyond job descriptions, which typically focus on work activities or duties, to focus on the measurable results or performance targets desired. They are also a way to link individual, team, department, or division results to the desired strategic objectives to be achieved by an organization. In most cases, the key performance indicators for individuals are linked to those for their teams, departments, divisions and the organization with due attention to a balanced scorecard that covers measurable results desired in financial, business process, customer, and learning/growth areas targeted (Kaplan and Norton, 1996).

The advent of KPIs has important implications for instructional designers. KPIs are a means by which to focus attention on desired performance targets. That establishes an accountability system. Training should seek to improve knowledge, skill and attitude that will help individuals, teams, departments, and divisions achieve their KPIs. Hence, performance measurements should be linked in some fashion to KPIs in training, and tests should seek to show how training has contributed to achieving KPIs and the organization's strategic objectives.

There is more to getting results than just achieving KPIs, however. How people behave influences their results. For that reason, many organizations establish performance management systems that include measuring KPIs and the behaviors linked to the competencies of successful or outstanding performers.

There is, and should be, a relationship between the behaviors desired in the organization to demonstrate competencies and the behaviors appearing in the objectives established for training programs. When there is transparency between behaviors desired for success and the desired, measurable results, it is easier for trainers to show learners "what is in it for them" to perform well in training. But when that relationship is not clear, learners are not likely to see how success in training will lead to success on the job and to the rewards promised for achieving KPIs.

Another important development in performance measurement is the growing interest in metrics generally. It has almost become an obsession. HR professionals are interested in scorecards for their work (Becker, Huselid, and Ulrich, 2001; Fitz-enz, 2000), and learning and performance professionals are also interested in measuring their results on a broad range of measures (Schmidt, 2003).

Finally, a third development in performance measurement is the growing interest in testing in all its forms. While it may be argued that it stems from the interest in testing children for schools, it is clear that employers are increasingly testing workers before and during their employment for many purposes. That includes drug tests, personality tests, physical tests, aptitude tests, honesty tests, and many others. It also includes testing in training (Hale, 2002; Shrock and Coscarelli, 2007). Employers should take care in using tests, ensuring that they are really related to the work to be performed and are necessary, ethical, and legally justifiable. When in doubt, employers should check with legal counsel.

Conclusion

As we noted at the beginning of this chapter, instructional designers should develop performance measurements during—or immediately following—preparation of performance objectives. In the chapter, we defined performance measurements, explained their importance, and provided advice about developing them, judging them, and explaining them. We also emphasized an important ethical issue in developing performance measurements and suggested how instructional designers can display cross-cultural sensitivity in developing those measurements. In the next chapter, we turn to sequencing performance objectives.

CHAPTER TEN

SEQUENCING PERFORMANCE OBJECTIVES

Sequencing instruction should usually occur after work tasks have been analyzed, performance objectives have been written, and performance measurements have been developed. It ensures that workers are introduced systematically to what they must know or do to perform competently (see Figure 10.1).

The resulting sequence of objectives becomes the basis for an instructional outline, sometimes called an instructional syllabus. It is a blueprint for choosing an instructional strategy and selecting, modifying, or preparing instructional materials. (It should be emphasized that a blueprint of some kind is essential regardless of the delivery media chosen–and is often quite helpful in integrating multimedia.) In this chapter, we will describe approaches to sequencing performance objectives, offer simple advice to instructional designers about judging and justifying sequencing decisions, and mention key ethical and cross-cultural issues in sequencing performance objectives.

Defining Key Terms

Sequence connotes the order in which learners are introduced, through planned instruction, to information and tasks essential to work performance. An instructional sequence ranges on a continuum from *inflexible* (a fixed sequence that

FIGURE 10.1. A MODEL OF STEPS IN THE INSTRUCTIONAL DESIGN PROCESS.

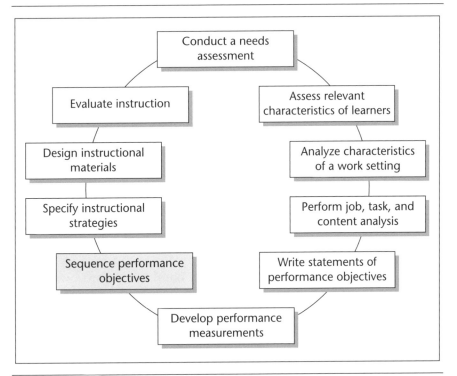

Source: Foshay, W., Silber, K., and Westgaard, O. *Instructional Design Competencies: The Standards.* Iowa City, IA: International Board of Standards for Training, Performance, and Instruction, 1986, p. 3. Copyright 1993 by the International Board of Standards for Training, Performance and Instruction. All rights reserved. Used with permission.

never varies across learners) to *flexible* (a varying sequence that is influenced by each learner's background, desired learning outcomes, and conditions in the learning environment).

Rules for sequencing instruction provide guidance for instructional designs. Some methods of sequencing instruction are simply more appropriate than others, depending on the performance objectives, the learner, and the learning environment. When these methods are clearly spelled out so that an instructional designer knows how to sequence performance objectives when furnished with information about the objectives, the learners, and the learning environment, the result is a rule for sequencing instruction.

The Importance of Sequencing

To find out about instructional sequencing, try an experiment. Ask several questions of the next five or six employed people you meet:

1. How were you first introduced to your job? Did you receive planned training, or were you forced to struggle to learn on your own, as best you could?
2. How clearly were you informed of performance expectations at the time you began your job? Did your supervisor explain to you, early on, what you should be able to do after you were trained? If you received planned on-the-job training, were you told how long the training period would last? How your progress would be assessed? How the training was organized—that is, sequenced—to help you acquire job-related information or build desired job skills?
3. How do you feel employees should be introduced to work activities? Is there an ideal way to organize information or build skills? How does this ideal match up to your experiences?

Instructional designers who carry out this experiment will no doubt hear some very interesting answers to these questions. The people who respond will probably say that they received minimal on-the-job training, that most learning had to be done on their own, and that nobody clarified what they should be able to do on completion of their job training. Most people are left to learn their jobs as best they can through the sink-or-swim method, and few are happy about that (Rothwell and Kazanas, 1994b; Rothwell and Kazanas, in press). In those rare cases when planned on-the-job training is available, it is often sequenced around crises or problems as they arise on the job (Rothwell and Kazanas, 1994b; Rothwell and Kazanas, in press).

However, effective instruction is rarely sequenced around the (sometimes random) order in which problems arise on learners' jobs. Nor does it necessarily match up to a convenient schedule for using equipment or trainer time. It should instead be sequenced so learners will be systematically introduced to work activities in ways appropriate to the performance objectives, the learners themselves, and the situations or conditions in which they must learn.

Approaches to Sequencing

There are at least nine approaches to sequencing performance objectives and the instruction planned to meet those objectives:

1. Chronological sequencing.
2. Topical sequencing.
3. Whole-to-part sequencing.
4. Part-to-whole sequencing.
5. Known-to-unknown sequencing.
6. Unknown-to-known sequencing.
7. Step-by-step sequencing.
8. Part-to-part-to-part sequencing.
9. General-to-specific sequencing.

Let us describe each one. It should be noted, however, that recent writings on instructional design have emphasized the importance of elaboration in which ideas are introduced at a basic level and then gradually built upon, much like a "pebble in a pond" (Merrill, 2002).

Chronological Sequencing

When performance objectives are sequenced chronologically, the content is arranged by time sequence with the presentation of later events preceded by discussion of earlier ones. Chronological sequencing is typically used with history. Many academic experts who write college textbooks favor a chronological approach, beginning with the history of their discipline. Instruction is sequenced from past to present to future.

Topical Sequencing

When performance objectives are sequenced topically, learners are immediately immersed in the middle of a topical problem or issue. For example, today's newspaper headline may be of topical significance to a given performance objective, and it could be used as a starting point for instruction. Learners are then led back in time to see how the problem originated. They may sometimes be led forward to see what will happen if the problem is not solved. This sequencing method is sometimes called in medias res, a Latin phrase meaning that instruction begins "in the middle of things."

Whole-to-Part Sequencing

When performance objectives are sequenced from whole to part, learners are first presented with a complete model or a description of the full complexities of a physical object (such as an automobile engine or the world globe), abstraction (such as steps in a model of instructional design), or work duty (such as writing a letter). Instruction is then organized around parts of the whole. For instance, learners are then led through each part of an automobile engine, each nation on a world globe, each step in a model of the instructional design process, or each task comprising the work duty.

This approach to sequencing was first advocated by Ausubel (1962), building on the work of Gestalt learning theorists (see the description in Rothwell and Sredl, 2000). Learners should be presented with an overarching logic to govern what they should know (Pucel, 1989). In this way, they can see how each part relates to a larger conceptual system.

Part-to-Whole Sequencing

When performance objectives are sequenced from part to whole, learners are introduced to each part of a larger object, abstraction, or work duty. By the end of instruction, they should be able to conceptualize the entire object or abstraction or perform the entire duty. For example, learners could be oriented to an organization by visiting, investigating, and charting work activities in each department. They should eventually be able to describe the activities of each organizational part and thus (presumably) the entire organization.

Known-to-Unknown Sequencing

When performance objectives are sequenced from known to unknown, learners are introduced to what they already know and are gradually led into what they do not know. Herbart (1898) was among the first to advocate this approach to sequencing desired results of instruction, arguing that learners bring their experience to bear on what they learn. Consequently, he concluded, it is essential for instruction to build on what the learner already knows.

Suppose, for example, that it is necessary to train a novice on how to make an overhead transparency on a copy machine. A trainer wishing to save time would first pose two questions: (1) Does the novice already know what an overhead transparency is? and (2) Does the novice already know how to make paper photocopies? If the answer to either question is no, instruction will have to begin by providing this essential prerequisite information. But if the answer to both questions is yes, the trainer can begin by explaining that transparencies are simply placed in the paper tray of a photocopier and an original sheet is copied. The result: an overhead transparency. In this way, the trainer has sequenced instruction from what the learner already knows about transparencies and photocopying to what the learner does not know about producing transparencies.

Unknown-to-Known Sequencing

When performance objectives are sequenced from unknown to known, learners are deliberately disoriented at the outset of instruction. In short, instructional designers consciously set out to "put the learners in over their heads." It is sometimes called discovery learning (see Allen, 2002). This approach dramatizes how little they really know about a subject or the performance of a task or work duty with which they already feel smugly familiar.

The aim of this approach is to motivate learners for a subsequent learning task. It gives them an uncomfortable experience that leads them to question their own knowledge, thereby demonstrating to them that they need to learn more. Perhaps the most obvious example is military boot camp, in which new recruits undergo an initial upending experience that clearly dramatizes how little they really know about their own physical and mental limitations.

Step-by-Step Sequencing

When performance objectives are sequenced step by step, learners are introduced to a task or work duty through either of two methods. The first method is based on the steps of the task or work duty itself. Instructional designers begin by analyzing how the task or duty is performed. They then sequence instruction around each step in the task or each task included in a work duty.

The second method is based on the knowledge that learners must already possess or they must have mastered the skills to be capable of learning the procedure. Instructional designers analyze how people learn the skill or process information. This analysis is conducted using techniques such as information processing analysis, information mapping, or learning hierarchy analysis. Performance objectives are then sequencing around each step ("chunk of knowledge" or "specific skill") that learners must possess to master a task or work duty. On occasion, training is not necessary for step-by-step learning to occur. Learners may be coached through a task by means of a job aid, such as a checklist or step-by-step description of a procedure. Alternatively, they may be coached through a task with a decision tool such as a flowchart, diagram, or electronic tool.

Part-to-Part-to-Part Sequencing

When performance objectives are sequenced part to part to part, learners are treated to a relatively shallow introduction to a topic, move on to another topic that is also treated superficially, move on to a third topic that is treated superficially, eventually return to the original topic for more in-depth exposure, and so on.

The aim is to ensure that learners are introduced to topics and then hear more about them gradually as they are elaborated on in subsequent rounds of the spiral.

General-to-Specific Sequencing

When performance objectives are sequenced from general to specific, all learners are introduced to the same foundation of knowledge of the same skills. Later, however, each learner specializes. This method of sequencing is sometimes called the pyramidal or core structure method. All learners are exposed to certain topics (the core) but may specialize (by exposing themselves to topics around the core).

Other Approaches to Sequencing

Other sequencing methods may, at times, be appropriate. The nine described in this section are not intended to be exhaustive. They are, instead, intended to be representative of possible ways to sequence instruction.

Making Decisions About Sequencing Performance Objectives

Instructional designers should be able to make decisions about sequencing performance objectives so as to identify and apply a sequencing approach that is appropriate for the learners and learning situation. Unfortunately, there are few absolute certainties when facing these decisions. Each situation may dictate its own rules. We have provided a flowchart in Figure 10.2 to aid instructional designers in making decisions about sequencing performance objectives.

Judging the Sequencing of Performance Objectives

Instructional designers should be capable of judging the sequencing decisions they and others have made about performance objectives. Such judgments can be made when instructional designers are furnished with performance objectives and with the results of learner, setting, and work analysis.

In earlier chapters, we pointed out the value of using a worksheet as an aid in judging work performed by instructional designers or their colleagues. A worksheet of the same kind can be helpful on these occasions as well. (Such a worksheet is shown in Exhibit 10.1.) Every time instructional designers must answer no to an item on the worksheet, they should go back and reexamine the sequence of performance objectives.

FIGURE 10.2. RULES FOR SEQUENCING
PERFORMANCE OBJECTIVES: A FLOWCHART.

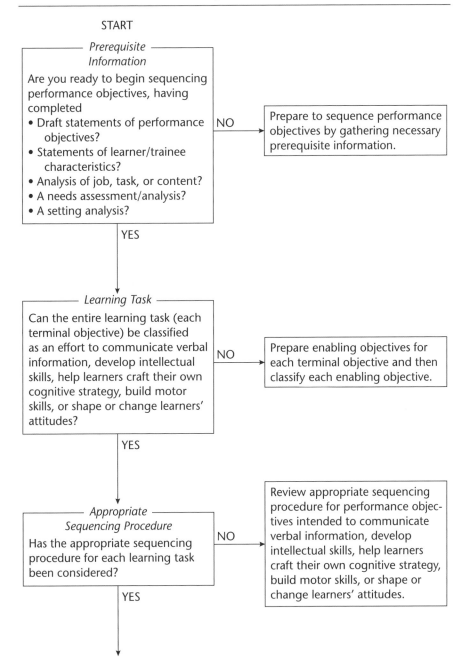

FIGURE 10.2. RULES FOR SEQUENCING
PERFORMANCE OBJECTIVES: A FLOWCHART, cont'd.

```
                              ┌─────── Reality Check ───────┐
                              │ Is there good reason to consider │              ┌────────────────────────────┐
                              │ other matters in making a decision │   NO       │ Sequence terminal and/or   │
                              │ about sequencing performance │ ────────────────►│ enabling performance objectives │
                              │ objectives?                  │              │ based on the learning task. │
                              └──────────────┬──────────────┘              └────────────────────────────┘
                                           YES
```

```
                                                               ┌──────────────────────────────────┐
                                                               │ Clarify the targeted learners and │
                                                               │ assess their existing knowledge/  │
                              ┌──────── Learners ────────┐      │ skill. If instruction is geared to │
                              │ Is it clear what learners already │  NO  │ novices and the learning task │
                              │ know and/or can do?          │ ──────────►│ warrants it, consider prerequisite │
                              └──────────────┬──────────────┘      │ knowledge or skill. Check to │
                                           YES                     │ ensure that the learners possess │
                                                               │ that prerequisite knowledge or │
                                                               │ skill. If they do not, backtrack to │
                                                               │ ensure that prerequisites are met │
                                                               │ before learners try to achieve │
                              ┌──────── Learners' ───────┐      │ these performance objectives. │
                              │        Attitudes          │      └──────────────────────────────────┘
                              │ Are the learners motivated to learn │
                              │ for any of the following reasons: │
```

- They are experiencing a
  "teachable moment"?
- They can readily see the
  importance of achieving the
  performance objectives for
  themselves and/or the
  organization?
- They believe the performance
  objectives are attainable?
- They favor—or are at least
  neutral to—change?
- They believe they will be
  rewarded, directly or
  indirectly, for achieving
  the results expressed in
  performance objectives?

NO → Consider methods of sequencing performance objectives so as to motivate the learners. Do that by demonstrating, before anything else, the importance of the instruction to them and to the organization.

YES

FIGURE 10.2. RULES FOR SEQUENCING
PERFORMANCE OBJECTIVES: A FLOWCHART, cont'd.

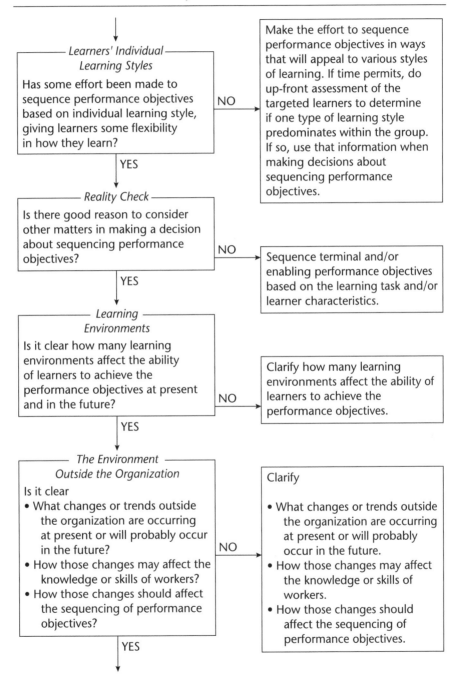

FIGURE 10.2. RULES FOR SEQUENCING
PERFORMANCE OBJECTIVES: A FLOWCHART, cont'd.

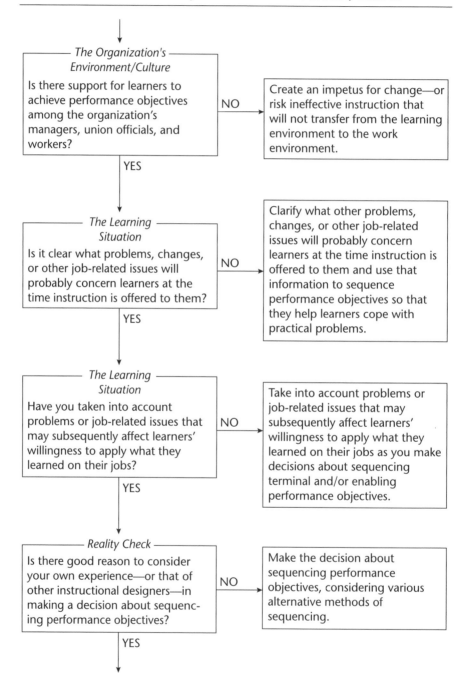

FIGURE 10.2. RULES FOR SEQUENCING PERFORMANCE OBJECTIVES: A FLOWCHART, cont'd.

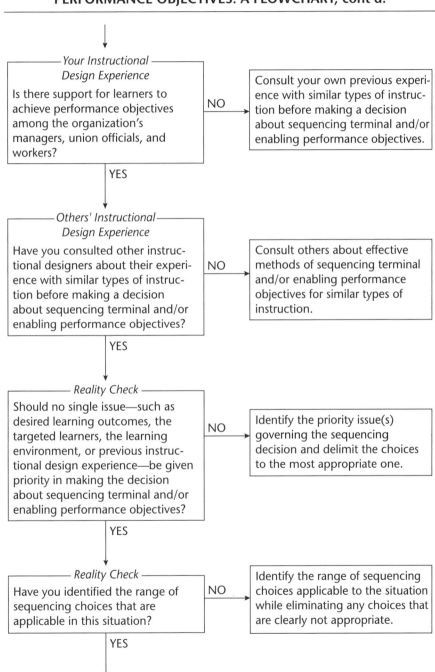

FIGURE 10.2. RULES FOR SEQUENCING
PERFORMANCE OBJECTIVES: A FLOWCHART, cont'd.

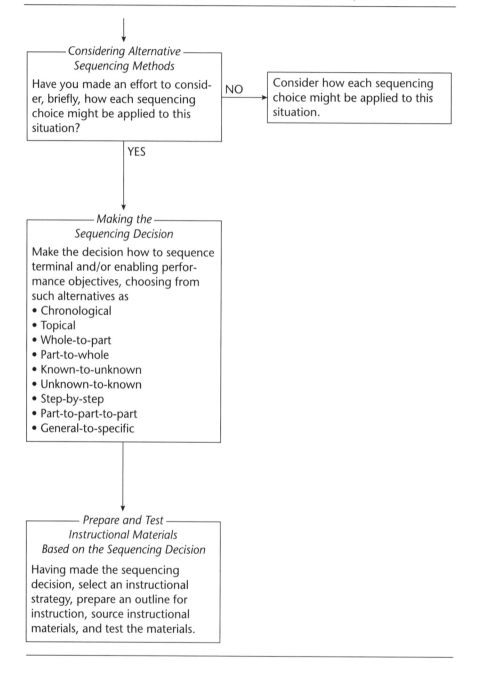

Considering Alternative Sequencing Methods

Have you made an effort to consider, briefly, how each sequencing choice might be applied to this situation?

NO → Consider how each sequencing choice might be applied to this situation.

YES

Making the Sequencing Decision

Make the decision how to sequence terminal and/or enabling performance objectives, choosing from such alternatives as
• Chronological
• Topical
• Whole-to-part
• Part-to-whole
• Known-to-unknown
• Unknown-to-known
• Step-by-step
• Part-to-part-to-part
• General-to-specific

Prepare and Test Instructional Materials Based on the Sequencing Decision

Having made the sequencing decision, select an instructional strategy, prepare an outline for instruction, source instructional materials, and test the materials.

EXHIBIT 10.1. A WORKSHEET FOR JUDGING THE SEQUENCING OF PERFORMANCE OBJECTIVES.

Directions: Use this worksheet to judge the sequencing of performance objectives.

First complete Part I to ensure that you have everything you need to judge the sequencing. For each question appearing in the left column, place a check (✓) in the center column to indicate an answer. If you are missing something, make notes to yourself in the right column.

Second, complete Part II to judge the sequencing decisions that have been made. For each question appearing in the left column below, place a check (✓) in the center column. You should be able to answer each question with a yes. If you must answer no to an item, (1) review the sequencing decision, and (2) be ready and able to state a rationale for it.

Make copies of this worksheet as necessary.

Part I. Conditions

Question	Response			Notes for Revision
	Yes	No	N/A	
Do you have available . . .	(✓)	(✓)	(✓)	
1. Statements of performance objectives?	( )	( )	( )	
2. Statements of learner characteristics?	( )	( )	( )	
3. Results of job, task, and/or content analysis?	( )	( )	( )	
4. Results of needs assessment/analysis?	( )	( )	( )	
5. Results of a setting analysis?	( )	( )	( )	

Part II. Decisions

Question	Response			Notes for Revision
	Yes	No	N/A	
In making the decision to sequence performance objectives, did you consider . . .	(✓)	(✓)	(✓)	
6. The nature of the performance objectives?	( )	( )	( )	
7. The learners?	( )	( )	( )	
8. The learning environment?	( )	( )	( )	
9. Your experience—or the experience of other instructional designers—with similar types of instruction?	( )	( )	( )	
10. Alternative methods of sequencing performance objectives?	( )	( )	( )	

Justifying the Sequencing of Performance Objectives

Instructional designers should be capable of explaining, when asked, why they decided on sequencing performance objectives in a certain way but not in others. More specifically, instructional designers should be prepared to answer the following questions as the need arises:

1. Why were performance objectives for instruction sequenced as they were?
2. What are the relative advantages and disadvantages of the approach to sequencing performance objectives that was selected?
3. Who should care about the decisions made about sequencing performance objectives?
4. Why should they care about sequencing?

Answer the foregoing questions as a starting point for justifying the decisions made about sequencing performance objectives.

Acting Ethically in Sequencing Performance Objectives

One key ethical issue in sequencing performance objectives is this: *How important are health and safety issues in sequencing objectives and instruction?* Effective instructional sequencing depends on what the learners already know or need to know to perform. In those cases where health and safety are at issue, however, learners should be instructed first about what they need to know about a topic to prevent injury or other accidents to themselves and others. For instance, when learners are oriented to a new machine, they are given a safety orientation first. In that way, decision makers ensure that learners are equipped first with what they need to know to avoid accidents or injuries. Such a policy places health and safety first; work procedures are thus secondary.

In Rothwell's (2003) survey, conducted in preparation for the third edition of this book, respondents pointed to the sequencing of objectives, and the instruction on which it is based, as a common problem. One respondent noted that "objectives [are] not sequenced in [an] intuitive fashion." Another indicated that this issue is "often overlooked." The result of this problem, noted one respondent, was that instructional experiences are "very limp in design." These notes, while admittedly sketchy, may suggest that sequencing instruction to help learners may not be given the focus it should be.

Applying Cross-Cultural Awareness to Sequencing Performance Objectives

What is the culture's preference for synchronicity? The answer to this question is most relevant to applying cross-cultural awareness to sequencing performance objectives. In this context, synchronicity means "occurring at the same time."

Western cultures tend to be synchronous societies (Hofstede, 1991; Odenwald, 1993). Time is viewed as a straight line. It exists outside individuals. Learners prefer to start on time and at the beginning, progress through instruction in logical sequence, and end on time.

In asynchronous cultures, however, time is viewed as a circle. It exists inside individuals. Scheduled starting and ending times are less important.

Consider, as a simple example, preferences about movie schedules, which can provide valuable clues about the culture. In the United States, movies start and end according to a fixed schedule. People usually want to watch a movie completely, so they appear at the movie theater when the show is scheduled to begin. This practice displays a preference for synchronicity.

However, in the Philippines, which is an asynchronous culture, movies run continuously. Viewers enter and leave movie theaters at any time. Their tolerance for asynchronicity is high, since individuals function according to their own internal schedules.

When sequencing instruction, instructional designers should be aware of these cultural preferences. Instruction designed for use in synchronous cultures should allow for the learners' (and clients') preferences for linearity and adherence to external schedules. By contrast, instruction designed for use in asynchronous cultures should allow for the learners' (and clients') preferences for circularity and tolerance for internal schedules.

Technological changes have made adaptations to these cultural differences easier. Many forms of e-learning and other forms of distance education are, by nature, asynchronous. Individuals can choose to start and end on their own schedules. As an alternative, however, they may participate in onsite or online group instruction in which schedules are followed.

What Is New in Sequencing Performance Objectives

What is new in how instructional designers start in sequencing learning experiences? The answer to that question is really the foundation for many different philosophies of instructional design. The chapter has described classic approaches to sequencing. But much experimentation is being conducted in academic and in business settings to sequence instruction in ways consistent with old and new ideas about various structures or organizational schemes (Reigeluth, 1983, 1999, and 2008).

One challenge for instructional designers is that learners are increasingly impatient. They want to access learning the way they can access websites—that is, jump from one topic to another to answer the questions that occur to them as they occur to them. Linear sequencing in training tends to frustrate impatient learners. What they seem to prefer increasingly is akin to random access based on the problems they face.

Conclusion

In this chapter, we described approaches to sequencing objectives. We also offered advice to instructional designers about judging and justifying sequencing decisions and emphasized key ethical and cross-cultural issues in sequencing performance objectives. This chapter was the last of three related chapters on performance objectives. Taken together, they have focused on the steps in the instructional design process that lay the foundation for planned learning experiences. In the next chapter, we turn to specifying instructional strategies—the process of planning learning experiences.

PART FOUR

DELIVERING THE
INSTRUCTION EFFECTIVELY

CHAPTER ELEVEN

SPECIFYING INSTRUCTIONAL STRATEGIES

Having written and sequenced performance objectives, instructional designers are ready to plan instruction. They should begin by asking this question: *How can the desired results of instruction be achieved?*

The answer is through instructional strategy. (See Figure 11.1.) While *instructional strategy* sometimes refers to the various methods, techniques, and devices for instructing, the term is used here to mean *strategies for instructing others— that is, how to go about the instructional process*. Methods, techniques, and devices for instructing are described in the next chapter.

In this chapter, we will define instructional strategy. We will also distinguish between two kinds of strategy (*macro-instructional* and *micro-instructional* strategy) and between instructional strategy and instructional tactics. In addition, we will describe how to conceptualize instructional strategy, choose strategy and tactics, choose media and delivery methods, and judge and justify strategy once chosen. We also provide an overview of cognitive strategy. Finally, we will identify ethical and cross-cultural issues in specifying instructional strategies.

According to *The Standards* (Richey, Fields, and Foxon, 2001, p. 51), one competency for instructional design is to "select and use a variety of techniques to define and sequence the instructional content and strategies." It is regarded as an essential competency. The performance statements associated with this competency indicate that instructional designers should be able to (Richey, Fields, and Foxon, 2001, p. 51):

a. Use appropriate techniques to identify the conditions that determine the scope of the instructional content (essential).

FIGURE 11.1. A MODEL OF STEPS IN THE INSTRUCTIONAL DESIGN PROCESS.

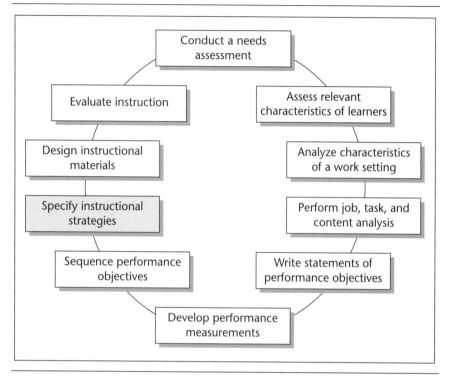

b. Use appropriate techniques to specify and sequence instructional goals and objectives (essential).

c. Select appropriate media and delivery systems (essential).

d. Analyze the learning outcomes and select appropriate strategies (essential).

e. Analyze the instructional context and select appropriate strategies (essential).

f. Select appropriate participation and motivational strategies (essential).

g. Select and sequence assessment techniques (essential).

h. Prepare a design document and circulate for review and approval (essential).

Great care should be taken in selecting the media–that is, the approach used to deliver instruction (Taylor, 2002). While much attention has focused on using e-learning and blended learning in recent years, there is still room for less technologically dependent methods (Barbian, 2002b).

Defining Instructional Strategy

In the most general sense, an instructional strategy is perhaps best understood as an overall plan governing instructional content (What will be taught?) and process (How will it be taught?). Any strategy consists of "decisions that result in a plan, method, or series of activities aimed at obtaining a specific goal. This definition is derived from its historical use as a term that represents an overall plan, for instance, to win a game" (Jonassen, Grabinger, and Harris, 1990, p. 31)—or to gain competitive advantage over business rivals (Rothwell and Kazanas, 1994a, 2003).

An instructional strategy is no different. It is a plan for systematically exposing learners to experiences that will help them acquire verbal information, establish cognitive strategy, or develop intellectual skills, motor skills, or new attitudes. Instructional strategy should grow out of an analysis of the work tasks that learners are being instructed to perform and from the corresponding performance objectives established to achieve those desired results. An instructional strategy is also "a translation of a philosophical or theoretical position regarding instruction into a statement of the way in which instruction should be carried out in specific circumstances" (Romiszowski, 1981, p. 292).

An instructional strategy is thus "like a blueprint; it shows what must be done" to achieve the desired outcomes of instruction (Jonassen, Grabinger, and Harris, 1990, p. 32). Once an instructional strategy has been decided on, it becomes "a product that can be used (1) as a prescription to develop instructional materials, (2) as a set of criteria to evaluate existing materials, (3) as a set of criteria and a prescription to revise existing materials, or (4) as a framework from which class lecture notes, interactive group exercises, and homework assignments can be planned" (Dick and Carey, 1990, pp. 175–176). Instructional strategy should usually be described in writing, although not in the detail typical of final instructional materials comprising a module, unit, or lesson. It should be prepared before instructional materials are designed or selected from other sources.

The aim of establishing an instructional strategy is, quite simply, to plan holistically. It helps instructional designers conceptualize, before they begin time-consuming and expensive preparation or selection of instructional materials, what must be done to facilitate learning. In the process of planning instructional strategy, instructional designers should take care to match the method with the objectives. They should also avoid the tendency—too often evident—to seize on using emerging instructional technologies for their own sake (Piskurich, 1993). Discussions in recent years have focused around the need to ensure *interactivity*, variously defined (see Haseman, Nuipolatoglu, and Ramamurthy, 2002), when using e-learning. Of greatest interest at the moment is so-called *blended learning*, which makes use of several media in a "blend." But ensuring that blend calls for skill in using each medium.

Distinguishing Between Two Kinds of Instructional Strategy

There are two kinds of instructional strategy. A *macro-instructional* strategy is, on the one hand, an overall plan governing a discrete learning experience, such as a course or module. It is the way instructional designers plan to help learners achieve terminal performance objectives. Think of it as a big-picture road map for an entire planned learning experience, akin to a syllabus for a college course. On the other hand, a *micro-instructional strategy* is a specific plan governing each part of the learning experience, such as a unit or lesson within a course or module. It is the way instructional designers plan to help learners achieve enabling objectives. An example would be an outline for one planned learning experience or course session. Macro-instructional strategy should typically be specified first.

Distinguishing Between Instructional Strategy and Instructional Tactics

An *instructional tactic* is related to, but more specific than, an instructional strategy. It is any instructional activity undertaken to facilitate a strategy. All grand instructional strategies are enacted through simple instructional tactics, just as any long-term strategy for winning a game is realized through many short-term plays or activities.

Conceptualizing Instructional Strategy

There are two ways to think about instructional strategy. The first stems from the philosophy of the instructional designer about learning and instructing; the second stems from events of instruction and conditions of learning. Each way provides some guidance when instructional designers find it necessary to identify the range of available instructional strategies.

Instructional Strategy Based on Philosophy of Learning and Instructing

Instructional designers have fought contentious battles, stemming from contrasting philosophical views, about the nature of learning and instructing. Two theoretical positions about learning and instructing seem to represent major anchor points on a philosophical continuum of instructional strategies, according to a classic description by Romiszowski (1981). Some instructional designers believe that all learning can be described best as resulting from a process of *reception*. This view leads to expositive instructional strategies. But other instructional designers believe that all learning is best described as resulting from a process of learner *discovery*. This view leads to experiential instructional strategies (Romiszowski, 1981).

To the behaviorist adherents of *reception learning*, learning centers around the communication process. Learning occurs through exposure to environmental variables outside the learner; instructing is a process of manipulating those variables to achieve predetermined ends. Learning occurs as people receive, understand, apply, and act on information directed to them by others. Learners are thus passive recipients of instructional messages, instructors or instructional designers are active transmitters of those messages, and instruction itself is synonymous with the message. When instructional designers believe that learning occurs through this communication process, they select an *expositive* instructional strategy (Romiszowski, 1981). Most traditional educators favor this approach. It is a four-step process in which the instructor should (1) present information to (passive) learners, (2) test learners on their recall or understanding of the message, (3) present opportunities for learners to practice or apply the message, and (4) present opportunities for learners to generalize what they have learned to real situations or problems (Romiszowski, 1981, p. 293).

At the other anchor point on the continuum is a different philosophy about learning and instructing. To adherents of *discovery learning*, learning is intensely personal. Set in the intimate mental world of the learner, it results not so much from manipulation of environmental variables outside the learner as from the learner's own internalized insight, reflection, and experience. When instructional designers believe that learning occurs through this experience-oriented process, they favor a discovery strategy for instruction. It is a four-step process in which the instructional designer will (1) structure opportunities for learners to receive important experiences and observe or reflect on them, (2) question the learners about the experiences and observe learner reactions, (3) help learners think about the general principles and significant emotional experiences they have experienced, and (4) structure opportunities for learners to apply what they have learned to actual situations and problems (Romiszowski, 1981, p. 294).

While expositive and discovery instructional strategies constitute more or less opposite anchor points on a continuum, there are many points in between. Instructional designers are thus free to select from numerous methods that are appropriate to achieve the desired outcomes of an instructional experience. Romiszowski's summary of these methods is given next (p. 180).

Strategy	*Description*
Impromptu discovery	Unplanned learning: no instruction was involved directly (for example, free use of a library or resource center).
Free exploratory discovery	Broad learning goals are fixed; otherwise the learner is free to choose how to achieve the desired outcomes.
Guided discovery	Objectives are fixed; the learner is guided as to appropriate methods, conclusion.
Adaptively programmed discovery	Guidance and feedback are given individually.
Intrinsically programmed discovery	Guidance and feedback are given according to a preplanned program, based on the "typical" student.
Inductive exposition	The trainer "talks through" the discovery process.
Deductive exposition	Lectures.
Drill and practice	Rote reception learning: instruction demonstrates what to do and provides practice. No conceptual understanding needs to be involved.

Other strategies have also been described by Clark (2003).

In recent years, much attention has focused around another form of instructional strategy called *action learning*, which may also be an approach to carrying out the instructional design process itself (Rothwell, 1999). When action learning is used, learners are given a real-world problem, assembled in teams to solve it, and are permitted the freedom to experiment to find solutions.

Instructional Strategy Based on Events of Instruction

Another way to think of instructional strategy is based on the events of instruction and the conditions of learning, not on the philosophy of the instructional designer. In this sense, instructional strategy is rooted in assumptions about what does—or should—happen during any planned learning experience and about what type of learning the instruction is intended to facilitate. In other words, different instructional strategies are required to help learners acquire verbal information, establish cognitive strategy, develop intellectual skills, build motor skills, or appreciate new attitudes (Gagné and Briggs, 1979).

To select instructional strategy, then, instructional designers start by examining performance objectives in order to determine what type of learning is to be facilitated. They should choose instructional strategy based on the type of learning. For example, if learners are to acquire verbal information, it will be necessary to discover a way to make that information meaningful to them. The instructional designer may adopt a strategy of fitting isolated information, like definitions, into some pattern, such as rhymes, mnemonics, or acronyms, that will be meaningful to learners and will improve their retention. If learners are to be aided in establishing a cognitive strategy or in changing their attitudes, they should be led through a process of discovery using the discovery strategies listed earlier. If learners are to develop intellectual or motor skills, expositive strategies are often appropriate.

Once the overall instructional strategy has been selected, instructional designers should focus attention on each event of instruction. "The events of instruction," note Gagné and Briggs (1979, p. 155) in a classic description, "are designed to make it possible for learners to proceed from 'where they are' to the achievement of the capability identified as the target objective." *Events of instruction* constitute what should be done in a planned learning experience: *instructional strategy*, a closely related notion, constitutes how they will or should be done. To plan instructional strategy for a learning experience, instructional designers begin by identifying each step in a learning experience. Then, bearing in mind the type of learning being planned, they pose the simple question, How can that be done?

Authorities on instructional design have devised many schemes for describing the events of instruction over a year. Pucel (1989), for example, has identified eight key instructional events based on a combination of his own independent research and the research of Ausubel (1962), Chase and Chi (1980), and Herbart (1898). To apply the results of their research, instructional designers should

1. State the performance objectives for the learning experience so as to clarify:
   a. What is to be learned
   b. How the learner can demonstrate the desired performance
   c. How performance will be judged

2. Explain the importance of the learning experience.
3. Provide crucial background information that the learner must have to achieve the performance objectives ("tell" the learner what to do and why).
4. Demonstrate the behavior ("show" the learner).
5. Guide practice (ask the learner to "do" it or apply it).
6. Allow for unguided practice (ask the learner to "do" it or apply it without benefit of extensive instructor feedback).
7. Evaluate the learner's performance and knowledge base ("follow up" with the learner).
8. Provide feedback and direction for future learning.

Possibly more widely known than these eight steps are the nine key instructional events identified in a classic treatment by Gagné and Briggs (1979) and summarized here:

1. Capture the attention of the learner.
2. Describe to learners what performance objectives are to be achieved.
3. Help learners recall prerequisite learning.
4. Present instruction to facilitate the learners' achievement of the performance objectives.
5. Guide the learners through the material so they begin to meet the objectives.
6. Prompt the performance desired from the instruction so learners meet the objectives.
7. Give the learners feedback, and make suggestions for improvement as appropriate, so learners sense how well they are beginning to meet the objectives.
8. Evaluate how well learners are beginning to achieve the objectives.
9. Work toward helping the learners retain what they have learned and apply it.

The appropriate instructional strategy for each event depends on the desired results. Hence, types of instruction aimed at helping learners acquire verbal information, establish cognitive strategy, or develop intellectual skills, motor skills, or new attitudes will require its own appropriate strategy within the planned learning experience. Those strategies are summarized in Table 11.1.

Choosing Instructional Strategy and Tactics

For instruction to be effective, instructional designers should be able to choose among many instructional strategies and tactics.

Choosing an Appropriate Instructional Strategy

Although authorities on reception and discovery learning have usually been interpreted as favoring a single instructional strategy for every learning situation, there really is no one universally appropriate strategy. For the most part, the authorities have been misinterpreted (Romiszowski, 1981). Any instructional strategy can actually be used to achieve any performance objective. Likewise, any instructional strategy can be used to carry out any instructional event. However, no one instructional strategy works uniformly well under all conditions. To choose the appropriate strategy, consider the learners, the desired learning outcomes, the learning and working environments, and constraints on the instructional design process.

If learners are inexperienced, instruction based on an expositive strategy is usually the most efficient approach. Exposition leads learners through a subject at a uniform rate, with the pace set more by the instructor than by the learner. On the other hand, learners who are already experienced will often rebel against an expositive strategy (Knowles, 1984). They often prefer a process of discovery that makes full use of their own experiences and allows them to become involved in, and committed to, learning.

The desired learning outcomes should also influence choice of instructional strategy. For example, learners should not be asked to acquire verbal information in precisely the same way that they are led to develop a cognitive strategy, intellectual skills, motor skills, or new attitudes (Gagné and Briggs, 1979). Learning experiences are of different kinds, and a different instructional strategy is appropriate for each kind.

The learning and working environments also influence the appropriate choice of instructional strategy. If the two environments are the same, as is the case with on-the-job training, an expositive strategy is usually most efficient; however, if they differ, a discovery strategy usually works best. Generally, the closer the relationship between conditions in the learning and working environments, the greater the likelihood that learners will be able to apply on the job what they learn during instruction (Baldwin and Ford, 1988).

Finally, constraints on the instructional design process should also be considered during selection of strategy. Of primary consideration are time and control factors. A discovery strategy simply requires more delivery than an expositive strategy. Learners must be led to reach their own discoveries. That takes time, since individuals learn at different rates. However, greater control is possible with an expositive strategy in which the instructor transmits the same information to all learners. There may be differences in how that information is received and interpreted. But an expositive strategy usually leads to greater

TABLE 11.1. INSTRUCTIONAL EVENTS AND THE CONDITIONS OF LEARNING THEY IMPLY FOR FIVE TYPES OF LEARNED CAPABILITIES.

Event	Capability		
	Intellectual Skill	Cognitive Strategy	Information
1. Capture the attention of the learner	Introduce a change in stimulus		
2. Describe to learners what performance objectives are to be achieved	Describe the performance to be achieved and give an example	Inform learners of the kind of solution that is expected	Describe what question is to be answered
3. Help learners recall prerequisite learning	Encourage learners to recall subordinate concepts and rules	Encourage learners to recall related strategies and intellectual skills	Encourage learners to recall the context of the information
4. Present instruction to facilitate the learners' achievement of performance objectives	Give examples of concepts or rules to be learned	Give unique problems to be solved	Give the information in the form of propositions
5. Guide the learners through the material so they begin to meet the objectives	Give cues to the learners	Hint at solutions	Link to a broader context
6. Prompt the performance	Have the learners apply the performance	Request solutions	Have the learners provide information or other examples
7. Give feedback to the learners	Affirm that the rule or concept has been applied correctly	Affirm that the solution to the problem is correct	Affirm that information has been stated correctly
8. Evaluate how well the learners are beginning to achieve the objectives	Learner demonstrates application of concept or rule	Learner originates a novel solution	Learner restates information in paraphrased form
9. Work toward helping the learners retain what they have learned and apply it	Review the material periodically with learners, giving them various examples	Give the learners opportunities to grapple with different solutions	Link the material to other information

TABLE 11.1. INSTRUCTIONAL EVENTS AND THE CONDITIONS OF LEARNING THEY IMPLY FOR FIVE TYPES OF LEARNED CAPABILITIES, cont'd.

Event	Capability	
	Attitude	*Motor Skill*
1. Capture the attention of the learner	Introduce a change in stimulus	
2. Describe to learners what performance objectives are to be achieved	Give an example of what action is called for	Demonstrate the expected performance
3. Help learners recall prerequisite learning	Encourage learners to recall information and other relevant skills	Help learners remember what to do
4. Present instruction to facilitate the learners' achievement of performance objectives	Give learners a choice in their actions	Give learners what they need to perform—such as appropriate tools, equipment, or other resources
5. Guide the learners through the material so they begin to meet the objectives	Give learners the opportunity to observe the model or choice of what to do	Give learners the chance to practice and the chance to receive feedback about their performance
6. Prompt the performance	Have the learners describe what they would do in real or simulated situations	Have the learners demonstrate performance
7. Give feedback to the learners	Give the learners reinforcement based on their choice	Give learners feedback on what they chose
8. Evaluate how well the learners are beginning to achieve the objectives	Learners choose the desired course of action as appropriate	Learners are capable of demonstrating the skill/ performance
9. Work toward helping the learners retain what they have learned and apply it	Give learners new opportunities to choose the desired course of action	Encourage learners to practice

Source: Adapted from the classic work of Gagné, R., Briggs, L., and Wager, W. *Principles of Instructional Design* (4th ed.). Fort Worth, TX: Harcourt Brace, 1992.

control over outcomes than a discovery strategy in which learners reach their own independent conclusions about their experiences.

Choosing Appropriate Instructional Tactics

Tactics are the ways instructional strategies are implemented. They are the detailed approaches and activities used by an instructional designer to accomplish a strategy. In this respect, they bear the same relationship to instructional strategy as daily operational tactics bear to corporate strategy. Just as a corporate strategy of growth is achieved through such tactics as increasing sales, decreasing expenses, increasing market share, or a combination of all these, so too can instructional strategies of reception or discovery learning be achieved through various methods (tactics).

The choice of instructional tactics has often been more art than science. Instructional designers should first identify the results they wish to achieve through instruction and then plot out how they will achieve those results. The process of choosing tactics has usually been left to instructional designers' creativity and imagination, whether they are working as individuals or on a team. Through systematic study of the events of instruction and writings about them, Jonassen, Grabinger, and Harris (1990, pp. 34–38) have identified five key instructional strategies and a range of instructional tactics for each strategy. Their classic research results are presented in Table 11.2. (Note that the list can be used effectively as a laundry list of tactics.)

Choosing Media and Delivery Methods

The variety of available media and delivery methods may present unique challenges to instructional designers. The choice should be made carefully and be based on the medium used.

According to *The Standards* (Richey, Fields, and Foxon, 2001, p. 50), one competency for instructional design is to "analyze the characteristics of existing and emerging technologies and their use in an instructional environment." It is regarded as an essential competency. The performance statements associated with this competency indicate that instructional designers should be able to (Richey, Fields, and Foxon, 2001, p. 50):

a. Specify the capabilities of existing and emerging technologies to enhance motivation, visualization, interaction, simulation, and individualization (essential).

TABLE 11.2. INSTRUCTIONAL STRATEGIES AND TACTICS.

1. Contextualizing instruction[a]

  1.1 Gaining the attention of the learner

      1.1.1 arouse learner with novelty, uncertainty, surprise
      1.1.2 pose question to learner
      1.1.3 learner poses question to be answered by lesson

  1.2 Relate the goals of instruction to the learner's needs

      1.2.1 explain purpose or relevance of content
      1.2.2 present goals for learners to select
      1.2.3 ask learners to select own goals
      1.2.4 have learner pose questions to answer

  1.3 State the outcomes of instruction

      1.3.1 describe required performance
      1.3.2 describe criteria for standard performance
      1.3.3 learner establishes criteria for standard performance

  1.4 Present advance organizers

      1.4.1 verbal expository: establish context for content
      1.4.2 verbal comparative: relate to content familiar to learner
      1.4.3 oral expository: establish context for instruction
      1.4.4 oral comparative: relate to content familiar to learner
      1.4.5 pictorial: show maps, globes, pictures, tables

  1.5 Present structured overviews and organizers

      1.5.1 outlines of content: verbal (see also 1.4.1, 1.4.2)
      1.5.2 outlines of content: oral (see also 1.4.3, 1.4.4)
      1.5.3 graphic organizers/overviews
      1.5.4 combinations of verbal, oral, and pictorial overviews

  1.6 Adapt context of instruction

      1.6.1 content adapted to learner preferences (different situations)
      1.6.2 content adapted to prior knowledge

2. Present and cue lesson content

  2.1 Vary lesson unit size

      2.1.1 large chunks
      2.1.2 small chunks

  2.2 Present vocabulary

      2.2.1 present new terms plus definitions
      2.2.2 student looks up list of new terms
      2.2.3 present attributes of rule, definition, concept, principle
      2.2.4 paraphrase definitions, present synonyms
      2.2.5 present definitions
      2.2.6 derive definitions from synonym list

[a]Key steps of instruction are in bold print; tactics are underlined.

TABLE 11.2. INSTRUCTIONAL STRATEGIES AND TACTICS, cont'd.

2.3   Provide examples

      2.3.1   prototypical examples
      2.3.2   matched example/non-example pairs
      2.3.3   divergent examples
      2.3.4   close-in non-examples
      2.3.5   vary the number of examples
      2.3.6   model appropriate behavior

2.4   Use cuing systems

      2.4.1   provide graphic cues: lines, colors, boxes, arrows, highlighting
      2.4.2   provide oral cues: oral direction
      2.4.3   provide auditory cues: stimulus change (e.g., music, sound effects, voice change)
      2.4.4   provide type style cues: font changes, uppercase, type size, headings, hierarchical numbering system, indentation
      2.4.5   present special information in windows

2.5   Advise learner

      2.5.1   instructional support needed: number of examples, number of practice items, tools, materials, resources
      2.5.2   learning strategies to use

3.   Activating learner processing of instruction

3.1   Elicit learner activities

      3.1.1   review prerequisite skills or knowledge
      3.1.2   learner selects information sources
      3.1.3   learner selects study methods
      3.1.4   learner estimates task difficulty and time
      3.1.5   learner monitors comprehension
      3.1.6   learner relates questions to objectives
      3.1.7   learner recalls elaborations
      3.1.8   learner evaluates meaningfulness of information

3.2   Elicit recall strategies

      3.2.1   underline relevant material
      3.2.2   rehearse/repeat/re-read
      3.2.3   use mnemonic strategies
      3.2.4   close reading activities
      3.2.5   identification with location (loci method)
      3.2.6   create summaries: hierarchical titles
      3.2.7   create summaries: prose
      3.2.8   create summaries: diagrammatic/symbolic (math)
      3.2.9   create summaries: mind maps

3.3   Facilitate learner elaborations

      3.3.1   imaging (creating images)
      3.3.2   inferring from information
      3.3.3   generating analogies
      3.3.4   creating story lines: narrative description of information

TABLE 11.2. INSTRUCTIONAL STRATEGIES AND TACTICS, cont'd.

3.4   Help learners integrate new knowledge

    3.4.1   paraphrase content
    3.4.2   use metaphors and learner-generated metaphors
    3.4.3   generating examples
    3.4.4   note-taking

3.5   Help learners organize information

    3.5.1   analysis of key ideas
    3.5.2   create content outline
    3.5.3   categorize elements
    3.5.4   pattern note techniques
    3.5.5   construct concept map
    3.5.6   construct graphic organizers

4.   **Assessing learning**

4.1   Provide feedback after practice

    4.1.1   confirmatory, knowledge of correct response
    4.1.2   corrective and remedial
    4.1.3   informative feedback
    4.1.4   analytical feedback
    4.1.5   enrichment feedback
    4.1.6   self-generated feedback

4.2   Provide practice

    4.2.1   massed practice session
    4.2.2   distributed practice session
    4.2.3   over-learning
    4.2.4   apply in real world or simulated situation (near transfer)
    4.2.5   change context or circumstances (far transfer)
    4.2.6   vary the number of practice items

4.3   Testing learning

    4.3.1   pretest for prior knowledge
    4.3.2   pretest for prerequisite knowledge or skills
    4.3.3   pretest for endpoint knowledge or skills
    4.3.4   embedded questions throughout instruction
    4.3.5   objective referenced performance
    4.3.6   normative referenced performance
    4.3.7   incidental information, not objective referenced

5.   **Sequencing instructional events**

5.1   Sequence instruction in logical order

    5.1.1   deductive sequence
    5.1.2   inductive sequence
    5.1.3   inductive sequence with practice

TABLE 11.2. INSTRUCTIONAL STRATEGIES AND TACTICS, cont'd.

5.2 Sequence instruction in learning prerequisite order

    5.2.1 hierarchical, prerequisite sequence
    5.2.2 easy-to-difficult
    5.2.3 concrete-to-abstract

5.3 Sequence instruction in procedural order

    5.3.1 procedural, job sequence
    5.3.2 information processing sequence (path sequencing)
    5.3.3 algorithmic presentation
    5.3.4 procedural elaboration

5.4 Sequence instruction according to content organization

    5.4.1 general-to-detailed (progressive differentiation)
    5.4.2 conceptual elaboration
    5.4.3 theoretical elaboration

5.5 Sequence instruction according to story structure

    5.5.1 narrative sequence

Source: Jonassen, D., Grabinger, S., and Harris, N. "Analyzing and Selecting Instructional Strategies and Tactics." *Performance Improvement Quarterly*, 1990, *3*(2), 34–38. Reprinted with permission of the International Society for Performance Improvement.

    b. Evaluate the capacity of a given infrastructure to support selected technologies (advanced).
    c. Assess the benefits of existing and emerging technologies (essential).

Choosing Media

To plan to achieve performance objectives, instructional designers should also choose a medium, or media, after selecting an instructional strategy. The term *medium* just means *the way an instructional message is communicated to the learner.* Although the term *media* has not always been used consistently by instructional designers, examples are easy enough to identify: books, programmed texts, computers, slides or tapes, videotape, and film.

A *media selection* model, sometimes called just a *media model*, is a decision-making aid. It is intended to guide selection of instructional media according to their instructional and cost effectiveness. Many media selection models have been devised to help instructional designers, such as the classics by Reynolds and Anderson (1992). However, it should be noted that "half a century of research on media has yielded little in the way of general guidelines for media selection. That is, we are not able to conclude that one medium or combination of media is more effective overall, or even that one medium works better for a particular type of learning or category of subject matter" (Gagné and Medsker, 1996, p. 181).

The Range of Media

Instructional media range from simple to complex. This distinction can be understood in two ways. First, a medium that does not require much advance preparation can be considered simple, while one requiring much preparation can be considered complex. For example, direct experience—possibly occurring on the job—is simple because it does not require much preparation. Second, a medium that appeals to only one sense can be considered simple; a medium appealing to more than one sense can be considered complex. The fewer the senses to which instruction is designed to appeal, the less need there is to be concerned about the effects on each sense and about how media can appeal to the learners' senses in combination.

The classification scheme below is listed from complex to simple media. The simplest media are placed at the bottom of the media "cone"; more complex media are placed at the top. This scheme is based on a classic list by Kemp (1985).

Media	*Examples*
Combinations of media	Interactive video
	Multi-image and sound computer-based training
	Multi-image/videotape
	Multi-image/audiotape
	Microfiche/audiotape
	Filmstrip/audiotape
	Slides/audiotape
	Print/videotape
	Print/audiotape
Projected motion pictures	Videotape
	Film
Projected still pictures	Computer programs (displayed)
	Overhead transparencies
	Slides
	Filmstrips
Audio recordings	Compact disk recordings
	Audiocassette recordings

Non-projected materials	Job aids
	Photographs
	Diagrams
	Charts
	Graphs
	Flip chart
	Chalkboard
	Print materials
Tangible objects	Models
	Objects/devices/equipment
	Instructors/speakers

Additional schemes for categorizing media are found in Piskurich and Sanders (1998). They distinguish among instructional methods, presentation methods, and distribution methods.

How do instructional designers decide just which medium is best to achieve performance objectives? Unfortunately, there is no one right answer to this question. Substantial research has been conducted over the years to determine which media are most appropriate for achieving desired instructional outcomes and supporting instructional strategy. But that research has not led to firm conclusions. (See Marx and Hudson-Samuels, 1999). Any medium can be used to achieve any performance objective. But not all media should be used in precisely the same ways.

Media selection decisions may improve in the future as artificial intelligence and expert systems are applied to the instructional design process. At present, however, the best approach to media selection is to make a primary media selection decision for an entire learning experience first. Then make secondary media selection decisions for each part of the experience. Do that by asking a series of questions and noting the answers.

When making a media selection decision, ask these questions first: What are the desired outcomes of instruction? Do they provide clues about what medium or media to choose? For example, suppose that instruction is being prepared so that learners "will be able to troubleshoot problems with a diesel engine when given diagnostic instruments and a diesel engine." Given that performance objective, what medium is appropriate? In this example, the performance objective itself specifies that the learner will be "given diagnostic instruments and a diesel engine." That phrase suggests that learners will be using tangible objects (as identified in the media classification scheme presented earlier). The objects may, however, range from real to simulated objects. The same principle applies to other performance objectives. Consult them first to determine whether they *imply* the appropriate medium (or media mix) to use during the planned learning experience.

When making a media selection decision, ask this question second: What constraints on time, equipment, staff skills, and costs affect this planned learning experience?

When making a media selection decision, ask this question third: How will the instruction be delivered? While that question cannot be answered until a delivery mode has been chosen (see the next section), instructional designers should bear in mind that some media are more appropriate than others for particular audiences. Overhead transparencies, for example, are frequently used in group presentations but are not very effective by themselves for individualized instruction.

When making a media selection decision, a fourth and final question to ask is this: How often will this planned learning experience have to be revised in the future? Obviously, it does not make much sense to invest large sums in a medium that will be difficult to revise. Yet that can happen to those who opt for video-based programs, when their organizations have no video production facilities. An expensive consultant is hired, the video is prepared and edited, and it is outdated by the time it is shown. Some media—print materials, slide shows, and overhead transparencies—are relatively easy to revise. Other media may not be that easy or inexpensive to revise at this time.

Selecting Delivery Modes

To plan performance objectives, instructional designers should also choose a delivery mode. A *delivery mode* means the choice made about the conditions under which instruction is to be offered. Not to be confused with media or instructional strategy, delivery mode is synonymous with the situation that confronts learners as they learn.

The range of delivery modes is not great. There are only four basic choices, according to a classic discussion of this issue (Ellington, 1985):

1. *Mass instruction* involving many learners.
2. *Group instruction* involving fewer learners.
3. *Individualized instruction* involving only one learner at a time.
4. *Direct experience* involving real-time learning, such as informal on-the-job training.

Make a selection of delivery mode based on the performance objectives to be achieved. (See Figure 11.2.) If many people share the same instructional need, select mass instruction. It is appropriate, for instance, when everyone in the same organization should receive the same instruction. If only some people, such as employees in one work unit, require instruction, select group instruction. It is often appropriate for introducing new work methods or new technology. If only one person experiences an instructional need, select individualized instruction. If the need is a minor one—not really enough of a "chunk" of information to warrant preparation of a planned learning experience—then rely on such direct experiential methods as supervisory coaching or on-the-job training to supply learners with what they need to perform competently (Rothwell and Kazanas, 1994b; Rothwell and Kazanas, in press).

Once the delivery mode for the entire learning experience has been selected on the basis of terminal performance objectives, reconsider media selection for each enabling objective (Ellington, 1985).

Allowing for Constraints on Choice of Delivery Mode

Instructional designers rarely enjoy complete freedom to choose whatever delivery mode they wish. They face the same constraints when choosing delivery mode that they face when choosing media. Limitations of time, equipment, staff skills, and costs can and often do affect choice of delivery mode. In addition, managers—and sometimes the learners themselves—will make their preferences about delivery modes known. For instance, middle managers in some organizational cultures dislike mass instruction delivered during working hours because it removes workers from the production process and results in too much lost production time. They may require that mass instruction be delivered after hours or on weekends, thus reducing the chances that all workers can participate in it. Likewise, some learners prefer individualized instruction because they have a storehouse of unpleasant memories from their formal schooling about classroom learning situations. When choosing delivery mode, then, be sure to consider *constraints* and *management and worker preferences*.

Appreciating the Learner's Perspective: A Brief Overview of Cognitive Strategies

Just as much attention should be devoted to appreciating the learner's perspective as the instructional designer's perspective. Savvy instructional designers will thus think about cognitive strategies for learners that will encourage their information processing. "Cognitive strategies," write Gagné and Medsker

FIGURE 11.2. ALGORITHM FOR SELECTION OF INSTRUCTIONAL MODE.

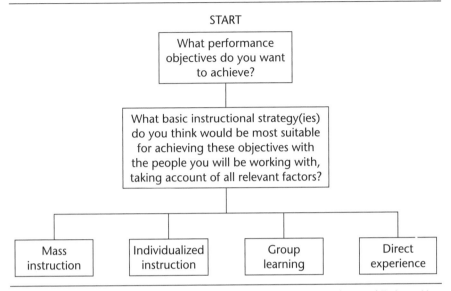

Source: Ellington, H. *Producing Teaching Materials: A Handbook for Teachers and Trainers.* New York: Nichols, 1985, p. 28. Used by permission of the publisher.

(1996, p. 72), "are the learned capabilities that enable us to manage our own thinking and learning processes."

While this book focuses primarily on what instructional designers do, it is important for readers to remember that cognitive strategies regulate how learning progresses. Individuals acquire cognitive strategies from their experience and schooling. While various taxonomies have been suggested to describe cognitive strategies (see, for instance, West, Farmer, and Wolff, 1991), Gagné and Medsker (1996) have skillfully described how to encourage the conditions of learning for training. One way to view cognitive strategy is through the lens of the open systems model (described in Chapter One), which includes input cognitive strategies, process cognitive strategies, output cognitive strategies, and feedback cognitive strategies.

Input Cognitive Strategies

An *input cognitive strategy* depends on what learners choose to pay attention to. Learners may be stimulated to pay attention by events external to them, by their own choice, or by a combination. An example of external stimulation might include job loss, which would create a significant emotional event for learners that would stimulate their learning on the job search. An example of internal stimulation might include remembrance of career goals, which could motivate individuals to seek out new approaches to meeting those goals.

Process Cognitive Strategies

A *process cognitive strategy* helps learners make sense of what they learn. Gagné and Medsker (1996, p. 75) list several:

- *Rehearsal*: trying out something new.
- *Elaboration*: associating something new with something previously learned.
- *Organization*: imposing a structure on what is newly learned through such methods as outlining, categorizing, or diagramming.

Output Cognitive Strategies

An *output cognitive strategy* means that learners acquire new knowledge or skill by applying what they have learned and making meaning of their experiences. An example would be asking learners to prepare instruction on something they would like to learn. The teaching (output) focuses the learners' attention on organizing the new knowledge or skill to teach it to others. That is an output-oriented cognitive strategy. Individuals could use the same approach to make sense of what they want to learn.

Feedback Cognitive Strategies

A *feedback cognitive strategy* means that learners acquire new knowledge or skill by giving feedback to others. An example would be asking learners to hear a speech and provide feedback to another person about that speech. The process of giving feedback focuses the learners' attention on organizing the new knowledge or skill to provide feedback to others. That is a feedback-oriented cognitive strategy. For more information on cognitive strategy—this discussion has been quite limited—see, as a starting point, Clark (1992; 2003).

Judging Instructional Strategy

Instructional designers should be capable of judging instructional strategies specified by themselves and their colleagues. Instructional designers can thus evaluate how appropriate the strategy is. Instructional designers may find it useful to rely on a worksheet, like that shown in Exhibit 11.1, when they are called on to judge a specified instructional strategy. Every time an answer of *no* must be given, the instructional designer should reexamine the instructional strategy.

Justifying Instructional Strategy

Instructional designers should be capable of justifying the instructional strategy they have chosen. As in most instructional design activities, they are held accountable by other stakeholders for what they do. Instructional designers should thus be prepared to answer questions such as the following:

1. Why was an instructional strategy chosen?
2. What assumptions guided the choice of strategy? More specifically, what did instructional designers assume about the nature of learning and instruction?
3. Who should care about the instructional strategy?
4. Why should stakeholders care about the instructional strategy?

Acting Ethically in Specifying Instructional Strategies

A key ethical issue in specifying instructional strategies can be expressed by this question: *Has as much emphasis in the instructional design process been placed on cognitive strategies as on instructional strategies?* A danger exists in placing too much emphasis on instructional strategies. Doing that may diminish the learner's role and lead to an overemphasis on glitzy technology rather than on the results. Instructional designers who act ethically will pay as much attention to learners as to instructors and as much attention to how learners can be helped to learn as to instructional strategies. The two issues are very much related.

Instructional designers are sometimes faced with clients who know what they want. However, their choices are problematic. It thus falls to designers to show them a better way—and the cost-benefit tradeoffs involved—of various instructional strategies.

In Rothwell's 2003 survey, conducted in preparation of the third edition of this book, respondents pointed to several ethical issues that come up when specifying instructional strategies. In the words of one, "Who do you believe *[about what media would be best to choose or combine]?*" A second respondent pointed to a classic dilemmas of reconciling [*what the*] "customer wants and what is good for [*the*] learner." A third respondent, commenting on the quality of the training staff in his or her organization, noted that "most people involved in training

EXHIBIT 11.1. A WORKSHEET FOR JUDGING THE APPROPRIATENESS OF A SPECIFIED INSTRUCTIONAL STRATEGY.

Directions: Use this worksheet to judge the appropriateness of an instructional strategy specified by yourself or other instructional designers.

First complete Part I to ensure that you have everything you need to judge the instructional strategy. For each question in the left column, place a check (✓) in the center column to indicate an answer. If you are missing something, make notes to yourself in the right column.

Second, complete Part II to judge the appropriateness of the instructional strategy that has been selected. For each question appearing in the left column below, place a check (✓) in the center column. You should be able to answer each question with a yes. If you must answer no to any item, (1) review the choice of instructional strategy in light of that answer, and (2) be ready to furnish justification for it.

Make copies of this worksheet as necessary.

Part I. Conditions

Question	Response			Notes for Revision
	Yes	No	N/A	
Do you have available a description of . . .	(✓)	(✓)	(✓)	
1. Learner characteristics?	( )	( )	( )	
2. Setting resources/constraints?	( )	( )	( )	
3. Desired learning outcomes in a sequence of instruction?	( )	( )	( )	

Part II. Judging the Appropriateness of a Specified Instructional Strategy

Question	Response			Notes for Revision
	Yes	No	N/A	
In judging the appropriateness of a specified instructional strategy, do you find evidence that each of the following issues has been considered during the process of specifying instructional strategy?	(✓)	(✓)	(✓)	
4. The instructional strategy based on the instructional designer's philosophical views of learning and instructing?	( )	( )	( )	
5. The instructional strategy based on conditions of learning?	( )	( )	( )	

EXHIBIT 11.1. A WORKSHEET FOR JUDGING THE APPROPRIATENESS OF A SPECIFIED INSTRUCTIONAL STRATEGY, cont'd.

6. The instructional strategy based on events of instruction?	( )	( )	( )
7. Appropriate media for the planned learning experience?	( )	( )	( )
8. Appropriate delivery mode for the planned learning experience?	( )	( )	( )
9. Other issues as necessary?	( )	( )	( )

here don't know [*to do*] this." Many instructional designers are thus relying on intuitive more than analytical approaches to selecting media.

Applying Cross-Cultural Awareness to Specifying Instructional Strategies

In a classic and well-known treatment, cross-cultural researcher Geert Hofstede (1991) has distinguished among cultures by describing four variables that are worth considering when specifying instructional strategies. Each variable in a culture may be ranked as "low" or "high." The four variables are

- *Power distance*, which refers to how much the less influential members of society accept power inequality.
- *Task orientation*, which refers to how much success and achievement are valued in the culture over relationships, caring for others, and the general quality of life.
- *Individualism*, which refers to the relative importance of the individual's role compared to the role of a group or family.
- *Uncertainty avoidance*, which refers to how much people feel threatened and unsettled by uncertainty, ambiguity, and the unknown.

Cultures characterized by low power distance minimize inequality; cultures characterized by high power distance are accepting of inequalities. In low power distance cultures, individuals have equal rights and change occurs by revolution; in high power distance cultures, power holders enjoy privileges denied to the common people. Cultures with a low task orientation work to achieve consensus among people. In contrast, cultures with a high task orientation focus around work, which becomes a central driving force in people's lives. Cultures characterized by low individualism seek togetherness, and relationships are valued more than tasks or achievements. Cultures characterized by high individualism are more self-oriented, with greater emphasis placed on individual consciousness and personal opinions. Finally, cultures characterized by low uncertainty avoidance are relaxed. In those settings emotions are hidden, hard work is not especially valued, dissent is accepted, and individuals are willing to take risks. Cultures characterized by high uncertainty avoidance are stressful. Individuals are driven to achievement, displays of emotion are accepted, conflict is viewed as threatening, and laws and rules predominate over individual and group sanctions.

Hofstede's four variables provide touchstones against which to consider the cross-cultural implications of instructional strategies. To cite one example, Sylvia Odenwald (1993, p. 54) notes that cultural differences "provide significant clues for the designer/trainer. Countries with high-power distance maximize individual status and are more comfortable with a known, well-laid-out approach using a more formal teacher-learner relationship. The low-power distance countries minimize individual status and encourage experimenting as a way of learning."

Odenwald offers six specific recommendations for cross-cultural instructional design. Instructional designers should (Odenwald, 1993, pp. 50–51): (1) "provide opportunities for the trainees to apply the material to their own cultural situation"; (2) "be empathetic to feedback from trainees" because that helps make course corrections to allow for cultural differences; (3) "look for opportunities to take advantage of cultural differences" when the trainer is from a culture different from that of the learners; (4) "be sensitive to a culture's methods of learning and working" because they will impact the success of the planned learning experience dramatically; (5) "learn about the local region and its technology" because the educational levels, experience base, and other variables about the learners will affect instruction; and (6) "most important, remember that, as an outsider, the trainer will never fully understand the communication styles, methods, constraints, and assets of the culture." A cultural informant can help. So, too, can the technique of establishing a cultural frame of reference at the outset of instruction by asking learners to present their views on the cultural implications of the training topic.

What Is New in Specifying Instructional Strategies?

Instructional designers continue to have a preoccupation with instructional media—and particularly new, emerging technology or modalities such as iPods, iPhones, wikiss, blogs, and many other novel approaches. Indeed, it seems that many academic and practitioner journals are replete with articles about unique, novel approaches to instructional delivery. Undoubtedly some experienced instructional designers are interested in not a single technology or modality but are curious about novel approaches to blended learning that draw on one or more media and methods to capture the interest of difficult-to-please, free agent learners.

Of course, iPods, iPhones and cell phones provide new modalities or vehicles by which to deliver instruction. These media pose unique challenges, since they are new and because delivery in these formats provide unique challenges to instructional designers. How much information can be packed on a tiny screen? How can learners be kept engaged and motivated when they find themselves amid the distractions of accessing instruction when in meetings, eating, standing in line, sitting in traffic, traveling on an elevator, or engaging in all other aspects of "real life."

A further challenge is that learners who have grown up with the challenge of video games and music videos expect rapid movement through training. Many of them enjoy learning in a game or simulation format, perhaps even with an opportunity to "play to learn" with other participants when online.

Social networking, such as YouTube or MyFace, introduce yet another new element. Instructional designers may be challenged to provide avenues for social networking—and will be faced with the issues of keeping learners focused on solving problems or visioning to leverage strengths rather than become distracted in social interactions with each other. Training cannot turn into a dating scene or a complaint session. Instructional designers are thus challenged to provide some control over those social interactions, although it is impossible to control it completely if participants are really interested in pursuing them.

Conclusion

In this chapter, we defined instructional strategy. We also distinguished between two kinds of strategy (macro-instructional and micro-instructional strategy), between instructional strategy and instructional tactics, and between instructional strategy and learning strategy. We then described how to conceptualize instructional strategy, choose strategy and tactics, and choose media and delivery methods. And we discussed what is important to understand about cognitive strategy. Finally, we emphasized the need to judge and justify strategy once chosen and reviewed important ethical and cross-cultural issues in specifying instructional strategies. In the next chapter, we turn to designing instructional materials.

CHAPTER TWELVE

SELECTING OR DESIGNING INSTRUCTIONAL MATERIALS

All the previous steps in the instructional design process culminate in instructional materials that will help learners achieve desired performance objectives. (See Figure 12.1.) Successful instructional materials share important attributes (McAlpine and Weston, 1994). In this chapter, we focus on selecting, modifying, or designing instructional materials, offer advice to instructional designers about judging and justifying instructional materials they or others have prepared, and identify key ethical and cross-cultural issues in designing instructional materials.

According to *The Standards* (Richey, Fields, and Foxon, 2001, pp. 51–52), one competency for instructional design is to "select or modify existing instructional materials." It is regarded as an essential competency. The performance statements associated with this competency indicate that instructional designers should be able to (Richey, Fields, and Foxon, 2001, pp. 51–52):

a. Identify existing instructional materials for reuse or modification consistent with instructional specifications (essential).
b. Select materials to support the content analyses, proposed technologies, delivery methods, and instructional strategies (essential).
c. Use cost-benefit analysis to decide whether to modify, purchase, or develop instructional materials (advanced).
d. Work with subject-matter experts to validate material selection or modification (essential).

FIGURE 12.1. A MODEL OF STEPS IN THE INSTRUCTIONAL DESIGN PROCESS.

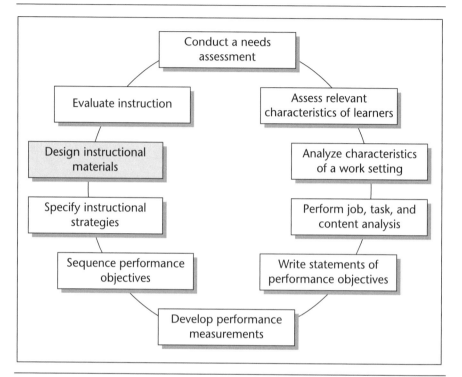

Source: Foshay, W., Silber, K., and Westgaard, O. *Instructional Design Competencies: The Standards.* Iowa City, IA: International Board of Standards for Training, Performance, and Instruction, 1986, p. 3. Copyright 1993 by the International Board of Standards for Training, Performance and Instruction. All rights reserved. Used with permission.

Another relevant competency mentioned in *The Standards* (Richey, Fields, and Foxon, 2001, p. 52) is to "develop instructional materials." It is described in *The Standards* as an essential competency. The performance statements associated with this competency indicate that instructional designers should be able to (Richey, Fields, and Foxon, 2001, p. 52):

a. Develop materials that support the content analyses, proposed technologies, delivery methods, and instructional strategies (essential).
b. Work with subject-matter experts during the development process (essential).
c. Produce instructional materials in a variety of delivery formats (essential).

These competencies and their related performance statements are relevant to the issues addressed in this chapter.

An Overview of Steps in Selecting or Designing Instructional Materials

Instructional designers take several steps to select, modify, or design instructional materials:

1. Preparing a working outline.
2. Conducting research.
3. Examining existing instructional materials.
4. Arranging or modifying existing materials.
5. Preparing tailor-made instructional materials.
6. Selecting or preparing learning activities.

We will describe these steps in the following sections of this chapter. These steps are followed regardless of whether the technology that is applied is print-based or electronically based, even though web-based training may require additional attention to the technology itself (Harris and Castillo, 2002). E-learning may have its own special standards of excellence (Delahoussaye and Zemke, 2001), and online learning may call for special actions to ensure interaction between learners and online facilitators (Kuchinke, Aragon, and Bartlett, 2001).

Step 1: Preparing a Working Outline

Preparing a working outline, sometimes called a syllabus, is the first step in designing instructional materials. A working outline summarizes the contents of the planned learning experience. This outline is based on the instructional strategy and on measurable, sequenced performance objectives that were written previously. An outline is useful because it reminds instructional designers of what they are doing and helps them plan how they will address each objective.

Recall from Chapter Eleven that all planned learning experiences should consist of certain clearly identifiable instructional events. For example, according to Gagné, Briggs, and Wager (1992), instructional designers should

1. Gain the learners' attention for the learning event.
2. Inform learners of the performance objectives to be achieved.
3. Stimulate recall of prerequisite learning so that learners have a frame of reference for addressing performance objectives.
4. Present the stimulus material to help learners achieve the objectives.
5. Provide "learning guidance" with the stimulus material so that learners begin to achieve the performance objectives.

6. Elicit desired performance so that learners achieve the desired performance objectives.

7. Provide feedback so that learners have a sense of how well they are progressing toward achievement of performance objectives—and can make corrections as necessary.

8. Assess learner performance toward achievement of the objectives.

9. Enhance retention and transfer so that learners will remember what they learned and can apply it when necessary.

These classic and still relevant events of instruction are reflected in the working outline. Special attention has been devoted to them for training applications (Gagné and Medsker, 1996).

Step 2: Conducting Research

Conducting research, the second step in designing instructional materials, is carried out to identify materials available inside or outside an organization. Suffice it to say that the cost of developing tailor-made materials is usually formidable. Instructional designers should not waste precious time, staff, and money preparing these materials if they can be obtained from other sources inside or outside the organization. It is possible to estimate the time needed to design and validate tailor-made instruction and to forecast the financial benefits resulting from the effort (Swanson and Gradous, 1988). (See Figure 12.2 for an algorithm to help decide whether to use existing materials.)

Begin research for instructional materials inside an organization by identifying knowledgeable people such as experienced workers, supervisors, union officials, top managers, human resource managers, or trainers. Ask them if they are aware of any unit, department, or division that might have had a past need (perhaps for on-the-job training purposes) for instructional materials like those necessary to meet the performance objectives.

Describing the materials carefully, ask the knowledgeable people three questions:

1. *Have you ever seen any procedure manuals, checklists, descriptive booklets, or training manuals on [subject name]?* By asking this question, instructional designers may uncover instructional materials already available within the organization. These may be suitable for immediate use or may lend themselves to modification. Procedure manuals and checklists are the most common materials used to support on-the-job training (Rothwell and Kazanas, 1994b; 2004). They provide a solid foundation on which to base instruction, particularly if they are current and have already been field-tested. Additionally, they have built-in credibility with operating management, especially if they have been used successfully.

FIGURE 12.2. AN ALGORITHM FOR DECIDING WHETHER TO PRODUCE YOUR OWN INSTRUCTIONAL MATERIALS.

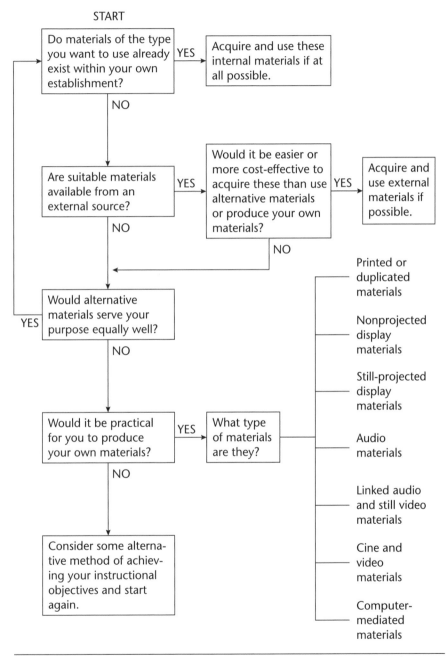

Source: Ellington, H. *Producing Teaching Materials: A Handbook for Teachers and Trainers.* New Jersey: Nichols, 1985, p. 32. Used with permission of the publisher.

261

2. *Who do you know in this organization who is especially knowledgeable about this subject?* Use this question to link up with in-house experts who may be aware of instructional materials already available inside the organization. Focus attention on employees who perform training at the operating level.

3. *What department might have needed, in the past, to do special training on the subject?* This question may help pinpoint the best places to look for materials in the organization. In some organizations, operating managers have authority to purchase their own training materials. Hence, useful instructional materials may be squirreled away somewhere, perhaps gathering dust, and they could be used, updated, or modified to meet other needs in the organization.

Even when instructional materials are not available inside an organization, instructional designers may still be able to transform existing work-related materials into instructional materials with minimal effort.

Begin research for materials outside the organization in a different way. First, network with instructional designers in other organizations. Find them by attending local, regional, and national meetings of organizations frequented by instructional designers.

Contact colleagues through these organizations to determine whether they have previously had occasion to design or select similar instructional materials. Ask to see their materials. Bear in mind, however, that some organizations consider their instructional materials proprietary, so be sure to comply with any organizational protocols that must be observed. If it is not possible to examine materials, then at least ask how they were prepared, focusing on the processes used rather than the products developed. Most instructional designers will share that information, even if they cannot share actual work products. (The favor may have to be reciprocated some day, of course.)

Searching print and computer-based references is another way to find existing instructional materials outside an organization. While few references will lead directly to instructional materials, many books and articles will be useful in sourcing them. In some cases, instructional designers may even be lucky enough to find off-the-shelf instructional materials. Numerous references can be invaluable in conducting such searches. For instance, begin looking for videos on the following websites:

- http://employeeuniversity.com/
- http://www.videotraining.com/
- http://www.trainingabc.com/
- http://trainerstoolkit.com/Merchant2/merchant.mvc
- http://www.search4careercolleges.com/?affiliateid=566

Numerous training materials can also be found for free, or for purchase, through searches on the web. (But note that copyright issues may sometimes be cloudy, so be sure to check with the website owner as to fairness in use of all materials.)

Step 3: Examining Existing Instructional Materials

Evaluating existing instructional materials is the third step in the process of designing instructional materials. When debating whether to use existing instructional materials, be sure they are consistent with the instructional strategy and performance objectives established for the planned learning experience. (Do not expect to use existing materials without making at least minor modifications.) Sometimes it is helpful to compare existing materials to a list of criteria on an evaluation checklist. When using such a checklist, think about these questions: (1) Can the existing instructional materials be used as they are, with minimal revisions? (2) What revisions, if any, must be made? and (3) Are the performance objectives to be met by learners so unique as to prevent use of anything except tailor-made materials?

Step 4: Arranging or Modifying Existing Materials

Arranging or modifying existing materials is the fourth step in the process of designing instructional materials. When existing instructional materials are appropriate to use, it may be necessary to secure copyright permissions and arrange or modify the materials in ways appropriate for satisfying the objectives.

Securing Copyright Permissions Copyright permissions must be secured for existing instructional materials whenever a copyright notice appears on the title page, or on a footer, of instructional materials. It is unethical for an instructional designer to do otherwise. (For an example of a copyright notice, see the page behind this book's title page.) As a rule of thumb, assume that any material purchased from a vendor or borrowed from another organization is copyrighted. Most government documents are not copyrighted.

To request permission to use the material, write directly to the copyright holder. Be sure to state where the material will be used (in-house only?), how much will be used (the entire document or only part of it?), and how it will be used (in-house training only?). Will the material be adapted in any way? Also indicate how soon it will be used (is there an urgent need for a response?), how many copies are to be made (will all participants in training be given a copy?), who will receive the copies (who are the learners?), why the material is needed (training only? promotional use?), and how often future requests will be made (how many times will the material be used each year?). Be prepared to pay a fee for the privilege of using the material.

Arranging Instructional Materials Even when existing instructional materials can be found to meet the needs of targeted learners, take care to arrange the materials suitable for the intended use. Do not assume that materials designed by other professionals will always be letter-perfect or suitable for specialized purposes. Be sure to modify the material, even if only cosmetically, so (1) it appears tailor-made to the industry and organization in which it will be used, and (2) it matches up exactly to the performance objectives established for the learning experience.

Begin by making the most obvious changes. Revise titles and case study settings so they match up to the organization and learners. (Be sure that changes to be made to copyrighted material are noted in the permission request.) Proceed to major changes, if they must be made. It is often helpful to record each change on a *point sheet*. The point sheet, a lined document resembling a page of footnotes, becomes a guiding document to help a team of instructional designers tackle revision. Finally, arrange the materials so their format matches up to any special requirements favored by the organization in which they will be used.

Step 5: Preparing Tailor-Made Instructional Materials

Preparing tailor-made instructional materials is the fifth step in the process of designing instructional materials. This step should be carried out only when it is not possible to use or modify existing materials from inside or outside the organization. When approaching the task of designing tailor-made instructional materials, think in terms of developing a complete instructional package.

Traditional Components of an Instructional Package An *instructional package* contains all the materials necessary to tell learners what they need to know, show them what to do or how to use that information, allow them to practice what they have learned, and follow up with learners to give them feedback on how well they have learned. A complete instructional package traditionally has four distinct components according to a classic discussion of that topic by Dick and Carey (1990):

1. *Learner directions or guidesheets* are instructions for learners. They explain how to use the instructional package. In print-based media they sometimes take the form of a student manual and are particularly important for individualized

instruction. They are usually unnecessary when instruction is delivered in a group setting, since the instructor can provide learner directions orally. However, most instructors do want to provide group participants with an organized manual, and that manual is a method of providing directions to learners. In electronically based media, the same purpose is served by instructions provided to learners.

2. *Instructional materials* contain the actual contents of instruction, including text and visual aids. They provide learners with the information they need to achieve the performance objectives. In electronically based media, they consist of lessons or all instructional "pages" or "frames."

3. *Tests* are student evaluation tools. The term "test" is used in a broad sense. Types of tests include pre-instructional assessments (*pre-tests*) to determine what learners know before they participate in planned learning experiences. Other types include self-check and instructor-check activities during instruction to determine how well learners are achieving enabling performance objectives (*progress tests*) and post-instructional assessments to determine how well learners have achieved the terminal performance objectives by the end of the planned learning experience (*post-tests*). Further examples include job-based assessments (*on-the-job performance tests*) to determine how well learners are applying on the job what they learned in the instructional setting.

4. *Instructor directions or guidesheets* are the instructors' counterparts of learner directions or guidesheets. They are procedural guides to aid instructors in delivering instruction or in supporting learners as they individually apply themselves to planned learning tasks. Examples range from one-page instructor guidesheets or content and procedure outlines or lesson plans to voluminous trainers' guides, trainers' manuals, or tutors' guides. Instructor directions or guidesheets are usually unnecessary in electronically based media, unless learners progress through instruction in groups, or instructors sit next to learners as they progress through computer-guided instruction.

Differences of Opinion About Components of an Instructional Package Authorities on instructional design sometimes differ in their opinions about what should be included in an instructional package. One reason for this difference of opinion is that the authorities do not agree on one philosophy of learning and instructing (see, for instance, a description of the theories in Reigeluth, 1987b, and classic examples provided in Reigeluth, 1987a). The instructional designers' underlying philosophies can have a major impact on how instruction is prepared, as numerous examples of widely diverse lesson plan formats clearly show. Another reason is that considerable flexibility exists in preparing instruction. Indeed, instructional materials should be prepared so that they are consistent with the type of learning and learners for which they will be used, as well as for the setting in which they will be used.

Preparing Instructional Materials for Individualized Use In most cases, instructional designers should prepare materials for individualized use first and then modify them, as necessary, for group use. One reason to take this approach is that instruction designed for individualized use, with minimal instructor guidance, can save valuable instructor time. This time can then be devoted to those learners needing special help. A second reason: since group-paced instruction drags along at the pace of the slowest learner, it may keep most learners from excelling. A third reason to begin with learner-centered, individually paced instruction is that it usually requires more complete learner instructions than group-paced instruction, making modification for group use relatively simple. A fourth reason is that individualized instruction encourages learners to accept responsibility for their own instruction. This is not always true in group settings, in which learners too often play passive roles, while an instructor plays an active role as transmitter of information.

How Should Instructional Materials Be Prepared and Formatted? Once instructional designers have decided what components of an instructional package should be used, they are ready to prepare and format the material.

Preparing instructional materials is the process by which a sketchy working outline is transformed into finished learner directions or guidesheets, instructional materials, tests, and instructor directions or guidesheets. This process is a highly creative one. On occasion, it can often be made more efficient and effective by techniques such as detailed outlining or storyboarding.

Detailed outlining is a step following preparation of a working outline or syllabus. A detailed outline summarizes the content of the planned learning experience— or series of related learning experiences—based on the instructional strategy and media that were selected earlier. Detailed outlining literally "adds details" to the simple working outline. Examples of such details might include visual aids, instructional material (handouts, text for the learner), and directions to the instructor or the learner. In this way, instructional materials are prepared directly from the working outline and are linked directly to performance objectives. At the end of this process, then, the working outline has been converted into a detailed outline and, from that, into even more detailed learner directions or guidesheets, instructional materials, tests, and instructor directions or guidesheets.

Storyboarding is a different method of preparing instructional materials. A storyboard is a visual representation, such as a series of pictures of major frames in a videotape accompanied by the script text and musical score to go with them. However, storyboarding is not limited solely to visual media, although it is frequently associated with them. To create a storyboard: (1) find a large blank wall that can serve as the backdrop for the storyboard, (2) fasten a picture of each step in a designated instructional experience to the wall, and (3) develop accompanying learner directions and guidesheets, instructional materials, tests, and instructor directions or guidesheets for each picture. Each step in the instructional experience must be represented visually in some way, although index cards or computer-generated overhead slides bearing text may serve this purpose as well as pictures or murals. Instructional materials are then created to support each step. The value of the storyboard is that it helps organize instructional design efforts, whether they are performed individually or on a team. It also tracks what must be done in every step of the planned learning experience.

Format means the print or audiovisual layout of instructional material in a given medium. Choosing format means making decisions about how the instructional message, as well as how instructor or learner directions and tests, will be organized and presented.

Formatting learner directions or guidesheets or student manuals is often of greatest concern when instruction is designed for individual use, since learners depend on this part of an instructional package to tell them what to do to progress through the learning experience.

To prepare learner directions, some instructional designers like to start out by thinking of themselves as "novices" who are approaching the subject for the first time. This mindset is helpful because it forces them to view the material as the least experienced learner will see it. They then ask themselves this question: What step-by-step guidance do the learners and the instructors need to approach the planned learning experience through which the instructional package is intended to guide them?

Begin the learner directions or guidesheet with a few carefully chosen, one-phrase or one-sentence descriptions of the purpose of the learning experience and its performance objectives. Other topics that should be covered include the importance of the learning experience to the learner, its relationship (if any) to other planned learning experiences or work tasks, prerequisites required, and necessary equipment or supplies. List, step by step, precisely what a learner must do to proceed through the instructional materials and tests. Once that is done, go back and list precisely what the instructor or tutor should do to prompt the learner through each step and place that information on an instructor (or tutor's) guidesheet. When finished, the directions should be so clear that they could guide anybody, without a need to ask further questions about how to proceed, through the entire planned learning experience. (A portion of a representative learner guidesheet appears in Exhibit 12.1.)

EXHIBIT 12.1. A PORTION OF A REPRESENTATIVE LEARNER GUIDESHEET.

SAMPLE 6-3	LEARNING GUIDE	E-02

AVTI
ANY VO-TECH INSTITUTE
1234 MASTERY LANE
ANYTOWN, U.S.A. 98765

AUTOMOTIVE MECHANICS

TASK:	Repair exhaust pipe, muffler, and tail pipe.

INTRODUCTION:

Since the exhaust pipe, muffler, and tail pipe are on the underside of the car, they take a terrific beating. If you can spot exhaust system parts that are corroded, cracked, or broken, you may save the customer more costly and inconvenient repairs later. Often, the exhaust pipe, muffler, or tail pipe must be replaced. If not replaced properly by the mechanic, the exhaust system may rattle or may leak deadly exhaust gases into the passenger compartment, causing sickness or even death.

TERMINAL PERFORMANCE OBJECTIVE

To Demonstrate Your Mastery of This Task, Do the Following:

GIVEN: Automobiles needing exhaust system repair and access to tools, equipment, and replacement parts.

YOU WILL: Remove and replace defective exhaust system components.

HOW WELL: Written test and performance test must be completed with 100% mastery.

ENABLING OBJECTIVES

This Learning Guide Is Divided into Several Parts to Help You:

(1) Describe function of and inspect exhaust system components.

(2) Remove and replace tail pipe.

(3) Remove and replace muffler.

(4) Remove and replace exhaust pipe.

School	Dept.	Prog.	Duty	Task	Preqt.	Avg.Hrs.		Dates Revised	
AVTI	Ind.	7291	E	02	E-01	36			

© Date AVTI

Program 7291 Task E-02: Replace exhaust pipe, muffler, and tail pipe.

Source: William E. Blank, *Handbook for Developing Competency-Based Training Programs.* © 1982, pp. 204–206. Reprinted by permission of Prentice-Hall, Inc., Englewood Cliffs, NJ.

EXHIBIT 12.1. A PORTION OF A REPRESENTATIVE LEARNER GUIDESHEET, cont'd.

AVTI	Follow the LEARNING STEPS listed below:	Task E-02
EO (1)	Describe function of and inspect exhaust system components.	

___✓___ 1. Read pages 171–174 in *Modern Auto Repair* describing the function of exhaust system components.

___✓___ 2. Read Instruction Sheet 1, enclosed, describing what to look for when inspecting the exhaust system.

___✓___ 3. See if you can describe parts of the exhaust system and determine which parts need replacing by completing Self-Check 1, enclosed.

EO (2)	Remove and replace tail pipe.

___✓___ 1. View slides 1–32 in slide-tape E-02, showing how to remove and replace tail pipe on automobile, all the way through.

___✓___ 2. While viewing slides 1–32 again, remove and replace the tail pipe from vehicle assigned by instructor.

_____ 3. Check your work using Self-Check 2, enclosed.

_____ 4. Have instructor check your work before going any further.

EO (3)	Remove and replace muffler.

_____ 1. View slides 33–50, showing how to remove and replace muffler, all the way through.

_____ 2. While viewing slides 33–50 again, remove and replace muffler on vehicle assigned by instructor.

_____ 3. Check your work using Self-Check 3, enclosed.

_____ 4. Have instructor check your work before going any further.

EO (4)	Remove and replace exhaust pipe.

_____ 1. While viewing slides 51–64, remove and replace exhaust pipe on assigned vehicle.

_____ 2. Check your work using Self-Check 4 enclosed, then have instructor check your work.

_____ 3. Now, practice replacing muffler, tail pipe, and exhaust pipe on customer's car assigned by shop foreman.

_____ 4. Have instructor check your work.

_____ 5. When you are ready, take the Written Test for Task E-02.

_____ 6. When ready, take the Performance Test for Task E-02.

Program 7291

EXHIBIT 12.1. A PORTION OF A REPRESENTATIVE LEARNER GUIDESHEET, cont'd.

AVTI	INSTRUCTION SHEET 1	Task E-02

Listed below are the steps to inspect the exhaust system. Make these checks both with and without the engine running. Caution: Exhaust system components are *hot!*

1. Identify vehicle—match car with work order—read it twice.

2. Raise vehicle on lift—be sure to follow rules for raising cars on lift. Review learning guide B-04 if needed.

3. Locate and inspect muffler. You will need to replace muffler if you find any of the following:

   a. Holes or cracks in body of muffler

   b. Breaks in either end of muffler where end is attached to body of muffler

   c. Excessive rust or corrosion

   d. Large dents or areas weakened by rust

   e. Loose, broken, or missing muffler clamps (check both ends—tighten or replace as needed)

4. Inspect the exhaust pipe. You will need to repair or replace if you find:

   a. Loose or missing nuts holding exhaust pipe to manifold (tighten)

   b. Missing or broken gasket (replace)

   c. Leaks in manifold/exhaust pipe connection. Feel for leaks with your hand (caution: exhaust pipe and manifold are *hot!*)

   d. Cracks or holes or split seams in pipe (replace)

   e. Loose connections at manifold or muffler (tighten)

   f. Dents or kinks that restrict flow of exhaust gases (replace)

5. Inspect tail pipe. You will need to repair or replace if you find:

   a. Loose connections (tighten)

   b. Cracks, holes, or split seams (replace)

   c. Dents or kinks (replace)

   d. Broken or frayed support brackets (replace brackets)

| | Program 7291 |

Student manuals tend to be formatted in two ways. One way is to set up the format so that the manual consists of many individualized learner guidesheets, each focusing on one lesson within a series of related learning experiences. The manual begins with a program description, a statement of program purpose, terminal performance objectives, relationships among lessons (organization of the series), equipment and supplies needed to complete instruction, and self-check activities or tests to assess student progress.

A second way to set up the format is to gear it toward participants in instructor-centered, group-paced instruction. In this format, the manual should also describe the program's purpose, terminal performance objectives, and organization. In addition, it should contain highlights of the program contents, handouts, activities, tests, space for notes, and other material. Both formats can be used on or off the job. One advantage of giving participants a student manual in off-the-job instruction is that they can take it back to the job with them and use it as a job aid. (For this reason, some instructional designers prefer to use three-ring notebooks for the manuals to make the task of revising material that much easier for them and the task of adding or revising material on the job that much easier for learners.)

Instructional materials have no one "right" format; rather, there are many possibilities. Examples may include lesson plans, audio or video scripts, and print-based or computer-based frames. The choice of format depends on the purpose of instruction, the performance objectives, who will use the instructional materials and why, how and where they are to be used, and what medium will be used for delivery of the instructional message.

Instructor directions or guidesheets frequently take the form of lesson plans, detailed outlines intended to guide instructors through group or individualized instructional activities. A *lesson* is the most detailed level of instructional planning. Focusing on what instructors should do to facilitate a single planned learning experience, such as a class or tutorial session, lesson plans are essential to establishing the link between learners' achievement of desired performance objectives and instructors' activities intended to foster that achievement. There is no one standardized format for a lesson plan. Many are acceptable. However, institutions may establish policies of their own on appropriate lesson plan format. A portion of a representative lesson plan appears in Exhibit 12.2.

A *lesson plan* should usually be developed directly from an outline describing instructional content. It should reflect previous decisions made about instructional strategy, media, and sequence of performance objectives. It should be organized in several distinct parts, reflecting necessary instructional events for learning and the directions necessary for an instructor to facilitate the planned learning experience. The necessary instructional events become a guide for the

EXHIBIT 12.2. A PORTION OF A REPRESENTATIVE LESSON PLAN.

(This lesson plan format is designed for group delivery.)

Suggested Procedures	Notes for the Instructor
	Welcome the participants to the Workshop on Employee Incentive Programs.
Display Visual 1.	Describe the purpose of the workshop:

> *Purpose of the workshop*
>
> To review methods of increasing employee involvement by tying rewards to work methods and results.
>
> ——————————— Visual 1 ———————

Display Visual 2.	Describe the terminal performance objectives of the workshop:

> *Objectives of the workshop*
>
> When you complete this workshop, you should be able to
>
> 1. Define the term Employee Incentive Program.
>
> ——————————— Visual 2 ———————

parts of the lesson. Lesson plans should also specify the instructional resources, supplies, equipment, facilities, and other support materials needed for the planned learning experience. In this way, instructors, who may not be the same as the instructional designers who prepared the material, know what to do and how to do it.

Scripts are similar to lesson plans in that they can be used to establish the link between learners' achievement of desired performance objectives and instructors' activities intended to foster that achievement. They may be word-for-word texts of what an instructor will say to learners in a group, what a tutor will say to learners individually, or what will be said in electronically based presentations on videotapes, films, slide and tape shows, or audiocassettes. Like lesson plans, effective instructional scripts should be organized into distinct parts reflecting the events of instruction. If instruction is presented in an electronic medium such as video, the script should also provide directions for camera and background music.

Formatting instructor directions or guidesheets or trainers' guides is of greatest concern when instruction is designed for group use, since trainers depend on this part of an instructional package to tell them how to facilitate a planned learning experience.

Any learning package requires some directions to let instructors or tutors know what support they should provide to learners. For learning packages geared to individualized use, simplified instructor directions are usually adequate. These directions should describe the purpose of the package, the performance objectives, the structure of the learning experience, the resources, equipment, and facilities necessary for the experience, and (most important) an overview of what learners must do to use the package. Instructor directions may be particularly useful when they identify the most common difficulties encountered by learners during their individualized experiences, as well as tips to guide instructors to help overcome those difficulties.

Trainers' guides are usually necessary for group-oriented classroom instruction. They may take any number of formats and range from simple two-page brochures or outlines to three-ring notebooks filled with detailed lesson plans and everything else a trainer needs to deliver a classroom presentation. Detailed trainers' guides, such as those published for workshops, typically contain more than one lesson. One excellent approach to formatting trainers' guides is to purchase and review several examples of them. The following is an overview of the parts of such a guide.

Section	*Contents*
Overview	Performance objectives
	Module outline
	Transparency/PowerPoint™ master list
	Handout master list
	Suggested training time
Introduction	Description of needs assessment
	Needs assessment questionnaire
	Training materials and aids
	Delivery preparation checklist
	Description of follow-up procedures
	Questionnaire for follow-up

Section	*Contents*
Related Materials	A list of books, articles, videotapes, and other aids to be used in delivering the workshop
Trainer's Lesson Plan for the Workshop	Lesson outline (points to be covered during the training session)
	Instructional notes (directions and information for the trainer)
Transparency Masters	Master copies of overhead transparencies or PowerPoint slides
Handout Masters	Master copies of all handouts for the workshop

Research on trainers' guides has shown that, under certain conditions at least, an outline format can be just as effective as a detailed format (McLinden, Cummings, and Bond, 1990). A *detailed format* is one in which an "instructor is provided with a picture of an overhead transparency, questions to ask, scripted statements to make, and directions as to when a discussion should be generated and what it should cover" (McLinden, Cummings, and Bond, 1990, p. 3). In contrast, an outline format is defined as one in which the instructor is "provided necessary content and sequence; however, scripted presentations, directions, and cues are kept to a minimum" (McLinden, Cummings, and Bond, 1990, p. 3). The outline format saves substantial time and expense in materials preparation, but it presupposes that the content of instruction is non-technical and that the instructors are prepared, highly experienced, and expert in their subject matter (McLinden, Cummings, and Bond, 1990).

Tests should be formatted on the basis of the learner assessment methods that have been chosen. While most novice instructional designers associate testing with paper-and-pencil or computerized assessment instruments, there are numerous ways to test knowledge, skills, and attitudes (Krieger, 1994; Lee and Mamone, 1995a, 1995b; Tenopyr, 1996). Testing may occur through one-on-one questioning of learners, one-on-one demonstrations of ability during or after instruction, or questionnaires to assess changes in learner attitudes. In short, considerable creativity should be exercised when formatting tests. One reason: the word test itself makes some representatives of management, union, or workers very nervous, since they wonder how test results will be used in subsequent personnel decision making.

Step 6: Selecting or Preparing Learning Activities

The sixth step in designing instructional materials is selecting or preparing learning activities. Materials selected from other sources will usually have learning activities included; tailor-made instructional materials will require selecting or preparing activities. Learners should be given the opportunity to discover or demonstrate what they have learned, and activities are intended for that purpose.

Selecting Existing Learning Activities It is possible to select existing learning activities from external sources for use in otherwise tailor-made instructional materials. These activities must, of course, support achievement of predefined performance objectives. The instructional designer must also comply with any copyright requirements.

Preparing Individual Learning Activities There are two general categories of learning activities: individual and group. Individual learning activities are geared to individualized instruction and informal learning. Compared to the wealth of writings available on group learning activities, relatively little has been written about preparing individual learning activities on or off the job. There are, however, time-honored sources to which instructional designers may refer when they undertake the task of preparing individual learning activities or helping people structure their own learning projects (Gross, 1977, 1982; Houle, 1961; Knowles, 1975; Tough, 1979). Another approach is to provide learners with strategies for "pulling" instruction out of unwilling co-workers or supervisors who are too busy to provide it (Rothwell, 1996d).

Almost any experience can be transformed into an individualized learning activity, provided that (1) outcomes are specified in advance, (2) the outcomes can be compared to pre-established performance objectives, and (3) the experience meets certain requirements from the standpoint of the learner or the instructor. It should furnish the learner with new information or skills, give the learner an opportunity to observe others applying a skill, allow a learner the opportunity to demonstrate knowledge or skill, or afford an instructor a chance to assess how well the learner has acquired information or skills. Examples of individualized learning activities may include the following:

- Reading a book
- Interviewing others
- Reviewing documents
- Addressing a group on a new topic
- Finding a problem
- Researching a subject
- Watching a videotape
- Observing others
- Demonstrating a skill
- Performing a new job

- Starting something new
- Solving a problem

Numerous others are possible. Even off the job, informal life experiences such as serving as a community volunteer, civic or church leader, parent or spouse can become learning experiences and may serve job-related instructional purposes.

To prepare individual learning activities, first decide how much instructor involvement will be necessary *during* the learning experience. If instructor involvement is necessary, supplement learner materials with instructor directions or guidesheets or "tutor aids" so that learners can be provided with instructor help as needed. For instance, instructor directions of some kind are important to support learners progressing through planned learning experiences in off-the-job, in-house learning centers.

However, if instructor support is unnecessary, then use contract learning to guide individualized learning experiences. *Contract learning* is defined, according to one classic source, as "an alternative way of structuring a learning experience: it replaces a content plan with a process plan. Instead of specifying how a body of content will be transmitted (content plan), it specifies how a body of content will be acquired by the learner (process plan)" (Knowles, 1986, pp. 39–40). To be effective, according to Knowles (1986, p. 38), a learning contract should specify

1. The knowledge, skills, attitudes, and values to be acquired by the learner (learning objectives).
2. How these objectives are to be accomplished (learning resources and strategies).
3. The target date for their accomplishment.
4. What evidence will be presented to demonstrate that the objectives have been accomplished.
5. How this evidence will be judged or validated.

Preparing Group Learning Activities Group learning activities are perhaps most frequently associated with experiential instructional methods in classroom settings. While results of research studies on the relative effectiveness of group learning activities in classroom instruction have proved largely inconclusive (see, for instance, Carroll, Paine, and Ivancevich, 1972; Newstrom, 1980), it appears that some group learning activities are better suited than others for meeting specific types of performance objectives. Indeed, the choice of what learning activity to use should stem from the match between the performance objective and the activity.

Numerous group learning activities can be identified. In fact, one enterprising author at one time catalogued and described over 350 (Huczynski, 1983). In the classic book *Approaches to Training and Development*, Laird (1985) points out that some group learning activities are superior to others for giving learners the chance to become involved in, and thus committed to, the learning process.

In the following paragraphs, we will provide brief descriptions of many common group learning activities, simple guidelines for developing them, notes about conditions when they are appropriate to use, and sources of additional information about them.

A panel discussion is an assembly of knowledgeable people who meet with learners to deliver short presentations or answer questions about issues with which the panelists are familiar. A panel discussion is appropriate for helping learners with verbal information; it is inappropriate for providing instruction on cognitive strategies or for changing attitudes.

To prepare a panel discussion, identify knowledgeable people who can speak on the issue and thus contribute toward achievement of the predefined performance objectives. Provide the panelists with a list of questions, or ask the participants to do so. Then identify an individual who can serve as panel leader to introduce panelists, pose questions to them, and keep the discussion on track.

A case study is a narrative description of a situation in which learners are asked to identify or solve a problem. It is particularly appropriate for instruction focused on cognitive strategy. Much has been written about it. See, for example, Alden and Kirkhorn (1996), Einsiedel (1995), Fidel (1984), Pfeiffer and Ballew (1988a), and Small (1994).

To prepare a case study, first identify its purpose, the performance objectives it is intended to support, and the targeted learners. Then conduct some research inside and outside the organization. Try to find existing case studies that have already been prepared and field-tested by others. Look for those in books and articles on the Web. If existing case studies cannot be located, then interview experienced workers in the organization to find examples of real situations demonstrating problems pertinent to the planned learning experience and supportive of its performance objectives. Use the interview guide appearing in Exhibit 12.3 to help structure questions that will produce the skeletal basis for a case study.

As a last resort, prepare a fictitious case to serve the intended purpose. Use settings and characters compatible with the organization in which the instruction will be delivered. Then present the draft case to supervisors and workers for their review. Revise it according to their suggestions so as to make it as realistic as possible. Occasionally, this approach will help the reviewers remember actual situations suitable for case study treatment. Actual situations may then be substituted for the fictitious ones. ("Actual situations," when labeled as such, tend to

⊕ EXHIBIT 12.3. AN INTERVIEW GUIDE FOR COLLECTING
CASE-STUDY INFORMATION.

Directions to the Instructional Designer: Use the questions appearing on this interview guide to help you collect information for a case study. First, find one or
more experienced workers from the targeted job class for which instruction is to
be designed. (Supervisors may also be used.) Then explain what kind of situation you are looking for—and why. When you find respondents who can think of
example(s), ask the following questions. Finally, write up the case study and ask
one or more respondents to review it for accuracy. Use disguised names, job titles,
locations, and other facts. Add questions at the end of the case, if you wish.

1. What was the background of the situation? Where and when did it occur?
    Who was involved? Why was it important?

2. What happened? ("Tell me the story.")

3. What caused the situation—or problem(s) in the situation—so far as you know?
    (Describe the cause.)

4. What were the consequences of the situation for the people in it? the work
    unit? the department? the organization? (Describe the consequences.)

5. What conclusions can be drawn from the situation? What should be learned
    from it? If it happened again, how would you handle it? Why?

Mastering the Instructional Design Process: A Systematic Approach, Fourth Edition. Copyright ©
2008 by John Wiley & Sons, Inc. Reproduced by permission of Pfeiffer, an Imprint of Wiley.
www.pfeiffer.com

have great credibility with learners. It is important, however, to conceal names
so as to avoid embarrassing anyone.)

An *action maze* is "a printed description of an incident, for analysis, followed
by a list of alternative actions" (Malasky, 1984, p. 9.3). As learners make suggestions about what actions to take, they are directed further in the action maze to
find out the consequences of their decisions. This approach is particularly effective for training people to troubleshoot problems and make decisions.

To construct an action maze, begin the same way you would in preparing a
case study. First, identify the purpose. Second, clarify how the action maze will
help learners achieve performance objectives, providing them with new information or affording them an opportunity to try out their skills and receive feedback about what they know or do. Third, select a situation requiring a series of
decisions to reach a conclusion, such as a procedure consisting of related tasks.
Fourth, write up each step of the procedure to a decision point in which learners must choose what to do. Fifth, give participants two, three, or four choices
only. Sixth, prepare a separate sheet describing what happened as a result of
that decision and leading the learners to another decision point. Seventh, complete enough sheets to reflect the entire procedure, with or without "detours"

made by novices. Eighth, request experienced workers to progress through the action maze to test how "realistic" it is. Ninth, revise the action maze based on the suggestions offered by experienced workers.

An in-basket exercise "is a variation of a case study. Each participant is provided with an in-basket, including correspondence, reports, memos, and phone messages, some of which may be important to the case or process under study, and some of which may be extraneous" (Malasky, 1984, p. 9.13). It is a timed exercise intended to discover how well each participant can manage details and withstand stress. Use an in-basket exercise only for "office skills" and supervisory practices. Do not use it for technical training focusing on use of heavy equipment or application of shop-floor procedures.

To prepare an in-basket exercise, begin in the same way preparation for a case study would begin. Identify the purpose. Then clarify how the exercise will help learners achieve performance objectives. Select or create memos, letters, or phone messages that require decision making and priority setting. Train experienced workers to observe participants and evaluate the quality of their decisions, providing feedback and coaching after the activity is completed.

A *role play* is a dramatic representation of a real situation. It is an umbrella term for a whole range of similar group-oriented experiential activities. A role play gives learners an opportunity to prepare for situations they may face, or have faced, on the job. This group learning activity is particularly useful for helping participants demonstrate and practice what they have learned during instruction. However, participants sometimes find role plays artificial and have trouble feeling and acting as they say they would on the job. For more information on role plays, see Greenberg and Eskew (1993), Pfeiffer and Ballew (1988c), Thiagarajan (1996), and Turner (1993).

Prepare a role play by writing a case study and then adding character descriptions to the case. Be sure to spell out exactly what learners should do during the role play. Use the framework for a role play presented in Exhibit 12.4 as the basis for preparing one. Simply fill in the blanks with information obtained from interviews with experienced workers. As in preparing case studies, base your role plays on actual situations confronted by workers, if possible. If that is not possible, then imagine realistic but fictitious situations.

A *simulation* is an artificial representation of real conditions. It may be computerized, or it may be prepared in print form. It should be used to assess previous learning or demonstrate technical ability. Simulations are advantageous because they provide hands-on experience and are engaging to participants in a planned learning experience. But they do have disadvantages. Among them: (1) they are usually expensive to develop, and (2) they may require an instructor to play the role of evaluator.

EXHIBIT 12.4. A FRAMEWORK FOR PREPARING A ROLE PLAY.

Introduction	Use this role play to help you _____ _____.
Purpose of the role play	To do _____.
Objectives of the role play	At the end of this role play, you should be able to:
Time required for the role play	Spend _____ minutes on this role play.
Number of people required for the role play	This role play is intended for groups of _____.
Equipment/seating required for the role play	To enact this role play properly, you will need a room with the following configuration and number of chairs:
Procedures	
Step 1	Assemble in groups of _____ for how long?
Step 2	Choose someone to play the part of each character. (Note how long that will take.)
Step 3	Read a description of the situation.
Step 4	Carry out the role play. (Indicate how long that will take.)
Step 5	Prepare for discussion. (Indicate how long that will take.)
Step 6	Ask participants to draw conclusions from what they learned and indicate how they will apply on their jobs what they have learned.

Prepare a simulation by preparing a case study and then creating detailed descriptions of characters in the simulation. Be sure to spell out the purpose and objectives first. Then set the parameters of the simulation: how long it will last, where the simulation is to be conducted, who will do what, and when the simulation should end. Allow participants a measure of freedom so that this extended role play feels realistic. Test out the simulation before using it to make sure it works. Revise it so that it has reasonably predictable outcomes that are pertinent to achieving the performance objectives of the learning experience.

The *critical incident technique* (CIT), sometimes called an incident process, is the production of a very brief narrative description of a problem or situation. Often compared to the case study method, the CIT is appropriate for developing learners' troubleshooting, decision-making, and questioning skills. It has been used in assessing needs as well as in delivering instruction. For more information about the CIT, see the classic description by Flanagan (1954).

To prepare a critical incident description, interview experienced job incumbents performing the same work as the targeted trainees. Ask them to identify the most common or the most important (*critical*) problem situations (*incidents*) that they have heard about or experienced in the past. Then ask (1) how the situation was handled, (2) what results were obtained, (3) how the situation should be handled in the future if it should come up again, and (4) what results should be obtained by using the recommended solution. From this information, create one- or two-sentence critical incidents based on real situations. Use the interview guide appearing in Exhibit 12.5 to help gather critical information.

Another approach to preparing descriptions of critical incidents is to ask experienced job incumbents or their supervisors to keep performance logs in order to identify common or serious problem situations encountered during the course of work. Use the performance log to identify how often specific problem situations are actually encountered by job incumbents and obtain detailed advice on how to handle them from exemplary job incumbents or their supervisors. Be sure to find

EXHIBIT 12.5. AN INTERVIEW GUIDE FOR GATHERING INFORMATION ON CRITICAL INCIDENTS.

Directions to the Instructional Designer: The questions appearing on this interview guide are intended to help you gather information about critical incidents for use in preparing experiential activities for instruction.

First, find one or more experienced workers—or supervisors of those workers—from the targeted group of trainees. Second, ask them the questions that follow. Third, use the results of a series of these interviews to prepare critical incident activities for the targeted trainees. If you wish, prepare a second sheet showing the answers or recommended solutions for each critical incident. Ask the trainees to work on the incidents individually or in a small group.

1. Think back to a time when you faced a difficult problem on the job, perhaps the most difficult situation you had ever faced. (Describe, briefly, the nature of that situation.)

2. What did you do in that situation? What solution or approach did you use? (Describe it briefly.)

3. What happened as a result of your solution or approach? (Describe the results.)

4. Suppose this situation arose again. What would you do now? Why? (Describe a recommended solution and reasons for suggesting it.)

5. What results would you expect from using the solution or the approach you suggested in response to question 4? (Describe what you would expect the consequences of your action to be.)

out (1) the circumstances of the problem, (2) how the situations are handled, (3) what happens as a result of that solution, (4) how the situation should be handled in the future if it should come up again, and (5) what results should be obtained by using the recommended solution.

Judging Instructional Materials

Instructional designers should be capable of evaluating instructional materials they or others have selected, modified, or prepared. Their judgments may be guided by three chief considerations (Foshay, Silber, and Westgaard, 1986). First, do the instructional materials contain explanations of the content, afford an opportunity for learners to practice the skill being learned, and provide measures of accomplishment? Second, are the instructional materials consistent with current principles of perception, visual literacy and visual design, text design and readability level, memory, cognitive or behavioral psychology, and adult or general learning theory? Third, do the materials conform to learner characteristics, setting constraints, results of work analysis, sequenced performance objectives, performance measurements, and instructional strategies? Instructional designers may rely on flowcharts as decision aids when they must judge instructional materials. Sample flowcharts appear in Figures 12.3 and 12.4. Consult them as necessary.

Justifying Instructional Materials

Instructional designers should be able to justify to others the decisions they make about selecting, modifying, or preparing instructional materials. As in most steps of the instructional design process, then, they should be prepared to explain to other stakeholders, such as operating managers and supervisors and targeted learners, what they have done.

More specifically, they should be prepared to answer questions such as the following:

1. Why was the decision made to use instructional materials selected from inside or outside the organization?
2. Why was the decision made to modify existing instructional materials?
3. Why was the decision made to prepare tailor-made instructional materials?
4. What is the estimated difference in cost between purchasing existing instructional materials (and possibly modifying them to meet present needs) and preparing tailor-made materials?

FIGURE 12.3. A FLOWCHART FOR JUDGING THE ACCURACY, COMPLETENESS, AND APPROPRIATENESS OF SELECTED INSTRUCTIONAL MATERIALS.

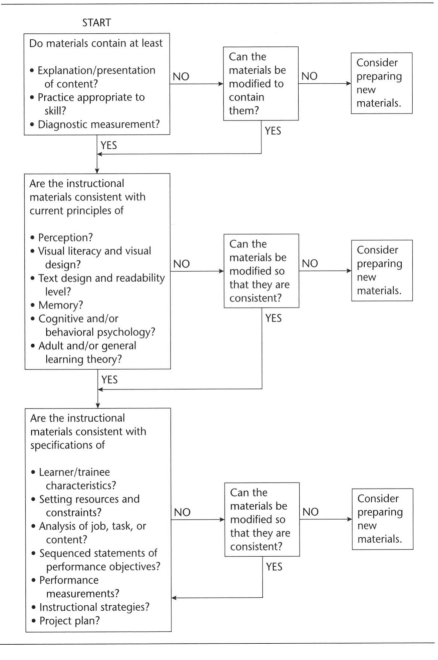

**FIGURE 12.4. A FLOWCHART FOR JUDGING THE ACCURACY,
COMPLETENESS, AND APPROPRIATENESS OF PREPARED
INSTRUCTIONAL MATERIALS.**

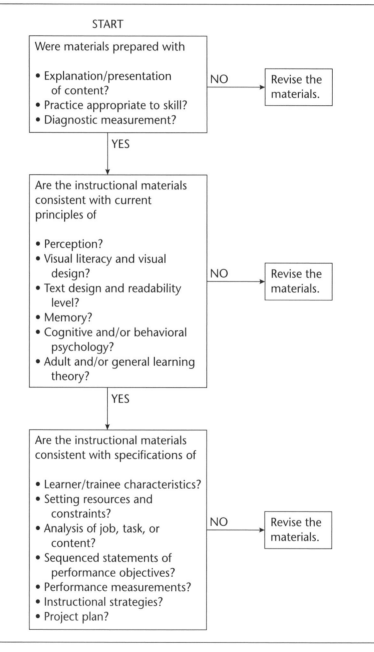

Instructional designers should be prepared to answer these questions after selecting, modifying, or preparing instructional materials. If they cannot do so, they may have to make further revisions.

Acting Ethically in Designing Instructional Materials

One important ethical issue in designing instructional materials can be expressed by this question: *Do the approaches used in instruction match up to actual work challenges and situations?* Instructional materials taken off the shelf (purchased externally) are not as effective in producing transfer of learning from instructional to application environments. There is one reason: learners have a more difficult time seeing how situations or settings that are not familiar to them, or even identical to their own, apply to them. To act ethically in designing materials, then, instructional designers must accept responsibility to ensure that learners can see the relationship between the instructional situation and workplace application. That may mean it is necessary to modify purchased materials for use in specific corporate or national cultures or work situations. Dishonesty in all these forms creates genuine ethical dilemmas. The best strategy, of course, is to tell the truth and take credit for one's own work only.

In Rothwell's (2003) survey, conducted in preparation for this third edition of this book, respondents pointed toward the classic tradeoff of time and quality as the chief ethical dilemma they encountered when trying to design or select instructional materials. In the words of one respondent, "deadlines limit quality." Another complained that "too much time [is] spent developing PowerPoint slides by us." A third bewailed the situation in which "time is not sufficient for quality design."

Applying Cross-Cultural Awareness to Designing Instructional Materials

As in specifying instructional strategies, designing instructional materials requires careful consideration of the cultures in which the materials will be used. To cite a few examples of the importance of doing that:

- In low-task-oriented cultures, group activities may take longer than in high task-oriented cultures simply because group members will seek consensus.
- In cultures characterized by low individualism, false agreement may be reached to appeal to those of higher perceived status in a group.

- In high power distance cultures, getting individuals of different status levels to function together in case study analyses or role plays may be difficult (if not impossible).

One way to meet the challenge of using materials cross-culturally is to develop "instructional shells" at a central location and then have them adapted to local cultures through regional tailoring. In particular, the examples used should be appropriate to the cultural context.

It is worth emphasizing that, according to *The Standards* (Richey, Fields, and Foxon, 2001, p. 52), one competency for instructional design is to "design instruction that reflects an understanding of the diversity of learners and groups of learners." It is described as an essential competency in *The Standards*. The performance statements associated with this competency indicate that instructional designers should be able to (Richey, Fields, and Foxon, 2001, p. 52):

a. Design instruction that accommodates different learning styles (essential).
b. Be sensitive to the cultural impact of instructional materials (essential).
c. Accommodate cultural factors that may influence learning in the design (essential).

What Is New in Selecting or Designing Instructional Materials?

Selecting instructional materials has been made somewhat easier by the web. Instructional designers can consult search engines, or even meta search engines (search engines that review multiple search engines at once), to identify material that may be reused to meet immediate organizational needs. Of course, copyright restrictions must be observed. Some instructional designers are unfortunately unaware that material on the web is not "free." However, only words can be copyrighted and not ideas. Hence, if reworded in the instructional designer's own words, material taken from the web can be used. (But it is ethically proper to identify the source.)

In designing instructional materials, an important development in recent years has been the advent of reusable learning objects. They are defined as essentially anything that can be reused for instructional purposes. While most often associated with e-learning (see "learning objects," and "the instructional use of learning objects," 2000), they can also appear as templates for classroom-based learning—including slides, participant materials, leader guides, activities, lesson plans, tests, and other materials. Using reusable learning objects can dramatically reduce the time it takes to write instructional materials or to customize those purchased or licensed from other sources. So too can using templates.

Templates may be focused on providing a format into which content is "poured." All instructional materials can be turned into templates. That permits even those with limited instructional design skills to be able to prepare instruction rapidly.

Conclusion

In this chapter, we focused on selecting, modifying, or designing instructional materials, offered advice to instructional designers about judging and justifying instructional materials they or others have prepared, and identified important ethical and cross-cultural issues in designing instructional materials. In the next chapter, we will focus on the last step in the instructional design process introduced in Chapter Four—formative evaluation.

CHAPTER THIRTEEN

EVALUATING INSTRUCTION

Instructional designers often believe that instruction is not finished until it is apparent that the targeted learners can learn from the material. Concerned with helping formulate instruction, this step in the instructional design process calls for formative evaluation. Usually distinguished from *summative evaluation*, which helps summarize results of instruction (Bloom, Hastings, and Madaus, 1971), *formative evaluation* is conducted before instructional materials are delivered to a majority of the targeted learners. Summative evaluation is conducted after instructional materials have been used with targeted trainees and results have been measured. Evaluation in all its forms has figured prominently in recent treatments of instruction as decision makers demand increasing accountability (Rothwell, Lindholm & Wallick, 2003).

Formative evaluation is the final step in the model of the instructional systems design (ISD) process we introduced in Chapter Four. (See Figure 13.1.) In this chapter, we clarify assumptions about formative evaluation and define key terms associated with it. We turn next to a case study that dramatizes issues in developing a formative evaluation plan. We also describe the steps in developing a formative evaluation plan and approaches to implementing the plan. We then offer advice to instructional designers about judging and justifying formative evaluations. We conclude the chapter by reviewing key ethical and cross-cultural issues affecting formative evaluation.

According to *The Standards* (Richey, Fields, and Foxon, 2001, pp. 52–53), one competency for instructional design is to "evaluate and assess instruction and its

FIGURE 13.1. A MODEL OF STEPS IN THE INSTRUCTIONAL DESIGN PROCESS.

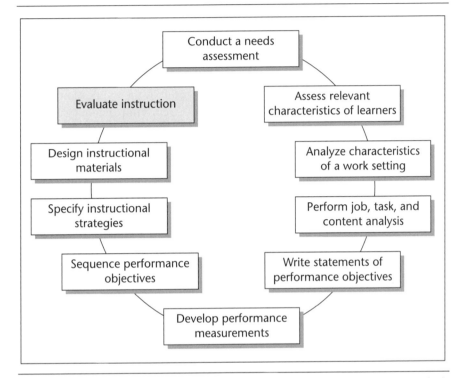

impact." It is regarded as an essential competency. The performance statements associated with this competency indicate that instructional designers should be able to (Richey, Fields, and Foxon, 2001, pp. 52–53):

a. Construct reliable and valid test items using a variety of formats (advanced).
b. Identify the processes and outcomes to be measured given the identified problem and proposed solutions (essential).
c. Develop and implement formative evaluation plans (essential).
d. Develop and implement summative evaluation plans (essential).
e. Develop and implement confirmative evaluation plans (advanced).
f. Determine the impact of instruction on the organization (advanced).
g. Identify and assess the sources of evaluation data (essential).

    h. Manage the evaluation process (advanced).

    i. Discuss and interpret evaluation reports with stakeholders (advanced).

Much attention has focused around evaluation in recent years. Instructional designers have been cautioned to do more than follow the well-known Kirkpatrick pyramid that focuses on assessing participant reactions, participant learning, on-the-job behavior change, and results (Kirkpatrick, 1996). They have, for instance, been advised to become thoughtful in the application of their evaluation approaches (Lee and Pershing, 2000), reinvent reaction evaluation (Lee and Pershing, 1999), forecast the financial benefits of training during performance analysis (Swanson, 2001), manage evaluation so that it can be done rapidly (Phillips and Burkett, 2001), apply a scorecard approach that establishes comprehensive evaluative criteria (Novak, 2000), integrate needs assessment and evaluation practices (Korth, 2001), consider applying econometric approaches to training evaluation (Wang, 2003), compare what they do against international benchmarks (Bassi and Ahlstrand, 2000; Van Buren and Erskine, 2002), use measures other than return on investment alone (Goldwasser, 2001; Simpson, 2002; Van Brakel, 2002), and apply a new approach to evaluation that goes beyond formative and summative evaluation and is confirmative (Moseley and Solomon, 1997).

Assumptions About Formative Evaluation

Instructional designers make three fundamental assumptions when evaluating instructional materials and methods.

First, they view evaluation as primarily a formative process. This assumption rests on the belief that instructional materials and methods should be evaluated—and revised—prior to widespread use to increase their instructional effectiveness. In this way, it is hoped, learner confusion will be minimized.

Second, instructional designers assume that evaluation means the process of placing value on something (Rothwell and Sredl, 2000). Evaluation is not completely objective and empirical; rather, it rests heavily on human judgment and human decisions. Human judgment, in turn, reflects the individual values of instructional designers and the groups they serve.

Third, instructional designers expect to collect and analyze data as part of the evaluation process. To determine how well instructional materials and methods work, instructional designers must try them out. It is then possible, based on actual experience with learners, to make useful revisions to the materials.

Defining Terms Associated with Formative Evaluation

Before undertaking a formative evaluation, instructional designers should take the time to familiarize themselves with at least two key terms: *formative product evaluation* and *formative process evaluation*. However, instructional designers should also minimize the use of this special terminology. Operating managers or clients will only be confused by it.

Formative Product Evaluation

The term *formative product evaluation* means the process of appraising instructional materials during preparation. Its key purposes are to provide instructional designers with descriptive and judgmental information about the value of instruction. Descriptive information outlines the value of instructional components. In contrast, judgmental information assesses how much learning results from the instructional materials when used with learners and places a value on those results.

Formative Process Evaluation

Formative process evaluation is related to formative product evaluation and means the appraisal of instructional methods, that is, how planned learning experiences are delivered or facilitated. Like product evaluation, it provides both descriptive and judgmental information about planned learning experiences.

The following case study dramatizes the key issues involved in developing a formative evaluation plan. Make notes as you read the case. Then read the section on developing a formative evaluation plan that follows the case.

Developing a Formative Evaluation Plan: A Case Study

Joan Richter has just completed a draft instructional materials package for a pre-retirement workshop. An experienced instructional designer, she has applied the instructional systems design model to technical training, but (until now) she has not applied it to "soft skills" instruction. Joan's pre-retirement package is intended for group-focused, instructor-led delivery. The learners will be employees of her client organization, and they will be screened so that only people within three years of retirement will participate in the workshop. The purpose of the workshop is to prepare learners emotionally for approaching retirement.

Joan has completed a thorough needs assessment. She has clarified the human performance problems that will be addressed by the workshop, prepared measurable and sequenced performance objectives, and crafted tailor-made instructional materials using relevant information about the learners and the setting. She is now ready to plan a formative evaluation.

Using a simple worksheet she constructed to help her remember what should be included in a formative evaluation plan, Joan prepares that plan. In this process she determines her workshop's purpose, objectives, audience, and subjects. She also assesses the information needs of the intended audiences of the evaluation, considers proper protocol, describes the populations to be studied, selects her subjects, ponders other variables of importance, formulates a design for the study, and formulates a corresponding management plan to guide the study. She makes sure that her formative evaluation plan includes the following (Foshay, Silber, and Westgaard, 1986, p. 74):

- A statement of purpose.
- A description of data collection plans.
- A description of procedures for analyzing data that are appropriate for them and the constraints imposed by the situation.
- Decision rules that will guide revisions based on the data.
- A description of the expected results consistent with the data collection techniques chosen and specified analysis plans.
- Time estimates for implementation of the evaluation plan.
- Plans for communicating results to appropriate decision makers.

Joan is now ready to implement her formative evaluation plan.

Developing a Formative Evaluation Plan

As the case study dramatizes, instructional designers should develop a formative evaluation plan that focuses attention on the instructional materials. There are seven steps in the process of developing a formative evaluation plan. We will describe them in the following sections.

Step 1: Determining Purpose, Objectives, Audience, and Subjects

The first step of formative evaluation is to determine the purpose, objectives, audience, and subjects of the formative evaluation. Begin by clarifying the purpose. Answer the question, Why is this evaluation being conducted? How much is the focus solely on the quality of the instructional materials or methods, and how much is it on other issues such as the following (Kirkpatrick, 1996):

1. How much will the targeted trainees enjoy the instructional materials, content, or methods?
2. How much will the participants learn?
3. How much impact will the learning experience have on the participants' job performance?
4. How much impact will the planned learning experience have on the organization?

As part of the first step, clarify the desired results of the formative evaluation. For each purpose identified, establish measurable objectives for the evaluation. In this way, instructional designers help themselves and others assess the results against planned intentions.

In addition, be sure to consider who wants the evaluation and why. Is it being conducted primarily for the benefit of instructional designers, key decision makers (top managers), immediate supervisors of the targeted learners, union representatives, or some combination of all these groups? Always clarify *who will review the results* of the formative evaluation and *what information they need* from it.

Identify who will participate in the formative evaluation. Will the evaluation be focused on representative targeted learners only, or will it also focus on learners with special needs or low abilities? Subject-matter specialists? Representatives of the supervisors of targeted trainees? Their managers? Top managers? There are reasons to target formative evaluation to each group of subjects, depending on the purpose and objectives of the evaluation.

Step 2: Assessing Information Needs

The second step in conducting formative evaluation is to assess the information needs of the targeted audiences. Precisely what information is sought from the results of the formative evaluation? In most cases, the targeted audiences will provide important clues about information needs:

- *Instructional designers* will usually be interested in how they can revise instructional materials or delivery methods to make them more effective for learners.
- *Key decision makers* will usually be interested in how well the materials meet previously identified instructional needs and solve human performance

problems. They may also want to assess how much and what kind of financial or managerial support is necessary to ensure instructional success or on-the-job application of what was learned.

- *The immediate supervisors* of targeted learners will usually be interested in familiarizing themselves with the instructional content so they can hold learners accountable on their jobs for applying what they learned.
- *Union representatives* may be concerned about how much the instruction increases productivity and thereby provides justification for future wage demands.
- *Representatives of the targeted learners* may be interested in how easy or difficult the instructional materials are and how test results will be used. In addition, consider the extent to which each group might be interested in determining how well instructional materials and methods present the content, allow participants to apply what they learn, measure accomplishment, and demonstrate learner achievement of performance objectives.

Step 3: Considering Proper Protocol

The third step in conducting a formative evaluation is to consider and observe proper protocol. Several questions about the protocol of conducting formative evaluation should be considered:

- How much do the targeted audiences expect to be consulted about a formative evaluation before, during, and after it is conducted?
- What permissions are necessary to carry out the study?
- Whose permissions are necessary?
- What formal or informal steps are necessary to secure the necessary permissions to conduct a formative evaluation, select subjects, collect data, and feed back results?

Protocol is affected by five key factors: (1) the decision makers' experience with formative evaluation, (2) labels, (3) timing, (4) participation, and (5) method of evaluation.

The *decision makers' experience with formative* evaluation is the first factor influencing protocol. If the decision makers have had no experience with formative evaluation, instructional designers should take special care to lay the foundation for it by describing to the key stakeholders what it is and why it is necessary. If decision makers have had experience with formative evaluation, determine what mistakes (if any) were made in previous evaluative efforts. Make it a point to avoid repeating them. Common mistakes may include forgetting to secure the right permissions, forgetting to feed back to decision makers information about evaluation results, and forgetting to use the results in a visible way to demonstrate that the evaluation was worth the time and effort.

Labels are a second factor affecting protocol. Avoid using the imposing term formative evaluation with anyone other than instructional designers, since it may only create confusion. Try less formidable and more descriptive labels such as walkthroughs, rehearsals, tryouts, or executive previews.

Timing is a third factor affecting protocol. Is it better to conduct a formative evaluation at certain times in the month or year than at other times, due to predictable work cycles or work schedules? Make sure that formative evaluations will not be carried out at times when they conflict with peak workloads or other events that may make it difficult for key stakeholders to approve or participate.

The *participation of key stakeholders* is a fourth factor affecting protocol. How essential is it to obtain permission from a few key individuals before conducting a formative evaluation? If so, who are they? How is their permission secured? How much time should be allowed for obtaining the necessary permissions?

The *method of evaluation* is the fifth and final factor affecting protocol. Given the organization's culture, should some instruments, methods of data collection, or analysis be used instead of others?

Instructional designers should never underestimate the importance of protocol. If protocol is forgotten, instructional designers can lose support for the instructional effort before it begins. Remember: any instructional experience is a change effort, and formative evaluation, like needs assessment, offers a valuable opportunity to build support for change. But if proper protocol is violated, it will militate against success. The audiences will focus attention on the violation, not instructional materials or methods.

Step 4: Describing the Population to Be Studied and Selecting the Subjects

The fourth step in conducting formative evaluation is to describe the population for study and to select participants.

Always describe from the outset the population to be studied. In most cases, of course, instructional materials or methods should be tried out with a sample, usually chosen at random, from the targeted group of learners. But take care to precisely clarify the kind of learners the materials will be tried out with. Should participants in formative evaluation be chosen, for any reason, on the basis of any specialized situation-related characteristics, decision-related characteristics, or learner-related characteristics, as those terms were described in Chapter Five?

There may be occasions when it is appropriate to try out instructional materials or methods with such specialized populations as exemplars (the top performers), veterans (the most experienced), problem performers (the lowest per-formers), novices (the least experienced), high-potential workers (those with great, but as yet unrealized, performance capabilities), or disabled workers. Formative evalu-ations conducted with each group will yield specialized information about how to adapt instructional materials to unique needs.

Once the learners have been identified, select a random sample. Use auto-mated human resource information systems for that chore, if possible. If a spe-cialized population is sought for the study, other methods of selecting a sample may be substituted. These could include announcements to employees or super-visors, word-of-mouth contact with supervisors, or appeals to unique represen-tatives. If specialized methods of selecting participants for formative evaluation must be used, be sure to consider the protocol involved in contacting possible participants, securing their cooperation, securing permission from their imme-diate supervisors or union representatives, and securing approval for any time off the job that may be necessary.

Step 5: Identifying Other Variables of Importance

The fifth step in conducting a formative evaluation is to identify other variables of importance. Ask these questions to identify the variables:

1. What settings should be used for the formative evaluation?
2. What specific program issues are particularly worth pre-testing before wide-spread delivery of instruction?
3. How much should the formative evaluation focus solely on instructional issues, and how much (if at all) should it focus on such other important but non-instructional issues as equipment needs, staff needs, financial resources required, facilities needs, and non-instructional needs of participants?
4. What positive but post-instructional outcomes of the planned learning expe-rience can be anticipated? What negative post-instructional outcomes can be anticipated?
5. What estimates should be made about expected costs of the instructional program?
6. How accurate are the prerequisites previously identified?

Step 6: Formulating a Study Design

The sixth step in conducting a formative evaluation is to formulate an evalua-tion design. At this point, the central question is this: How should the formative evaluation be conducted?

An evaluation design is comparable in many respects to a research design (Campbell and Stanley, 1966), except that its purpose is to judge instructional materials and methods rather than make new discoveries. An evaluation design is thus the "plan of attack"—the approach to be used in carrying out the evaluation. In formulating a design, be sure to (1) define key terms; (2) clarify the purpose and objectives of the evaluation; (3) provide a logical structure or series of procedures for assessing instructional materials and methods; (4) identify the evaluation's methodologies, such as surveys, trial runs or rehearsals, and interviews; (5) identify populations to be studied and means by which representative subjects will be selected; and (6) summarize key standards by which the instructional materials and methods will be judged.

Step 7: Formulating a Management Plan to Guide the Study

The seventh and final step in conducting a formative evaluation is to formulate a management plan, a detailed schedule of procedures, events, or tasks to be completed in order to implement the evaluation design. A management plan should specify due dates and descriptions of the tangible products resulting from the evaluation. It should also clarify in detail how information will be collected, analyzed, and interpreted in the evaluation.

The importance of a management plan should be obvious. When a team is conducting a formative evaluation, the efforts of team members must be coordinated. A management plan helps avoid the frustration that results when team members are unsure of what must be done, who will perform each step, and where and when the steps will be performed.

There are essentially two ways to establish a management plan. One way is to prepare a complete list of the tasks to be performed, preferably in the sequence they are to be performed in. This list should be as complete and as detailed as possible, since this task-by-task management plan becomes the basis for dividing up the work of instructional designers, establishing timetables and deadlines, holding staff members responsible for their segments of project work, and (later) assessing individual and team effort.

A second way is to describe the final work product of the project and the final conditions existing on project completion. What should the final project report contain? Who will read it? What will happen as a result of it? How much and what kind of support will exist in the organization to facilitate the successful introduction of instruction? Ask team members to explore these and similar questions before the formative evaluation plan is finalized, using their answers to organize the steps to achieve the final results.

Four Major Approaches to Conducting Formative Evaluation

Although there are many ways to conduct formative evaluation (Bachman, 1987; Chernick, 1992; Chinien and Boutin, 1994; Dick and King, 1994; Gillies, 1991; Heideman, 1993; Russell and Blake, 1988; Tessmer, 1994; Thiagarajan, 1991), four major approaches will be discussed here. Each has its own unique advantages and disadvantages. These approaches may be used separately or in combination; they are as follows:

1. Expert reviews.
2. Management or executive rehearsals.
3. Individualized pre-tests and pilot tests.
4. Group pre-tests and pilot tests.

We will describe each approach briefly.

Expert Reviews

There are two kinds of expert reviews: (1) those focusing on the *content of instruction* and (2) those focusing on *delivery methods*. Most instructional designers associate expert reviews with content evaluation.

Expert reviews focusing on content are, by definition, conducted by subject-matter experts (SMEs), individuals whose education or experience with respect to the instructional content cannot be disputed. Expert reviews ensure that the instructional package, often prepared by instructional design experts (IDEs) who may not be versed in the specialized subject matter, is consistent with current or desired work methods or state-of-the-art thinking on the subject matter.

A key advantage of the expert review is that it ensures that materials are current, accurate, and credible. On the other hand, expert reviews may be difficult and expensive to conduct if "experts" on the subject matter cannot be located easily.

Begin an expert review by identifying experts from inside or outside the organization. Do that by accessing automated human resource information systems (skill inventories), contacting key management personnel, or conducting surveys. Identify experts outside the organization by asking colleagues, accessing automated sources such as the American Society for Training and Development's Membership Information Service, or compiling a bibliography of recent printed works on the subject and then contacting authors.

Once the experts have been identified, prepare a list of specific questions for them to address about the instructional materials. Use open-ended questions like those appearing in Exhibit 13.1. To ensure that the experts address every key question you want considered, use a highly structured checklist like that appearing in Exhibit 13.2. Expert reviews are rarely conducted in group settings; rather, each expert prepares an independent review. The results are then compiled and used by instructional designers to revise instructional materials.

Expert reviews that focus on delivery methods are sometimes more difficult to conduct than expert reviews focusing on content. The reason: experts on delivery methods are not that easy to find. One good approach is to ask "fresh" instructional designers, that is, those who have not previously worked on the project, to review instructional materials for the delivery methods that are used.

For each problematic issue the reviewers identify, ask them to note its location in the instructional materials and suggest revisions. Another good approach is to ask experienced instructors or tutors to review an instructional package. If the package is designed for group-paced, instructor-led delivery, offer a dress rehearsal and invite experienced instructors to evaluate it. If the package is designed for individualized, learner-paced delivery, ask an experienced tutor to try out the material.

Management or Executive Rehearsals

Management or executive rehearsals are different from expert reviews. They build support by involving key stakeholders in the preparation and review of instructional materials prior to widespread delivery. In a management rehearsal, an experienced instructor describes to supervisors and managers of the targeted trainees—or even to top managers—what content is covered by the instructional materials and how they are to be delivered. No attempt is made to "train" the participants in the rehearsal; rather, the focus is on familiarizing them with its contents so they can hold their employees accountable for on-the-job application. Rehearsals are advantageous for building management support for job-related application. However, they are problematic when key managers insist on presenting instruction consistent with their own idiosyncratic preferences rather than with current job methods or thinking on the subject.

To conduct a management or executive rehearsal, begin by identifying and inviting key managers to a short (thirty-minute to one-hour) overview of the materials. Some instructional designers prefer to limit invitations to specific job categories, such as top managers or middle managers. Others prefer to offer several different kinds of rehearsals.

Be sure to prepare a special agenda for the rehearsal. Make it a point to cover at least (1) the purpose of the instructional materials, (2) the performance objectives, (3) the business needs, human performance problems, challenges, or

EXHIBIT 13.1. A WORKSHEET ON INSTRUCTIONAL MATERIALS AND METHODS FOR EXPERT REVIEWERS.

Directions for Reviewers: Use this worksheet to record your comments about the strengths and weaknesses of the instructional package with which you have been provided. (You should also have received information about the performance problem to be addressed and relevant information regarding the organization in which the instruction must operate.) For each question appearing in the left column below, provide an answer in the right column. When you are finished, return the completed worksheet to_____ at

(name)

_____by _____ .

(address)   (date).

Your comments will be helpful in revising, and thereby improving, the instructional package prior to widespread use. Attach more paper, if necessary.

Questions	Answers
1. How clearly do the instructional materials state the desired outcomes of instruction? (Consider the instructional objectives for completeness, sequence, and priority.)	
2. How well do the materials appear to match learner/trainee characteristics? (Consider the clarity with which those characteristics are described and/or used.)	
3. How well are the instructional materials based on the instructional objectives? (Consider the match between objectives and materials.)	
4. How complete and up to date is the content of the instructional package? (Consider whether the instructional package is adequate for delivery in an individualized or group format and whether it reflects the latest thinking on the topic.)	
5. How well are learners given opportunities to be informed of content, practice or apply what they learn, and receive feed-back on how well they practiced or applied what they learned? (Consider the sequence of instructional events within each part of the instructional package.)	
6. What other issues did you notice that should be considered during revision?	

EXHIBIT 13.2. A CHECKLIST ABOUT INSTRUCTIONAL MATERIALS AND METHODS FOR EXPERT REVIEWERS.

Directions for Reviewers: Use this checklist to review the instructional package with which you have been provided. For each question appearing in the left column below, check (✓) yes, no, or not applicable in the right column. If you check no, attach separate sheets to describe the problem and possible ways to revise the materials to address that problem. (Along with the instructional package, you should have also received information about the performance problem to be addressed and relevant information regarding the organization in which the instruction will be used.) When you are finished, return the completed checklist to

_____ at _____

       (name)   (address)

by _____ .

      (date)

    By completing this checklist, you will help identify the means by which the instructional package can be improved prior to widespread delivery to the targeted learners.

	Response		
	Yes	No	Not Applicable
Question	(✓)	(✓)	(✓)
1. Do the instructional materials clearly state the desired outcomes of instruction?	( )	( )	( )
2. Do the instructional materials appear to match learner/trainee characteristics?	( )	( )	( )
3. Are the instructional materials clearly based on the instructional objectives?	( )	( )	( )

4. Is the content of the instructional package
  a. Complete?
  b. Up to date?
	( )	( )	( )

5. Are learners given adequate opportunities to
  a. Receive information about the content?
  b. Practice or apply what they learn?
  c. Receive feedback on how well they practiced or applied what they learned?
	( )	( )	( )

6. Are there other issues you noticed that should be considered during revision?	( )	( )	( )

    If yes, describe:

issues to be addressed by the instruction, (4) a description of targeted trainees, (5) evidence of need, (6) an overview of the instructional materials, (7) steps taken so far to improve the instruction, and (8) steps that members of this audience can take to encourage application of the learning in the workplace. Ask a colleague to attend the rehearsals to take notes about suggested revisions that stem from the discussions with participants.

Individualized Pre-Tests and Pilot Tests

Individualized pre-tests, conducted on-site or off-site, constitute another approach to formative evaluation. Frequently recommended as a starting point for trying out and improving draft instructional materials, they focus on learners' responses to instructional materials and methods, rather than those of experts or managers. Most appropriate for individualized instructional materials, they are useful because they yield valuable information about how well the materials will work with the targeted learners. However, pre-tests and pilot tests do have their drawbacks: they can be time-consuming, and they require learners to take time away from work and may thus pose difficulties for supervisors and co-workers in today's lean-staffed, right-sized organizations.

Individualized pre-tests are intensive "tryouts" of instructional materials by one learner. They are conducted to find out just how well one participant fares with the instructional materials. A pre-test is usually held in a non-threatening or off-the-job environment, such as in a corporate training classroom or learning center. Instructional designers should meet with one person who is chosen randomly from a sample of the target population. That person should preferably be a lower-than-average performer, since average or better-than-average performers may succeed with instructional materials despite their poor quality. Begin the session by explaining that the purpose of the pre-test is not to "train" the participant but, instead, to test the material. Then deliver the material one-on-one. Each time the participant encounters difficulty, encourage the person to stop and point it out. Note these instances for future revision. Typically, instructional designers should direct their attention to the following issues: (1) How much does the participant like the material? (2) How much does the participant learn (as measured by tests)? (3) What concerns, if any, does the participant express about applying what he or she has learned on the job? Use the notes from this pre-test to revise the instructional materials.

The individualized pilot test is another approach to formative evaluation. It is usually conducted after the pre-test, focusing on participants' reactions to instructional materials in a setting comparable to that in which the instruction is to be delivered. Like pre-tests, pilot tests provide instructional designers with valuable information about how well the instructional materials work with representatives from the group of targeted trainees. However, their drawbacks are similar to those for pre-tests: they can be time-consuming, and they require learners to take time away from work.

Conduct a pilot test in a field setting, one resembling the environment in which the instructional materials are intended to be used. Proceed exactly as for a pre-test: (1) select one person at random from a sample of the target population; (2) begin by explaining that the purpose of the pilot test is not to train the participant but to test the material; (3) progress through the material with the participant in a one-to-one delivery method; (4) note each instance in which the participant encounters difficulty with the material; (5) focus attention on how much the participant likes the material, how much the participant learns as measured by tests, and what concerns, if any, the participant raises about applying on the job what he or she has learned; and (6) use the notes from the pilot test to revise instructional materials prior to widespread use.

Group Pre-Tests and Pilot Tests

Group pre-tests resemble individualized pre-tests but are used to try out group-paced, instructor-led instructional materials. Their purpose is to find out just how well a randomly selected group of participants from the targeted trainee group fares with the instructional materials. Held in an off-the-job environment, such as in a corporate training classroom or learning center, the group pre-test is handled precisely the same way as an individualized pre-test.

A group pilot test resembles an individualized pilot test but is delivered to a group of learners from the targeted trainee group, not to one person at a time. Typically the next step following a group pre-test, it focuses on participants' reactions to instructional materials in a field setting, just like its individualized counterpart. Administer attitude surveys to the learners about the experience, as well as paper-and-pencil, computerized assessments or demonstration tests to measure learning. Realize in this process that a relationship does exist between attitudes about instruction and subsequent on-the-job application (Dixon, 1990).

Using Approaches to Formative Evaluation

Each approach to formative evaluation is appropriate under certain conditions. Use an expert review to double-check the instructional content and the recommended delivery methods. Use a management or executive rehearsal to build support for instruction, familiarize key stakeholders with its contents, and establish a basis for holding learners accountable on the job for what they learned off the job. Use individualized pre-tests and pilot tests to gain experience with, and improve, individualized instructional materials prior to widespread delivery; use group pre-tests and pilot tests to serve the same purpose in group-paced, instructor-led learning experiences.

Providing Feedback from Formative Evaluation

One final issue to consider when conducting formative evaluation is how to provide feedback to key stakeholders about the study and its results. Generally speaking, the shorter the report, the better. One good format is to prepare a formal report with an attached, and much shorter, executive summary.

The report should usually describe the study's purpose, key objectives, limitations, and any special issues to be addressed. It should also describe the study methodology (including methods of sample selection) and instruments prepared and used during the study, and should summarize the results. Include copies of the instructional materials that were reviewed, or at least summaries of them. Then describe the study's results, including descriptions of how well learners liked the material, how much they learned as measured by tests, what barriers to on-the-job application of the instruction they identified, and what revisions will be made to the materials.

An executive summary should list the study's key results first and then briefly describe the study's background, purpose, objectives, and sample selection. It should be limited to no more than three pages, and it should preferably be one or two pages.

Formative product evaluation results are rarely presented to management, since their primary purpose is to guide instructional designers in the process of improving instructional materials. However, instructional designers can feed back the results of formative evaluation to management as a way of encouraging management to hold employees accountable on the job for what they learned.

Judging Formative Evaluations

Instructional designers should be capable of judging the quality of a formative evaluation plan prepared by themselves or other designers. They should base their judgments on the contents of the plan, its implementation, and the revisions subsequently made to instructional materials. As in judging other steps of the instructional design process, a checklist (like the one shown in Exhibit 13.3) can be a useful decision aid.

EXHIBIT 13.3. A CHECKLIST FOR JUDGING THE APPROPRIATENESS, COMPREHENSIVENESS, AND ADEQUACY OF STATEMENTS OF THE EVALUATION PLAN AND REVISION SPECIFICATIONS.

Directions: After preparing a written evaluation plan and revision specifications for instructional materials, do a quality check by completing the following checklist. Answer each question appearing in the left column below by checking an appropriate response in the middle column. If necessary, make notes for revising materials in the right column.

Questions	Response		Notes for Revision
	Yes	No	
Does the . . .	(✓)	(✓)	
1. Evaluation plan include			
a. A clear statement of purpose that is appropriate to the given situation?	( )	( )	
b. Data collection plans that are consistent with the purpose of the evaluation and the instruction and that are appropriate for the given situation?	( )	( )	
c. Data collection procedures that yield data as reliable and as valid as possible under the constraints imposed by the given situation?	( )	( )	
d. Plans that reflect the relative importance of different objectives within the instruction being evaluated?	( )	( )	
e. Plans for the analysis of the data that are appropriate for the type of data collected and the constraints imposed by the situation?	( )	( )	
f. Decision rules that will guide revisions based on the data?	( )	( )	
g. A description of the expected results consistent with the data collection techniques chosen and the specified analysis plans?	( )	( )	
h. Time estimates for the implementation of the evaluation plan that are realistic and appropriate for the given situation?	( )	( )	

(Continued)

EXHIBIT 13.3. A CHECKLIST FOR JUDGING
THE APPROPRIATENESS, COMPREHENSIVENESS,
AND ADEQUACY OF STATEMENTS OF THE EVALUATION
PLAN AND REVISION SPECIFICATIONS, cont'd.

Questions	Response		Notes for Revision
	Yes	No	
Does the ...	(✓)	(✓)	
i. Plans for communicating results to appropriate decision makers that are effective, efficient, consistent with the types of dat and congruent with the particulars of the given situation?	( )	( )	
2. Specification for revision: a. Directly reflect the data?	( )	( )	
b. Appear in the order recommended for implementation?	( )	( )	
c. Contain specific instructions for implementation?	( )	( )	

Mastering the Instructional Design Process: A Systematic Approach, Fourth Edition. Copyright © 2008 by John Wiley & Sons, Inc. Reproduced by permission of Pfeiffer, an Imprint of Wiley. www.pfeiffer.com

Justifying Formative Evaluations

Instructional designers should be capable of justifying the formative evaluations they conduct. As in other steps of the instructional design process, they are accountable to other stakeholders such as operating managers, learners, and other designers, and they should be prepared to answer questions posed about formative evaluation by key stakeholders. Four questions are perhaps most often posed.

Question 1: Why Is It Necessary to Conduct Formative Evaluation?

To answer this question, be prepared to provide—and stand behind—the purposes of the formative evaluation. Try to anticipate, if possible, any objections to the purposes that may be raised. (One common objection is that formative evaluation takes people away from their work for an uncertain payoff and is thus tough to quantify.) Have responses prepared for on-the-spot justification.

Question 2: What Valuable, Measurable Results Will Stem from the Study?

Be sure to clarify the performance objectives of instruction for the benefit of the audiences. Explain the value of the formative evaluation results in terms of their relationship to the performance objectives.

Question 3: How Much Will the Study Cost?

Be prepared to justify the formative evaluation on the basis of costs and benefits. Be sure to prepare a budget for the evaluation following preparation of the management plan to guide it. But go a step further: prepare to discuss why each step in the formative evaluation is necessary. And be ready to point out that, without formative evaluation, instructional delivery may be pointless because the learners may waste valuable time with untested materials.

Question 4: How Soon Will the Evaluation Be Completed?

Use the task-by-task estimates provided in the management plan to prepare a realistic time frame for study completion. Be prepared to say when the instructional materials will be ready to deliver following the evaluation.

In short, be prepared to justify every step taken in planning the formative evaluation, carrying it out, and taking actions based on it.

Acting Ethically in Evaluating Instruction

Key ethical issues in evaluating instructional materials can be expressed by these questions: *Did the instruction lead to intended changes?* and *Did those changes meet the needs of the learners and the client?* It is difficult for instructional designers to evaluate their own materials, methods, and results because their credibility may be as suspect as bookkeepers who audit their own accounts (Rothwell, Lindholm and Wallick, 2003). The reason: both instructional designers and bookkeepers may be regarded as self-interested parties in the process and may be accused of acting to manipulate results to promote or protect themselves. To avoid that charge, evaluation should be conducted by others when that is possible and when others can be found who are willing to serve in that role. In organizations that use training councils, members of that group may serve as watchdogs, auditors—and instructional evaluators—though they may require special training and assistance to serve in that capacity.

Similarly, it is unethical for instructional designers to manipulate evaluation results for their own benefit. Do not take such actions as censoring comments on participant evaluations, passing out post-tests for learners to consult as they progress through instruction, or waiting until instruction is completed to assess how results will be measured on the job.

Often, instructional designers feel that they cannot win when it comes to evaluation: they may have to convince management that evaluation data are worth collecting. At the same time, they may be required to supply return-on-investment information, but only after instruction has been designed and delivered.

To address these problems, instructional designers must work to build a case for using evaluation data to improve instruction continuously. Only when evaluation data have been collected before instruction is designed and delivered is it genuinely persuasive to the critics who may surface later.

In Rothwell's (2003) survey, conducted in preparation for the third edition of this book, respondents pinpointed several ethical challenges they face when conducting evaluation. As one wrote, "Most managers and executives see measurement and evaluation as important, but they are not willing to pay for it. Yet, they want to measure ROI." A second indicated that he or she faces a problem because evaluation is "often overlooked." These comments underscore two problems that are sometimes forgotten in evaluation. First, it does cost money and time to conduct evaluation. There is also an opportunity cost involved, since time devoted to evaluation is not devoted to design, delivery, or application. Second, too many instructional designers wait until they are asked for evaluative information to mount an effort to collect it. A better approach is to plan for it from the beginning, integrating it with the needs assessment process.

Applying Cross-Cultural Awareness to Evaluating Instruction

Cross-cultural sensitivity is as important to successful evaluation as it is to other activities in the instructional design process. As in specifying instructional strategies and designing instructional materials, evaluating instruction effectively calls for consideration of the cultures in which the evaluation will be carried out. To cite a few examples of the importance of remaining sensitive to the cross-cultural implications of evaluation:

- In low task-oriented cultures, group evaluation efforts such as focus groups may take longer than in high task-oriented cultures simply because group members will seek consensus on what they think of instruction.

- In cultures characterized by low individualism, participants in formative evaluations may falsely agree to statements about their opinions. In other words, they may say that instruction is effective when, in fact, it is not. The reason: they aim to please an instructional designer of higher perceived status. For this reason, double-checks may have to be instituted in the process, or else formative evaluations should be carried out by those of the same status as the targeted participants of the formative evaluation.

One way to meet the challenge of conducting formative evaluation cross-culturally is, as in other situations, to rely on cultural informants. They can suggest ways to achieve results when cultural differences may otherwise lead to unexpected complications during formative evaluation.

What Is New in Evaluating Instruction?

Evaluation has been a perennially popular topic with trainers and instructional designers. The reason is simple: Instructional designers are under pressure, perhaps as never before, to justify what they do, how they do it, and what results are obtained from it. Unfortunately, there is no such thing as foolproof approaches to instructional evaluation.

Sugrue (2003) reported in the ASTD *2003 State of the Industry Report* that "78 percent of training organizations were evaluating training at Level 1 [how much people liked the training]; 46 percent were evaluating at Level 2 [how much people learned in the training]; 27 percent were evaluating at Level 3 [how much people took back and applied on their jobs in changed behavior]; and 11 percent were evaluating at Level 4 [how much measurable change occurred for the organization as a result of the training]" (p. 2). That means that, despite increasing pressure to demonstrate results from training, instructional designers often have too little time, money and effort to devote to evaluation practices. There is a cost to evaluation, since nothing in organizational life is "free." To devote time to evaluation often means to subtract time from designing or delivering other training.

The holy grail of the instructional design field is to find a simple, cost-effective, and foolproof way to demonstrate the value of instruction. But, even after decades of working on it, instructional designers are no closer than ever to reaching that holy grail. There are, after all, many factors that influence human performance. It is more difficult than it seems to pinpoint precisely what results were obtained from instruction alone.

Conclusion

The final step in the model of the instructional design process we unveiled in Chapter Four, formative evaluation provides a means by which to improve instructional materials before they are released for widespread use. In this chapter, we clarified assumptions about formative evaluation, defined key terms associated with it, provided a case study to dramatize important issues in developing a formative evaluation plan, described the steps in developing a formative evaluation plan and approaches to implementing the plan, offered advice about judging and justifying formative evaluations, and reviewed key ethical and cross-cultural issues affecting formative evaluations.

In the remaining chapters of this book, we turn to competencies linked to managing and communicating about instructional design projects. In the next chapter, we focus on the instructional management system that is essential to ensure that learners can receive the training, that they can begin in the proper place, and that their progress can be appropriately tracked.

PART FIVE

MANAGING INSTRUCTIONAL DESIGN PROJECTS SUCCESSFULLY

CHAPTER FOURTEEN

DESIGNING THE INSTRUCTIONAL MANAGEMENT SYSTEM

Good training is not adequate by itself. It must be reinforced by an effective logistical support system, known as an instructional management system. An effective instructional management system ensures that (Foshay, Silber, and Westgaard, 1986):

- Entrance into the instruction is quick and easy.
- Learners entering instruction are diagnosed as to their readiness.
- Learners are directed to appropriate sections with a minimum of time and effort.
- Each step, section, or experience within the instruction is provided with transitions and references.
- Each instructional element is easily identified.
- Competence is documented so that management and learners know precisely what is required.
- The learner's exit from the instruction is diagnostic of future needs.
- Record keeping is adequate for both individual and organizational purposes.

More recently, seven capabilities have been identified as key to an effective learning management system (LMS): (1) a gateway; (2) classroom courses; (3) online learning; (4) virtual classroom; (5) community learning; (6) skills and competency management; and (7) back office administration ("Capabilities to Look for When Purchasing or Renting an LMS," 2001). Both learning management systems and learning content management systems are likely to figure increasingly in discussions of instructional design in the future (Oakes, 2002).

The most recent edition of *The Standards* also emphasizes the importance of designing instructional management systems. According to *The Standards* (Richey, Fields, and Foxon, 2001, p. 54), one competency for instructional design is thus to "design instructional management systems." It is regarded as an essential competency. The performance statements associated with this competency indicate that instructional designers should be able to (Richey, Fields, and Foxon, 2001, p. 54):

a. Establish systems for documenting learner progress and course completion (advanced).
b. Establish systems for maintaining records and issuing reports of individual and group progress (advanced).
c. Establish systems for diagnosing individual needs and prescribing instructional alternatives (advanced).

Of course, related to an instructional management system is a curriculum or program.

According to *The Standards* (Richey, Fields, and Foxon, 2001, p. 49), one competency for instructional design is to "design a curriculum or program." It is regarded as an essential competency. The performance statements associated with this competency indicate that instructional designers should be able to (Richey, Fields, and Foxon, 2001, p. 54):

a. Determine the scope of the curriculum or program (essential).
b. Specify courses based upon needs assessment outcomes (essential).
c. Sequence courses for learners and groups of learners (essential).
d. Analyze and modify existing curricula or programs to insure adequate content coverage (essential).
e. Modify an existing curriculum or program to reflect changes in society, the knowledge base, technology, or the organization (advanced).

A learning management system is thus closely related to the strategy for training and learning in an organization (Rothwell and Kazanas, 2003). *Curriculum design*, sometimes called program design, has to do with establishing a long-term plan for training and learning in an organization that integrates on-the-job training, off-the-job training, and incidental training that stems from the work experience that individuals gain in their jobs (Rothwell and Kazanas, 2003; Rothwell and Sredl, 2000). It also requires instructional designers to consider the delivery media that strike a balance between learner impact and cost (Cowan, 2000).

But how are these requirements of an effective instructional management system put in place? In this chapter, we answer that question for each requirement listed. We begin with a brief case study to dramatize key issues and then address each requirement. Finally, we offer advice to instructional designers about judging and justifying instructional management systems.

Designing an Instructional Management System: A Case Study

Georganna Smithson is an instructional designer employed by a private vendor under contract to a small manufacturing firm. Smithson's client has recently established a series of planned instructional experiences using the model of instructional systems design described in this book. It is now time to design an instructional management system.

Smithson reads this chapter and prepares a worksheet (see Exhibit 14.1) to help her structure her thinking. She uses the worksheet as an agenda in a meeting with representatives of client management and other instructional designers on her team. They find that, by answering the questions posed on the worksheet, they are able to meet the minimum criteria for an effective instructional management system.

Ensuring That Entrance into Instruction Is Quick and Easy

By following the steps in the model of the instructional design process, instructional designers should have ensured that the instruction is useful and can have a demonstrated impact on improving employee performance. But practicality is not enough. The targeted learners must be attracted to the instruction, and participation must be made as convenient as possible for them. In other words, instructional designers must be able to market their products and services. To that end, they should start by paying keen attention to four key and classic issues (McCarthy, 1978): place, promotion, product, and price. Each provides clues to the appropriate marketing of instruction.

Place

To make it easy for targeted participants to enter instruction, instructional designers should consider this question: *How can instruction be delivered at a location, or locations, convenient to the targeted learners?* To answer that question, first identify

EXHIBIT 14.1. A WORKSHEET ON THE INSTRUCTIONAL MANAGEMENT SYSTEM.

Directions: Use this worksheet to help you, your client, and other instructional designers on your team structure your thinking. For each criterion for an effective instructional management system described in the left column below, jot down some ideas in the right column about how you can meet the criterion. There are no right or wrong answers in any absolute sense, though some answers may be more right or wrong, depending on the organization.

Criteria for effective instructional management systems	What ideas do you have about how to meet the criteria?
1. Entrance into instruction should be quick and easy.	
2. Entering learners should be diagnosed as to their readiness for the instruction.	
3. Learners should be directed to appropriate sections of instruction with minimum time and effort.	
4. Each step, section, or experience within the instruction should be provided with transitions and references.	
5. Each instructional element should be easily identified in terms of both content and purpose.	
6. Competence should be documented in such a way that both management and learners know precisely what is required, when, and the standards applicable.	
7. Exit from the instruction should be well documented and diagnostic of future needs.	
8. Recordkeeping should be adequate for both individual and organizational purposes.	

Mastering the Instructional Design Process: A Systematic Approach, Fourth Edition. Copyright © 2008 by John Wiley & Sons, Inc. Reproduced by permission of Pfeiffer, an Imprint of Wiley. www.pfeiffer.com

the geographical locations of the learners by doing some rudimentary market research. Are most of the learners grouped closely together in one work location or in several identifiable work locations? Are they spread all over the map?

Next decide how to make the instruction available conveniently. There are, of course, a range of options. For instance, group-oriented, instructor-led, or individually oriented, learner-directed instruction can be offered in one or more locations: (1) on-site at key work locations where prospective participants are centralized, (2) off-site at key work locations, (3) on-site at key locations that are geographically positioned between other locations, (4) off-site at key locations that are geographically positioned near other locations, and (5) on a regional basis.

Remember one important principle: *The more delivery formats in which instruction is made available, the greater the likelihood that the broadest audience will be attracted.* There are at least two reasons why this is true. First, learners differ in their learning styles and preferences and therefore differ in the formats—group-oriented or individual-oriented—that they prefer (Kolb, 1984). Second, individual learners face different constraints on their time, both on and off the job. Some have time to progress through instruction on the job and prefer to do so. Some have time to progress through instruction off the job, and prefer that. However, others have no time to progress through instruction on or off the job or have no desire to do it at all. By making instruction available in multiple delivery formats, instructional designers increase the likelihood that the unique constraints each targeted learner must cope with are minimized.

Promotion

To make it easy for targeted participants to enter instruction, consider promotion next. Promotion, of course, means communicating with targeted participants so they are aware that the right kind of instruction to meet their needs is available at a convenient location and at a reasonable cost. To consider promotion, pose this question: *How can participants be alerted to the availability of instruction in ways that will attract them?* To answer this question, begin by identifying the learning needs. For instance: (1) What exactly is the need? Is the aim to correct past performance deficiencies, address present human performance problems, or avert future human performance problems? Are people being initially trained, retrained, or educated for future advancement? How might the participants view the need? How would they answer the question, What's in it for me? (2) How important is the need? Is it particularly keen for everyone in the organization or only for workers in specific departments or work units? (3) How much time is available to meet the need? Is time an important issue? Are there good reasons, from the standpoint of individuals or the organization, that instruction be delivered before, during, or after some planned change effort such as the introduction of new equipment, work methods, new leaders, or new products and services? When these questions about time have been answered, consider how the targeted participants can best be reached. For instance, what methods might work best: personal selling? organizational selling? sales promotion methods? online notices? a blend of two or more promotion methods?

Personal selling is direct, face-to-face contact between instructional designers—or other representatives of a human resource development department—and prospective learners or their immediate supervisors. Quite expensive since it usually involves travel to identifiable work locations of targeted learners, personal selling is appropriate when immediate feedback from the targeted learners about instruction must be secured.

As in all promotion, there are essentially three basic steps to personal selling. First, secure the willingness of learners to participate in the instruction by pointing out to them and to their immediate supervisors the advantages of participation. Second, help learners through the enrollment process by coaching them on how to complete any necessary forms. Make sure they actually enroll. Third, support them so that they do participate. Continue to stress the advantages of participation to them before, during, and after the planned learning experiences.

Organizational selling is geared to large groups of people in the organization. Less expensive than personal selling, it relies on advertising devices like instructional catalogues, brochures, newsletter articles, bulletin board notices, announcements by supervisors, specially prepared newsletters issued by the human resource development department, electronic mail or electronic bulletin board announcements, and other methods. Appropriate for reaching large groups of learners in the shortest time, it is particularly useful when the targeted participants are geographically scattered.

Sales promotion methods are, for the most part, much neglected in instructional marketing. They include displays and shows. They are akin to organizational selling in that they secure much attention very quickly.

To carry out sales promotion methods for marketing instruction, consider sponsoring "information fairs" about instruction in-house, one-time "walkthroughs" of instruction for groups within the organization, and giveaway items such as mugs, Thermos® bottles, matchboxes, and pens. If they will not work, try a small-scale lottery. Use giveaway items and lotteries as vehicles to advertise instruction. While some instructional designers might say that giveaways or lotteries are hokey, realize that they can, and do, work!

Product

To attract targeted participants, always consider the product. By product, of course, we do not mean instruction by itself. We are referring to the capacity of instruction to help learners rectify past human performance problems, meet present work performance requirements, prepare for future work needs, and prepare for increasing responsibility and advancement. In other words, *product refers to everything having to do with an instructional experience.* This includes the opportunity provided to employees and their supervisors during sign-up to discuss each employee's future and the organization's goals, the social experience of group instruction, the challenge of individualized instruction, and the valuable feedback that post-instructional evaluation provides to individuals.

Pose this question when considering product: *How can instruction be packaged in a way that will appeal to the needs of learners and the organization?* Consider that question relative to the types of learners who may participate in instruction.

Recall that individual learners can be classified into three basic types (Houle, 1961; Knowles, 1984): (1) *the goal-oriented,* who use instruction to satisfy an immediate need; (2) *the activity-oriented,* who use instruction to find social support while they struggle with problems; and (3) *the learning-oriented,* who seek instructional experiences for their own sake. Each category of individual learner provides clues about how to market instruction, since each suggests what learners seek from it.

Supervisors of targeted learners may be classified as learners are. Goal-oriented supervisors use instruction instrumentally as a tool to help them prepare their people for present or future change or to cope with past change. Activity-oriented supervisors use instructions as a reward, a way of giving their people a "break" for work well done. While instructional designers may strongly reject activity-oriented motives, be aware that they do exist. This should be considered when marketing instruction. Learning-oriented supervisors encourage their employees to participate in instructional experiences for the sake of learning itself, to give them a chance to familiarize themselves with new ideas.

In team-based organizations, co-workers serve the same purpose as supervisors in more traditional settings. In those organizations, co-workers may also be categorized as goal-oriented, activity-oriented, and learning-oriented. In team-based organizations, particularly those in which teams are self-directed, prospective learners may need to secure the permission of their co-workers to attend off-the-job training. After all, time away from the job may affect collective team results.

Learners and supervisors are thus prospective instructional consumers whose needs and wants must be satisfied if they are to be attracted to instruction and participate in it, or support it, willingly. Instructional designers face the challenge of appealing to all types of learners and supervisors. To that end, the following questions must be addressed to market instruction: (1) How does instruction meet a demonstrable need of the organization or the learners? (2) What opportunities for social support or networking will the instructional experience open up to participants? and (3) How does the instructional experience furnish new ideas to learners, even those who may feel they are familiar with the subject matter?

Price

It has been said that nothing in life is free, so the price of instruction is always an issue in marketing it. Even when instruction is free to all learners, there are organizational costs associated with instructor time, learner time, facilities, equipment, and supplies. When considering price, pose this question: How can instruction be priced at a level that will attract participation? To address this question, identify possible competitors, that is, organizations that offer comparable instruction. Locate competitors by scanning the catalogues of local colleges and vocational schools and by accessing such computerized databases as the American Society for Training and Development's TRAINET or the Seminar Information Service (SIS) to identify seminars offered by profit-making vendors. Then compare the content of offerings and their prices to in-house experiences. If in-house price and content compare favorably to those of competitors, publicize that fact in marketing efforts. Let prospective participants research the differences themselves, if they wish. In fact, help them do so to demonstrate that the price of in-house instruction compares favorably to other sources.

Ensuring That Learners Entering Instruction Are Diagnosed for Their Readiness

Once learners have been enrolled, turn attention to diagnosing their readiness for instruction. Diagnose learner readiness by making sure that they have satisfied prerequisites and that they are motivated to learn.

Have Learners Satisfied Prerequisites?

For an instructional management system to work effectively, there must be a means in place to assess how well learners have satisfied the prerequisites *before* they participate in instruction. One way to do that is to screen learners during formal enrollment. Use an enrollment form or application blank, and ask learners to document how they have met the prerequisites. Prerequisites may include minimum levels of education, experience, or past training. Learners may also be required to provide testimonials from knowledgeable people to attest that prerequisites have been met.

Another way to screen for prerequisites is to administer proficiency examinations to learners. These examinations measure the learners' mastery of prerequisites. Examinations may be administered by using the paper-and-pencil method or the electronic media, or by demonstrating correct performance.

How Motivated Are the Learners?

It is folly to ignore learners' willingness to participate in instruction, since there is a direct and undeniable relationship between learner motivation and achievement (Brown, 1989). The trouble is that assessing and influencing learner motivation is by no means quick or easy (Wlodkowski, 1985). However, several approaches can be used. These approaches can be classified by timing. Some may be used before the instructional experience, some may be used during the experience, and some may be used after it.

Before the experience, simply ask the learners how interested they are in participating in the instruction and what they hope to gain through participation. Do that by including a question on training applications or enrollment forms. As an alternative, send them an attitude questionnaire to complete and return before they begin instruction. (An example of such a questionnaire appears in Exhibit 14.2.) Use the results to assess the level of learner motivation and to determine methods by which to increase it.

During the instructional experience, ask learners what they hope to gain from the instructional experience and then, as instruction is presented, tie each major point to learner interests (Knowles, 1980). Alternatively, ask learners how much the key points are useful to them—and why they are. These approaches will help to crystallize the value of the instruction to the learners.

After the instructional experience, ask learners whether their interest in the subject has increased and how they can apply what they learned on their jobs. Use their responses to assess the learners' motivation. If the instructional experience is subsequently repeated, describe to learners how previous individuals or groups of learners reacted to the instruction, perceived its value, and subsequently applied it to their jobs. Use these testimonials, then, to motivate learners by stressing the value of instruction to them.

Ensuring That Learners Are Directed to an Appropriate Section with Minimum Time and Effort

If learners have demonstrated sufficient mastery of the subject matter, they may have to complete only a portion of it. A *section* is part of an instructional experience—either one unit or lesson. Use print- or electronic-based instructional flowcharts, decision charts, advanced organizers, enabling objectives, proficiency examinations, or a combination of these methods to direct learners to appropriate sections of an instructional experience, depending on their level of subject mastery.

EXHIBIT 14.2. A SURVEY QUESTIONNAIRE TO ASSESS LEARNER MOTIVATION.

Directions to Participants: You are enrolled in instruction on (topic description). As part of your preparation, please complete the questionnaire that follows. Read each statement in the left column and then circle a number appearing in the right column that best summarizes your feelings. Use this scale:

1 = Strongly disagree
2 = Disagree
3 = Neutral
4 = Agree
5 = Strongly agree

When you finish, please return the completed questionnaire to _____
                                                                    (name)
at _____ by _____.
              (address)   (date)

Thank you for your cooperation!

Question	Response				
	Strongly Disagree 1	Disagree 2	Neutral 3	Agree 4	Strongly Agree 5
1. I am highly enthusiastic about participating in this instructional experience.	1	2	3	4	5
2. Based on my past experience, I am sure the instructor or tutor will help increase my interest in this subject.	1	2	3	4	5
3. I find that I enjoy participating in any instructional experience just for the sake of learning something new.	1	2	3	4	5
4. I once experienced a job-related problem that is associated with the subject of this instruction.	1	2	3	4	5
5. I am now experiencing a job-related problem that is associated with the subject of this instruction.	1	2	3	4	5
6. I soon expect to be experiencing a problem, on or off the job, that is related to the subject of this instruction.	1	2	3	4	5
7. Whenever I attend instruction, I find that I learn more from other participants than from the instructor or handouts.	1	2	3	4	5
8. I really find it helpful to discuss job-related problems I face with other people.	1	2	3	4	5

EXHIBIT 14.2. A SURVEY QUESTIONNAIRE TO ASSESS LEARNER MOTIVATION, cont'd.

	Response				
Question	Strongly Disagree 1	Disagree 2	Neutral 3	Agree 4	Strongly Agree 5
9. Whenever I attend instruction, I always have a clear sense of what I "need."	1	2	3	4	5
10. Whenever I attend instruction, I ask questions until my need for help on a problem is satisfied.	1	2	3	4	5

11. If I don't learn anything else, the one thing I do want to learn when I participate in this instructional experience is (fill in the blank): _____

12. The one thing that really interferes with my learning is (fill in the blank): _____

Thank you for your cooperation!

Mastering the Instructional Design Process: A Systematic Approach, Fourth Edition. Copyright © 2008 by John Wiley & Sons, Inc. Reproduced by permission of Pfeiffer, an Imprint of Wiley. www.pfeiffer.com

An *instructional flowchart* illustrates the flow of lessons or topics in an instructional experience. It is frequently used by advocates of Gestalt learning theory to provide learners with an overview of an entire instructional experience before they proceed sequentially through individual parts (Rothwell and Sredl, 2000). An example of such a flowchart appears in Figure 14.1.

A *decision chart* presents prospective learners with an array of choices for entering instruction, based on their demonstrated proficiency. It allows the learner to decide quickly where to begin instruction. An example of such a decision chart appears in Table 14.1.

An *advanced organizer* can be understood as a narrative summary or overview of instruction, although other interpretations are possible. By giving learners advanced organizers for each unit or lesson, they can draw their own conclusions about whether they need to proceed through it.

An *enabling objective* is, of course, directly related to a terminal (or end-of-instruction) performance objective. It enables the learner to master part of a terminal objective. Learners or instructors may use enabling objectives to guide entry to instruction. Learners who have demonstrated mastery of some, but not all, enabling objectives may be channeled to begin instruction at the point they need to through successful completion of proficiency examinations or other methods.

Proficiency examinations are pre-tests, often administered prior to instructional entry, that assess a learner's level of knowledge, skill, or ability and that are specifically intended to channel a learner through instruction to begin at an appropriate point. They are frequently used at the outset of computer-based or text-based programmed instructional lessons, although they may also be used at the outset of group-paced, instructor-led instruction. Administer the proficiency examination immediately following the statement of each lesson's terminal performance objectives. Establish an arbitrary cutoff score, based on formative evaluation, so that learners who achieve all items correctly can move on to the next lesson. In this way, learners can be directed to appropriate sections of instruction.

Of course, you may wish to combine two or more approaches—instructional flowcharts, decision charts, advanced organizers, enabling objectives, or proficiency examinations—to direct learners to appropriate sections of an instructional experience. While that will require expenditure of more up-front effort for an instructional designer, it is likely to ensure that learners will be effectively channeled to the point at which they should begin instruction.

Ensuring That Each Step, Section, or Experience Within the Instruction Is Provided with Transitions and References

Instructional designers should ensure that each step, section, or experience within instruction is provided with transitions and references. A *transition* is a link from past to future learning.

Appropriate transitions depend, for the most part, on how performance objectives have been sequenced. Recall that performance objectives may be sequenced in several ways. Some sequencing possibilities and corresponding transitions are listed below.

Sequencing	*Appropriate Transitions*
Chronologically	Use time as the basis for transitions. Clarify when each task, step, or procedure should occur.
Topically	Simply explain how one topic relates to another.
Whole-to-part	Remind learners of the whole (model, procedure) before proceeding to a description of each individual part.
Part-to-whole	Remind learners of previous parts before proceeding into descriptions of subsequent parts.
Known-to-unknown	Use learner knowledge and skill in building-block fashion.

FIGURE 14.1. AN EXAMPLE OF A SIMPLIFIED INSTRUCTIONAL FLOWCHART.

Structure of the Instruction

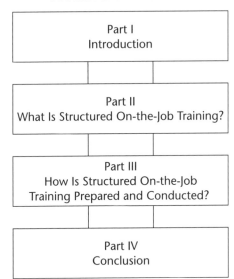

TABLE 14.1. AN EXAMPLE OF A SIMPLIFIED DECISION CHART.

If you already know, or have demonstrated proficiency with, the following	THEN	Move on to this part
1. Familiarity with the difference between structured and unstructured on-the-job training (lesson 1)		Lesson 2
2. Knowledge of the four steps in structured on-the-job training (lesson 2)		Lesson 3
3. How to "tell" learners (lesson 3)		Lesson 4
4. How to "show" learners (lesson 4)		Lesson 5
5. How to ask learners to "do" the task to demonstrate competency with it (lesson 5)		Lesson 6
6. How to "follow up" with learners, providing them with feedback on how well they perform (lesson 6)		Lesson 7
7. How to demonstrate all four steps of structured on-the-job training (lesson 7)		Skip the entire instructional experience

Sequencing	*Appropriate Transitions*
Unknown-to-known	Begin with an upending or unsettling experience, using it to stimulate learner interest in a search for solutions.
Step-by-step	Remind learners of the last step before proceeding to a description of each subsequent step.
Part-to-part-to-part	Relate each part to other parts.
General-to-specific	Begin with a very general description, moving to specialized parts based on learner interests.

Instructional sequence may thus provide important clues about appropriate transitions.

A *reference* is a link to materials outside those of the instructional experience. (In computer-based training it is usually associated with "hot buttons," "hot links," or "context-sensitive help.") For instance, learners may be furnished with up-to-date bibliographies of books, articles, videotapes, and other material in case they wish to pursue learning on their own. Be sure to clarify whether the materials are available through the organization or whether learners must seek out the materials on their own time or at their own expense.

Ensuring That Each Instructional Element Is Easily Identified

Be sure to identify each part of instruction, clarifying its purpose (Why is it there?) and its content (What does the instruction cover?). If the instruction is to be delivered in print media, use headings effectively to identify each instructional element. If instruction is delivered in other media, be sure to clarify purpose and summarize content briefly before presenting it to learners.

Ensuring That Competence Is Documented

Be sure to document that learners have successfully completed the instruction. Do that by testing them and then keeping records of the test scores. Alternatively, instructional designers may wish to have designated subject-matter experts, line managers, or union officials question or observe the learners' performance and then document in writing that the learners have reached a predefined, acceptable level of competence, based on performance measures.

Ensuring That the Learner's Exit from Instruction Is Diagnostic of Future Needs

Instructional designers should make an effort to ensure that each learner's completion of instruction is recognized and used diagnostically in assessing future needs.

First, establish some means by which to recognize or reward learners for successful completion of instructional experiences. For example, prepare training certificates or, if the budget allows, elaborate engraved plaques for each learner. Issue them routinely in a graduation ceremony on completion of instruction. In this way, learners feel encouraged, and they may display the certificates or plaques, thereby providing free promotion for the instruction.

In addition, diagnose future learner needs. Plan to do that at the time learners complete each instructional experience. More specifically, determine whether a future need will exist for each learner, depending on expected changes in organizational strategy, job requirements, or technology. One method: perform a strategic needs assessment at the end of the instructional experience (Rothwell and Kazanas, 1994a). Another method: ask learners to have a follow-up discussion with their supervisors about the value of the instruction.

Ensuring That Record Keeping Is Adequate for Individuals and the Organization

Without information about the individual instructional needs of each learner in the organization, much time and effort can be wasted. After all, learners may be routinely scheduled to participate in instruction that is unnecessary for them.

There are several ways of keeping records of individual participation in instructional experiences. One is through personnel records or human resource information systems. In some organizations, managers prefer to keep all records—job applications, information about salaries, training, off-the-job education, performance appraisals, disciplinary notices, and others—together in one place.

Personnel records have traditionally been paper files. Indeed, the government-prompted necessity for keeping these files was one of the earliest factors that led organizations to establish human resource management departments (Eilbirt, 1959). However, not all organizations keep personnel records of employee participation in off-the-job or on-the-job training, off-the-job educational courses, and conferences.

Human resource information systems are developed to systematically collect, store, maintain, retrieve, and validate data needed by an organization about its human resources. They typically include information about employee security, recruiting, education and training, human resource planning, employee skills, employment records, benefits, wages and salaries, labor relations, medical concerns, and safety. They may, therefore, be used to retain records about employee completion of instruction.

Skill inventories are systematic lists of employee skills (or competencies) in organizational settings. They customarily provide information about individuals' work experiences, educational attainment, proficiency in foreign languages, performance appraisal ratings, employment dates, and other information. Although they have been frequently used, they are by no means easy to develop or maintain. They can be used to keep records of employee participation in instructional experiences—and, most recently, on what competencies individuals have documented track records in demonstrating.

Training record systems may be maintained separate from, or as part of, personnel files, human resource information systems, or skill inventories. Three parts of a comprehensive record-keeping system may exist. The first part—the training center—provides course and cost data and class equipment requirements, class rosters, and enrollment status by class. The second part—the student center—provides information for prospective trainees. It gives them the ability to search for available courses, obtain information on specific courses, enroll in instruction, check on their enrollment status, change their enrollment status, or even review the evaluations of courses. The third part contains information about instructional participants from their human resource files.

Various formats can be used to maintain instructional records. At minimum, most organizations will want to have one system to keep employee information and a separate system to keep course and instructor information. Of course, they should be integrated such that a user can find a direct relationship between participation in various courses and individual employees.

In some organizations, there may be reasons to tie together personnel records, skill inventories, and training record systems, and thus to use a combination of the approaches just mentioned. Instructional designers must lay the foundation for record keeping by systematically analyzing intended uses for records of instruction.

Judging an Instructional Management System

Instructional designers should be capable of judging an instructional management system. This judgment should be based on how well the system meets the criteria for an effective instructional management system described previously in this chapter.

Instructional designers may find it helpful to use a checklist as a decision aid on those occasions when they must judge the appropriateness, comprehensiveness, and adequacy of an instructional management system. An example of such a checklist appears in Exhibit 14.3.

Justifying an Instructional Management System

Instructional designers should be capable of justifying decisions they have made when constructing or judging an instructional management system. To that end, they should be prepared to explain to other people, such as other instructional designers, operating managers, or learners, why the instructional management system was established as it was. For this reason, instructional designers should keep notes about what they have done, and why, so that they can justify their decisions to others when necessary.

What Is New in Designing the Instructional Management System?

In recent years, *instructional management systems* have been renamed as *learning management systems* (LMS) or as *learning content management systems* (LCMS). A learning management system helps in managing learning experiences; a learning content management system helps to do more than that by permitting access to learning objects and instructional applications that can be re-used or re-purposed. A learning content management system permits easy instructional authoring, However, some authorities still use the old term *instructional management systems* to describe any system that helps enroll participants in instruction, market the value of programs to prospective participants and their immediate supervisors, provide support to deliver instruction, provide support for measuring learner achievement through testing, help facilitate evaluation of learning experiencees through online participant evaluations and learner tests, and keep records of learners. The value of an LMS is that it permits learners the freedom to access learning experiences, online instructional games, and instructional records at any time and from almost any place. It is a growing market.

As in any electronically mediated instruction, LMSs have been changing quickly. They are growing to include broadcast quality online video from the desktop, and even social networking such as MyFace and YouTube that allows individuals to trade information or even collaboratively work on problems in real

EXHIBIT 14.3. A CHECKLIST FOR JUDGING THE APPROPRIATENESS, COMPREHENSIVENESS, AND ADEQUACY OF THE INSTRUCTIONAL MANAGEMENT SYSTEM.

Directions: Judge the appropriateness, comprehensiveness, and adequacy of an instructional management system using this checklist. Answer each question appearing in the left column below by checking (✓) an appropriate response in the middle column. If necessary, make notes in the right column on any aspect of the instructional management system that, in your opinion, deserves improvement.

Question	*Response*		*Notes for Improvement*
Does the organization have in place an instructional management system that ensures that . . .	Yes (✓)	No (✓)	
1. Entrance into the instruction is quick and easy?	( )	( )	
2. Entering learners are diagnosed as to their readiness for the instruction?	( )	( )	
3. Learners are directed to appropriate sections with a minimum of time and effort?	( )	( )	
4. Each step, section, or experience within the instruction is provided with transitions and references?			
5. Each instructional element is easily identified in terms of both content and purpose?	( )	( )	
6. Competence is documented in such a way that both management and learners know precisely what is required, when, and the standards applicable?	( )	( )	
7 Exit from the instruction is well documented and diagnostic of future needs?	( )	( )	
8. Recordkeeping is adequate for both individual and organizational purposes?	( )	( )	

time. Social networking is likely to revolutionize instruction, since it facilitates an online learning community in which people can learn from each other.

The same is also true of *instant messaging*, which has already been used for real-time coaching online. Already individuals are meeting through instant messaging, face-to-face through inexpensive webcams, and can trade information in real time. Such technology even facilitates globalization by permitting virtual teams to meet online and collaborate around problem solving.

A third revolutionary technology is *Second Life* (see, for instance, http://secondlife.com/), which permits individuals to adopt a three-dimensional image representing themselves (called an *avatar*). Second Life gives individuals the freedom to try out new things without being bound by their real-world personas. Learning by experience takes on a whole new meaning when individuals can adopt a persona other than their own to interact with other people. That facilitates experimentation and also reduces resistance that stems from always "considering the source" (see "Learning Management System," 2007). Already the evidence suggests that workers are spending much time in social networking sites while at work, and it is a challenge for employers to figure out how to make social networking improve—rather than distract from—productivity (Krell, 2007). Social networking and Second Life both offer the promise of completely new ways to encourage worker interaction and participation (Frauenheim, 2007).

The future is likely to include workers talking to each in real time by video and even using personal digital assistants (PDAs) to do that, making coaching and even planned instruction available almost anywhere that a signal can reach.

Conclusion

In this chapter, we began with a brief case study to dramatize issues associated with instructional management systems. We then described how to address each key requirement for an effective system. Finally, we offered a few words of advice about judging and justifying such a system. In the next chapter, we turn to a related subject: planning and monitoring instructional design projects.

CHAPTER FIFTEEN

PLANNING AND MONITORING INSTRUCTIONAL DESIGN PROJECTS

Instructional design projects can grow complex. Simple ones may involve only a few people; complicated ones may involve teams of many people to oversee instructional design, subject matter, graphic design, and delivery systems. It is therefore important to develop a plan as a basis for monitoring the progress of each project.

Project planning has never been more important. That is particularly true in large-scale multimedia projects where runaway costs (and runaway staff) can drive up the costs and lead to long delays if projects are not forcefully managed. That is most true when many experts must be coordinated in an instructional design team (Beer, 2000; Conrad and TrainingLinks, 2000; Driscoll, 1998).

In this chapter, we will describe how to develop a project management plan for an instructional design project, beginning with a brief discussion about the background of project management and planning. We will then describe key issues to consider when planning and monitoring projects. We will conclude the chapter with a few words about judging and justifying project plans.

According to *The Standards* (Richey, Fields, and Foxon, 2001, p. 53), one competency for instructional design is to "plan and manage instructional design projects." It is regarded as an advanced competency. The performance statements associated with this competency indicate that instructional designers should be able to (Richey, Fields, and Foxon, 2001, p. 53):

a. Establish project scope and goals (advanced).
b. Use a variety of techniques and tools to develop a project plan (advanced).
c. Write project proposals (advanced).
d. Develop project information systems (advanced).
e. Monitor multiple instructional design projects (advanced).
f. Allocate resources to support the project plan (advanced).
g. Select and manage internal and external consultants (advanced).
h. Monitor congruence between performance and project plans (advanced).
i. Troubleshoot project problems (advanced).
j. Debrief design team to establish lessons learned (advanced).

Also important, according to *The Standards* (Richey, Fields, and Foxon, 2001, p. 54), is the competency for instructional design to "apply business skills to managing instructional design." It is regarded as an advanced competency. The performance statements associated with this competency indicate that instructional designers should be able to (Richey, Fields, and Foxon, 2001, p. 54):

a. Link design efforts to strategic plans of the organization (advanced).
b. Establish strategic and tactical goals for the design function (advanced).
c. Use a variety of techniques to establish standards of excellence (advanced).
d. Develop a business case to promote the critical role of the design function (advanced).
e. Recruit, retain, and develop instructional design personnel (advanced).
f. Provide financial plans and controls for the instructional design function (advanced).
g. Maintain management and stakeholder support of the design function (advanced).
h. Market services and manage customer relations (advanced).

Two other competencies are also relevant to this chapter, focused on project management.

According to *The Standards* (Richey, Fields, and Foxon, 2001, p. 50), one competency for instructional design to "reflect upon the elements of a situation before finalizing design solutions and strategies." It is an essential competency. The performance statements associated with this competency indicate that instructional designers should be able to (Richey, Fields, and Foxon, 2001, p. 50):

a. Generate multiple solutions to a given problem situation (advanced).
b. Remain open to alternative solutions until sufficient data have been collected and verified (essential).

c. Assess the consequences and implications of design decisions on the basis of prior experience, intuition, and knowledge (advanced).

d. Revisit selected solutions continuously and adjust as necessary (advanced).

Also important is the competency to "select, modify, or create a design and development model appropriate for a given project" (Richey, Fields, and Foxon, 2001, p. 51). It is an advanced competency. The performance statements associated with this competency indicate that instructional designers should be able to (Richey, Fields, and Foxon, 2001, p. 51):

a. Consider multiple design and development models (advanced).

b. Select or create a model suitable for the project based on an analysis of model elements (advanced).

c. Modify the model if project parameters change (advanced).

d. Provide a rationale for the selected design and development model (advanced).

The Background of Project Management and Planning

Project management as it is known today was introduced as an efficient and effective way to assemble, in a short time, a team of people whose combined knowledge and expertise matched up to unique situational and technical demands posed by a given work assignment (Cleland, 1964). Since that time, project management has been widely used whenever it has been necessary to assemble groups of technical or professional employees, such as groups of medical doctors, lawyers, engineers, accountants, or combinations of all these. Within the last few years, project management and planning has been facilitated through project software that has automated many routine project management issues and project management certification that has professionalized project management.

Differences Between Project Management and Traditional Management

Project management differs in key respects from traditional management, which is typified by a line and staff organization. In a traditional organizational structure, *line managers* exert direct authority over people. They are action-takers who are responsible for getting the work out. They issue orders, make decisions, and allocate rewards. A production manager in manufacturing exemplifies line management. Staff managers, on the other hand, support and advise line managers. In the simplest sense, they are idea makers and are responsible for seeing to it that decisions made by line managers are well advised. They do not have the authority to issue orders, make decisions, or allocate rewards; rather, their social power stems from expert knowledge of their specialty (French and Raven, 1959). A human resource manager exemplifies staff management. Conflict frequently arises between line and staff managers, particularly because staff managers have historically tended to be younger, less experienced, and better educated than their line management counterparts (Dalton, 1969).

Unique Challenges Posed by Project Management

Project management poses unique challenges unlike those encountered in traditional line and staff organizations.

First, project managers are selected on the basis of their ability to grapple with a temporary problem or complete a unique work assignment. Team members may not have worked with each other before and may never work with each other again. The team leader must be skillful in facilitating group dynamics and team building, helping members of the group proceed quickly through the forming and storming stages in which all groups progress.

Second, project managers lack the long-term authority over people that is effectively wielded by supervisors in line and staff organizations. They are only temporary bosses. Hence, project managers must be very skillful in negotiating with people and influencing them.

Third, project managers exercise greater control and enjoy greater flexibility over their work assignments than most traditional managers do. As the workload necessitates, they can add or subtract team members, sharing expertise with other project managers. That is usually difficult in line and staff organizations.

Project planning and managing thus poses its own challenges and frustrations. Its unique strengths make it well-suited to the demands of instructional design work, in which it is usually necessary to pair up experts in instructional design with experts in subject matter and instructional media production.

Projects can spin out of control, however, for many reasons. It is not always the fault of a bad plan. Consider the following vignette described by a respondent to Rothwell's (2003) survey, undertaken for the third edition of this book:

"In 2001 I was involved in developing a CD for supervisory training. I was one of an eclectic team of instructional systems specialists working on this project. The skills varied, and many of the areas for training were apt to change significantly in the short term. On top of this a test was developed. No real analysis was done, [and] no gaps were identified beyond anecdotes. Learning objectives were developed, but they were not adequate for writing test questions over. The stakeholders for the various topics were not available or support materials such as policies and procedures had yet to be developed. The program was to be passed on to the field and updated as needed. We subsequently needed updates but had no funds for updating the CD and for reproduction costs. Poor quality of content and poor planning led to the program being passed on in a questionable condition."

This passage underscores some real-world dilemmas that instructional designers face in doing project work.

For more information on project management as it applies to instructional design, consult Halprin and Greer (1993); Harvey (1993); Hennessy and Hennessy (1989); Jackson and Addison (1992); Lowe (1993); Mohler (1993); Molenda, Pershing, and Reigeluth (1996); Murphy (1994); Schulz, (1993); and Wallace (1991).

Key Features of Project Planning and Controlling

All projects share certain common features: they must be planned, scheduled, and controlled. Figure 15.1 illustrates key project tasks, means of accomplishing tasks, and timing of tasks.

As part of project planning, instructional designers must also prepare a time line or chart and a budget, establish a control system to monitor the time of instructional designers and track project accomplishments, establish methods for allocating funds, and plan equipment and facility requirements. Each activity deserves closer consideration.

Preparing a Time Line

When developing a project management plan, instructional designers usually prepare a time line or project chart with milestones and deadlines. Such time lines or charts serve several purposes.

First, they focus attention on identifying procedures—and specific tasks and subtasks within procedures—that are to be performed during the project. Second, they help allocate responsibilities by identifying *who is to do what by when.* Third, they provide the basis for controlling project time, budgeting money, and estimating staffing requirements. Fourth, they minimize the work needed to complete the project successfully, since they allow the project manager to identify efficient ways to cut corners while achieving effective results. Fifth, they provide a basis for estimating project duration. Hence, preparation of a project

FIGURE 15.1. PLANNING, SCHEDULING, AND CONTROLLING INSTRUCTIONAL DESIGN PROJECTS.

FUNCTIONS	→PLAN —————→	SCHEDULE ————→	CONTROL →
What are the activities?	• Identify the resources needed to carry out the project and the times when they are needed	• Prepare guidelines for each resource that indicate when they are needed	• Establish means to track resource utilization and occasions when resources are not being efficiently or effectively used

How are the activities to be accomplished?	• Track expenditures
	• Track use of human resources
	• Track time
	• Track milestone charts
		• Charts
		  • People
		  • Money
		  • Equipment
		  • Facility use
		  • Dates
			• Budget reports
			• Activity reports
			• Time reports
			• Other reports

When are the activities to be carried out?	• Before the project begins • As changes occur in the project	• Slightly before the beginning of the project • Continuous monitoring during the project	• During the project

Source: Adapted from the classic work by Gaither, N. *Production and Operations Management: A Problem-Solving and Decision-Making Approach.* Hinsdale, IL: Dryden Press, 1980, p. 311.

time line or chart requires project managers and/or members of an instructional design team to think through project activities before they begin.

Instructional design work usually involves separate teams working on different, but related, projects. However, there are different types of projects. Each requires an appropriate time line or chart, designed especially for the project. For example, *performance analysis* is one type of instructional design project. Described at length in Chapter Two, performance analysis clarifies what the performance problem is and what alternative performance improvement strategies can be used to address the problem. In carrying out a performance analysis project, a team of instructional designers conducts a background investigation. That means they clarify what is happening, identify what should be happening, assess the difference, consider the importance of that difference, identify possible causes of the problem, identify possible performance improvement strategies, and select a strategy. Other steps may be added.

The second type of project is *needs assessment,* described at length in Chapter Four. Sometimes it is conducted by the same team that conducted the initial performance analysis. But since needs assessment is often a massive undertaking and is crucial for providing information about the instruction necessary to address a performance problem, it is more often carried out by a team different from the one conducting the initial performance analysis. As a result, needs assessment becomes a separate project in which the following question should be addressed:

1. What results are desired from the needs assessment?
2. Whose needs are to be assessed?
3. What methods will be used to select a representative group of people from the target audience?
4. By what means will information be collected?
5. What management approvals are necessary to collect that information?
6. How will the information collected during the needs assessment be analyzed?
7. How will instructional needs be identified from results of data collection and analysis?

Some needs assessment projects may encompass assessments of relevant characteristics of learners (Chapter Five), analysis of relevant characteristics of the work setting (Chapter Six), and job, task, or content analysis (Chapter Seven).

The third project type takes up where needs assessment leaves off. Called *pre-instructional planning* and described in Chapters Eight to Eleven, such projects have a fourfold purpose: (1) preparation of performance objectives, (2) development of performance measurements, (3) sequencing of performance objectives, and (4) specification of instructional strategies.

The fourth type of project takes up where pre-instructional planning leaves off. It involves the *preparation of instructional materials.* Members of the instructional design team work together, using the blueprints prepared in earlier steps, to create the materials that will help narrow or close an identified performance gap. The steps in this type of project were described in Chapter Twelve.

The fifth type of project is *evaluation*. It may be combined with the design of an instructional management system, although that may be a sixth type of project in its own right. The steps in these projects are outlined in Chapters Thirteen and Fourteen.

To prepare a time line or chart, instructional designers must first clarify the scope of the project. In other words, what results or tangible products (deliverables) must the project produce? Next, identify questions or issues to be addressed by the project. Arrange them in a logical order. Then ask team members to think through how the questions are to be answered. In other words, what procedures—and tasks or subtasks within the procedures—must be carried out to answer the questions or address the issues? Next, estimate the number of staff members and types of expertise they must possess to carry out the procedures. Allocate the workload (procedures, tasks, and subtasks) and assign responsibility to individuals on the team, describing who must do what by when.

When these steps have been carried out, instructional designers have established the basis for a time line or chart that will set forth, in a visual format, who does what by when. Although it may be subject to eventual revision, it provides the basis for estimating project requirements and establishing direction for conducting the project. (It should be noted that, in the real world, sometimes the final deadline is fixed and the project steps are backed into to meet the deadline.)

Over the years, several different techniques have been suggested for preparing project time lines or charts. They include scheduling and control charts, the critical path method, and the program evaluation and review technique. Although they deserve more attention than we will devote to them here, instructional designers should have some awareness of what these techniques are and how they can be used in planning, scheduling, and controlling instructional design projects.

Scheduling and control charts are commonly used in instructional design work, as they are in manufacturing. A variation of the original chart prepared at the beginning of this century by Henry Gantt, the chart is formatted with project activities along the left margin, dates along the top, and bars representing time lines. By consulting the one-page chart, which is updated during the project as progress on activities is made, members of an instructional design team can receive simple and instant feedback about their progress.

The *critical path method* (CPM) was developed by Remington Rand in 1957. It is appropriate for complex instructional design projects in which timely completion of each procedure, task, or subtask is imperative. Since it is relatively expensive to use, CPM should be reserved for those occasions when it is really justified by the costs involved or by the importance of retaining client good will. Like scheduling and control charts, CPM allows for continual updating as a project unfolds. Also like scheduling and control charts, CPM requires a complete list of project activities (procedures, tasks, and even subtasks). Unlike scheduling and control charts, however, CPM requires instructional designers to describe the interrelationships between activities carefully. The time necessary for each activity must be specified. Using a CPM chart, members of an instructional design team identify what tasks must be performed in what sequence. Moreover, it is possible to identify the most efficient methods of conducting tasks.

The *program evaluation and review technique* (PERT) closely resembles CPM. Indeed, PERT and CPM are frequently confused. The chief difference is that CPM requires only one time estimate per activity; PERT, on the other hand, requires three. PERT relies on probabilistic estimates of each activity's duration; CPM relies on a single estimate. In all other respects, PERT and CPM are identical. Both are valuable tools for planning, scheduling, and controlling instructional design projects.

Budgeting Projects

When developing a project management plan for an instructional design project, instructional designers should not only be capable of devising some form of time line or chart but should also be capable of preparing a budget that considers project expenses. A budget is a key to planning and controlling in many organizations. The budget is prepared as a financial plan and serves as a means by which to monitor project operations through costs. For instructional designers functioning as external consultants, the budget that is provided in the proposal for a project is often the key feature determining whether a profit or loss will result from the project, so estimating a project budget in a proposal is one of the most important skills that can be learned by a consultant. (Without first-rate budgeting skills for proposals, a person will be out of business quickly by either setting a price so high that competitors will get the business or so low that no profit can be realized.)

Most organizations have some budgeting process. Budgets are tools for translating organizational plans into action. In business firms, organizational budgets are usually based on, and constrained by, projections of sales and production levels. In government agencies, on the other hand, budgets are based on (and constrained by) projections of tax and other revenues.

Budgeting for instructional design projects, however, poses a somewhat different challenge than is typically encountered by managers who budget for long-term, continuing operations.

First of all, instructional design projects are usually one of a kind. As a consequence, they do not provide a historical record of activities. By way of contrast, a production manager in a manufacturing firm may enjoy the luxury of many years' past budgets, providing valuable clues about (1) what to budget for, (2) how much to budget based on expected levels of production activity, and (3) what areas in the production budget have been most difficult to estimate. Instructional designers rarely enjoy the luxury of an extended project history.

Second, instructional design projects are temporary. Although they can and often do spill across annual budgeting cycles, they do come to an eventual conclusion. In this respect, they differ from (for example) departmental budgeting in line and staff organizations. Project budgets stem directly from detailed descriptions of planned project activities. In other words, instructional designers must first have very detailed descriptions of what they plan to do before they can prepare a budget of what resources are needed to do it. This detailed description should at least set forth the expected project duration, project tasks, staffing requirements, staff travel, equipment needs, facility needs, and other resources necessary for conducting the project. Project budgets should also provide estimates of how much financial support will be needed to enact the project plan and when that support will be needed. For this reason, instructional designers must think through, before the project begins, how much money will be required to obtain the desired results and when that money is likely to be expended.

Third, budgets for instructional design projects require as much—if not more—control than is typical for departmental budgets. After all, budgets are only useful if there is a reliable way to keep track of spending, linking budgeted estimates (*plans*) with expended dollars and project outcomes (*results*). It is thus important to establish a budgeting control system that keeps track of expenditures and ties them to budget estimates originally made through an *audit* or *paper trail*. In this way, instructional designers can see how well the budget estimates eventually compare to expended funds and project results.

How is a project budget developed? First, learn the budgeting system and budgeting cycle of the client organization. Budgeting systems and cycles are not all the same. How does the budgeting process work in the organization? What special forms, if any, are used in the budgeting process? What special charts of accounts providing ready-to-go budget categories already exist? What key dates must be met to submit a budget in the organization? How do decision makers want to handle project budgets relative to the human resource development department's budget? What special audit requirements are tied to organizational budgets? What other special requirements, such as governmental record keeping, must be established and maintained for the budget?

When these difficult questions have been answered, then prepare a detailed project plan that describes what procedures, tasks, and subtasks will be performed and what resources will be needed to perform them. Use this plan as the basis for the budget. Above all, be sure to estimate how many staff members will be needed at different stages of the project, how long they will be needed, and how much they will cost to maintain by way of salary, benefits, and equipment. (The expenses for staff are usually the greatest.) An excellent approach is to budget for each step, or in a large project each task, of a project separately and then roll them up into such categories as salaries, fringe benefits, indirect overhead charges, equipment, supplies, communication requirements, and others to create a master budget for the entire project. It may also be necessary to estimate benefits resulting from a project as well as expenses to maintain a continuing cost-benefit analysis for the project.

In some organizations, there is an overall budget for the human resource development department but separate budgets for each instructional design project. There may, in fact, be other budget centers as well. For a new instructional designer, the relationship between the department budget and one or more complicated project budgets may be difficult to understand.

Probably the best way to integrate project and departmental budgets is to use a bottom-up approach to the budgeting process. Instructional designers budget separately for each project, based on their project plans, and then submit them to become part of the human resource development department budget.

Monitoring the Time of Instructional Designers

Instructional design projects are often successful when they are completed on a timely basis. For this reason, when a project plan is developed, instructional designers need a system to track the time and timeliness of instructional designers on a project team.

One effective way to track the time of instructional designers is to develop a chart at the outset of a project and update it on a regular basis as milestones are achieved. For instance, a *scheduling and control chart* can be prepared with activities listed along the left margin, dates along the top, and bars representing time lines. Each bar is then color-coded to indicate which instructional designer on a team is primarily responsible for that task or activity. If posted online or in a prominent location, the chart provides feedback to all team members about project progress. Color coding can also designate individual responsibility on a PERT or CPM chart.

Another effective way to track time is to request a regular (usually weekly) *progress report* from each instructional designer. These reports may be submitted in a simple memo format, or the project leader can supply team members with a simple standardized format to save time (see Exhibit 15.1). Reports can uncover short-term or intermediate-term project problems, allowing the project leader to intervene when help is needed. Particularly useful for helping to manage different teams operating at geographically scattered locations, they provide documentation of progress that can later contribute valuable information for project performance appraisals of each team member.

A third way to track the time of instructional designers is to conduct *regular weekly meetings* with all team members. These meetings provide opportunities for sharing information across the team; the lack of information can cause problems in a project when team members are working on different activities simultaneously. Most staff meetings are held with groups of no more than twelve people. The project leader opens the meeting with a project summary and any news affecting the entire project team. Groups or individuals assigned to different activities then report briefly on their status, explaining how they are progressing compared with deadlines, what special difficulties they have encountered, and how they are coping with those difficulties. Meetings usually conclude after in-depth discussion of special project-related problems affecting individuals or the entire project team. Of course, such meetings may be held face-to-face or virtually.

Tracking Project Accomplishments

Just as instructional design projects are often successful only when they are completed on a timely basis, instructional design work is often successful in an organization only when instructional designers can track and publicize project successes.

EXHIBIT 15.1. A STANDARDIZED FORMAT FOR A PROGRESS REPORT.

Progress Report

Name _____ Date _____
Location _____ Project Number_____

1. Duties and Activities. (*Describe briefly what activities you have been assigned and pertinent deadlines.*)

2. Progress. (*Describe briefly how much progress you have made over the past week. Cite specifics and results acheived, if any.*)

3. Problems. (*Describe any special problems you are encountering on the project.*)

Small change efforts often build an impetus for larger and more successful efforts. For this reason, be sure to establish a means of tracking project accomplishments. There are two ways to do that: by documenting success cases and change.

A *success case* is a description of something that worked out well. For instructional designers, it is an anecdote that captures the essence of a project and describes a successful result (Brinkerhoff, 1983). Despite everything that has been said about the weight placed on profits in business and industry, human nature is such that telling a story about a success often has more emotional and persuasive impact on listeners than pages of financial reports or complex statistics. People have a natural interest in others, and a success case is a powerful way to tell a story about what happened to others during an instructional project.

Set out to collect success cases during each instructional design project. Ask team members to keep their eyes peeled for individuals whose scores on pre-tests and post-tests are phenomenal; appeal to participants during instruction to report any successes they subsequently experience when they apply on the job what they learned in instruction. Classify these cases as individual or departmental successes. Then report them when there is a need to build, or keep, support for an instructional project in the organization or when attracting members of the targeted audience to participate in instruction.

If facts and figures are preferable to emotionally appealing success stories, track instructional design project accomplishments by documenting measurable change resulting from them. *Documented change* can be arrived at in several ways, perhaps in a way consistent with Kirkpatrick's hierarchy of evaluation (1996).

Document participant reaction by collecting information about participant attitudes, perhaps through an attitude survey, before the instructional experience. Then administer an identical attitude survey as a participant reaction questionnaire following the instructional experience. Compare the differences. Use the results to demonstrate attitudinal change among participants.

Document learning by administering pre-tests and post-tests. Compare the results. Use them to demonstrate changes in knowledge or skills of participants, being sure to comply with standard statistical requirements for data analysis. Document post-instructional results by tracking the turnover and relative performance of participants. If possible, compare participants over an extended time period to a comparable control group of individuals who, for one reason or another, did not participate in the instruction. Use positive results to make the case that participation in instruction benefits individuals and the organization.

Establishing and Using Methods to Reallocate Funds

When developing a project plan, be sure to establish ways to redistribute funds, within existing project constraints, to manage differences between planned and actual project performance to meet project obligations. For instance, match the project budget to deadlines. If deadlines are not reached, or are reached sooner than expected, be prepared to compensate by making adjustments to the budget. Establish a regular schedule to review the budget and expenses compared to project deadlines. Find out, too, what procedures are used in the organization to justify budget variances, that is, differences between planned and actual expenditures.

Planning and Monitoring Equipment and Facility Requirements

Consider equipment and facility requirements when preparing a plan for an instructional design project. Each project necessitates specialized planning for equipment and facilities. For instance, during a performance analysis, members of an instructional design team will typically need desks, chairs, lights, computers, and telephones. Although there is a temptation for the management of a client organization to supply whatever spare space and equipment may already be available, the project leader should see to it that necessary equipment and facilities are requested before they are needed and are available when needed.

To plan equipment and facilities, begin with a master scheduling and control chart for the project. For each activity listed on the chart, estimate equipment and facility needs. Be sure to consider, of course, what will be needed, how much will be needed, and when it will be needed. Then allow time for the equipment and facility requests to be reviewed, approved, and acted on.

Establish a sign-up system for allocating equipment and facilities, since they may face conflicting demands. Make sure that the project leader resolves conflicting demands as they arise. Monitor equipment and facilities against the master scheduling and control chart. Each time a piece of equipment or a facility is used, ask instructional designers to track it. Then review equipment and facility use periodically.

Judging a Project Plan

Instructional designers should be capable of judging the quality of a project plan. This judgment should be based on whether the plan includes a time line or chart, a budget, a control system to monitor time and track project accomplishments, methods for allocating funds, or descriptions of equipment and facility requirements.

Judge the appropriateness and comprehensiveness of a project plan by using a checklist as a decision aid. An example of such a checklist appears in Exhibit 15.2.

The results of a 1993 survey shed light on critical attributes of instructional design projects. They are worth bearing in mind when judging such projects. The survey results revealed that instructional designers should take seven key actions in any instructional design project (Halprin and Greer, 1993):

- Conduct a front-end analysis.
- Complete a time estimate and project schedule.
- Define the roles and responsibilities of project team members.
- Identify clearly the target audiences for the instruction as well as the skills to be taught and the content.
- Complete a detailed blueprint (plan) to guide the project.
- Complete and review drafts that meet material specifications.
- Create, assemble, and store high-quality masters and copies of all instructional materials.

Justifying a Project Plan

Instructional designers should be prepared to explain to colleagues on the instructional design team and managers what elements have been included in the project plan, what elements have been omitted, and the reasoning underlying the choices made. As always, instructional designers should be prepared to address challenges to their judgment by others. Be prepared, then, to answer each of the following questions:

- How was project time planned and monitored?
- How was the budget prepared, and what variances resulted?
- How was the control system established to monitor time and track project accomplishments?
- How were funds allocated?
- How was equipment planned? How were facility requirements planned?

Be prepared to answer—and justify the answers to—each of these questions.

Problems often occur on projects when events take unexpected turns and not everyone involved is clued in to what is happening. Consider the following

EXHIBIT 15.2. A CHECKLIST FOR JUDGING THE APPROPRIATENESS AND COMPREHENSIVENESS OF A PROJECT PLAN.

Directions: Judge the appropriateness and comprehensiveness of a project plan using this checklist. Answer each question appearing in the left column below by checking (✓) an appropriate response in the middle column. If necessary, make notes in the right column on any aspect of the project plan that, in your opinion, deserves improvement.

Question	Response		Notes for Improvement
	Yes	No	
Does this project plan include . . .	(✓)	(✓)	
1. Some form of timeline or chart that includes key development milestones and interim and final deadlines?	( )	( )	
2. A budget that			
a. Considers project expenses?	( )	( )	
b. Considers the total amount available for the project?	( )	( )	
c. Is broken down into generally acceptable budget categories?	( )	( )	
3. Some system that keeps track (weekly) of the			
a. Designer's time?	( )	( )	
b. Budgets?	( )	( )	
c. Timelines?	( )	( )	
d. Measurable impact?	( )	( )	
4. Some mechanism for identifying discrepancies between the project plan and actual progress?	( )	( )	
5. Some procedure for reallocating funds (within project constraints) to resolve discrepancies between actual and planned project performance to meet project commitments?	( )	( )	
6. Equipment requirements?	( )	( )	
7. Facility requirements?	( )	( )	

situation described by a respondent to Rothwell's (2003) survey, which was conducted in preparation for the third edition:

> "A client asked for assistance on an interesting instructional design and development project where her former boss was the lead developer and a team was to do most of the content development. Once the project began, the lead explained that he knew nothing about the instructional design process but instead should be considered a subject-matter expert (SME). He expressed confidence that I could do the job. The team said they couldn't really write anything. I was given kudos for the work I had done in running the meeting and in organizing an approach. I agreed to capture all of the data, design the training, and begin to develop the material. I had to keep the lead knowledgeable about what I was doing but do all of the work myself. He agreed to review the material. The lead expressed confidence in the work after reviewing it. The time line was extremely short. My contractual agreement was for a limited role and for my labor alone. The lead agreed to allow me to use my office staff for assistance in order to meet the deadline and since he and the committee were unavailable to do any work other than review. My accounting branch submitted bills for labor hours expended. I drafted some material roughly in order to get an okay before proceeding. I sent a copy to the lead and to the client. In the cover letter, I acknowledged that the product was not heavily edited and I stressed in the disclaimer that I was looking for agreement on approach and format before proceeding. Some pages just had display text so the page layout could be evaluated. The lead reviewed it and said he understood what I was trying to do and agreed with it. The client called me and said that I was to stop work immediately and that I had committed fraud. She said that my office had billed for the labor of people (some who were editors) who were not in the original agreement (although I had not exceeded any amount) for labor. She further explained that the submittal was considered unacceptable because it contained too many errors. All invoices were returned unpaid."

What Is New in Planning and Monitoring Instructional Design Projects?

The process of planning and monitoring instructional design projects is changing most due to the easy availability of new technology and growing sophistication in project management.

New technology makes it easier for supervisors, coaches, and even virtual team members to meet in real time through a host of media, such as cell phones, personal digital assistants, BlackBerries, video applications, instant messaging, and many more. Instructional designers can receive almost instant help to deal with on-the-spot challenges. That ready availability of supervisors may lead to growing stress as it makes it easier for supervisors to micromanage and builds stress in supervisors who find that they may need to be available nearly at all times to offer advice, coaching, and support to workers who need it or who want it.

Project management competence is critically important to instructional designers. Much of what they do is managed in a project format. The prevalence of designations to certify project managers has encouraged growing sophistication among instructional designers, their supervisors, and managers in guiding instructional design projects. See, for instance, online descriptions of the Master Project Manager (MPM), the Certified International Project Manager (CIPM), the Master Project Manager (MPM), and the Certified Project Manager (CPM).

The challenge in many work settings today, however, is managing across many projects—that is, multi-tasking. Some people compare this challenge to juggling. Many projects must be overseen at the same time, which builds stress and increases the chance that important issues will be lost in the shuffle across many different projects and clients. That leads to growing interest in whole systems transformational change (WSTC), which involves a fundamental re-examination of all goals and projects at once with a goal of bringing them all together around a larger unity of goals (Holman, Devane, and Cady, 2007). In many cases, WSTC requires many stakeholders—and sometimes the whole organization—to come together to re-examine the change projects underway and to find ways to unify them.

Conclusion

In this chapter, we described key issues to consider when planning and monitoring instructional design projects. We concluded the chapter with a few words about judging and justifying project plans. Now we turn to the first of three chapters focused on the importance of communication in instructional design.

CHAPTER SIXTEEN

COMMUNICATING EFFECTIVELY

Instructional designers should be proficient in written, oral, and visual communication. That means, of course, they should be able to read, write, speak, listen, and express themselves effectively with visual aids. Unfortunately, few people—whether high school or college graduates—bring to their jobs the polished communication skills expected by many managers today. However, effective communication is as essential to success in the field of instructional design as it is in many other fields.

According to *The Standards* (Richey, Fields, and Foxon, 2001, p. 46), one competency for instructional design is to "communicate effectively in visual, oral, and written form." The performance statements associated with this competency indicate that instructional designers should be able to (Richey, Fields, and Foxon, 2001, p. 46):

a. Create messages that accommodate learner needs and characteristics, content, and objectives (essential).
b. Write and edit text to produce messages that are clear, concise, and grammatically correct (essential).
c. Apply principles of message design to page layout and screen design (essential).
d. Create or select visuals that instruct, orient, or motivate (essential).
e. Deliver presentations that effectively engage and communicate (essential).
f. Use active listening skills in all situations (essential).
g. Present and receive information and ideas among individuals with diverse backgrounds and roles (essential).

  h. Seek and share information and ideas among individuals with diverse backgrounds and roles (essential).
  i. Facilitate meetings effectively (essential).

Cutting-edge approaches to thinking about effective communications go beyond traditional views, stressing the value of networking, communities of practice, rotational assignments across organizations, and communal space (Galbraith, Downey, and Kates, 2002).

This chapter briefly reviews principles of effective communication as they apply to instructional design. Its purpose is to provide useful information to sharpen and improve communication skills. It is worth noting that, while an increasingly virtual world leads to less frequent face-to-face interaction, communication skills remain critically important to success in any field.

Using Effective Visual Communication

Instructional designers should be able to communicate their ideas in powerful ways. That may include visually appealing documents or other written material.

The Power of Visual Communication

Of all modes of communication, visual communication may be the most powerful. In describing the efficiency of visual communication, Peoples (1988, p. 66) writes, "Of the total inventory of knowledge you have in your head, 75 percent came to you visually, 13 percent through hearing, and a sum total of 12 percent through smell, taste, and touch. In fact, if I show you a pictorial presentation of a key point and say nothing, the comprehension and retention will be 3 1/2 times greater than if I just say the words without a picture. And if I do both—give you the words and the picture—the comprehension and retention will be six times greater than just saying the words." The sense of sight can thus lead to significantly increased learner comprehension and retention. As Wileman (1980, p. 16) points out in a classic treatment of the topic, visualization is a powerful communication tool for three major reasons: (1) a visual message can be attention-getting, (2) a visual message can be efficient, and (3) a visual message can be effective. Instructional designers should thus be skilled in using techniques of effective visual communication so they can take full advantage of its power to increase learner comprehension and retention.

Appropriate Uses of Visualization in Communication

According to a classic treatment by Wileman (1980), visual messages can be appropriate for presenting or reinforcing any of the following kinds of information:

1. *Concrete facts* (such as the types of energy particles in elementary physics).
2. *Directions* (such as steps in preparing spaghetti).
3. *Processes* (such as steps in conducting strategic business planning).
4. *Bits of data* (such as the age distribution of the U.S. population).
5. *Comparative data* (such as the relative temperature averages between Miami and Chicago).
6. *Data recorded over time* (such as the average annual rainfall in New Zealand).
7. *Organizational structure* (such as reporting relationships at IBM).
8. *Places* (such as a map of Washington, D.C.).
9. *Chronologies* (such as the history of industrial training).
10. *A generalization* (such as the rate of return on investments in human capital).
11. *A theory* (such as Einstein's theory of relativity).
12. *Feelings or attitudes* (such as sadness, love).

Each occasion imposes its own demands on the instructional designer, prompting a different type of visual representation.

Identifying Types of Visual Images

Wileman (1980) identifies seven types of visual images, ranging from the purely verbal to the purely visual (see Figure 16.1). At the lowest level (Type I), the visual image is simply a representation of the printed word. At the highest level (Type VII), information is conveyed through pictorial or graphic symbol, is highly abstract, and is purely visual. For Wileman, the choice of appropriate visual imagery is not absolute; rather, it depends on the occasion.

Using Cues

A *cue* is a signal for action. In visual communication, a cue is a signal to the viewer that an object, represented on a visual, is worthy of special note (Wileman, 1980). Suppose, for example, that a visual shows a group of people representing all age categories, but an arrow is drawn to a small child in the group. That arrow is a cue, since it draws attention to one person in the picture. To "cue" the significance of a visually depicted object to a viewer, use various techniques. One technique is to superimpose writing on the object itself. Other methods of adding

FIGURE 16.1. TYPES OF VERBAL-VISUAL IMAGE RELATIONSHIPS.

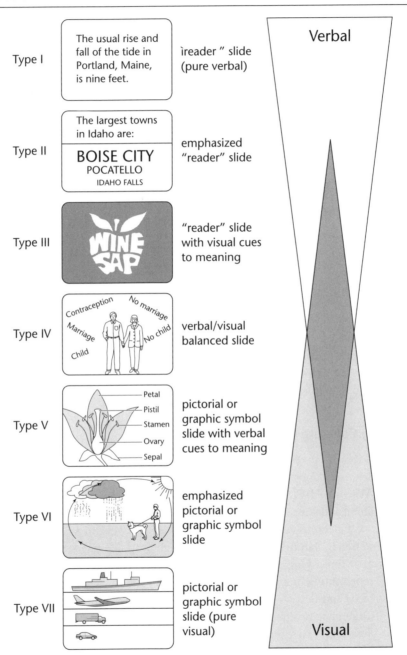

emphasis also work. These can include using colors, decorations, or symbols such as stars or arrows. In visual media, a cue can also be provided by doing a close up of one image.

Highlighting Key Attributes in a Visualization and Minimizing Irrelevant Attributes

An *attribute* is an essential quality or feature. Since the visual medium does not lend itself well to verbal discourse, instructional designers should be able to highlight key attributes of a message for visual representation. As evidence of the importance of selectivity in the visual medium, consider that many audio-visual experts recommend including no more than twenty-four words on an overhead transparency or a still slide (Wileman, 1980). The reason: more information than that will diminish the value of such a Type I visual representation, simply confusing the viewer with too many stimuli.

Develop images and visual reinforcements by starting with the instructional materials. Identify key ideas for presentation or reinforcement. Use three criteria by which to judge: (1) Is the idea essential to achieving performance objectives? (2) Does the occasion lend itself to visual representation because an idea can be effectively presented visually? and (3) Is the idea important enough, relative to other ideas presented in the instructional materials, to warrant special reinforcement through visual representation? If all three questions can be answered by yes, use visual representation; if the answer to any question is no, devote attention to highlighting other ideas visually.

Selecting Concrete Concepts for Visualization

A *concrete concept* is usually equated with phenomena found in everyday life. There are three kinds: (1) plans and organization charts, (2) maps, and (3) chronologies (Wileman, 1980). Each lends itself to concrete representation, "an attempt to be literal and realistic in the presentation of information" (Wileman, 1980, p. 12).

Concrete concepts can be illustrated in several ways. For instance, each step in a plan may be conveyed through graphic images associated with time or activities. As an example, a time line running through a year may show symbols representing four seasons. (Examples of symbols might include snow for winter, birds and flowers for spring, falling leaves for fall, and a hot sun for summer.) Organization charts lend themselves easily to visual representation through lines and boxes, representing positions of authority and reporting relationships. Maps may be presented three-dimensionally, proportionally, or by other means. Chronologies, like steps in a plan, may be conveyed through graphic images.

Select concrete concepts for visualization by examining instructional materials. Highlight plans, reporting relationships, maps, or chronologies. Then decide, based on the relative importance of the concepts, whether they warrant visual presentation or reinforcement. If they do, decide what kind of visual representation to use.

Selecting Abstract Concepts for Visualization

An *abstract concept* is the same as an invisible concept. It is equated with complex or highly abstract phenomena. There are three kinds: (1) generalizations, (2) theories, and (3) feelings and attitudes (Wileman, 1980). A generalization is "a conclusion or 'truth' underlying a field of inquiry" (Wileman, 1980, p. 12). A theory is "a verified or conjectured formulation about an underlying artistic or scientific principle" (Wileman, 1980, p. 12). Feelings and attitudes are expressions of subjective emotions, not as easily depicted visually as tangible facts. Each does not lend itself easily to concrete representation, since no visual object is closely associated with the concept (Wileman, 1980).

If an abstract concept must be visually represented, seize the chance to exercise considerable creativity. Abstract concepts usually require visualization through pictorial or graphic symbols, sometimes highly abstract ones. Use essentially the same approach to select abstract concepts for visualization that would be used to select concrete concepts for visualization. Begin by examining instructional materials and identifying abstract concepts. Highlight generalizations, theories or feelings, and attitudes. Then, based on the relative importance of the concepts, decide whether they warrant visual representation. If so, use graphic or pictorial displays for this purpose. For more information on visual literacy, see Moore and Dwyer (1994).

Using Effective Oral Communication

Instructional designers should be able to communicate orally in powerful ways.

Principles of Effective Oral Communication

Perhaps the first principle of effective oral communication is the use of correct grammar. The English word grammar is derived from the Greek word for "letters," *grammatikos*. Appropriate use of grammar is expected in everyday conversation and in formal group presentations. When grammar is used inappropriately, however, speakers lose credibility. Indeed, an audience may discount the speaker's message simply because its presentation is faulty. The reasoning, fair or unfair as it might be, is that speakers who cannot use appropriate grammar probably also have faulty thinking or a flawed message. Use of appropriate grammar is important for establishing and maintaining credibility.

Spoken language is rarely scrutinized for grammatical correctness in the same way that written language often is. (However, spoken language may give rise to comment when words are mispronounced.) One reason is that spoken language is fleeting; written language is enduring. The receiver of a spoken message also has less time to subject the message to scrutiny. In addition, spoken language relies in part on the speaker's body language and tone of voice to establish meaning. In written language, the words stand alone and must convey the message.

Grammatical mistakes do occur in speech, however. They are likely to occur when speakers engage in heated debate and thus make statements without thinking about them carefully first, make use of convoluted sentence structure in an effort to impress others, or for some other reason use nonstandard syntax.

Use the following tips to help improve grammar while speaking. First, think through what will be said before saying it. If unsure of subject-verb agreement or pronunciation, then recast the sentence so as to avoid using a problematic construction. Second, use simple sentences. Avoid trying to impress listeners. Simply say what should be said. There is elegance in simplicity. Third, become familiar with books on English usage. Purchase at least one good dictionary, a thesaurus, and a book on specialized usage.

Using an Appropriate Understandability Level

To make oral communication understandable, always plan the presentation. Make the effort to do that, even when the occasion is informal and the presentation will be made to just one other person or to a small group. Decide whether the aim is to inform or persuade. Whenever preparing to speak, perform an audience analysis. Such an analysis should include a review of the objectives for the presentation, the speaker's relationship to the audience, the length of that relationship with the audience, the audience's vocabulary level, and the willingness of the audience to accept the ideas that will be presented. As part of the audit, analyze specific members of the audience to whom the presentation will be addressed. Classify their knowledge of the subject, their opinions, any reasons why they may have a special interest in the subject, and any attention-getting techniques such as stories, demonstrations, or statistical information that may make a favorable impression. Base the presentation on the results of that analysis.

Using Acceptable Organization

Organizing conversation, whether it is formal or informal, is very much like sequencing performance objectives. In fact, the very same principles of organization may be applied in both cases. An oral presentation may thus be organized based on time or topic. It may also flow from whole to part, part to whole, known to unknown, unknown to known, step by step, part to part to part, or general to specific. (We will not describe these organizing principles here, as they were described at length in Chapter Ten.)

The important point is to choose the organization of the presentation based on the objectives (*What results are to be achieved?*), the audience (*What do they think of the desired results?*), and the subject matter (*What is the subject?* and *What does the audience know about it?*). In the broadest sense, any conversation may be classified as informative or persuasive. An informative presentation is geared to instructing an audience. It begins with background information and then moves into topical, timely, or detailed descriptions. A persuasive presentation is intended to convince an audience that an idea or belief has value. The presentation is usually organized in such a way that audience interests are described first, followed by a description of an idea that will satisfy those interests.

Using an Acceptable Presentation Format

Presentation format refers to the way messages are delivered to an audience. In oral communication, presentation format may include one-on-one (dyadic) meetings, small-group meetings, and large-group meetings. Choose a presentation format based on the communication climate, situation, expectations of others, and expectations of the presenter.

Communication climate refers to how people behave, what they perceive, how they respond to each other, what their expectations are, what conflicts exist among them, and what opportunities exist for development. It is thus related to perceptions of organizational members about the ways in which they are expected to act and behave. In using communication climate to choose presentation format, consider these questions adapted from the classic questions posed by Waters, Roach, and Batlis (1974): (1) How are important messages typically presented in the organization? (2) How are important decisions typically made? (3) How is technology used in the organization's communication processes? and (4) How do lower-level members of the organization influence decision making at the top? The answers to these questions should provide useful clues about what presentation format is appropriate for a given occasion.

Situation means the relative willingness of people in the organization to accept change. Situations range from highly favorable to highly unfavorable. The more unfavorable the situation, the greater the likelihood that the presentation format will have to be highly persuasive; the more favorable the situation, the greater the likelihood that the presentation format should be informative.

Expectations of others are influenced, to a great extent, by organizational climate and culture. Consider: How have instructional designers presented their ideas in the past? How do others expect them to present their ideas now?

Expectations of presenters are also influenced by organizational climate, culture, and expectations of others. Consider: How do instructional designers feel they should present their ideas? Why? Choose the presentation format based on answers to these questions.

Answering Questions Posed by Others

Be prepared to field questions posed by others. Indeed, it should be possible to anticipate the questions others will pose, based on an advance analysis of audience members' self-interests. Fielding questions may be viewed as a process, and answers to questions may be arranged in a taxonomy of difficulty loosely adapted from the Bloom (1956) taxonomy of educational objectives. The taxonomy of answer categories is as follows (Sanders, 1966, p. 3):

1. *Memory.* Be prepared to answer questions requiring listeners to recall information.
2. *Translation.* Be prepared to answer questions in such a way as to change existing information into something new.
3. *Interpretation.* Be prepared to answer questions so as to help listeners discover relationships between facts, generalizations, values, and skills.
4. *Application.* Be prepared to answer questions so as to lead listeners to solve a problem requiring identification of an issue and selection and use of appropriate generalizations and skills.
5. *Analysis.* Be prepared to answer questions so as to help listeners solve a problem in light of conscious knowledge of parts and forms of thinking.
6. *Synthesis.* Be prepared to answer questions requiring original thought and insight.
7. *Evaluation.* Be prepared to answer questions requiring judgments of what is good and bad, right or wrong, according to predefined standards.

Use a worksheet like the one shown in Exhibit 16.1 to help anticipate questions that may be posed by others and to choose the types of answers appropriate to the occasion.

EXHIBIT 16.1. A WORKSHEET FOR ASSESSING APPROPRIATE ANSWERS TO QUESTIONS.

Directions: Use this simple worksheet to help you anticipate questions that you may be asked by others and to formulate appropriate answers to them. Assume, for purposes of this worksheet, that you have prepared a presentation and that you intend to give it to one or more people. In the first part of the worksheet, summarize your audience analysis. In the second part, describe the questions you fully expect to be asked by your audience, based on your analysis of their interests. In the third part, consider the taxonomy of answers and select one answer category appropriate for addressing the concerns of your audience.

Part I: Audience Analysis

1. *Describe the results of your audience analysis.* Consider: What is your relationship to your audience? How is the audience likely to receive your message? What does the audience know about the subject? What are their opinions on the subject likely to be? What interest will the audience have in the subject? How important is the subject likely to be to the audience, considering members' present problems and concerns? In what ways have you tried to secure and retain their attention during the presentation?

Part II: Questions Expected from the Audience

2. *List the questions you expect from the audience about your presentation.* What are they likely to want to know more about, considering their self-interests?

Part III: Answer Categories

3. Select answer categories for each question listed in response to Part II. Recall that the answer categories are as follows: (1) memory, (2) translation, (3) interpretation, (4) application, (5) analysis, (6) synthesis, and (7) evaluation.

Using Rules or Standards of Conduct Accepted as Appropriate by an Authentic Source

Rules and standards of conduct should be considered when planning and delivering oral messages. How do people communicate orally in the organization? The answer depends, of course, on culture—"the way we do things around here"—and on individual preferences. Be sure to ask others how people communicate. Is it necessary to make an appointment with someone, or does an open door policy make it possible for instructional designers to meet with people informally and on the spur of the moment? What are the expectations of decision makers in the organization about appropriate ways to conduct oral communication? Is anything in particular (such as profane language) not permitted?

If instructional designers have occasion to communicate orally, particularly if they must make formal presentations, they may wish to polish their oral communication skills. Books on public speaking are available through professional societies, libraries, and bookstores. Obtain one and study it carefully.

To learn more, observe effective speakers in action. Note their techniques closely. What do they do? Practice those techniques. Instructional designers who desire eventual promotion should be aware that special competencies (platform skills) are expected of classroom instructors, whose positions are sometimes a rung above instructional designers on the career ladder. As described by another competency study sponsored by the International Board of Standards for Training, Performance, and Instruction (Hutchison, Stein, and Shepherd, 1988), instructors should at least be able to

1. Analyze course materials and learner information.
2. Assure preparation of the instructional site.
3. Establish and maintain instructor credibility.
4. Manage the learning environment.
5. Demonstrate effective communication skills.
6. Demonstrate effective presentation skills.
7. Demonstrate effective questioning skills and techniques.
8. Respond appropriately to learners' needs for clarification or feedback.
9. Provide positive reinforcement and motivational incentives.
10. Use instructional methods appropriately.
11. Use media effectively.
12. Evaluate learner performance.
13. Evaluate delivery of instruction.
14. Report evaluation information.

These competencies are described in detail in King, King, and Rothwell (2000).

To improve communication skill, perhaps in anticipation of becoming an instructor, instructional designers should examine each competency described. Then they should rate themselves on them, identifying strengths and weaknesses. They should ask their supervisors, and perhaps their professional peers as well, to do the same. Finally, they should solicit opinions about how they may overcome identified weaknesses through formal or informal learning.

Using Effective Written Communication

Instructional designers should be able to communicate in written form effectively. Of course, software can be used to check—and enhance—writing. (See www.whitesmoke.com/landing_flash/grammar.html?d=9&a=5&r=21&gclid=CPHm_oiF8JICFQhusgodFRFx4Q)

Principles of Effective Written Communication

The key grammatical rules for effective written communication with which instructional designers should be familiar are summarized succinctly in a classic book by Strunk and White (1979). Writing has never been more important, as it is a medium that is often key to success in online instruction as well as in preparing classroom materials (Ko and Rossen, 2001). Instructional designers may use the worksheet appearing in Exhibit 16.2 to assess examples of their writing against the grammatical rules offered by Strunk and White. If they identify a discrepancy between what they have written and a rule of grammar, they should review the appropriate section in Strunk and White (1979) or a simliar source or discuss the discrepancy with a more seasoned instructional designer whose writing is considered clear and concise by others. Training on writing can also help improve writing skills.

Using an Appropriate Understandability Level

Instructional designers should gear their messages to their readers' level, using language that is likely to be understood. However, they should remember that the message is more likely to be read when it is easy to read, short and succinct, answers all the key questions of importance to the reader, makes clear what action (if any) is required by the reader, and has been revised several times for clarity.

First, make the message easy to read. Readers are more likely to understand written communication best when it does not use many multi-syllabic words, lengthy sentence structure, or passive constructions in which nobody ever takes any action. Unfortunately, we have found that it is far easier to get people to criticize the writing of others than to view their own writing with a critical eye.

EXHIBIT 16.2. A WORKSHEET FOR ASSESSING YOUR WRITING FOR GRAMMATICAL CORRECTNESS.

Directions: Select an example of your writing. Compare it to the rules stated below. You should be able to answer every question by checking (✓) yes. If you must check no, then review your writing for grammatical correctness. If you do not understand the question, then read the section in the classic by Strunk and White (1979) or a simliar work to understand it.

Questions **Have you . . .**	*Yes* (✓)	*No* (✓)
1. Formed the possessive singular of nouns by adding 's?	( )	( )
2. Used a comma, in a series of three or more terms, after each term except the last?	( )	( )
3. Enclosed parenthetical expressions between commas?	( )	( )
4. Placed a comma before a conjunction introducing an independent clause?	( )	( )
5. Taken care not to join independent clauses by a comma?	( )	( )
6. Avoided breaking sentences in two?	( )	( )
7. Used colons appropriately to introduce		
a. A list of particulars?	( )	( )
b. An appositive?	( )	( )
c. An amplification?	( )	( )
d. An illustrative quotation?	( )	( )
8. Used a dash to set off an abrupt break and to announce a long appositive or summary?	( )	( )
9. Used the number of the subject to determine the number of the verb?	( )	( )
10. Used the proper case of each pronoun?	( )	( )
11. Made sure that each participial phrase at the beginning of a sentence refers to the grammatical subject?	( )	( )
12. Chosen a suitable design for your composition and held to it?	( )	( )
13. Made the paragraph the clear unit of composition?	( )	( )
14. Used the active, rather than passive, voice?	( )	( )
15. Made an effort to state ideas positively?	( )	( )
16. Used definite, specific, and concrete language?	( )	( )
17. Omitted needless words?	( )	( )
18. Avoided instances in which there are successions of loose sentences without clear logical connections between them?	( )	( )
19. Expressed coordinate ideas in similar form?	( )	( )
20. Kept related words together?	( )	( )
21. Used a consistent tense?	( )	( )

Source: Excerpt pp. v–vi from *The Elements of Style,* 4th ed. by William Strunk, Jr. and E.B. White. Copyright ©2000 by Allyn & Bacon. Reprinted by permission of Pearson Education, Inc.

One tool may be useful for this purpose—the readability formula. A readability formula measures the relative difficulty of writing, often expressing it in the form of a grade-level equivalent. Although such a formula does not help a writer detect grammatical errors, it may improve the ease with which readers can comprehend a written message. More than one hundred such formulas exist (Klare, 1979; Torrence and Torrence, 1987).

Perhaps the most popular and still widely used readability formula is the Gunning Fog Index (Gunning, 1952). To apply the Gunning Fog Index: (1) select three passages of one hundred words each; (2) count one hundred words from each passage; (3) count the number of sentences in each passage; (4) divide the number of sentences by 100 to determine average sentence length; (5) count the words of three or more syllables, excluding capitalized words and verbs ending in -ing or -ed; (6) add average sentence length and number of three-syllable words; and (7) multiply the sum of (6) by 0.4 to obtain a *grade-level equivalent* (Drew, Mikulecky, and Pershing, 1988). The theory is that the lower the grade-level equivalent, the easier the material should be to read. Of course, some word-processing programs have built-in ways to examine readability.

Second, make the message short and succinct. Some managers routinely place any memo or report longer than one or two pages at the bottom of their in-baskets, where the document remains to collect dust for some time. Bear that expectation for brevity in mind whenever writing to learners or to managers. Long written messages often receive the same treatment as bottles cast in the ocean.

Third, answer key questions of significance to the reader. It is just as important to conduct an audience analysis audit before writing as it is to do so before speaking. Try to anticipate the questions that the readers will want to have answered. Be sure to answer them. One way to measure the effectiveness of written communication is surprisingly simple: count the number of people who have to ask questions after reading the message. Less effective messages produce many people who have to ask follow-up questions.

Fourth, make clear what action is required from the reader. Always ask this question: Is it clear to the reader what he or she must do after reading this correspondence or this memo? Be sure to ask for that action in the final paragraph. If no action is required, ponder whether a written message is warranted at all.

Fifth, be willing to revise the writing for clarity. Some people who seldom write have the impression that revision is a sign of weakness or mental inefficiency. That is just not true. Effective writers prepare a draft, then (if time allows) they lay it aside for a while. When they return to it, they are able to revise it for clarity with a fresh eye. Revision often economizes writing, making it more powerful and succinct.

Using Acceptable Organization

Many instructional design projects culminate in a letter, report, memo, instructional text, or script. As in speaking, writing should be organized based on objectives (*What results are to be achieved?*), the audience (*What do they think of those desired results?*), and the subject matter (*What is the subject?* and *What does the audience know about it?*). There are no simple and clear-cut rules.

When organizing written communication, be sure to grapple with at least one major issue: Should sufficient detail be provided to answer all the questions that might be posed by interested readers, or should brevity be the guiding factor? Unfortunately, the answer to this question is not always clear. But it is possible to strike a balance. Do that by providing *both completeness and brevity*. How is that possible? First, write a complete report of the project; second, write a very brief *executive summary* addressing key points. Apply other rules to preparation of instructional materials themselves (Carter, 1985).

Organize the report chronologically, reflecting the progress of the project itself. First, describe the background, explaining why the project was initiated and how its objectives were clarified. Second, describe the investigation, detailing how the problem was researched. Third, summarize results of the investigation. Fourth, make recommendations for action, supporting them by appropriate estimates of costs and benefits. A fifth but optional section can address possible difficulties that may arise in implementing the recommendations, suggesting steps that can be taken to minimize negative side effects that may stem from taking action (Rothwell, 1996a).

Reverse this order in an executive summary. First, make recommendations for corrective action. Second, summarize results of the investigation so that the reasons for taking action are clear. Third, describe briefly how the investigation was conducted. Fourth, remind readers why the project was initiated. Keep the executive summary as short as possible. One or two pages is usually the right length. Refer interested readers of the summary to details in the report, or offer to make an oral presentation to them.

Using an Acceptable Presentation Format

Should a letter, memo, formal report, electronic mail message, World Wide Web site, or some combination of these be written to present the results of the project to management? Choose the presentation format based on the same three questions that guided the organization: (1) What results are to be achieved? (2) What do they think of those desired results? (3) What is the subject, and what does the audience know about it?

Follow some simple guidelines. In most cases, it is a good idea to use a letter or memo to make a short proposal, express a simple idea, or summarize and follow up on meetings. Memos are particularly useful for making simple and non-controversial progress reports or expressing a simple idea for broad distribution to others. Write a formal report when describing the results of an in-depth investigation. Use electronic mail for short, timely messages that do not require immediate answers, such as those that may be obtained by telephone or personal visit.

Answering Questions Posed by Others

Use a written message when there is good reason to prompt others to reflect on an issue before giving an answer or directions. Written messages may also help instructional designers crystallize their own thinking. The process of composing written language demands thought and reflection; spoken language, spontaneous as it is, does not require the same degree of thoughtful consideration and planning. Likewise, the process of reading prompts people to reflect on an issue or idea in a way that they may not when a message is communicated orally.

Using Rules or Standards of Conduct Accepted as Appropriate by an Authentic Source

Refer to a definitive source such as a dictionary, thesaurus, and usage manual whenever there is an occasion to write. Remember that the writer's credibility depends as much on how a message is written as on what is written. Spelling errors, word usage mistakes, typographical errors, and grammatical faults will detract from the writer's credibility, leading others to question the quality of the message and the writer's competence. On occasion, instructional designers may wish to ask colleagues to read what they have written before they send it to its intended audience. In this way they can test its effects.

What Is New in Communicating Effectively?

There are many ways to communicate. But research by consulting company Watson Wyatt (2003/2004) has found that:

- "Companies that communicate effectively have a 19.4 percent higher market premium than companies that do not.

- Shareholder returns for organizations with the most effective communication were over 57 percent higher over the last five years (2000–2004) than were returns for firms with less effective communication.
- The 2005/2006 study found evidence that communication effectiveness is a leading indicator of financial performance.
- Firms that communicate effectively are 4.5 times more likely to report high levels of employee engagement versus firms that communicate less effectively.
- Companies that are highly effective communicators are 20 percent more likely to report lower turnover rates than their peers.
- Two-thirds of the firms with high levels of communication effectiveness are asking their managers to take on a greater share of the communication responsibility, but few are giving them the tools and training to be successful.
- Global firms are not customizing their messages to meet local needs or cultural sensitivities.
- On average, firms within the financial and retail trade sectors rank among the most effective communicators. Health care, basic materials, telecommunications and other service companies rank among the least effective communicators."

Communication—broadly defined—is thus increasingly important. New technology opens up many new avenues for communication, though many people feel burned out using email and other impersonal forms of communication that do not facilitate face-to-face interpersonal interaction. Improving communication may require starting with an assessment of it, which usually takes the form of a *communication audit*. It measures the quantity and quality of communication in an organization, division, department or team. And it provides a foundation to pinpoint areas for possible improvement in communication.

For instructional designers, communication is—and remains—a critical competency area. How people are approached is as important as the content of any message delivered to them. When important decisions are to be made, it usually helps to reduce the issues to writing to focus time and reflection on the thoughtful answers. But if give-and-take interaction is important, then meetings may remain essential.

Conclusion

In this chapter, we briefly reviewed principles of effective communication as they apply to instructional design. In the next chapter, we turn to another topic that is also related to effective communication—successful interpersonal skills.

CHAPTER SEVENTEEN

INTERACTING WITH OTHERS

Instructional design is not a solitary pursuit. Instead, it requires relations with many different people such as training managers, managers of operating departments, subject-matter experts, media production people, graphic artists, and trainees. When designing instruction, interaction with others is not always easy because it may require people to think or act in new ways and function under high stress.

Yet interpersonal skills are crucial to success in the instructional design field. In this chapter, we will describe how instructional designers should establish rapport, state the purpose of an interaction, ask questions, provide explanations, listen actively, deal with friction, handle resistance to change, keep people on track, secure commitment, and select appropriate behaviors for effective interpersonal interaction.

According to *The Standards* (Richey, Fields, and Foxon, 2001, pp. 53–54), one competency for instructional design is to "promote collaboration, partnerships, and relationships among the participants in a design project." It is regarded as an advanced competency. The performance statements associated with this competency indicate that instructional designers should be able to (Richey, Fields, and Foxon, 2001, pp. 53–54):

a) Identify how and when collaboration and partnerships should be promoted (advanced).
b) Identify stakeholders and the nature of their involvement (advanced).

c) Identify subject-matter experts to participate in the design and development process (advanced).
d) Build and promote effective relationships that may impact a design project (advanced).
e) Determine how to use cross-functional teams (advanced).
f) Promote and manage the interactions among team members (advanced).
g) Plan for the diffusion of instructional or performance improvement products (advanced).

Establishing Rapport

Establishing rapport is essential for instructional designers. *Rapport,* in its simplest sense, can be understood to mean interpersonal trust. Hence, establishing rapport means creating a trusting relationship with another person or group of people. It is perhaps best understood as synonymous with effective interaction, meaning the interpersonal skills leading to mutual trust.

Perhaps the most important single element in working as an instructional designer is this ability to inspire (and keep) trust. Trust has been the focus of much attention in recent years. For instance, McLagan (2003) found it to be key to a "change-capable" organization. Successful CEOs are those who can establish and keep employee trust (Finley, 2002). Effective executive coaches inspire client trust (David, 2001). Work on virtual teams requires trust (Guillot, 2002), and trust is essential in groups demonstrating emotional intelligence (Druskat and Wolff, 2001). But volatile working conditions, prevalent in so many workplaces today, undermine trust because face-to-face relationships are essential to it (Prusak and Cohen, 2001).

Kirkpatrick (1978, p. 46), in a classic description, listed the key conditions of rapport as follows:

"(1) There is mutual respect between sender and receiver; (2) Friendly relationships exist between sender and receiver; (3) The sender encourages questions and feedback from the receiver; (4) The receiver doesn't hesitate to say, 'I don't understand'; (5) When [the] sender says 'Do you have any questions?,' the receiver feels free to ask questions without fear of being embarrassed or ridiculed; (6) The sender is willing to accept responsibility for the receiver's understanding or lack of understanding; and (7) The sender compliments [the] receiver for understanding and blames self if the receiver misunderstands."

To these conditions we can add several listed in Foshay, Silber, and Westgaard (1986, p. 92) that are still relevant today:

"(1) The dialogue should continue as long as the instructional designer wants, (2) information is not withheld from or by the instructional designer, (3) false assumptions about the instructional designer are not made, and (4) information given to the instructional designer is not changed to meet the individual's or group's assumptions about what kind of person the instructional designer is."

But how are these conditions established? The instructional designer's affiliation is the first consideration in creating and maintaining rapport. Conditions for establishing rapport differ, depending on whether you are an instructional designer working as an internal or external consultant. Insiders, working as internal consultants, are employed by the same organization as their potential clients. They have usually established a reputation by which group members may predict their behavior. However, outsiders working as external consultants or simply as vendors are not employed by the same organization.

Instructional designers who work within organizations sometimes enjoy an advantage over outsiders in that they may have more understanding of the organization's culture as well as the key beliefs and values of its leaders. They can thus have unique insight into the causes and ramifications of a problem. Yet they may also experience difficulties in initiating contact with others, since insiders are so familiar that their expertise may not be fully appreciated, they may lack authority or access within the organization's chain of command, or they may have experienced past problems with others so that their ability to help is compromised.

Instructional designers working as external consultants, however, may not have interacted with members of the client organization's management before and thus may lack social ties. And members of the organization have had no experience—as they may have had with insiders—by which to predict the instructional designer's behavior or assess how the designer may interact with others. Yet instructional designers who work as external consultants do enjoy certain advantages: they are (sometimes) accorded expert status in a way that insiders rarely are; they might enjoy a special reporting relationship with or access to top managers; and they might be able to look at a problem with a fresh perspective, one that is not colored by in-house politics or organizational traditions and culture.

The outsider sometimes experiences difficulties in establishing credibility. Outsiders must therefore work to establish, to the satisfaction of their clientele, that they are trustworthy, knowledgeable, and diligent. By trustworthy, we mean that instructional designers must demonstrate that they are not mere pawns of top managers. By knowledgeable, we mean that they must demonstrate enough knowledge about the organization, industry, and problem that they are viewed as credible. By diligent, we mean that instructional designers must be perceived by insiders as capable of researching problems in all their complexity and as capable of following up or implementing the solutions they propose. To establish rapport when working as an outsider, instructional designers must demonstrate thoughtfulness, a willingness to listen to what others have to say, and the ability to function within the norms of the organization's culture.

The situation is the second issue affecting interaction. Instructional designers typically initiate relationships with potential clients under two possible sets of circumstances. In the first situation, help is requested by a prospective client, and instructional designers are asked to research a problem, assess needs, or otherwise investigate and take appropriate action. In this situation, they do not initiate the relationship. They are asked for help, and they meet with a representative or group of representatives from the organization requesting that help. In the second situation, instructional designers request help from others. In this situation, then, they initiate the interaction and the relationship. Others are asked for information or for permission to obtain information.

Both situations may be encountered in the same instructional design project. For instance, top managers or key middle managers may request assistance to analyze a human performance problem or design instruction. In the process of conducting performance analysis, the instructional designer may also need to initiate contact with others in the organization to obtain information.

The basic steps in establishing and maintaining rapport are outlined in Table 17.1. Study that table carefully. As you do so, you may wish to consider that establishing good rapport has important cross-cultural implications. As Odenwald (1993, p. 44) notes, "The strong task orientation of Western culture does not play well in many Asian cultures that regard establishing good rapport as the first order of business." For that reason, instructional designers should also remain vigilant to the importance of rapport in some cultures–and adapt accordingly as project requirements necessitate.

Stating the Purpose of an Interaction

Instructional designers should be able to explain why an interaction must occur. Purpose simply means the reason for an interaction with another person. Agenda refers to the sequence of events that will occur during an interaction.

TABLE 17.1. A MODEL FOR SELECTING TECHNIQUES TO ESTABLISH AND MAINTAIN RAPPORT IN INSTRUCTIONAL DESIGN PROJECTS.

| | *Affiliation* | |
Situation	Insider	Outsider
Request Initiated by Others	*Before initial meeting* Ask for advance information about the problem. Research the in-house politics of the problem, if possible. Research the person who requested assistance, if possible. Dress to make a good first impression. Prepare some questions in advance.	*Before initial meeting* Ask for advance information about the organization and problem. Find out what you can. Dress to make a good impression. Prepare some questions in advance. Prepare biosketch and list of references who can provide information about your skills/abilities.
	During initial meeting Allow the initiator of the meeting to set agenda. Take notes. Demonstrate attending skills. Ask "how can I help?" Determine purpose of meeting, nature of help required. Clarify your reporting relationship. Ask key questions. Clarify next steps.	*During initial meeting* Allow the initiator of the meeting to set agenda. Take notes. Ask "how can I help?" Determine purpose of meeting and nature of help required. Clarify your reporting relationship. Ask key questions. Clarify next steps.
	After initial meeting Follow up, summarizing help requested and next steps.	*After initial meeting* Follow up, summarizing help requested and next steps.
	In subsequent interaction Demonstrate thoughtfulness, keeping others informed.	*In subsequent interaction* Demonstrate thoughtfulness, keeping others informed.
Request Initiated by Instructional Designer	*Before initial meeting* Clarify protocol for contacting people and follow it. Make advance contact, clarifying nature of request. Try to arrange for another person in the organization to contact the individual, requesting his or her cooperation (when appropriate). Dress to make a good first impression. Prepare questions in advance. Prepare an agenda for the meeting in advance.	*Before initial meeting* Clarify protocol for contacting people and follow it. Make advance contact, clarifying nature of request and who has approved the meeting. Ask your "contact" in the organization to help arrange the meeting, when appropriate, to help lay the groundwork for cooperation and show evidence that the request for information has been approved by key managers in the organization.

TABLE 17.1. A MODEL FOR SELECTING TECHNIQUES TO ESTABLISH AND MAINTAIN RAPPORT IN INSTRUCTIONAL DESIGN PROJECTS, cont'd.

Situation	Affiliation	
	Insider	**Outsider**
		Dress to make a good first impression. Prepare questions in advance. Prepare an agenda for the meeting in advance.
	During initial meeting	*During initial meeting*
	Run the meeting. Begin the meeting with small talk to set the individual at ease. Clarify who you are, where you come from, what you want, why you want it, how the information you request will be used, and who will see the results of any investigation you conduct. Establish your own credibility. Listen actively. Make your request specific and (if possible) show how providing information could benefit the individual to whom the request is being made. Encourage participation by the individual who will provide the information. Clarify next steps.	Run the meeting. Begin the meeting with small talk to set the individual at ease. Clarify who you are, where you come from, what you want, why you want it, how the information you request will be used, and who will see the results of any investigation you conduct. Establish your own credibility. Listen actively. Make your request specific and (if possible) show how providing information could benefit the individual to whom the request is being made. Encourage participation by the individual who will provide the information. Clarify next steps.
	After initial meeting	*After initial meeting*
	Thank the individual for his or her time and effort. Summarize the meeting and next steps.	Thank the individual for his or her time and effort. Summarize the meeting and next steps.
	In subsequent interaction	*In subsequent interaction*
	Remain thoughtful and considerate of others' viewpoints and feelings.	Remain thoughtful and considerate of others' viewpoints and feelings.

When deciding how to state the purpose or agenda of an interaction, instructional designers should always ask themselves three questions: (1) Have good relations already been established with the individual or group with whom interaction is necessary? (2) Is the nature of the interaction structured or unstructured?

(3) How much authority do instructional designers have to enforce cooperation from others? These questions, based on Fiedler's time-tested contingency theory of leadership, can provide practical guidance about how to state the purpose or agenda of an interpersonal interaction (Fiedler, 1967; Fiedler and Chemers, 1974). While Fiedler's views on leadership have not escaped criticism, they are quite practical and can be applied in specific situations as instructional designers confront situations while performing their work.

Relations Between Instructional Designer and Individual or Group Members

How well have instructional designers been able to establish and maintain good rapport with the clients? How much trust, respect, and confidence exists in this relationship? When little or no rapport has been successfully established between instructional designers and others within the organization—an unfortunate situation that does happen—instructional designers should work on improving their interaction. They can do that by spending more time face-to-face with others or by giving them opportunities to participate in the process of collecting or interpreting information.

Nature of the Interaction

What is the nature of the interaction? In other words, how easily can instructional designers explain to others the tasks to be performed during their project? How clear-cut is the range of possible strategies that can be used to identify or address human performance problems? How easily can instructional design decisions be justified? When the nature of the activities to be performed in the interaction is easily understood, the range of possible strategies is limited, and instructional designers can justify their actions and decisions without too much difficulty, the situation is structured. When activities are difficult to explain, the range of solutions is not limited, and instructional designers find it difficult to justify their actions and decisions, the situation is unstructured.

When the situation is structured, instructional designers should find interaction easy enough. They need only explain their reasons (purposes) and describe what steps they must take to collect information or find a solution. On the other hand, unstructured situations are more difficult. In those cases, they should try to find an "idea champion" from the organization to help reassure those who may be concerned about the project and to function as a liaison with others. To reduce the likelihood of misunderstandings that could destroy rapport, instructional designers should take pains to brief managers at the outset of the project about their need for information, the steps in the project, and key assumptions underlying those steps. They are thus able to facilitate decisions and interaction. Much has been written about the importance of facilitation (Bentley, 1994; Driskell, Olmstead, and Salas, 1993; Kinlaw, 1993, 1996; Schwarz, 1994).

Instructional Designers' Position Power

Position power refers to the ability, perceived or real, to exact obedience from others. When instructional designers begin an assignment with full support from top managers and easy access to them, their position power is said to be high; when they begin an assignment without full support from top managers or without access to them, their position power is said to be low.

When position power is high, ask that a top manager or sponsor send out a memo or email to solicit support and cooperation during data collection. (Instructional designers may have to draft the memo themselves for the top manager's initials.) That should provide an adequate introduction to those who must be contacted within the organization. When position power is low, base information requests on the problem itself. Explain why the information is needed and how it can help solve the problem or prepare instruction. In other words, point out the problem, state what information needs have to be met to solve it, and ask others pointedly for their cooperation. Use influence effectively to intervene in the inner workings of the organization (Tosti and Jackson, 1992).

Asking Questions

Instructional designers should be able to "ask questions of individuals or groups so that they (1) gather all the information that is required for their purpose; (2) gather the information accurately; [and] (3) phrase and sequence questions so the individual or groups provide the information they have" (Foshay, Silber, and Westgaard, 1986, p. 94). Of course, questions are powerful tools for data gathering. They can shed new light on perceptions of problems, people, or events. Instructional designers may use questions to collect information about existing human performance problems, identify performance criteria or managerial expectations, pinpoint causes of performance problems, and determine the significance of those problems. They can also use questions to consider possible solutions to address those problems, select one or more solutions, anticipate negative side effects that may stem from implementing solutions, establish goals for learners, test learners' knowledge, manage classroom instruction, and for other purposes (Leeds, 1988).

Questions may be categorized in two ways. First, they may be open or closed. Second, they can be externally or internally focused.

Open questions invite people to talk; closed questions tend to shut off or redirect responses. *Open questions* begin with words like who, what, when, where, why, and how. Instructional designers may ask open questions such as these: When did you first notice this performance problem? Who is affected by the problem? Where is it most and least evident? Open questions can also begin with such words as could or would, as in the question, Could you tell me a little more about . . . ? As a matter of fact, questions beginning with could tend to prompt the most talking and offer the fewest number of clues about what the interviewer is looking for in an answer. Use open questions to explore and investigate problems, probe what others have said, and prompt creative thinking by learners.

Closed questions begin with such words as is, are, was, were, do, did, have, and has. Instructional designers can ask closed questions such as these: Is that an accurate description? Was that always the work standard? Do you have ideas about the cause of the problem? Have you taken steps to investigate this problem in greater depth? Use closed questions to guide a conversation, that is, by verifying information or tactfully shutting off further talk.

Externally focused questions are directed to conditions in the outside world; *internally focused questions* are directed to conditions in the inside (mental) world. Externally focused questions are appropriate for collecting objective or factual information. Examples include any of the following questions: How would you describe the human performance problem your organization is experiencing? When was it first noticed? In what locations is it most apparent? Use externally focused questions to collect descriptive information. However, internally focused questions are appropriate for assessing attitudes, opinions, beliefs, and perceptions. Examples include any of the following: How do you feel about this problem? What do you think others feel about this problem? What is your perception of this problem's cause or causes? Use internally focused questions to collect interpretive information.

The newest development in questioning centers around the *tone* of questions. With the advent of appreciative inquiry as a new development in organization development, many practitioners are rethinking their approach. Instead of focusing around "solving problems" and "eliminating gaps," appreciative inquiry centers around discovering strengths so as to build on them. Questions based around this approach focus on the positive—what works, what makes people feel good, what strengths an organization can leverage, and so forth. Whitney, Cooperrider, Trosten-Bloom, and Kaplin (2002) have assembled a book full of questions that can be used along these lines.

Providing Explanations

Instructional designers should be able to "explain information to individuals or groups so that the presentation of information is done clearly, accurately, and so the individuals or groups can act on it appropriately" (Foshay, Silber, and Westgaard, 1986, p. 95). Explanation is simply a description of facts, conclusions, decisions, judgments, or actions. It includes clarification and paraphrase, responses to feelings and emotions, summarization, and justification. A good explanation anticipates, and addresses, questions of interest to the prospective audience.

Before taking action, instructional designers should always ask themselves, Who should know about it? Use the answer to identify those who deserve explanation. Then try to anticipate what they will need or want to know. Plan an explanation to provide them with information they will view as important.

Listening Actively

Instructional designers should be able to "listen to individuals or groups so that they gather sufficient information for the purpose, the individuals or groups feel listened to, and the individuals or groups continue to provide information for as long as you want them to" (Foshay, Silber, and Westgaard, 1986, p. 96). Instructional designers should, of course, distinguish projects appropriate for instructional design from those that are not, conduct needs assessment, and carry out many other activities. Listening may require at least 48 percent of project time. However, when people are not trained to listen, their listening efficiency can dip as low as 25 percent of a complete message (Nichols, 1957). Part of the problem is that most people speak at a rate of about 125 words per minute, yet an average listener is capable of thinking at a rate of about 400 words per minute. Hence, there is a significant amount of extra time that can be wasted as one person listens to another. It is easy to fall into the trap of listening passively or spending time planning what to say next rather than hearing what others are saying. However, listening should be an active endeavor, one in which the listener devotes as much attention to the *feeling* (emotional) components as to the *content* (meaning) components of the message.

There are several keys to active listening. First, instructional designers should focus on what is being said on more than one level. In other words, they should ask themselves not only, What does the speaker mean? but also, How does the speaker feel about the subject at hand? Body language, tone of voice, and any other clues to meaning and feeling should be noted.

Second, instructional designers should work at listening. They should ask questions, show interest, and use body language that encourages rather than discourages speakers. The key is to remain self-conscious, aware of how a listener's actions influence speakers, while simultaneously focusing attention on a speaker's content and feelings.

Dealing with Friction

Instructional designers should be able to "deal with friction among members of the group in a way that facilitates, or at least does not impede, attaining the purpose of the interaction by either (1) controlling the friction, or (2) recognizing when it is out of control and minimizing the damage by 'cutting the losses and running'" (Foshay, Silber, and Westgaard, 1986, p. 97). Friction is synonymous with conflict, and conflict is perhaps best understood simply as any situation in which people disagree.

How Does Friction Arise?

Friction arises whenever individuals or groups disagree about philosophy, values, goals, measurement methods, or results. It also stems from differences in personal styles, communication problems, competition, association, interdependence, expectations, and change. As Hensey (1983, p. 52) points out in a classic comment, "Conflict is often a result of changes, actual or perceived, and conflict is a very legitimate way of managing change, though not the only way. Planning, collaboration, problem-solving, and co-existence are some other ways of dealing with change."

Whenever people work together, undergo change, or experience interdependence, the potential for friction exists, and instructional designers work with many different kinds of people: colleagues, operating managers, media production people, learners, learners' supervisors, and others. Naturally, change and learning are synonymous (Rothwell and Sredl, 2000), and instructional design projects typically require interdependence among team members. Very real differences of opinion can arise about instructional design projects. Moreover, personality conflicts can arise between members of an instructional design team and between instructional designers and operating managers.

How Should Friction Be Managed?

Before attempting to manage friction, instructional designers should first clarify their assumptions about it. Second, they should try to determine its cause. They should then apply one of many available approaches to manage it.

The starting point for managing conflict is to *clarify assumptions about it*. Many people tend to view any disagreement as something to be avoided. "Conflict," as Baker and Morgan (1989, p. 151) point out in a still-relevant passage, "is often viewed negatively, although it is neither good nor bad in itself. If properly handled, conflict can become a positive source of energy and creativity; if mishandled, it can become dysfunctional, draining energy and reducing both personal and organizational effectiveness."

Each instructional designer should begin by clarifying his or her own views about friction. If that is difficult, then he or she should think back to the last time in which he or she observed, or was a party to, a disagreement. It could have been a disagreement with a supervisor, co-worker, team member, or even a spouse. What feelings did it evoke? How was the conflict handled? Were any of the following ineffective conflict resolution strategies used to cope with it?

- Moralizing (My way is right!)
- Submitting (I'll give up just to keep the peace, even though I still think this is wrong.)
- Denying (Maybe we don't disagree after all.)
- Coercing (You better do it my way or else.)
- Bribing (If you do it my way this time, I'll see to it you get your way on something else.)

Reflect on past actions in conflict situations at work or at some other location. Determine what assumptions were made about the conflict. Was it handled as though it were best avoided? If so, rethink how it was handled, realizing that conflict is a natural part of social life and can be a stimulus for new ideas.

The second step in managing conflict is to *identify its causes*. To that end, apply essentially the same techniques used in performance analysis. Never be misled by symptoms alone. Of course, symptoms of conflict may include arguments between people, name calling, malicious gossiping, the formation of cliques among team members, and (when friction is at its worst) absenteeism, turnover, or even sabotage. These problems result from more than simple personality conflicts and may reflect much deeper causes stemming from differing philosophies, values, goals, or work methods. Consider: When did the conflict first appear? What are its consequences? Who is involved? Is it a difference between individuals or groups? What do the conflicting parties believe the causes of the conflict to be? Probe for answers, just as you would do in performance analysis.

The third step in managing conflict is to *apply a conflict resolution approach*. Use collaboration, which means working with others to find a mutually satisfactory, if not mutually beneficial, solution to a problem. If conflict exists between two people, use classic interpersonal peacemaking techniques to help them resolve destructive differences (Walton, 1969). If the conflict is between two groups of people, use team-building techniques to mediate the dispute and build esprit de corps.

Handling Resistance to Change

Instructional designers should be able to "deal with resistance from an individual or group in a way that indicates recognition of the existence of resistance, manages or controls the resistance, or minimizes the damage by 'cutting losses and running'" (Foshay, Silber, and Westgaard, 1986, p. 98). Each step in the instructional design process implies change. As human resource professionals, instructional designers should understand their roles as change agents. Here are some questions worth pondering:

Step in Instructional Design	*Change Issue*
1. Determining projects appropriate for instructional design	1. Is change warranted to address a human performance problem?
2. Conducting a needs assessment	2. What kind of individual change is appropriate? What should people know, do, or feel that is different from what they presently know, do, or feel?
3. Assessing relevant characteristics of learners	3. What learner characteristics can affect the intended change effort?
4. Analyzing characteristics of a work setting	4. What characteristics of the settings can affect the intended change effort?
5. Performing job, task, or content analysis	5. What characteristics of the job, task, or subject should be a focus of change with prospective learners?
6. Writing statements of performance objectives	6. What results are desired from a change effort?
7. Developing performance measurements	7. How will individual change be assessed?
8. Sequencing performance objectives	8. In what order should changes in individual knowledge, skills, or attitudes be introduced?

Step in Instructional Design	*Change Issue*
9. Specifying instructional strategies	9. What are the best ways to introduce change?
10. Designing instructional materials	10. What materials can help introduce or guide the change effort?
11. Evaluating instruction	11. How can change efforts be assessed?
12. Designing the instructional management system	12. How can the change effort be supported?
13. Planning and monitoring instructional design projects	13. How can efforts to introduce change be effectively managed among the change agents themselves?
14. Communicating effectively	14. How can effective communication facilitate a change effort?
15. Interacting with others	15. How can effective interpersonal communication facilitate the change effort?
16. Promoting the use of instructional design	16. How can this approach to identifying the need for change and to designing and implementing it be passed on to others?

How Do People React to Change?

There are essentially three possible reactions to change among learners, their immediate superiors, and others with whom instructional designers must interact: individuals may resist it, favor it, or remain neutral to it. However, most managers, like most instructional designers, probably find resistance to change the most noticeable reaction, if only because it appears to stymie success in a way that the other reactions do not.

Why Do People Resist Change?

Before instructional designers can deal effectively with resistance to change, they should make an attempt to understand its causes. Kirkpatrick (1985), in a classic treatment, enumerated most of the reasons people resist change, and these reasons remain valid today. One reason is that they fear they will lose security, money, pride, satisfaction, friends and contacts, freedom, responsibility, authority, good working conditions, or status. A second reason is that they see no need for change. They are comfortable with the way things are and do not experience a deep need to depart from the known into the realm of the unknown. A third reason is that they perceive that change will produce more harmful than useful consequences. Other reasons for resisting change are easily identifiable: people lack respect for those making the change, feel the change has been introduced in an objectionable manner, and experience negative attitudes about the organization (or people running it). They may also feel powerless, dislike criticism of existing conditions implicit when the need for change is identified, sense that the change will place additional burdens on them, and anticipate that additional effort will be required of them to cope with the change. They might feel, too, that the change is poorly timed, wish to challenge authority, dislike receiving information about the change from secondhand sources, and dislike their own lack of input in the change process.

Of course, people can also welcome change. They may do so for reasons that are exactly the reverse of those producing resistance (Kirkpatrick, 1985). For instance, people may favor change when they feel it will lead to increased security, money, pride, satisfaction, friends and contacts, freedom, responsibility, or authority, or in better working conditions or status. Likewise, they may be experiencing a problem that change could solve. In addition, they may be restless with the way things are and experience a deep personal need to depart from existing conditions. They may also perceive that change will produce consequences leading to benefits that outweigh their costs. Finally, they may welcome change because they have deep respect for those making it, feel the change has been introduced in an exemplary manner, or experience strong loyalty and commitment to the organization (or people running it). They might also feel that the change makes them more powerful, like the criticism of existing conditions implicit when the need for change is identified, and sense that the change will reduce the burdens and stress placed on them. In addition, they might feel that the change is well timed, wish to support authority, and like the opportunity for input in the change process that they may be afforded.

How Should Instructional Designers Deal with Resistance to Change?

Adopt different strategies for dealing with resistance to change, depending on the stage of the change effort and the sources of resistance. Each stage of the change effort implies a different role for the instructional designer. During the earliest stages in which the need for change is being recognized, adopt the role of advertiser of the need for change. Once the need for change has been recognized, plan on serving as a counselor to help decision makers decide on appropriate performance improvement strategies, depending on the causes of the problems that change is intended to rectify. Once decision makers have fixed on a course of action, be prepared to function as demonstrator of that action, helping conceptualize what to do and how to do it. As the change process unfolds, be prepared to function as instructor and technical assistant to show others appropriate ways to act to facilitate implementation of change.

Each source of resistance should be considered when planning the change effort. Like anyone involved in a change effort, instructional designers should try to identify individuals or groups likely to resist change. They should also plan specific strategies to anticipate and head off each source of resistance.

Keeping People on Track

Instructional designers should be able to "keep an individual or group on track so that the interaction returns quickly to its purpose and the individual or group does not feel slighted" (Foshay, Silber, and Westgaard, 1986, p. 99). They should be able to enact this performance when "an individual or group wanders from the purpose of the interaction" (Foshay, Silber, and Westgaard, 1986, p. 99). Keeping people on track thus means achieving desired results from interactions with others while being spared distractions of peripheral interest or concern.

Why Do People Lose Track of Purpose?

Any interaction between people can lose focus. Individuals are driven by different wants, needs, and goals. Moreover, they often have different priorities. A meeting expressly called to address instructional needs can turn into a platform for a handful of vocal participants to launch into a tirade against the organization's selection, promotion, pay, or retirement practices. Likewise, an individual who is being interviewed about training needs may offer advice about what or who to believe in the organization. These sometimes frustrating (and sometimes amusing) mismatches between the goals and outcomes of an interaction occur because some issues weigh more heavily than others on the minds of the participants. Without exercising control and exerting influence over interactions with others, instructional designers may find themselves wasting valuable time and effort or struggling to establish priorities among a myriad of competing interests.

How Should People Be Guided Back on Track?

Instructional designers may use several approaches in exercising control over interactions. But first they should clarify in their own minds what results they seek from a meeting, interview, or discussion. When an interaction will be lengthy and formalized, as is often the case with meetings or interviews, instructional designers should prepare an agenda or list of questions in advance. They should then send it to the participants as a place to start discussion and as a control mechanism in case others turn to tangential issues.

Second, instructional designers should restate the purpose of the meeting or discussion when others begin to wander off the topic. In one meeting, for example, a participant wanted to discuss the organization's pay practices rather than employees' instructional needs. (The latter topic was the reason for the meeting.) The instructional designer noted, "What you have said is most interesting and possibly true. However, I am neither qualified to judge or knowledgeable enough on the subject to respond. Could we turn back for now to the subject of instructional needs?" That remark brought a prompt apology from the wanderer and renewed attention to the subject of the meeting from other participants.

Third, if all else fails, an instructional designer should begin speaking at the same time as the individual who has wandered off the topic. While that may seem rude and socially unacceptable, it can turn a discussion back on track. The trick is to keep talking, even when the inclination is not to do so. Other people will usually stop to listen, and at that point the discussion can be guided back to the subject.

Fourth, use periodic feedback to keep people on track. End each meeting or discussion by asking participants, How well did we stay on the subject of the meeting? How well did we interact as a group? This is an approach borrowed from process consultation, defined in a classic description by Edgar Schein (1969, p. 9) as "a set of activities . . . which helps the client to perceive, understand, and act upon process events which occur in the client's environment."

Securing Commitment

Instructional designers should be able to "obtain commitment from an individual or group so that the commitment facilitates [the project's] goals, both parties feel the commitment is binding, both parties are willing to follow through on it, and both parties feel there is value in it" (Foshay, Silber, and Westgaard, 1986, p. 100). Obtaining commitment simply means that people support the instructional design project. They are thus willing to provide information, resources, facilities, and their own time to ensure that the project's goals are achieved.

Why Is Commitment Important?

Instructional designers, by virtue of the work they perform, must work with—and often through—others. If they are unable to secure cooperation and commitment, they will probably waste much time, effort, and organizational resources as they analyze human performance problems, conduct needs assessment, and carry out other steps in the instructional design process. Hence, commitment from key decision makers and other affected groups and individuals is essential to project success.

How Is Commitment Obtained?

Obtain and maintain commitment to an instructional design project by practicing empathy about the project, communicating with individuals or groups affected by the project, and encouraging participation in the project by those affected by it. These are also three key methods for managing change according to the classic view of Kirkpatrick (1985).

Practicing empathy means looking at a project, problem, or issue from another person's viewpoint. It is an appreciation of the viewpoints and feelings of others. To practice empathy, instructional designers must first have some information about the individual or group with which they must interact. For instance, in preparing to deal with individuals, instructional designers may find it useful to learn about their education, experience, outside hobbies and activities, and other issues. Instructional designers might also find it useful to know what others think about instructional design projects generally, the present project specifically, the organization, their prospects within the organization, and any other matters that could affect their support of the project. In this way, it is possible to bring out hidden agendas and address individual concerns at the project's outset.

Communicating leads to understanding. To obtain and maintain commitment to an instructional design project, be sure to identify who will be affected by it, select appropriate timing to communicate about it, pick appropriate methods of communicating, and establish methods by which to obtain feedback (Kirkpatrick, 1985).

Encouraging participation means "getting involvement from those concerned with and affected by change" (Kirkpatrick, 1985, p. 133). It is the third and final key to obtaining and maintaining commitment to an instructional design project.

Since the late 1940s, numerous authors have emphasized the crucial importance of participative decision making in planning, implementing, and sustaining change (Coch and French, 1948; Likert, 1967; Marrow, 1972; Myers, 1970; Rothwell, Sullivan, and McLean, 1995). Subsequent research has even demonstrated that participation is of critical importance in instructional design efforts in particular (Rothwell and Kazanas, 1987). Surprisingly, corporate planners and instructional designers alike feel that strategic business planning activities, typically carried out by top managers only, are more open to participative decision making than most instructional design efforts.

To obtain commitment, instructional designers should begin by identifying those affected by the instructional design process. They should then use the following techniques to encourage participation in this process (Kirkpatrick, 1985, p. 144): (1) ask for input before and during each step of the project; (2) consider and evaluate the input received; (3) give credit to those who contributed useful ideas; (4) thank those who contributed ideas that were not used, and explain why they were not used.

Participation may be solicited during each step of the instructional design process. Indeed, there are good reasons for instructional designers to encourage participation by others, even after instruction has been designed: different groups may be involved, and members of those groups may have their own ideas about present and future instruction.

Selecting Behaviors for Effective Interpersonal Interaction

Instructional designers should be able to "select and tailor appropriate behaviors for specific interactions with other people" (Foshay, Silber, and Westgaard, 1986, p. 100). While it is important for instructional designers to establish rapport, state the purpose of an interaction, ask questions, provide explanations, listen actively, deal with friction, handle resistance to change, keep people on track, and secure commitment, it is equally important to be able to select appropriate behaviors for effective interpersonal interaction.

When to Establish Rapport

Establishing rapport is usually associated with the beginning of a relationship; maintaining it is associated with preserving a relationship. Establishing rapport is frequently an issue when you have been contacted for help and are meeting, for the first time, with a prospective client or clients. The need to maintain rapport will continue as long as instructional designers meet new people in the organization while seeking information, present results of investigations such as performance analyses or needs assessments, and work on subsequent instructional design steps.

When to State the Purpose of an Interaction

State the purpose of, or establish an agenda for, each interpersonal interaction at the outset. Repeat the purpose or remind people of the agenda whenever it appears that the interaction may shift to unrelated topics.

When to Ask Questions

Ask questions to collect information or exercise control over interactions with others. Remember that open questions are suitable for exploring opinions and collecting information. Closed questions are appropriate for controlling interactions and closing off discussion.

When to Provide Explanations

Try to avoid misunderstandings with others by providing explanations and justifications of actions taken and decisions made.

When to Listen Actively

Listen actively to hear what others say and how they feel. In this way, instructional designers can collect the maximum amount of information about the subject under investigation and about those from whom the information is collected.

When to Deal with Friction

Use conflict resolution techniques to deal with friction whenever it appears to threaten the objectives of the instructional design project. Remember that conflict can be both constructive and destructive. Encourage issue-oriented conflict leading to creative solutions; discourage—and work to alleviate—destructive, unproductive conflict.

When to Deal with Resistance

Realize that some people will resist change, some will welcome it, and some will not care about it. Try to identify, in advance, who is likely to resist change because of their fear of real (or perceived) loss of security, money, pride, satisfaction, friends and contacts, freedom, responsibility, authority, good working conditions, or status, or for other reasons. Then try to mount convincing arguments in favor of the change. Allow others the opportunity to participate in the instructional design project, since participation often builds ownership and reduces resistance.

When to Keep People on Track

Take steps to keep people on track when they attempt to deviate from the stated purpose of an interaction.

When to Secure Commitment

Take steps to secure and maintain commitment during all steps in an instructional design project.

Judging Interactions with Others

Instructional designers should be capable of "judging the appropriateness and effectiveness of behaviors used in specific interactions with other people" (Foshay, Silber, and Westgaard, 1986, p. 102). Use a checklist as a decision aid when it becomes necessary to make such judgments. An example of such a checklist appears in Exhibit 17.1.

Justifying Behaviors Used in Interactions with Others

Instructional designers should also be capable of justifying "the selection and tailoring of appropriate behaviors for specific interactions with other people" (Foshay, Silber, and Westgaard, 1986, p. 103). This justification should include:

"(a) An explanation of the logic of the plan for the selection and tailoring of appropriate behaviors for that interaction; (b) A plan for dealing with, rather than avoiding, friction or resistance; (c) An explanation of how well the selection and tailoring worked; (d) An explanation of any deviations from the plan during the actual interaction; (e) A description of the instructional designer's perception of the effectiveness of the interaction; and (f) An explanation of any specific behaviors asked about."

In other words, instructional designers should be prepared to explain their actions and behaviors and be able to justify why they acted as they did. Realize that not everyone involved with the project may be trusting, share the natural

EXHIBIT 17.1. A CHECKLIST FOR JUDGING THE APPROPRIATENESS AND EFFECTIVENESS OF BEHAVIORS USED IN SPECIFIC INTERACTIONS WITH OTHER PEOPLE.

Directions: Use this checklist to judge the appropriateness and effectiveness of the behaviors used on a project by instructional designers. Answer each question appearing in the left column below by circling an appropriate numeral in the center column. Use the following scale in the center column:

1 = Needs substantial improvement
2 = Needs some improvement
3 = Adequate
4 = Better than adequate
5 = Excellent

In the right column, make notes about project behaviors that instructional designers could improve.

Behavior	How Well Is The Behavior Exhibited on the Project by Instructional Designers?					Notes for Improvement
	Needs . . .		Adequate	Excellent		
How well do instructional designers . . .	**1**	**2**	**3**	**4**	**5**	
1. Establish rapport with individuals and groups?	1	2	3	4	5	
2. State the purpose and/or agenda of each interaction?	1	2	3	4	5	
3. Ask questions of individuals or groups?	1	2	3	4	5	
4. Explain information to individuals or groups?	1	2	3	4	5	
5. Listen actively to individuals or groups?	1	2	3	4	5	
6. Deal with friction among members of a group?	1	2	3	4	5	
7. Deal with resistance from an individual or group?	1	2	3	4	5	
8. Keep an individual or group on track?	1	2	3	4	5	
9. Obtain commitment from an individual or group?	1	2	3	4	5	
10. Select and tailor appropriate behaviors for specific interactions with other people?	1	2	3	4	5	

enthusiasm of the designer, understand what is being done, or appreciate why it should be done. As a result, they may become anxious about the designer's methods, behaviors, credentials—and whatever else they can become anxious about. As agents of change, instructional designers do occasionally feel that they are placed squarely in the role of lightning rod for controversy. Be patient enough with the clients and others with whom interaction is necessary to explain the need for each step in the instructional design process. Plan to state those reasons at each step of a project and on each occasion when interaction with others is necessary.

What Is New in Interacting with Others?

Interpersonal interaction is more important than ever before. Virtual technology has made it easier to reach people, including those at great distances. But finding the time for interpersonal interaction is a challenge. Much interaction in organizational settings occurs in meetings. And yet meetings can also be frustrating and can become time-wasters.

The common problems with meetings is that they are not planned, are not kept on track, do not lead individuals to step forward to volunteer for doing work for the good of the group, and encourage some people to take an active role while others do not. These are just examples of the problems. Many more exist as well. In fact, many people today feel that they spend all their time in meetings. And yet they may also feel that they accomplish nothing.

Meetings are important for creating common goals and facilitating discussion among members of a group or organization. But they are not appropriate when action can be taken faster and more effectively without a meeting. After all, meetings can lead to no progress if some groups resist change and thereby discourage clarity about who should do what after the meeting.

To manage interpersonal interactions effectively, group members should adopt a list of rules to govern how they will interact and how they will treat each other.

Some organizations are adopting the techniques of process consultation to encourage interaction (Schein, 1998). In process consultation, an individual watches the group interact and counts the number and quality of interactions they demonstrate in a group setting. Then, usually at the end of the meeting, the process consultant facilitates a group discussion to challenge the group members to find more effective ways of interacting. Another approach is for the group leader to ask, usually at the end of a meeting, a question like "How are we interacting as a group, and how could we encourage that interaction in future meetings?" That question—and similar ones that a process consultant could pose—can lead the group to focus on improving how they interact.

Conclusion

In this chapter, we described how instructional designers establish rapport, state the purposes of an interaction, ask questions, provide explanations, listen actively, deal with friction, handle resistance to change, keep people on track, secure commitment, and select appropriate behaviors for effective interpersonal interaction. Such day-to-day behaviors are critical to the success of each instructional design project. However, instructional designers also have an obligation to promote the use of instructional design over the long term, extending beyond a single project. That is the topic of the next chapter.

CHAPTER EIGHTEEN

PROMOTING THE USE OF INSTRUCTIONAL DESIGN

Instructional designers bear a responsibility to promote the use of instructional design. After all, some people honestly believe that instruction should not be designed rigorously or according to any systematic approach. Some know just enough to be dangerous. Others know little, if anything, about instructional design or wish to avoid the hard work involved. For these reasons, instructional designers have a responsibility to demonstrate the value of what they do and to explain and even promote it to others.

We begin this chapter with a brief case study to dramatize important issues in promoting instructional design. We then turn to describing ways to make others aware of instructional design. We conclude the chapter with a few words of advice about justifying these promotional efforts.

Promoting the Use of Instructional Design: A Case Study

George McDonald is the director of human resource development for a large insurance company. He was hired not long ago to establish formal training in a one-hundred-year-old company that has never before offered it to employees.

An experienced specialist who is quite familiar with current professional approaches to instructional design, George wants to introduce a performance-based approach as he establishes his new workplace learning and performance (WLP) department.

George reports to an advisory committee that was created shortly before he was hired. Its purpose is to provide advice about the direction of WLP activities in the organization. The committee consists of representatives from first-line supervision, middle management, and top management. George has decided that, if he can inform and persuade members of that committee to support adoption of a rigorous approach to instructional design from the outset, it will be much easier for him to implement it as the organization's instructional efforts grow in number.

George prepares a short (two-page) white paper on the topic of instructional design for the next meeting of the advisory committee. At the meeting, he makes a brief presentation on the white paper, with the dual goals of informing and persuading his listeners to support the introduction of a rigorous instructional design process. George is fully aware that, as a newcomer to the organization, he is accorded a certain amount of license to introduce whatever innovations he feels are appropriate. He takes advantage of that license with committee members to ensure that this innovation is adopted. He is even successful in soliciting their support for persuading others in the organization to adopt the approach.

Making Others Aware of Instructional Design

As the case study has illustrated, instructional designers who set out to promote a rigorous and systematic approach to instructional design should begin by targeting key decision makers. After all, they are the ones who should be informed of the importance of such an approach. Moreover, decision makers should be the target of goals and a strategy formulated to guide the promotion effort. Of course, the promotional strategy chosen should be attuned to the organization's and the WLP department's stage in adopting the instructional design model.

In one sense at least, every organization can be viewed as composed of different market segments or interest groups. As in classifying learners, individuals in any organization may be segmented on the basis of their experience, education, job responsibilities, level within the organizational hierarchy, and other characteristics. In each organizational market segment there are opinion leaders who are regularly consulted by others for their ideas about issues affecting the organization. Some opinion leaders are positioned in management, some are positioned in unions, and some informal opinion leaders are affiliated with neither one. Opinion leaders wield considerable social power arising from their positions, extraordinary knowledge of the work, personal charisma, or other characteristics are noted in the classic work of French and Raven (1959).

As a first step in making others aware of instructional design, identify key market segments in the organization (Gilley and Eggland, 1992). Then identify opinion leaders for each market segment. Target such key decision makers and opinion leaders as colleagues in the WLP department, professional or organizational superiors, line managers, union representatives, and others. Finally, for each organizational market segment, ask three questions:

1. What special interests exist in this group that might lead its members to explore—and perhaps support—a rigorous, professional approach to instructional design?
2. How might the members of this group benefit from a rigorous approach to instructional design?
3. What would opinion leaders in this group need to know to be persuaded to support such an approach?

Use the answers to these questions in establishing goals for promoting a professional approach to instructional design in an organization.

Establishing Goals

Make a list of goals for promoting a professional approach to instructional design for each organizational market segment. Goals may vary. For instance, instructional designers may choose any or all of the following goals:

1. Inform opinion leaders of the advantages of a professional approach to instructional design.
2. Answer any questions or address any concerns that opinion leaders may have about the application of the instructional design model in an organization.
3. Persuade opinion leaders that a rigorous and systematic approach to instructional design can produce results superior to less rigorous approaches. (Such benefits may include reduced training time, reduced long-term costs, increased production, decreased scrap rates, increased or improved customer service.)
4. Prompt opinion leaders to back the application of a rigorous and systematic approach to instructional design by the organization or the ROI, WLP department, perhaps supplanting an existing but less rigorous approach.
5. Convince decision makers to reconsider an earlier rejection of a systematic approach to instructional design.

When opinion leaders are not sophisticated, instructional designers will usually want to establish goals in more or less the order listed. First, inform opinion leaders about the options; then convince them that a professional approach to instructional design deserves to be adopted. Other goals may, of course, be established. For instance, some instructional designers may wish to convince decision makers to commit resources to experimentation with instructional design.

Selecting a Promotional Strategy

Once instructional designers know what goals to seek from their promotional efforts, they will be well-positioned to decide how to accomplish them. Each goal implies possible promotional strategies. Here are some examples.

Goal

1. Inform opinion leaders about professional approaches to instructional design.

Possible Promotional Strategies

Route articles about instructional design to opinion leaders; describe instructional design in management, professional, and technical training sponsored by the organization; take advantage of windows of opportunity by describing what to do when decision makers ask for help to address immediate human performance problems confronting them; invite outside speakers to address managers about instructional design; write articles on instructional design for in-company publications; write articles about instructional design for professional journals in the field, and then route the articles to key opinion leaders in the organization; build support informally for rigorous approaches to instructional design by discussing the issue with opinion leaders who may be possible supporters (try members of a training advisory committee first); describe how a rigorous approach to instructional design can help implement the organization's strategic business plan.

2. Persuade opinion leaders that the benefits of a rigorous, systematic approach to Instructional design outweigh Its costs.	Gather testimonials from colleagues in other organizations; collect information about the application of rigorous approaches to instructional design by key competitors; prepare a detailed proposal for using a rigorous approach to instructional design in the organization; be sure to describe the relative costs and benefits of the approach, preferably compared to methods of instructional design already in use.
3. Prompt adoption of a rigorous, systematic approach to instructional design by the organization or the WLP department.	Press the issue, since persistence often leads to success; make a simple, straightforward presentation to key decision makers, ending with a plea for adopting the approach in the future and identifying specifically what each member of the audience would need to do.
4. Prompt reconsideration of a rigorous systematic approach to instructional design if such an approach has previously been considered but rejected.	Monitor reasons for initial rejection of the approach. If conditions change, raise the issue again. Identify which decision makers resisted the approach. If the organization experiences a change in leadership, raise the issue again with the new decision-makers. Then select appropriate promotional strategies. Generally speaking, it is better to select at least two such strategies at the same time so that the chances of success are doubled.

Ensuring That Promotional Strategies Are Appropriate for the Stage of Adoption of the Client

Numerous authors have noted that organizations and WLP departments progress through predictable stages called life cycles (Rothwell and Sredl, 2000). In many respects, theories of life cycle development are comparable to classic theories of innovation (Rogers and Shoemaker, 1971). Each deserves brief review.

Each life cycle stage of an organization or WLP department corresponds to an individual's stage of development. Whereas empirical proof of organizational life cycles is elusive, and those who accept the idea completely tread perilously close to personifying an abstraction, the notion of organizational life cycles has a strong intuitive appeal. Moreover, useful clues can be offered about appropriate leadership strategies for each stage of development. In many ways, organizational life cycle theories bear close resemblances to similar notions of product life cycles in marketing, individual life cycles in psychology, group formation life cycles in organizational dynamics, and diffusion theory in anthropology, sociology, and communications.

In each stage of a life cycle, an organization confronts critical issues in much the same way that individuals confront critical issues in each phase of their development. To address those issues, different leadership strategies should be employed, just as different counseling strategies should be used in guiding individuals through various stages in their development.

During the conception and birth stage, entrepreneurs have an idea for a profitable venture. The challenge they face, however, is making the idea a reality. The appropriate leader must be an innovator; management is usually a one-person operation; the organization's central focus is a struggle for existence; and the leader devotes energy to the new and unusual. Entrepreneurs have to arrange for necessary growth capital, locate adequate physical facilities, and secure the other resources necessary to establish their organization. They must also enter their market, create a vision of the organization's future, and maximize profits.

The same general principles hold true for the conception and birth of a WLP department, even though the WLP function's genesis does not always coincide with that of the host organization (Rothwell, 1983). Appropriate leaders must be innovators and entrepreneurs (Pinchot, 1985), willing to seize opportunities to create highly visible successes through the application of instructional design. A key issue that leaders must confront: Can they persuade decision makers to provide adequate support for the function? They must also be masterful in competing for scarce resources with other—and usually established—parts of the organization.

During the infancy stage, an organization must maximize the opportunities with which it is confronted. Leaders must be opportunists, willing to make the most of environmental conditions. The focus must be on achievement. Planning is typically catch-as-catch-can. Management consists of a small group of people. The central concern is continued survival.

The same general principles hold true for the infancy stage of a WLP department. The operation is limited in scope. Attention is focused on activities in which maximum success can be demonstrated quickly and visibly, and with minimal expenditure of money, energy, and staff time. The central concern is continued survival, since few decision makers are necessarily convinced that the function is worthwhile. The staff size of the department is limited and must be highly leveraged to achieve maximum results.

During the adolescent stage of an organization, decision makers focus on accelerated growth. Appropriate leaders function as consultants, that is, those who provide advice to others but do not necessarily impose their own opinions. Managers at this stage want to establish a reasonable market share, and their planning methods reflect that preoccupation. However, managers increasingly seek planned profits in ways they did not seek them in earlier stages of the organization's development.

WLP departments also progress through adolescence. Appropriate leaders are knowledgeable about the relevant professional practices. They function as consultants. Staff members of the department should devote their attention to meeting specific and identifiable instructional needs. Departmental planning reflects a preoccupation with establishing an identifiable market niche within the organization, that is, with serving justifiable learning needs in a cost-effective manner.

During an organization's middle age, the focus of management attention is on sustained, balanced, and systematic growth. Appropriate leadership styles vary, although most organizations have nurtured those who are professionally trained and knowledgeable about the business, industry, and market. Planning methods may be sophisticated.

During a WLP department's middle age, the leaders are usually professionally trained. The work is divided up by function or organizational component. The methods used are adequate, if not sophisticated.

During an organization's old age, leaders devote their attention to the continued existence of the enterprise. They are administrators, preoccupied with preserving existing conditions rather than introducing innovations. The organization's self-image is complacent, and a central problem is preservation of stability, often through bureaucratic rules. By this time the organization's culture has become quite strong and tradition-bound. Managers defend their turf.

During a WLP department's old age, leaders also devote their attention to the continued existence of the function. They, too, are preoccupied with preserving the status quo, tend toward complacency, and worry about preserving stability and tradition.

Of course, the life cycle of organizations and departments may be renewed through efforts to change the culture by changing the leadership, policies, procedures, work methods, rewards, and structure.

Appropriate goals and strategies for promoting rigorous, professional approaches to instructional design may vary by life cycle stage of the organization or department. Here are some examples.

Life Cycle Stage	Goal	Promotion Strategy
Conception and birth	Inform others about professional approaches to instructional design.	Apply performance analysis to identify improvement opportunities. Describe a current, rigorous approach to instructional design.
Infancy	Persuade others to adopt a professional approach to instructional design.	Train opinion leaders. Train assigned WLP staff.
Adolescence	Apply the approach.	Advertise successes. Enlist supporters who can offer testimonials.
Middle age	Refine the approach.	Continue to advertise successes. Keep in close contact with supporters so that continuing refinements can be made. Hire individuals skilled in up-to-date professional approaches to instructional design.
Old age	Identify complaints, problems, or concerns about applications of professional approaches to instructional design in the organization and reenergize support.	Call in outsiders to interview learners and operating managers, providing advice about improving the approach adopted.

Efforts to promote the use of rigorous, professional approaches to instructional design in organizations are comparable to other efforts to introduce innovation. In *Communication of Innovations,* Rogers and Shoemaker (1971) provide a classic framework by which to guide the introduction of innovation and change in any social system. They distinguish between invention, defined as "the process by which new ideas are created or developed," and diffusion, defined as "the process by which these new ideas are communicated to the members of a social system" (p. 7).

In most organizations, innovation usually begins as a result of some crisis, large or small. An active search for new approaches stems from dissatisfaction with existing conditions by advocates of change called idea champions (McCall and Kaplan, 1985). Hence, innovation is rarely serendipitous; rather, it stems from vague but uncomfortable feelings about existing conditions (Hassinger, 1959).

Rogers and Shoemaker (1971), in their time-tested treatment of the subject, describe four key stages in the adoption of organizational innovations following exploration: knowledge, persuasion, decision, and confirmation. Their paradigm of the innovation-decision process is complex and encompasses many variables.

During the knowledge stage, the first stage in innovation, an individual or group is exposed to a new idea and becomes aware of what it means. This stage is influenced by receiver and social system variables. Receiver variables include the decision makers' attitudes about change, their receptiveness to new ideas, and the perceived need for the change. Social system variables are functions of the organizational culture, including group norms and tolerance for nonconformity, among other issues.

To introduce an innovation to an organization, such as a rigorous and systematic approach to the instructional design, years of organizational research suggest the best way to identify key decision makers who are early adopters of innovation. Like their consumer counterparts who adopt new products or services before others do, they are the first to consider new ideas and are willing to introduce change if they can readily see benefits from it. Their interest can be piqued by providing them with information, such as articles, white paper descriptions, or one-on-one briefings. Their support will increase when they can see a use for the approach in helping them address their immediate problems.

During the persuasion stage, the second stage in innovation, individuals or groups form a favorable or unfavorable impression of an idea. Of crucial importance for innovation to be successfully introduced, the persuasion stage is influenced by a host of factors. To consider these factors, instructional designers should ask themselves the following questions: (1) How much will decision makers view a possible innovation as offering distinct advantages and relatively few disadvantages when compared to existing conditions? (2) How compatible is the proposed innovation with the organization's present ways of doing things? (3) How easily can the proposed innovation be explained to others? (4) How easily does the proposed innovation lend itself to trial tests? (5) How easily observable are the consequences of the innovation? Use the answers to these questions to identify ways to persuade decision makers to accept a rigorous, systematic approach to the instructional design process.

During the decision stage, the third stage in innovation, key decision makers either adopt or reject a new idea. This stage is heavily influenced by how the innovation was introduced. Participation of affected parties is of crucial importance to success in this stage. If an idea is adopted, it may either be retained in its original form or gradually supplanted, over time, by refinements. If an idea is rejected, it may either be adopted at a later time or dropped forever from consideration. Both adoption and rejection over time are influenced by decision makers, problems confronting the organization, or prospects for future challenges confronting the organization.

During the confirmation stage, the fourth and final stage in innovation, key decision makers either remain committed to the innovation or grow disenchanted with it. If experience leads to complete acceptance, then additional resources may be devoted to it, or else the idea may be further refined; if experience with the idea leads to rejection, then resources may be removed from it. Of course, a rejected innovation can be revived when key decision makers change through retirement, removal, or reorganization or when changing conditions make the innovation appealing.

Ensuring That Promotional Strategies Are Congruent with the Value Systems of Decision Makers

Each organization is governed by a dominant coalition, consisting of its key decision makers (Cyert and March, 1963; March, 1962). Each organization's culture is influenced, to a great extent, by that coalition. Members of the dominant coalition are responsible for allocating work assignments and distributing rewards. They are also advocates and apologists for the culture, since their own rise to authority can be traced to their adherence to values implicit in the culture. Although that is not always true, it often is.

To promote rigorous, planned approaches to instructional design, then, instructional designers should make sure that the methods they use are congruent with the value systems of the dominant coalition. But how is that done? First, identify members of the dominant coalition. Just who are the movers and shakers? When that question has been answered, the members of the dominant coalition have been identified. These are the people who make things happen. Every organization has them. They are not always members of top management. Sometimes they are high-potential managers located in middle or lower management.

Second, clarify the values, goals, and aspirations of the dominant coalition. According to Rokeach's classic definition (1973, p. 5), a value is "an enduring belief that a specific mode of conduct or end-state of existence is personally or socially preferable to an opposite or converse mode of conduct or end-state of existence." A goal is simply a desired end-state. It is usually not capable of measurement, as an objective is (Rothwell and Kazanas, 1994a). An aspiration is comparable to a vision, that is, a view of what the future should look like.

To clarify the values, goals, and aspirations of the dominant coalition, audit the culture. Observe the setting carefully to see what is rewarded. Watch for any existing rituals, backed by tradition, that receive attention from important individuals. (Rituals include holiday parties, going-away parties, or retirement dinners.) In addition, listen to what members of the dominant coalition talk about and say they want. Compare what they talk about to what they do, what they spend their time on, and what they reward. Listen also to stories told about members of the dominant coalition and their predecessors. If possible, administer a value survey to members of the organization (see Francis and Woodcock, 1990; Rokeach, 1973).

Rokeach distinguishes between two kinds of values: instrumental and terminal. Instrumental values are those leading to a desired end state; terminal values are equated directly with the end state itself. Values include expressions or actions pertaining to any of the following, as described in a classic treatment by Schmidt and Posner (1982).

Values	*Descriptions of the Values (Relative Importance)*
Organizational effectiveness	How well the organization achieves desired results
High productivity	The ratio of inputs to outputs
Organizational leadership	Top management's ability to meet challenges facing the organization
High morale	High job satisfaction among members of each work group and in the organization as a whole
Organizational reputation	The organization's standing in the industry and in all industries
Organizational efficiency	How well the organization is able to use its resources to achieve desired results
Profit maximization	The ratio of profits to expenses

Values	*Descriptions of the Values (Relative Importance)*
Organizational growth	The organization's ability to grow in assets, staff, or market share
Organizational stability	The organization's ability to cope with change created by conditions in the environment
Organizational value	The organization's relative contributions to the quality of life in each community of which it is a part

Generally speaking, supervisors and executives place different values on different activities and results.

Selecting Strategies for Promoting Instructional Design Consistent with the Values of the Dominant Coalition

Efforts to promote a professional approach to instructional design must be geared to the values, goals, and aspirations of the dominant coalition. For instance, if members of the dominant coalition seem to value organizational effectiveness most highly, then instructional designers should describe how a rigorous approach to instructional design can improve that effectiveness. However, if members of the dominant coalition wish to increase organizational efficiency, a rigorous approach to instructional design can help achieve that end. In short, promotion efforts should be based on the values and goals of the dominant coalition (Duncan and Powers, 1992).

Justifying Promotional Strategy and Tactics

Instructional designers should be capable of justifying the methods they use to promote a rigorous, systematic approach to instructional design. As in most activities, instructional designers should be prepared to explain what they have done and why they have done it to such interested stakeholders as other instructional designers, operating managers, supervisors, and targeted learners. The same holds true for their efforts to promote instructional design. However, they will usually find that, in most cases, they will be asked to justify their methods of promoting instructional design only to other instructional designers. They tend to be most interested in this subject.

When justifying the strategy used to promote instructional design, be prepared to answer the following questions:

1. What key decision-makers were targeted, and why were they selected rather than others?
2. What goals were established for the promotional effort? Why were they selected?
3. What consideration was given to the organization's life cycle stage? What consideration was given to its stage in adopting a rigorous, systematic approach to instructional design?
4. What consideration was given to the personal value systems of key decision makers?

By answering these questions, instructional designers should be able to explain why and how they chose to promote a rigorous, systematic approach to instructional design.

What Is New in Promoting the Use of Instructional Design?

Although many readers of this book take for granted the definition and value of instructional design, that is not universally true in the world—even now. If you do not believe that, try telling your friends or relatives that your occupation is "instructional designer." There is a good chance that they will ask "What is *that*?" Many people—and, indeed, many managers in many companies in both the United States and in other countries—have never heard of the field, have no idea why it is needed, and may even question its value.

Some managers of my acquaitance have said things like "Why should we hire instructional designers? What is there to training—just outline a book and offer the course?" In short, the level of awareness of what the field is and why it is necessary should not be taken for granted.

In the last few years, both ISPI and ASTD have launched professional certification programs. (Visit the websites of ISPI and ASTD to learn more about professional certifications.) Participating in those programs is a good way to promote the use of instructional design. One reason is that, upon achieving certification, instructional designers will usually be recognized for achievement by their employers. That will promote the use of instructional design by making employers more aware of what instructional design is, what competencies are essential to master it, and why it is valuable.

Instructional designers are also well-advised to take what opportunities they can to inform managers and workers about the field. Building awareness of the field is more likely to build the credibility of instructional designers in their own organizations and in the business world generally.

Conclusion

This chapter began with a brief case study to dramatize important issues in promoting instructional design. We then described ways to make others aware of instructional design. Our final notes were about justifying these promotional efforts.

CHAPTER NINETEEN

DEVELOPING YOURSELF

In this book we have emphasized key competencies that are essential to the professional practice of instructional design. However, instructional designers have a responsibility to keep their skills current. According to *The Standards* (Richey, Fields, and Foxon, 2001, p. 47), an instructional designer has an obligation to "update and improve [*his or her*] knowledge, skills, and attitudes pertaining to instructional design and related fields." It is an essential competency. The performance statements associated with this competency indicate that instructional designers should be able to (Richey, Fields, and Foxon, 2001, p. 47):

a. Apply developments in instructional design and related fields (advanced).
b. Acquire and apply new technology skills to instructional design practice (essential).
c. Participate in professional activities (essential).
d. Document one's work as a foundation for future efforts, publications, or professional presentation (advanced).
e. Establish and maintain contacts with other professionals (essential).

Also important, according to *The Standards* (p. 47), instructional designers should "apply current research and theory to the practice of instructional design." It is an advanced competency. The performance statements associated with this competency indicate that instructional designers should be able to (Richey, Fields, and Foxon, 2001, p. 47):

a. Promote, apply, and disseminate the results of instructional design theory and research (advanced).

b. Read instructional design research, theory, and practice literature (essential).

c. Apply concepts, techniques, and theory of other disciplines to problems of learning, instruction, and instructional design (advanced).

In a sense, professional development is primarily the individual's responsibility. For that reason, we have included a tool to begin your process in Appendix I of this book. Use it to self assess yourself. Then identify some mentors other than your immediate supervisor who are familiar with who you are and with how well you perform. Ask for their advice about professional development.

Developing Yourself Professionally

We define *professional development* as an individual's gradual and continuing mastery of a field's body of knowledge, methods, and procedures. In addition, it also implies that practitioners adhere to ethical standards appropriate to the field.

In a very real sense, then, professional development is never finished. It requires constant effort. Even the most experienced instructional designers, like the most experienced professionals in other fields, should continuously strive to build their knowledge, maintain their awareness of new developments and approaches, and preserve their adherence to ethical standards.

It has been our experience that many instructional designers, even the most ambitious and dedicated, are sometimes unwilling or unable to make time for such professional development activities as reading, participating in local chapters of organizations like ISPI or ASTD, attending professional conferences, or taking college courses.

It is not uncommon to hear a plethora of excuses when staff members are asked about their professional development. Lack of time is frequently cited. Here is a sample of typical excuses we have heard:

- "If the company thinks professional development is important, then the company can send me on work time. Otherwise, I have to get my kids to school every day. I also need to be home at night."
- "It is worthwhile attending chapter meetings. But I do not like to travel at night [or *during the day*] to these meetings. I just do not have time for it."
- "I would enroll in school to continue my education, but I just don't have the time for commuting, attending classes, and doing the homework."

It is ironic that these and similar excuses are also offered frequently by the learners that instructional designers work so hard to satisfy in the workplace.

To address these excuses, we find it helpful to counsel employees one-on-one. The purpose of the counseling is to reemphasize the importance of professional development and to convey the message that it is not entirely the company's or the boss's responsibility to address professional development needs. The lion's share of that responsibility always belongs to the individual. Indeed, in the future, the ability of individuals to master their own learning will set exemplary performers apart from the average (Rothwell, 2002).

Lack of motivation is also a barrier to professional development. We see it often enough among seasoned instructional designers who feel so smug about their experience or educational credentials that they see no reason to pursue further development unless there is an obvious or immediate personal gain to be had. If asked about their professional development, those lacking motivation are likely to make statements like these:

- "I don't really feel a need. The articles and books I look at seem too superficial. The conferences I have attended waste time and are geared to novices. Chapter meetings always seem to be dominated by a clique of insiders. I feel I am doing pretty well without these time wasters."
- "Experience is the best teacher. I feel that I am developing professionally by working in the field every day."

Managers of instructional designers should address these objections by pointing out that everyone, no matter how experienced, can and should develop professionally. If need be, managers should ask these instructional designers how they would address similar objections raised by trainees who attend courses they designed. Then managers should be quite obvious about turning the approach around, applying it directly to the instructional designer who offers excuses!

Finally, very real barriers to professional development can stem from organizations rather than from instructional designers themselves. Chief among these barriers is what instructional designers perceive to be lack of support for professional development activities. It is a barrier most keenly felt by the most ambitious staff members.

Lack of funding is one way that organizations show lack of support. Some cost-conscious organizations pinch pennies on journal subscriptions, association membership fees, and book purchases. Likewise, many organizations limit attendance at professional conferences and chapter meetings. Employees interpret such miserly practices as direct assaults on their efforts to develop themselves professionally. Worse yet, managers of instructional designers are not always capable of single-handedly reversing these trends because final budgetary decisions are made by others.

What managers can do, however, is make sure they encourage professional development in spite of the circumstances. One approach that may work is to poll staff about the journals they would like the organization to subscribe to, the associations they wish to belong to, the books that should be purchased, and the conferences they would like to be sent to. The managers should then make the budget requests based on this information. Each item should be justified for a work-related reason.

As an alternative when that strategy fails, managers in large organizations may find that there is a possibility of forming networks of instructional designers internal to the organization. That can be an inexpensive vehicle for professional development. It can also have a payback in other ways because it forges ties to other instructional designers in the organization.

Instructional designers in small or medium-sized organizations may find that they simply have to absorb more of the funding for their own professional development without expecting their employers to do so. While that is a bitter pill to swallow—it does amount to a pay cut—it preserves participation in professional development activities, even when employers cut expenses and undergo downsizing or rightsizing. For innovative and committed people, no barrier is so insurmountable that they are unable to find the means to fuel their learning.

Lack of supervisory encouragement is the single worst barrier to professional development. Instructional designers will not participate in professional development activities when they feel that their bosses do not support them. The best way for managers of instructional design to foster professional development is to set the example, not by just talking about it but also by participating. It is also quite important to establish a learning climate that fosters and supports professional development, and at least one tool is available to measure that climate (see Rothwell, 2002).

While there is no simple solution to lack of supervisory encouragement, some instructional designers are honest enough to confront their bosses when they encounter this issue. In those cases, instructional designers may have to undertake the delicate task of pointing out to their bosses that the example they set is the one many people will be influenced to follow.

What Is New in Developing Yourself?

As mentioned at the end of the previous chapter, many professional associations in fields related to instructional design have been introducing professional certifications in the field. ISPI has introduced the Certified Performance Technologist (CPT) designation. ASTD has introduced the Certified Professional in Learning and Performance (CPLP) designation. Both designations are demonstrations of more than instructional design, although they also include traditional instructional design components as well as the broader role of the human performance improvement or technologist.

The first step in developing yourself is to pursue one or more of these designations. That is particularly important to do if you regard yourself as a professional in the field who plans to remain in the field rather than seek alternative career paths into management, human resources, or other fields.

Once you achieve the designation or designations, you will be required to accumulate continuing education credits. You should do that anyway if you wish to set the right example with workers and managers in your organization. If instructional designers are unwilling to develop themselves, then they will hardly be positioned to advocate it to managers and workers. It is important to "walk the walk" as well as "talk the talk" of professional development.

Other strategies can also be used to develop oneself. These include seeking out a mentor to give advice about next steps in your professional development. These can also include taking initiative to develop yourself more by initiating and implementing individual learning projects. You are the master of your own career development, and you should therefore be willing to take initiative to satisfy your curiosity, acquire more visibility in the organization or the field, and leverage your own talents.

Conclusion

This chapter has focused on professional development. *Now is the time to take action to keep yourself up-to-date!*

CHAPTER TWENTY

BEING AN EFFECTIVE INSTRUCTIONAL DESIGNER

Lessons Learned

In a classic article titled "The Most Important Lessons I've Learned as a Consultant About the Systems Approach to Instructional Design," Eric Davidove (1991) advises instructional designers to "prepare answers to tough questions" posed by clients (p. 11), "identify results valued by your client" (p. 12), "make your client self-sufficient" (p. 12), "document everything" (p. 13), and "develop detailed work and staff plans" (p. 13).

Following Davidove's lead, we feel it is fitting to close the book with some personal reflections, gained through our experience, about what it takes to be effective as an instructional designer. In the items to follow, we will share lessons we have learned, our personal opinions, and our thoughts about professional development.

According to *The Standards* (Richey, Fields, and Foxon, 2001, p. 55), one competency for instructional design is to "provide for the effective implementation of instructional products and programs." It is regarded as an essential competency. The performance statements associated with this competency indicate that instructional designers should be able to (Richey, Fields, and Foxon, 2001, p. 55):

a) Use evaluation data as a guide for revision of products and programs (advanced).
b) Update instructional products and programs as required (essential).

c) Monitor and revise the instructional delivery process as required (essential).

d) Revise instructional products and programs to reflect changes in professional practice or policy (essential).

e) Revise instructional products and programs to reflect changes in the organization or the target population (essential).

f) Recommend plans for organizational support of instructional programs (advanced).

Key to success in instructional design is the ability to "follow through." That is really what this competency is all about. First and foremost, we believe that "follow through" in any form often spells the difference between success and failure.

Being an Effective Instructional Designer

The following ten points sum up what we feel are the keys to success in instructional design.

Point 1: Emphasize Performance Analysis

We have found over the years that conducting a first-rate performance analysis is central to the professional practice of instructional design. Indeed, we feel it is the single most important competency for success in this field.

In many cases, however, operating managers will pressure you to take a shortcut. More often than not, we have found, they would like you to skip the analysis, jump into action, and do what they want you to do. There is a bias, in the United States at least, toward highly visible action but not necessarily toward thoughtful analysis.

The lesson we have learned, and that we would like to share with you, is to beware of giving customers what they want but not what you are genuinely convinced they need. Too often, that path leads down blind alleys fraught with perils on every side. Even worse, it can eventually damage the credibility of instructional designers if operating managers misdiagnose the causes of human performance problems, the solutions they offer are ill-advised, or they are simply seeking trendy solutions to otherwise complex problems. Remember that the ultimate responsibility for failures will quickly return to you, but that many people will help you take credit for successes.

Point 2: Exercise Performance Analysis Creatively

Although we emphasized performance analysis in point 1, we have to admit that we often feel that present-day models of performance analysis are too simplistic. Our opinion is that, since it is sometimes difficult to be clear in print, writers on the subject have sometimes erred on the side of clarity rather than bringing out the true complexity that may be involved in analyzing human performance problems. In practice, we do not always limit ourselves, as popular models of performance analysis suggest you should, to the simple pigeonholing of all human performance problems into those stemming from skill deficiencies— what Gilbert (1996) in his classic work calls *deficiencies of execution*—and those stemming from nonskill deficiencies—what Gilbert calls *deficiencies of environment*. We find that, too often, such pigeonholing does not reflect the actual complexity of problems. Indeed, many human performance problems stem from both deficiencies of environment and deficiencies of execution.

Nor is it the dizzying complexity of the problems alone that poses a challenge. There is a broad range of potential solutions, instructional and non-instructional, to address human performance problems. To make matters more interesting, each solution can be combined with others (Rothwell, 1996b).

The lesson we have learned is that it is our own inability to be creative enough that often stymies our search for effective solutions. So our advice to you is this: *hold nothing sacred*. Be willing to experiment. Think about "crazy" ideas. Challenge assumptions others blithely take for granted in your quest for the causes of human performance problems and innovative solutions. As examples of what we mean, consider: Is it really necessary to structure an organization into jobs rather than groups or teams? Must all organizations have pay structures? Is an organization chart essential? Should every group in an organization have a "boss"? Are performance appraisals or job descriptions always necessary if other means can be found to provide feedback, document performance, or outline responsibilities? What competencies should *clients* possess for instructional design to be used successfully? Always be willing to ask, Why? Listen carefully to the answers you receive.

Our thinking is that the instructional design field has already begun to move beyond performance analysis, with its problem-oriented focus, and to concentrate on designing work systems themselves. Productivity can be directly affected by such strategies as spreading more work across fewer workers, broadening the responsibilities of work groups, or linking up groups more closely to those supplying them or distributing for them. As we confront such challenges, we should direct our attention more often to anticipating, and avoiding, human performance problems before they arise rather than troubleshooting them after they become apparent.

Point 3: Take Steps to Educate Managers About Performance Analysis

Although the instructional design field is moving away from performance analysis toward actual work systems design, we remain staunch defenders and believers in performance analysis. We also believe that instructional designers should not be content to practice performance analysis as a solitary pursuit, something treated as sacrosanct and as a well-kept professional secret. They should, instead, work energetically to educate operating managers about it and build *client* competencies into it. They can do that by offering training on performance analysis, writing and circulating organizational white papers, holding executive briefings, writing articles for company publications, and talking to management groups.

It has been our experience that many benefits can flow from these efforts. First, frivolous or ill-advised requests for instruction will diminish as managers become more sophisticated. (Initially, though, you will receive many requests for help in applying performance analysis to special situations or in unusual conditions.) Second, publicizing performance analysis is a subtle way to educate others about the importance of instructional design itself. Third, training others to do troubleshooting may eventually lead to a day when you can devote more time to solving the most important problems than to analyzing less important ones.

Point 4: Pay Attention to the Future and to the Consequences of Solutions

Looking back, we feel that most of the operating managers we have encountered are a bright, impressive group of people. Yet we have found, in too many cases, that they tend to think in a linear chain like this:

1. We have a problem.
2. We search for a solution and, having identified a solution,
3. We implement it.

Think of this approach as akin to problem solving on a staircase, because the conditions giving rise to problems and the conditions affecting solutions do not move. As are the steps on a staircase, conditions are stationary. If an implemented solution introduces new problems not initially considered, managers repeat anew the steps listed earlier.

But you should do better than that if you are to save your clients time and spare yourself grief. We find that the following approach works better:

1. We have a problem or can anticipate one before it manifests itself.
2. We search for a solution while trying to find out whether any conditions presently affecting the problem will change in the future.
3. We tentatively identify a solution and consider how future changes in the organization's environment or in the organization itself may affect it.
4. We play a game called "If . . . what" (If we implement the solution, what is likely to happen?).
5. We step back into the present and modify the solution to avert or minimize the negative side effects that we expect will arise during implementation.
6. We implement the solution.
7. We follow up continuously to ensure that the solution works as expected as the future unfolds.

Think of this approach as akin to problem solving on an escalator. Unlike the stationary steps on a staircase, here conditions affecting the problem and solution are capable of moving. What is more, the consequences of solutions are considered before implementation.

We cannot stress too much the importance of (1) scanning the future to see if anything will change the conditions causing a human performance problem, (2) considering future consequences of steps taken in the present to address problems, (3) scanning the future to see if anything will change the assumptions we make about a problem's solution, and (4) following up continuously to ensure that the solution works as expected.

Point 5: Be Flexible When Applying a Model of Instructional Systems Design

Although we have devoted much time to instructional systems design (ISD), we do not want you to come away from reading this book with the impression that instructional design is inflexible and never lends itself to modification. To apply it properly, you must be creative, not mechanical, in your approach. You must be willing to add, modify, or subtract steps in the process to match up with the culture of the organizations in which you use it. That may require spur-of-the-moment decisions or quick-witted action. *You simply must avoid thinking of the instructional design process as a paint-by-the-numbers activity, with each step to be performed mindlessly and in lockstep fashion.*

Point 6: Changing Environmental Conditions Will Prompt Modifications in the Instructional Design Process and in the Competencies Required for Instructional Designers

We want to stress that instructional design is not a static field; rather, like so many other things, it is influenced by trends in the economy, government, technology, and demographics. To maintain professional competence and adapt to changing conditions, you should willingly revisit the steps in the instructional design process and periodically reassess your own competencies relative to it.

Point 7: Beware of Pursuing New Technology for Its Own Sake

The authors examined the literature published in the field of learning and performance since 2003. One clear conclusion was that much of it focused on emerging technology that could be applied to instruction. That included all forms of media by which instruction could be delivered, such as iPods, cell phones, BlackBerries, personal digital assistants (PDAs), blogs, wikis, and much more. While it is encouraging to see that instructional designers are keenly aware of how new media might be turned to instructional advantage, it is not good that publications on these topics far exceeded the number of articles and books about ways to align instruction to achieve business goals. One possible conclusion is that instructional designers have a love affair with new technology but tend to miss the basics and tend to overlook what business leaders are demanding—that is, to show how instruction such as training (or even other performance improvement interventions) helps the organization achieve its goals. That goes beyond a preoccupation with demonstrating return on investment for training. Indeed, business leaders want to feel assured that their investments in instruction are worthwhile.

Sometimes, low-tech solutions, such as simple job aids or one-on-one training (on the job training), would meet instructional needs faster and less expensively than technology-dependent methods. That is worth remembering.

Point 8: Take Pains to Build Awareness and Show Linkages to the Contribution of Instructional Design Efforts with the Organization's Business Needs and Strategic Plans

At every stage of the instructional design process, instructional designers should ask themselves this question: "What has been done to communicate how this step in the instructional design process will help the organization achieve its goals and reassure managers that it is worth the time and money invested in it?" Instructional designers should not take it for granted that everyone sees the results of their hard work. They do not. It is essential to prepare a communication strategy at each step—and most importantly during the delivery phase, since that is what learners remember most—to demonstrate how training meets business needs. One idea is to require that topic to be treated at the opening of every planned instructional experience.

Point 9: Remember That Instructional Designers Are Expected to Provide Solutions, Not Just Instruction

Managers want results. If they face human performance problems, they do not necessarily want training. Instead, they want results. While it is true that managers sometimes ask for solutions because they think they already know the root causes, they usually do not. More often than not, they complain about symptoms of performance problems, not their root causes. And, when they ask for solutions, they have usually not considered the full range of options that may actually solve a human performance problem by addressing its root cause. Instructional designers should do that. In many cases, solving a human performance problem may actually require both management action and instruction. Instructional designers must ensure that both interventions are synergistic, yielding results better than their individual contributions.

Point 10: Do Everything Possible to Facilitate Self-Directed Learning

The half life of all human knowledge is now less than ten years—and it is falling. In our lifetimes there will come a time when all human knowledge turns over during the four years that a college student attends school. Increasingly, instructional designers must build in strategies to encourage learners to take initiative for planning, implementing, and evaluating their own individual and group learning experiences.

That starts by building the right expectations. Workers should be briefed during orientation programs about what role is expected of them in their own learning. They should be empowered to take initiative to learn on their own—and see that their efforts will correlate to future promotion and performance decisions.

Conclusion

This chapter closed the book with some personal reflections, gained through our experience, about what it takes to be effective as an instructional designer. We offered ten key lessons for you to consider as you embark on the challenge of working as an instructional designer.

ONLINE INSTRUCTIONAL DESIGN RESOURCES

This appendix is not intended to be exhaustive. However, it is intended to point the reader to a few useful online resources. Many of these resources will take you to other useful resources.

The following websites provide comprehensive information about recent instructional design theories and innovations.

- http://carbon.cudenver.edu/~mryder/itc_data/idmodels.html
- http://tip.psychology.org/index.html
- http://web.mala.bc.ca/lizhk/IDesign/ISDresources.htm
- www.student.seas.gwu.edu/~sbraxton/ISD/design_models.html

The wikipedia entry on instructional design. It defines what ISD is and provides links to many useful resources.

- http://en.wikipedia.org/wiki/Instructional_design

This link provides links to other online resources. That includes current instructional design models, online learning articles, learning activities for the web, and blogs.

- www.utoronto.ca/cat/whatson/presentation_notes/ID3X_f krauss/tsld029.htm

This link provides a comprehensive summary of instructional design models.

- http://carbon.cudenver.edu/~mryder/itc_data/idmodels.html

This link describes the so-called ADDIE model.

- www.fbe.unsw.edu.au/learning/instructionaldesign/materials.htm

The Encyclopedia of Educational Technology provides a large number of links to online resources.

- http://coe.sdsu.edu/eet/

This link provides tips for online learners and instructors.

- www.immaculata.edu/GeneralInformation/CampusServices/Technology%20Services/faculty_center/faculty_guide/teaching.htm

This link is to the Northern Educational Technology. It provides links to many useful resources.

- www.it.onu.edu/etdl/instruc_design/index.html

This link is to the learning guru. It is a good storehouse of material relating to e-learning. It contains articles about developing e-learning, a glossary and many links to other web resources.

- www.e-learningguru.com/articles.htm

This link is to a good collection of links to other sites with discussions of instructional theories from Action Research to Mind Tools. Some articles are much easier to read than others.

- http://carbon.cudenver.edu/~mryder/itc_data/idmodels.html

This link leads the user to a good, and relatively easy to read, explanation of three major learning theories—behaviorism, cognitivism, and constructivism.

- www.usask.ca/education/coursework/802papers/mergel/brenda.htm

This website has much good information about using the ISD model.

- www.nwlink.com/~donclark/hrd/sat.html

At this website you will find an entire book about ISD online.

- www.nwlink.com/~donclark/hrd/sat.html

This website is the Canadian Core Learning Object Metadata Application Profile. The site is the official home for documents, presentations, and other resources related to the Canadian Core Learning Object Metadata Application Profile. The CanCore Profile is intended to facilitate the interchange of records describing educational resources and the discovery of these resources both in Canada and beyond its borders. CanCore is based on and fully compatible with the IEEE Learning Object Metadata standard and the IMS Learning Resource Meta-data specification.

- www.cancore.ca/en/

The University of Texas at San Antonio's Learning Object Repositories has a list of websites and organizations that either have generated learning objects and host their own repository (e.g., Wisc-Online) or have provided guidelines, templates, or frameworks for objects that are stored in their repository (such as Apple Learning Exchange).

- http://elearning.utsa.edu/guides/LO-repositories.htm

This tutorial has been created for Learning Object Trick or Treat, a Techlearn 2001 event in which participants find learning objects (SCOs) in a virtual pumpkin patch, create a content package by adding their own SCO, and load and launch the package in an LMS.

- www.eduworks.com/LOTT/tutorial/

Macromedia Learning Objects Development Center provides software, white papers, and news about Learning Objects.

- www.macromedia.com/resources/elearning/objects/

The New York Public Library Digital Gallery provides access to over 275,000 images digitized from primary sources and printed rarities in the collections of The New York Public Library, including illuminated manuscripts, historical maps, vintage posters, rare prints and photographs, illustrated books, printed ephemera, and more.

• http://digitalgallery.nypl.org/nypldigital/index.cfm

The Learning Resources Unit of the British Columbia Institute of Technology was created by the Learning Resources Unit of the British Columbia Institute of Technology to support and recognize innovative practice in distributed learning at BCIT, and in the greater educational community.

• http://online.bcit.ca/sidebars/02november/inside-out-1.htm

The Academic Advanced Distributed Learning (ADL) Co-Lab: Wisconsin On-Line Resource Center is a collaborative virtual center of web-based teaching and learning resource options, technical and peer support. The sixteen two-year colleges of the Wisconsin Technical College System and the State Board Office have partnered to develop high-quality, interactive online learning resources to support the statewide development of core general education course offerings on the Internet. As a national model, the project goal is to accelerate the development of quality on-line offerings while minimizing the cost of development and the time for faculty training and course implementation while preserving faculty control of the course design.

• www.academiccolab.org/projects/learning_objects/wisc-online.html

The websites below focus on project, problem- and inquiry-based learning.

• http://score.rims.k12.ca.us/problearn.html
• www.eduscapes.com/tap/topic43.htm
• www.imsa.edu/team/cpbl/cpbl.html

This website focuses on inquiry-based assessment.

• http://inquiry.uiuc.edu/index.php3

This website focuses on the phases of ISD.

• www.student.seas.gwu.edu/~tlooms/ISD/general_phases.html

This website provides tips for developing web-based learning activities.

• www.sonoma.edu/CTPD/webtips.html

Converge Magazine is an online educational technology magazine that is one of the best.

• www.convergemag.com/index.php

The Chronicle of Higher Education is an online magazine that deals with many issues.

• http://chronicle.com/

T.H.E. Journal Magazine is mostly aimed at k-12, but it addresses industry information also.

• http://thejournal.com/

Innovate is the journal of online education.

• http://innovateonline.info/

WHAT IS KNOWLEDGE MANAGEMENT (KM), AND HOW DOES KM RELATE TO INSTRUCTIONAL DESIGN?

This appendix defines knowledge management, defines key terms associated with it, explains why it is important, shows how it relates to instructional design, briefly describes how instructional design can contribute to KM in organizations, and points readers toward additional resources useful for future research on KM.

What Is KM?

No widely accepted definition of knowledge management exists. In practical terms, though, it means the process by which organizations create and leverage value from the knowledge possessed by members of the organization ("ABC," 2007). It involves identifying, capturing, and preserving knowledge about an organization.

What Key Terms Are Associated with KM, and What Do They Mean?

There are differences between *information* and *knowledge* and between *explicit* and *tacit knowledge*. These key terms are worthy of definition.

- *Information*: Information consists of facts, figures, procedures, processes, and anything that can be thought, written or said about an organization's practices.
- *Knowledge*: Information that is especially useful in operating an organization's operations. It is a subset of information.
- *Explicit knowledge*: A subset of all knowledge, it is that which can be conveyed about an organization's policy, plans, procedures, or processes by written or oral means.
- *Tacit knowledge*: A subset of all knowledge, that knowledge that people carry around in their heads. It is acquired from experience. It contains lessons learned from experience.
- *Technical succession planning*: The process of capturing tacit knowledge and institutional memory and passing it on to successors in the future (Rothwell and Poduch, 2004).

Why Is KM Important?

Most work in most organizations today depend on knowledge. That is aptly captured by using the phrase "knowledge economy." It means businesses—and other organizations—are heavily dependent on knowledge for present and future success. Knowledge itself is the basis of competitive advantage in the knowledge economy.

As many baby boomers prepare to retire, organizational leaders are becoming increasingly interested in technical succession planning (Rothwell and Poduch, 2004).

How Does KM Relate to Instructional Design?

As defined in this book, "instructional design is (1) an emerging profession, (2) focused on establishing and maintaining efficient and effective human performance, (3) guided by a model of human performance, (4) carried out systematically, (5) based on open systems theory, and (6) oriented to finding and applying the most cost-effective solutions to human performance problems and discovering quantum leaps in productivity improvement through human ingenuity" (Rothwell and Kazanas, 2008, p. 28). By that definition, instructional design (ID) is a means of improving human productivity. That often involves identifying useful knowledge, essential to human performance, and transmitting it to those who need. In some cases, ID also includes facilitating a process of creating new knowledge and transmitting to facilitate improved human performance.

How Can Instructional Design Contribute to KM in Organizations?

Instructional design can contribute to KM by assisting in the process of identifying, capturing, distilling, and transferring useful explicit and tacit knowledge from those possessing it to those needing it at present and in the future. When regarded in this way, ID becomes an essential component of KM and is an important means to an end.

What Resources Are Useful for Future Research on KM?

"ABC: An Introduction to Knowledge Management (KM)," downloaded on 2 November 2007 from www.cio.com/article/40343/ABC_An_Introduction_to_Knowledge_Management_KM.

Davenport, T., and Prusak, L. *Working Knowledge: How Organizations Manage What They Know* (2nd ed.). Boston: Harvard Business School Press, 2000.

Frappolo, C. *Knowledge Management* (2nd ed.). Mankato, MN: Capstone, 2006.

Groff, T., and Jones, T. *Introduction to Knowledge Management: KM in Business.* Burlington, MA: Butterworth-Heinemann, 2003.

O'dell, C., and Grayson, C. *If Only We Knew What We Know: The Transfer of Internal Knowledge and Best Practice.* New York: The Free Press, 1998.

Rothwell, W. (2004). Knowledge transfer: 12 strategies for succession management. *IPMA-HR News,* pp. 10–12.

Rothwell, W., and Poduch, S. (2004). Introducing technical (not managerial) succession planning. *Public Personnel Management, 33*(4), 405–420.

Conclusion

In the future it is likely that ID and KM will become even more closely associated than they are now. For that reason, ID professionals must become more aware of KM and stand ready to contribute to KM efforts. ID's contribution to KM can go well beyond instructional approaches to include a full range of methods by which to transfer knowledge from those possessing it to those needing it.

LEARNING THEORY AND INSTRUCTIONAL DESIGN

What Is Learning Theory?

A *learning theory* is simply a theory about how people learn.

What Is the Relationship Between Learning Theory and Instructional Design?

To the extent that instructional designers use instruction to prompt changes in performance, they must be interested in learning theory because theories about how people learn become a foundation for designing learning experiences that will have the greatest impact on individual performance.

There are many different learning theories. Some websites are devoted simply to summarizing a large number of them and pointing readers to places to learn about those learning theories. A few, but by no means all, key learning theories are summarized in the table below. Note that behaviorism, cognivitism and constructivism are summarized in an earlier chapter of this book. Hence, the theories summarized below are in addition to the "big three" learning theories of behaviorism, cognitivism and constructivism.

Learning Theory	Summary of the Theory	What the Theory Means for Instructional Design	Resources to Consult to Learn More About the Theory
Social learning theory	Albert Bandura is usually credited to be the father of social learning theory. Learning can take place simply by having people watch what other people do and then imitating it. People thus learn by watching others and trying it out.	Encourage learners to watch others demonstrate good and bad examples, since learning can occur both by watching the right way and the wrong way. Then encourage "behavioral modeling" so that individuals try to imitate what they saw demonstrated.	Bandura, A. (1997). *Self-efficacy: The exercise of control.* New York: W.H. Freeman. Bandura, A. (1986). *Social Foundations of Thought and Action.* Englewood Cliffs, NJ: Prentice-Hall. Bandura, A. (1973). *Aggression: A Social Learning Analysis.* Englewood Cliffs, NJ: Prentice-Hall. Bandura, A. (1977). *Social Learning Theory.* New York: General Learning Press. Bandura, A. (1969). *Principles of Behavior Modification.* New York: Holt, Rinehart and Winston. Bandura, A., and Walters, R. (1963). *Social Learning and Personality Development.* New York: Holt, Rinehart and Winston. Huitt, W. (2004). "Observational (Social) Learning: An Overview." *Educational Psychology Interactive.* Valdosta, GA: Valdosta State University.
Gestalt theory	The key argument of gestalt theory is that the whole is greater than the sum of its parts. People strive to see patterns. That is why they hear a melody rather than one note at a time.	Present learners with a picture of the "whole"—such as a model that shows all the parts—and then proceed to describe each part and how it contributes to the whole.	"Origins and Development of Gestalt Theory" at www.aagt.org/html/origins_and_development_of_ges.html

| Information processing theory | There are three modes of learning, according to Rumelhart and Norman (1978): accretion, structuring, and tuning. Accretion means adding new knowledge to memory. Structuring has to do with forming new schema or ways of organizing knowledge. Tuning simply means adjusting knowledge based on practice. | Find ways to focus instruction around the three modes of learning. | Norman, D. (1982). *Learning and Memory.* San Francisco: Freeman.

Rumelhart, D., and Norman, D. (1978). "Accretion, Tuning and Restructuring: Three Modes of Learning." In. J.W. Cotton and R. Klatzky (Eds.), *Semantic Factors in Cognition.* Hillsdale, NJ: Lawrence Erlbaum Associates.

Rumelhart, D., and Norman, D. (1981). "Analogical Processes in Learning." In J.R. Anderson (Ed.), *Cognitive Skills and Their Acquisition.* Hillsdale, NJ: Lawrence Erlbaum Associates. |
| Situated learning | Learning occurs as a function of what is to be learned, in what setting it is learned, and the cultural context in which it is to be learned. Social interaction is critical in learning. | Encourage people to learn gradually by having novices learn from experts in the settings where they must apply what they learn. | Brown, J.S., Collins, A., and Duguid, S. (1989). "Situated Cognition and the Culture of Learning." *Educational Researcher,* 18(1), 32–42.

Cognition and Technology Group at Vanderbilt (March 1993). "Anchored Instruction and Situated Cognition Revisited." *Educational Technology,* 33(3), 52–70.

Lave, J. (1988). *Cognition in Practice: Mind, Mathematics, and Culture in Everyday Life.* Cambridge, UK: Cambridge University Press.

Lave, J., Wenger, E. (1990). *Situated Learning: Legitimate Periperal Participation.* Cambridge, UK: Cambridge University Press.

McLellan, H. (1995). *Situated Learning Perspectives.* Englewood Cliffs, NJ: Educational Technology Publications.

Suchman, L. (1988). *Plans and Situated Actions: The Problem of Human/Machine Communication.* Cambridge, UK: Cambridge University Press. |

(continued)

Learning Theory	Summary of the Theory	What the Theory Means for Instructional Design	Resources to Consult to Learn More About the Theory
Theory of multiple intelligences*	Howard Gardner (1983) suggested a new way of regarding intelligence that expanded what it means. He suggested that intelligence has seven aspects: (1) **Logical-Mathematical Intelligence**: ability to note patterns, reason deductively and think logically; (2) **Linguistic Intelligence**: mastery of language. People who possess this form of intelligence can manipulate language to express themselves; (3) **Spatial Intelligence**: gives people the ability to manipulate and create mental images to solve problems; (4) **Musical Intelligence**: recognize and compose music; (5) **Bodily-Kinesthetic Intelligence**: the ability to use mental abilities to coordinate body movements; (6) **Interpersonal intelligence**: understand and discern the feelings of others; and (7) **Intrapersonal intelligence**: understand one's own feelings and motivations.	Gardner's Theory of Multiple Intelligences has many implications for instructional designers. All seven are needed by learners to perform effectively. They are thus equally important. Instructional designers should organize learning to encourage as many intelligences as possible.	Gardner, H. (1983). *Frames of Mind.* New York: Basic Books. Gardner, H. (1991) *The Unschooled Mind: How Children Think and How Schools Should Teach.* New York: Basic Books. Gardner, H., and Hatch, T. (1989). "Multiple Intelligences Go to School: Educational Implications of the Theory of Multiple Intelligences." *Educational Researcher, 18*(8), 4–9. Kornhaber, M., and Gardner, H. (1993, March). *Varieties of Excellence: Identifying and Assessing Children's Talents. A Series on Authentic Assessment and Accountability.* New York: Columbia University, Teachers College, National Center for Restructuring Education, Schools, and Teaching. (ERIC Document Reproduction Service No. ED 363 396) Lazear, D. (1991). *Seven Ways of Teaching: The Artistry of Teaching with Multiple Intelligences.* Palatine, IL: IRI Skylight Publishing Inc. (ERIC Document Reproduction Service No. ED 382 374) (highly recommended)

Subsumtion theory	David Ausubel's theory focuses on how people learn much information—particular from verbal/textual presentations in a school setting. "A primary process in learning is subsumption in which new material is related to relevant ideas in the existing cognitive structure on a substantive, non-verbatim basis. Cognitive structures represent the residue of all learning experiences; forgetting occurs because certain details get integrated and lose their individual identity." ("Subsumtion theory," http://tip.psychology.org/ausubel.html)	Ausubel's subsumtion theory is primarily focused on expository learning in formal learning settings. For Ausubel, instructional designers should: (1) present the most general ideas of a subject first and then move on to more detail; (2) build on previous material. Ausubel is most famous for advocating so-called advance organizers that help learners see all the major parts of information first and permit them to focus on what they most need to know.	Ausubel, D. (1963). *The Psychology of Meaningful Verbal Learning.* New York: Grune & Stratton. Ausubel, D. (1978). "In Defense of Advance Organizers: A Reply to the Critics." *Review of Educational Research, 48,* 251–257. Ausubel, D., Novak, J., and Hanesian, H. (1978). *Educational Psychology: A Cognitive View* (2nd ed.). New York: Holt, Rinehart and Winston.

REFERENCES

Alden, J. A *Trainer's Guide to Web-Based Instruction: Getting Started on Intranet- and Internet-Based Training*. Alexandria, VA: The American Society for Training and Development, 1998.

Alden, J., and Kirkhorn, J. "Case Studies." In R. Craig (Ed.). *The ASTD Training and Development Handbook: A Guide to Human Resource Development* (4th ed.) (pp. 497–516). New York: McGraw-Hill, 1996.

Allen, E. (Ed.). *Needs Assessment Instruments*. Alexandria, VA: The American Society for Training and Development, 1990.

Allen, E. "Information Resources." In R. Craig (Ed.), *The ASTD Training and Development Handbook: A Guide to Human Resource Development* (4th ed.) (pp. 947–963). New York: McGraw-Hill, 1996.

Allen, M. "Discovery Learning: Repurposing an Old Paradigm." *e-Learning*, 2002, *3*(1), 18–20.

"A Nation Online: Entering the Broadband Age." Washington, DC: U.S. Department of Commerce, 2004. Downloaded 23 October 2007 from www.ntia.doc.gov/reports/anol/NationOnlineBroadband04.htm.

Andrews, D., and Goodson, L. "A Comparative Analysis of Models of Instructional Design." *Journal of Development*, 1980, *3*(4), 2–16. (ED EJ 228 351)

Annett, J., and Stanton, N. *Task Analysis*. New York: Taylor & Francis, 2001.

Antaki, C. *Analyzing Everyday Explanation: A Casebook of Methods*. Newbury Park, CA: Sage, 1988.

Appelbaum, E., and Batt, R. *The New American Workplace: Transforming Work Systems in the United States*. Ithaca, NY: ILR Press, 1994.

Arvey, R., and Faley, R. *Fairness in Selecting Employees*. (2nd ed.). Reading, MA: Addison-Wesley, 1988.

ASTD Multicultural Forum. *Elements of Competency for Diversity Work*. Alexandria, VA: The American Society for Training and Development, 1996.

Atwater, L., and Waldman, D. "Accountability in 360 Degree Feedback." *HRMagazine*, 1998, *43*(6), 96–104.

Ausubel, D. "A Subsumption Theory of Meaningful Verbal Learning and Retention." *Journal of General Psychology,* 1962, *66,* 213–214.

Bacal, R. *Performance Management.* New York: McGraw-Hill, 1999.

Bachman, L. "Pilot Your Program for Success." *Training and Development,* 1987, *41*(5), 96–97.

Bader, G., and Rossi, C. *Focus Groups: A Step-by-Step Guide* (3rd ed.). San Diego, CA: The Bader Group, 2002.

Baker, G., Mohammed, T., and Boyle, M. "A Three-Axis Model for Conceptualizing the Relevant Elements Involved in Cross-Cultural Training." *Performance Improvement Quarterly,* 1994, *7*(2), 27–37.

Baker, H., and Morgan, P. "Building a Professional Image: Handling Conflict." In F. Stone (Ed.), *The American Management Association Handbook of Supervisory Management.* (Originally printed in *Supervisory Management,* September 1980.) New York: AMACOM, 1989.

Baldwin, T., and Ford, J. "Transfer of Training: A Review and Directions for Future Research." *Personnel Psychology,* 1988, *41*(1), 63–105.

Barbian, J. "Blended Works: Here's Proof." *Online Learning,* 2002a, *6* (6), 26–31.

Barbian, J. "No-Tech Still Matters." *Training,* 2002b, *39*(2), 56–60.

Barksdale, S., and Lund, T. *Rapid Needs Analysis.* Alexandria, VA: The American Society for Training and Development, 2001.

Barron, T. "Learning Object Approach Is Making Inroads." *Learning Circuits,* 2002, *3*(5). See www.learningcircuits.org/2002/may2002/barron.html

Bartlett, C., and Ghoshal, S. *Cross-Border Management.* Homewood, IL: Business One Irwin, 1992.

Bassi, L., and Ahlstrand, A. *The 2000 ASTD Learning Outcomes Report.* Alexandria, VA: The American Society for Training and Development, 2000.

Bassi, L., Gould, E., Kulik, J., and Zornitsky, J. *Thinking Outside the Lines: High Performance Companies in Manufacturing and Services.* Cambridge, MA: ABT, 1993.

Becker, B., Huselid, M., and Ulrich, D. *The HR Scorecard.* Boston: Harvard Business School Press, 2001.

Beckhard, R., and Pritchard, W. *Changing the Essence: The Art of Creating and Leading Fundamental Change in Organizations.* San Francisco: Jossey-Bass, 1992.

Beckshi, P., and Doty, M. "Instructional Systems Design: A Little Bit of ADDIEtude, Please!" In G. Piskurich, P. Beckshi, and B. Hall (Eds.), *The ASTD Handbook of Training Design and Delivery* (pp. 28–41). New York: McGraw-Hill, 2000.

Beer, V. *The Web Learning Fieldbook: Using the World Wide Web to Build Workplace Learning Environments.* San Francisco: Pfeiffer, 2000.

Belasco, J. *Teaching the Elephant to Dance: Empowering Change in Your Organization.* London: Random House, 1990.

Bell, B., and Kozlowski, S. "A Typology of Virtual Teams." *Journal of Group and Organization Management,* 2002, *27*(1), 14–49.

Bengtson, B. *An Analysis of CEO Perceptions Concerning Trainer Roles in Selected Central Pennsylvania Manufacturing Firms.* Unpublished doctoral dissertation. University Park, PA: The Pennsylvania State University, 1994.

Bentley, T. *Facilitation: Providing Opportunities for Learning.* London: McGraw-Hill, 1994.

Berger, M. "A Market-Led Training Needs Analysis: Is the Training Needs Analysis Outmoded?" *Industrial and Commercial Training,* 1993, *25*(1), 27–30.

Bernardez, M. "From e-Training to e-Performance: Putting Online Learning to Work." *Educational Technology,* 2003, *43*(1), p. 6–11.

Bernthal, P., Colteryahn, K., Davis, P., Naughton, J., Rothwell, W., and Wellins, R. *Mapping the Future: Shaping New Workplace Learning and Performance Competencies.* Alexandria, VA: The American Society for Training and Development, 2004.

Berry, L. "Instructional Message Design: Evolution and Future Directions." In B. Seels (Ed.), *Instructional Design Fundamentals: A Reconsideration* (pp. 87–98). Englewood Cliffs, NJ: Educational Technology Publications, 1995a.

Berry, L. *On Great Service: A Framework for Action.* New York: The Free Press, 1995b.

Bishop, H. "Accurate Job Descriptions: First Things First." *Performance and Instruction*, 1988a, *27*(2), 15–18.

Bishop, H. *Employment Testing and Incentives to Learn.* Ithaca, NY: State University of New York and School of Industrial and Labor Relations, Cornell University, 1988b.

Black, J., and Mendenhall, M. "Cross-Cultural Training Effectiveness: A Review and a Theoretical Framework for Future Research." *Academy of Management Review*, 1990, *15*(1), 113–136.

Blalock, R. "Using Development 'Shells' for Fast and Creative Multimedia Development at American Airlines." *Journal of Instruction Delivery Systems*, Summer 1995, pp. 3–9.

Blank, W. *Handbook for Developing Competency-Based Training Programs.* Englewood Cliffs, NJ: Prentice-Hall, 1982.

Bloom, B. *Taxonomy of Educational Objectives, the Classification of Educational Goals—Handbook I: Cognitive Domain.* New York: McKay, 1956.

Bloom, B., Hastings, J., and Madaus, G. (Eds.). *Handbook of Formative and Summative Evaluation.* New York: McGraw-Hill, 1971.

Bogan, C. "Benchmarking for Best Practices." In R. Craig (Ed.). *The ASTD Training and Development Handbook: A Guide to Human Resource Development* (4th ed.) (pp. 394–414). New York: McGraw-Hill, 1996.

Borman, R. "Training a Global Audience." *e-Learning*, 2001, *2*(7) 12–15.

Brake, T., Walker, D., and Walker, T. *Doing Business Internationally: The Guide to Cross-Cultural Success.* Burr Ridge, IL: Irwin Professional Publishing, 1995.

Brandenburg, D., and Binder, C. "Emerging Trends in Human Performance Interventions." In H. Stolovitch and E. Keeps (Eds.), *Handbook of Human Performance Technology: A Comprehensive Guide for Analyzing and Solving Performance Problems in Organizations* (pp. 651–671). San Francisco: Jossey-Bass, 1992.

Brandenburg, D., and Smith, M. *Evaluation of Corporate Training Programs.* TME report 91. Princeton, NJ: Educational Testing Service, 1986.

Brannick, M., and Levine, E. *Job Analysis: Methods, Research, and Applications for Human Resource Management in the New Millennium.* Beverly Hills, CA: Corwin Press, 2002.

Bredo, E. "Reconstructing Educational Psychology: Situated Cognition and Deweyian Pragmatism." *Educational Psychologist*, 1994, *17*(1), 23–35.

Brennan, J. *Applications of Critical Path Techniques.* New York: Elsevier, 1968.

Bridges, W. *Job Shift.* Reading, MA: Addison-Wesley, 1994.

Brien, R., and Eastmond, N. *Cognitive Science and Instruction.* Englewood Cliffs, NJ: Educational Technology Publications, 1994.

Briggs, L. "Designing the Strategy of Instruction." In L. Briggs (Ed.), *Instructional Design: Principles and Applications.* Englewood Cliffs, NJ: Educational Technology Publications, 1977.

Brinkerhoff, R. "The Success Case: A Low-Cost High-Yield Evaluation." *Training and Development*, 1983, *37*(8), 58–61.

Brinkerhoff, R., and Dressler, D. *Productivity Measurement: A Guide for Managers and Evaluators.* Newbury Park, CA: Sage, 1989.

Broad, M., and Newstrom, J. *Transfer of Training: Action-Packed Strategies to Ensure High Payoff from Training Investments.* Reading, MA: Addison-Wesley, 1992.

Brown, J. (Ed.). *An Investigation of Motivation's Role in Postsecondary Vocational Training Programs for At-Risk Learners and Their Entry into the Work Force.* St. Paul, MN: Minnesota Research and Development Center for Vocational Education, 1989.

Brown, K. "Strategic Performance Measurements." *CPA Journal,* 1995, *65*(10), 65.

Brown, M. "Human Capital's Measure for Measure." *Journal for Quality and Participation,* 1999, *22*(5), 28–31.

Bruner, J. *Towards a Theory of Instruction.* New York: W.W. Norton, 1966.

Buchanan, D. *The Development of Job Design Theories and Techniques.* New York: Praeger, 1979.

Bureau of Law and Business. *How to Write Job Descriptions—The Easy Way.* Madison, CT: Bureau of Law and Business, 1982.

Burk, J., and Birk, T. "The Art and Science of Personnel Selection." *Performance Improvement,* 2001, *40* (1), 32–37.

Business Research Publications. *The Encyclopedia of Managerial Job Descriptions.* Plainville, NY: Business Research Publications, 1976.

Byham, W. "Recruitment, Screening, and Selection." In W. Tracey (Ed.), *Human Resources Management and Development Handbook* (3rd ed.) (pp. 190–203). New York: AMACOM, 1994.

Byrne, J. "Management Meccas: Everyone Seems to Be Studying U.S. Corporate Stars." *Business Week,* September 18, 1995, pp. 122–132.

Campbell, A., and Luchs, K. *Core Competency-Based Strategy.* London: International Thomson Business Press, 1997.

Campbell, D., and Stanley, J. *Experimental and Quasi-Experimental Designs for Research.* Chicago: Rand-McNally, 1966.

Campion, M., and McClelland, C. "Follow-Up and Extension of the Interdisciplinary Costs and Benefits of Enlarged Jobs." *Journal of Applied Psychology,* 1993, *78*(3), 339–351.

Carlisle, K. *Analyzing Jobs and Tasks.* Englewood Cliffs, NJ: Educational Technology Publications, 1986.

Carnevale, A., Gainer, L., and Meltzer, A. *Workplace Basics: The Skills Employers Want.* Alexandria, VA: American Society for Training and Development and Washington, DC: Employment and Training Administration, U.S. Department of Labor, 1988.

Carnevale, A., Gainer, L., and Villet, J. *Training in America: The Organization and Strategic Role of Training.* San Francisco: Jossey-Bass, 1990.

Caropreso, F. (Ed.). *Managing Globally: Key Perspectives.* Report No. 972. New York: The Conference Board, 1991.

Carr, C. "Designing Systems for the 90s." *Performance Improvement Quarterly,* 1990, *3*(1), 14–26.

Carroll, S., Jr., Paine, F., and Ivancevich, J. "The Relative Effectiveness of Training Methods—Expert Opinion and Research." *Personnel Psychology,* 1972, *25*(3), 495–509.

Carter, J. "Lessons in Text Design from an Instructional Perspective." In T. Duffy and R. Waller (Eds.), *Designing Usable Texts.* San Diego, CA: Academic Press, 1985.

Charness, N., and Czaja, S. *Older Worker Training: What We Know and Don't Know.* Downloaded 23 October 2007 from www.aarp.org/research/work/issues/2006_22_worker.html, Washington, DC: AARP, 2006.

Chase, R., and Tansik, D. "The Customer Contact Model for Organization Design." *Management Science,* 1983, *29*, 1037–1050.

Chase, W., and Chi, M. "Cognitive Skill: Implications for Spatial Skill in Large-Scale Environments." In J. Harvey (Ed.), *Cognition, Social Behavior, and the Environment*. Hillsdale, NJ: Lawrence Erlbaum, 1980.

Chernick, J. "Keeping Your Pilots on Course." *Training and Development*, 1992, *46*(4), 69–73.

Chew, I., and Chong, P. "Effects of Strategic Human Resource Management on Strategic Vision." *International Journal of Human Resource Management*, 1999, *10* (6), 1030–1045.

Chinien, C., and Boutin, F. "A Framework for Evaluating the Effectiveness of Instructional Materials." *Performance and Instruction*, 1994, *33*(3), 15–18.

Choi, I., and Jonassen, D. "Learning Objectives from the Perspective of the Experienced Cognition Framework." *Journal of Educational Technology*, 2000, *40*(6), 36–40.

Clark, R. "Defining the 'D' in ISD: Part 2: Task-Specific Instructional Methods." *Performance and Instruction*, 1986, *25*(3), 12–17.

Clark, R. "How the Cognitive Sciences Are Shaping the Profession." In H. Stolovitch and E. Keeps (Eds.), *Handbook of Human Performance Technology: A Comprehensive Guide for Analyzing and Solving Performance Problems in Organizations* (pp. 688–700). San Francisco: Jossey-Bass, 1992.

Clark, R. "The New ISD: Applying Cognitive Strategies to Instructional Design." *Performance Improvement*, 2002, *41*(7).

Clark R. (2003). *Building Expertise: Cognitive Methods for Training and Performance Improvement* (2nd ed.). Silver Springs, MD: International Society for Performance Improvement.

Cleland, D. "Why Project Management?" *Business Horizons*, 1964, *7*(Winter), 81–88.

Clifford, J. "Job Analysis: Why Do It, and How Should It Be Done?" *Public Personnel Management*, 1994, *23*(2), 321–340.

Coch, L., and French, J., Jr. "Overcoming Resistance to Change." *Human Relations*, August 1948, pp. 512–532.

Cole, P. "Constructivism Revisited: A Search for Common Ground." *Educational Technology*, 1992, *32*(2), 27–34.

The Conference Board. *Organization Designs for the '90s*. New York: The Conference Board, 1989.

Connor, D. *Managing at the Speed of Change*. New York: Villard Books, 1992.

Conrad, K., and TrainingLinks. *Instructional Design for Web-Based Training*. Amherst, MA: Human Resource Development Press, 2000.

Cooper, K. *Effective Competency Modeling and Reporting*. New York: AMACOM, 2000.

Cooper, P. "Paradigm Shifts in Designed Instruction: From Behaviorism to Cognitivism to Constructivism." *Educational Technology*, 1993, *33*(5), 12–19.

Cowan, S. Alternatives to Classrooms. *Info-Line*, No. 250209. Alexandria, VA: The American Society for Training and Development, 2002.

Cooperrider, D., and Whitney, D. *Appreciative Inquiry: A Positive Revolution in Change*. San Francisco: Berrett-Koehler, 2005.

Crabtree, S. Getting Personal in the Workplace: Are Negative Relationships Squelching Productivity in Your Company? *The Gallup Management Journal*, downloaded on 22 October 2007 from http://www.govleaders.org/gallup_article_getting_personal.htm, 2007.

Crowe, M., Hettinger, L., Weber, J., and Johnson, J. *Analysis of Students' Basic Skills Performance in Selected Instructional Delivery Systems: Final Report*. Columbus, OH: National Center for Research in Vocational Education, Ohio State University, 1986.

Cyert, R., and March, J. *A Behavioral Theory of the Firm*. Englewood Cliffs, NJ: Prentice-Hall, 1963.

Dalton, G., Thompson, P., and Price, R. "The Four Stages of Professional Careers: A New Look at Performance by Professionals." *Organizational Dynamics*, Summer 1977, pp. 19–42.

Dalton, M. "Conflict Between Staff and Line Managerial Officers." In A. Etzioni (Ed.), *A Socio-logical Reader on Complex Organizations* (2nd ed.). Troy, MO: Holt, Rinehart and Winston, 1969.

David, M. Guide to Successful Executive Coaching. *Info-Line*, No. 250204. Alexandria, VA: The American Society for Training and Development, 2002.

Davidove, E. "The Most Important Lesson I've Learned as a Consultant About the Systems Approach to Instructional Design." *Performance and Instruction*, 1991, *31*(10), 11–13.

Davis, R., Alexander, L., and Yelon, S. *Learning Systems Design*. New York: McGraw-Hill, 1974.

Dean, P. "A Selected Review of the Underpinnings of Ethics for Human Performance Technology Professionals—Part One: Key Ethical Theories and Research." *Performance Improvement Quarterly*, 1993, *6* (4), 3–32.

Dean, M., and Dean, P. "Competency-Based Performance Feedback." In P. Dean (Ed.), *Performance Engineering at Work* (pp. 129–142). Batavia, IL: International Board of Standards for Training, Performance and Instruction, 1994.

"Defense Contractors Create Gold Standard for Ethics Training and Compliance." *IOMA's Report on Managing Training and Development*, 2002, *2*(7), 1, 6–7, 10–11.

Delahoussaye, M., and Zemke, R. "10 Things We Know for Sure." *Training*, 2001, *38*(9), 48–59.

Denis, J. "A Base(ic) Course on Job Analysis." *Training and Development*, 1992, *46* (7), 67–70.

Dervarics, C. "What's a 'Good' Needs Assessment?" *Technical and Skills Training*, 1994, *5*(4), 22–26.

Deterline, W. "Feedback Systems." In H. Stolovitch and E. Keeps (Eds.), *Handbook of Human Performance Technology: A Comprehensive Guide for Analyzing and Solving Performance Problems in Organizations* (pp. 294–311). San Francisco: Jossey-Bass, 1992.

Dick, W. "Enhanced ISD: A Response to Changing Environments for Learning and Performance." *Educational Technology*, 1993, *33*(2), 12–16.

Dick, W., and Carey, L. *The Systematic Design of Instruction* (3rd ed.). New York: HarperCollins, 1990.

Dick, W., and King, D. "Formative Evaluation in the Performance Context." *Performance and Instruction*, 1994, *33*(9), 3–8.

DiConsiglio, J. "Trainers Look to Parlez Business in Different Languages." *Workforce Training News*, October 1994, p. 7.

The Dictionary of Occupational Titles (4th ed.). Hawthorne, NJ: The Career Press, 1991.

Dillman, D. *Mail and Internet Surveys: The Tailored Design Method* (2nd ed.). Hoboken, NJ: John Wiley & Sons, 1999.

Dixon, N. "The Relationship Between Trainee Responses on Participant Reaction Forms and Posttest Scores." *Human Resource Development Quarterly*, 1990, *1*(2), 129–137.

Dosher, R. "Records and Information Systems." In R. Craig (Ed.), *Training and Development Handbook: A Guide to Human Resource Development* (3rd ed.). New York: McGraw-Hill, 1987.

Drew, R., Mikulecky, L., and Pershing, J. *How to Gather and Develop Job-Specific Literacy Materials for Basic Skills Instruction*. Bloomington, IN: Office of Education and Training Resources, School of Education, Indiana University, 1988.

Driscoll, M. *Web-Based Training: Using Technology to Design Adult Learning Experiences*. San Francisco: Pfeiffer, 1998.

Driscoll, T. "Chronicling the Emergence of Human Performance Technology." *Performance Improvement*, 2003, *42*(6), 9–18, 20–22.

Driskell, J., Olmstead, B., and Salas, E. "Task Cues, Dominance Cues, and Influence in Task Groups." *Journal of Applied Psychology*, 1993, *78*(1), 51–60.

Drucker, P. *Management: Tasks, Responsibilities, Practices*. New York: HarperCollins, 1973.

Druskat, V., and Wolff, S. "Building the Emotional Intelligence of Groups." *Harvard Business Review*, 2001, *79*(3), 80–90.

Dubois, D. *Competency-Based Performance Improvement: A Strategy for Organizational Change.* Amherst, MA: Human Resource Development Press, 1993.

Dubois, D., and Rothwell, W. *Developing the High-Performance Workplace Organizational Assessment Package: Administrator's Handbook and Data Collection Instrument.* Amherst, MA: Human Resource Development Press, 1996.

Dubois, D., and Rothwell, W. *Competency-Based Human Resource Management.* Palo Alto, CA: Davies-Black, 2004.

Dubois, D., and Rothwell, W. *The Competency Toolkit* (2 vols.). Amherst, MA: Human Resource Development Press, 2000.

Dubois, D., and Rothwell, W. *Competency-Based Human Resource Management.* Palo Alto, CA: Davies-Black, in press.

Duncan, D. "Organization Design." In W. Tracey (Ed.), *Human Resources Management and Development Handbook* (3rd ed.) (pp. 161–180). New York: AMACOM, 1994.

Duncan, J., and Powers, E. "The Politics of Intervening in Organizations." In H. Stolovitch and E. Keeps (Eds.), *Handbook of Human Performance Technology: A Comprehensive Guide for Analyzing and Solving Performance Problems in Organizations* (pp. 77-94). San Francisco: Jossey-Bass, 1992.

Eder, R., and Ferris, G. *The Employment Interview: Theory, Research, and Practice.* Newbury Park, CA: Sage, 1990.

Edmonds, G., Branch, R., and Mukherjee, P. "A Conceptual Framework for Comparing Instructional Design Models." *Educational Technology Research and Development*, 1994, *42*(4), 55–72.

Edwards, M., and Ewen, A. *360-degree Feedback: The Powerful New Model for Employee Assessment.* New York: AMACOM, 1996.

Egan, K. "What Is Curriculum?" *Curriculum and Inquiry*, 1978, *8*(1), 65–72.

Eilbirt, H. "The Development of Personnel Management in the United States." *Business History Review*, 1959, *33*(3), 345–364.

Einsiedel, A., Jr. "Case Studies: Indispensable Tools for Trainers." *Training and Development*, August 1995, pp. 50–53.

Ellington, H. *Producing Teaching Materials: A Handbook for Teachers and Trainers.* New York: Nichols, 1985.

Erikson, E. *Identity and the Life Cycle.* New York: International Universities Press, 1959.

Ertmer, P., and Quinn, J. *The ID Casebook: Case Studies in Instructional Design* (2nd ed.). Englewood Cliffs, NJ: Prentice-Hall, 2002.

Eugenio, V., and Habelow, E. "Is All Multimedia Created Equal? Differentiating Between Four Types of Multimedia Products." *Journal of Instruction Delivery Systems*, 1994, *8* (1), 20–24.

Falcone, P. "Motivating Staff Without Money." *HRMagazine*, 2002, *47*(8), 105–108.

Fidel, R. "The Case Study Method: A Case Study." *Library and Information Science Research*, 1984, *6* (3), 273–288.

Fiedler, F. *A Theory of Leadership Effectiveness.* New York: McGraw-Hill, 1967.

Fiedler, F., and Chemers, M. *Leadership and Effective Management.* Glenview, IL: Scott-Foresman, 1974.

"A Field Guide to Learning Objects." *Learning Circuits*, 2002, *3*(7), at www.learningcircuits.org/2002/jul2002/smartforce.pdf.

Finley, M. "All for One, but None for All? Why CEOs Make Lousy Team Players." *Across the Board*, 2002, *39*(1), 45–48.

Finnegan, G. "Job Aids: Improving Employee Performance in Healthcare." *Performance and Instruction Journal*, 1985, *24*(6), 10–11.

Finnerty, M. "Coaching for Growth and Development." In R. Craig (Ed.), *The ASTD Training and Development Handbook: A Guide to Human Resource Development* (4th ed.) (pp. 415–436). New York: McGraw-Hill, 1996.

Fitz-Enz, J. *How to Measure Human Resources Management.* New York: McGraw-Hill, 1984.

Fitz-Enz, J. *The ROI of Human Capital.* New York: AMACOM, 2000.

Flanagan, J. "The Critical Incident Technique." *Psychological Bulletin*, 1954, *51*, 327–358.

Fleishman, E. "On the Relationship Between Abilities, Learning, and Human Performance." *American Psychologist*, 1972, *27*, 1017–1032.

Ford, D. "Benchmarking HRD." *Training and Development*, 1993, *47*(6), 36–41.

Ford, D. "Introduction to This Volume." In D. Ford (Ed.), *In Action: Designing Training Programs* (pp. xiii-xxi). Alexandria, VA: The American Society for Training and Development, 1996.

Foshay, W., Silber, K., and Westgaard, O. *Instructional Design Competencies: The Standards.* Iowa City, IA: International Board of Standards for Training, Performance, and Instruction, 1986.

Francis, D., and Woodcock, M. *Unblocking Organizational Values.* Glenview, IL: Scott-Foresman, 1990.

Frantzreb, R. (Ed.). *The ASTD Training Support Software Directory.* Alexandria, VA: The American Society for Training and Development, 1993.

Frauenhemi, E. "Social Networking a Wire to Hire." *Workforce Management*, 2007, *86*(18), 28–32, 34, 36–37.

French, J., Jr., and Raven, B. "The Bases of Social Power." In D. Cartwright (Ed.), *Studies in Social Power.* Ann Arbor, MI: University of Michigan Press, 1959.

Gagné, R. "Analysis of Objectives." In L. Briggs (Ed.), *Instructional Design: Principles and Applications.* Englewood Cliffs, NJ: Educational Technology Publications, 1977a.

Gagné, R., Briggs, L., and Wager, W. *Principles of Instructional Design* (4th ed.). Fort Worth, TX: Harcourt Brace Jovanovich, 1992.

Gagné, R., and Medsker, K. *The Conditions of Learning: Training Applications.* Fort Worth, TX: Harcourt Brace, 1996.

Galbraith, J., Downey, D., and Kates, A. *Designing Dynamic Organizations: A Hands-On Guide for Leaders at All Levels.* New York: AMACOM, 2001.

Galbraith, J., Downey, D., and Kates, A. "How Networks Undergird the Lateral Capability of an Organization—Where the Work Gets Done." *Journal of Organizational Excellence*, 2002, *21*(2), 67–78.

Galosy, J. "Curriculum Design for Management Training." *Training and Development Journal*, 1983, *37*(1), 48–51.

Gery, G. Electronic *Performance Support Systems: How and Why to Remake the Workplace Through the Strategic Application of Technology.* Boston, MA: Weingarten, 1991.

Gibbons, A. *A Review of Content and Task Analysis Methodology.* San Diego, CA: Courseware, 1977. (ED 143 696)

Gibson, J., Ivancevich, J., and Donnelly, J., Jr. *Organizations: Behavior, Structure, Processes* (5th ed.). Plano, TX: Business Publications, 1985.

Gilbert, T. *Human Competence: Engineering Worthy Performance.* New York: McGraw-Hill, 1978.

Gilbert, T. *Human Competence: Engineering Worthy Performance* (tribute ed.). Washington, DC: The International Society for Performance Improvement, 1996.

Gilley, J., and Eggland, S. *Marketing HRD Within Organizations: Enhancing the Visibility, Effectiveness, and Credibility of Programs.* San Francisco: Jossey-Bass, 1992.

Gillies, D. "Fine-Tuning Nurse Management Education Through Formative Evaluation." *Journal of Continuing Education in the Health Professions*, 1991, *11*(3), 229–242.

Goldhaber, G., and Rogers, D. *Auditing Organizational Communication Systems: The ICA Communication Audit*. Dubuque, IA: Kendall/Hunt, 1979.

Goldwasser, D. "Beyond ROI." *Training*, 2001, *8*(1), 82–90.

Gordon, J., and Zemke, R. "The Attack on ISO." *Training*, April 2000.

Green, P. *Building Robust Competencies: Linking Human Resource Systems to Organizational Strategies*. San Francisco: Jossey-Bass, 1999.

Greenberg, J., and Eskew, D. "The Role of Role Playing in Organizational Research." *Journal of Management*, 1993, *19*(2), 221–241.

Gross, R. *The Lifelong Learner*. New York: Simon & Schuster, 1977.

Gross, R. (Ed.). *The Independent Scholar's Handbook*. Reading, MA: Addison-Wesley, 1982.

Grote, D. *The Complete Guide to Performance Appraisal*. New York: AMACOM, 1997.

Guillot, T. Team Building in a Virtual Environment. *Info-Line*, No. 250205. Alexandria, VA: The American Society for Training and Development, 2002.

Gunning, R. *The Technique of Clear Writing*. New York: McGraw-Hill, 1952.

Gupta, K. *A Practical Guide to Needs Assessment*. San Francisco: Pfeiffer, 1999.

Gustafson, K. "Instructional Design Fundamentals: Clouds on the Horizon." *Educational Technology*, 1993, *33*(2), 27–32.

Hagberg, J., and Leider, R. *The Inventurers*. Reading, MA: Addison-Wesley, 1982.

Hale, J. *Performance Based Evaluation: Tools and Techniques to Measure the Impact of Training*. San Francisco: Pfeiffer, 2002.

Hallowell, E., and Ratey, J. *Driven to Distraction*. New York: Pantheon, 1993.

Halprin, M., and Greer, M. "Critical Attributes of ID Project Success: Part II—The Survey Results." *Performance and Instruction*, July 1993, pp. 15–21.

Halson, B. "Teaching Supervisors to Coach." *Personnel Management*, 1990, *22*(3), 36–39, 53.

Hannafin, M. "Emerging Technologies, ISD, and Learning Environments: Critical Perspectives." *Educational Technology Research and Development*, 1992, *40*(1), 49–63.

Harless, J. "Performance Technology and Other Popular Myths." *Performance and Instruction Journal*, 1985, *24*(6), 4–6.

Harless, J. "Guiding Performance with Job Aids." In M. Smith (Ed.), *Introduction to Performance Technology*. Washington, DC: National Society for Performance and Instruction, 1986.

Harris, P., and Castillo, P. Instructional Design for WBT. *Info-Line*, No. 250202. Alexandria, VA: The American Society for Training and Development, 2002.

Hartley, D. Job *Analysis at the Speed of Reality*. Amherst, MA: Human Resource Development Press, 1999.

Harvey, F. "A Process Model for Managing Large-Scale Hypermedia Training Development Projects." *Journal of Interactive Instruction Development*, 1993, *6* (2), 25–32.

Haseman, W., Nuipolatoglu, V., and Ramamurthy, K. "An Empirical Investigation of the Influences of the Degree of Interactivity on User-Outcomes in a Multimedia Environment." *Information Resources Management Journal*, 2002, *15* (2), 31–48.

Hassinger, E. "Stages in the Adoption Process." *Rural Sociology*, 1959, *24*, 52–53.

Hatcher, T. "Legal or Right?" *Training and Development*, 2002, *56* (8), 62–64.

Hatten, K., and Rosenthal, S. "Why—and How—to Systematize Performance Measurement." *Journal of Organizational Excellence*, 2001, *20* (4), 59–73.

Havighurst, R. *Developmental Tasks and Education* (2nd ed.). New York: McKay, 1970.

Heideman, J. "The Team Approach to Formative Evaluation." *Technical and Skills Training*, 1993, *4* (3), 9–12.

Heinich, R., Molenda, M., Russell, J., and Smaldino, S. *Instructional Media and Technologies for Learning* (7th ed.). Englewood Cliffs, NJ: Prentice Hall., 2002.

Hennessy, D., and Hennessy, M. *Instructional Systems Development: Tools and Procedures for Organizing, Budgeting, and Managing a Training Project from Start to Finish.* Frederiksted, St. Croix, U.S. Virgin Islands: TRC Press, 1989.

Hensey, M. "Conflict: What It Is and What It Can Be." In D. Cole (Ed.), *Conflict Resolution Technology.* Cleveland, OH: Organization Development Institute, 1983.

Herbart, J. *The Application of Psychology to the Science of Education.* (Beatrice C. Mulliner, trans.) New York: Charles Scribner's Sons, 1898.

Hofstede, G. *Cultures and Organizations: Software of the Mind.* New York: McGraw-Hill, 1991.

Hogan, C. "Course Design in Half the Time: How to Generate Ideas Using a Network of Computers. *Training and Management Development Methods,* 1994, *8*(2), 5.01–5.14.

Holman, P., Devane, T., and Cady, S. *The Change Handbook: The Definitive Resource on Today's Best Methods for Engaging Whole Systems* (2nd ed.). San Francisco: Berrett-Koehler, 2007.

Holstein, J., and Gubrium, J. (Eds.). *Handbook of Interview Research: Context and Method.* Thousand Oaks, CA: Sage, 2001.

Horabin, I., and Lewis, B. "Algorithms." In *The Instructional Design Library* (Vol. 2). Englewood Cliffs, NJ: Educational Technology Publications, 1978.

Houle, C. *The Inquiring Mind.* Madison, WI: University of Wisconsin Press, 1961.

"How to Produce High Quality Course Materials—FAST." *The Microcomputer Trainer,* March 1993, pp. 7–11.

Huczynski, A. *Encyclopedia of Management Development Models.* London: Gower, 1983.

Heum Lee, S., and Pershing, J. "Evaluation of Corporate Training Programs: Perspectives and Issues for Further Research." *Performance Improvement Quarterly,* 2000, *13*(3), 244–260.

Hultman, K. *Balancing Individual and Organizational Values: Walking the Tightrope to Success.* San Francisco: Pfeiffer, 2002.

Hutchison, C. "A Performance Technology Process Model." *Performance and Instruction,* 1990, *29*(2), 18–21.

Hutchison, C. "What's a Nice P.T. Like You Doing . . . ?" *Performance and Instruction,* 1990, *29*(9), 1–6.

Hutchison, C., Stein, F., and Shepherd, J. *Instructor Competencies Volume I: The Standards.* Batavia, NY: The International Board of Standards for Training, Performance, and Instruction, 1988.

"Instructional Designer." *News and Notes,* 1988, *1*(2), 6.

Instructional Objective Helper. Downloaded 24 October 2007 from www.cogsim.com/idea/forms/Inst_obj2.htm, 2007.

The Instructional Use of Learning Objects. Downloaded 24 October 2000 from www.reusability.org/read/, 2000.

Isaac, S., and Michael, W. *Handbook of Research and Evaluation for Education and the Behavioral Sciences* (2nd ed.). San Diego, CA: EDITS, 1984.

Ives, B., and Forman, D. "Winning over the Bean Counters." *CBT Directions,* 1991, *4*(6), 10–18.

Jackson, S. "Task Analysis." In M. Smith (Ed.), *Introduction to Performance Technology.* Washington, DC: National Society for Performance and Instruction, 1986.

Jackson, S., and Addison, R. "Planning and Managing Projects." In H. Stolovitch and E. Keeps (Eds.), *Handbook of Human Performance Technology: A Comprehensive Guide for Analyzing and Solving Performance Problems in Organizations* (pp. 66–76). San Francisco: Jossey-Bass, 1992.

Jacobs, R. *Human Performance Technology: A Systems-Based Field for the Training and Development Profession.* Columbus, OH: ERIC Clearinghouse on Adult, Career, and Vocational Education, National Center for Research in Vocational Education, Ohio State University, 1987.

Jacobs, R. *Effects of Feedback for Training and Development: Selected Research Abstracts.* Columbus, OH: College of Education, Ohio State University, 1988. (ED 305 464)

Jaffee, C., Frank, F., and Mulligan, C. "Assessing Potential." In W. Tracey (Ed.), *Human Resources Management and Development Handbook* (3rd ed.) (pp. 204–226). New York: AMACOM, 1994.

Janis, I. *Victims of Groupthink: A Psychological Study of Foreign Policy Decisions and Fiascos.* Boston, MA: Houghton Mifflin, 1973.

Jette, R., and Wertheim, E. "Performance Appraisal." In W. Tracey (Ed.), *Human Resources Management and Development Handbook* (3rd ed.) (pp. 274–302). New York: AMACOM, 1994.

Jewell, S., and Jewell, D. "Organization Design." In H. Stolovitch and E. Keeps (Eds.), *Handbook of Human Performance Technology: A Comprehensive Guide for Analyzing and Solving Performance Problems in Organizations* (pp. 211–232). San Francisco: Jossey-Bass, 1992.

Job Genie. 12,741 job descriptions. Downloaded 24 October 2007 from www.stepfour.com/jobs/, 2007.

Johnson, R. "Trainers Grapple with Education Needs of 'Contingent Workers.'" *Training Directors' Forum Newsletter,* April 1994, pp. 1–3.

Johnson, S. "Critical Incident." In F. Ulschak (Ed.), *Human Resource Development: The Theory and Practice of Need Assessment.* Reston, VA: Reston Publishing, 1983.

Johnson, S. "Cognitive Analysis of Expert and Novice Troubleshooting Performance." *Performance Improvement Quarterly,* 1988, *1*(3), 38–54.

Joinson, C. "Employee Sculpt Thyself . . . With a Little Help." *HRMagazine,* 2001, *46*(5), 60–64.

Jonassen, D. "Thinking Technology: Toward a Constructivist View of Instructional Design." *Educational Technology,* 1990, *30*(9), 32–34.

Jonassen, D. "Objectivism Versus Constructivism: Do We Need a New Philosophical Paradigm?" *Educational Technology Research and Development,* 1991, *39*(3), 5–14.

Jonassen, D., Grabinger, S., and Harris, N. "Analyzing and Selecting Instructional Strategies and Tactics." *Performance Improvement Quarterly,* 1990, *3* (2), 29–47.

Jonassen, D., Hannum, W., and Tessmer, M. *Handbook of Task Analysis Procedures.* New York: Praeger, 1989.

Kanter, R. *World Class: Thriving Locally in the Global Economy.* New York: Simon & Schuster, 1995.

Kaplan, R. *Measures for Manufacturing Excellence.* Boston, MA: Harvard Business School Press, 1990.

Kaplan, R., and Norton, D. *The Balanced Scorecard.* New York: Random House, 1996.

Katz, D., and Kahn, R. *The Social Psychology of Organizations* (2nd ed.). Hoboken, NJ: John Wiley & Sons, 1978.

Kaufman, R. "Assessing Needs." In M. Smith (Ed.), *Introduction to Performance Technology.* Washington, DC: National Society for Performance and Instruction, 1986.

Kaufman, R. "Auditing Your Needs Assessments." *Training and Development,* 1994, *48*(2), 22–23.

Kaufman, R. *Strategic Thinking: A Guide to Identifying and Solving Problems.* Alexandria, VA: The American Society for Training and Development, 1996.

Kaufman, R., and English, F. *Needs Assessment: Concept and Application.* Englewood Cliffs, NJ: Educational Technology Publications, 1979.

Keller, J. "Motivational Systems." In H. Stolovitch and E. Keeps (Eds.), *Handbook of Human Performance Technology: A Comprehensive Guide for Analyzing and Solving Performance Problems in Organizations* (pp. 277–293). San Francisco: Jossey-Bass, 1992.

Kemmerer, F., and Thiagarajan, S. "What Is an Incentive System?" *Performance and Instruction*, 1989, *28*(3), 11–16.

Kemmerer, F., and Thiagarajan, S. "Incentive Systems." In H. Stolovitch and E. Keeps (Eds.), *Handbook of Human Performance Technology: A Comprehensive Guide for Analyzing and Solving Performance Problems in Organizations* (pp. 312–330). San Francisco: Jossey-Bass, 1992.

Kemp, J. *Instructional Design: A Plan for Unit and Course Development.* Belmont, CA: Lear Siegler, 1971.

Kemp, J. *The Instructional Design Process.* New York: HarperCollins, 1985.

Kerr, S. "On the Folly of Rewarding A, While Hoping for B." *Academy of Management Journal,* 1975, *18*, 769–783.

Kerr, S. "Organizational Rewards: Practical, Cost-Neutral Alternatives that You May Know, But Don't Practice." *Organizational Dynamics*, 1999, *28*(1), 61–70.

Kerr, J., and Slocum, J. "Managing Corporate Culture Through Reward Systems." *Academy of Management Executive,* 1988, *1*(2), 99–109.

Khalifa, M. "A Graphical Task Analysis Language." *INFOR*, 1993, *31*(2), 65–79.

Kiger, P. "Frequent Employee Feedback Is Worth the Cost and Time." *Workforce*, 2001, *80*(3), 62–63, 65.

King, S., King, M., and Rothwell, W. *The Complete Guide to Training Delivery: A Competency-Based Approach.* New York: AMACOM, 2000.

Kinlaw, D. *Team-Managed Facilitation: Critical Skills for Developing Self-Sufficient Teams.* San Francisco: Pfeiffer, 1993.

Kinlaw, D. *Facilitation Skills.* Alexandria, VA: The American Society for Training and Development, 1996.

Kirkpatrick, D. *No-Nonsense Communication* (2nd ed.). Elm Grove, WI: K & M Publishers, 1978.

Kirkpatrick, D. *How to Manage Change Effectively: Approaches, Methods, and Case Examples.* San Francisco: Jossey-Bass, 1985.

Kirkpatrick, D. *Evaluating Training Programs: The Four Levels.* San Francisco: Berrett-Koehler, 1996.

Kish, L. *Survey Sampling.* New York: Wiley-Interscience, 1995.

Klare, G. *Readability Standards for Army-Wide Publications.* Evaluation Report 79–1. Fort Benjamin Harrison, IN: U.S. Army Administrative Center, 1979.

Knowles, M. *Self-Directed Learning: A Guide for Teachers and Learners.* New York: Cambridge Book Company, 1975.

Knowles, M. *The Modern Practice of Adult Education: Andragogy Versus Pedagogy.* New York: Association Press, 1980.

Knowles, M. *The Adult Learner: A Neglected Species* (3rd ed.). Houston, TX: Gulf, 1984.

Knowles, M. *Using Learning Contracts: Practical Approaches to Individualizing and Structuring Learning.* San Francisco: Jossey-Bass, 1986.

Knowles, M., Swanson, R., and Holton, E. *The Adult Learner: The Definitive Classic in Adult Education and Human Resource Development.* (6th ed.). San Francisco: Berrett-Koehler, 2005.

Knox, A. *Adult Development and Learning.* San Francisco: Jossey-Bass, 1977.

Ko, S., and Rossen, S. *Teaching Online: A Practical Guide.* New York: Houghton-Mifflin, 2001.

Kochan, T., Katz, H., and McKersie, A. *The Transformation of American Industrial Relations.* Ithaca, NY: ILR Press, 1994.

Kolb, D. *Experiential Learning: Experience as the Source of Learning and Development.* Englewood Cliffs, NJ: Prentice- Hall, 1984.

Korth, S. "Consolidating Needs Assessment and Evaluation." *Performance Improvement*, 2001, *40*(1), 38–43.

Krell, E. "HR Challenges in Virtual Worlds," *HRMagazine*, 2007, *52*(11), 85–88.

Krieger, G. *"Constructing and Validating Tests."* In W. Tracey (Ed.), *Human Resources Management and Development Handbook* (3rd ed.) (pp. 1239–1252). New York: AMACOM, 1994.

Krueger, R., and Casey, M. *Focus Groups: A Practical Guide to Applied Research* (3rd ed.). Thousand Oaks, CA: Sage, 2000.

Krohe, J., Jr. "The Productivity Pit." *Across The Board*, 1993, *30*(8), 16–21.

Krueger, R, and Casey, M.A. *Focus Groups: A Practical Guide for Applied Research* (3rd ed.). Newbury Park, CA: Sage, 2000.

Kruger, M. "How to Make a Management Advisory Committee Work for You." *Training and Development*, 1983, *37* (6), 86–90.

Kuchinke, K., Aragon, S., and Bartlett, K. "Online Instructional Delivery." *Performance Improvement*, 2001, *40* (1), 19–27.

Lahti, R., Darr, E., and Krebs, V. "Developing the Productivity of a Dynamic Workforce: The Impact of Informal Knowledge Transfer." *Organizational Excellence*, 2002, *21*(2), 13–21.

Laird, D. *Approaches to Training and Development* (2nd ed.). Reading, MA: Addison-Wesley, 1985.

Lamos, J. "Programmed Instruction to Computer-Based Instruction: The Evolution of an Instructional Technology." In R. Bass and D. Lumsden (Eds.), *Instructional Development: The State of the Art*. McAlester, OK: Best Books, 1984.

Langdon, D. "Objectives? Get Over Them." *Training and Development*, 1999, *53*(2), 54–58.

Langdon, D., and Marrelli, A. "A New Model for Systematic Competency Identification." *Performance Improvement*, 2002, *41*(4), 14–21.

Langdon, D., Whiteside, K., and McKenna, M. (Eds.). *Intervention Resource Guide: 50 Performance Improvement Tools*. San Francisco: Jossey-Bass, 1999.

Laroche, L. "Beyond Translation." *Training and Development*, 2000, *54* (12), 72–73.

Lawler, E., III. *"Reward Systems."* In J. Hackman and J. Suttle (Eds.), *Improving Life at Work*. Santa Monica, CA: Goodyear, 1977.

Lawler, E. III. *From the Ground Up: Six Principles for Building the New Logic Corporation*. San Francisco: Jossey-Bass, 1996.

Lawson, T. *Formative Instructional Product Evaluation: Instruments and Strategies*. Englewood Cliffs, NJ: Educational Technology Publications, 1974.

Lazer, R. "Performance Appraisal: What Does the Future Hold?" *Personnel Administrator*, 1980, *25*(7), 69–73.

Learning Management System. Downloaded 27 October 2007 from the Wikipedia definition found at http://en.wikipedia.org/wiki/Learning_Management_System, 2007.

"Learning Objects." Downloaded 24 October 2007 from www.hi.is/~joner/eaps/cs_lobj.htm, 2007.

Lee, S., and Pershing, J. "Effective Reaction Evaluation in Evaluating Training Programs." *Performance Improvement*, 1999, *38*(8), 32–39.

Lee, W., and Mamone, R. "Design Criteria That Make Tests Objective." *Journal of Instruction Delivery Systems*, Summer 1995a, pp. 18–22.

Lee, W., and Mamone, R. *Handbook of Computer Based Training: Assessment, Design, Development, Evaluation*. Englewood Cliffs, NJ: Educational Technology Publications, 1995b.

Lee, W., and Owens, D. "Rapid Analysis Model." *Performance Improvement*, 2001, *40* (1), 13–18.

Lee, S., and Rothwell, W. "Exploring HRD Competencies in Taiwan: The Results of a Cross-Cultural Study." *International Journal of Vocational Education and Training*, 1995, *3*(2), 5–20.

Leeds, D. *Smart Questions*. New York: McGraw-Hill, 1988.

Lei, D., Slocum, J., and Pitts, R. "Designing Organizations for Competitive Advantage: The Power of Unlearning and Learning." *Organizational Dynamics*, 1999, *27* (3), 24–38.

Leibman, M., and Weinstein, H. "Money Isn't Everything." *HRMagazine*, 1990, *35* (11), 48–51.

Levinson, D. *The Seasons of a Man's Life*. New York: Knopf, 1978.

Lewis, T., and Bjorkquist, D. "Needs Assessment—A Critical Reappraisal." *Performance Improvement Quarterly*, 1992, *5* (4), 33–54.

Likert, R. *The Human Organization*. New York: McGraw-Hill, 1967.

Lineberry, C., and Bullock, D. "Job Aids." In *The Instructional Design Library* (Vol. 25). Englewood Cliffs, NJ: Educational Technology Publications, 1980.

Lowe, R. *Creating Instructional Diagrams*. London: Kogan Page, 1993.

Lowe, T., Funk, F., and Altreche, W. "Measuring Customer Satisfaction with Public Schools." *Performance Improvement*, 1996, *35* (10), 18–21.

Lucia, A., and Lepsinger, R. *The Art and Science of Competency Models: Pinpointing Critical Success Factors in Organizations*. San Francisco: Jossey-Bass, 1999.

McAlpine, L., and Weston, C. "The Attributes of Instructional Materials." *Performance Improvement Quarterly*, 1994, *7* (1), 19–30.

McArdle, G. "What Is Training?" *Performance and Instruction*, 1989, *28* (6), 34–35.

McCall, M., Jr., and Kaplan, R. *Whatever It Takes: Decision Makers at Work*. Englewood Cliffs, NJ: Prentice-Hall, 1985.

McCarthy, E. *Basic Marketing: A Managerial Approach* (6th ed.). Homewood, IL: Irwin, 1978.

McClelland, D. "Testing for Competence Rather Than for 'Intelligence.'" *American Psychologist*, 1973, *28* (1), 1–14.

McClelland, D. *A Guide to Job Competency Assessment*. Boston, MA: McBer and Co., 1976.

McClelland, S. "Training Needs Assessment Data-Gathering Methods: Part 1—Survey Questionnaires." *Journal of European Industrial Training*, 1994a, *18* (1), 22–26.

McClelland, S. "Training Needs Assessment Data-Gathering Methods: Part 2—Individual Interviews." *Journal of European Industrial Training*, 1994b, *18* (2), 27–31.

McClelland, S. "Training Needs Assessment Data-Gathering Methods: Part 3—Focus Groups." *Journal of European Industrial Training*, 1994c, *18* (3), 29–32.

McClelland, S. "Training Needs Assessment Data-Gathering Methods: Part 4—On-Site Observations." *Journal of European Industrial Training*, 1994d, *18*(5), 4–7.

McCormick, E. *Job Analysis*. New York: AMACOM, 1979.

McLagan, P. "The Change-Capable Organization." *Training and Development*, 2003, *57* (1), 50–58.

McLinden, D., Cummings, O., and Bond, S. "A Comparison of Two Formats for an Instructor's Guide." *Performance Improvement Quarterly*, 1990, *3* (1), 2–13.

Mager, R. *What Every Manager Should Know About Training*. Belmont, CA: Lake Publishing Co., 1992.

Mager, R. *Goal Analysis: How to Clarify Your Goals So You Can Actually Achieve Them* (3rd ed.). Atlanta, GA: The Center for Effective Performance, 1997a.

Mager, R. *How to Turn Learners On . . . Without Turning Them Off: Ways to Ignite Interest in Learning* (3rd ed.). Atlanta, GA: The Center for Effective Performance, 1997b.

Mager, R. *Measuring Instructional Results: Or "Got a Match?" How to Find Out If Your Instructional Objectives Have Been Achieved* (3rd ed.). Atlanta, GA: The Center for Effective Performance, 1997c.

Mager, R. *Preparing Instructional Objectives: A Critical Tool in the Development of Effective Instruction* (3rd ed.). Atlanta, GA: The Center for Effective Performance, 1997d.

Mager, R., and Pipe, P. *Analyzing Performance Problems or "You Really Oughta Wanna"* (3rd rev. ed.). Atlanta, GA: The Center for Effective Performance, 1999.

Malasky, E. *"Instructional Strategies: Nonmedia."* In L. Nadler (Ed.), *The Handbook of Human Resource Development*. New York: Wiley-Interscience, 1984.

March, J. "The Business Firm as a Political Coalition." *Journal of Politics*, 1962, *24*(2), 662–678.

Marelli, A. "Determining Training Costs, Benefits, and Results." *Technical and Skills Training*, 1993a, *4*(7), 35–40.

Marelli, A. "Ten Evaluation Instruments for Technical Training." *Technical and Skills Training*, 1993b, *4*(5), 7–14.

Marquardt, M., and Engel, D. "HRD Competencies for a Shrinking World." *Training and Development*, 1993, *47*(5), 59–65.

Marquardt, M., King, S., and Ershkine, W. *International Comparisons: ASTD's Annual Accounting of WorldWide Patterns in Employer-Provided Training*. Alexandria, VA: The American Society for Training and Development, 2002.

Marrow, A. *The Failure of Success*. New York: AMACOM, 1972.

Marshall, H., and Weinstein, R. *Classroom Dimensions Observation System Manual*. Berkeley, CA: Department of Psychology, University of California, 1982.

Maslak, G. "The Performance Improvement Dilemma." *Performance Improvement*, 2003, *42*(4), 13–15.

Martinez, M. "Creative Ways to Employ People with Disabilities." *HRMagazine*, 1990, *35*(11), 40–44, 101.

Martinko, M., and Gepson, J. "Nominal Grouping and Needs Analysis." In F. Ulschak (Ed.), *Human Resource Development: The Theory and Practice of Need Assessment*. Reston, VA: Reston Publishing, 1983.

Marx, R., and Hudson-Samuels, K. *The ASTD Media Selection Tool for Workplace Learning*. Alexandria, VA: The American Society for Training and Development, 1999.

Maul, J., and Krauss, J. "Outsourcing in Training and Education." In R. Craig (Ed.). *The ASTD Training and Development Handbook: A Guide to Human Resource Development* (4th ed.) (pp. 1008–1030). New York: McGraw-Hill, 1996.

Merrill, M. "Instructional Transaction Theory: Instructional Design Based on Knowledge Objects." *Educational Technology*, 1996, *36* (3), 30–37.

Merrill, M. "A Pebble-in-the-Pond Model for Instructional Design." *Performance Improvement*, 2002, *41*(7), 41–46.

Merrill, M., Li, Z., and Jones, M. "Limitations of First Generation Instructional Design." *Educational Technology*, January 1990, pp. 7–11.

Meyer, G. *Job Performance Analysis Practices As Perceived by Members of the International Society for Performance Improvement*. Unpublished Doctoral Dissertation. University Park, PA: The Pennsylvania State University, 1995.

Michalko, M. *Thinkertoys: A Handbook of Business Creativity for the 90s*. Berkeley, CA: Ten Speed Press, 1991.

Mink, O., Owen, K., and Mink, B. *Developing High Performance People: The Art of Coaching*. Reading, MA: Addison-Wesley, 1993.

Mohler, L. "Project Management for Instructional Development: Phase I—Planning." *Performance and Instruction*, May-June 1993, pp. 15–18.

Molenda, M., Pershing, J., Reigeluth, C. *"Designing Instructional Systems."* In R. Craig (Ed.). *The ASTD Training and Development Handbook: A Guide to Human Resource Development* (4th ed.) (pp. 266–293). New York: McGraw-Hill, 1996.

Moore, D., and Dwyer, F. (Eds.). (1994). *Visual Literacy: A Spectrum of Visual Learning.* Englewood Cliffs, NJ: Educational Technology Publications.

Morabito, J., Sack, I., and Bhate, A. *Organization Modeling: Innovative Architectures for the 21st Century.* Englewood Cliffs, NJ: Prentice-Hall, 1999.

Morgan, D. *Focus Groups as Qualitative Research.* Newbury Park, CA: Sage, 1988.

Morical, K., and Tsai, B. "Adapting Training for Other Cultures." *Training and Development,* 1992, *46*(4), 65–68.

Moseley, J., and Dessinger, J. *Training Older Workers and Learners: Maximizing the Performance of an Aging Workforce.* San Francisco: Pfeiffer, 2007.

Moseley, J., and Heaney, M. "Needs Assessment Across Disciplines." *Performance Improvement Quarterly,* 1994, *7*(1), 60–79.

Moseley, J., and Solomon, D. "Confirmative Evaluation: A New Paradigm for Continuous Improvement." *Performance Improvement,* 1997, *36* (5), 12–16.

Mullins, B. "The Cultural Repertoire of Adult Learning." *Adult Learning,* 2000, *11*(1), 3–5.

Murphy, C. "Utilizing Project Management Techniques in the Design of Instructional Materials." *Performance and Instruction,* 1994, *33* (3), 9–11.

Nadler, D. *Feedback and Organization Development: Using Data-Based Methods.* Reading, MA: Addison-Wesley, 1977.

Naisbitt, J. *The Global Paradox.* New York: Avon Books, 1994.

"National Skills Standards Project for Advanced High Performance Manufacturing." Washington, DC: National Coalition for Advanced Manufacturing, 1995.

Nelson, B. *1001 Ways to Reward Employees.* New York: Workman Publishing, 1994.

Newstrom, J. "Evaluating the Effectiveness of Training Methods." *Personnel Administrator,* January 1980, pp. 55–60.

Newstrom, J., and Lilyquist, J. "Selecting Needs Analysis Methods." *Training and Development,* 1979, *33* (10), 52–56.

Nichols, R. *Successful Management.* New York: Doubleday, 1957.

Nonaka, I., and Takeuchi, H. *The Knowledge-Creating Company.* New York: Oxford University Press, 1995.

Novak, C. HPI Balanced Scorecard. *Info-Line,* No. 250010. Alexandria, VA: The American Society for Training and Development, 2000.

Nystrom, P., and Starbuck, W. *Handbook of Organizational Design* (2 vols.). New York: Oxford University Press, 1983.

Oakes, K. "LCMS, LMS—They're Not Just Acronyms but Powerful Systems for Learning." *Training and Development,* 2002, *56* (3), 73–75.

Oakes, K., and Rengarajan, R. "An Objective View of Learning Objects." *Training and Development,* 2002, *56* (5), 103–105.

Odenwald, S. *Global Training: How to Design a Program for the Multinational Corporation.* Homewood, IL: Business One Irwin, 1993.

Odiorne, G. *MBO II: A System of Managerial Leadership for the 80s.* Belmont, CA: Fearon-Pitman, 1979.

Olson, E., and Eoyang, G. *Facilitating Organizational Change.* San Francisco: Pfeiffer, 2001.

O*NET. Downloaded 24 October 2007 from www.doleta.gov/programs/onet/

Osterman, P. "How Common Is Workplace Transformation and Who Adopts It?" *Industrial and Labor Relations,* 1990, *47* (2), 173-188.

O'Toole, M. "Training in a Second-Language Environment." *Journal of European Industrial Training,* 1994, *18* (1), 4–9.

Parmenter, D. *Key Performance Indicators: Developing, Implementing, and Using Winning KPIs.* Hoboken, NJ: John Wiley & Sons, 2007.

Patterson, M. *Accelerating Innovation.* New York: Van Nostrand Reinhold, 1993.

Pearce, J., II, and David, F. "A Social Network Approach to Organization Design—Performance." *Academy of Management Review,* 1983, *8,* 436–444.

Peoples, D. *Presentations Plus: David Peoples' Proven Techniques.* Hoboken, NJ: John Wiley & Sons, 1988.

Pfeiffer, J., and Ballew, A. "Using Case Studies, Simulations, and Games in Human Resource Development." In *The Training Technologies Series* (Vol. 5). San Francisco: Pfeiffer, 1988a.

Pfeiffer, J., and Ballew, A. "Using Instruments in Human Resource Development." In *The Training Technologies Series* (Vol. 2). San Francisco: Pfeiffer, 1988b.

Pfeiffer, J., and Ballew, A. "Using Role Plays in Human Resource Development." In The Training Technologies Series. (Vol. 4). San Francisco: Pfeiffer, 1988c.

Phillips, J. (Ed.). *In Action: Performance Analysis and Consulting.* Alexandria, VA: The American Society for Training and Development, 2000.

Phillips, J., and Holton, E., III (Eds.). *In Action: Needs Assessment.* Alexandria, VA: The American Society for Training and Development, 1995.

Phillips, P., and Burkett, H. Managing Evaluation Shortcuts. *Info-Line,* No. 250111. Alexandria, VA: The American Society for Training and Development, 2001.

Pinchot, G., III. *Intrapreneuring: Why You Don't Have to Leave the Corporation to Become an Entrepreneur.* New York: HarperCollins, 1985.

Pine, J., III. *Mass Customization.* Boston, MA: Harvard Business School Press, 1993.

Piskurich, G. "The Possible Futures of Instructional Technology." *Training and Development,* 1993, *47* (3), 50–53.

Piskurich, G., and Sanders, E. *ASTD Models for Learning Technologies: Roles, Competencies, Outputs.* Alexandria, VA: The American Society for Training and Development, 1998.

Prahalad, C., and Hamel, G. "The Core Competence of the Corporation." *Harvard Business Review,* May–June 1990, pp. 79–91.

ProComp 2005. Downloaded 24 October 2007 from www.procompfce.com/

Prusak, L., and Cohen, D. "How to Invest in Social Capital." *Harvard Business Review,* 2001, *79* (6), 86–93.

Pucel, D. *Performance-Based Instructional Design.* New York: McGraw-Hill, 1989.

"Quick, Consultative Approach to Training Needs Assessment." *IOMA's Report on Managing Training and Development,* 2001, *1*(10), 1, 12–14.

Rae, L. *How to Measure Training Effectiveness.* New York: Nichols, 1986.

Rath, G., and Stoyanoff, K. "The Delphi Technique." In F. Ulschak (Ed.), *Human Resource Development: The Theory and Practice of Need Assessment.* Reston, VA: Reston Publishing, 1983.

Reddout, D. "What Is a Task?" *Performance and Instruction,* 1987, *26* (1), 5–6.

Reigeluth, C. *Instructional Design Theories and Models: A New Paradigm of Instructional Theory.* Mahwah, NJ: Lawrence Erlbaum Associates, 1999.

Reigeluth, C. *Instructional Theories in Action: Lessons Illustrating Selected Theories and Models.* Hillsdale, NJ: Lawrence Erlbaum, 1987a.

Reigeluth, C. "Introduction." In C. Reigeluth (Ed.), *Instructional Theories in Action: Lessons Illustrating Selected Theories and Models.* Hillsdale, NJ: Lawrence Erlbaum Associates, 1987b.

Reigeluth, C. (Ed.). *Instructional Design Theories and Models: An Overview of Their Current Status.* London: Lawrence Erlbaum Associates, 1983.

Reigeluth, C. (Ed.). *Instructional-Design Theories and Models: A New Paradigm of Instructional Theory* (Vol. 2). London: Lawrence Erlbaum Associates, 1999.

Reigeluth, C. (Ed.). *Instructional-Design Theories and Models* (Vol. 3). London: Lawrence Erlbaum Associates, 2008.

Regalbuto, G. "Targeting the Bottom Line." *Training and Development*, 1992, *46* (4), 29–38.

"Rethinking Rewards." *Harvard Business Review*, 1993, *71*(6), 37–49.

Reynolds, A. "The Basics: Exporting Technical Training." *Technical and Skills Training*, May–June 1993, pp. 32–33.

Reynolds, A., and Anderson, R. *Selecting and Developing Media for Instruction.* New York: Van Nostrand Reinhold, 1992.

Richey, R.C. "Instructional Design Theory and a Changing Field." *Educational Technology*, 1993, *33* (2), 16–1.

Richey, R. C. "Trends in Instructional Design: Emerging Theory-Based Models." *Performance Improvement Quarterly*, 1995, *8*(3), 96–110.

Richey, R., Fields, D., and Foxon, M. *Instructional Design Competencies: The Standards* (3rd ed.). Syracuse, NY: ERIC Clearinghouse on Information and Technology, 2001.

The Road to High Performance Workplaces. Washington, DC: Office of the American Workplace, U.S. Department of Labor, 1995.

Robinson, A. *"Incentives and Rewards."* In W. Tracey (Ed.), *Human Resources Management and Development Handbook* (3rd ed.) (pp. 591–606). New York: AMACOM, 1994.

Robinson, D., and Robinson, J. *Performance Consulting: Moving Beyond Training.* San Francisco: Berrett-Koehler, 1995.

Robson, R. "SCORM Steps Up." *e-Learning*, 2002, *3*(8), 48–50.

Robson, R., Rogers, E., and Shoemaker, F. *Communication of Innovations: A Cross-Cultural Approach* (2nd ed.). New York: The Free Press, 1971.

Rogers, R. *The Political Process in Modern Organizations.* New York: Exposition Press, 1971.

Rokeach, M. *The Nature of Human Values.* New York: The Free Press, 1973.

Romiszowski, A. *Designing Instructional Systems: Decision Making in Course Planning and Curriculum Design.* New York: Nichols, 1981.

Rosow, J., and Hickey, J. *Strategic Partners for High Performance: Part I: The Partnership Paradigm for Competitive Advantage.* Scarsdale, NY: The Work in America Institute, 1994.

Ross, L. "Seven Performance Drivers." *Performance Improvement*, 2003, *42*(4), 26–29.

Rossett, A. *Training Needs Assessment.* Englewood Cliffs, NJ: Educational Technology Publications, 1988.

Rossett, A. "Overcoming Obstacles to Needs Assessment." *Training*, 1990, *27*(3), 36–41.

Rossett, A. "Analysis of Human Performance Problems." In H. Stolovitch and E. Keeps (Eds.), *Handbook of Human Performance Technology: A Comprehensive Guide for Analyzing and Solving Performance Problems in Organizations* (pp. 97–113). San Francisco: Jossey-Bass, 1992.

Rossett, A. *First Things Fast: A Handbook for Performance Analysis.* San Francisco: Pfeiffer, 1999.

Rossett, A., and Gautier-Downes, J. *A Handbook of Job Aids.* San Francisco: Pfeiffer, 1991.

Rothwell, W. "Conducting an Employee Attitude Survey." *Personnel Journal*, 1983, *62*(4), 308–311.

Rothwell, W. *Effective Succession Planning: Ensuring Leadership Continuity and Building Talent from Within* (2nd ed.). New York: AMACOM, 2000.

Rothwell, W. *Identifying and Solving Human Performance Problems: A Survey.* Unpublished survey results. University Park, PA: The Pennsylvania State University, 1995a.

Rothwell, W. "Performance Technology: Isn't It Time We Found Some New Models?" In E. Holton (Ed.), *The 1995 Conference Proceedings of the Academy of Human Resource Development.* Austin, TX: The Academy of Human Resource Development, 1995b.

Rothwell, W. *ASTD Models for Human Performance Improvement: Roles, Competencies, Outputs.* Alexandria, VA: The American Society for Training and Development, 1996a.

Rothwell, W. *Beyond Training and Development: State-of-the-Art Strategies for Enhancing Human Performance.* New York: AMACOM, 1996b.

Rothwell, W. *The Just-In-Time Training Assessment Instrument.* Amherst, MA: Human Resource Development Press, 1996c.

Rothwell, W. *The Self-Directed On-the-Job Learning Workshop.* Amherst, MA: Human Resource Development Press and Minneapolis, MN: Lakewood Publications, 1996d.

Rothwell, W. *The Action Learning Guidebook: A Real-Time Strategy for Problem-Solving, Training Design, and Employee Development.* San Francisco: Pfeiffer, 1999.

Rothwell, W. *The Analyst.* Alexandria, VA: The American Society for Training and Development, 2000a.

Rothwell, W. (Ed.). *ASTD Models for Human Performance: Roles, Competencies, Outputs* (2nd ed.). Alexandria, VA: The American Society for Training and Development, 2000b.

Rothwell, W. *The Workplace Learner: How to Align Training Initiatives with Individual Learning Competencies.* New York: AMACOM, 2002.

Rothwell, W. *A Survey About Current Issues in Instructional Design.* Unpublished report on survey results. University Park, PA: The Pennsylvania State University, 2003.

Rothwell, W., and Brandenburg, D. "Solutions to Literacy Deficiencies in the Workplace: A Survey of Current Practices." *Performance and Instruction,* 1990a, *3* (2), 16–28.

Rothwell, W., and Brandenburg, D. *The Workplace Literacy Primer: An Action Manual for Training and Development Professionals.* Amherst, MA: Human Resource Development Press, 1990b.

Rothwell, W., and Cookson, P. *Beyond Instruction: Comprehensive Program Planning for Business and Education.* San Francisco: Jossey-Bass, 1997.

Rothwell, W., and Dubois, D. (Eds.). *In Action: Improving Performance in Organizations.* Alexandria, VA: The American Society for Training and Development, 1998.

Rothwell, W., Hohne, C., and King, S. *Human Performance Improvement: Building Practitioner Performance* (2nd ed.). Boston: Butterworth-Heinemann, 2007.

Rothwell, W., Jackson, R., Knight, S., Lindholm, J. with Wang, W., and Payne, T. *Career Planning and Succession Management: Developing Your Organization's Talent—for Today and Tomorrow.* Westport, CT: Greenwood Press, 2005.

Rothwell, W., and Kazanas, H. "Participation: Key to Integrating Planning and Training?" *Performance and Instruction,* 1987, *26* (9 & 10), 27–31.

Rothwell, W., and Kazanas, H. "Curriculum Planning for Training: The State of the Art." *Performance Improvement Quarterly,* 1988, *1*(3), 2–16.

Rothwell, W., and Kazanas, H. *The Complete AMA Guide to Management Development.* New York: AMACOM, 1993a.

Rothwell, W., and Kazanas, H. "Developing Management Employees to Cope with the Moving Target Effect." *Performance and Instruction,* 1993b, *32* (8), 1–5.

Rothwell, W., and Kazanas, H. *Human Resource Development: A Strategic Approach* (rev. ed.). Amherst, MA: Human Resource Development Press, 1994a.

Rothwell, W., and Kazanas, H. *Improving On-The-Job Training.* San Francisco: Jossey-Bass, 1994b.

Rothwell, W., and Kazanas, H. *The Strategic Development of Talent.* [Second edition of *Human Resource Development: A Strategic Approach.*] Amherst, MA: Human Resource Development Press, 2003.

Rothwell, W., and Kazanas, H. *Improving On-the-Job Training* (2nd ed.). San Francisco: Pfeiffer, 2004.

Rothwell, W., and Kazanas, H. *Planning and Managing Human Resources: Strategic Planning for Personnel Management* (3rd ed.). Amherst, MA: Human Resource Development Press, 2003.

Rothwell, W., and Lindholm, J. "Competency Identification, Modeling and Assessment in the USA." *International Journal of Training and Development*, 1999, *3* (2), 90–105.

Rothwell, W., Lindholm, J., and Wallick, W. *What CEOs Expect from Corporate Training: Building Workplace Learning and Performance Initiatives That Advance Organizational Goals.* New York: AMACOM, 2003.

Rothwell, W., Prescott, R., and Taylor, M. *Human Resource Transformation.* Palo Alto, CA: Davies-Black, 2008.

Rothwell, W., Prescott, R., and Taylor, M. *Strategic HR Leader.* Palo Alto, CA: Davies-Black, 1998.

Rothwell, W., Sanders, E., and Soper, J. *ASTD Models for Workplace Learning and Performance: Roles, Competencies, Outputs.* Alexandria, VA: The American Society for Training and Development, 1999.

Rothwell, W., and Sredl, H. *The American Society for Training and Development Reference Guide to Workplace Learning and Performance* (3rd ed.) (2 vols.). Amherst, MA: Human Resource Development Press, 2000.

Rothwell, W., and Sullivan, R. (Eds.). *Practicing Organization Development: A Guide for Consultants* (2nd ed.). San Francisco: Pfeiffer., 2005.

Rothwell, W., Sullivan, R., and McLean, G. (Eds.). *Practicing OD: A Guide for Consultants.* San Francisco: Pfeiffer, 1995.

Rowland, G. "What Do Instructional Designers Actually Do? An Initial Investigation of Expert Practice." *Performance Improvement Quarterly*, 1992, *5* (2), 65–86.

Rummler, G. "The Performance Audit." In R. Craig (Ed.), *Training and Development Handbook: A Guide to Human Resource Development* (2nd ed.). New York: McGraw-Hill, 1976.

Rummler, G. "Human Performance Problems and Their Solutions." In L. Baird, C. Schneier, and D. Laird (Eds.), *The Training and Development Sourcebook.* Amherst, MA: Human Resource Development Press, 1983.

Rummler, G. "Organizational Redesign." In M. Smith (Ed.), *Introduction to Performance Technology.* Washington, DC: The National Society for Performance and Instruction, 1986.

Rummler, G., and Brache, A. *Improving Performance: How to Manage the White Space on the Organization Chart* (2nd ed.). San Francisco: Jossey-Bass, 1995.

Russell, J., and Blake, B. "Formative and Summative Evaluation of Instructional Products and Learners." *Educational Technology*, 1988, *28* (9), 22–28.

Sanders, N. *Classroom Questions: What Kinds?* New York: HarperCollins, 1966.

Sayre, S. "Content Analysis as a Tool for Consumer Research." *Journal of Consumer Marketing*, 1992, *9* (1), 15–25.

Schechter, S., Rothwell, W., and McLane, S. "Think Tank Uses Reverse Delphi Process to Reach Consensus on Top Trends/Competencies." *Issues and Trends in Personnel*, June 19, 1996, *382*, 8–9.

Schein, E. *Process Consultation: Its Role in Organization Development.* Reading, MA: Addison-Wesley, 1969.

Schein, E. *Process Consultation Revisited: Building the Helping Relationship.* Reading, MA: Addison-Wesley, 1998.

Schein, E. *Organizational Culture and Leadership: A Dynamic View.* San Francisco: Jossey-Bass, 1985.

Schmidt, L. (Ed). *In Action: Implementing Training Scorecards.* Alexandria, VA: The American Society for Training and Development, 2003.

Schmidt, W., and Posner, B. *Managerial Values and Expectations: The Silent Power in Personal and Organizational Life*. New York: American Management Association Membership Publications Division, 1982.

Schmitt, N., and Robertson, I. "Personnel Selection." *Annual Review of Psychology*, 1990, *41*, 289–319.

Schulz, R. "Time Management Hints." In R. Golembiewski (Ed.), *Handbook of Organizational Consultation* (pp. 663–668). New York: Marcel Dekker, 1993.

Schwarz, R. *The Skilled Facilitator: Practical Wisdom for Developing Effective Groups*. San Francisco: Jossey-Bass, 1994.

Shrock, S., and Coscarelli, W. *Criterion-Referenced Test Development: Technical and Legal Guidelines for Corporate Training*. San Francisco: Pfeiffer, 2007

Senge, P. *The Fifth Discipline: The Art and Practice of the Learning Organization*. New York: Currency Doubleday, 1990.

"7 Capabilities to Look for When Purchasing or Renting an LMS." *IOMA's Report on Managing Training and Development*, 2001, *1*(7), 3–5.

Shank, P. "Dreadful! Ick! Here's What Patti Abhors About the State of E-learning." *Lakewood Report on Technology for Learning*, 2001, *7*(1), 1, 4–5.

Shapiro, E. *Fad Surfing in the Boardroom: Reclaiming the Courage to Manage in the Age of Instant Answers*. Reading, MA: Addison-Wesley, 1996.

Sheehy, G. *Passages: Predictable Crises of Adult Life*. New York: Dutton, 1974.

Sherman, A., Bohlander, G., and Snell, S. *Managing Human Resources (10th ed.)*. Cincinnati, OH: South-Western College Publishing, 1996.

Short, D., and Opengart, R. "It's a Free Agent World: Training and Retraining Employees." *Training and Development*, September 2000. Downloaded 23 October 2007 from http://findarticles.com/p/articles/mi_m4467/is_9_54/ai_65579214

Simpson, L. "Taking the High Road." *Training*, 2002, *39*(1), 36–38.

Sink, D. "ISD—Faster, Better, Easier." *Performance Improvement*, 2002, *41*(7).

Sitze, A. "Lost in Translation." *Inside Technology Training*, 2000, *4*(2), 16–22.

"Skills Inventories: Companies Identifying, Tracking Where Employee Talent Lies." *Workforce Strategies*, 2002, *20*(3), WS13.

Small, R. "Adding Value to the Case Study Method: The Potential of Multimedia." *Journal of Instruction Delivery Systems*, 1994, *8*(1), 18–19.

Smillie, R. *"Design Strategies for Job Performance Aids."* In T. Duffy and R. Waller (Eds.), *Designing Usable Texts*. San Diego, CA: Academic Press, 1985.

Smith, J., and Merchant, S. "Using Competency Exams for Evaluating Training." *Training and Development*, 1990, *44*(8), 65–71.

Smith, P., and Reinertsen, D. *Developing Products in Half the Time*. New York: Van Nostrand Reinhold, 1991.

Smith, V. "The Invisible Disability." *Human Resource Executive*, August 1994, pp. 48–49.

Spaulding, K. *The Effect of Paper-Based Job Aids in Facilitating Student Cognitive Development*. Unpublished Doctoral Dissertation. University Park, PA: The Pennsylvania State University, 1997.

Spector, M. "The IBSTPI Code of Ethical Standards for Instructional Designers." In R. Richey, D. Fields, and M. Foxon (Eds.), *Instructional Design Competencies: The Standards* (pp. 203–205) (3rd ed.). Syracuse, NY: ERIC Clearinghouse on Information and Technology, 2001.

Spencer, L., Jr., and Spencer, S. *Competence at Work: Models for Superior Performance*. Hoboken, NJ: John Wiley & Sons, 1993.

Springer, J. *Job Performance Standards and Measures.* Alexandria, VA: American Society for Training and Development, 1980.

Stacey, R. *Managing Chaos: Dynamic Business Strategies in an Unpredictable World.* London: Kogan Page, 1992.

Steele, F. *Physical Settings and Organization Development.* Reading, MA: Addison-Wesley, 1973.

Stolovitch, H., and Keeps, E. (Eds.). *Handbook of Human Performance Technology: A Comprehensive Guide for Analyzing and Solving Performance Problems in Organizations.* San Francisco: Jossey-Bass, 1992.

Stowell, S., and Starcevich, M. *The Coach: Creating Partnerships for a Competitive Edge.* Salt Lake City, UT: Center for Management and Organization Effectiveness, 1987.

Strandberg, J. "Instant answers.com." *Training,* 1999, *36*(5), 40–44.

Strunk, W., Jr., and White, E. *The Elements of Style* (3rd ed.). New York: Macmillan, 1979.

Sugrue, B. *State of the industry: ASTD's Annual Review of U.S. and International Trends in Workplace Learning and Performance.* Alexandria, VA: The American Society for Training and Development, 2003.

Sullivan, R., and Elenburg, M. "Performance Testing for Technical Trainers." *Training and Development,* 1988, *42*(11), 38–40.

Swanson, R. *Assessing the Financial Benefits of Human Resource Development.* San Francisco: Berrett-Koehler, 2001.

Swanson, R. *Analysis for Improving Performance.* San Francisco: Berrett-Koehler, 1994.

Swanson, R., and Gradous, D. *Performance at Work: A Systematic Program for Analyzing Work behavior.* New York: Wiley-Interscience, 1986.

Swanson, R., and Gradous, D. *Forecasting Financial Benefits of Human Resource Development.* San Francisco: Jossey-Bass, 1988.

Swinburne, P. "How to Use Feedback to Improve Performance." *People Management,* 2001, *7*(11), 46–47.

Swindall, C. *Engaged Leadership: Building a Culture to Overcome Employee Disengagement.* Hoboken, NJ: John Wiley & Sons, 2007.

Syrett, M., and Lammiman, J. "Developing the 'Peripheral' Worker." *Personnel Management,* July 1994, pp. 27–31.

Taylor, C. "The Second Wave." *Training and Development,* 2002, *56*(10), 25–31.

Tenopyr, M. *"Testing."* In R. Craig (Ed.), *The ASTD Training and Development Handbook: A Guide to Human Resource Development* (4th ed.) (pp. 342–356). New York: McGraw-Hill, 1996.

Tessmer, M. "Formative Evaluation Alternatives." *Performance Improvement Quarterly,* 1994, *7*(1), 3–18.

Thiagarajan, S. "Formative Evaluation in Performance Technology." *Performance Improvement Quarterly,* 1991, *4*(2), 22–34.

Thiagarajan, S. "Instructional Games, Simulations, and Role Plays." In R. Craig (Ed.), *The ASTD Training and Development Handbook: A Guide to Human Resource Development* (4th ed.) (pp. 517–533). New York: McGraw-Hill, 1996.

Thompson, S. *Sampling* (2nd ed.). Hoboken, NJ: John Wiley & Sons, 2002.

Thompson, T., Felce, D., and Symons, F. (Eds.). *Behavioral Observation: Technology and Applications in Developmental Disabilities.* Baltimore, MD: Paul H. Brookes, 1999.

Thorndike, E., and Woodworth, R. "The Estimation of Magnitudes." *Psychological Review,* 1901a, *8,* 384–395.

Thorndike, E., and Woodworth, R. "Functions Involving Attention, Observation, and Discrimination." *Psychological Review,* 1901b, *8,* 553–564.

Thorndike, E., and Woodworth, R. "The Influence of Improvement in One Mental Function upon the Efficiency of Other Functions." *Psychological Review*, 1901c, *8*, 247–261.

Thornton, G. *Assessment Centers in Human Resource Management.* Reading, MA: Addison-Wesley, 1992.

Tilaro, A., and Rossett, A. "Creating Motivating Job Aids." *Performance and Instruction*, 1993, *32*, 13–20.

Titcomb, T. Chaos and Complexity Theory. *Info-Line*, No. 259807. Alexandria, VA: The American Society for Training and Development, 1998.

Torrence, D., and Torrence, J. "Training in the Face of Illiteracy." *Training and Development*, 1987, *41*(8), 46.

Tosti, D. *"Feedback Systems."* In M. Smith (Ed.), *Introduction to Performance Technology.* Washington, DC: National Society for Performance and Instruction, 1986.

Tosti, D., and Jackson, S. "Influencing Others to Act." In H. Stolovitch and E. Keeps (Eds.), *Handbook of Human Performance Technology: A Comprehensive Guide for Analyzing and Solving Performance Problems in Organizations* (pp. 551–563). San Francisco: Jossey-Bass, 1992.

Tough, A. *The Adult's Learning Projects* (2nd ed.). Toronto, Ontario: Institute for Studies in Education, 1979.

Townsend, P., and Gebhardt, J.E., *The Executive Guide to Understanding and Implementing Employee Engagement Programs: Expand Production Capacity, Increase Revenue, and Save Jobs.* American Society for Quality, 2007.

Tracey, W. *Training Employees with Disabilities.* New York: AMACOM, 1995.

Tripp, S., and Bichelmeyer, B. "Rapid Prototyping: An Alternative Instructional Design Strategy." *Educational Technology Research and Development*, 1990, *38*(1), 31–44.

Troha, F. "The Right Mix." *e-Learning*, 2002, *3* (6), 34–37.

Turner, D. *Role Plays: A Sourcebook of Activities for Trainers.* London: Kogan Page, 1993.

Tyre, M., and Orlikowshi, W. "Exploiting Opportunities for Technological Improvement in Organizations." *Sloan Management Review*, 1993, *35*(1), 13–26.

Ulrich, D., and Lake, D. *Organizational Capability: Competing from the Inside Out.* Hoboken, NJ: John Wiley & Sons, 1990.

Ulrich, D., and Smallwood, N. *Why the Bottom Line ISN'T!: How to Build Value Through People and Organization.* Hoboken, NJ: John Wiley & Sons, 2003.

Ulschak, F., Nathanson, L., and Gillan, P. *Small Group Problem Solving: An Aid to Organizational Effectiveness.* Reading, MA: Addison-Wesley, 1983.

U.S. Air Force. *Handbook for Designers of Instructional Systems.* Washington, DC: U.S. Air Force, 1973.

U.S. Department of Labor and U.S. Department of Education. *The Bottom Line: Basic Skills in the Workplace.* Washington, DC: Government Printing Office, 1988.

"United States vs. France: Vacation Time What Will You Leave Behind?" Downloaded 23 October 2007 from www.thinkandask.com/2005/10191vacations.html, 2005.

Uretsky, M. "Simulated Reality—The Key to More Effective Training." *Employment Relations Today*, 1989/1990, *16*(4), 305–314.

Van Brakel, R. "Why ROI Isn't Enough." *Training and Development*, 2002, *56*(6), 72–74.

Van Buren, M., and Erskine, W. *Learning Outcomes: ASTD's Fourth Annual Report on Standards for Evaluating Organizations' Investments in Training.* Alexandria, VA: The American Society for Training and Development, 2002.

Van den Berghe, M. *Application of ISO 9000 Standards to Education and Training.* Thessaloniki, Greece: European Centre for the Development of Vocational Training, 1997.

Van Gundy, A. *Techniques of Structured Problem Solving.* New York: Van Nostrand Reinhold, 1981.

VanLeeuwen, E. "Quick Donkey Bridge." *Training and Development*, 2001, *55*(11), 84–85.

Vazquez-Abad, J., and Winer, L. "Emerging Trends in Instructional Interventions." In H. Stolovitch and E. Keeps (Eds.), *Handbook of Human Performance Technology: A Comprehensive Guide for Analyzing and Solving Performance Problems in Organizations* (pp. 672–687). San Francisco: Jossey-Bass, 1992.

Vroom, V. *Work and Motivation.* Hoboken, NJ: John Wiley & Sons, 1964.

Walker, J. *Human Resource Planning.* New York: McGraw-Hill, 1980.

Wallace, G. "Costing out a Training Project." *Technical and Skills Training*, 1991, *2*(4), 29–33.

Wallace, J., III. "Participation's Effects on Performance and Satisfaction: A Reconsideration of the Research Evidence." *Academy of Management Review*, 1994, *19*(2), 312–330.

Walton, R. *Interpersonal Peacemaking: Confrontations and Third Party Consultation.* Reading, MA: Addison-Wesley, 1969.

Wang, G. "Valuing Learning: The Measurement Journey." *Educational Technology*, 2003, *43*(1), 32–37.

Waters, L., Roach, D., and Batlis, N. "Organizational Climate Dimensions and Job-Related Attitudes." *Personnel Psychology*, 1974, *27*, 465–476.

Watkins, R., and Kaufman, R. "An Update on Relating Needs Assessment and Needs Analysis." *Performance Improvement*, 1996, *35*(10), 10–13.

Watkins, K., and Marsick, V. *Sculpting the Learning Organization: Lessons in the Art and Science of Systemic Change.* San Francisco: Jossey-Bass, 1993.

Watson, D., and Llorens, L. *Task Analysis: An Occupational Performance Approach.* Bethesda, MD: American Occupational Therapy Association, 1997.

Watson Wyatt. Connecting Organizational Communication to Financial Performance—2003/2004 Communication ROI Study™. Downloaded 27 October 2007 from www.watsonwyatt.com/research/resrender.asp?id=w-868&page=1, 2003/2004.

Webb, E., Campbell, D., Schwartz, R., and Sechrest, L. *Unobtrusive Measures.* Chicago: Rand-McNally, 1966.

Wederspahn, G. "Expat Training." *Training and Development*, 2002, *56*(2), 67–70.

Weech, W. "Training Across Cultures: What to Expect." *Training and Development*, 2001, *55*(1), 62–64.

Weisbord, M. "Diagnosing Your Organization: Six Places to Look for Trouble with or Without a Theory." In R. Golembiewski (Ed.), *Handbook of Organizational Consultation* (pp. 753–766). New York: Marcel Dekker, 1993.

Weiss, D. *Coaching and Counseling in the Workplace.* New York: AMACOM, 1993.

Wellins, R. *Empowered Teams: Creating Self-Directed Work Groups That Improve Quality, Productivity, and Participation.* San Francisco: Jossey-Bass, 1991.

Wellins, R., and Rioux, S. "The Growing Pains of Globalizing HR." *Training and Development*, 2000, *54*(5), 79–85.

Wernick, S. "Self-Directed Work Teams and Empowerment." *Journal for Quality and Participation*, 1994, *17*(4), 34–36.

Werther, W., and Davis, K. *Personnel Management and Human Resources* (2nd ed.). New York: McGraw-Hill, 1985.

West, C., Farmer, J., and Wolff, P. *Instructional Design: Implications from Cognitive Science.* Englewood Cliffs, NJ: Prentice-Hall, 1991.

Wheatley, M. *Leadership and the New Science: Learning About Organization from an Orderly Universe.* San Francisco: Berrett-Koehler, 1992.

Whiteley, R. *The Customer Driven Company: Moving from Talk to Action*. Reading, MA: Addison-Wesley, 1991.

Whitmore, J. *Coaching for Performance: A Practical Guide to Growing Your Own Skills*. San Francisco: Pfeiffer, 1994.

Whitney, D., Cooperrider, D., Kaplin, B., and Trosten-Bloom, A. *Encyclopedia of Positive Questions, Volume I: Using AI to Bring Out the Best in Your Organization* (Tools in Appreciative Inquiry Series, Volume 2). Lakewood, IL: Lakeshore Communications, 2001.

Whitney, D., Cooperrider, D., Trosten-Bloom, A., and Kaplin, B. *Encyclopedia of Positive Questions: Using Appreciative Inquiry to Bring Out the Best in Your Organization*. Euclid, OH: Lakeshore Communications, 2002.

Wilcox, J. (Ed.). *ASTD Trainer's Toolkit: More Needs Assessment Instruments*. Alexandria, VA: The American Society for Training and Development, 1994.

Wileman, R. *Exercises in Visual Thinking*. New York: Hastings House, 1980.

Wilson, T. *Innovative Reward Systems for the Changing Workplace*. New York: McGraw-Hill, 1995.

"Win New Allies with a Training and Education Committee." *Training*, 1982, *19*(2), 67.

Winer, L., and Vázquez-Abad, J. "The Present and Future of ID Practice." *Performance Improvement Quarterly*, 1995, *8*(3), 55–67.

Winn, W. "Instructional Design and Situated Learning: Paradox or Partnership?" *Educational Technology*, 1993, *33*(3), 16–21.

Wlodkowski, R. *Enhancing Adult Motivation to Learn: A Guide to Improving Instruction and Increasing Learner Achievement*. San Francisco: Jossey-Bass, 1985.

Wlodkowski, R. *Enhancing Adult Motivation to Learn: A Comprehensive Guide to Teaching All Adults*. (rev. ed.). San Francisco: Jossey-Bass, 1999.

You, Y. "What Can We Learn from Chaos Theory? An Alternative Approach to Instructional Systems Design." *Educational Technology Research and Development*, 1993, *41*(3), 17–32.

Zemke, R., and Kramlinger, T. *Figuring Things Out: A Trainer's Guide to Needs and Task Analysis*. Reading, MA: Addison-Wesley, 1982.

Zingheim, P., and Schuster, J. "Pay It Forward." *People Management*, 2002, *8*(3), 32–34.

NAME INDEX

A

Addison, R., 336
Ahlstrand, A., 290
Alden, J., 277
Alexander, L., 175
Allen, M., 215
Anderson, R., 244
Annett, J., 72
Appelbaum, E., 122
Aragon, S., 259
Arvey, R., 26, 29, 108
Atwater, L., 21
Ausubel, D., 214, 235

B

Bacal, R., 21, 39
Bachman, L., 298
Bader, G., 72
Baker, H., 378
Baldwin, T., 119, 237
Ballew, A., 277, 279
Barbian, J., 60, 230
Barksdale, S., 61
Bartlett, K., 259
Bassi, L., 122, 290

Batlis, N., 357
Batt, R., 122
Beckshi, R., 60
Becker, B., 209
Beer, V., 332
Bell, B., 6
Bengtson, B., 61
Bentley, T., 374
Bhate, A., 30
Birk, T., 26
Bishop, H., 24, 28
Bjorkquist, D., 61, 63
Blake, B., 298
Blank, W. E., 91, 92, 180, 268
Bloom, B., 177, 288, 358
Bond, S., 274
Borman, R., 53
Boutin, F., 298
Brandenburg, D., 196
Brannick, M., 132
Bridges, W., 29, 132
Briggs, L., 143, 174, 175, 235, 236, 237, 239, 259
Brinkerhoff, R., 344
Broad, M., 119
Brown, J., 321
Brown, M., 190

Bullock, D., 23
Burk, J., 26

C

Cady, S., 349
Campbell, A., 155
Campion, M., 30
Carey, L., 174, 175, 176, 264
Carlisle, K., 145
Carnevale, A., 93
Carr, C., 30
Carroll, S., Jr., 276
Carter, J., 364
Casey, M.A., 72
Castillo, P., 10, 259
Charness, N., 110
Chase, R., 30, 235
Chemers, M., 373
Chernick, J., 298
Chew, I., 25
Chi, M., 235
Chinien, C., 298
Choi, I., 169
Chong, P., 25
Clark, R., 15, 104, 147, 149, 234, 250

Cleland, D., 334
Clifford, J., 132
Coch, L., 385
Cohen, D., 368
Conrad, K., 332
Cookson, P., 59
Cooper, K., 154
Cooper, P., 105
Cooperrider, D., 54, 55, 375
Coscarelli, W., 209
Cowan, S., 314
Crabtree, S., 122, 128
Craig, R., 38
Crowe, M., 117, 119
Cummings, O., 274
Cyert, R., 400
Czaja, S., 110

D

Dalton, G., 98
Darr, E., 19
David, 368
Davidove, E., 410
Davis, K., 132
Davis, R., 175
Dean, M., 18
Dean, P., 18, 49
Delahoussaye, M., 259
Denis, J., 132
Dennen, V., 15
Dessinger, J., 94
Deterline, W., 18
Devane, T., 349
Dick, W., 15, 174, 175, 176, 264, 298
Dillman, D., 72
Dixon, N., 193, 303
Donnelly, J., Jr., 30
Doty, M., 60
Downey, D., 30, 351
Drew, R., 363
Driscoll, M., 332
Driskell, J., 374
Drucker, P., 91
Druskat, V., 368
Dubois, D., 21, 39, 40, 74, 88, 114, 122, 155, 156, 158
Duncan, D., 30
Duncan, J., 402
Dwyer, F., 355

E

Eggland, S., 393
Eilbirt, H., 327
Einsiedel, A., Jr., 277
Elenburg, M., 199
Ellington, H., 247, 248, 261
English, F., 63
Eoyang, G., 12
Erickson, E., 97
Erskine, W., 290
Eskew, D., 279

F

Falcone, P., 24
Faley, R., 26, 29, 108
Farmer, J., 249
Felce, D., 72
Fidel, R., 277
Fielder, F., 373
Fields, D., 4, 36, 50, 51, 61, 62, 89, 112, 146, 147, 229, 240, 257, 258, 286, 288, 289, 314, 332, 333, 334, 350, 367, 405, 410
Finlay, J., 46–47
Finley, M., 368
Finnegan, G., 22
Fitz-enz, J., 209
Flanagan, J., 281
Fleishman, E., 119
Ford, J., 119, 237
Foshay, W., 60, 65, 90, 113, 170, 211, 230, 258, 282, 289, 292, 313, 369, 374, 376, 382, 383, 385, 387
Foxon, M., 4, 36, 50, 51, 61, 62, 89, 112, 146, 147, 229, 240, 257, 258, 286, 288, 289, 314, 332, 333, 334, 350, 367, 405, 410
Francis, D., 401
Frauenheim, E., 331
French, J., Jr., 385, 393

G

Gagné, R., 143, 174, 175, 235, 236, 237, 239, 248, 249, 250, 259, 260
Gainer, L., 93
Gaither, N., 337
Galbraith, J., 30, 351

Gantt, H., 339
Gautier-Downes, J., 22
Gebhardt, J. E., 128
Gibbons, A., 146, 147, 148
Gibson, J., 30
Gilbert, T., 41, 42, 46, 56, 88, 183
Gillan, P., 151
Gilley, J., 393
Gillies, D., 298
Goldwasser, D., 290
Gordon, J., 15
Gould, E., 122
Grabinger, S., 240, 244
Gradous, D., 142, 145, 146, 149, 151, 260
Greenberg, J., 279
Greer, M., 336, 346
Gross, R., 275
Gubrium, J., 71
Guillot, T., 368
Gunning, R., 363
Gupta, K., 61
Gustafson, K., 15

H

Hale, J., 209
Hallowell, E., 91
Halprin, M., 336, 346
Hamel, G., 155
Hannum, W., 136
Harless, j., 22
Harris, N., 240, 244
Harris, P., 10, 259
Hartley, D., 132
Harvey, F., 336
Hassinger, E., 399
Hastings, J., 288
Hatcher, T., 85
Hatten, K., 190
Havighurst, R., 97
Heiderman, J., 298
Heinich, R., 188
Hennessy, D., 336
Hennessy, M., 336
Hensey, M, 377
Herbart, J., 214
Hettinger, L., 117, 119
Hofstede, G., 225, 253
Hohne, C., 3, 10, 18, 63
Holman, P., 349
Holstein, J., 71

Holton, E., 97
Horabin, I., 23, 142
Houle, C., 99, 275
Huczynski, A., 277
Hudson-Samuels, K., 246
Hultman, K., 50
Huselid, M., 209
Hutchinson, C., 360

I

Isaac, S., 78
Ivancevich, J., 30, 276

J

Jackson, R., 98
Jackson, S., 143, 144, 145, 336, 374
Jacobs, R., 3, 23, 31, 42, 136
Janis, I., 48
Jewell, D., 30
Jewell, S., 30
Johnson, J., 117, 119
Johnson, S., 74, 143
Joinson, C., 20
Jonassen, D., 136, 169, 240, 244
Jones, M., 14, 15

K

Kahn, R., 11
Kaplan, B., 55, 375
Kaplan, R., 37, 199, 208
Kates, A., 30, 351
Katz, D., 11
Kaufman, R., 62, 63, 83
Kazanas, H., 64, 98, 101, 134, 135, 178, 179, 180, 204, 212, 248, 260, 314, 385, 401
Kemmerer, F., 25
Kemp, J., 147, 148, 181, 182, 201, 245
Kerr, J., 24
Kerr, S., 24, 25
Khalifa, M., 136
Kiger, P., 18
King, D., 298
King, M., 360
King, S., 3, 10, 18, 63, 360
Kinlaw, D., 374
Kirkhorn, J., 277
Kirkpatrick, D., 193, 290, 344, 368, 380, 381, 384, 385

Kish, L., 69
Klare, G., 363
Knight, S., 98
Knowles, M., 97, 101, 237, 275, 276, 321
Knox, A., 97
Kolb, D., 317
Korth, S., 290
Kozlowski, S., 6
Kramlinger, T., 138, 150
Krebs, V., 19
Krell, E., 331
Krieger, G., 201, 274
Krueger, R., 72
Kuchinke, K., 259
Kulik, J., 122

L

Lahti, R., 19
Laird, D., 64, 277
Lake, D., 155
Lamos, J., 103
Langdon, D., 18, 35, 154, 169
Laroche, I., 53
Lawler, E., III, 24, 30
Lee, S., 290
Lee, W., 61, 191, 274
Lei, D., 25
Lepsinger, R., 154
Levine, E., 132
Levinson, D., 97
Lewis, B., 23, 142
Lewis, T., 61, 63
Li, Z., 14, 15
Likert, R., 385
Lilyquist, J., 76, 77, 197
Lindholm, J., 13, 61, 98, 130, 288, 307
Lineberry, C., 23
Llorens, L., 72
Lorch, G., 99
Lowe, R., 336
Luchs, K., 155
Lucia, A., 154
Lund, T., 61

M

Madaus, G., 288
Mager, R., 42, 47, 56, 169, 171, 172, 178, 179

Malasky, E., 278, 279
Mamone, R., 191, 274
March, J., 400
Marelli, A., 154
Marrow, A., 385
Marsick, V., 114
Marx, R., 246
Maslak, G., 53
McArdle, G., 13
McCall, M., Jr., 37, 399
McCarthy, E., 315
McClelland, C., 30
McClelland, D., 155
McCormick, E., 28, 132, 139, 141
McKenna, M., 18, 35
McLagan, P. A., 158, 368
McLean, G., 385
McLinden, D., 274
Medsker, K., 248, 249, 250, 260
Meltzer, A., 93
Merchant, S., 199
Merrill, M., 14, 15, 213
Meyer, G., 39
Michael, W., 78
Michalko, M., 173, 200
Mikulecky, L., 363
Mohler, L., 336
Molenda, M., 188, 336
Moore, D., 355
Morabito, J., 30
Morgan, P., 378
Moseley, J., 94, 290
Mullins, B., 53
Murphy, C., 336
Myers, 385

N

Nadler, D., 18
Nathanson, L., 151
Nelson, B., 26
Newstrom, J., 76, 77, 119, 197, 276
Norton, D., 208
Novak, C., 290
Nystrom, P., 30

O

Oaks, K., 314
Odenwald, S., 370
Odiorne, G., 38
Oldenwald, S., 254

Olmstead, B., 374
Olson, E., 12
Opengart, R., 110
Osterman, P., 122
Owens, D., 61

P

Paine, F., 276
Payne, T., 98
Peoples, D., 351
Pershing, J., 290, 336, 363
Pfeiffer, J., 277, 279
Phillips, J., 40
Pinchot, G., III, 396
Pipe, P., 42, 47, 56
Piskurich, G., 246
Pitts, R., 25
Posner, B., 401
Powers, E., 402
Prahalad, C., 155
Price, R., 98
Prusak, L., 368
Pucel, D., 214, 235

R

Ratey, J., 91
Raven, B., 393
Reddout, D., 140, 143
Reigeluth, C., 226, 265, 336
Reynolds, A., 244
Richey, R., 4, 10, 11, 13, 15, 36, 50,
  51, 61, 62, 89, 112, 146, 147,
  229, 240, 257, 258, 286, 288,
  289, 314, 332, 333, 334, 350,
  367, 405, 410
Richter, J., 291–292
Roach, D., 357
Robinson, A., 26
Robson, R., 152
Rogers, R., 395, 398, 399
Rokeach, M., 97, 401
Romiszowski, A., 233, 234, 237
Rosenthal, S., 190
Ross, L., 39
Rossett, A., 15, 22, 23, 37, 71
Rossi, C., 72
Rothwell, W., 3, 10, 13, 18, 21, 23,
  33, 36, 39, 40, 50, 52, 59, 61,
  63, 66, 74, 85, 88, 98, 101, 107,

108, 114, 119, 122, 125, 126,
  130, 134, 135, 155, 156, 162,
  176, 178, 179, 180, 187, 204,
  206, 212, 214, 224, 234, 248,
  251, 260, 275, 285, 288, 290,
  307, 308, 314, 335, 348, 360,
  364, 377, 385, 395, 396, 401,
  407, 408
Rummler, G., 9, 10, 18, 30, 31, 38,
  39, 42, 43
Russell, J., 188, 298

S

Sack, I., 30
Salas, E., 374
Sanders, E., 50, 246
Sayre, S., 147
Schein, E., 97, 383, 389
Schmidt, L., 209
Schmidt, W., 401
Schulz, R., 336
Schuster, J., 25
Schwarz, R., 374
Senge, P., 114
Sheehy, G., 97
Shepherd, J., 360
Shoemaker, 395, 398, 399
Short, D., 110
Shrock, S., 209
Sibler, K., 60, 90
Silber, K., 65, 113, 170, 211,
  230, 258, 282, 289, 292,
  313, 369, 374, 376, 382,
  383, 385, 387
Simpson, L., 50, 290
Sitze, A., 53
Slocum, J., 24, 25
Smaldino, S., 188
Small, R., 277
Smallwood, N., 50
Smillie, R., 23
Smith, J., 199
Smith, M., 196
Smith, V., 91
Smithson, G., 315
Solomon, D., 290
Soper, J., 50
Spaulding, K., 22
Sredl, H., 23, 61, 63, 66, 119, 214,
  290, 314, 377, 395

Stanton, N., 72
Starbuck, W., 30
Starcevich, M., 19
Steele, F., 114
Stein, F., 360
Stowell, S., 19
Strandberg, J., 23
Strunk, W., Jr., 361, 362
Sugrue, B., 309
Sullivan, R., 125, 199, 385
Swanson, R., 97, 142, 145, 146,
  149, 151, 260, 290
Swinburne, P., 18
Swindall, C., 128
Symons, F., 72

T

Tansik, D., 30
Taylor, C., 230
Tenopyr, M., 201, 274
Tessmer, M., 136, 298
Thiagarajan, S., 25, 279, 298
Thompson, P., 98
Thompson, S., 69
Thompson, T., 72
Thornton, E., 75
Throndike, E., 119
Tilaro, A., 23
Torrence, D., 363
Torrence, J., 363
Tosti, D., 18, 374
Tough, A., 275
Townsend, P., 128
Tracey, W., 91
Troha, F., 10
Trosten-Bloom, A., 55, 375
Turner, D., 279

U

Ulrich, D., 50, 155, 209
Ulschak, F., 151

V

Van Brakel, R., 290
Van Buren, M., 290
Van Gundy, A., 151
VanLeeuwen, E., 53
Vroom, V., 24, 25

W

Wager, W., 143, 174, 175, 239, 259
Waldman, D., 21
Walker, J., 134
Wallace, G., 336
Wallace, J., III, 122
Wallick, W., 61, 288, 307
Walton, R., 379
Wang, G., 290
Wang, W., 98
Waters, L., 357
Watkins, K., 114
Watkins, R., 63
Watson, D., 72
Weber, J., 117, 119

Wederspahn, G., 53
Weech, W., 53
Weisbord, M., 116
Werther, W., 132
West, C., 249
Westgaard, O., 60, 65, 90, 113, 170,
    211, 230, 258, 282, 289, 292,
    313, 369, 374, 376, 382, 383,
    385, 387
White, E. B., 361, 362
Whiteside, K., 18, 35
Whitney, D., 54, 55, 375
Wileman, R., 351, 352, 353, 354,
    355
Wlodkowski, R., 128, 321
Wolff, P., 249

Wolff, S., 368
Woodcock, M., 401
Woodworth, R., 119

Y

Yelon, S., 175
You, Y., 12

Z

Zemke, R., 15, 138, 150, 259
Zingheim, P., 25
Zornitsky, J., 122

SUBJECT INDEX

A

Abstract concepts
    definition of, 355
    selecting visualization, 355
Action maze, 278–279
Action task, 140–141
Active listening, 376, 386
Activity-oriented learners, 319
Activity-oriented supervisors, 319
"Actual situations," 277–278
Adaptive subsystem, 11
ADDIE model, 59–60
Advanced organizer, 323
Affective domain
    performance objectives levels
        of, 179fig
    verbs associated with objectives
        in, 182t
Algorithms
    for deciding to produce
        instructional materials,
        261fig
    for delivery mode selection,
        249fig
    description and use of, 23
    See also Decision making

American Society for Training and
        Development (ASTD)
    Certified Performance and
        Learning Professional
        (CPLP) of, 5, 403, 408
    job search information from
        website of, 4
    Membership Information
        Service, 298
    professional development
        through, 406
    State of the Industry Report
        (2003) by, 309
    TRAINET database of, 320
Americans with Disabilities Act,
        91, 164
*Analyzing performance Problems or 'You
        Really Oughta Wanna'* (Mager
        and Pipe), 42
Approaches to Training and Development
        (Laird), 277
Assessment centers
    data collection using, 75, 77t
    external, 204
Assessments
    grammatical correctness, 362e
    learner, 89–111

learner motivation,
        322e–323e
    See also Evaluation; Needs
        assessment
ASTD. *See* American Society for
        Training and Development
        (ASTD)
Attitude survey, 204
Attitudes, 13
Attributes
    definition of, 354
    highlighting key visualization,
        354
Audience
    delivery mode for attracting
        broadest, 317
    needs assessment to identify
        target, 68–69
    See also Learner assessment
Audit (or paper trail), 341

B

Bebo.com, 15
Behavioral events interviewing
        (BEI), 155, 161
Behaviors

for effective interpersonal
interaction, 385–387
human performance problems
from responsive, 10
instructional objectives/
test items on specified,
201*t*–202*t*
justifying interactional, 387–389
standards of conduct for
communication, 360–361,
365
See also Interactions
Borrowed approach, 156, 157
Borrowed-and-tailored approach,
156, 157
Budgeting projects, 340–342
Burnout, 128–129

C

Case study, 277
Cause of problem
deficiencies as, 39–40
definition of, 38*fig*
CD-ROM
checklist about instructional
materials and methods for
expert reviewers, 301*e*
checklist for judging behaviors
used in interactions, 388*e*
checklist for judging evaluation
plan and revision, 305*e*–306*e*
checklist for judging
instructional management
system, 330*e*
checklist for judging interaction
behaviors, 388*e*
checklist for judging project
plan, 347*e*
framework for preparing a role
play, 280*e*
interview guide for collecting
case-study information, 278*e*
interview guide for gathering
information on critical
incidents, 281*e*
portion of representative lesson
plan, 272*e*
survey questionnaire assessing
learner motivation, 322*e*–323*e*
worksheet for assessing answers
to questions, 359*e*

worksheet for assessing
appropriate answers to
questions, 359*e*
worksheet for judging
appropriateness of specified
instructional strategy,
252*e*–253*e*
worksheet for judging
performance measurements,
206*e*–207*e*
worksheet for judging
performance objectives, 186*e*
worksheet for judging
sequencing of performance
objectives, 223*e*
worksheet for preparing
instructional objectives, 184*e*
worksheet on instructional
management system, 316*e*
worksheet on instructional
materials and methods for
expert reviewers, 300*e*
worksheet on learner
characteristics, 100*e*
Certified International Project
Manager (CIPM), 349
Certified Performance and Learning
Professional (CPLP), 5, 408
Certified Performance Technologist
(CPT), 5, 408
Certified Project Manager (CPM),
349
Change
commitment and managing,
384–385
documented, 344
handling resistance to, 379–382,
386–387
organizational innovation
adoption stages, 399–400
positive change theory on,
54–55
situation and, 358
trust as key to, 368
Checklists
description and use of, 23
instructional materials and
methods for expert
reviewers, 301*e*
judging behaviors used in
interactions, 388*e*

judging evaluation plan and
revision, 305*e*–306*e*
judging instructional
management system, 330*e*
judging project plan, 347*e*
Chronological sequencing,
213, 324
CLO (Chief Learning Officer), 5
Closed questions, 375
Cluster analysis, 176
Coaching
executive, 19
feedback in the form of, 19
Cognitive domain
performance objectives levels
in, 178*fig*
verbs associated with objectives
in, 181*t*
Cognitive strategies
learner perspective and,
248–249
types of, 249–250
Cognitive task, 140
Cognitivism
constructivism critique of,
105–106
description of, 103–104
instructional design process use
of, 105
knowledge categories of,
104–105
on learner instruction
interpretation, 104
Collaboration. *See* Interactions
Commitment
importance of, 384
securing, 383–385
Communication
active listening component of,
376, 386
using effective oral, 355–361
using effective visual, 351–355
using effective written,
361–365
understanding and commitment
through, 384
what is new in effective,
365–366
See also Messages
Communication audit, 366
Communication climate, 357

Company performance, description of, 6

Competencies
definition of, 155
increasing interest in study of, 156
organizational core, 155–156
See also Instructional designer competencies; *The Standards* (Richey, Fields, and Foxon)

Competency assessment, 74–75, 77*t*

Competency modeling
conducting behavioral events interviewing (BEI) for, 161
methodologies for, 156–161

Competency modeling methodologies
borrowed approach, 156, 157
borrowed-and-tailored approach, 156, 157
EGDSS (group decision-support system) software used with, 161, 164–165
invented approach, 159
outputs-driven approach, 156, 157–159
process-driven approach, 156, 157, 159
rapid results assessment approach, 160–161
trends-driven approach, 159

Competency models
description of, 154–155
key definitions associated with, 155–156

Complexity theory, 12–13

Comprehensive human performance model
description of, 7*fig*–9*t*
Gilbert's performance matrix as, 41–42, 43*t*
See also Instructional design process model

Concepts
abstract, 355
concrete, 354–355

Concrete concepts
definition of, 354
visualization use of, 354–355

Concurrent instructional design, description of, 34

Condition
definition of, 38*fig*
gap between criterion and, 38–39

Conflict
clarifying assumptions about, 378
managing, 377–379
origins of, 377
when to deal with, 386

Conflict resolution approach, 378–379

Constructivism, 105–106

Content
expert reviews of, 298–299
learning content management systems (LCMS) for, 329

Content analysis
assumptions underlying, 148–149
cross-culturally applying, 163–164
definitions and examples of, 149*t*
description of, 146–147
ethical issues of, 162–163
importance of, 147–148
performance objectives derived from, 172–177
steps in performing, 149–152
timing of, 147

Contract learning, 276

Convenience (or judgmental) sampling, 69–70

Copyright permissions, 263–264

CPT (Certified Performance Technologist), 5, 408

Criteria
performance objective component of, 179–180
process and product, 180–181

Criterion
definition of, 38*fig*
gap between condition and, 38–39

Critical incident method, 74, 77*t*

Critical incident technique (CIT), 280–282

Critical path method (CPM), 339–340, 342

Cross-cultural issues
evaluation, 308–309
instructional material preparation and, 285–286
instructional strategy, 253–254
of job, task, content analysis, 163–164
learner assessment, 108–109
needs assessment, 86
performance analysis, 53
performance measurements, 208
performance objectives, 188
performance objectives sequencing, 225
work setting analysis, 126–127
See also Value systems

Cues
definition of, 352
visual communication of, 352, 354

Culture
expectations of others/presenters influenced by, 358
learning affected by values of, 126–127
low and high variables of, 253–254
synchronicity preferences of, 225

Curriculum design competency, 314

Customer surveys, 21

D

Data analysis, 78–79

Data collection
determining needs assessment, 71–76
strengths and weaknesses of selected, 77*t*
See also Interviews; Questionnaires

Decision chart, 323, 325*t*

Decision makers
key, 293–294
promotional strategies congruent with value systems of, 400–402

Decision making

EGDSS software methodology
for, 161, 164–165
key decision makers and,
293–294
learner characteristics related
to, 92
participative, 384–385
performance objectives
sequencing, 216
See also Algorithms
Declarative knowledge, 104–105
Deficiency of environment, 39, 45
Deficiency of execution, 39
Deficiency of knowledge, 39
Delivery modes
algorithm for selection of, 249*fig*
allowing for constraints on
choice of, 248
assessing environment of,
117–119
expert reviews of, 298–299
relationship between attracting
broadest audience and,
317
selecting, 247–248
See also Media
Delphi procedure, 73, 77*t*
Descriptions Now (software), 164
Descriptive learner characteristic
profile, 103
Detailed formats, 274
Detailed outlining, 266
The Dictionary of Occupational Titles
(1991), 28, 134, 164
Direct observation of work,
72, 77*t*
Disabled learners, 91
Discovery learning, 233–234
Discussions
group discussion method, 204
panel, 277
Documentation
adequate record keeping,
327–328
ensuring that competence
is, 326
progress report, 342–343*e*
tracking project
accomplishments, 343–344
Documented change, 344

E

E-learning, 286
Economic suprasystem, 12
Educational Testing Service, 199
Effectiveness
definition of, 6
instructional designer, 411–416
Efficiency, 6
EGDSS (electronic group decision
support system), 161,
164–165
Empathy, 384
Employee burnout, 128–129
Employee engagement, 127–128
Employee selection practices
addressing performance
problem using, 27–29
description of, 26–27
job analysis, 28
recruitment, 27–28
selection tools, 28–29
Enabling objective, 323
Enron scandal, 50
Environment
deficiency of, 39
facilitating instruction through
changing, 415
instruction application, 119–123
instruction delivery, 117–119
work setting, 39, 45, 112–129
See also Work setting
Equal Employment Opportunity
Commission, 97
Equipment requirements, 345
Ethical issues
evaluation, 307–308
IBSTPI Code of Ethical
Standards for Instructional
Designers, 51*e*
instructional materials, 285
instructional strategy, 252–253
of job, task, and content
analysis, 162–163
learner assessment, 108
needs assessment, 85
performance analysis, 49–53
performance objectives,
187–188
performance objectives
sequencing, 224

work setting analysis, 125–126
Ethics
definition of, 49
as instructional designer
competency area, 49–50
Evaluation
cross-cultural issues of,
308–309
description as project type, 339
ethical issues of, 307–308
formative, 288, 290–307
Kirkpatrick's hierarchy of, 344
summative, 288
testing used for, 265
what is new in, 309
See also Assessments
Events of instruction
definition of, 235
instructional strategy based on,
234–236
learning capabilities, learning
and, 238*t*–239*t*
Executive coaching, 19
Executive (or management)
rehearsals, 299, 302
Exit interviews, 75, 77*t*, 204–205
Expectations of others, 358
Expectations of presenters, 358
Experience, 95
Expert reviews, 298–299,
300*e*–301*e*
External assessment centers, 204
Externally focused questions, 375

F

Facebook.com, 15
Facility requirements, 345
FedEx, 156
Feedback
addressing performance
problem using, 18–19
customer surveys for, 21
definition and types of, 18
inadequate or nonexistent, 10
solving performance problems
through, 19–21
summative evaluation, 304
360-degree, 21
Feedback cognitive strategies, 250
Financial issues

budgeting projects, 340–342
equipment and facility
requirements, 345
reallocating project funds, 345
Focus groups (or key informant
groups), 72–73, 77t
Formative evaluation
assumptions about, 290
defining terms associated
with, 291
description of, 288
expert reviews approach to,
298–299, 300e–301e
group pre-tests and pilot tests
for, 303
individualized pre-tests and
pilot tests for, 302–303
judging, 304–306e
justifying, 306–307
management or executive
rehearsals approach to,
299, 302
providing feedback from, 304
Formative evaluation plan
case study on developing,
291–292
steps in developing, 292–297
Formative process evaluation, 291
Formative product evaluation, 291
Formats
definition of, 267
detailed, 274
instructional record, 327–328
portion of representative lesson
plan, 272e
presentation, 357, 364–365
progress report, 342–343e
variety of instructional
materials, 271
Formatting
instructor directions or
guidesheets, 273
learner directions or
guidesheets, 267–270e
Friction
clarifying assumptions about
conflict or, 378
managing, 377–379
origins of, 377
when to deal with, 386
Friendster.com, 15

G

Gallup Management Journal's semi-
annual employee engagement
index (2007), 128
General-to-specific sequencing,
216
Gilbert's performance matrix,
41–42, 43t, 46
Goal analysis
defining, 172
performance objectives derived
from, 172–177
Goal-oriented learners, 319
Goal-oriented supervisors, 319
Goals
description of, 32
distinguishing performance
objectives from, 170–171
establishing instructional design
promotion, 393–394
instructional and organizational,
170–171
See also Objectives
Governmental-legal suprasystem, 12
Grade-level equivalent readability,
363
Grammatical correctness
worksheet, 362e
Group decision-support software,
161, 164–165
Group discussion method, 204
Group post-tests, 303
Group pre-tests, 303
Guidesheets
instructor directions, 265,
271–272e, 273
learner directions, 267,
268e–270e
trainers,' 273–274
Gunning Fog Index, 363

H

Hay/McBer, 157
hi5.com, 15
Hierarchical analysis, 175–176
High Performance Workplace
(HPW), 121
Historical learner characteristic
profile, 103

Human performance
description of, 6
instructional design guided by,
6–10
Human performance models
comprehensive, 7fig–9t, 41–42,
43t
situation-specific, 7, 9–10fig, 41,
42, 44–46
Human performance problems
caused by performers, 9–10fig
components of, 38fig
comprehensive model on causes
of, 7fig–9t
defining and labeling parts of,
37–40
feedback used to address and
solve, 18–21
instructional design solutions
to, 13–14
job performance aids to address,
22–24
practicing empathy regarding,
384
reward systems to address,
24–26
situation-specific model on
causes of, 7, 9–10fig
See also Performance analysis
models; Performance
problems
Human resource information
systems, 327–328

I

IBM, 156
IBSTPI Code of Ethical Standards
for Instructional Designers,
50, 51e
ID$_1$ (First Generation Instructional
Design), 14, 15
ID$_2$ (Second Generation Instruction
Design), 1446
In-basket exercise, 279
Incentives
performance problem addressed
through reward and, 25–26
performance problems and role
of, 39
Incidental feedback, 18

Indirect examinations of performance, 72, 77*t*
Individualism, 253, 254
Individualized post-tests, 302–303
Individualized pre-tests, 302–303
Industry suprasystem, definition of, 12
Information gathering competency, 374–376
Innovation adoption stages, 399–400
Input cognitive strategy, 249–250
Inputs, 11
Instruction
  changing environmental conditions to facilitate, 415
  delivery modes of, 117–119, 247–249*fig*, 298–299
  marketing of, 315–320
  media used for, 244–247
  See also Lessons; Pre-instructional planning
Instructional design
  carried out systemically, 10
  cognitivism used in, 105
  criticisms of traditional, 14–16
  description of, 3–4
  as emerging profession, 4–5
  human performance focus of, 5–6
  human performance solutions through, 13–14
  linkages between organization needs and, 415–416
  new alternatives to, 33–35
  open systems theory on, 11*fig*–13
  promoting use of, 391–404
  reflecting before finalizing solutions/strategies for, 333–334
  ten key assumptions about, 4*e*
  See also Project management/planning
Instructional design alternatives
  concurrent instructional design as, 34
  rapid prototyping as, 34
  substituting another instructional design model for ISD, 33–34
Instructional design experts (IDEs), 298
  See also Instructional designers

Instructional design problems
  judging match between needs assessment data and, 84
  needs assessment identifying, 83
  See also Instructional design solutions
Instructional design process model
  analyze characteristics of a work setting, 113
  assessing relevant characteristics of learners, 90*fig*
  components and overview of the, 6–10
  conduct a needs assessment, 60*fig*
  design instructional materials, 258*fig*
  develop performance measurements, 191*fig*
  evaluate instruction, 289*fig*
  flexibility when applying, 414
  perform job, task, and content analysis, 131*fig*
  sequence performance objectives, 211*fig*
  specify instructional strategies, 230*fig*
  write statements of performance objectives, 170*fig*
  See also Comprehensive human performance model
Instructional design promotion
  case study on, 391–392
  ensuring strategies are congruent with value systems, 400–402
  ensuring that strategies are appropriate, 395–400
  establishing goals for, 393–394
  as marketing strategy, 317–318
  questions to ask for, 393
  selecting strategy for, 394–395
  what is new in the use of, 403–404
Instructional design solutions
  alternatives to ISD as, 33–35
  awareness regarding consequences of, 413–414
  determining projects appropriate for, 36–56
  management solutions as, 17–35

provided by instructional designers, 416
  See also Instructional design problems
Instructional designer competencies
  for analyzing relevant work setting, 112–113
  for business skills to manage instructional design, 333
  for collaboration and relationships, 367–368
  for communicating effectively, 350–351
  for conducting needs assessment, 36–37, 61–62
  for designing curriculum, 314
  for designing instructional management systems, 314
  for determining instructional content, 146–147
  for effective instructional design, 410–411
  for evaluating instruction, 288–290
  IBSTPI study (1988) on, 360
  for learner assessment, 89–90
  for planning/monitoring instructional design projects, 332–334
  for professional development, 405–406
  for reflecting before finalizing design strategies, 333–334
  for selecting or designing instructional materials, 257–258*fig*, 286
  for specifying instructional strategies, 229–230, 240
  ten key assumptions about, 4*e*
  See also Competencies
Instructional designers
  ability to ask questions/gather information by, 374–375
  ability to provide explanations, 376
  active listening by, 376–377
  approach to handling resistance to change by, 381–382, 386–387
  competency as effective designer, 411

criteria for being an effective,
411–416
dealing with friction, 377–379,
387
establishing rapport, 368–370,
371*t*–372*t*
interactions between clients
and, 373–374
monitoring time of, 342–343
position power of, 374
regular weekly meetings held
by, 343
securing commitment, 383–385
self-directed learning facilitated
by, 416
solutions to be provided by, 416
See also Instructional design
experts (IDEs)
Instructional events
definition of, 235
instructional strategy based on,
234–236
learning capabilities, learning
and, 238*t*–239*t*
Instructional flowchart, 323, 325*fig*
Instructional goals. *See* Goals
Instructional management system
case study on designing, 315
competency for designing,
313–314
definition of, 329
ensuring adequate record
keeping, 327–328
ensuring diagnoses of future
learner needs, 327
ensuring easily identified
instructional elements, 326
ensuring instruction transitions
and references, 324–326
ensuring learner diagnosis for
readiness, 320–321
ensuring learners are directed
to appropriate section, 321,
323–324
ensuring that competence is
documented, 326
instructional flowchart, 323,
325*fig*
judging, 328–330
justifying, 329
for quick and easy entrance into
instruction, 315–320

simplified decision chart, 323,
325*t*
what is new in designing,
329–331
worksheet on, 316*e*
See also Learning management
system (LMS)
Instructional marketing
place, 315–317
price, 320
product, 318–319
promotion, 317–318
Instructional material preparation
steps
1: preparing working outline,
259–260
2: conducting research, 260,
262–263
3: examining existing
instructional materials, 263
4: arranging or modifying
existing materials, 263–264
5: preparing tailor-made
materials, 264–274,
266–267
6: selecting or preparing
learning activities, 274–282
Instructional materials
algorithm for decisions on
producing, 261*fig*
copyright permissions for,
263–264
cross-cultural issues regarding,
285–286
description as project type, 338
differences of opinion on
components of, 265–266
ethical issues in designing, 285
judging, 282, 283*fig*–284*fig*
justifying, 282, 285
overview of, 257–258
prepared for individualized
use, 266
steps in selecting or designing,
259–260, 262–265
what is new in selecting or
designing, 286–287
Instructional package, 264
Instructional strategies
choosing media and delivery
methods, 240, 244–248
chosing tactics and, 236–240

cognitive, 248–250
conceptualizing, 232–236
cross-cultural issues of, 253–254
defining, 231–232
distinguishing between tactics
and, 232
ethical issues of, 251–253
judging, 250–253*e*
justifying, 251
listed, 241*t*–244*t*
macro- and micro- types of, 232
overview of, 229–230*fig*
as pre-instructional planning
project, 338
what is new in specifying, 255
Instructional tactics
choosing appropriate, 240
distinguishing between strategy
and, 232
listed, 241*t*–244*t*
Instructor directions (or
guidesheets), 265, 271–272*e*,
273
Instruments
preparing performance
measurement, 198–204
specifying needs assessment,
76–77
Intentional feedback, 18
Interactions
behaviors for effective, 385–387
establishing rapport for,
368–370, 371*t*–372*t*, 385
gathering information through,
374–375
handling friction during,
377–379
handling resistance to change,
379–382
between instructional designer
and clients, 373–374
keeping people on track during,
382–383
listening actively during,
376–377
providing explanations during,
376
securing commitment during,
383–385
stating purpose of, 370, 372–373
what is new in, 389
See also Behaviors

Internally focused questions, 375
International Board of Standards
for Training, Performance,
and Instruction Code of
Ethical Standards, 50, 51*e*
International Board of Standards
for Training, Performance,
and Instruction (IBSTPI),
3, 360
International Society for
Performance Improvement
(ISPI), 4, 39, 403, 406
Interviews
behavioral events interviewing
(BEI), 155, 161
critical incidents information
gathered through, 281*e*
exit, 75, 77*t*, 204–205
group discussion, 204
item format measurement used
in, 200–201
planning needs assessment,
71–72
strengths and weaknesses of, 77*t*
See also Data collection
Invented approach, 159
ISPI (International Society for
Performance Improvement),
4, 39, 403, 406
Item format measurement,
200–201

J

Job analysis
cross-cultural application of,
163–164
definition of associated terms
and, 132
as employee selection practice,
28
ethical issues of, 162–163
importance of, 132–133
of relevant work setting,
112–129
steps in performing, 133–138
timing of, 133
Job analysis steps
1: identifying jobs to be
analyzed, 134
2: clarifying results derived from
analysis, 134–137

3: preparing plan to guide job
analysis, 137–138
4: implementing job analysis
plan, 138
5: analyzing and using results,
138
Job category, 96–97
Job description, 135, 136
Job performance aids
description of, 22
designing and using, 22–24
performance problems
addressed through, 22
types of, 23–24
Job setting. *See* Work setting
Job situation
change and, 358
performance problems caused
by, 9, 10*fig*
Job specification, 135–136
Judgmental (or convenience)
sampling, 69–70

K

Keeping on track, 382–383, 387
Key decision makers, 293–294
Key informant groups (or focus
group), 72–73, 77*t*
Key performance indicators (KPIs),
208–209
Key results areas (KRAs), 208
Knowledge
deficiency of, 39
definition of, 13, 177
as learner characteristic, 95
procedural and declarative,
104–105
See also Learning
Known-to-unknown sequencing,
214, 324

L

Learner assessment
case study example of, 99
cognitivism approach to,
103–106
cross-cultural, 108–109
description of, 89
determining methods for,
99–102

developing profile of learner
characteristics, 102–103
ethical issues of, 108
instructional designer
competency regarding,
89–90
judging, 106–107
justifying, 107–108
new issues in, 109–110
selecting characteristics for,
90–99
See also Audience; Target
population
Learner characteristics
case study on selecting, 99
decision-related, 92
demographic, 93–94
developing profile of, 102–103
experience and knowledge
as, 95
geographical location as, 96
job category as, 96–97
learner-related, 92–93
physiological conditions and
attitudes, 94–96
situation-related, 91–92
when and how to assess, 99, 102
Worksheet on Learner
Characteristics, 99, 100*e*
Learner characteristics profiles
normative, descriptive, and
historical, 103
what to include in, 102
Learner directions (or guidesheets),
267, 268*e*–270*e*
Learners
cognitive strategies in context of,
248–250
diagnosed for readiness,
320–321
ensuring adequate record
keeping for individual,
327–328
motivation of, 24, 321,
322*e*–323*e*
performance measurement
development role of,
205–206
three basic types of, 319
Learning
contract, 276
discovery, 233–234

facilitating self-directed, 416
instructional events, learning
capabilities and, 238*t*–239*t*
reception, 233
See also Knowledge
Learning activities
definition of, 171
preparing group, 276–282
preparing individual, 275–276
selecting existing, 275
Learning competence, 95–96
Learning content management
systems (LCMS), 329
Learning management system
(LMS)
capabilities key to effective, 313
curriculum design relationship
to, 314
description and functions of,
329–331
See also Instructional
management system
Learning objects, 286
Learning style, 95
Learning tasks, 174
Learning-oriented learners, 319
Learning-oriented supervisors, 319
Legislation
Americans with Disabilities Act,
91, 164
Sarbanes-Oxley Act, 164
Lesson plans
description of, 271–272
portion of representative, 272*e*
Lessons
definition of, 271
efficient directing of learners to,
321, 323–324
portion of representative plan
for, 272*e*
providing transitions and
references in, 324, 326
See also Instruction; Sections
Library of Congress Subject
Index, 150
Line managers, 334

M

Machine performance, description
of, 6
Macro-instructional strategy, 232

Mager and Pipe's performance
engineering model (PEM),
42, 44–46, 47
Mail surveys. *See* Questionnaires
Maintenance subsystem, 11
Management (or executive)
rehearsals, 299, 302
Management solutions
description of, 17–18
employee selection practices,
26–29
feedback options, 18–21
job performance aids, 22–24
organizational redesign, 30–35
reward systems, 24–26
Managerial subsystem, 11–12
Managers
activity-oriented supervisors
and, 319
goal-oriented supervisors and,
319
learning-oriented supervisors
and, 319
line, 334
performance analysis education
for, 413
staff, 334–335
Marketing competitive
suprasystem, 12
Master Project Manager (MPM), 349
Materials. *See* Instructional
materials
McBer (now Hay/McBer), 157
Media
definition of, 244
range of instructional, 245–247
selecting instructional, 244–245
See also Delivery modes
Medium, 244
Memorandum feedback, 20
Messages
organization of, 357
presentation format of, 357–358
See also Communication
Methodology. *See* Competency
modeling methodologies
Micro-instructional strategy, 232
"The Most Important Lessons I've
Learned as a Consultant
About the Systems
Approach to Instructional
Design" (Davidove), 410

Motivation
definition of, 24
incentives and, 25–26, 39
learner, 321
Motorola, 156
MyFace, 255, 329
MySpace.com, 15

N

National Skills Standards Board,
199
The Nature of Human Values
(Rokeach), 97
Needs
definition of, 62
ensuring diagnoses of future
learner, 327
linkages between instructional
design and organization,
415–416
Needs analysis, 63
Needs assessment
competency in conducting,
36–37, 61–62
cross-cultural issues of, 86
definition of, 63
description as project type, 338
developing plan for, 65–80
ethical issues of, 85
formative evaluation, 293–294
identifying instructional
problems through, 83
identifying target audience of,
68–69
recent developments in, 86–87
solving problems in conducting,
81–82
what is new in conducting,
87–88
See also Assessments
Needs assessment planning
definition of, 64
determining data collection
strategy and tactics, 71–76,
77*t*
determining methods of data
analysis, 78–79
establishing objectives of a,
67–68
establishing sampling
procedures, 69–71

Needs assessment planning
  (continued)
  questions related to, 66–67
  specifying instruments and
    protocols, 76–78
Needs assessment plans
  assessing feasibility of, 79–80
  case study in developing, 80–81
  definition of, 65
  judging, 83–84
  justifying, 84–85
  steps in developing, 65–80
Netlog.com, 15
Nominal group technique (NGT),
  73, 77*t*
Noninstructional (or non-learning)
  solutions. *See* Management
  solutions
Normative learner characteristic
  profile, 103

O

O*NET, 164
Objectives
  Bloom's taxonomy of
    educational, 358
  description of, 32
  distinguishing goals from,
    170–171
  enabling, 323
  See also Goals; Performance
    objectives
Office of the American Workplace,
  39, 122
On-the-job performance tests, 265
Open questions, 375
Open systems
  basic components of
    organization as, 11*fig*
  description of, 11
Open systems theory
  on basic components of
    organization, 11
  instructional design based on,
    11–13
Operations, 11
Oral communication
  using acceptable organization
    for, 357
  using acceptable presentation
    format for, 357–358

answering questions posed by
    others, 358–359*e*
  presentation for
    understandability of, 356
  principles of, 355–356
  using rules or standards of
    conduct in, 360–361
Organizational goals, 170–171
Organizational redesign
  addressing performance
    problems using, 30–33
  description of, 30
Organizational selling, 318
Organizations
  basic components as open
    system, 11*fig*
  ensuring adequate record
    keeping for, 327–328
  innovation adoption stages by,
    399–400
  linkages between instructional
    design and needs of, 415–416
  trust as key to "change-
    capable," 368
orkut, 15
Output cognitive strategies, 250
Outputs, 11
Outputs-driven approach, 156,
  157–159

P

Panel discussion, 277
Paper trail (or audit), 341
Part-to-part-to-part sequencing,
  215–216
Part-to-whole sequencing, 214, 324
Participative decision making,
  384–385
Performance
  description of, 5–6
  developing measurements of,
    190–209
  efficiency and effectiveness
    aspects of, 6
  factors affecting individual,
    work-group and
    organizational, 8*t*–9*t*
  objectives of, 169–189
Performance analysis
  acting ethically in applying, 49–53
  creative exercise of, 412–413

criticism of, 54
cross-cultural application of, 53
description as project type,
  337–338
educating managers about, 413
effective instructional designer's
  emphasis on, 411
example of application of,
  46–47
judging, 47–48
justifying, 49
positive change theory impact
  on, 54–55
Performance analysis models
  comprehensive and situation-
    specific categories of, 41
  described, 40
  Gilbert's performance matrix,
    41–42, 43*t*, 46
  Mager and Pipe's performance
    engineering model (PEM),
    42, 44–46, 47
Performance appraisal, 205
  feedback through, 20
Performance engineering model
  (PEM), 42, 44–46, 47
Performance improvement potential
  (PIP), 88
Performance management, 21
Performance matrix, 41–42, 43*t*, 46
Performance measurements
  cross-cultural issues of, 208
  deciding method of, 197–198
  definition of, 190–191*fig*
  ethical issues of, 205–207
  importance of, 191–192
  judging and justifying, 205,
    206*e*–207*e*
  other methods of taking,
    204–205
  as pre-instructional planning,
    338
  preparing instruments for,
    198–204
  purposes of, 192–193, 194*t*–195*t*
  sources of information for
    developing, 193, 196–197
  what is new in developing,
    208–209
Performance objectives
  affective domain levels and
    associated verbs, 179*fig*

classifying, 177–178*fig*
cognitive domain levels and
    associated verbs, 178*fig*, 181*t*
cross-cultural issues of, 188
deriving from goal, task, or
    content analysis, 172–177
describing parts of, 178–183
distinguishing goals from,
    170–171
ethical issues regarding,
    187–188
function of, 169
instructional design process step
    on, 170*fig*
judging and justifying, 184–187
as pre-instructional planning
    project, 338
psychomotor domain levels and
    associated verbs, 180*fig*
sequencing, 210–226, 324, 326
what is new in writing, 188–189
work activities linked to,
    176–177
worksheet for preparing, 184*e*
writing, 183–184
See also Objectives
Performance objectives sequencing
approaches to, 212–216
cross-cultural issues of, 225
defining key terms related to,
    210–211*fig*
ethical issues of, 224
flowchart on rules for,
    217*fig*–222*fig*
importance of, 212
judging, 216, 223*e*
justifying the, 224
making decisions about, 216
as pre-instructional planning
    project, 338
transition and, 324, 326
what is new in, 225–226
See also Sequence
Personal selling, 318
Personnel records, 327
PERT (program evaluation and
    review technique), 340, 342
Pilot tests, 303
Place, 315–317
Planning. *See* Pre-instructional
    planning; Project
    management/planning

Playscript technique, 23–24
Point sheet, 264
Positive change theory, 54–55
Post-tests
    description of, 265
    group, 303
    individualized, 302–303
Power distance, 253–254
Practicing empathy, 384
Pre-instructional planning
    description as project type, 338
    performance measurements,
        192–209, 338
    performance objectives,
        169–188, 338
    performance objectives
        sequencing, 210–226, 324,
        326, 338
    specification of instructional
        strategies, 231–255, 238
    See also Instruction
Pre-tests
    description of, 265
    group, 303
    individualized, 302–303
    proficiency examinations as,
        323–324
Presentation formats
    oral communication, 357
    written communication,
        364–365
Price, 320
Problems. *See* Human performance
    problems; Instructional
    design problems
Procedural analysis, 176
Procedural knowledge, 104
Procedure manuals
    description and use of, 23
    playscript technique used in,
        23–24
Process cognitive strategies, 250
Process criteria, 180–181
Process-driven approach, 156,
    157, 159
ProComp, 164
Product, 318–319
Product criteria, 180–181
Production subsystem, 11
Production wall charts, 19–20
Productivity improvement potential
    (PIP), 183

Professional development
    competency in, 405–406
    excuses for failure to pursue,
        406–407
    importance of, 406–408
    what is new in, 408–409
Proficiency examinations, 323–324
Program evaluation and review
    technique (PERT), 340, 342
Progress report, 342–343*e*
Project management/planning
    budgeting, 340–342
    competencies for, 332–334
    differences between traditional
        and, 334–335
    different types of, 338–339
    equipment and facility
        requirements components
        of, 345
    key features of planning and,
        336–340
    monitoring time of instructional
        designers, 342–343
    practicing empathy as part of, 384
    reallocating funds for, 345
    time line for, 336–340
    tracking accomplishments of,
        343–344
    unique challenges posed by,
        335–336
    what is new in, 348–349
Project plans
    issues to be covered in, 334–346
    judging, 345–346, 347*e*
    justifying, 346, 348
Promotion. *See* Instructional design
    promotion
Protocols
    formative evaluation,
        294–295
    specifying needs assessment,
        77–78
Psychomotor domain
    performance objectives levels
        of, 180*fig*
    verbs associated with objectives
        in, 182*t*

Q

Questionnaires
    description of, 72, 77*t*

Questionnaires *(continued)*
 item format measurement used
  in, 200–201
 Learner Motivation, 322*e*–323*e*
 See also Data collection
Questions
 assessing appropriate answers to
  questions worksheet, 359*e*
 instructional design promotion,
  393
 instructional designer's ability to
  ask, 374–375
 oral communication for
  answering, 358–359*e*
 related to needs assessment
  planning, 66–67
 types and categories of, 375
 when to ask, 386
 written communication to
  answer, 365

R

Rapid prototyping, 34
Rapid results assessment approach,
 160–161
Rapport
 definition of, 368
 establishing, 368–370
 model for techniques to
  establish, 371*t*–372*t*
 when to establish, 385
Readability formula, 363
Reception learning, 233
Reception process, 233
Record keeping formats, 327–328
Recruitment practices, 27–28
References
 providing instructional, 326
 providing lesson and section,
  324, 326
Regular weekly meetings, 343
Relationships. *See* Interactions
Remington Rand, 339
Resistance to change, 379–382,
 386–387
Response. *See* Behaviors
Reward system
 description and uses of, 24–25
 performance problem addressed
  through incentive and,
  25–26

Role plays
 definition of, 279
 framework for preparing, 280*e*

S

Sales promotion methods, 318
Samples/sampling
 convenience or judgmental,
  69–70
 establishing procedures for,
  69–71
 simple random, 70
 stratified, 70
 systematic, 70–71
Sarbanes-Oxley Act, 164
Scheduling and control charts,
 339, 342
Scripts, 272–273
SCROM (sharable content object
 reference model), 152
Second Life, 331
Sections
 efficient directing of learners to,
  321, 323–324
 providing transitions and
  references in, 324, 326
 See also Lessons
Self-directed learning, 416
Seminar Information Service
 (SIS), 320
Sequence
 cultural preference for
  synchronicity and, 225
 definition of, 210
 inflexible and flexible,
  210–211
 See also Performance objectives
  sequencing
Simple random sampling, 70
Simulation
 definition of, 279
 preparing, 280
Situation
 change and, 358
 performance problems and job,
  9, 10*fig*
Situation-specific human
 performance model
 description of, 7, 9–10*fig*
 Mager and Pipe's performance
  analysis, 42, 44–46

Skills
 definition of, 13
 inventories of, 328
Social networking sites, 15, 255, 331
Solutions. *See* Instructional design
 solutions
Staff managers, 334–335
Stakeholders
 advisory committee made up
  of, 204
 definition of, 193
 formative evaluation
  participation of, 295
 performance measurement
  information from, 193, 196
Standards
 definition of, 32
 performance problems and role
  of, 39
Standards of conduct
 for oral communication,
  360–361
 for written communication, 365
The Standards (Richey, Fields, and
 Foxon)
 on analyzing relevant work
  setting competency, 112
 on being an effective
  instructional designer,
  410–411
 on business skills
  competency, 333
 on collaboration and
  relationships competency,
  367–368
 on communicating effectively
  competency, 350–351
 on creating design and
  development model
  competency, 334
 on designing instructional
  management systems
  competency, 314
 on determining instructional
  content competency,
  146–147
 on evaluation competency,
  288–290
 on identifying target
  population/learner
  assessment competency,
  89–90

on instructional design material competency, 258, 286
on needs assessment competency, 61–62
on planning/managing instructional design projects competency, 332–333
on professional development competency, 405–406
on reflection before finalizing design strategies competency, 333–334
on selecting/designing instructional materials competency, 257
on specifying instructional strategies, 229, 240
See also Compentencies; Instructional designer competencies
State of the Industry Report (2003) [ASTD], 309
Step-by-step sequencing, 215
Storyboarding, 266–267
Stratified sampling, 70
Student manuals, 271
Subject-matter experts (SMEs), 298, 348
Success case, 344
Summative evaluation, 288
Supervisors types, 319
Supplier suprasystem, 12
Suprasystem
complexity theory on, 12–13
definition of, 11
types and interrelativeness of, 11–12
Symptoms of problem
definition of, 38fig
list of typical, 40
Synchronicity cultural preferences, 225
Systematic sampling, 70–71

T

Tacking project accomplishments, 343–344
Tactics. See Instructional tactics
Target population
competency in identifying, 89

formative evaluation, 292–293, 295–296
marketing of instruction to, 315–320
See also Learner assessment
Task analysis
cross-culturally application of, 163–164
defining associated terms and, 139–142
description of, 72, 77t
ethical issues of, 162–163
performance objectives derived from, 172–177
steps in performing, 142–145
summary of approaches to, 146t
Task analysis steps
1: identifying tasks to be analyzed, 142–143
2: clarifying the desired results, 143
3: preparing plan to guide the tasks analysis, 143–145
4: implementing task analysis plan, 145
5: using results, 145
Task orientation, 253, 254
Tasks
action, 140–141
classification of learning, 174
cognitive, 140
work, 174
Taxonomy of Education Objectives (Bloom), 177
Team meetings, 20
Technological suprasystem, 12
Technology
caution in pursuing new, 415
EGDSS (electronic group decision support system), 161, 164–165
instructional project planning/ monitoring, 348–349
Tests
evaluation using, 265
on-the-job performance, 265
pilot, 303
pre- and post-, 265, 302–303, 323–324
proficiency examinations, 323–324
360-degree feedback, 21

Time monitoring methods
progress reports, 342–343e
project time lines, 336–340
regular weekly meetings, 33
scheduling and control charts, 339, 342
Topical sequencing, 213, 324
Trainers' guides, 273–274
TRAINET database (ASTD), 320
Training record systems, 328
Training requirements planning, definition of, 63–64
Transition
definition of instructional, 324
performance objective sequencing and, 324, 326
Trends-driven approach, 159

U

Uncertainty avoidance, 253, 254
Unknown-to-known sequencing, 215
U.S. Air Force, 139
U.S. Department of Labor, 121

V

Value systems
definition of, 97
learning affected by cultural, 126–127
promotional strategies congruent with, 400–402
See also Cross-cultural issues
Visualization
appropriate uses of, 352
using cues in, 352, 354
highlighting key attributes in, 354
identifying types of images used in, 352, 353fig
power of, 351
selecting abstract concepts for, 355
selecting concrete concepts for, 354–355

W

Watson Wyatt, 365
Web-based surveys. See Questionnaires

Websites
  American Society for Training
    and Development, 4
  Bebo.com, 15
  CPT (Certified Performance
    Technologist), 5
  Facebook.com, 15
  Friendster.com, 15
  hi5.com, 15
  instructional material
    sources, 262
  International Society for
    Performance Improvement, 4
  MySpace.com, 15
  Netlog.com, 15
  orkut, 15
  Second Life, 331
  social networking, 15,
    255, 331
"What Is a Task?" (Reddout), 140
Whole-to-part sequencing,
    213–214, 324
Work activities-performance
    objectives link, 176–177
Work analysis
  content analysis component of,
    146–152
  cross-cultural application of,
    163–164
  description of, 130–131*fig*
  ethical issues of, 162–163
  job analysis component of, 28,
    112–138
  judging, 152–153
  justifying, 154

performance objectives derived
    from, 172–177
  task analysis component of, 72,
    77*t*, 139–145
  what is new in, 164–165
  See also Competency models
Work samples, 24
Work setting
  deficiency of environment,
    39, 45
  employee engagement
    characteristic of, 127–128
  High Performance Workplace
    (HPW), 121
  See also Environment
Work setting analysis
  cross-cultural, 126–127
  ethical issues of, 125–126
  identifying factors and carrying
    out, 114–123
  importance of, 114
  instructional designer
    competency for, 112–113
  judging a, 123–124
  justifying, 124–125
  what is new in, 127–129
Work tasks, 174
Worksheets
  assessing appropriate answers to
    questions, 359*e*
  Instructional Management
    System, 316*e*
  judging appropriate
    instructional strategy,
    252*e*–253*e*

judging performance
    measurements, 206*e*–207*e*
  judging performance objectives,
    186*e*
  judging sequencing of
    performance objectives,
    223*e*
  Learner Characteristics, 99,
    100*e*
  preparing instructional
    objectives, 184*e*
Written communication
  acceptation presentation format
    for, 364–365
  answering questions posed by
    others, 365
  appropriate understandability
    level of, 361, 363
  assessing grammatical
    correctness of, 362*e*
  Gunning Fog Index for, 363
  principles of effective, 361
  readability formula for, 363
  using rules or standards of
    conduct for, 365
WSTC (whole systems
    transformational change),
    349

Y

YouTube, 255, 329

CONTENTS OF THE WEBSITE

You are invited to view and download the supplementary materials listed below. The materials are available FREE with the purchase of this book at www.pfeiffer.com/go/masteringid

Syllabus for an Introductory Course in Instructional Design

Activities to Support the Text

Activity 1–1:   What Is Instructional Design?

Activity 1–2:   What Is Performance?

Activity 2–1:   Discriminating Between Situations Requiring Instructional Design Solutions and Those Requiring Other Solutions

Activity 2–2:   Judging the Appropriateness and Accuracy of Instructional Design Project Selection Decisions

Activity 2–3:   Stating a Rationale for Instructional Design Decisions

Activity 3–1:   Using Feedback to Improve Performance

Activity 3–2:   Using Discipline/Corrective Action to Improve Performance

Activity 3–3:   Using Employee Reward Systems to Improve Performance

Activity 3–4:   Using Organizational Redesign to Improve Performance

Activity 4–1:   Developing a Needs Assessment Plan

Activity 4–2:   Conducting a Needs Assessment

Activity 4–3:   Identifying Instructional Problems

Activity 4–4:   Judging Needs Assessment Plans

Activity 4–5:   Stating a Rationale

Activity 5–1:   Selecting Learner Characteristics Appropriate for Assessment

Activity 5–2:   Determining Methods for Assessing Learner Characteristics

Activity 5–3:   Developing a Profile of Learner Characteristics

Activity 5–4:   Judging Learner Characteristics

Activity 5–5:   Explaining Assessment of Learner Characteristics

Activity 6–1:   Determining Resources and Constraints of the Environments

Activity 6–2:   Judging a Setting Analysis

Activity 6–3:   Stating a Rationale for Selection of Resources and Constraints

Activity 7–1:   Defining Job, Task, and Content Analysis

Activity 7–2:   Judging the Adequacy of an Analytical Method and Its Results

Activity 7–3:   Stating a Rationale for Selection, Analysis, or Judgment

Activity 8–1:   Stating Objectives in Performance Terms

Activity 8–2:   Judging Whether Performance Objectives Are Stated in Performance Terms and Are Accurate, Comprehensive, and Appropriate

Activity 8–3:   Stating a Rationale for the Objectives Written or for Judgments Made

Activity 9–1:   Generating Performance Measures

Activity 9–2:   Stating a Rationale for the Way the Measurement Instrument Is Constructed or How the Judgment Is Made

Activity 10–1:   Stating Rules for Sequencing Performance Objectives

Activity 10–2:   Deviating from Decisions Made About Sequencing Performance Objectives

Activity 10–3:   Judging the Accuracy, Completeness, and Appropriateness of a Given Sequence of Performance Objectives

Activity 10–4:   Stating a Rationale for the Rules, Sequence, or Judgment

Activity 11–1:   A Worksheet for Specifying the Instructional Strategy

Activity 11–2:   Judging the Appropriateness of a Specified Instructional Strategy

Activity 12–1:   Questions About Designing Instructional Materials

Activity 13–1:   Developing a Formative Evaluation Plan

Activity 13–2:   Conducting a Formative Evaluation

Activity 14–1:   Designing an Instructional Management System

Activity 15–1:   Developing a Project Management Plan for an Instructional Design Project

Activity 15–2:   Monitoring an Instructional Design Project

Activity 16–1:   Using Effective Visual Communication

Activity 16–2:   A Role Play on Using Effective Oral Communication: Preparing and Delivering a Presentation

Activity 17–1:   Establishing and Maintaining Rapport

Activity 17–2:   Critical Incidents: Keeping an Individual or Group on Track

Activity 18–1:   Specifying Ways to Make Others Aware of Instructional Design

Activity 19–1:   Thinking It Through

Activity 20–1:   Thinking It Through

Worksheets, Checklists, and Other Resources

Exhibit 5.1:   A Worksheet on Learner Characteristics

Exhibit 8.1:   A Worksheet for Preparing Instructional Objectives

Exhibit 8.2:   A Worksheet for Judging Performance Objectives

Exhibit 9.1:   A Worksheet for Judging Performance Measurements

Exhibit 10.1:   A Worksheet for Judging the Sequencing of Performance
                  Objectives

Exhibit 11.1:   A Worksheet for Judging the Appropriateness of a
                  Specified Instructional Strategy

Exhibit 12.2:   A Portion of a Representative Lesson Plan

Exhibit 12.3:   An Interview Guide for Collecting Case-Study
                  Information

Exhibit 12.4:   A Framework for Preparing a Role Play

Exhibit 12.5:   An Interview Guide for Gathering Information on
                  Critical Incidents

Exhibit 13.1:   A Worksheet on Instructional Materials and Methods for
                  Expert Reviewers

Exhibit 13.2:   A Checklist About Instructional Materials and Methods
                  for Expert Reviewers

Exhibit 13.3:   A Checklist for Judging the Appropriateness,
                  Comprehensiveness, and Adequacy of Statements of the
                  Evaluation Plan and Revision Specifications

Exhibit 14.1:   A Worksheet on the Instructional Management System

Exhibit 14.2:   A Survey Questionnaire to Assess Learner Motivation

Exhibit 14.3:   A Checklist for Judging the Appropriateness,
                  Comprehensiveness, and Adequacy of Statements of the
                  Instructional Management System

Exhibit 15.2:   A Checklist for Judging the Appropriateness and
                  Comprehensiveness of a Project Plan

Exhibit 16.1:   A Worksheet for Assessing Appropriate Answers to
                  Questions

Exhibit 17.1:   A Checklist for Judging the Appropriateness and
                  Effectiveness of Behaviors Used in Specific Interactions
                  with Other People

PowerPoint Presentation

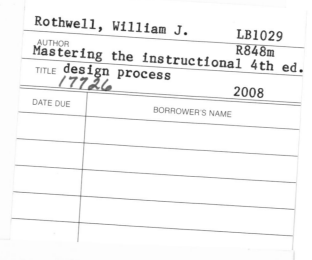